Politics and Parentela in Paraíba

Manaus
AMAZONAS
PARÁ
Belém
São Luís
Fortaleza
MARANHÃO
CEARÁ
RIO GRANDE
DO NORTE
Teresina
Natal
PIAUÍ
PARAÍBA
Parahyba
PERNAMBUCO
Recife
TER. OF ACRE
Maceió
Rio Branco
ALAGOAS
SERGIPE
Aracajú
MATO GROSSO
BAHIA
GOIÁS
Salvador
Cuiabá
Goiás
MINAS GERAIS
Belo Horizonte
ESPÍRITO SANTO
Vitória
SÃO PAULO
RIO DE JANEIRO
São Paulo
Niterói
Rio de Janeiro
(FEDERAL DISTRICT)
PARANÁ
Curitiba
SANTA CATARINA
Florianópolis
RIO GRANDE
DO SUL
Porto Alegre
BRAZIL 1930

LINDA LEWIN

Politics and Parentela in Paraíba

A CASE STUDY OF FAMILY-BASED OLIGARCHY IN BRAZIL

PRINCETON UNIVERSITY PRESS

PRINCETON, NEW JERSEY

Published by Princeton University Press, 41 William Street,
Princeton, New Jersey 08540
In the United Kingdom: Princeton University Press, Guildford, Surrey

Library of Congress Cataloging in Publication Data will be
found on the last printed page of this book

ISBN 0-691-07719-3

Publication of this book has been aided by a grant from the
Whitney Darrow Fund of Princeton University Press

This book has been composed in Linotron Trump

Clothbound editions of Princeton University Press books
are printed on acid-free paper, and binding materials are
chosen for strength and durability. Paperbacks, although satisfactory
for personal collections, are not usually suitable for library rebinding

Printed in the United States of America by Princeton University Press
Princeton, New Jersey

For Mario and Iracema Rosas

CONTENTS

LIST OF ILLUSTRATIONS

For acknowledgments for the use of these photographs, see page xix.

LIST OF MAPS AND FIGURES

LIST OF TABLES

ACKNOWLEDGMENTS

While doing the research for this book, I incurred an enormous debt to Brazilians without whom the work could never have been completed. I can mention only a few who assisted me in the course of three trips to Brazil during the 1970s. First, I am grateful to the members of the Instituto Histórico e Geográfico Paraibano in João Pessoa, Paraíba, particularly to its former president, Dr. Humberto Carneiro da Cunha Nóbrega, who in 1970 first permitted me to use the archives of Coronel Antônio da Silva Pessoa and João Pessoa Cavalcanti de Albuquerque, which belong to the IHGP. Members Celso Mariz, Deusdedit Leitão, Rosilda Cartaxo, Wilson Seixas, Waldice Porto, and José Leal, as local historians of Paraíba, offered much early help and advice. To Dr. Maurílio Augusto de Almeida, who placed his splendid library at my disposal in the summer of 1975, I am especially grateful. Among informants who contributed oral and family history, I would like to thank particularly Donas Maria de Lourdes de Toledo Lins, Júlia Lins Vieira de Melo, Antónia do Monte (Montinha) Lins, Clóris Vieira, Maria das Neves Falcão Pessoa, and Dr. Normando Guedes Pereira. Dra. Diana Soares de Galliza shared archival lore. Although I have taken great care that the genealogical information and relationships described in this book are accurate, errors may appear. If they do, they are in no way the responsibility of the informants mentioned here but my own.

In nearby Recife, D. Lúcia Nery of the Arquivo Público do Estado assisted considerably with newspapers and documents. Dr. Ariano Suassuna graciously shared family memories and genealogy, recounting useful details about his father's political career. Marc and Judith Hoffnagel not only have always been my most resourceful guides to Pernambuco's rich historical resources but also have repeatedly hosted and befriended me in many visits to their adopted city of Recife.

In Rio de Janeiro, the list of those who offered me scholarly assistance is too lengthy to mention in its entirety. I can only single out a very few by name. I am particularly grateful to the late Irmã Maria Regina do Santo Rosário (Laurita Pessoa Raja Gabaglia), the daughter of President Epitácio da Silva Pessoa. I owe her special thanks for facilitating my access to her father's archive at the Instituto Histórico e Geográfico Brasileiro. Irmã Maria Regina recounted a number of valuable anecdotes about the roles of both her father and her cousin, Governor João Pessoa Cavalcanti de Albuquerque, that provided otherwise unobtainable insights about the 1930 crisis. Dr. Pedro Calmon, the late president of the IHGB, who permitted me to use Epitácio's archive, deserves special thanks for the assistance he and his staff offered. Like many North American researchers, I benefited enormously from his willingness to make all of the resources of the IHGB available to me. Sr. Antônio Quintela of the Biblioteca Nacional, Sr. Gabriel da Costa Pinto of the Arquivo Nacional, and D. Martha Maria Gonçalves of the Itamaraty Archives offered valuable advice on where to search for additional documents as well as individual assistance with their own institutions' collections. My generous neighbor, the late Dr. Horácio de Almeida, the Areiense historian who transplanted himself from Paraíba to Copacabana after the Revolution of 1930, most willingly opened his private collection of Paraibana to me, oriented me considerably in the early stages of my work, and imparted some of the flavor of the Old Republic's politics to me during conversational Sundays with his family.

Joseph L. Love, Warren Dean, John Schultz, Michael Hall, and Ralph Della Cava, as veteran researchers, offered me further orientation and advice drawn from their extensive experience in the archives of Rio de Janeiro, São Paulo, and the Northeast. To Robert M. Levine, I owe a special word of thanks for bringing to my attention the existence of the Arquivo do Epitácio Pessoa and for suggesting its untapped potential value. Herbert S. Klein, my dissertation director at Columbia University, gave me the benefit of a very valuable critique of my original dissertation, suggestions about my use of quantitative data, and additional encouragement later for the project of this book. Karen Spalding, my dissertation co-director, carefully criticized my use of anthropology and guided me further in the direction of my growing interest in political anthropology and kinship studies. Warren Dean, as a member of my dissertation committee, also provided suggestions incorporated in this book. More recently, in preparing the revised draft of this book, I have again received help from Joe Love, as well as Stanley J. Stein, Jason Clay, and a number of my new colleagues at Berkeley, among whom I would particularly like to thank Tulio Halperín-Donghi and Richard Herr, whose careful criticism I have tried to address.

Institutional support was indispensable for the completion of this book. Columbia University awarded me an NDFL Fellowship in Portuguese and the Woodrow Wilson Foundation a Dissertation Fellowship that enabled me to spend 1970–1971 in Brazil undertaking the original research. A summer travel grant for research in Paraíba in 1978, as well as supplemental funds for the typing of a first draft of the manuscript, were provided by Princeton University's Committee on Research in the Humanities and Social Sciences. I received very generous support both from the History Department and the Center for Latin American Studies, University of California, Berkeley, for the preparation of the revised manuscript including maps, glossaries, and photographs. More than the material support, I would like to acknowledge my deeper appreciation for the personal interest and encouragement that a number of colleagues at Berkeley have shown in this book. I would particularly like to thank Richard Herr of the History Department and David Collier, director of the Center for Latin American Studies in 1982, whose enthusiasm for this study initially welcomed me to Berkeley. Sheldon Rothblatt, chairman of the History Department, very kindly arranged for supplementary assistance with part of the typing, when I was obliged to turn to dictation after surgery on my wrist. This enabled me to continue writing. Two of my graduate students offered special contributions—Richard Parker for carefully compiling the glossaries, and Cynthia Forster for meticulously checking many of the notes and text and then preparing the bibliography for typing. Clara Imada, always patient and competent in typing manuscripts, also offered, along with corrections of my Portuguese, her Brazilian *simpatia*.

Finally, I would like to try to express how much I owe to Dr. Mario Rosas, his wife Iracema Jenner Rosas, and their children, Norma, Eric, Rosalina, Roberta, Fernanda, Maria Euthalia, Luluca—and Gerusa, who, although she could not be there, in spirit was always present in the Rosas's home. The members of their extended family in João Pessoa, especially Amaury Falcone and Maria Luiza Jenner Falcone, Nelson Rosas and Alayde Souto Maior Rosas, have always been part of my fond memories of that northeastern city. This is a debt words must fail to express adequately. Most providentially, they gave me a second home while I worked in Paraíba throughout the seventies, integrating me into their family life after I appeared on their doorstep in December 1970 as a perfect stranger from the South of Brazil. Like the proverbial cousin who appears from a distant place, they invited me into their home without hesitation and made me feel welcome. Even more, they sustained me by offering me a great deal of personal support, affection, and humor, not to mention their delicious regional cuisine and admirable toleration for my North American foibles as a guest. I am sure that only the friendship and love that came from sharing their family life made it possible to continue pursuing the lonely tasks of archival research and to set aside the inevitable disappointments that accompany it. The supportive ambience of their household helped me to find both the physical and the emotional resources to transcend the mounds of documents and venture into the interior of Paraíba. In the United States, their letters, telegrams and announcements of graduations, marriages, and the births of grandchildren (which means now a third generation is too numerous to mention here by name) have continued to encourage me in the "conquest" of this project. So I thank particularly Mario and Iracema for forgiving my lapses in a tropical environment—as when I unknowingly carried into their home a colony of *"bichinhos"* that live in the pages of books purchased in *sebus*—and for tolerating my early deficiencies in their beautiful language, while at the same time teaching me to speak *nordestino*. Even now, I cannot imagine a human context more perfectly suited for initiating me as a foreigner into the impressive expansiveness of that highly developed and wonderfully complex social institution, the Brazilian extended family. Their kindness, like that of all my other informants and collaborators in Paraíba, enabled me to experience what they meant when they said, *"A Paraíba é pequena e boa!"*

Berkeley, California
March 1986

ACKNOWLEDGMENTS FOR PHOTOGRAPHS

THE AUTHOR wishes to thank the following individuals and institutions for permission to reproduce photographs for this book:

Américo Jocobina Lacombe, president of both the Instituto Histórico e Geográfico Brasileiro and the Fundação Casa de Rui Barbosa, Rio de Janeiro, for 7 and 14, which came from the Arquivo do Epitácio da Silva Pessoa at the IHGB, and for 15, which came from the Seção de Iconografia of the FCRB.

Herwig Strolz, director of the International Textile Manufacturers' Federation, Zurich, Switzerland, for permission to reproduce 3 from Arno Pearse, *Brazilian Cotton* (Manchester: International Federation of Master Cotton Spinners & Manufacturers' Association, 1923), p. 167.

Humberto da Nóbrega, of Tambaú, Paraíba, former president of the Instituto Histórico e Geográfico Paraibano, João Pessoa, Paraíba, for 9, 12, 18, 19, 20, 21, 22, and 23, which came from his private collection, the Acervo Humberto Nóbrega.

José de Nazareth Rodrigues, for permission to reproduce a photograph from his *2 séculos da cidade; passeio retrospectivo—1870–1930* (João Pessoa: Gráfica Iterplan, 1978), which appears as 13. This photograph comes from his father's collection, the Acervo Walfredo Rodriguez.

José Joffily, of Londrina, Paraná, for permission to reproduce 11, which appears in his *Entre a Monarquia e a República; ideas e lutas de Ireneo Joffily* (Rio de Janeiro: Livraria Kosmos, 1982), p. 288.

Maria Augusta de Sales Souza, of João Pessoa, Paraíba, for permission to reproduce 5, which appears in her father Celso Mariz's *Evolução econômica da Paraíba* (João Pessoa: *A União* Editora, 1939), p. 58.

Maria de Lourdes de Toledo Lins, of João Pessoa, Paraíba, for permission to reproduce 10, which comes from her personal collection.

Maria do Socorro Silva de Aragão, president of the Fundação Casa de José Américo, Tambaú, Paraíba, for permission to reproduce 1, 2, 16, 17, and 24 from the Arquivo Fundação José Américo.

Renato Domingues da Silva, of João Pessoa, Paraíba, for permission to reproduce 4, which comes from his brother Alpheu Domingues's *Relatorio da Delegacia do Serviço do Algodão na Parahyba apresentado ao Superintendente F. L. Alves Costa, anno de 1929* (Parahyba: Imprensa Oficial, 1930), p. 28.

For 6 and 8, to Carlos Dias Fernandes, *Politicos do Norte, III: Epitacio Pessôa* (Rio de Janeiro: Conde Pereira Carneiro Editora, 1919), pp. 96 and 108.

The author especially wishes to thank Dr. Humberto Nóbrega for his generosity both in making his photographic collection available to her and in spending his time assisting her with the selection and identification of photographs. Bob Tarr, director of the Multimedia Services of the University of California, Berkeley, very kindly made photographic laboratory facilities available. Jerome Crump, the photographer who labored long and diligently to improve very considerably the quality of the prints, also deserves special thanks.

NOTE ON PORTUGUESE USAGE AND STYLE

REGARDING Portuguese usage and style, several comments are necessary. All Portuguese words have been defined in the text for the general reader and grouped in a glossary. Classificatory kinship terminology, however, appears in a separate glossary for consultation by readers with special scholarly interest in it. Where relevant, it has also been defined in the legal language of the Brazilian Civil Code. Because this is a study emphasizing family and kinship, Brazilian names have received special attention in the text. Following standard usage, individuals are often referred to only by their given names. However, when an individual is first mentioned in the text his or her full family name is used. Since the context where a name appears often implies relationships of blood and marriage between politicians, full family names occasionally have been reintroduced in order to underscore kin connections that otherwise a reader unfamiliar with them would not notice. For instance, Epitácio Pessoa, Paraíba's oligarchical patriarch, is referred to as "Epitácio Lindolfo da Silva Pessoa," his full legal name, when first mentioned. Subsequently, "Epitácio" is usually a sufficient referential name, although "Epitácio Pessoa," his official name, also appears. Usage prefers the given name only where an individual possesses a sufficiently different name not susceptible to ambiguity. Thus, President Hermes da Fonseca universally was "Hermes" and Sen. Octacílio de Albuquerque, "Octacílio." But since around two-thirds of all Brazilian men are named João, José, or Antônio, in those instances usually a single family name was substituted. Federal Deputy João Tavares de Melo Cavalcanti thus became merely "Tavares" and João Pessoa Cavalcanti, "João Pessoa." (Due to Pessoa's ambiguity—the word means "person"—he could not be called merely "Pessoa.") Occasionally, when an individual's name reappears after not having been mentioned for several chapters, the full name has been repeated to remind the reader of the family affiliation. Readers should keep in mind that first-name references such as these are standard and carry a formal connotation absent in English. In addition, nicknames have sometimes been included, when they were the standard form of referential name employed. Thus, Col. José Pereira Lima also appears as Col. "Zé" Pereira. Several living informants have also been identified by their contemporary nicknames in footnotes for recognition in Paraíba.

Portuguese orthography has been modified frequently in this century. Therefore, authors' names, titles of books, and publication information have been left in the original spelling in the footnotes and the bibliography in order to assist readers who wish to consult them. Except for a few, well-known historical figures who preferred not to modify the spelling of their names during their lives, names that appear in the text conform to current spelling rules, as do geographical place names. The one exception is "Parahyba." The archaic orthography for the capital of the state of Paraíba has been retained in order to distinguish it from the province or the state of the same name, which until 1930 was officially named "Parahyba do Norte." Usually, however, Parahyba has been referred to as "the Capital," following contemporary usage. In commemoration of assassinated Gov. João Pessoa, the Capital was renamed "João Pessoa" in 1930. It should also be kept in mind that during the Empire (1822–1889) the chief executive of a province was called a "president" (*presidente*), as he was during the Old Republic (1889–1930). In order to avoid confusion with the national executive, however, provincial and state executives are referred to here as "governors."

A few extremely common terms in Brazilian history have been left in Portuguese because translation is impossible or would significantly alter the contextual meaning. The word *município* has been left in the original, for example, because to translate it as "county" would be to alter its contextual meaning. Brazilian municípios possess legal prerogatives not associated with the Anglo-American county. In addition, a município includes both a city or seat (*sede*) and considerable surrounding territory, encompassing a unit of urban local administration as well as a rural environs. "*Prefeito*" has likewise been left in the original, for "mayor" implies an exclusively urban executive. Similarly, Brazilian political concepts, like "*coronelismo*" or *política de família*, have been thoroughly explained but rendered in Portuguese. Although "Supreme Court" is an accurate translation of "Supremo Tribunal Federal," Brazil's highest court, the translation of "(Supremo) Tribunal de Justiça" as "State Supreme Court" is rather misleading. The latter tribunal was part of the federal court system and therefore functioned in more respects like a federal appeals court. Nevertheless, the commonly used English equivalent of "State Supreme Court" has been retained since many readers will already be familiar with the term.

The common adjectival endings in Portuguese indicating a native or resident of a place have been extensively employed in the text, following standard usage in works published in English. Thus, "*ano,* as in *Paraibano,* and "*-ense,* as in *Areiense,* denote either the adjectival form of Paraíba and Areia or a native of them. Personalistic factions or their members are designated by attaching the standard Portuguese suffix "*-ista*" to the name of the leader of the faction, as in "Epitacista," "Alvarista," "Valfredista," referring to Epitácio's Álvaro's, or Valfredo's followings. Occasionally, the plural of *coronel, coronéis,* or of *bacharel, bacharéis,* appears in the text, but elsewhere Portuguese plurals terminate in "s."

One modification of English usage has been employed to avoid ambiguity regarding a word that frequently appears in the text. Capitalized, the word "State" refers to the concept; in lower case, "state" refers to either the state of Paraíba or the state government.

Finally, the monetary unit of the Empire and Old Republic was the *mil-réis,* written 1$000. The *conto* equaled 1,000 mil-réis and was written 1:000$000. A table of U.S. dollar equivalencies appears in Appendix A. Measurements have been either retained in the metric system or converted to it.

LIST OF ABBREVIATIONS

ABNRJ *Anais da Biblioteca Nacional do Rio de Janeiro*

ACAP Arquivo do Coronel Antônio da Silva Pessoa

AEP Arquivo do Epitácio da Silva Pessoa

AI Arquivo Histórico do Itamaraty [Foreign Ministry]

Boletim do DNOCS *Boletim do DNOCS [Departamento Nacional das Obras Contra as Sêcas]*

CIFTA Centro das Indústrias de Fiação e Tecelagem do Rio de Janeiro (today, SINTA, or Sindicato das Indústrias de Fiação e Tecelagem do Rio de Janeiro)

CSSH *Comparative Studies in Society and History*

HAHR *Hispanic American Historical Review*

IHGB Instituto Histórico e Geográfico Paraibano

PRO Public Record Office, London

RGB *Revista Genealógica Brasileira*

RGL *Revista Genealógica Latina*

RIHGB *Revista do Instituto Histórico e Geográfico Brasileiro*

RIHGP *Revista do Instituto Histórico e Geográfico Paraibano*

Footnote citations to the AEP and ACAP use diagonals to separate *pasta* (*livro*), or bound file-book, from document number. Thus, AEP/12/102 refers to Arquivo do Epitácio Pessoa, Pasta 12, document (or page—there are inconsistencies) 102. The ACAP had few page or document numbers and consists of only four pastas, so most citations read merely ACAP/3, etc. Readers who consult the author's dissertation should be aware that those citations also include reference to the tin boxes in which the pastas were stored, sometimes two to a box.

Politics and Parentela in Paraíba

Introduction

> I did not condone in silence the formation of an oligarchy in my native state. . . . I protested at the right time and place. . . . I was the first politician to register his dissent, in 1890, against the first oligarchy founded in Brazil: The oligarchy of the Neivas of Paraíba do Norte.
>
> —Sen. João Coelho Gonçalves Lisboa, May 7, 1908

On the 5th of July 1919, the U.S.S. *Idaho* sailed from New York, bound for Rio de Janeiro on a voyage of state. It carried as its special passenger the president-elect of Brazil, Epitácio Lindolfo da Silva Pessoa. He traveled as President Wilson's personal guest, for the two men had been diplomatic colleagues at the Paris Peace Conference, where they had developed a relationship of mutual admiration and respect. Epitácio was the first Brazilian head of state to visit North America since the Emperor Dom Pedro II attended the Philadelphia Centennial Exposition, almost half a century earlier. Epitácio, his wife, Mary Sayão Pessoa, and his eldest daughter Laurita had made official visits to Boston and Washington, D.C., and Secretary of the Treasury Carter Glass presided over a full state dinner given in his honor at the Pan American Union on the eve of his departure for New York.

Before his United States visit, Epitácio had toured Europe, paying official visits to Italy's Parliament and King Victor Emmanuel, the pope, and the reigning monarchs of Belgium and Great Britain. Having first attracted international attention as the head of the Brazilian delegation to the Versailles Conference, he played a crucial role there as a spokesman for Latin American and non-Western nations, in addition to presenting Brazil's claims against a defeated Germany. Quite unexpectedly, his national political career reached its culmination while he was advancing Brazil's diplomatic goals. At Versailles he learned that he had been elected president.[1]

Epitácio's political career had been one of the most distinguished of his generation, the generation of the 1880s. Briefly serv-

[1] *New York Times*, 1, 2, 4, 5, and 12 July 1919.

ing as a federal deputy in Brazil's Constituent Congress between 1891 and 1893, when he was only twenty-six, he attracted national attention with his maiden speech boldly denouncing the dictatorship of Marshal Floriano Peixoto. From 1898 to 1901, he held the important cabinet post of minister of justice, culture, and education under President Manuel Ferraz de Campos Sales, supervising the revision of Brazil's ancient Portuguese civil code as the nation moved toward adopting jurisprudential principles more attuned to its recently adopted identity as a republic.

Forced to resign because of his firm stand on educational reform, Epitácio returned to public service in 1902 as attorney general; shortly after, he was conjointly appointed a justice of the Supreme Court. Beginning in 1905, he served exclusively on the Court, where his brilliant jurisprudential expertise was enlisted by Brazil's foreign minister, the Baron of Rio Branco (José Maria da Silva Paranhos). As a key adviser on international boundary disputes, Epitácio contributed several legal opinions that served to further Brazil's acquisition of a slice of territory the size of France.

Resigning from the Supreme Court in 1911 because of illness, Epitácio undertook a senatorial career on his recovery later the same year. In 1912, he was elected senior senator for the small northeastern state of Paraíba, his birthplace and childhood home. In late 1918, he was appointed to lead the Brazilian delegation to the Paris Peace Conference. Brazil had just plunged into a national crisis because President Francisco de Paula Rodrigues Alves had become ill in November, and died in January, only two months into his term. The three most powerful states then became hopelessly deadlocked over the selection of a successor. By March, however, Epitácio emerged as the preferred "neutral" candidate. As the head of Paraíba's congressional delegation, Epitácio possessed the advantage that he did not belong to the nation's major power blocs, which were led by the states of São Paulo, Minas Gerais, and Rio Grande do Sul. Epitácio's political gifts also recommended him highly for the presidency. As good-looking and urbane as his official photographs suggested, Paraíba's senior senator also possessed the elegant manners and cosmopolitan polish that periodic travel to Europe had refined. He had been a brilliant student in law school, his intelligence was keen, his reasoning sagacious, and his judgment well-considered. On only rare occasions did he display the outbursts of choleric temper that were said to be a family trait. On the contrary, patience was one of his greatest political assets. He was a consummate orator in the nineteenth-century tradition of his alma mater, the Recife Law School, and the legalistic reasoning of his written opinions conveyed the tone of a magistrate. Epitácio had embraced liberalism and republicanism in his youthful days in Recife. Their ideological appeal appears to have been traceable to his fiery individualism, which also explained his courage in making unpopular political decisions.

Those who placed Epitácio in the presidency did not foresee that he would be as strongly independent as he proved. Between 1919 and 1922, he managed to leave his personal stamp on Brazil. Subsequently, both political contemporaries and historians would remember him as a fervent constitutionalist whose presidential propensity for an all-civilian cabinet made him unique.[2] Above all, the tremendous personal dignity he brought to Brazil's presidency during the final, tumultuous decade of the Old Republic placed him in a class to himself in the eyes of the generation that had made the transition from Empire to Republic.

Before reaching its destination of Rio de Janeiro, the U.S.S. *Idaho* dropped anchor in Brazilian waters at Cabedêlo, an obscure spot only an hour from the Northeast's major port of Recife. Little more than a lone wharf that interrupted the coconut palms lining Paraíba's tropical coastline, Cabedêlo was a point of entry into Epitácio's other political world—one to which the world press had made only tangential and usually inaccurate reference. Stepping ashore in the State of Paraíba for a few hours, the new president-elect of Brazil paid homage to his power base in national politics. Even before his triumphant election as senator in 1912, the huddle of politicians who proudly embraced Epitácio on the wharf had long supported him, sometimes against incredible obstacles. For them, as the saying went, Epitácio "wore another hat": that of state party boss of Paraíba (chefe do partido).

For his loyal supporters in Paraíba, Epitácio's rise to chief executive confirmed their euphoric expectations. By no means did his new role prove incompatible with his more enduring and fundamental one as the political patriarch of Paraíba's ruling oligarchy. Epitácio's political role in Paraíba, ignored by the world press covering the Versailles Conference, would have offered a fascinating contrast to newspaper readers in Paris, Rome, London, and Washington who were accustomed to reading the Brazilian senator's

[2] Epitácio was the only civilian northeasterner to be elected to the Brazilian presidency. His best biography remains the one written by his daughter Laurita Pessôa Raja Gabaglia [Irmã Maria Regina do Santo Rosário], *Epitacio Pessôa*, 2 vols. (São Paulo: José Olýmpio Editôra, 1951).

name among those of the world's most distinguished diplomats. His behavior as state party boss would have been incomprehensible to many of them—a contradiction of the liberalism he espoused. Brazilians, however, took Epitácio's dual role for granted. Indeed, the ability to live two highly divergent political lives that were nevertheless intimately connected was the sine qua non of a successful politician in Brazil's "era of the oligarchies."

Paraíba as a Case Study of Oligarchy

The Scholarly Focus

This is a book about the political system in Senator Epitácio Pessoa's Paraíba during the Old Republic, especially the impressive electoral machine he and his oligarchical following controlled between 1912 and 1930. Closed to all but the small elite who determined its political fortunes, Paraíba's oligarchy reflected a pattern of organization both Brazilian and northeastern. Brazil's era of the Old Republic witnessed "the oligarchies" exercising political power at the state and national levels of government according to a new federal system imposed by the Constitution of 1891. The First (or Old) Republic opened in 1889 after the forced abdication of Emperor Dom Pedro II ended the Brazilian monarchy that had ruled the nation since independence from Portugal in 1822. The Republic closed in 1930 as the national coffee economy fell victim to world depression and an institutional crisis of the ruling political elite reached a climax. In spite of the Revolution of 1930, which ushered in the era of Getúlio Vargas, oligarchical politics in many respects outlived the era of the oligarchies and continued to be a significant force even at the national level. More recently, urbanization, industrialization, and the imposition of military rule have restricted oligarchical politics to the local level. Oligarchy's roots, therefore, have remained far from vestigial even in the 1980s. In many rural localities where the massive capitalization of agriculture and the eviction of the tenant population characteristic of Brazil since the 1960s have not challenged older agrarian structures, the political arrangements historically associated with those structures have often endured.[3]

[3] The extent to which oligarchical politics survives at the município level is still a matter of historiographical debate. See, for example: Gláucio Ary Dillon Soares, *Sociedade e política no Brasil* (São Paulo: Difusão Européia do Livro, 1973), pp.

In focusing on the Pessoa oligarchy from 1912 to 1930 under Epitácio's leadership, this case study reflects the author's advantageous access to the extensive record that the Pessoas left for historians.[4] The documents in the archives of Senator Epitácio, his brother Col. Antônio da Silva Pessoa, and their nephew, Gov. João Pessoa Cavalcanti de Albuquerque, provided abundant evidence for reconstructing the history of the Paraíba oligarchy throughout the Old Republic. Although on one level this book can be considered an effort to write Paraíba's oligarchical history during that era, more narrowly, its purpose is to relate the story of Senator Epitácio Pessoa's efforts to protect and expand a family base of oligarchical power in his native state. From the late 1890s, when he reentered national politics as President Campos Sales's minister of justice and education, Epitácio demonstrated that the trajectory of his brilliant political career was indeed related to successful oligarchical organization and leadership. Thanks to him, the Pessoa oligarchy also presents a special historical twist, for, unlike many of his contemporaries in the Senate—who also headed the ruling oligarchies in their states—Epitácio eventually commanded the machinery of national politics as president of Brazil. On a different plane, however, his oligarchical triumph in Paraíba essentially remains the success story of his political family. Without reference to the web of relationships woven by its members, especially the intermarried branches of Pessoas, Lucenas, and Neivas, it would be impossible to account for either Pessoa political control of the state or Epitácio's exceptional national career. Consequently, in many respects this book attempts to interpret Epitácio as the creation of his political family.

123–35; Eul-Soo Pang, "*Coronelismo* in Northeast Brazil," in *The Caciques*, ed. Robert Kern (Albuquerque: University of New Mexico Press, 1973), pp. 87–88; and Antônio Olavo Cintra, "Traditional Brazilian Politics: An Interpretation of Relations between Center and Periphery," in *The Structure of Brazilian Development*, ed. Neuma Aguiar (New Brunswick, N.J.: Transaction Books, 1979), pp. 154–55.

[4] The Pessoa archives consulted for this study included the following: Arquivo do Epitácio Lindolfo da Silva Pessoa (henceforth, AEP), Instituto Histórico e Geográfico Brasileiro (henceforth, IHGB), Rio de Janeiro; Arquivo do Coronel Antônio da Silva Pessoa (henceforth, ACAP), Instituto Histórico e Geográfico Paraibano (henceforth, IHGP), João Pessoa, Paraíba; and Arquivo do João Pessoa Cavalcanti de Albuquerque (henceforth, AJP), IHGP, João Pessoa, Paraíba. Duplicates or typescripts of much of the contents of the AJP are part of the AEP (pastas 8 and 9). Documents from the AJP cited herein are therefore cited in terms of the AEP, pastas 8 or 9. (The author verified copies and duplicates with the originals filed in the AJP at the IHGP.)

Paraíba's Neiva–Pessoa oligarchy enjoyed the dubious distinction—according to a native-son senator who opposed it—of having been the first oligarchy founded in Brazil.[5] However exaggerated the charge, Paraíba's oligarchy certainly proved to be one of the most resilient in the history of the Old Republic, for it survived with the same leadership longer than most. And the assertion that it was one of the oldest could be appropriately laid at the Pessoas's door. Their family had been closely associated with the ruling oligarchy from the moment they joined the *coup d'état* to force Dom Pedro II to relinquish his throne, in late 1889.[6]

On the most elementary level, this book analyzes oligarchy as factional politics. Undeniably, a factional perspective is essential for understanding not only Paraíba's political organization during the Old Republic but also how national politics was structured. In addition, approaching politics as a factional system avoids a certain tendency in the scholarly literature to condemn Brazil's political organization during the Old Republic in pejorative terms as "anarchic," "atavistic," or even "tribal." Finally, a factional interpretation of oligarchical politics exposes its crucial systemic dependence on clientism and patronage, although political mobilization was based on a wide spectrum of group motives ranging from economic interests to goals of personal status and family position.

Yet appraising Paraíba's oligarchy as a factional system is inadequate for understanding either the organizational basis or the raison d'être of politics in a state such as Paraíba. Clearly, politics in Paraíba had to be analyzed beyond the boundaries defined by the formal institutions of power, particularly because factions operated in closed-door contexts. They relegated decision-making, electoral strategies, and dramatic schisms within their own ranks to private encounters and communications. Factional politics therefore was best appreciated by examining the factions themselves—the composition of specific personal factions and the process by which they built alliances or fragmented into competing elements. And, as oligarchy's organizational basis was revealed in its smallest units, those units revealed characteristics analogous to other patterns of social organization. In short, the small groupings of the factions to which Paraíba's politicians gave their loy-

[5] João Coelho Gonçalves Lisbôa, *Oligarchias, seccas do norte e clericalismo* (Rio de Janeiro: Imprensa Nacional, 1909), p. 11.

[6] L. Pessôa, *Epitacio Pessôa,* 1:53.

alty were congruent with the segmental organization of their own extended families.

It follows from such a coincidence of group identity that merely offering a factional perspective on oligarchy had to remain a secondary purpose of this book. Instead, its primary goal is to examine the historical relationship between kinship and political organization implicit in the units of factional affiliation characteristic of the Old Republic. The role of kinship ties in oligarchical politics has received rather cursory, although almost universal, note in the historical literature on Empire and Republic. Most scholars have merely mentioned the traditional dependence of Brazilian political organization on family and kinship ties without giving central consideration to the implications of that relationship over time. This study brings to the foreground of analysis the central Brazilian institution of the extended family or *parentela*. It connects elite family organization to complementary economic, political, and social structures, with the intention of making Brazilian kinship organization itself a subject worthy of analysis in the transition from Empire to Republic.

Twenty years ago, anthropologist Charles Wagley called attention to the fact that, "while the patriarchal family type of the agrarian past may have disappeared, a larger network of relatives[,] . . . the *parentela*, has persisted with modifed but important functions in Brazilian society, economy, and even political life."[7] Rejecting the notion that surviving reliance on kinship ties was "antagonistic" to the emergence of "modern institutions," he observed that, to date, comparative studies in Brazil had not "made an exhaustive analysis of the parentela and its functions."[8] Wagley pointed out that American anthropologists had overlooked many aspects of the Brazilian parentela's organization and functioning because, from their perspective, the kinship system was neither strange nor exotic. Cultural blinders, in other words, had prevented them from unraveling the intricacies of this fundamental Brazilian social institution.

Wagley's observation would yield an analogous conclusion in the historical literature. Scholars of Brazilian oligarchy and the era of the Old Republic have usually been concerned with questions

[7] Charles Wagley, "Luso-Brazilian Kinship Patterns: The Persistence of a Cultural Tradition," in *The Politics of Change in Latin America*, ed. Joseph Maier and Richard W. Weatherhead (New York: Praeger, 1964), p. 175.

[8] Ibid.

and problems stressing new historical variables. Attention has been directed, for instance, to urbanization, immigration, industrialization, and nationalism rather than to those aspects of social organization that conserved historical patterns of political life. Scholars have merely noted, in most cases, that the force of kinship declined in a linear fashion at some point in the nineteenth century without considering its high adaptability to change over time or even its survival in otherwise "modern" contexts.[9] This case study, consequently, attempts to contribute to the scholarly literature by delineating, with reference to Paraíba, how the force of kinship in Brazilian politics underwent complex change and, rather than evidencing an abrupt and rapid linear decline, survived well into the present century. So sophisticated was its adaptation to change that kinship continued to influence politics in ways that were not always easily detectable.

The Organization and Comparative Significance of This Case Study

This book attaches significance to an *informally* organized system of politics, one underlying the formally defined institutions of political power. The analysis seeks to link the institutions of the State to indispensable, informal structures maintained by bonds of kinship, political friendship, and personal association. It reexamines the formal features of key institutions—political office, elections, the police power, and the legal norms or sanctions vital to the State's authority—in an effort to draw a comprehensive picture of politics during Brazil's era of the oligarchies.

Paraíba offers a model. Reliance on bonds of blood and marriage survived with particular vigor in political life there, accentuating in the early part of this century a dependence on kin and family ties that had once characterized more obviously political organi-

[9] The sociological and anthropological literature reflects greater awareness of the adaptability of Brazilian kinship organization in the face of urbanization and industrialization. See: Takashi Maeyama, *Familialization of the Unfamiliar World: The Família, Networks and Groups in a Brazilian City* (Ithaca: Cornell University Press, 1975), pp. 32–34, 138–40; Manuel Tosta Berlinck, *The Structure of the Brazilian Family in São Paulo* (Ithaca: Cornell University Press, 1969), pp. 137–38; Charlotte Miller, "The Function of Middle-Class Extended Family Networks in Brazilian Urban Society," in *Brazil*, ed. Maxine L. Margolis and William E. Carter (New York: Columbia University Press, 1979), pp. 305–15; and Antônio Candido, *Os parceiros do Rio Bonito* (Rio de Janeiro: José Olýmpio Editôra, 1964), pp. 184–209.

zation throughout Brazil.[10] By 1910, the Paraíba oligarchy was making a transition in its reliance on a family-based system of politics. This evolutionary shift is relevant to changing patterns of political organization in other Brazilian states, even where the historical reliance on kinship and family already had eroded more rapidly than in Paraíba.

It is important to apprehend that Paraíba's organization was not exclusively grounded in family ties of membership, but rather family-*based*. In other words, informal ties of oligarchical association were based on political friendship as well as on kinship. Both types of associational ties wove crucial institutional and personal connections into a single political web that insured oligarchy's survival. This is why the term "family-based group" is preferred to "elite family" when this study discusses the units of oligarchical mobilization. By the advent of the Republic, family ties alone could not provide an adequate nexus for local political organization and mobilization. Even earlier, ties of kinship had ceased to be relied upon as narrowly as they had been for securing an elite parentela's vital interests, and indeed, they never had been the exclusive connecting bonds in politics that the term "family system of politics" connotes in the anthropological literature.[11] By the ar-

[10] On the historical importance of kinship and family for Brazilian society, see Stuart Schwartz, *Sovereignty and Society in Colonial Brazil* (Berkeley and Los Angeles: University of California Press, 1973); Eni de Mesquita Samara, "A família na sociedade paulista do século XIX (1800–1860)" (Ph.D. diss., University of São Paulo, 1980); idem, "Uma contribuição ao estudo da estrutura familiar em São Paulo durante o período colonial: A família agregada em Itú de 1780 a 1830," *Revista de História* [São Paulo] 105 (1976):33–45; Donald Ramos, "Marriage and the Family in Colonial Vila Rica," *Hispanic American Historical Review* (henceforth, *HAHR*) 55 (May 1975):200–225; Maria Luiza Marcílio, *A cidade de São Paulo: Povoamento e população, 1750–1850* (São Paulo: Livraria Pioneira Editôra, 1974); Luís de Aguiar Costa Pinto, *Lutas de família no Brasil* (São Paulo: Cia. Editôra Nacional, 1949); Caio Prado Junior, *The Colonial Background of Modern Brazil*, trans. Suzette Macedo (Berkeley and Los Angeles: University of California Press, 1969), pp. 410–11; and Alcântara Machado, *Vida e morte do bandeirante* (São Paulo: Editôra Itatiaia, 1980); Gilberto Freyre, "The Patriarchal Basis of Brazilian Society," in *Politics of Change*, ed. Maier and Weatherhead, pp. 155–70.

[11] Darrell E. Levi, *A família Prado* (São Paulo: Livraria Editôra, 1977), pp. 62–66; John Wirth, *Minas Gerais in the Brazilian Federation, 1889–1937* (Stanford: Stanford University Press, 1977), pp. 67–76; Fernando Uricoechea, *The Patrimonial Foundations of the Brazilian Bureaucratic State* (Berkeley and Los Angeles: University of California Press, 1980), pp. 57–58; Nestor Duarte, *A ordem privada e a organização política nacional*, 2nd ed., Brasiliana 172 (São Paulo: Cia. Editôra Nacional, 1939), pp. 70–71; Billy Jaynes Chandler, *The Feitosas and the Sertão dos Inhamuns* (Gainesville: University Presses of Florida, 1972), pp. 77–78.

rival of the Republic dependence on kinship in politics had lessened markedly.

In analyzing the historical relationship between kinship and politics in Paraíba, this book poses two broad sets of questions. The first set concerns the pattern of connections between kinship organization and political organization within the state oligarchy. Its purpose is largely descriptive, for the questions seek to illuminate the oligarchy's family and factional divisions, detailing the process of family-based politics as it was revealed in the formal institutions of local, state, and national government. By what means and for what motives did family-based groups mobilize in politics? How did the state oligarchy's party boss devise a strategy for forming a winning coalition? What were the cohesive and fragmenting consequences of kinship divisions for oligarchical politics? In connection with the last question, how did matrimonial patterns reflect the concerns of political organization? Finally, how did family-based politics span the local, state, and federal levels of government?

The second set of questions assesses changes in the kin and family base of political organization in Paraíba. The answers offer readers conclusions about the relationship of kinship and family to politics over time in Paraíba, but they hold implications for Brazil at large. They also suggest why family-based politics endured longer in regions such as the Brazilian Northeast than in the Center-South, raising implicit comparisons with the organization of other state oligarchies in Brazil. Analysis connects changes in elite family organization in Brazil with changes in the wider society. Because the central organizational change in the elite extended family after mid-century concerned preferred matrimonial patterns, that associative bond is scrutinized: What were the political implications of preferred patterns of consanguineous marriage? What were the limits of their political utility and why did they yield to a greater reliance on exogamous bonding by the close of the last century? How did the shift away from endogamy reflect political, economic, and social change in the wider society? Historical change affected not only the elite family's matrimonial strategies but also the group basis of the wider society. The second set of questions therefore attempts to elucidate at what point and why reliance on kinship ties for group affiliation in politics weakened, due to either competition from new groups or simply the family-based group's failure to represent a particular interest.

In addressing these sets of questions, this book adopts a thematic format that emphasizes the state oligarchy's organization as a family-based system of politics. Chapters are grouped into three parts: Political Economy, the Politics of Parentela, and Oligarchical Politics. This organization corresponds roughly to oligarchy's economic, social, and political dimensions. Such a framework avoids excessive historical narrative devoted to Paraíba and permits analytical focus on the history of the state oligarchy. The major thread throughout is the Pessoa oligarchy's rise to political power and its eventual demise. However, Parts One and Two pursue the evolution of oligarchical power in Paraíba more broadly.

Part One examines the oligarchy as an economic elite within the state's political economy over the long run. It describes the historical structures that accounted for perpetuation of family-based power from the earliest conquest and settlement in the sixteenth and seventeenth centuries and the eighteenth-century emergence of the cotton export economy so crucial to the rise of the Pessoa oligarchy. Part Two approaches oligarchy as a social elite and places it within Brazilian kinship organization. The informal group basis of oligarchical organization is discussed and major attention is paid to the central concepts of the family-based group and the family-based network. In Part Three, oligarchical politics is considered largely in terms of Epitácio's efforts to construct a successful political machine in Paraíba. Narrative discussion seeks to integrate the conclusions offered in Parts One and Two with an appraisal of the formal political system's institutional linkages between local, state, and federal levels of government. Thus, it offers a concluding view of oligarchical politics as a convergence of informal and formal systems of power.

From the broadest perspective, this case study treats issues related to politics and parentela raised earlier by Brazilian scholars concerned with either the evolution of "the great families" as political entities or the emergence of a strong, centralizing State. Specifically, it pushes further a number of points raised by the political sociologists or historians Nestor Duarte, Oliveira Vianna, Costa Pinto, Nunes Leal, and Caio Prado Junior, examining their arguments from the vantage point of an empirical case study.[12]

[12] Duarte, *Ordem privada*, pp. 70–71; [Francisco José de] Oliveira Vianna, *Instituições políticas brasileiras*, 2 vols. (Rio de Janeiro: José Olýmpio Editôra, 1955), 1:259–60; Costa Pinto, *Lutas de família*, pp. 25–33; Vitor Nunes Leal, *Corone-*

However, it pays more attention to the changing role of kinship organization within oligarchical politics, in both the late Empire and the Old Republic. Because the pattern of kinship organization among Paraíba's elite extended families was universally distributed in Brazil, the empirical data surveyed here were representative of a cluster of important features that shaped elite family organization throughout the nation. Consequently, while regional differences imposed important variations on kinship organization, the process of long-term change this case study details was by no means unique to Paraíba or even the Northeast.

It is tempting, as Costa Pinto observed, to regard many of the patterns described in this book as "an archeological diagram of Brazilian society that preserved in stagnation the early forms of social life" in colonial Brazil.[13] But such an assumption would miscast the nature of the problem. Instead, one would do better to heed the caveat laid down by Vitor Nunes Leal at the beginning of his classic study of coronelismo (the Brazilian term used to describe local boss rule). The structural underpinnings of coronelismo, he warned, were not fossils of the colonial past buried within the Old Republic. On the contrary, coronelismo, with its family base of power—as the local-level expression of oligarchy—was an amalgam of a recently imposed "representative regime resting on a backward [*inadecuada*] socioeconomic structure."[14] Because this book shares Nunes Leal's conviction of the importance of the more immediate past of the Second Empire for understanding historical change during the Old Republic, brief comment about the meaning of oligarchy and the nature of political organization during the Empire is necessary. The varieties of oligarchy that characterized Brazil's political organization during the Old Republic possessed in common their dependence on a federal system of government that in important respects contrasted with the preceding Empire's system of rule.

---

lismo, enxada e voto, 2nd ed. (São Paulo: Editôra Alfa-Omega, 1975), pp. 19-57. Caio Prado, *Colonial Background*, pp. 410–11. In addition, two classic articles by anthropologists guided the initial research: Emílio Willems, "The Structure of the Brazilian Family," *Social Forces* 31, 4 (1953):339–45; and Antônio Candido, "The Brazilian Family," in *Brazil*, ed. T. Lynn Smith and Alexander Marchant (New York: The Dryden Press, 1951), pp. 291–312.

[13] Costa Pinto, *Lutas de família*, p. 34. See also Oliveira Vianna, *Instituições políticas*, 1:24–50 and 326.

[14] Nunes Leal, *Coronelismo*, p. 20.

Oligarchy in Brazil

The Imperial Background

Historians have compared the centralization of the Second Empire (1840 to 1889) favorably with the politically decentralized Old Republic that followed. From the time the fourteen-year-old Dom Pedro II assumed his majority, in 1840, the Second Empire witnessed significant national consolidation under a sole emperor. The sovereign, as a constitutional monarch, enjoyed considerable authority, by virtue of the Moderating Power, which enabled him to dismiss the bicameral legislature and call new elections for the House of Deputies. The Senate consisted of his appointees, who served for life. Particularly following the national crisis of the War with Paraguay, from 1865 to 1870, he employed the Moderating Power in ways that contradicted parliamentary rule based on majoritarian consensus. While such a trend fueled the criticism that eventually led to his abdication, it also indicated the monarchy's potential for centralization, one even more evident in its military suppression of regional revolt. The emperor's power of appointment extended to naming the provincial governors and imperial district judges (*juíz de direito*) for the national judiciary. By rotating appointees recruited from a national pool of career administrators and magistrates, the monarchy sought to curb the local interests of familialism and personalism. Provincial governors therefore experienced frequent transfers, and the key national official in município politics—the imperial district judge—often found himself an outsider among the local politicians of his judicial district.[15]

An electoral system was introduced in 1835 for both the provincial assemblies and the House of Deputies. The fact that suffrage was extremely restricted helps to explain the higher degree of administrative and political centralization before 1889 than af-

[15] On state-building and the elaboration of a national bureaucracy over the long run, see Duarte, *Ordem privada*, pp. 125–26; João Camilo de Oliveira Torres, *A democracia coroada; teoria política do Imperio do Brasil*. 2nd ed. rev. (Petrópolis: Editôra Vozes, 1963), pp. 379–98; Raimundo Faoro, *Os donos do poder*, 2 vols. (São Paulo: Editôra Globo/Editôra do USP, 1975), 2:621–22; and José Murillo de Carvalho: "Barbacena: A família, a política e uma hipótese," *Revista Brasileira de Estudos Políticos* 20 (Jan. 1966):153–94; idem, "Elite and State-Building in Imperial Brazil" (Ph.D. diss., Stanford University, 1974), esp. chs. 6–8.

terward. During the Empire, a more restricted electorate also meant that the political parties had greater capacity for controlling elections. Relatively speaking, the electorate tended to be those who were better off—the more substantial property owners and those with sizable incomes. The fact that elections were indirect, based on a system of electors chosen by voters, also made electoral outcomes more susceptible to control by either of the two national parties. The emergence of Conservative and Liberal Parties at national, provincial, and município levels of government by 1840 contributed to national consolidation in the late Empire. During the 1870s, the appearance of a Republican Party complicated politics, but the fact that it did not become a national party meant that a bipartisan division and significant political cohesion prevailed.[16]

Two other national institutions, the military and the civil service, reinforced the monarchy's central authority. Although the army emerged after the War with Paraguay as a major political actor nationally—a role retained during the Old Republic—its personnel and resources were never sufficient to police Brazil's vast hinterland. However, the emperor could use it to impose central political authority where regional revolt or unrest threatened the State's power. The 1824 Constitution granted him the right to occupy militarily any part of the country. The creation of a civil administration in the 1840s directly reflected the monarchy's aim of undercutting deeply entrenched localism in the municípios and instituting compliance with the central government's laws and edicts. In the absence of a sufficient military presence in the provinces, however, a locally recruited National Guard was created in 1831 to strengthen the central power by complementing the authority of the civil service.[17] This arrangement was, as a number of scholars have recognized, a compromise, for the National Guard depended on the local landowners to serve as its officer corps and recruit the rank and file. It thus strengthened the police power in

[16] Voter registration in the Empire required an annual liquid income of 200 mil réis until 1881, when the Saraiva Law raised the minimum amount to 400 mil réis. The same law abolished indirect elections, which previously had not required voters—only electors—to demonstrate literacy. Henceforth, literacy was mandatory for registering to vote. In 1872, with a population of 8.9 million (of whom 1.5 million were literate), Brazil had 1,089,659 registered voters and 20,006 electors. Faoro, *Donos do poder*, 1:374 and 2:756.

[17] Uricoechea, *Patrimonial Foundations*, pp. 57, 268; Faoro, *Donos do poder*, 2:621–22 and 736–37.

the municípios on behalf of local interests. Yet, in joining and leading the National Guard, powerholders in município politics also accepted a national bureaucracy, however tenuous its presence. Hence the importance of the emperor's imperial district judge, whose decisions the National Guard was expected to enforce. As an outsider, supposedly without local kin and family ties, he was charged with the responsibility of upholding imperial law and overruling the localistic interests of the family blocs controlling the municípios in his district. In reality, however, his decisions reflected yet another compromise between conflicting local and national interests.[18]

Oligarchy, although directly associated with the Old Republic, emerged in the Second Empire.[19] As Oliveira Vianna correctly perceived, it resulted from the wedding of a national electoral system with what he called "extended family clans" (*clãs parentais*), which had, by the close of the colonial period, expanded aggressively "like oil stains," absorbing rural society's great landed estates and their dependent client populations.[20] The emergence of political parties in the 1840s pushed powerful extended families into the public sphere of the município, transforming "extended clans" into "electoral clans."[21] "Like the Lins of (Pilar) Paraíba," he noted, the great families began to encompass entire municípios and became "the major segments" of the national political parties at the local level.[22] The intermingling of public and private power, due to the expansion of both elected offices and the civil service, led to the widespread phenomenon of "*empreguismo*," or nepotistic control of public office and employment by ruling elite families.[23]

Although oligarchy emerged where the national parties re-

[18] On the coexistence of private, family motives and a "rational" bureaucracy in the Empire, see Thomas Flory, *Judge and Jury in Imperial Brazil, 1808–1871* (Austin: University of Texas Press, 1981), p. 194; in more recent times, see Simon Schwartzman, "Back to Weber: Corporatism and Patrimonialism in the Seventies," in *Authoritarianism and Corporatism*, ed. James M. Malloy (Pittsburgh: University of Pittsburgh Press, 1977), pp. 19–20.

[19] Oliveira Vianna, *Instituições políticas*, 1:332–40.

[20] Ibid., 1:271. The *clã parental* referred to an extended family distributed over many households and properties whose members were related by blood, marriage, and fictive kinship (1:299). Its meaning was identical with the use of "parentela" and "extended family" in this book.

[21] Ibid., 1:271–300.

[22] Ibid., 1:332–40.

[23] Nunes Leal, *Coronelismo*, pp. 38–39, 43(n. 45).

mained only superficially implanted, its local manifestation of coronelismo was universally distributed throughout Brazil. Thus, the local party boss, very often a *coronel* (colonel) in the National Guard, functioned locally as the crucial broker between elite family interests and the national government.[24]

Oligarchy in the Old Republic

Constitutional changes introduced in the Old Republic, however, explained the crystallization of oligarchy as a national system of rule.[25] By rewriting the rules of electoral politics, taxation, and the police power, the framers of the 1891 Constitution restructured the national polity in accordance with federal principles. Because the regional interest of the State of São Paulo provided the impetus for the *coup d'état* that ended the monarchy, it is not surprising that Brazil's subsequent organization reflected a centripetal shift, one placing the economic interests of the wealthiest states before the broader interest of a national economy. Consequently, the 1891 Constitution stripped the national government of much of its power to tax, leaving to the states the revenues produced by export taxes and granting them the right to contract foreign loans independently of the federal government. Thanks to this provision, the federal army was matched in size by the collective police forces of the states. As late as 1932, the wealthiest state, São Paulo,

[24] "We conceive of coronelismo as, above all, a compromise, an exchange of advantages between public power, progressively envigorated, and the decadent social influence of the local bosses, particularly the landowners." Nunes Leal, *Coronelismo,* p. 20. "Besides being an economic group, the parentela was a political group whose internal solidarity guaranteed the loyalty of its members to their chieftains." Maria Isaura Pereira de Queiroz, *O mandonismo local na vida política brasileira e outros ensaios*, 2nd ed. (São Paulo: Editôra Alfa-Omega, 1976), p. 179. "A big coronel generally was also the head of a parentela, and, consequently, its apex . . ." ibid., p. 183.

[25] In this respect, Paul Cammack's recent criticism of Nunes Leal for conceiving of the landowning coronel as primarily a politician and the rural population as an electorate has missed the central importance of the issue that Nunes Leal placed at the heart of his study: the long-term nature of município government vis-à-vis the changing role of the State in the national political system. "O 'coronelismo' e o 'compromisso coronelista': Uma crítica," *Cadernos DCP* [Universidade Federal de Minas Gerais, Faculdade de Filosofia e Ciências Humanas] 5 (Mar. 1979):10. See the excellent refutation offered by Amilcar Martins Filho: "Clientelismo e representação em Minas Gerais durante a Primeira República: Uma crítica a Paul Cammack," *Revista de Ciências Sociais* [Rio de Janeiro] 27, no. 2 (1984):175–97, esp. pp. 187–88. The author is grateful to Joseph L. Love for bringing the latter article to her attention.

possessed sufficient military capacity to challenge the federal government by armed revolt—and nearly succeeded in defeating the national army. Although the Constitution conferred on the president the right to intervene militarily in a state and to replace its governor with his interventor, throughout the Old Republic the federal government played such a role only in weaker states.

The collapse of the national parties following the emperor's abdication led to a partisan vacuum that was never filled during the Old Republic. What President Campos Sales called "the politics of the states"—and what has been known subsequently as "the politics of the governors"—attempted to counterpose a national executive envigorated through extraconstitutional means, to the extreme federalism mandated by the Constitution of 1891.[26] Although the politics of the governors did enable the president to discipline the oligarchies of the weaker states, it enhanced decentralization at the state and município levels because it accorded state governors wide latitude of action in the purely internal affairs of their states. At least until the second half of the Old Republic, when the national government began to play a larger role in state politics, both constitutional and extraconstitutional arrangements explained why the Old Republic became synonymous with the era of the oligarchies.

In referring to the Old Republic as the era of the oligarchies, historians had in mind the state oligarchies whose political parties determined the outcome of national politics. The tightly organized oligarchical elites who controlled the state parties dominated the electoral process in Brazil by virtue of their delivery of votes to the national presidential machine. Prior to 1910, national politics directly reflected the undisputed leadership of the two most powerful states in Brazil, São Paulo and Minas Gerais. In that election year, however, the southernmost state, Rio Grande do Sul, challenged their control over nomination of the winning presidential candidate. São Paulo and Minas continued to rotate the Brazilian presidency between them, but thereafter they were obliged to admit Rio Grande do Sul directly into their nomination deliberations. Rio Grande do Sul could now cast a swing vote, were either of the other two to veto a candidate. Politicians referred to this informal arrangement, a "gentleman's agreement" among states, by the term "the politics of *café com leite*" (*café au lait*) in recogni-

[26] The genesis of the politics of the governors is discussed in Chapter V, in connection with the role the Paraíba oligarchy played in its enunciation.

tion of São Paulo and Minas as coffee and dairy states respectively. The pact continued unbroken until the 1930 election, when São Paulo refused to accept the candidate of both Minas and Rio Grande do Sul, Riograndense Governor Getúlio Vargas. By insisting that outgoing President Washington Luis, a Paulista, should be followed in the presidency by yet another Paulista, Júlio Prestes, São Paulo provoked the national crisis that precipitated the Revolution of 1930.[27]

Throughout the Old Republic, national politics focused every four years on construction of a winning presidential coalition for the November elections. In the absence of true political parties at the national level, every winning coalition had to be forged anew from a majority of the state oligarchies and their official parties. Consequently, once every four years the three most powerful states extracted electoral support from the other seventeen for nomination of the candidate who enjoyed the outgoing president's backing.[28] The "oligarchies" that indirectly governed Brazil during the Old Republic therefore consisted of the small group of men who monopolized political office in each state, normally the governor and elected representatives to Congress and the state legislature. (Paraíba was one of the two states with a unicameral legislature. Elsewhere, states had a senate and a house of deputies.) The local powerholders, from whom the party bosses were recruited at the município level, were the lowest rung of the oligarchical ladder and bore responsibility for delivering the vote.

[27] On the political history of the Old Republic, see José Maria Bello, *História da República*, 3rd ed., rev. and exp. (São Paulo: Cia. Editôra Nacional, 1956); and Edgard Carone, *A República Velha (Instituições e classes sociais)* (São Paulo: Diffusão Européia, 1970); idem, *A Primeira República (1889–1930): Texto e contexto* (São Paulo: Diffusão Européia, 1969). On oligarchical politics in specific states, see Eul-Soo Pang, *Bahia in the First Brazilian Republic* (Gainesville: University Presses of Florida, 1979); Ralph Della Cava, *Miracle at Joaseiro* (New York: Columbia University Press, 1970); and the series on Brazilian regionalism published by Stanford University Press: Joseph L. Love, *Rio Grande do Sul and Brazilian Regionalism* (1971); idem, *São Paulo in the Brazilian Federation, 1889–1937* (1980); John D. Wirth, *Minas Gerais in the Brazilian Federation, 1889–1937* (1977); and Robert M. Levine, *Pernambuco in the Brazilian Federation, 1889–1937* (1978).

[28] According to President Campos Sales, "true political power" resided in the states, not in a national party system. [Manoel Ferraz de] Campos Salles, *Da propaganda à presidencia* (São Paulo: n.p., 1908), p. 352. The Federal Republican Party, or PRF (Partido Republicano Federal), the major but abortive attempt to form a national party prior to 1910, he termed "a large aggregation of antagonistic elements" (p. 234). It lacked "all the essential elements of a well-constituted party: uniformity of doctrine, leadership, and a national orientation" (p. 230).

Any oligarchy's leadership clique could be readily identified, for it consisted of men who directed the official party of their state. Almost invariably, the latter was known by a label affixing the name of the state to a variation of "Republican Party," although no national Republican party formally survived throughout the Old Republic. Beginning in 1892, Paraíba's Machado–Leal oligarchy controlled the Paraíba Republican Party, or PRP (Partido Republicano Paraibano). In 1917, after Epitácio succeeded to its direction, he changed the name to the Republican Party of Paraíba, or PR do P (Partido Republicano do Paraíba) to distinguish his own factional coalition from the one formed by his predecessor. Theoretically, the official state party, which signified the party of the incumbent coalition recognized by the president of Brazil, could deliver the state's vote to whichever candidate it chose, and hence, considerable bargaining for votes occurred between the president of Brazil and the state oligarchies, whose leadership occupied seats in the Senate and the House of Deputies. Commitments of federal resources for the states were routinely extracted. Patronage was vital to the oligarchies because it gave them immense economic leverage in their respective states.[29] Typically, oligarchy's economic roots lay in the agrarian export economy, although the commercial sector in many states also exercised significant political influence.

The oligarchy's political identity also derived fundamentally from yet another connotation of the term. "Oligarchy," as the Old Republic's most knowledgeable historian has emphasized, implied more than an identity as a political or an economic elite: "to the original meaning of the term . . . 'government by the few' can be added a more specific connotation in the Brazilian context: Government based on the patriarchal family structure."[30] Whether, in fact, oligarchy always rested on a patriarchal base of family power is a question raised by this case study; however, the notion that family power played an integral role in the Old Republic's oligarchical organization is basic to the scholarly literature.

Sílvio Romero, the distinguished intellectual, historian, and po-

[29] Campos Sales justified the implementation of his "politics of the governors" on the grounds that true political parties did not exist: "I did not destroy the parties because they had not existed, nor did I concern myself with their formation because I did not find evident the elements I deemed indispensable [for their formation]." *Propaganda à presidencia*, p. 263.

[30] Carone, *República Velha*, p. 267. "Every state had its owner, a person or a family or a closed group" (Faoro, *Donos do poder*, 2:568).

litical pundit of the Old Republic, summed up, in 1910, oligarchy's organizational dependence on a family base that interwove kin relationships with those of clientage: "The truth is we are divided into clans [*clãs*] with their masters [*donos*], into groups [*grupos*] with their chieftains [*chefes*], into bands [*bandos*] with their headmen [*cabecilhas*]: Politically, socially, economically, that is the general spectacle Brazil presents."[31]

Romero erred in dissecting the root causes of Brazilian oligarchy, but his insistence that its characteristics were responsible for what he deplored as Brazil's "disunity" was not wide of the mark. For many of his contemporaries as well, so-called "clan" organization explained the unsavory and retrograde aspects of Brazilian politics: "the nepotism, the denial of justice, the disregard for the legal rights of political adversaries, the oppression of political opponents, the malfeasance of all types, the siphoning off of the public revenues, the poverty of entire populations . . . and the simulacrity of elections made fraudulently."[32]

In criticizing oligarchy's operational style, Romero likened Brazil to a "mastodon divided into twenty pieces" and attacked its formation "as a collection of true clans of several types." The dependence of politics on kinship led, he asserted, to relations of clientage that disposed "all of them to live under a boss [*chefe*], a patron, a protector, a guide—everyone has 'his man'!"[33]

Varieties of Oligarchy

Romero was the first to refer to "modalities" of oligarchy in Brazil and subsequent commentators have retained his emphasis on oligarchy's grounding in familial or personalistic ties, even if they have discarded his reliance on a continuum of greater to lesser dependence on ties of kinship and clientism.[34] More recently, typologies of oligarchy have tended to be connected to variations in either regional and subregional economies or, secondarily, to the organization of a state's political party: according to Edgard Ca-

[31] Sylvio Romero, "As oligarchias e sua classificação," in *Provocações e debates* (Porto: Livraria Chardron de Lello & Irmãos, 1910), p. 410. The Portuguese terms retained in brackets suggest the kinship flavor of contemporary political vocabulary that Romero wanted to emphasize.

[32] Ibid., p. 407.

[33] Idem, "As zonas sociais e a situação do povo," in *Provocações*, p. 222.

[34] Idem, "Oligarchias," p. 412. More recently, Eul-Soo Pang has proposed four oligarchical categories for the Old Republic that also reflect a continuum along family lines: familiocratic, tribal, collegial, and personalistic. *Bahia*, pp. 19–25.

rone, whose assessment is the best, a "geography of oligarchy" existed during the Old Republic that associated specific regions and subregions of Brazil with a high reliance on either family or kinship ties or an "impermeable group" based on personalistic ties. Family-based oligarchies, consequently, were to be found in Brazil's most underdeveloped regions: in the "less wealthy states the control of one group or family was almost absolute."[35]

Regional disparities in wealth came clearly into focus during the Old Republic. In fact, only in the era of the oligarchies did Paraíba and its five neighbors acquire a regional identity as "the Northeast." By the close of the nineteenth century, the widespread benefits of urbanization and industrialization began to appear in the Center-South—what in northeastern speech was referred to as "the South." The gap between states in the latter region and the Northeast widened as the twentieth century progressed.[36] Drastic contrasts in living standards did not go unnoticed by the members of Paraíba's oligarchy when they journeyed to Rio de Janeiro to take their seats in the national legislature. By the early twentieth century, northeastern politicians saw the regional disparity in wealth and the poverty of their states as political issues.

In the geography of oligarchy, extreme underdevelopment and poverty were associated with exercise of a near monopoly by one or several families. This pattern embraced the largest number of states. In the northern and western states of the Amazon Basin, where open frontiers, large estates, and a dispersed population characterized human settlement, central authority tended to be

[35] Carone, *República Velha*, p. 275. "The geography of oligarchy showed itself all over Brazil."

[36] Brazil's literacy rate of 16 per cent, for instance, had been virtually at a standstill from 1872 to 1890. But by 1920 it had jumped to 25 per cent. In Paraíba, however, literacy rose only from 11 per cent in 1872 to 13 per cent in 1920, the second lowest rate in Brazil. Infant mortality rates have a similar pattern. The 1920 Census showed that in the nation's Federal District (Rio de Janeiro) infant deaths had fallen to 154 per thousand, while in Paraíba's capital they stood at 217, well in excess of the national rate of 175 (Brazil, Ministerio da Agricultura, Industria e Commercio, Directoria Geral de Estatistica, *Recenseamento do Brazil realizado em 1 de setembro de 1920*, vols. 1–5 in 17 vols. [Rio de Janeiro: Typografia de Estatistica, 1922–1928], vol. 4, pt. 2, pp. xlvi–lii). An absence of urban improvements suggested the growing disparity between the Northeast and the Center-South. In 1922, for instance, only 5 per cent of the households in Paraíba's capital had indoor sanitary facilities ; 85 per cent still used oil or kerosene for illumination, and the average inhabitant lived in a mud house with a straw roof, for only 12,000 of the city's 63,000 residents lived within walls of brick roofed with tile (José Joffily, *Revolta e revolução: Cinqüenta anos depois* [São Paulo: Paz e Terra, 1979], pp. 135–36).

intermittent at best. Geography enhanced the political decentralization of the Old Republic. Not surprisingly, the economic roots of these so-called political clans lay in the landed economy. In Amazonas, the Nery family's domination rose to legendary proportions; in Mato Grosso rival families disputed political control for decades; and in Pará, Antônio Lemos and his relatives governed.[37]

In the Northeast, where local family bases of power had been implanted in the patterns of settlement dictated by motives of early exploration as well as Crown policy, virtually every state political party was associated with either the rule of one family or one individual's personalistic domination. Consequently, the state of Rio Grande do Norte adjoining Paraíba had its Pedro Velho, while the state of Alagoas was synonymous with the Malta family; and Paraíba was identified with "the iron rule of the Machados, reigning successors to the Neivas."[38] In Ceará, the control of the Acioli family was so ubiquitous, Carone pointed out, that Sílvio Romero facetiously coined the term "Aciolismo" to describe his modality of family oligarchy.[39]

The Aciolis exercised power in Ceará through their political machine, the Republican Party of Ceará, the PRC (Partido Republicano Cearense). As Carone and other commentators have pointed out, the nature of the Aciolis' party organization made them the "classic case of family domination."[40] They staffed the PRC with either members of their own family or persons who enjoyed the Aciolis' "highest confidence." Like all family-based oligarchies, they relied on two pillars of institutional support: opportunistic reform of electoral law and federal intervention on their behalf. Through rewriting electoral laws that prohibited reelection of the same individual to the same office, they monopolized key public office; through appeal to the police power of the federal government, they secured their position against local armed op-

[37] Carone associated Brazilian oligarchy with specific, regional export crops: latex (Amazonas), sugar (the Northeast), stockraising (western São Paulo), coffee (Paraíba Valley of Rio de Janeiro), maté (Mato Grosso and Paraná), and cacao (Bahia). Ibid., p. 152.

[38] Romero, "Oligarchias," p. 414.

[39] " '*Aciolismo oikoarquico*' was the most widespread type of oligarchy in Brazil" (ibid., p. 413). Familialistic and personalistic oligarchies together were the political organization of the majority of states for Carone as well. *República Velha*, pp. 274–75.

[40] Carone, *República Velha*, p. 275. See Della Cava, *Miracle Joaseiro*, for a detailed study of the Aciolis' downfall in Ceará.

position. And by resorting to election-rigging, they validated their public authority as well as fulfilled their pact to deliver the vote to the national presidential machine. Thus, the PRC became synonymous with their family name and interests.[41]

Paraíba's oligarchy reflected a blend of strong personalistic loyalties and familial recruitment and mobilization. Organizationally, it more resembled Ceará than Pernambuco. The changing nomenclature by which the public referred to the Paraíba oligarchy over the forty-year era of the Old Republic illustrated this blending. The Neiva–Lucena oligarchy assumed control of Paraíba when the national government named Venâncio Neiva governor in 1889. Venâncio's oligarchy was referred to as the Neiva–Lucena oligarchy because his brother was married to a sister of the Baron of Lucena, a minister in the new republican government. Because the baron's nephew, Epitácio Pessoa, served as Venâncio's secretary and a federal deputy, their successors referred to their brief administration as the Neiva–Lucena–*Pessoa* oligarchy. Only the opposition employed the term "oligarchy" to describe the coalition in power; the incumbents routinely denied they were an oligarchy and referred to their predecessors—if the opposition had previously controlled the state government—as an oligarchy.

The oligarchy that followed Venâncio reflected fewer ties of kinship at its highest level. Álvaro Lopes Machado led the Paraíba oligarchy from 1892 to 1912, in tandem with Monsig. Valfredo dos Santos Leal, a nonkinsman. They illustrated a partnership based on political friendship, what Sílvio Romero would call "friendly groupism."[42] Both came from Areia, both had belonged to the former Liberal Party, and their family backgrounds were closely connected. The Machado–Leal oligarchy included Alvaristas and Valfredistas, just as their opposition embraced Venancistas and Epitacistas. Partisan designations, in other words, confirmed the personalistic character of political affiliations.

In 1908, Epitácio and Venâncio struck a strategic bargain with Álvaro for representation, and the Paraíba oligarchy occasionally was even referred to as the "Machado–Pessoa–Leal" oligarchy. By 1911, the Machado–Leal oligarchy's days were numbered. Following Álvaro's sudden death in 1912, his name remained attached to the oligarchy only briefly, by virtue of a claim put forward by his

[41] Carone, *República Velha*, pp. 269, 272.

[42] Romero, "Oligarchias," p. 414. "Friendly groupism" was for Romero an alternative designation for a "semi-familial" oligarchy, which others have called "personalistic."

younger brother, Sen. João Lopes Machado. Once Valfredo and Epitácio withdrew their support from João Machado and his "Machadista" faction, each alignment schemed independently to capture political leadership. For a short time, the incumbents were identified solely as the Machado oligarchy. But, when Epitácio definitively assumed leadership in 1912, the "Neiva–Pessoa" oligarchy reappeared. Because Venâncio had already receded to a subordinate position, the "Pessoa oligarchy" soon became the preferred designation used by the opposition.

Although intermarried Neivas, Lucenas, and Pessoas formed the Paraíba oligarchy's leadership level, it was in its broader membership that the family base was evident. The leadership echelon was connected to the oligarchy's rank and file by two basic units of oligarchical organization: the family-based group and the family-based network. The first was the fundamental unit of the informal political system, and it originated at the lowest level, the município.[43] The membership core of the family-based group derived from a politician's extended family or parentela but was not perfectly congruent with it. Due to residence patterns associating specific branches of a parentela with the same or adjoining municípios, the family-based group also carried a spatial connotation. The inner core of this unit of political recruitment and mobilization contained the closest kinsmen of its politician-head: his brothers, sisters' husbands, his wife's brothers, his wife's sisters' husbands, and his father, uncles, and nephews. It also included political friends who had long been loyal to the leader, conferring on them quasi-kin status. Epitácio's family-based group managed his home município of Umbuseiro, where he had been born. He visited Paraíba only three times after 1910 and never returned to Umbuseiro. This very successful politician's family-based group governed his home município although he never resided there, a common pattern for officeholders at the federal level. On the other hand, even in 1920, the majority of the state assemblymen still resided in their home municípios for most of the year.

[43] "Family-based group" is not to be equated with *grupo*, used in Portuguese to designate a faction, not a group. (*Fação*, also faction, was used very rarely.) Factions consisted of at least several family-based groups. The term "family-based" avoids confusion with what in the anthropological literature is a system of "family rule," i.e., one relying exclusively on the kin group for recruitment and mobilization in politics. Thus it is incorrect to refer to Paraíba's form of political organization during the Old Republic as a "family oligarchy" or as a "family system of rule," since it depended on indispensable nonkin relationships to function.

Any faction (*grupo*, and only rarely, *façāo*) worthy of the name depended on several family-based groups. Often, ties of marriage connected them. Epitácio's faction, for instance, drew on the Pessoas and their political friends in Umbuseiro, such as the Lucenas, Cavalcanti de Albuquerques, Barbosas, Neivas, and Pereiras, who enjoyed more distant kinship with him and each other. The ruling oligarchy, in other words, was no more than a coalition (*agglomeração*) of several factions. Each was identified by the personal name of its leader, in adjectival form. This strongly familial cast to factions explained their organizational vulnerability, because segments were susceptible to realignments.

A more complex unit, the family-based network, held together individual factions and factional coalitions. It derived from the kinship ties that cemented various family-based groups to produce a ruling factional coalition. By spanning different levels of government, family-based networks offered the political ligatures binding the ruling oligarchy together. In addition, family-based networks bound the oligarchy's leadership stratum to family-based groups in the municípios. In contrast to family-based groups, which appeared at the state level as discrete units, networks were unbounded. They therefore linked local, state, and federal levels to government in a common social field. They also served as channels of communication between individuals at complementary levels of government. Finally, a family-based network possessed a core membership of kin, but was also valuable for crucial members who were nonkin.[44]

Although the scholarly literature about kinship and politics leaves many questions unanswered, Paraíba's model of organization appears to have been typical for the Northeast of Brazil and similar to most other extremely underdeveloped states. While variations arose in the degree of familialism or personalism that any state oligarchy reflected, a conservative count of the twenty state oligarchies governing Brazil in the Old Republic revealed that at least ten were organized much the way Paraíba was.[45] All

[44] This concept of network draws on J. A. Barnes's analysis. The family-based network, as employed in this book, is very close to what he distinguishes as a "partial network," i.e., an extract of a total network such as "an easily identifiable cognatic web of kinship." "Networks and Political Process," in *Local-Level Politics*, ed. Marc J. Swartz (Chicago: Aldine Publishing Co., 1968), pp. 111–12.

[45] The standard list of familial oligarchies during the Old Republic included Rio Grande do Norte (Pedro Velho), Alagoas (the Maltas), Paraíba (Neiva–Pessoas and Machados), Maranhão (the Leites), Pará (the Lemos or Montenegros), Ceará (the

tended to be rural and oriented around simple, usually monocrop, export economies. Their social structures were highly stratified, predominantly along vertical lines, not the horizontal ones of class. The state governments that these oligarchies directed lacked the material resources to impose political authority throughout their territories. Not surprisingly, group formation remained very limited, if nonexistent, during the first decades of the Old Republic. The simplicity of economic arrangements and the rigidity of the social structure, in addition to the strength of the already entrenched family-based groups, accounted for the slow emergence of formally organized groups. Furthermore, political culture forestalled the appearance of more functionally specific groups because it reinforced the corporate bonds of family, clientism, the church, and the military.

Is this case study of the Paraíba oligarchy relevant to Brazilian states that were less underdeveloped and whose oligarchical patterns were not family-based? The answer requires consideration of several points raised in the scholarly literature on oligarchy. Usually, commentators have not made rigid distinctions between familialistic and personalistic oligarchies, preferring instead to contrast both with more bureaucratically or collegially organized oligarchies. For instance, probably the most well known personalistic oligarchy in the Old Republic was the one directed in Pernambuco by Senator Rosa e Silva between 1896 and 1911. Several scholars who studied its organization have stressed that Rosa e Silva preferred to rely on political friends rather than on the members of his own family for staffing political offices and bureaucratic posts.[46] Nevertheless, the Pernambuco oligarchy displayed at its base a strong dependence on family and kinship ties for defining its political organization and support. At the state level, or the apex of its leadership, politicians placed considerable reliance on vertically defined family-based groups in key municípios.[47]

Aciolis), Amazonas (the Nerys), Mato Grosso (the Ponces), and, in a more intermediate situation, Bahia (the Viannas). Sergipe and Espírito Santo were also included. Carone, *República Velha*, p. 274; Romero, "Oligarchias," pp. 413–14; Leôncio Basbaum, *História sincera da República*, 4th ed. (São Paulo: Editôra Alfa-Omega, 1976), p. 190. Piauí (Barão da Parnaíba) and Sergipe (the Almeida Bottos) were cited by Oliveira Vianna as the first oligarchies in Brazil. *Instituições políticas*, 1:217–26.

[46] Carone, Romero, and Levine express firm consensus on this point: *República Velha*, pp. 278–79; "Oligarchias," p. 414; and *Pernambuco*, p. 108.

[47] Levine, *Pernambuco*, p. 108. Pernambuco's "freewheeling" state Republican

Furthermore, officeholders in Pernambuco had more kinship ties among themselves than in either São Paulo or Minas Gerais. This suggests why Pernambuco has long offered fertile ground for studies of so-called "clan" politics in Northeast Brazil. Family-based networks enabled the major family-based groups to consolidate their political ties across state lines, much as their feuding patterns also reached into neighboring states.[48] Eul-Soo Pang's study of the Bahia oligarchy also noted the major role family-based groups played in the politics of a personalistic oligarchy, although Pang did not classify its pattern as family-based.[49] Personalistic oligarchies, consequently, still demonstrated the vigorous collaboration of family-based groups on the level of state–local relations. The blending of the personalistic and the familialistic varied not only according to the state but also to the chronological point, depending on which set of ins controlled the state government. In Rio de Janeiro, Bahia, and Pernambuco, frequent federal interventions brought in successive oligarchies with wide oscillations in their proportions of personalism or familialism. Paraíba's case study can thus illuminate important characteristics of the political process at the regional level even in personalistic oligarchies.

Is the study of the Paraíba oligarchy relevant to states with considerable urbanization and economic differentiation? At first glance, it appears that the oligarchies of São Paulo, Minas Gerais, and Rio Grande do Sul—the "big three" of the Old Republic's politics—do not deserve to be assessed according to the same set of organizational characteristics as the oligarchies of the less developed states. In the big three, economic growth, urbanization, industrialization, and foreign immigration already had made considerable inroads on agrarian society's economic pursuits, interest group base, and social and political values, expectedly eroding the family base of oligarchy. Competing economic interests cut deeply into family lines of group formation, often reinforcing personalistic allegiances. Yet, even in those cases, the historical literature makes clear, the imprint of family and kinship in political organization and style was evident. A much more limited argu-

Party was "but a pale shadow" of its "disciplined and hierarchical counterparts in São Paulo, Minas, and Rio Grande do Sul," for it was "always dependent on a system of personal linkages" (pp. 89–90).

[48] Ibid., p. 108.

[49] Pang, *Bahia*, p. 25. Pang appraised Bahia's oligarchy during 1919 and 1924 as personalistic. It closely resembled Max Weber's charismatic rule and was a transitional type to either"collegial" or "tribal oligarchy" (pp. 24–25).

ment can be made for Rio Grande do Sul, but all three states bore witness to a slow retreat of the historical influence the great families had exercised in their politics.

While tinged with histrionic exaggeration, Sílvio Romero's accusations that a few families controlled Brazil's most economically advanced states contained a kernel of truth. His remarks called attention to an essential complementarity between kinship and partisan organization. Romero poked fun at industrializing São Paulo, pointing a rhetorical finger at its "presidentially powerful Glicério, Rodrigues Alves, Bernardino de Campos, and Tibiriçá" families for not "being satisfied with ruling in their own territories." He charged that, "raised high on their heaps of coffee beans and foreign loans, [they] had seized [the Republic] by means of their electoral machines" (i.e., through the 'herd' vote).[50] He rebuked Minas Gerais, claiming that ". . . the Pena, Bias Fortes, Sales, Pinheiro, Peixoto, and Veiga [families] had gone so far as to compete with São Paulo, rivaling it in the rule of Brazil."[51] Even Santa Catarina's relatively innocuous oligarchy elicited Romero's derision, because "the Hercílios and the Lauros and other refined little bosses [there] know how to divide the cheese fraternally."[52]

The comparative literature on Brazilian state and regional politics has made clear the importance of family networks of power in the Republican parties of São Paulo and Minas Gerais, even though they by no means resembled Paraíba's model of a family-based oligarchy. In contrast to the states in the Northeast, North, and West of Brazil, the Republican Party of São Paulo, the PRP (Partido Republicano Paulista), had been formed in the Empire, as early as 1871. Its original commitment to abolition and republicanism meant that it evolved very differently from either the family-based or the personalistic parties that characterized most Brazilian states. Calling attention to the vigorous party organization of the PRP, Joseph L. Love has noted that it achieved both internal cohesion and discipline. Unlike almost all other political parties of the Old Republic, the PRP's Executive Committee of nine members represented a statewide spectrum of interests. Collectively, the Executive Committee played a major role in decision-making, although after 1916 the governor's role became stronger due to the steady rise in state revenues. Henceforth, dramatic change was reflected in the power of the State as personified by the

[50] Romero, "Oligarchias," p. 414.

[51] Ibid.

[52] Ibid., p. 415.

governor.[53] In contrast, in Paraíba the state party boss, either Álvaro Machado or Epitácio Pessoa, concentrated decision-making in his own hands, signifying that the official state party was fused with the person of the leader. In such cases, as Carone has explained, "the party represented private interest and not the equilibrium of various factions."[54]

Love has also called attention to the role of powerful parentela groups within São Paulo's PRP, arguing, with Carone, that as late as 1924 key splits within its ranks occurred along family lines. He concluded, however, that the PRP was "clearly something more than an elaborate network of parentelas and clientelas." In fact, he qualified his use of "party" with respect to the PRP, evaluating it as an "intermediate" case because it fell between a modern "horizontally" organized party—one that was functionally or ideologically cohesive—and a "vertically organized clientele network."[55] Clearly, the PRP had moved away from a highly familialistic or personalistic model; yet vertical family and clientele networks continued to characterize it.

Minas Gerais offered a second contrast to Paraíba. Minas appeared not to have attained the degree of corporate decision-making and multiple interest representation associated with São Paulo. Scholarly assessments of Minas' oligarchical organization vary considerably in the significance they accord to family ties. Edgard Carone, for instance, stressed the "accentuated and stratified hegemony" that prominent families in Minas enjoyed even during the Empire. Those families helped explain the impressive number of monarchist groups active in Minas after 1889. In contrast to São Paulo, Carone argued, the Republican Party of Minas, the PRM (Partido Republicano Mineiro) contributed to the survival of prerepublican values and attitudes because of its own internal weaknessess. Consequently, the competing oligarchical groups in Minas continued, throughout the Republic, to vie for control of the state, precisely because an institutionalized party like São Paulo's never developed. Rival oligarchical groups im-

[53] Love, *São Paulo*, pp. 115–16; and personal communication with the author, 15 Oct. 1984. After 1916, the PRP's Executive Committee became more oligarchically inclined because the members became gubernatorial appointees and self-perpetuating. Ibid., p. 116. See also Carone, *República Velha*, p. 271.

[54] Love, *São Paulo*, p. 115. The Executive Committee, which represented the most powerful local bosses, mitigated factional divisions by mediating between the governor and the local bosses, and performed as a broker of party patronage. Ibid. See also Carone, *República Velha*, p. 272.

[55] Love, *São Paulo*, p. 115.

posed their personalistic and familialistic views on official party conventions as they alternated in control of the PRM's Executive Committee.[56]

John Wirth came to a different conclusion, appraising Minas' oligarchical organization as more convergent with São Paulo's than with either familial or personalistic oligarchies in the majorities of states. He conceded that the traditional elite family in Minas sustained social and economic power for its members and imparted a "sense of place and stability" to "the political mosaic of the state" in the Old Republic.[57] Nevertheless, he deemed the elite family "a weaker institution than is commonly supposed," for, in his view, economic change and urbanization had exerted significant influence. The great families of Minas had been ceding power slowly to highly mobile urban elites long before 1930. Family groups and their vertical divisions of clientism were less solidly defined as a result, according to Wirth. They deserved to be contrasted with the Northeast, where sugar baronies formed a patrimonial oligarchy. Yet Wirth recognized that an important element of vigorous family politics endured.[58]

Rio Grande do Sul had even less in common with Paraíba's family-based oligarchy than did São Paulo or Minas Gerais. Its uniqueness derived broadly from the role militarism had played in its history since colonial times, when border conflicts with Spanish America had characterized its settlement. However, a bloody civil war in 1893–1895 crystallized partisan allegiances and rendered the state's party evolution unique until 1930. Rio Grande do Sul was the only state where the ruling Republican Party, the PRR (Partido Republicano Riograndense) projected a definite ideology. Likewise, it was the only state with a well-organized opposition party aligned along an ideological axis. As a result, Riograndense politics had a distinctive authoritarian cast. Because a strong, positivistic orientation belonged to the victors in the civil war, both the state constitution and the organization of the PRR institutionalized authoritarian structures. Of all Brazil's state oligarchies, Rio Grande do Sul's least revealed a reliance on family-based ties at the state level.

Joseph L. Love's exemplary analysis of Rio Grande do Sul's politics during the era of the oligarchies demonstrated that the PRR acquired a monolithic structure not duplicated elsewhere in Bra-

[56] Carone, *República Velha*, pp. 272–75.
[57] Wirth, *Minas Gerais*, pp. 70–71.
[58] Ibid., p. 70.

zil.[59] During the formative decade of the nineties, state party boss Júlio de Castilhos, as head of the PRR, imposed his decisions on the local party organization through an authoritarian and bureaucratic structure. Borges de Medeiros, his successor, continued the trend. The local bosses, or coronéis, became disciplined executors of party policies, unlike their counterparts in other Brazilian states, who enjoyed considerable local autonomy as long as they delivered their municípios' votes to the state party machine at election time. The Riograndense local boss functioned as a "bureaucratic" coronel.[60] Furthermore, the ideological content of state politics, grounded in the tenets of positivism, permeated political culture even locally, significantly undercutting the claims of family ties.

This brief survey of oligarchy in the Old Republic places Paraíba's case in a national context and identifies how this book addresses issues or themes common to Brazilian history. As the scholarly literature suggests, all state oligarchies depended on family-based groups and networks to some extent. However, one group of states clearly demonstrated a primary dependence on the ties of family in their political organization. Ceará, Amazonas, Alagoas, and Paraíba best illustrated this category of family-based oligarchy. Another group, in which Rio de Janeiro, Bahia, Pernambuco, and—with reservation—Minas Gerais, were the most important examples, can be characterized as personalistic oligarchies, although personal ties closely dovetailed with kinship bonds. São Paulo was distinct, because of the emergence there of a true party organization—however immature.[61] Finally, Rio Grande do Sul was unique, due to the impressive degree of bureaucratization in its organizational structure.

Viewed against this array of oligarchical types, Paraíba is germane to the broad scholarly literature on the politics of the Old Republic precisely as a less powerful state. Thus, much of the value of this book lies in the fact that it inverts the conventional focus on the triumvirate of states that dominated the politics of the Old Republic. That focus, while appropriate, obscured a basic historical reality: Seventeen other state oligarchies were also ac-

[59] Love, *Rio Grande do Sul*, pp. 76–77.

[60] Ibid., p. 77.

[61] The oligarchies of populous Bahia, Rio de Janeiro, and Pernambuco played leadership roles in regional voting blocs. They lined up support for the national presidential machine among their "satellite" states and defined a second tier of oligarchical power in Congress, which fell below the three states at the top and above the majority of states at the bottom.

tors in federal politics. Rio Grande do Sul, São Paulo, and Minas were always obliged to contend with them on the national level, where politics centered on mobilizing voting blocs in Congress. The majority of state Republican parties were little more than electoral machines, especially in contrast to Rio Grande do Sul's centralized PRR, and therefore highly dependent on transacting patronage at the federal level with the three most powerful states. Paraíba's model of political organization was fairly typical of the other seventeen states and thus deserves appraisal, in spite of its small size. References to "tiny Paraíba" in the historical literature are misleading because they have suggested that Paraíba was particularly small. In fact, in both population and territorial size, Paraíba was a middle-rank state among the seventeen states subordinated to the big three.[62]

In offering an oligarchical contrast to Brazil's more powerful states, therefore, this case study provides a perspective characteristic of the weak political position most Brazilian states occupied until 1930. Three interconnected aspects of their historical situation receive comparative attention. First, by underscoring the political domination of the most populous and wealthiest states, this book reveals the limitations the national political system imposed on the aspirations of the majority of Brazilian states. More specifically, the analysis emphasizes the dependence of northeastern states on relationships with the more powerful states of the Center-South for receiving the resources of the national government. Paraíba's peripheral position in the nation must therefore be considered in terms of national political patterns, not merely regional economic cycles of "boom and bust."

Second, by adopting as a central theme one essential aspect of the "North–South" gap in Brazil, namely, the longer survival of family-based oligarchies in the Northeast, this book addresses a phenomenon intrinsically Brazilian. Kinship was an important force in politics, in varying degrees throughout Brazil, during the era of the oligarchies and despite regional differences. Coronelismo, oligarchy's lowest common denominator, enjoyed nationwide distribution as a system of local boss rule. Until 1930, the national political system, consequently, rested on political means

[62] Instituto Histórico e Geográfico Brasileiro, *Diccionario historico, geografico e ethnografico do Brasil*, 2 vols. (Rio de Janeiro: Imprensa Oficial, 1922), 1:247. On the role of the other seventeen states in national politics, see Steven Topik's reassessment: "State Intervention in a Liberal Regime: Brazil, 1889–1930," *HAHR* 60 (Nov. 1980):593–616.

that were customarily violent, fraudulent, and nepotistic.[63] Coronelismo displayed more similarities than differences across the nation. Above all, however, it wedded family power to political power locally and perpetuated the force of kinship in national politics by defining the vertical divisions on which every oligarchical party rested. Those vertical divisions so integral to the preservation of family-based politics deserve comment in view of nationwide similarities.

Although Paraíba undeniably represented a mode of oligarchical organization more directly connected to the structures of the agrarian past, certain features of its family-based system of politics had recently also been prominent in the industrializing Center-South. The state oligarchies that ruled Brazil between 1889 and 1930 were similar more than they differed. Throughout Brazil "the shift from plantation to city" did not "shatter the verticality of social relations"—mass immigration and rising social mobility notwithstanding.[64] Everywhere, the "Conservative classes" that governed Brazil relied on sharp vertical divisions to militate against the demands of an expanding working class in the cities, just as rural landlords relied on those divisions to check rebellion in the countryside. The oligarchies shared an elitist world view whose paternalism logically derived from society's corporatistic organization. The political system's dependence on patronage relationships, strong bonds of clientism, and face-to-face relationships at the national level enhances the broad relevance of this case study.[65]

[63] Carone, *República Velha*, p. 267. "At the state level, the political system was defined not only by the formation of oligarchies—more or less broad coalitions comprising either a large group of kin or a more heterogeneous group—but also by the actual institutionalization of colonelism [coronelismo], that is, the pact between the public powers and [the] leaders of the interior who controlled and supplied votes from their local domains" (Cintra, "Traditional Politics," p. 132).

[64] Michael Conniff has observed that "the paternalism of the upper class and the mediating action of the traditional professions allowed city life to adopt plantation manners." *Urban Politics in Brazil* (Pittsburgh: University of Pittsburgh Press, 1981), p. 150. Maria Isaura Pereira de Queiroz has also argued that traditional, family-group ties were reinforced during the urbanization of the mid-nineteenth century and that the family group survived as an economic group in the early phase of industrialization. "Singularidades sócio-culturais do desenvolvimento brasileiro," in her *Cultura, sociedade rural, sociedade urbana no Brasil* (São Paulo: Livros Técnicos e Científicos Editôra, S.A. & Editôra da Universidade de São Paulo, 1978), pp. 73 and 81. For contrasts between elite family behavior styles by region or zone, see [Francisco José de] Oliveira Vianna, *Populações meridionais do Brasil*, 2 vols. (Rio de Janeiro: Paz e Terra, 1973), 2:95, 108, 137, and 143–45.

[65] "Conservative classes" embraced both rural landowners and those in the ur-

Finally, in focusing on the process of state-building, this book addresses a theme that is important at the national level. The historical process by which family power either became absorbed and legitimated as part of the public interest or was removed from that arena is one very much at the center of scholarly attention today. Private family power underwent historic defeat in Brazil only when confronted by an aggressive central State. Thus, this study of politics and parentela in a typical state offers valuable empirical demonstration for the process of the State's expansion vis-à-vis the remarkable survival of family power in the public realm.

---

ban population who possessed substantial property or income. On clientism after 1930, see Robert W. Shirley, "Patronage and Cooperation: An Analysis from São Paulo State," in *Structure and Process in Latin America*, ed. Arnold Stricken and Sidney M. Greenfield (Albuquerque: University of New Mexico Press, 1972), pp. 139–58; Roberto da Matta, "As raizes da violência no Brasil: Reflexões de um antropólogo," in *Violência brasileira*, ed. Roberto da Matta et al. (São Paulo: Brasiliense, 1982), pp. 11–44; Kenneth Paul Erickson, *The Brazilian Corporative State and Working-Class Politics* (Berkeley and Los Angeles: University of California Press, 1977), chs. 2–3.

PART ONE

Political Economy

· I ·

Land and Population

> This valuable plant has now become of more importance in Pernambuco than even the sugar cane, owing to the great demand for the cotton of that province, and of those adjoining it, in the British markets.
>
> —Henry Koster, *Travels in Brazil*, 1817

> Can we, in view of the threatened supply of long-staple cotton . . . afford to neglect any possible source . . . ? Does it not behoove all, Lancastershire in particular, to look around in good time for new fields? From what I have seen in the north-eastern part of Brazil, I maintain that we have a stretch of country able to come to our help; all that is required is administration and the initiation of a few elementary reforms.
>
> —Arno Pearse, *Brazilian Cotton*, 1923

LAND AND POPULATION in Paraíba reflected geographical patterns common to the Brazilian Northeast. However modest its territory, Paraíba occupied the geographical heartland of the region. Brazil's seventh smallest state, it shared with its neighbors the two major ecological zones of the Northeast: a coastal sugar belt that had originally opened the region and the colony to sixteenth-century European expansion, and an agro-pastoral hinterland that subsequently maintained coastal export production. Strategically placed in the very center of Brazil's northeastern "hump," Paraíba's political boundaries encompassed all of the topographical and climatic features considered typical of the region. (See Map I.1.) In addition, its population had always participated in the major events of regional history. From the very first contact that both French and Portuguese dyewood gatherers had with the indigenous inhabitants in the early 1500s, historical developments in Paraíba paralleled those elsewhere in colonial Brazil. Later, land and population would also reveal Paraíba's regional uniqueness and hint at the rebellious historical role the Northeast would eventually play, first in the Portuguese colony and then in the independent nation.

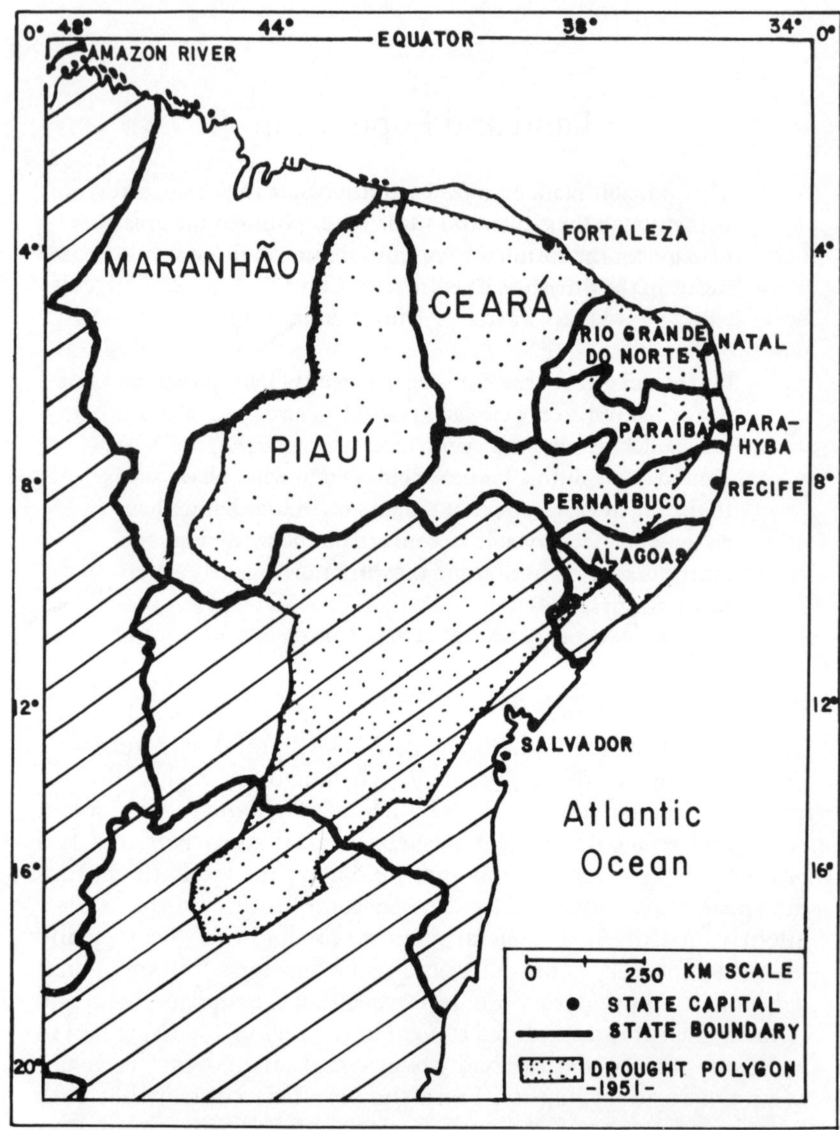

Map I.1: The States of Northeast Brazil (1930) with Subsequent Drought Polygon
Source: Adapted from Stefan Robock, *Brazil's Developing Northeast: A Study of Regional Planning and Foreign Aid* (Washington, D.C.: The Brookings Institution, 1963), p. 71.

GEOGRAPHY

The Regional Context

Although physical differences existed within the six states that originally defined the Northeast, they remained subordinated to overwhelming similarities of geographical accident. In Euclydes da Cunha's immortal enunciation, topography, climate, and settlement patterns had molded the population of the Northeast's interior into "the bedrock of the Brazilian race."[1] Features of geography and settlement patterns did indeed forge a distinctive regional type, one that as a racial mixture still retains predominantly Portuguese and Amerindian features while conserving a decidedly more muted African ancestry.[2] Historically, the interior's population turned not toward the commercial and administrative centers of the coast but toward the empty and vast heartland of the region. Natural barriers, coupled with the limitations that distance imposed on Crown authority, nurtured early tendencies toward independence and local rule. If that circumstance was by no means unique in Brazil's history, two other features of regional evolution would distinguish Paraíba and its neighbors from the rest of Brazil.

First, declining comparative advantage in producing sugar for a world market meant that eventually Brazil's growing Center-South would economically surpass the Northeast as the colony's most dynamic region. By independence, what had once been the world's richest sugar colony bowed to the ascendance of coffee.[3]

[1] Euclides da Cunha, *Rebellion in the Backlands (Os Sertões)*, trans. Samuel Putnam (Chicago: University of Chicago Press, 1944), p. 481.

[2] See Waldice Mendonça Porto, *Paraíba em preto e branco* (João Pessoa: *A União*, 1976); Billy Jaynes Chandler, "The Role of Negroes in the Ethnic Formation of Ceará: The Need for a Reappraisal," *Revista de Ciências Sociais* 4, no. 1 (1973):31–43; José Américo de Almeida, *A Parahyba e seus problemas* (Parahyba: Imprensa Oficial, 1923), p. 197; and Diana Soares de Galliza, *O declínio da escravidão na Paraíba, 1850–1888* (João Pessoa: Editora da Universidade Federal da Paraíba, 1979).

[3] Celso Furtado, *The Economic Growth of Brazil*, trans. Ricardo W. Aguiar and Eric Charles Drysdale (Berkeley and Los Angeles: University of California, Press, 1968), pp. 16–19, 57–58, 67–68, 95–98, and 155–56; Caio Prado Junior, *História econômica Brasil*, 21st ed. (São Paulo: Brasiliense, 1978), pp. 84, 157–59; Nathaniel H. Leff, "Economic Development and Regional Inequality: Origins of the Brazilian Case," *Quarterly Journal of Economics* 86 (May 1972):245–47 and 262; José Ribeiro Junior, *Colonização e monopólio no nordeste brasileiro* (São Paulo: Hucitec, 1976), pp. 25–60.

Second, the absence of significant foreign immigration to the Northeast—except for the continual traffic in African slaves throughout the three centuries preceding 1850—caused the region to evolve more conservatively than the Center-South. The Northeast retained its homogenous population throughout the Old Republic, at a time when many familiar features of Brazilian life were being discarded or modified elsewhere under the influence of mass immigration and rapid industrialization. Long before the collapse of the Empire, the region had ceased to play a pivotal role in national development, for long-term, irreversible decline had taken hold by 1750. By 1889, the Northeast's role in the political economy of the nation had been subordinated to the industrializing core of São Paulo–Rio de Janeiro in two respects. First, although the Northeast still exported raw materials, chiefly cotton, to transatlantic markets, the Center-South had become the major customer for its sugar and an important buyer of its cotton. Second, the Northeast increasingly exported its own population as cheap labor—by the 1870s to exploit rubber riches in the Amazon and by the 1890s to work in factories or staff middle-class households in the Center-South. Among all social classes in the underdeveloped Northeast, outmigration remains the most reasonable individual solution to the region's endemic poverty and lack of economic opportunity.[4]

Geography, both physical and human, only partly explains why underdevelopment has persisted in the Brazilian Northeast. More comprehensive attempts to account for the region's human misery would place greater emphasis on historical patterns of political and economic organization, especially the changing position of the Northeast in the world economy. Even though geography has too often been made the scapegoat for the region's poverty, it is nevertheless true that topography and climate have imposed crucial limitations on the forms of social organization possible in the region.[5]

Variations in Paraíba's physical geography explained the state's

[4] Anthony Hall, "Irrigation in the Brazilian Northeast: Anti-Drought or Anti-Peasant?" in *The Logic of Poverty*, ed. Simon Mitchell (London, Boston, and Henley: Routledge & Kegan Paul, 1981), pp. 160–61; Albert Hirschman, "Northeast Brazil," in *Journeys Through Progress* (New York: W. W. Norton & Co., Inc., 1973), p. 28.

[5] Furtado, *Economic Growth of Brazil*, pp. 268–69; Stefan Robock, *Brazil's Developing Northeast: A Study of Regional Planning and Foreign Aid* (Washington, D.C.: The Brookings Institution, 1963), pp. 18–44.

historical subordination to neighboring Pernambuco and its political role as Pernambuco's satellite during the Old Republic. Even more strikingly, variations in Paraíba's geography directly influenced the political distribution of power among the five geoeconomic zones that had emerged in Paraíba by the advent of the Republic. Until the close of the eighteenth century, geography had defined only two zones for Paraíba's inhabitants—the coast and the interior. But because zonal divisions ran according to vertical or north–south axes, they ignored the political boundaries established during the colonial period, which ran on east–west axes oblivious to the natural features imposed by geography. This simple fact allowed Pernambuco to control Paraíba for centuries, because topography remarkably integrated Paraíba within its boundaries. In addition, Pernambuco had the splendid harbor of Recife, which had caused the original colonists to establish the administrative capital of the region there. Its early suitability as a zone for sugar cultivation and unrivaled geographical position as the regional entrepôt for the transatlantic trade gave it political hegemony over the Northeast. Not only Paraíba but also Alagoas, Ceará, Rio Grande do Norte, Piauí, and southern Maranhão fell within Recife's commercial and political orbit as so-called satellite states.[6] (See Map I.1.) Because Paraíba remained incorporated politically within Pernambuco for much of the colonial period, many of its founding families, both on the coast and in the backlands, were Pernambucano pioneers.

Geographical accident, on the other hand, defined one important difference, for it deprived Paraíba of a large sugar zone and bestowed on Pernambuco one of Brazil's two most productive cane-growing centers. North of the capital city of Parahyba, the verdant coastal belt narrows and then disappears upon reaching Rio Grande do Norte. At that point, the landscape of the backlands

[6] Only in the last half of the nineteenth century, when drought emerged as a political issue, did the term "Northeast" begin to designate a regional identity. Formerly, it had been implicit in the term "the North," which had embraced Amazonas, Pará, and Maranhão, in addition to the six states that first became historically identified as "the Northeast": Piauí, Ceará, Rio Grande do Norte, Paraíba, Pernambuco, and Alagoas. Maranhão sometimes was added as a seventh. With the establishment of the "drought polygon" in 1936, the Northeast acquired an official regional identity that the Brazilian Congress progressively expanded. Since 1951, the drought polygon has embraced the original six (or seven) and a periphery circumscribing parts of Bahia, Sergipe, and Minas Gerais. Manoel Correia de Andrade, "História regional: Nordeste" (Paper presented at the XI° Simpósio Nacional de História de ANPUH, João Pessoa, Paraíba, 19–24 July 1981) pp. 1–2 and 7.

meets the sea. This geographical circumstance encouraged the interior to play a more important role in Paraíba's politics. By comparison, in Pernambuco the coastal belt has always been the preponderant political force, even during the Old Republic. In Paraíba, on the other hand, the political emergence of the intermediate zones known as the *brejo* and the *caatinga-agreste* had coincided with the introduction of provincial legislatures throughout Brazil in 1835. From the beginning, the intermediate zones, together with the two backlands zones, possessed a significant voice in Paraíba's unicameral legislature, the Provincial Assembly.[7]

Physical Features

Paraíba's landscape, like that of its neighbors, revealed an astonishing diversity of topography and climate, which fostered the emergence of five geoeconomic zones within the state by the close of the Empire. A long, narrow, and very irregular slice of territory, Paraíba cuts inland due west from the Atlantic Ocean for slightly over 600 kilometers. (See Map I.2.) When the Portuguese arrived, the approximately 150 kilometers of the coastal belt was densely forested with tropical hardwoods. Alluvial soils, rich in organic material and mineral salts, explained its conversion into a sugarcane zone in the second half of the sixteenth century. Two-thirds of the state's surface area, however, spans the backlands or *sertões*, a vast, semi-arid zone originally exploited for stockraising. This pastoral hinterland, though socially isolated, always had economic connections with the coastal zone because geography had provided routes that ran from the Paraíba backlands directly to the regional entrepôt of Recife. Where it aligned with Rio Grande do Norte and Pernambuco, Paraíba's irregular and pinched north–south boundaries registered an ancient pattern of economic dependence on regional market routes. The jagged profile on the map reflected favorable openings that nature had created, for key river valleys permitted passage across most of the imposing barrier of the Serra do Borborema.

The rugged Planalto (Plateau) of the Serra do Borborema—a dry, elevated backlands that extended inland once its eastern escarpment had been scaled—was Paraíba's principal topographical feature beyond the coast. A forbidding divide, the Borborema united Paraíba, Pernambuco, and Rio Grande do Norte in a common geographical and commercial subregion. The trade routes that criss-

[7] Pernambuco's coastal *mata* contained 50.3 per cent of the state's population in 1890 and 48.5 per cent of it in 1935. Levine, *Pernambuco*, p. 19. (Cf. Table I.2.)

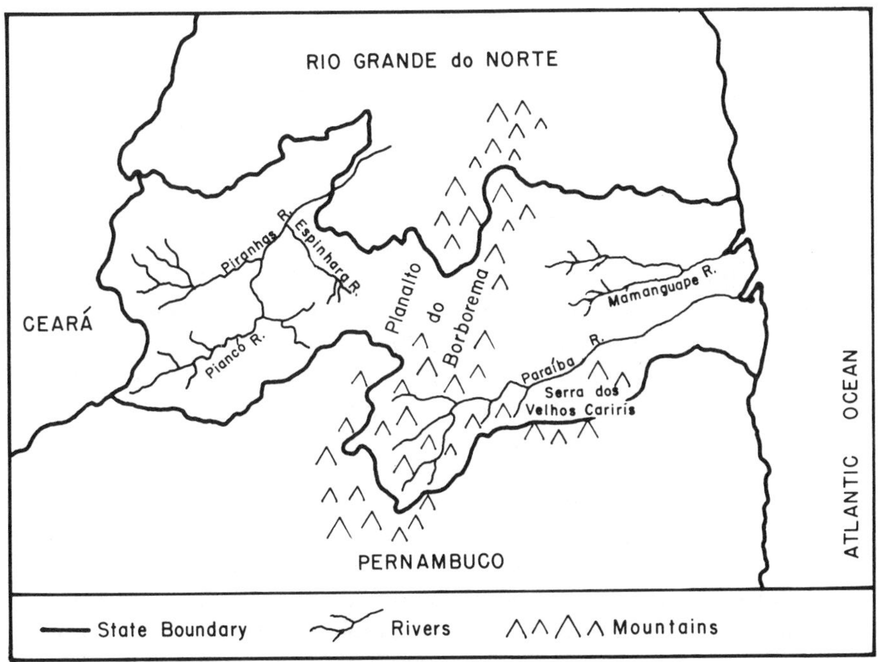

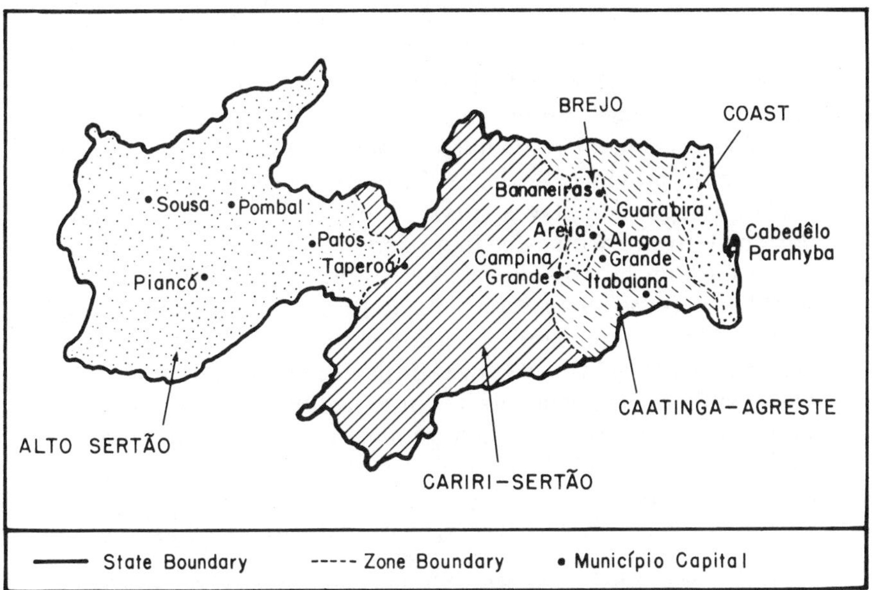

MAP I.2: Paraíba: Principal Physical Features, Geoeconomic Zones, and Market Centers (Scale: 1 inch = 180 km)

SOURCES: State of Paraíba, Departamento de Estradas e Rodagem, *Mapa rodoviário 1950 (Based on the work of Engineer L.F.R. Clerot)* (João Pessoa: Imprensa Oficial, n.d.), p. 1; "Mapa do Estado da Paraíba," organized under the direction of Engineer Guilherme Lane, Chief Topographer, IFOCS, in Delmiro Pereira de Andrade, *Evolução histórica da Paraíba do Norte* (Rio de Janeiro: Editôra Minerva, 1946), overleaf.

crossed its rugged heights connected zones beyond the western ridges of the mountain range to points nearer the Atlantic. Cutting across Paraíba on a northeasterly axis, the plateau originally had confined population to the coastal belt, forming an extensive barrier to early settlement in the interior. Until the end of the eighteenth century, it was the reason why only two zones—the coast and the interior—existed. However, when cotton cultivation spread into the river valleys lying to the west of the Serra do Borborema after 1860, then the plateau exerted a new influence in the economy of the far backlands. Only when world prices rose substantially, would planters receive sufficient compensation for sending their cotton over the steep gradients of the Piancó Valley and through the Pernambuco backlands to distant Recife.

Two major river basins complemented the geographical division between coast and backlands. Together they etched out the earliest zones of economic wealth and the key riparian routes to Paraíba's unexplored interior. The coast's major river system, the Paraíba, originated 500 kilometers upstream, in the eroded metamorphic rock slopes of the Cariris Velhos, a southwesterly spur of the Borborema Plateau. As the lower Paraíba River flowed toward the sea, it created the broad floodplain of the coastal zone that surrounded the capital city and gave it its name. Further north, this coastal belt adjoined a second floodplain formed by the river Mamanguape, which similarly drained the Borborema Plateau on its northeastern slopes. From the sixteenth to the nineteenth centuries, these contiguous floodplains contained the political seat of power in the province. By the 1890s, however, the coast's opulence based on sugar and slaves survived among only a few families. They had shrewdly invested in modern *usinas*, steam-powered refineries, either buying out or foreclosing on their less fortunate neighbors. In the 1930s, José Lins do Rêgo, a scion of the ruined Lins de Albuquerque family, described the melancholy silence of the dead hearths of the old sugar mills lining the Paraíba's banks. The nostalgic cycle of novels he wrote testified as much to the decline of the planters' political hegemony in Paraíba as it did to the economic "decadence" of the coastal plantation society into which he had been born.[8]

Paraíba's other major river system, the Piranhas Basin, origi-

[8] José Lins do Rêgo's fictional portrayal of Paraíba's coastal sugar "aristocracy" in decline faithfully chronicles the history of his home município of Pilar and draws its political characters from his own relatives: *Menino de engenho* (1932), *Doidinho* (1933), *Bangüe* (1934), *O moleque Ricardo* (1935), and *Usina* (1936).

nated in the far backlands near Ceará. The ecological conditions it supplied were uniquely favorable for growing tree cotton. Flowing northeasterly as the Espinhara or the Espinharas, the Piranhas then forked in a parallel course southwest of the city of Pombal and carved out the Piancó Valley. (See Map I.2.) Depositing a rich strip of black bottomland for 240 kilometers south to Pernambuco, this tributary eventually connected with the San Francisco Basin. Except for a few, very fertile pockets, it became completely dry during the long summers, offering perfect growing conditions for the backlands' long-staple arboreal cottons. The chain of rich agricultural oases that the Piranhas implanted in the otherwise dessicated far backlands attracted seventeenth-century pioneers to settle along its tributaries. The concatenated pattern these early clusters of cattle ranches outlined along the riverbanks revealed the propensity for the interior's population to gravitate to sources of water. By 1900, the Piranhas Basin emerged as Paraíba's major zone of tree cotton cultivation. Not surprisingly, its planters began to challenge the political monopoly which zones nearer the coast had exercised until the late 1890s.

Zonal Divisions

By the middle of the nineteenth century, the original division between coast and backlands had given way to five geographical zones, each with an economic specialization.[9] Except for the coast, each bore the mark of cotton's advance into the interior. The coastal zone extended only 20 to 68 kilometers inland from the sea. The landscape beyond its white beaches of coconut palms originally had contained the densely forested *zona da mata*, whose primeval stands of trees had been exploited for their brazilwood. After centuries of deforestation, most of the zona da mata had been rendered an extensive floodplain of green canefields. Further inland, the coastal zone changed to sandy tableland before

[9] This geographical classification of Paraíba's zones draws on the official one used by the Instituto Brasileiro de Geografia e Estatística (IBGE). See *Estudos de desenvolvimento regional (Paraíba)* (Rio de Janeiro: Campanha Nacional de Aperfeiçoamento de Pessoal de Nível Superior, 1959), pp. 17–78. Topographical description came from Irinêo Joffily, *Notas sobre a Parahyba*, 2nd ed. (Brasília: Thesaurus Editôra, 1977), pp. 87–103, 125, 136; Manoel Correia de Andrade, *A terra e o homem no nordeste*, 2nd ed. (São Paulo: Editôra Brasiliense, 1969), pp. 175–84; Kempton Webb, *The Changing Face of Northeast Brazil* (New York: Columbia University Press, 1974), pp. 112–24; *Atlas geográfico da Paraíba* (João Pessoa: Universidade Federal da Paraíba, 1965), pp. 27–59.

yielding to a second, intermediate zone known as the *caatinga-agreste (agreste acaatingada)*. The caatinga-agreste consisted of a very fertile strip of agricultural land 26 kilometers wide known as the *agreste*, which was surrounded by a drier belt of *caatinga*. Partly named for the zerophytic vegetation, or caatinga, that blanketed its outer ring of landscape, this zone straddled the territory between coast and backlands. The ubiquitous *caatingueira*, a low-lying creeper particularly prominent in this zone, announced that one had entered the bleak interior, where all plant life was dedicated to conserving water. Thorn trees, hardy fibrous plants, scrub, and gigantic cacti created the caatinga's dry and twisted summer landscape. As one moved upward to the higher elevation of the Borborema Plateau, this vegetation continued indefinitely, its water-storing bulbous roots offering travelers an emergency source of liquid when drought caused rivers and streams to disappear.

The agreste, a small subhumid pocket in the caatinga's northeastern corner at the beginning of the nineteenth century, possessed ideal conditions for agriculture. Historically, the drier caatinga surrounding the agreste had been developed as an adjunct pastoral zone for the coastal sugar belt. Isolated ranches, which were mere camps in the bush, began to appear there during the late sixteenth and early seventeenth centuries. They supplied charky (*carne do sol*) and the oxen and horses that served as motor power for the coastal sugar mills during the cane-grinding season. Beginning in the late eighteenth century, the relationship of economic complementarity between the caatinga and the coastal zone changed. Agriculture—cereals and cotton—began to steal the forage resources of the pastoral economy. The uniqueness of the caatinga-agreste, consequently, lay in its emergence as a zone of polyculture. By the 1820s, the agricultural agreste had become a man-made landscape, thanks to creeping enclosure, and by the era of the Old Republic it was challenging successfully the adjoining *brejo* zone as the major market center in Paraíba. Cereals, tobacco, and a remarkable variety of both herbaceous and arboreal cottons accounted for the agreste's burgeoning productivity. Not surprisingly, by 1900, the caatinga-agreste usurped the position the brejo had enjoyed as Paraíba's wealthiest zone of agriculture. In the same year, the ginning center of Campina Grande, which dominated the economy of the caatinga-agreste, became the largest market in the state. Cotton had made Campina "the gateway to the sertão." Thanks also to cotton, the politicians of the caatinga-agreste, who formerly had aligned themselves with the brejo's merchant and landowning elite, found new allies in the local bosses of the backlands zones, where the cotton boom redirected their commercial endeavors.

The brejo, or "brejos," was a second intermediate zone northeast of the agreste. Surrounded by caatinga on the east and the south, the brejo rested on eroded northeasterly fingers of the Borborema massif. Advantageous elevation made it an even more fertile zone of polyculture, and it extended almost 200 kilometers north to south and spanned 100 kilometers east to west. Cotton and cereals had created the brejo in the second half of the eighteenth century, but by the arrival of the Old Republic the zone had passed its productive peak of the 1860s and 1870s and was already sinking into slow and irreversible decline. During the Old Republic, the brejo's economic wealth came from tobacco, coffee, aguardiente, and *rapadura* (unrefined sugar). Until the 1890s, the brejo contained Paraíba's most prosperous commercial city (Areia) and the largest cluster of market centers. The strategic position that the brejo commanded, overlooking the eastern slopes of the Borborema, enabled it to cradle Paraíba's key interprovincial and interzonal markets: Areia, Guarabira, Bananeiras, and Alagoa Nova. They furnished the politicians who, along with several sugar families, had dominated the provincial oligarchy of Empire. Thanks to a generational lag, the brejo's political ascendance endured into the early Republic and survived the loss of economic preeminence its market centers suffered after 1900.

The backlands, or sertão, began in the foothills of the Borborema, where the caatinga's harsh vegetation moved further inland toward even drier conditions. In reality, it comprised two interior zones; colloquial speech still carefully distinguishes between them. The first, the *cariri-sertão* or "sertão of the cariri," began exactly at the western edge of the City of Campina Grande, where travelers leaving "the gateway of the sertão" looked upward and westward toward the Borborema's heights. The classic backlands of Euclydes da Cunha's literary epic *Os sertões (Rebellion in the Backlands)*, the cariri-sertão zone covered all of Borborema's elevated plateau. Its rugged landscape contained the driest municípios in Paraíba, and for that matter in Brazil. The second backlands zone was the *alto sertão*, or the far backlands. As "the beyond the Borborema" (*o alem do Borborema*), this most distant zone began where the escarpment's western edge left the cariri-sertão and sloped downward into the vastness of the Piranhas Basin. As a

zone of lower elevation, the far backlands received more rainfall than the cariri-sertão. A mild humidity, as well as the water-retaining sandiness of the soil along the riverbanks, provided optimum natural conditions for cultivating tree cottons and made the alto sertão the largest producer of long-staple cottons during the Old Republic. Finally, backlands geography also determined that both the alto sertão and the cariri-sertão would remain commercially integrated with neighboring states and disconnected from the coastal capital of Parahyba.

The fact that Paraíba's municípios were rarely congruent with one geographical zone injected an element of political and economic conflict into local life. The major family groups contending for control of political office frequently reflected different agrarian emphases. Neat classifications based on zones therefore distorted the reality of economic interests. Sometimes a município was an anomalous pocket of one zone firmly planted in the midst of another. At other times, nature imposed a landscape that required a complex and variegated set of productive endeavors. More frequently, geography encouraged common agrarian pursuits that stretched political alliances across município lines. Geographical differences within the same município often gave local strife an internecine character. On the other hand, the economic survival of food-producing zones of polyculture—the caatinga-agreste and the brejo—depended directly on the exports of the pastoral backlands as well as the imports of the coastal zone. The need to maintain a complex balance of commercial relations in the intermediate zones worked to mitigate local violence. Thus a mutual dependence between zones, along with features of the kinship and inheritance systems, tended to limit conflict within tacitly acknowledged boundaries.

Drought

Climate was yet another crucial variable that contained the seeds of both conflict and cooperation. If topography shaped a município's economic and political fortunes, then rainfall offered the most critical determinant of its fate. Plentiful rainfall watered only the coastal belt with regularity. Beyond the littoral, periodic droughts exercised a decisive influence on the evolution of the political economy. In 1922 the federal government declared 60 percent of Paraíba—45,000 square kilometers—within the unofficially acknowledged "drought polygon" of the Brazilian Northeast. (See Map I.1.) Today, over 95 per cent of the state is so classified.[10] Especially in the two backlands zones, drought occurred with cyclical regularity and determined much of the underlying scarcity characteristic of the rural economy. During "great droughts," those of maximum intensity and range, the livestock herds would be decimated. Even the otherwise resilient tree cottons died. From the first penetration of the backlands, which coincided with the Great Drought of 1692, Paraíba's history was intimately bound to drought cycles. Seemingly predictable events in the political economy and folklore of the population, droughts appeared in a variety of forms. Either they affected only a few municípios or struck several states simultaneously. With cyclic regularity, every century "great droughts" embraced the backlands of the entire region and persisted for two or three winters. Usually, however, their parching devastation visited a confined territory, lasted only one winter, and left agricultural and pastoral activity uninterrupted elsewhere.[11]

The Old Republic opened during the final year of the great drought known as "the triple-eights." Beginning in 1888, the rains failed to arrive and dessication of the interior persisted until 1890. The result was particularly disastrous because the population and the economy had not yet recovered from the worst drought of the century, which had lasted from 1877 to 1879. Uncharacteristically, the province's remaining centers of food production in the brejo felt the blow. In Brejo de Areia, Paraíba's wealthiest commercial city, an eyewitness reported:

> Drought in this area is terrible. There is no more hope of saving the last crops planted, given that a plague of caterpillars has destroyed everything. The foodstuffs that rush through the market are priced extremely high and are snatched up by the backlanders whose countenances reflect the misfortune of their own granaries. And the indigent population of the city wanders aimlessly through the streets without work, begging . . . public charity. The proletarian suffers, [but] the wealthiest landowner suffers even more. The lack of any recourse in the city or the surrounding countryside has produced a shocking stream of farmers and artisans headed for the provinces of

[10] Zenon Fleury Monteiro, *A margem dos Carirys* (São Paulo: Editôra Helios, 1926), pp. 26 and 197; Correia de Andrade, *Terra nordeste*, p. 25.

[11] J. A. de Almeida, *Parahyba*, unnumbered chart ("Observações pluviometricas nas localidades do Estado da Parahyba do Norte"), n.p.

Pará and Amazonas. Entire families have left . . . for those destinations.[12]

Outmigration affected all classes, although the poorest usually first took the initiative to search for either new employment or a refugee camp. Refugees set out on foot for the urban centers of the coast and intermediate zones, following the same trails that the preconquest inhabitants of the interior had used when they had been forced to abandon the backlands in search of food and water:

> The journey begins. The head of the family leads the march, carrying on his back the knapsack with the last rations of *macambira* [a root] and the saddlebags of clothing. Perched on top is the littlest child who does not yet know how to walk. Behind him comes his wife, who has their newborn infant at her breast; after her, the others, each carrying his bundle, according to age. It is an almost Biblical picture, this scene of a family of drought refugees on the first day of their journey . . . to the unknown.[13]

Many never reached their destinations, and many more—like those who took ship to Amazonia and its rubber boom—never returned. Population decimation of the entire region followed as an economic as well as a social consequence. By conservative estimates, at least one-third of the Northeast's inhabitants either perished or never returned to the backlands after each of the great droughts of 1877–1879 and 1888–1890.

The mass misery induced by drought had important political consequences for Paraíba's elite families. Historically, they organized themselves to confront the social and economic disruption that prolonged drought always imposed. In spite of their determination, the control that rural landlords exercised over their agricultural tenants loosened considerably during such natural calamities. Violent rivalry for foodstuffs or water received a new impetus during the drought of 1877–1879. For the first time, the national government implemented a policy of sending precious supplies of food and water to relieve starvation and thirst in the backlands. But the distribution of the supplies fell to powerful local landlords who, thanks to their political affiliation with the dominant party in provincial politics, kept them to be dispensed

[12] *Gazeta do Sertão* [Campina Grande, Paraíba], 18 May 1889, cited in I. Joffily, *Notas*, p. 29.

[13] I. Joffily, *Notas*, pp. 176–77.

1. During the Great Drought of 1932, a family of refugees in the alto sertão faced conditions similar to those of the earlier Great Drought of 1877. However, the presence of José Américo de Almeida (at right, in sunglasses) evidenced the federal government's stronger role after 1930 in alleviating starvation. (Courtesy of the Arquivo Fundação Casa de José Américo)

2. Food distribution centers like this one built on the Patos-Sousa highway fed thousands, particularly orphaned children. (Courtesy of the Arquivo Fundação Casa de José Américo)

as patronage among their own tenant clinets. Banditry, endemic in the region since the seventeenth century, increased during times of drought. Wealthy landowners therefore preferred to remain on their estates, understandably reluctant to abandon their properties to pillaging by well-armed brigands or desperate attacks by the hordes of refugees who roamed the countryside. Barricading their household members and loyal retainers safely behind heavily planked doors and windows, they exposed only their gunbarrels to any uninvited visitors who approached too closely.[14]

Droughts posed tests of family solidarity for the elite families who ruled locally. As natural catastrophes, they revealed a major parentela's ability to tap resources beyond its own município. They also issued a direct challenge to elite families' local monopoly on violence. Powerful extended family networks accommodated themselves to drought by owning properties distributed throughout several ecological zones, often spanning state boundaries. In the pastoral zones, geographical circumstances necessitated transhumance: normally, families accustomed themselves to travel annually between upland and lowland properties in order to accompany their livestock herds. Migration between zones coincided with patterns of social visiting for weddings and livestock roundups. Regular contact could thereby be maintained between members of the same extended family who were widely scattered, while seasonal migration insulated them from drought. Seasonal migration also contained a political dimension, for the itinerant pattern of backlands life provided an important opportunity for political caucusing among local bosses whose family groups were allies.

A final political consequence of drought concerned the Northeast's position in the nation. By the dawn of the Republic, drought itself had become a political issue. The mass starvation and economic desolation left in its wake also revealed the region's declining influence in national politics. In summing up the desperate plight of the survivors of the "drought of the triple eights," even a small backlands newspaper in the Paraíba brejo could critically articulate the regional dissatisfaction that was widespread on the eve of the Republic:

[14] Prior to 1877–1879, great droughts of maximum intensity occurred during the last century in 1803–1804, 1824–1825, and 1844–1845. "Sínopse das seccas do nordeste desde 1692 a 1932," *Revista do Instituto Histórico e Geográfico Paraibano* (henceforth, *RIHGP*) 7 (1928):166–67. However, the major bandit groups active in Paraíba in the 1870s and 1880s preceded the great droughts of those decades. J. A. de Almeida, *Parahyba*, pp. 136–37.

> The large part of the backland's population is suffering horrible hunger, feeding itself macambira, *xiquexique* [a root of a spiney cactus], *potó* [a beetle], and other poisonous roots that produce horrible consequences. . . . Give work to the starving people. The country spends millions of contos on foreign immigrants, leaving the Brazilians of the Northeast to die of hunger for lack of employment.[15]

Like no other issue, drought dramatically juxtaposed the region's underdevelopment to the dynamic growth economy whose industrializing hub lay in São Paulo and Rio de Janeiro. Eventually, Paraíba's congressional delegation would attempt to join delegations from other northeastern states in lobbying nationally for a program of federal regional assistance. The creation in 1909 of a federal drought relief agency known as the IFOCS (Inspetoria Federal de Obras Contras as Sêcas) signaled a modest beginning.[16] After 1888–1889, major droughts returned to plague Paraíba more briefly and only in 1899, 1915, and 1919. Their relative absence contributed significantly to the almost uninterrupted cotton boom the state experienced during the first three decades of this century. Not until 1932 did a drought comparable to those of 1877–1879 and 1888–1890 again visit the region. Although the new federal commitment to drought relief little alleviated either the human suffering or the economic disruption imposed by cycles of drought, the presence of the national government at the state level of politics after 1909 introduced an important new variable in the oligarchical politics of Paraíba and the region.[17]

Conquest and Settlement Patterns

Settlement as Commercial Colonization

Historical patterns of conquest and settlement, in conjunction with climate and geography, continued to shape Paraíba's political

[15] *Gazeta do Sertão* [Campina Grande, Paraíba], 10 Jan. 1890, cited in I. Joffily, *Notas*, p. 48.

[16] Originally the IOCS (Inspetoria de Obras Contra as Sêcas), the Inspetoria's name was changed to IFOCS during Epitácio's presidency. In 1945, it became the DNOCS (Departamento Nacional Contra as Sêcas).

[17] The major beneficiaries of what is known in Brazil as the "drought industry" (*a indústria das sêcas*) have been not the landowners but "the members of the vast federal bureaucracy and consulting firms preparing their feasibility studies." Hall, "Irrigation," pp. 159–60 and 163.

economy during the Old Republic. The most important legacy of the frontier experience came from the period of initial colonization, when commercial routes were carved out to connect coast and backlands. As a result, Paraíba's backlands became more closely integrated with neighboring Pernambuco by virtue of an economic dependence on the Recife emporium. Market centers nearer the coast in Paraíba later emerged as aggressive rivals of the coastal capital.

The original donatary grant of 1534 creating Paraíba, known then as the Captaincy of Itamaracá, placed it under the administrative supervision of Pernambuco. Effective settlement began only in the 1580s and was undertaken largely by Pernambucano settlers and Spanish soldiers. Beginning with the Dutch invasion and occupation of the Capital in 1635, the captaincy was absorbed as Pernambuco's administrative dependency; it regained independent status only in 1684. From 1755 to 1799 Pernambuco again absorbed its northern neighbor. Paraíba's settlement and colonization paralleled efforts elsewhere in Brazil, for warfare with the French privateers for control of the brazilwood trade on the coast initially impeded Iberian colonization attempts. The Portuguese were kept at bay until 1579, when they finally evicted the French commercial interlopers from their trading factories on the Itamaracá coast. Thanks to a military alliance with the indigenous Tabajaras, conquest of the coast proceeded almost peacefully. The provincial capital of Filipéia, later Parahyba, was established in 1585, just after Portugal came under Spanish rule.

In founding the first settlement on the mainland near the mouth of the Paraíba River, the Portuguese colonists inadvertently guaranteed that economic tension would trouble commercial relations in the nineteenth and twentieth centuries. The Capital's geographical location eventually proved antagonistic to exporters in both the regional emporium at Recife and the backlands emporium at Campina Grande. Since Filipéia had been built at the point where the Paraíba River's wide mouth formed a sheltered basin with the confluence of one of its tributaries, the Sanhauá, the Capital possessed an inland port. However, eighteen kilometers downstream, the peninsular settlement of Cabedêlo posed a potential point of rivalry. An ocean anchorage situated precisely where the Paraíba river met the sea, Cabedêlo was unaffected by the Sanhauá River's shifting sandbars. In contrast, access for seagoing vessels to the Capital's riparian port of Varadouro remained totally dependent on the favorable conjuncture of the daily tides. Natural circumstances also meant that Cabedêlo enjoyed direct access by sea to the regional emporium at Recife.

For these reasons, during the nineteenth century the powerful Recife merchants who controlled the region's coastal trade as far north as southern Maranhão, acting in concert with the small group of merchants who monopolized the Capital's trade in Varadouro, deliberately prevented Cabedêlo's development as a deepwater port. The lone anchorage on the Atlantic served as a symbol of what local historians and politicians began to call "the tutelage" of Recife, for that port retained control over the Parahyba customs house until 1890. Merchants in Parahyba thereby remained subordinated to the Pernambuco trading houses and to Recife's regional political domination. However, they acquired expectations of economic independence with the arrival of the Old Republic, for a national policy of economic decentralization suggested that a deepwater port for the Capital could become a reality:

> Situated between those two ports [Cabedêlo and Recife], her fortunate location should have given [Parahyba] great commercial development. But up to now her growth has been slow. During the . . . three hundred years she has existed, she cannot count even one notable era of prosperity that enabled her to escape the tutelage of the neighboring Recife market—one in which she has always found and still finds herself.[18]

Once the customs house was officially transferred from Recife to Parahyba, the Capital's merchants and politicians continued to appreciate Cabedêlo's even greater potential for dominating their own commerce. That threat became real only when they challenged Recife for control of the interior's commerce after 1920.

As conquest and colonization turned inland in the 1660s, coastal Parahyba became strikingly detached from the hinterland, where trade was oriented directly toward the Recife emporium. Just as the original settlement of the coastal belt had followed from rising demand for sugar and dyestuffs in Europe's commercial revolution, the effective occupation of the interior depended upon the complementary economic activities of coast and hinterland. The earliest efforts to settle the land beyond the littoral assumed the objective of founding primitive cattle ranches. Backlands trade, in addition to flowing to Recife, became oriented

[18] I. Joffily, *O Academico Parahybano* [Recife] 4 (4 July 1886), cited in idem, *Notas*, p. 18.

toward Salvador in Bahia because the Piancó Valley's streams drained into the São Francisco River Basin in the Pernambuco backlands. Rivers also linked the alto sertão of Paraíba to coastal São Luis in distant Maranhão. The capture of the local Amerindian population for sale as slaves and the exploitation of alluvial gold deposits in the Piancó Valley also fueled the colonization of the hinterland.

By the 1690s, pioneering cattle drovers from Bahia and Pernambuco had already carved out the major commercial arteries that in the twentieth century would become the principal highways for exporting Paraíba's cotton to Atlantic ports. The backlands' network of cattle trails, integrated within a regional market web, demonstrated the fact that the settlement of the interior "proceeded as much from the backlands to the coast as from the coast toward the backlands."[19] Two separate routes connected the backlands with the coastal entrepôts of Recife and Salvador. A third route, via either the Seridó or Espinharas Roads, struck due west from Campina Grande and favored that town as "the meeting point of the major arteries of the sertão."[20] Lying in the eastern foothills of the Borborema, Campina Grande had easier and more rapid communication with Recife than with Parahyba. By the early nineteenth century, Campina had become the major terminus for the long-distance cattle drives that tapped livestock zones as far away as Ceará and Piauí. In 1889, a backlands journalist prophesied the city's new historical role, just before the arrival of the twentieth century's great cotton boom: "There is no doubt that by virtue of her topographical location Campina Grande is destined to be the emporium of the sertão—and in certain respects she already is."[21]

Settlement as a Family Business

Brief consideration of Paraíba's frontier formation will clarify the colonial family roots of political organization and behavior evident during the First Republic. As in the case of commercial routes, local patterns of political organization can be traced to the

[19] Horácio de Almeida, *Brejo de Areia* (Rio de Janeiro: Ministério da Educação e Cultura, Serviço de Documentação, 1958), p. 10.

[20] I. Joffily, *O Academico Parahybano* 4 (4 July 1886), cited in idem, *Notas*, p. 143.

[21] *Gazeta do Sertão*, 8 Mar. 1889.

initial period of conquest and settlement. The exercise of political power therefore remained wedded to the fact that the first settlers had subjugated and peopled both the coast and the hinterland as family military endeavors. The political economy they bequeathed to their descendants continued to reflect a high dependence on family membership and kinship ties despite unprecedented rural change after 1800. Three aspects of this frontier legacy had important consequences for the kin underpinnings of Paraíba's political economy after 1889: 1) violent and endemic family feuding as a means of resolving conflict; 2) reliance on lineage claims as a basis for political authority; and 3) family membership as a foundation for rights in land. All three conferred political legitimacy on the oligarchy at the local level and preserved violence as a sanctioned means of resolving conflict.

In the first place, the seventeenth-century *entradas*, or expeditions of frontiersmen seeking Amerindian slaves, gold, and cattle ranches in the interior, were the historical starting point for the reliance of politics on kinship organization throughout Brazil. Eventually, most of the leaders of entradas sought and obtained land grants in the vast interior, where their bands formed the first colonizing nuclei. The size of an entrada varied considerably, from as few as a dozen members to as many as a thousand. As a rule, it included the leader's sons or his father, his brothers and brother-in-law, and often his uncles or nephews. Not only the leader's family dependents and Amerindian or African slaves accompanied him but large numbers of free fighting men and random adventurers of either European or Brazilian ancestry also joined his ranks. The majority were Brazilians and *mamelucos*, persons of mixed Portuguese-Amerindian ethnicity. Ties of a patron–client nature bound all of them to the leader, whose paternalistic control of the entrada frequently depended on his identity as a ruthless patriarch. Almost always acting independently of Crown authority, the bellicose chieftains of the entradas opened the Northeast's interior to settlement under the auspices of their self-sufficient bands of frontiersmen; later they appealed to the political authorities on the coast for grants of land and military titles that would confer political legitimacy. In Paraíba's case, for instance, the earliest entradas penetrated the backlands under the private sponsorship of Brazilian outsiders from other regions. Their chieftains included members of the Garcia d'Avila and Oliveira families of Bahia, as well as the notorious *bandeirante* Jorge Domingos Velho, whose frontier army of over one thousand mameluco warriors had been raised in distant São Paulo.[22]

The brutal and even genocidal warfare that accompanied the confrontation between the indigenous population and the seventeenth- and eighteenth-century conquerors of the Northeast's backlands served to perpetuate the violent raiding patterns of two semi-nomadic cultures, the Iberian and the native Cariri. Frontier warfare became inseparably linked to the fusion of the races, although the published genealogies of many traditional families of the backlands later played down this important socio-racial aspect of settlement patterns.[23] Violent and endemic feuding evolved from the bellicosity the entradas had first spawned. As the native population faced extinction or withdrew to more inaccessible redoubts, the tradition of blood vendettas that the conquerors carried as part of their Mediterranean culture merged with analogous indigenous patterns. The native population having been first despoiled and then obliterated, the grandsons of the seventeenth-century conquerors of the backlands turned to preying upon smaller propertyowners.[24] The descendants of the first violent unions between Europeans and Amerindians might fight each other over points of honor or shame, but they would claim lands, livestock, and tenant clients as the spoils of victory, seizing these from neighbors who had become ethnically indistinguishable from themselves.

Geographical isolation from Crown authority, which gave the strongest families a local monopoly on violence, also perpetuated the internecine pattern of feuding so closely associated with Northeast Brazil. Because the power of a central State was exerted only sporadically, the colonizing families disputed land and grazing rights among themselves with impunity. Otherwise, they engaged in armed rivalries challenging the State's recognition of

[22] Capistrano de Abreu, cited in I. Joffily, *Notas*, pp. 31–61; ibid., pp. 117–35; Maximiano Lopes Machado, *História da Província da Paraíba (Reprodução da edição de 1912 . . .)*, 2 vols. (João Pessoa: Editôra Universitária, UFPb, 1977), 2:35–83.

[23] For example, Custódia de Almorim Valcáçar, grandmother of the Nóbrega kindred's legendary "seven sisters" and its founding mother, rarely is identified as an Amerindian woman in local histories and genealogies. See Epaminondas Câmara, *Datas campinenses* (João Pessoa: Departamento de Publicidade, 1947), pp. 13, 29, and 30 (n. 1). On Teixeira's first families' racially mixed origins, see Pedro Baptista, *Cônego Bernardo* (Rio de Janeiro: Civilização Brasileira, [1933]), pp. 12–13.

[24] Baptista, *Cônego Bernardo*, p. 33.

their competing claims to local military and administrative offices. Central authority could easily be countermanded locally, thanks to the private armies that large landowning families mustered in crisis. Not surprisingly, first royal officials and then their Brazilian imperial successors found themselves transformed into the political creatures of the very families whose conflicts they were sent to adjudicate. As Chandler has shown for Ceará's Inhamuns district, Crown officials who intervened locally in backlands family conflicts tended to become avid partisans; if they did not, they often had to seek physical safety beyond the immediate arena of warfare. In several respects, this situation endured in much of rural Brazil, as well as in Paraíba, until the present century.[25]

Reliance on lineage claims for the exercise of political authority was another aspect of Paraíba's political system bequeathed by the conquest and settlement period. Such claims, which were usually inseparable from claims to landed property, asserted political prerogatives by virtue of membership in a "first" or a "traditional" family. In the first place, this meant invoking racial criteria to demonstrate a politician's "whiteness"—his real or putative Portuguese descent. Given the increasing mobility of the nineteenth century, and especially the more frequent appearance of the mulatto in the nation's social and political life after 1850, those belonging to the oligarchies sought to separate themselves from the darker-skinned majority they ruled. The concept of the "traditional family" defined a class and color bar against entry to state politics. Although a chosen few were permitted to cross that barrier, as late as 1930 the grandson of an imperial politician observed that people of color were conspicuous for their absence at the Paraíba oligarchy's civic celebrations and social fêtes.[26] In the second place, by establishing lineage connections with a traditional family, a politician could claim political authority on the ground that he was descended from a kin grouping that historically had exercised considerable political and military authority. Descendants of the pioneering Oliveira Ledos, for example, still revered and manipulated their lineage claims in the nineteenth and twentieth century. They boasted of their "noble" blood derived from either

[25] Chandler, *The Feitosas*, ch. 2. The standard treatment of colonial feuding patterns in Brazil is Costa Pinto's *Lutas de família*.

[26] J. Joffily, *Revolta e revolução*, p. 147. Only one Paraíba politician from the Old Republic was identified as "mulatto" in the relevant biographical and memoir literature. J. A. de Almeida, *Parahyba*, p. 463.

Antônio or Teodósio de Oliveira Ledo and the latter's long-lived granddaughter, the legendary Dona Adriana Oliveira Ledo of Santa Rosa.

As leaders in opening the Paraíba backlands to settlement between the 1660s and the 1720s, and the founders of Pombal, Campina Grande, and a score of other interior settlements, the Oliveira Ledos formed the most important ancestral pool for the "first families of the sertão." The Portuguese Crown named their earliest trailblazer, Antônio Oliveira Ledo, military governor of the backlands. His title, Capitão Môr of the Piranhas, Cariri, and Piancós, suggested the territorial domain he commanded. First his brother, Custódio de Oliveira Ledo, then Custódio's son Constantino de Oliveira Ledo, and finally Constantino's famous brother, Teodósio de Oliveira Ledo, succeeded him. Agnatic ties—the bonds between brothers, between father and son, or between uncle and nephew—defined a family business of conquest, settlement, and politico-military rule for the Oliveira Ledos until the close of the eighteenth century. Their military conquests left a family imprint in the special privileges enjoyed by the local bosses in both the Empire and the Republic. Coupled with local officeholding, the bosses' patents in the National Guard conferred plenary grants of military authority similar to what their Oliveira ancestors had received from the Portuguese Crown.[27]

Although exceedingly useful resources in politics, lineage claims alone could not guarantee a politician an influential position in Paraíba's oligarchical elite or give a family political control of its home município. Possession of land, combined with a prestigious lineage, conferred the crucial entitlement to local rule. Legal rights to land rested on an informal oral tradition that linked landowners, either legitimate or putative, to the huge land grants, or *sesmarias*, that the backlands' first families had obtained from the Crown. Crown policy had granted land only to family heads, frequently to sibling sets—either to brothers or to brothers and their married sisters and their sisters' husbands—in addition to family heads and their married male offspring. The Oliveira Ledos, for example, received their first grant of 4,000 square kilometers as a family unit when the Crown simultaneously bestowed deeds

[27] Câmara, *Datas campinenses*, pp. 35–38. See Eul-Soo Pang, "The Politics of Coronelismo in Brazil: The Case of Bahia, 1890–1930" (Ph.D. diss., University of California, Berkeley, 1970), ch. 1, for an excellent history of the Brazilian National Guard.

on their patriarch Antônio de Oliveira Ledo, his brother, Custódio, his sister Barbara, his wife's sister and her husband, his son Francisco, his nephew Constantino, and finally on his four sons.[28] Because the Oliveiras remained the largest landowners in Paraíba until the close of the eighteenth century, possession of one of their family deeds conferred great proprietary legitimacy. Even in the 1890s, a "deed of the Oliveiras" was the best proof of land ownership that one could produce.[29]

Changing Demographic Patterns

Two striking demographic changes signaled the reorganization of Paraíba's political economy by the close of the Empire. First, throughout the nineteenth century an unprecedented shift of population inland testified to the economic changes taking place. Second, pronounced urban growth in the interior resulted, once agrarian production increased. The dynamic peopling of Paraíba's hinterland could be traced directly to the expansion of cereals and cotton in its four interior zones. This trend stood in marked contrast to more populous Pernambuco, where the sugar coast continued to be the most densely populated zone and the state's economic hub until 1930. A 1782 parish census showed that almost two-thirds of Paraíba's population had been concentrated in the small coastal zone by that date. A century later, the Empire's 1872 census revealed that only one-quarter of the province's population still lived there. (See Table I.1.) And by 1890 the coast's population had dropped to a mere 17 per cent of the population.

The shift of population inland represented a direct response to the emergence of the brejo and the caatinga-agreste. In 1782, the territory that would develop into those zones had contained approximately 8 per cent of the province's population, but a century later one-third of Paraíba's residents lived there. By 1890 the expansion of zones further west was challenging the preeminence of

[28] João de Lyra Tavares, *História territorial da Parahyba*, 2 vols. (Parahyba: Imprensa Oficial, 1909–1911) and Horácio de Almeida, *História da Paraíba*, 2 vols. (João Pessoa: Editôra Universitária/UFPb, 1978), 2:23, 27–31. Lyra Tavares's work was supplemented by Irinêo Joffily's *Sinopse das sesmarias da Capitania da Parahyba*, Vol. 1 (Parahyba: Typografia M. Henriques, 1894). See also the index of Lyra Tavares's comprehensive history, compiled by Genny da Costa e Silva: *Sesmeiros da Paraíba* (João Pessoa: Universidade Federal da Paraíba, 1965).

[29] I. Joffily, *Notas*, p. 40.

Table I.1: Paraíba Population Growth by Geographical Zone (1782–1930)

Geographic Zone	1782 N	1782 %	1872 N	1872 %	1890 N	1890 %	1920 N	1920 %	1930 N	1930 %
Coast	33,606	(64%)	93,051	(25%)	75,995	(17%)	173,019	(18%)	241,147	(18%)
Brejo Caatinga-agreste	4,322	(8%)	116,671	(31%)	71,992 121,251	(16%) (26%)	150,306 237,686	(16%) (25%)	211,593 334,588	(16%) (25%)
Cariri Alto Sertão	14,540	(28%)	165,512	(44%)	187,994	(41%)	194,321 205,774	(20%) (21%)	273,534 289,633	(20%) (21%)
Total	52,468	(100%)	375,234	(100%)	457,232	(100%)	961,106	(100%)	1,350,495	(100%)

Sources: I. Joffily, *Notas*, p. 253; Brazil, Ministerio da Agricultura e Commercio, Directoria Geral de Estatistica, *Recenseamento da população do Imperio do Brazil a que se procedeu no dia 1° de agosto de 1872*, 21 vols. (Rio de Janeiro: Leuzinger & Filhos, 1873–1876), 11:116; Brazil, Ministerio da Agricultura, Industria e Commercio, Directoria Geral de Estatistica, *Sexo, raça e estado civil, nacionalidade, filiação culto e analphabetismo da população recenseada em 31 de dezembro de 1890* (Rio de Janeiro: Oficina da Estatistica, 1898), pp. 86–89; State of Paraíba, Repartição de Estatistica e Arquivo Publico, *Annuario estatistico do Estado da Parahyba de 1916* (Parahyba: Imprensa Oficial, 1918), pp. 112–13; State of Paraíba, Secção de Estatistica do Estado, *Annuario estatistico do Estado da Parahyba de 1931* (João Pessoa: Imprensa Oficial, 1934), pp. 55–56; Brazil, Ministerio da Agricultura, Industria e Commercio, Directoria do Serviço de Estatística, *Divisão administrativa em 1911 da Republica dos Estados Unidos do Brazil* (Rio de Janeiro: Tipografia anexa a Directoria do Serviço de Estatistica, 1913), pp. 140–141.

Note: Before 1920, statistics collected according to parish boundaries did not admit the distinction of either brejo and caatinga-agreste or cariri and alto sertão. Hence population data is combined in those cases until 1890. Population according to zone has been estimated for 1782 based on the division of the province into only three parishes which closely corresponded to coast, brejo (with caatinga-agreste), and sertão (both cariri and alto sertão). The 1872 census data, which were collected according to many more parishes, have been reconstituted to correspond to those three zones. In 1890 and 1920, census data could be reconstituted by município according to, respectively, four and five zones. Throughout this work, the 1911 national definition of municípios has been used for data categorized according to zone. Thus in Paraíba's case the thirty-nine municípios recorded for 1911 provided the base list. The breakdown of municípios according to zones is as follows: *Coast*—Cabedêlo, Capital (Parahyba), Espírito Santo, Mamanguape, Pedras de Fogo, Santa Rita; *Brejo*—Alagoa Nova, Areia, Bananeiras, Serraria; *Caatinga-Agreste*—Alagoa Grande, Araruna, Caiçara, Campina Grande, Guarabira, Ingá, Itabaiana, Pilar; *Cariri-Sertão*—Alagoa do Monteiro, Cabaceiras, Picuí, Santa Luzia, São João do Cariri, Soledade, Taperoá, Umbuseiro; *Alto Sertão*—Brejo do Cruz, Cajazeiras, Catolé do Rocha, Conceição, Misericórdia, Patos, Piancó, Pombal, Princesa, São João do Rio do Peixe, São José de Piranhas, Sousa, Teixeira. (See also Map II.2, which indicates the location of municípios.)

the brejo and caatinga-agreste, whose population had increased to 42 per cent of the state's total. By the same date, the combined cariri-sertão represented 41 per cent of the state's residents. After 1889, the exhaustion of open land and the stability of the export sector's expansion maintained a static pattern of population for the next four decades.

Marked urban growth in the interior was the second major demographic change in Paraíba's nineteenth-century political economy. The appearance of new settlements and the expansion of existing ones testified to the urban revolution taking place beyond the coast. The Capital had been the only legally constituted city (*cidade*) in the province from 1585 until 1846, when it was joined by Areia. After mid-century, however, a new group of market centers concentrated in the brejo collectively challenged the Capital's commercial ascendancy. Areia, Guarabira, Bananeiras, and Alagoa Nova had originated as exchange points between coastal and backlands markets because they straddled the easternmost slopes of the Borborema. The exchange of backlands cattle, hides, and long-staple cotton for the foodstuffs of the brejo and caatinga-agreste underlay the new dynamic role the interior played in Paraíba's political economy. As early as the 1860s, nevertheless, a second set of fairs or markets in the caatinga-agreste—Fagundes, Itabaiana, Alagoa Grande, and especially mushrooming Campina Grande—became new urban competitors. They would overtake the brejo's commercial lead during the first decade of the Old Republic.

The importance of new urban centers in the interior found confirmation in the large number of them that received official recognition as legally constituted towns between 1800 and 1889. Previously, only three legally constituted towns had existed in Paraíba: Pilar (1758), Pombal (1772), and Campina Grande (1790). Between 1800 and 1845, all four (Areia, Bananeiras, Alagoa Nova, and Guarabira) of the brejo's market centers, in addition to coastal Mamanguape, became legal towns. Between 1846 and 1855, they were elevated to cities. In addition, six backlands settlements that legally had been mere villages—*aldeas*—became towns between 1800 and 1860. One, Sousa, became a city prior to the cotton boom of the 1860s. Following the cotton boom, however, Paraíba had twenty-five towns and nine cities. During the Old Republic only two more cities were legally created. Thus urbanization beyond the coast preceded the advent of the Republic and reinforced the zonal divisions that were crucial to the conflict which characterized oligarchical politics after 1889.

Agrarian Organization

The Cotton Export Economy, 1780–1920

The roots of the small-scale urban revolution that was apparent in Paraíba's hinterland by the 1850s reached back to the 1770s and 1780s, when a new crop, cotton, dramatically appeared beyond the coast for the first time. As an immediate consequence, the interior's economic orientation toward production for the coastal export sector shifted toward the production of cotton for the transatlantic economy. Henceforth, the livestock economy competitively shared land and water with agriculture. As a result, by the 1870s, Paraíba's political economy had undergone fundamental transformation. Britain's late eighteenth-century Industrial Revolution, with its voracious appetite for nature's white fiber, exerted an immediate impact on agriculture in the "cotton arc" of the Brazilian Northeast, especially in the Pernambuco–Paraíba hinterland and Maranhão.

Beginning in 1796, the apparently deliberate introduction of several foreign species of cotton—and not the exploitation of indigenous tree cotton, as commonly assumed—explained the pivotal role the Northeast would sporadically play as a major world supplier. During the first regional cotton boom, which lasted from the 1780s to around 1810, cotton displaced all of Brazil's commodities except sugar as the colony's leading export.[30] Production zones in the Paraíba interior played a major role from the start. In the first essay on Brazilian cotton cultivation, published in 1799, an eyewitness to the rapid spread of cotton cultivation beyond the coast wrote:

> The information regarding the great profits that cotton would pay those who cultivated it slowly penetrated the interior and awakened the planters. During the years 1777 to 1781 the people exerted new effort, and then it was that the interior became more densely inhabited and better cultivated, and cotton culture and the cotton trade increased wonderfully.[31]

[30] Prado Júnior, *História econômica,* p. 82; Visconde de Porto Seguro [Francisco Adolfo Varnhagen], *História geral do Brasil . . . antes de sua separação e independencia de Portugal,* 2 vols., 2nd ed. (Rio de Janeiro: E. & H. Laemmert, 1877), 2:1073–74 and 1078, cited in John C. Branner, *Cotton in the Empire of Brazil,* Department of Agriculture Miscellaneous Report, no. 8 (Washington, D.C.: U.S. Government Printing Office, 1885), p. 28.

[31] Manoel de Arruda da Camara, *Memoria sobre a cultura dos alogodoeiros, e*

British interest in the direct export of raw cotton from Paraíba dated from 1819, when four English commercial houses from Recife moved to the Capital's sole wharf at Varadouro in the lower city.[32] An unbroken series of cotton export statistics beginning in 1836 shows that Paraíba's commercial production for foreign markets gradually increased during the 1840s and averaged around 1 million kilos annually for the decade after 1836. (See Table I.2.) During the 1850s, exports steadily rose to an average of nearly 3 million kilos annually and then soared after 1865, thanks to the Civil War in the United States. Paraíba's annual exports of raw cotton averaged 4 million kilos for the decade after 1865, but they peaked at 5.9 million kilos in the 1874–1875 harvest. In his annual message of 1862, the provincial governor identified the factors that made Northeast Brazil's cotton arc a natural supplier to the British mills during the notorious Lancashire cotton "famine" of the 1860s. The factors he singled out to explain Paraíba's export success would appear again during the Old Republic, when they defined analogous demand conditions for the post-1910 peak of the boom:

> The war that is raging between the Southern States and those in the North of the Republic of the United States has opened a new and important era of advantageous consequence for our farmers and for the wealth of the nation. The planting of cotton in our country, which was being replaced by sugar, is regaining ground that had been lost. . . . Cotton from this province always deserves a good price in the markets of Europe by virtue of its strength and the length of its fiber. The struggle that is taking place in those American States is responsible for a rise in the price of this product favorable to farmers and to the revenues of the nation. . . . Cotton trees will be seen greening our countryside and once again taking the most favored place in the efforts . . . of our planters. The most important gains they could achieve will be reaped from the cultivation of herbaceous [*arbusto*] cotton, so important for its precious and generous yields.[33]

---

sobre o método de o escolher, e ensacar, etc. . . . (Lisbon: Casa Litteraria do Arco do Cego, 1799), p. 7.

[32] Lyra Tavares, *A Parahyba*, 2 Vols. (Parahyba: Imprensa Oficial, 1910), Vol. 1, pp. 13–18, 23–24.

[33] Annual Message of Gov. Francisco Araújo Lima, 1862, published in Irineu Ferreira Pinto, *Datas e notas para a história da Paraíba (Reproducção da edição de 1908)*, 2 vols. (João Pessoa: Editôra Universitária/UFPb, 1977), 2:293.

TABLE I.2: Cotton Exported from Paraíba during the Empire (1836/37 to 1875/76)

Year	Kilos	Year	Kilos
1836/37	1,793,115	1856/57	4,212,262
1837/38	1,635,375	1857/58	2,745,323
1838/39	—	1858/59	2,257,651
1839/40	883,050	1859/60	3,222,647
1840/41	1,058,400	1860/61	2,592,989
1841/42	881,445	1861/62	2,674,909
1842/43	1,445,150	1862/63	2,936,712
1843/44	1,471,620	1863/64	2,351,971
1844/45	1,921,905	1864/65	3,606,982
1845/46	—	1865/66	5,851,476
1846/47	—	1866/67	4,013,221
1847/48	1,360,815	1867/68	4,650,153
1848/49	2,819,115	1868/69	4,956,291
1849/50	—	1869/70	3,651,664
1850/51	—	1870/71	1,628,907
1851/52	3,120,015	1871/72	4,859,861
1852/53	2,703,869	1872/73	2,758,670
1853/54	1,947,331	1873/74	4,404,944
1854/55	2,860,582	1874/75	5,907,392
1855/56	3,730,836	1875/76	3,748,272

SOURCES: Irineu Ferreira Pinto, *Datas e notas para a história da Paraíba (Reprodução da edição de 1908)*, 2 vols. (João Pessoa: Editôra Universitária/UFPb, 1977), 2:137–300; Branner, *Cotton in the Empire of Brazil*, pp. 47–48.

NOTE: Branner's pounds, derived from arrobas, have been converted on the basis of his formula: thirty-two pounds per arroba or fifteen kilograms, per arroba, as have the arrobas taken from *Datas e notas*. Harvests span December–January and therefore overlap years.

The abrupt contraction in world prices during the early 1870s, as the American South resumed production for the Lancashire textile mills, caused a severe crisis in Brazilian cotton exports. Paraíba's exports fell less precipitously than elsewhere in the region, probably because its fine-quality, long-staple cotton was in higher demand. "Bust," however, was undeniable by 1873. Then at the end of the decade, natural catastrophe struck in the Great

Drought of 1877–1879. Production was devastated for three harvests, and even the deeply rooted tree cottons of the backlands failed to survive the century's worst drought. Recovery was rapid, although the trees needed five to seven years to reach maturity. The 1886–1887 harvest produced 9.6 million kilos of ginned cotton, the highest ever recorded. But this remarkable upsurge was abruptly curtailed the following year by the Great Drought of 1888–1890.

With the advent of the Republic in 1889, new factors of domestic and world demand for raw cotton asserted themselves. Although they had appeared as early as the 1880s, it was not until the first decade of this century that they called forth another dramatic period of expansion, one that was sustained throughout the Northeast until the Great Depression. By the late 1880s the textile center of Brazil had shifted from Salvador to Rio de Janeiro and São Paulo. The mills became dependent on either São Paulo or the Northeast's cotton-growing arc for supplies of the raw fiber. World demand, on the other hand, was still satisfied by the United States, the Nile Valley, and India. A republican form of government in Brazil, in tandem with the coffee boom in the Center-South, created domestic conditions favorable to the expansion of northeastern production. As Stanley J. Stein has pointed out, a number of factors were at work. Above all, the coffee boom led to capital formation that stimulated investment in the domestic market. Initially, tariff policy in the 1890s raised the import duties on coarse cotton goods and thus nationalistically protected the market for Brazilian manufacturers. In the long run, however, relatively low wages enabled a national textile industry to expand at the expense of foreign manufactures.[34]

The third and final cotton boom in the Northeast rested on a different factor: worsening shortages of long-staple cottons in virtually every major production zone around the world. Like the 1780s and the 1860s, the period from 1910 to 1930 disclosed the Northeast's essentially marginal role as a world producer: only during special periods of worldwide cotton dearth, when excep-

[34] Stanley Stein, *The Brazilian Cotton Manufacture: Textile Enterprise in an Underdeveloped Area, 1850–1950* (Cambridge: Harvard University Press, 1957), pp. 14–23. For a critique of the conventional emphasis placed on tariff policy as the primary stimulant of Brazilian self-sufficiency in textiles by the 1920s, see Albert Fishlow, "Origins and Consequences of Import Substitution in Brazil," in *International Economics and Development: Essays in Honor of Raúl Prebish*, ed. Luís Eugenio de Marco (New York: Academic Press, 1972), pp. 318–22.

tionally high prices prevailed, did production boom. The boll weavil's inexorable destruction of crops in the United States, beginning in the 1890s, resulted in a global shortage of Sea Island (Georgia or Bourbon) and other long-staple varieties that by 1917 reached crisis proportions.[35] World manufacturers correctly perceived that their supplies of long-staple cottons would be severely curtailed for another decade at least, and when production in Barbados and the Nile Valley plummeted following World War I, they became desperate. In 1921, Arno Pearse, the secretary general of the Manchester-based International Federation of Master Cotton Spinners and Manufacturers' Association, undertook his historic survey of Brazil's production zones. After stating that the supply of long-staple cotton was likely to remain below demand for another decade, he concluded that the Northeast of Brazil could offset the shortfall.[36] In default of the key traditional suppliers, Brazil's cotton arc became the most important production zone of long-staple cottons in the world.

Patterns of Land Use, 1870–1930

The political significance of the Northeast's identity as a world production zone for raw cotton lay in the change the new export crop had imposed on patterns of land use and labor by the era of the Old Republic. First in "boom" and then in "bust," cotton's advance into the hinterland between the late 1850s and the early 1870s reorganized the political economy there. Unclaimed land ceased to be available after mid-century. The more liberal arrangements that had prevailed between landlords and their free tenant cultivators earlier in the century tightened into an onerous system of servitude. Changes in agrarian organization, particularly the dispossession of small holders, strengthened old patterns of family feuding. By maintaining effective control over their tenant clients, landlords rendered insignificant any challenge from the laboring population in the countryside. As land itself became a scarce resource, highly exploitative rural labor arrangements directly contributed to the agrarian oligarchy's profitable investment in the cotton export economy.

[35] William W. Coelho de Souza, *Possibilidades da cultura algodoeira no Brasil* (Rio de Janeiro: Ministerio da Agricultura, Industria e Commercio, 1922), pp. 21–23.

[36] Arno Pearse, *Brazilian Cotton* (Manchester: International Federation of Master Cotton Spinners & Manufacturers' Association, 1923) p. 54.

A survey of land use in Paraíba published in 1907 noted that virtually no unclaimed land remained. Where land lay uncultivated, the survey's politician-author knowingly observed, owners invariably were large proprietors. And large proprietors proved remarkably adept at acquiring land by pressing spurious claims and using illegal or extralegal methods of taking effective possession. In his scholarly analysis of rural life in Paraíba, José Américo de Almeida also could comment knowingly on the fact that latifundia in his native state had failed to break up. Alleging that inheritance patterns alienated very little land from the control of traditional families, he observed: "Their sesmaria [legal] constitution is a matter of great discord. Almost all [large properties] remain undivided. Conflicts over land . . . rarely have juridical solutions."[37] What could not be accomplished legally, or by means of consanguineous marriage strategies that circumvented the partible inheritance system, could be achieved by judicial chicanery and forced eviction. In practice, either the private retainers of powerful rural magnates or the state police acting on their behalf customarily acted as arbiters of property rights.[38]

Armed clashes over land use occurred with astonishing regularity as soon as agriculture challenged the stockraising economy for grazing resources. After 1860 new economic incentives for cotton and cereal production in the polyculture zones placed a higher premium on land values. By 1907 extensive deforestation testified to agriculture's victorious advance:

> Virgin forest does not exist, and the original trees can be found only in the *capoeirões*, those strips of land that have gone for a number of years without the cultivator's destructive axe.

[37] J. A. de Almeida, *Parahyba*, p. 548. Antonio Botto de Menezes describes how Col. José Lins de Albuquerque, a wealthy sugar planter, squeezed out a modest neighbor in Pilar by manipulating the legal process. *Minha terra* (Rio de Janeiro: ESPA, 1944), pp. 106–107. Thanks to manipulation of the legal system, in 1980, the Brazilian newsweekly *Veja* (São Paulo) noted that "[in] no country in the world does one find the same piece of land registered so many times. Judging from the written registries in the public record offices, Brazil's territorial size is much larger than the eight million square kilometers established by international treaty during the colonial era." 13 Feb. 1980, pp. 21–22.

[38] Robert Shirley offers an anthropologist's view of the persisting tensions between the Brazilian judiciary and powerful landlords in the countryside of São Paulo in recent decades: "Law in Rural Brazil," in *Brazil: Anthropological Perspectives*, ed. Maxine Margolis and William E. Carter (New York: Columbia University Press, 1979), pp. 343–61.

> The farmer is a prisoner of the regimen [*a rotina*] of traditional agriculture and he knows only how to devastate the woods.[39]

In the município of Campina Grande, the gradual westward movement of a *travessão*, a man-made barrier for preventing livestock from entering the agricultural agreste, symbolized the challenge that the expanding cereal and cotton economy had posed to stockraisers since the 1830s. In the 1890s the conflict over the travessão's presence still persisted: "In the agreste and the caatinga two industries, stockraising and agriculture, are always in conflict, in spite of the municipal laws that prescribe limits to each one, as well as penalties for breaking them."[40]

It is impossible to assess precisely the impact of cotton's expansion on land tenure patterns in Paraíba. Reliable analyses, and perhaps even the sources from which to construct them, do not exist. From José Américo's firsthand observations, however, it appears that the concentration of land apparently increased during the Old Republic and accelerated more rapidly in the 1930s.[41] The first attempt to survey land on a comprehensive basis in Paraíba, the 1920 national census, assessed only about one-half of the state's existing properties. But for these properties at least, it revealed patterns of agrarian organization that directly affected the political organization of family-based rule. Two-thirds of Paraíba's rural properties were medium to small in size, less than 101 hectares. Their value per hectare was nevertheless five times greater than that of the remaining one-third of the properties over 101 hectares. The larger properties tended to be vast, semi-arid livestock estates in the interior, except for a small proportion of them on the coast that, as former sugar plantations, had recently been consolidated as commercial land belonging to a few usinas, or modern sugar refineries. In other words, the small to medium holdings characteristic of the caatinga-agreste and brejo, and devoted to polyculture, including intercropped cotton, represented the state's richest land resource. This circumstance suggests why in the intermediate zones local violence so dramatically escalated beginning in the late 1880s. Campina Grande, for instance, was the município with the largest number of medium to small properties and the wealthiest in agricultural land. Not surprisingly, internecine family war-

39 Lyra Tavares, *A Parahyba*, 2:600.

40 I. Joffily, *Gazeta do Sertão*, 9 Nov. 1888, cited in I. Joffily, *Notas*, p. 29.

41 J. A. de Almeida, *Parahyba*, p. 548; I. Joffily, *Notas*, p. 29; and Celso Mariz, *Evolução econômica da Paraíba* (João Pessoa: *A União Editôra*, 1939), p. v.

fare expanded more dramatically in Campina than in any other município. The sound of gunfire echoed in the streets of its county seat throughout the entire Old Republic.

The oligarchy's local political organization directly reflected Paraíba's pattern of land tenure. Above all, patterns of ownership reinforced the fragmentary nature of coronelismo, the system of local boss rule. Unlike many larger states in the Center-South, or even in Pernambuco—where a single boss often wielded great power over an entire zone—local power in Paraíba remained spatially restricted and highly segmented. Political bosses continued to be dependent on the personal alliances cemented by intermarriage that transcended município boundaries. The "super coronel" that Joseph L. Love identifies in Rio Grande do Sul during the Old Republic never appeared in Paraíba, where local bosses acquired domination over one município at best.[42] And what Jean Blondel points out as a feature of the post-1945 era really had existed much earlier: the "collegial" organization he associated with coronelismo in Paraíba can be traced to the fragmented pattern of land ownership based on multiple ownership of land by allied families.[43] Of course, the 1920 Census underrepresented land concentration. Comparison of the lists of property owners by município established that the same individual owned properties adjacent to each other in different municípios—or individuals, in tandem with their siblings and other close relatives, owned land in close proximity as co-heirs.[44] True latifundia emerged only in the sugar zone, where one "monolithic" family, the Ribeiro Coutinhos, dominated politics. Elsewhere, however, two or three families exercised political influence according to a delicate balance, which land tenure and inheritance patterns eventually rendered precarious.[45]

[42] Love, *Rio Grande do Sul*, p. 80. The exception to the rule that the power of a local boss did not encompass more than one município was Col. José Pereira Lima of Princesa.

[43] Jean Blondel, *As condições da vida política no Estado da Paraíba* (Rio de Janeiro: Fundação Getúlio Vargas, 1957), pp. 42–51.

[44] Brazil, Ministerio da Agricultura, Industria e Commercio, Directoria Geral de Estatistica, *Recenseamento do Brazil realizado em 1 de setembro de 1920, Relação dos proprietarios dos estabelecimentos ruraes recenseados no Estado da Parahyba* (Rio de Janeiro: Typografia da Estatistica, 1928), pp. 17–54, 85–109, 128–62, 223–28. See also Jason Clay, "The Articulation of Non-Capitalist Systems of Exchange with Capitalist Systems of Exchange: The Case of Garanhuns, 1845–1917" (Ph.D. diss., Cornell University, 1977), p. 198.

[45] Wirth found that the "extended clans of Minas" relied on their kinship ties for spanning municípios to form zonal power bases in the second half of the nine-

Landlord–Tenant Relationships Transformed, 1870–1930

New patterns of land use reflecting a demographic shift inland and a rising concentration of land led to the appearance of a "new" peasantry in the 1870s. Cotton's strongest impact beyond the coast resulted in the reorganization of the rural population within a new labor system. Although legally free, the Northeast's agricultural tenants became incorporated within a subordinate arrangement that they themselves referred to as *a sujeição*—literally, submission or subjugation. In more recent times, this system has become universally familiar as *cambão* labor, after the hobble used to control a team of oxen.[46]

Sujeição labor predominated as either sharecropping or a quasi-rental arrangement throughout the hinterland of the Northeast following the 1860s cotton boom. An exploitative means of insuring cheap and compliant labor for landlords, the sujeição arrangement represented a divergence from earlier landlord-tenant relationships in two respects. First, it exacted labor under much more onerous and impoverishing terms. Second, its existence depended on the disappearance or deliberate obliteration of the middle peasantry and on the conversion of that stratum of freeholders into a group of landless agricultural tenants. Henry Koster's detailed observations on the organization of cotton production in Paraíba, Pernambuco, and Rio Grande do Norte between 1811 and 1816 made these points very clear. He noted that landlords "sometimes" required peasants to labor in their fields in lieu of paying money rents. The only limitation on the quantity of land farmed by peasant families, however, had been their capacity to cultivate it.[47] The arrangements Koster described appeared strikingly more generous than the sujeição labor that critical journalists and government agronomists condemned a century later.

What had caused labor arrangements to change so adversely for the peasantry? In the early 1870s, as Jason Clay points out, falling earnings from bumper crops, due to lower world prices and demand, caught the middle peasantry of the Northeast in a scissors

---

teenth century. *Minas Gerais*, pp. 68–69. See also Cid Rebelo Horta, "Famílias governamentais de Minas Gerais," in *Segundo, Seminário de Estudos Mineiros* (Belo Horizonte: Universidade de Minas Gerais, 1956), pp. 58–61, on the same phenomenon.

[46] Francisco Julião, *Cambão—The Yoke* (Baltimore and Middlesex: Penguin Books, 1972), p. 13.

[47] Henry Koster, *Travels in Brazil*, 2 vols. (Philadelphia: M. Carey & Son, 1817), 1:137.

effect.[48] While export earnings continued to fall, domestic cereals remained relatively high in price. Consequently, debts could not be repaid and credit disappeared. Foreclosure, sale, and presumably the bargaining away of more liberal land and labor arrangements followed. Historically more generous arrangements for obtaining local credit from wealthier landlords also collapsed. "Subjugation" therefore emerged from local agriculture's structural dependence on exports and from the parallel dependence of peasants on landlords for credit. The 1870s and 1880s present a painful paradox: just when abolition of the slave trade and gradual emancipation was draining the Northeast of its captive population for work in the coffee fields of western São Paulo, free peasants in the interior found themselves laboring under a new yoke of poverty and submission.

The widespread institutionalization of this labor system carried important political consequences for the era of the oligarchies. The imposition of sujeição labor had coincided with the last great regional revolt challenging the rural landlords' control of the countryside—the Quebra-Quilo (Smash the Kilos) Revolt. A major *jacquerie*, this uprising took its name from popular opposition to the imperial government's introduction of the metric system of weights and measures in 1874. The revolt sent tremors throughout five provinces after its eruption in the market town of Fagundes, a few kilometers outside Campina Grande. Spreading from an epicenter in Paraíba's caatinga-agreste as far south as the province of Bahia and as far north as Rio Grande do Norte, the Quebra-Quilo testified to the militancy of the peasantry. Brutally suppressed by imperial forces in early 1875, after three months of unchecked popular attacks on commercial houses, markets, and government offices, the Quebra-Quilo would be Paraíba's last popular rebellion. The revolt's historical significance for the Old Republic lay in the rebels' political failure to prevent the imperial government from setting aside the ancient system of Portuguese measurements and to check the aggressive regulation of weekly markets by the government, which included the implementation of more determined efforts to collect taxes. Above all, the singular brutality with which the imperial and provincial authorities in Paraíba crushed the revolt offered a powerful object lesson to future peasant rebels.[49]

[48] Clay, "Garanhuns," pp. 57, 114, 134–36, 157–60, and 177–79.

[49] Ibid., p. 179. See also Roderick J. Barman, "The Brazilian Peasantry Reexamined: The Implications of the Quebra-Quilo Revolt, 1874–75," *HAHR* 57, 3

Following the cotton bust and the Quebra-Quilo, labor arrangements between landlords and tenants account for the largely unchallenged political control that landlords in the oligarchy exercised over their rural clients until the 1920s. Considerable fragmentation within the rural labor force facilitated local landlords' control of their tenants. Divisions existed between lessees (*foreiros*), sharecroppers (*meeiros*), and specially favored squatters or small holders who enjoyed greater privileges (*moradores*). In addition, a small semi-migratory stratum of rural wage labor found employment in the coastal and intermediate zones. These distinctions, based on specific arrangements for exchanging land and labor, posed severe obstacles to peasant cohesion and rendered collective action highly unlikely. Sujeição labor colloquially applied to both lessees and sharecroppers. Strictly speaking, it was a Brazilian variant of corvée labor that was widespread and did not come under frontal attack until the 1960s. In exchange for access to a plot of land, a tenant entered a sujeição arrangement in order to perform unpaid labor service for his landlord. His "submission" implied great relevance for political control, because the deferential behavior that the sujeição relationship demanded placed him in a clearly subordinate role as the landlord's client. In the mid-1920s, the popular poet José Camelo protested this humiliating servitude in his native state. His outcry, written a generation after sujeição labor had hardened into a widespread system, disclosed that for the ordinary cultivators of cotton the "boom" brought only misery. Entitled "The Subjugation of the Brejos of Paraíba do Norte," the poem circulated as a "hit" in the chapbooks that were popular reading material throughout the Northeast:

Hoje o Brasil quasi todo Vae ficando escravizado, Mas na Parahyba o jugo Ja se acha habilitado.	In Brazil almost everyone today Is falling under slavery. But in Paraíba one can find That the yoke is already customary.
Portanto eu solto clamores, Por ser filho deste Estado. Pois é mais na Parahyba.	That's why I'm making my outcry, Because I'm a native son. Because it's worse in Paraíba.
. . . .	. . . .
E creio que augmentará Si não encontrar barreira.	And I believe that it will get worse As long as nothing stops it.[50]

(1977):401–24; and Geraldo Joffily, *O Quebra-Quilo (A revolta dos matutos)* (Brasília: Thesaurus, 1977).

[50] José Camello de Mello Rezende, *A sujeição da zona brejeira da Parahyba do*

Large landowners usually subcontracted their cotton production, occasionally ceding fenced areas to tenants or small independent proprietors. They advanced credit in exchange for first option on purchase of the crop. In the caatinga-agreste, where *mata* or herbaceous cottons predominated, the most common system of subcontracting land and labor was *aforamento*, the annual leasing of land to lessees known as foreiros. Because of the need to replant herbaceous cottons every year, annual contracts, almost always oral, prevailed. Thus, tenants could easily be dismissed when their labor was no longer needed. The system of credit also insured that landowners would retain labor when it was needed. After the First World War, large proprietors advanced credit for planting at annual interest rates of 20 to 40 per cent, so that any unpaid balance accumulated as debt in succeeding years. They also maintained the notorious company store, or *barracão*, another feature common to the Northeast that survived until the 1960s.[51]

Rodrigues de Carvalho, a journalist, folklorist, and part-time politician, concurred with the poet José Camelo about the misery of the rural tenants. His caustic comment, included in a 1916 report he wrote for the federal government, revealed his personal and professional familiarity with rural conditions:

> Small-scale agriculture is composed of the most humble proletarians in the world. These are the uneducated peasants who lease: illiterate, without houses—because they inhabit an open-air lean-to covered only with straw—without a piece of land, without even a cow or animal to ride, and without comfort or rights. Almost always the lessee is the head of a numerous progeny—a progeny raised in nakedness, anemic, starving, [and] semi-barbaricized. The peasant [*matuto*] of the Northeast has become subjugated to the owners of land.[52]

True sharecropping (*meiação*) prevailed in both backlands zones, where perennial tree cottons predominated. Sharecroppers, or meeiros, received seeds for both cotton and cereals from landlords; in some cases, interest-free loans with which to purchase

Norte (Guarabira, Paraíba: Livraria e Typografia Lima, 1925), pp. 8–9, cited in J. Joffily, *Revolta*, p. 130.

51 Diogenes Caldas, "Algodão da Parahyba," *Annaes da Primeira Conferencia Algodoeira (1916)*, 2 vols. (São Paulo: [Sociedade Nacional da Agricultura], 1916), 2:290. Claudio Gouveia, "O algodão na Parahyba," pamphlet no. 4 in *Algodão* [Miscellaneous collection of Brazilian government pamphlets] (n.p., n.d.), pp. 2 and 8.

52 [José] Rodrigues de Carvalho, "A cultura do algodoeiro no Estado da Parahyba—O problema da pequena lavoura," *Annaes Algodoeira (1916)*, 2:318.

them were made available. In exchange, the sharecropper worked two or three days a week in the landlord's fields and pledged a predetermined portion of his own cotton harvest, usually one sack of raw cotton. Weighing about thirty-four kilos, the notorious sack symbolized why, for one government agronomist, the meiação arrangement was "a type of sharecropping in which the tenant farmer was always the suffering Christ."[53] If disaster struck and the harvest failed, the sharecropper became his landlord's prisoner: the following year, not one but two sacks of raw cotton would be demanded. Debt peonage thus was implicit in the arrangement.[54]

The most favored rural tenants fell into the morador category, whose members ranged from the small, independent proprietor to the squatter who enjoyed quasi-permanent residence rights on a large estate. Moradors comprised a stratum indispensable to the landed oligarchy's control because it was from their ranks that the personal retainers of the powerful were recruited. They advertised their higher social status through the coveted privilege to bear firearms. Those who performed sujeição labor were permitted only cudgels and the long knives known in the Northeast as *parnaíbas*. The landlord's favorite henchman—the *cabra do coronel* so celebrated in Brazilian popular poetry, fiction, and Western movies—was usually a morador. As the landlord's right hand, the cabra disciplined and policed the tenant population, and even executed those who proved unsubmissive. Above all, he delivered the vote for the rural and urban bosses at election time, protecting those who voted for his patron and intimidating the local political opposition.

Throughout the Old Republic, the impressive vertical control exercised by the agrarian oligarchies everywhere rested fundamentally on the relationships they maintained with the tenant cultivators who comprised the majority of the nation's population.[55] Strong ties of clientage, often strengthened by quasi-famil-

[53] Caldas, "Algodão na Parahyba," p. 290.

[54] Eviction operated as a powerful coercive measure: "The livestock of the landowner enjoy immunity. They break the fences [of the tenants], destroy the crops, but everything stays that way because if the unlucky tenant complains, he will not be long in being expelled, his crops fed to the catttle, and his lean-to burned down. And if the coronel, the landowner, is also political boss, or even the local law officer . . . [then] the unfortunate man will go to the nearby jail to be purgued of his rage." Rodrigues de Carvalho, "Pequena lavoura," p. 318.

[55] Forman and Riegelhaupt have analyzed the phenomenon of patron–client relationships from the perspective of the political economy of the Brazilian nation-

ial bonds, enabled the oligarchies to resist challenge from below in many rural areas. Particularly in the Northeast, the patron–client relationships universal to town and countryside forestalled the appearance of political divisions along sharply horizontal or class lines. A corporatist and paternalistic world view subsumed both familial and client–patron relationships.

To maintain their superior position in the hierarchy of power, members of the oligarchy relied equally on their horizontal ties with each other. They could invoke a tacit social pact among themselves that rewarded a tenant's defiance with swift eviction at the very least. Thus grinding poverty, extreme economic dependence on landlords, and the reciprocal bonds of patron-client relationships all reinforced the landed oligarchy's control of the countryside. Rural tenants could seek redress or revenge only in individual revolt. Not until the 1920s did this situation change.

Rural Change and Family-Based Oligarchy

Historical patterns of land, labor, and population distribution, coupled with the commercialization of rural production imposed after 1880, directly affected the course of Paraíba's oligarchical politics throughout the Old Republic. These factors represented the key elements in political conflict at the local level and, to a large extent, explained the fragility inherent in the ruling oligarchy's coalition statewide. The progressive expansion of cotton production until 1930, however, provided an economic foundation of unprecedented prosperity for oligarchical consolidation, one that facilitated the hegemony the Pessoas exercised between 1912 and 1930. Unprecedented urbanization in the interior and emergence of an agro-exporting economy of growth based on "*ouro branco*" (white gold) nevertheless reinforced Paraíba's historical orientation toward major regional markets in neighboring Pernambuco, Ceará, and Rio Grande do Norte. Although Paraíba's own "gateway to the sertão"—Campina Grande—assumed historical importance as the state's principal entrepôt for backlands cotton, after 1889 the determination to develop Cabedêlo as a deepwater port for backlands production planted the seeds of future political conflict on an interzonal basis. By etching five zones of

---

state in Shepard Forman and Joyce F. Riegelhaupt, "The Political Economy of Patron–Clientship: Brazil and Portugal Compared," in *Brazil*, ed. Margolis and Carter, pp. 379–400, esp. 384–90.

distinct geoeconomic interest within Paraíba's boundaries, patterns of settlement and land use introduced a powerful impetus toward fragmentation, because family blocs of power were wedded to local bases of interest which competed for the same resources.

In spite of almost uninterrupted boom conditions during the Old Republic, a fundamental truth of Paraíba's politics always had to be taken into account: the landed economy remained an economy of extreme scarcity, even for the prospering family-based groups that managed it. Economic growth favored only a narrow slice of the population. Outward dependence on an international—and, after 1915, national—demand for cotton, hides, and sugar meant that the leading sector of growth would remain vulnerable and limited as a means for generating broad development of the state economy. Declining economic and political importance of the Northeast in the nation further restricted opportunity for the state oligarchy to use economic growth to alter Paraíba's historically persistent poverty. Furthermore, the ruling oligarchy viewed economic growth as opportunity for expanding both patronage and export infrastructure on behalf of the key family-based groups controlling the municípios, not as a means of alleviating poverty or addressing its causes.

When, in the 1970s, octogenarian survivors of the era of the oligarchies in Paraíba turned to reminisce, they still recalled the early decades of this century as "*a época da alta*"—the era of the boom. The fact that Paraíba's family-based oligarchical system enjoyed its greatest power during the boom years of cotton production is more than a coincidence. It suggests that the powerful family-based groups that formed the oligarchy's basic units rose and fell, just as agriculture passed through cycles of boom and bust, because their perpetuation in power remained closely linked to the political economy. The economy of growth that had emerged by the turn of the century, however, did more than merely signal the rise of some family-based groups and the fall of others. It introduced new elements of change that after the First World War would challenge the historical reliance oligarchy had placed on those informal groups as a foundation for political cohesion.

· II ·

The Agrarian Oligarchy and Its Export Economy in an Era of Change, 1889–1922

I lived in the typical sertão that is now disappearing. . . . In the old days cotton had not killed the fields and the cattle could range throughout the hinterland. . . . [They] were herded together only for the annual division of the newborn calves among the cowhands during festive roundups. . . . Now even the cotton planters themselves come to the Capital to oversee the delivery of their bales . . . everything is done by automobile. . . . With the "boom" in cotton and sugar, former planters have ordered houses to be constructed for themselves in the cities on the coast. They go to the sertão only at harvest. . . . All of this revolution came after 1911.

—Luis da Câmara Cascudo,
Vaqueiros e cantadores, 1939

More economic growth occurred in Paraíba during the forty-one years of the Old Republic than had taken place in the preceding three centuries. The unprecedented expansion of the export sector could be measured in an impressively rising volume of cotton shipped abroad and to domestic ports, a larger capital investment in infrastructure, and a higher proportion of land planted in cotton. Together, these indicators of growth defined a boom economy that would have important effects on Paraíba's system of family-based oligarchy. The agrarian oligarchy depended directly on the export economy not only for its livelihood but also for its control of politics. The cotton boom meant that the state government acquired greater significance for Paraíba's ruling families, because as the export sector expanded between 1900 and 1930, the role of government in fostering economic growth assumed more critical proportions. Oligarchy's essence lay in the near monopoly that the dominant party machine exercised over the formal institutions of the State and in the economic power that flowed from this monopoly. Elite families engaged more frequently in violent competition for control of local markets. For that reason, the ability of the more powerful family-based groups to monopolize local officeholding or to exclude their rivals from representation in the Assembly also acquired a new urgency.

Public policy consistently reflected the landed and commercial interests of the most important family-based groups. Several dozen powerful parentelas and their local factional groupings exercised preponderant control over the landed economy in each of Paraíba's five geoeconomic zones. As the ruling oligarchy at the state level, they represented largely overlapping economic interests spanning land ownership, agricultural production and processing, and commerce. All these endeavors rested firmly on the expanding cotton export economy, although most parentelas invested in a wide spectrum of productive activities. Besides producing cotton, cotton seeds, cakes, oil, and paste, they also manufactured sugar and aguardiente, or raised cattle, goats, horses, and sheep for the export of meat, hides, skins, and wool. Coffee, coconut, and indigenous plant fibers and waxes rounded out the list of their commodities.

Far from being merely a planter group, the families who comprised Paraíba's wealthiest and politically most powerful landowners represented an emerging agrarian bourgeoisie. By 1910 the oligarchy's most influential members were entrepreneurially oriented landowners. Typically, cotton planters who had invested in agricultural processing equipment or in commercial and industrial ventures that were linked to the export sector formed the powerful core of this class. Mutual interest in an expanding export economy, one that amounted to a tenet of economic faith, provided the basis for an underlying consensus and reinforced the homogeneity of political goals at the leadership level. In large part, this consensus explains the relative absence of serious divisions within the elite until the late 1920s. The similarity in the working relationship that both the Machado–Leal oligarchy and the Pessoa oligarchy established with the State is evident where the linkages between the State and the expanding export economy are examined. Both the group basis of oligarchy and its grounding in agrarian export production depended on the existence of a patronage State.

Growth and Oligarchical Divisions

An Economic Periodization of Oligarchy

Broadly speaking, events at the national level determined the political chronology in Paraíba throughout the Old Republic. They imposed basic limits to change and introduced new factors that would modify family-based politics. In addition, they reveal why oligarchical organization could remain highly adaptive in the face of challenges from the state government. National political events also influenced the stages of Paraíba's economic growth, which corresponded to three political subperiods of oligarchical leadership. Each subperiod ended with a crisis that could be linked to the changing role of the federal government and framed against the expansion or contraction of the boom economy.

The first subperiod, that of the Machado–Leal oligarchy (1892–1912), witnessed accelerating economic growth accompanied by relatively little infrastructure elaboration, since significant federal resources were absent. Technological modernization of agricultural processing plants and equipment increased only modestly, for private capitalists financed investment. This period acquired political identity as one of Alvarista "anarchy"; it ended in an armed insurrection in the backlands. The second subperiod, that of a cohesively maintained Pessoa oligarchy (1912–1922), witnessed a comparatively greater amount of infrastructure expansion, due to the role the federal government assumed in investment, which took place during years of high export-led growth. Politically, contemporary language referred to this decade as one of Epitacista "order," one that exemplified the Pessoas' smooth coordination of a statewide electoral machine. The third and final subperiod, that of the Pessoas' oligarchical decline and disintegration (1922–1930), coincided on the one hand with the apogee of cotton's export expansion, and on the other with a drastic reduction in federal patronage. It closed with the arrival of economic "bust" imposed by the world crisis of 1929–1930. The long-term impact of economic growth on Paraíba's family-based politics, however, became evident only in this last stage, as more complex interest groups, social differentiation, and intraregional competition developed. As a consequence, the final subperiod ended in rising elite fragmentation, realignment, and another armed insurrection. Nationally, the denouement of Pessoa rule coincided with the victory of Getúlio Vargas's Revolution of 1930.

Export Growth and Oligarchical Rivalry

Although the president of Brazil decided who would lead the Paraíba oligarchy as its state party boss, his decision was influenced by the ability of rival contenders to build a successful, well-organized, statewide electoral machine. In Paraíba the first competitors for oligarchical control, Venâncio Neiva and Álvaro Machado, each had their respective political fates decided by national military coups. Having been named by Marshal Deodoro da Fonseca in 1889 as Paraíba's first republican governor, Venâncio only briefly exercised executive power and oligarchical leadership. Marshal Floriano Peixoto replaced him with Álvaro Machado in 1892. However, thanks to the wishes of Floriano's civilian presidential successor, Álvaro remained Paraíba's oligarchical boss after 1894. For the next eighteen years, he served alternately as either governor or senior senator. Venâncio, meanwhile, as leader of the opposition, headed a coalition composed of several factions formerly loyal to the defunct Conservative Party. By the close of the turbulent 1890s, Álvaro's oligarchical leadership had become transformed into a political partnership. In 1894 he had recruited the highly popular Monsig. Valfredo Leal as an oligarchical ally, and until 1912 they would rotate the offices of governor and senator between them, drawing their votes from the former Liberals.

The Machado–Leal oligarchy depended on more than the endorsement of Brazil's presidents for its exceptionally long hegemony, for it competed in the local arena of politics, as well as at the state-federal level of oligarchical relations, with its Nevia–Pessoa challengers. In reality, therefore, the capacity to deliver the state vote to the president of Brazil determined an oligarchy's tenure in office. Decisions at the federal level confirmed what was fundamentally a local consensus.

The competition between Álvaro and Epitácio played itself out against the backdrop of the cotton cycle's favorable upward swing. Expansion of export infrastructure became the central political issue, as the local elites reflected a stronger identification with cotton cultivation at the expense of more traditional economic pursuits, especially stockraising. Better equipped in the long run to respond positively to the cotton producers, the Neiva–Pessoa opposition returned to power gradually. Its reintegration with the dominant Alvarista machine, which began shortly after 1900 and was formalized by 1908, eventually enabled the Pessoas to assume power during the crisis of 1912. Once an increasing number of local bosses withdrew their support from Álvaro and Valfredo and pledged themselves to Epitacismo, the Neiva–Pessoa revanche succeeded.

Nevertheless, the personal connections that Álvaro and Valfredo maintained with the national political elite had proved crucial for preserving their oligarchy in power. Both men devoted themselves rather narrowly to the special interests of the brejo zone where they had been born and brought up. Secondarily, they favored the Capital. Álvaro and Valfredo recruited their oligarchical lieutenants and colleagues in the federal delegation largely from the two wealthy commercial centers of Areia and Guarabira, but they particularly associated their government with a small clique of politicians drawn from Areia. (See Map I.2.) The men in the Areia clique possessed strong ties to the last generation of imperial politicans who still controlled Brazil's national government. Their talent and experience confirmed Areia's well-deserved nineteenth-century reputation as Paraíba's intellectual capital.

The brejo's dominant families usually were descendants of Portuguese immigrants who had originally settled in Areia between the 1780s and the 1830s. They had quickly grown prosperous as merchants engaging in an import–export trade between the coast and the backlands. Although Areia's economic life blood was commerce, the município's elite families also took pride in their sugar and coffee estates, and in the smaller number of tobacco properties they owned and managed in the fertile mountain valleys outside the city of Areia. Their economic connections with both the backlands and the coast contributed to the electoral support that the Machado–Leal oligarchy received from other geoeconomic zones. In the backlands zones, former Liberal Party local bosses, who in the 1890s still maintained a skeletal partisan organization, delivered the winning vote to the dominant oligarchy. On the coast, a small group of sugar families, as former Liberals, delivered their votes to Álvaro and Valfredo, but the commercial sector in the Capital played a crucial secondary role in elections. Thanks again to brejo merchants, who had maintained strong contacts with foreign—usually Portuguese—import–export firms in coastal Parahyba, the Machado–Leal oligarchy received backing from that city's still modest commercial sector.[1]

[1] On the genealogical and commercial ties among Areia's merchants, see H. de Almeida, *Brejo de Areia*, pp. 147–202, 215, and 234. On foreign businessmen, see Mariz, *Evolução econômica*, pp. 51–66 and 75–84.

Although Álvaro's oligarchical machine claimed important blocs of electoral support in each of Paraíba's five zones, its fulcrum in the brejo rested on a precarious economic base. By the late 1890s, both Areia and Guarabira had passed the peak of their commercial expansion and faced strong competition from market centers further west. During that decade, the brejo's four market cities, together with the Capital, contained both the largest urban populations in Paraíba and the largest number of commercial establishments. However, after 1900 the rapidly expanding caatinga-agreste surrounding the brejo assumed the demographic and commercial lead. The caatinga-agreste's economic life rested on cotton cultivation and complementary ginning and exporting activities, for one-half to two-thirds of all backlands cotton production passed through its warehouses. Between 1900 and 1910, therefore, the expansion of cotton production in that zone drove a fatal wedge into the loose coalition that Álvaro's brejo-based oligarchy had been mobilizing since the early 1890s. During the late Empire, many Old Liberal families loyal to Álvaro or Valfredo after 1892 had failed to invest deeply in cotton cultivation, leaving to their Conservative rivals the initiative in that respect. Thus after 1900 the Old Conservatives benefited from the economy's accelerating boom, while the Alvaristas and Valfredistas appeared less frequently among the ranks of the so-called cotton lords of the sertão.

Because Epitacismo stood for a commitment to an expansion of export infrastructure and a greater role for the State in stimulating cotton production, it eventually gained statewide support in Paraíba. Many backers of the Epitacista opposition at the turn of the century came from local elite families that had been Conservative and primarily agricultural. But more than their partisan identity, the fact that by the late 1880s they had curtailed livestock production and begun to invest heavily in cotton cultivation set them apart. During the late Empire agricultural interests in the caatinga-agreste had tended to favor the Conservative Party, and the Liberals had drawn greater support from the stockraising sector, which had assumed the economic defensive as a result of creeping enclosure. However, both groups could be found in each of the major parties. This distinction became less significant by 1908, the year that Epitácio's opposition gained formal representation on the Alvarista party machine's Executive Committee. By 1908, cotton trees so heavily covered the landscape of both the cariri-sertão and alto sertão that Epitacismo was attracting the most aggressive and successful commercialized cotton producers regardless of their party alliances in the 1880s.

The caatinga-agreste's political significance in the early Republic lay in its potential as a swing zone in electoral contests. Whether the state oligarchy would find its political pivot closer to the coast or further west depended eventually on how its votes were cast. With around 20 per cent of Paraíba's population by 1900, the caatinga-agreste was balanced between the 40 per cent of the population living on the coast and in the brejo and the equal proportion living in the two backlands zones. By the 1890s, the demographic shift inland had transformed the caatinga-agreste into an arena of fierce competitive struggle between Alvaristas and their Venancista and Epitacista opposition. But after 1900, the political and economic future lay with the backlands, not the brejo and the coast, and the caatinga-agreste made its new commercial importance felt in oligarchical politics during the first decade of the century.

The Expansion of the Agrarian Economy

Railroads and Roads

Not surprisingly, the extension of the railroad westward provided the issue that enabled the caatinga-agreste to flex its new political muscle effectively and to expose the incapacity of the incumbent oligarchy to deliver infrastructure beyond the coast and brejo. Even before the railroad reached the intermediate zones, its coastal construction in the 1880s had dramatically altered existing trade patterns between the coast and the interior.[2] When the Conde d'Eau Railway Company had first connected the anchorage of Cabedêlo and the nearby Capital to the brejo market in 1886, interprovincial centers on the coast north of Cabedêlo immediately entered a period of rapid decline. (See Map II.1.) Once a branch line to Alagoa Grande opened in 1901, however, that caatinga-agreste center gained direct access to the Capital and Cabedêlo. Areia and Guarabira, consequently, lost their monopoly on

[2] Information on rail routes comes from Câmara, *Datas campinenses*, pp. 99–100; Mariz, *Evolução econômica*, pp. 46–48; and Estevão Pinto, *História de uma estrada-de-ferro do nordeste* (Rio de Janeiro: José Olýmpio Editôra, 1949), pp. 115–17.

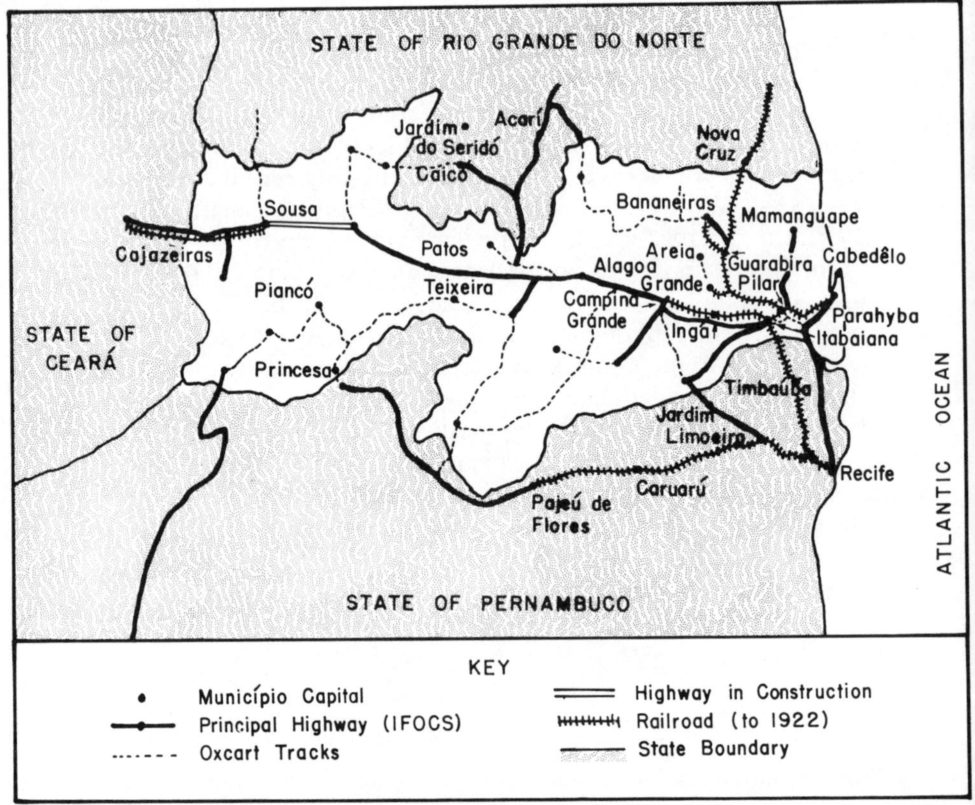

MAP II.1: Paraíba's Transport Infrastructure and Município Capitals with Connections to Major Out-of-State Markets (1928) (Scale: 1 inch = 180 km)

SOURCES: H. E. Williams and Roderic Crandall, *Mappa dos Estados do Ceará, Rio Grande do Norte e Parahyba* (Rio de Janeiro: Ministerio da Viação e Obras Publicas, 1910); Engineer Guilherme Lane, *Mapa do Estado da Parahyba Organizado pelo Engenheiro Robert Miller* (Rio de Janeiro: Secção Cartografica da Companhia Litografica Ipiranga, 1926); Estevão Pinto, *História de uma estrada-de-ferro do nordeste* (Rio de Janeiro: José Olýmpio Editôra, 1949); *The Great Western of Brazil Railway Co., Ltd.* (London: Waterlow & Sons, 1903).

trade between the coast and the backlands. More seriously, the railroad's capacity to integrate the Capital with market towns in the brejo and production zones further west quickly faded. Instead, the railroad's arrival in the caatinga-agreste accelerated commercial competition between Alagoa Grande and its nearby neighbor, Campina Grande. Within a few years, Campina emerged the victor and possessed its own direct rail link to the regional emporium in Recife.

The arrival of the railroad in Campina Grande in 1907 assured that the city's strategic commercial identity as "the gateway to the sertão" would endure. Moreover, it was not mere coincidence that the politician who secured the rail extension and thereby embarrassed the Machado–Leal oligarchy for its neglect of the interior also owned the Casa Inglêsa, Campina's largest cotton buying and ginning establishment. Cristiano Lauritzen lobbied hard for such a goal after he became both *prefeito* and political boss of Campina in 1902–1903 thanks to ties of political loyalty to Epitácio Pessoa. He defeated the strategy that would have subordinated his adopted city to nearby Alagoa Grande, by making Campina's railroad a branch line of that município's direct rail connection to the Capital.[3] In 1902, Cristiano journeyed to Rio de Janeiro to obtain federal appropriations for constructing a direct link with both the Capital and Recife, via Itabaiana. (See Map II.1.) Exporters in Campina Grande thus found themselves equidistant from both ports, but market circumstances led them to prefer trading with Recife, where they could get higher prices for their ginned cotton and pay less for imported goods, because it cost more to handle cargo between Parahyba's port of Varadouro and Cabedêlo.

The Machado–Leal oligarchy confirmed its neglect of the interior's need for infrastructure by sponsoring public spending on highly visible urban improvements in the Capital (and secondarily in Areia and Guarabira). By 1912, Parahyba's main streets had been paved, illuminated, and outfitted with an electric trolley service. A new governor's palace, a state normal school, and an ostentatious train station topped the list of important construction projects. The city's famous Santa Rosa Theatre was completely refurbished, and became an elegant monument to civic pride and the leisurely pursuits of the oligarchical elite. The railroad figured only tangentially in the Capital's new ambience of modernity. As Gov. Valfredo Leal explained in his annual message of 1908, the modification of the Parahyba–Cabedêlo line in order to accommodate a new stop at Tambaú provided access to an "important bathing beach station and recreational spot" for the Capital's residents. Tambaú, the picturesque tropical beach only six kilometers outside the city, he pointed out, would now offer "comfort to

[3] In a memorandum to Recife's Commercial Association, Col. Cristiano Lauritzen rebutted the arguments of merchants from Parahyba, who favored a railroad connection with Alagoa Grande at the expense of Campina Grande. *Relatorio da Associação Commercial Beneficiente de Pernambuco* (Recife: n.p., 1903), pp. 247–52, quoted in Brazil, Ministerio da Viação e Obras Publicas, *Relatorio apresentado ao Presidente Artur da Silva Bernardes . . . anno de 1922* (Rio de Janeiro: Imprensa Nacional, 1924), p. 135.

the population of the Capital and even [that] of the interior, when they went to swim in the ocean and rest from the cares of life during the [agricultural] dead season."[4]

The Machado–Leal oligarchy's emphasis on the brejo and the Capital eventually placed a winning card in the hands of its Epitacista and Venancista rivals. Like Col. Cristiano, the cotton lords of the backlands did not intend to stand by passively while the strategic potential of Campina Grande's market was ignored. Once the railroad there had been opened, they resumed an interest in building roads between their production zones and Campina's rail head. Meanwhile, Gov. João Machado, Álvaro's brother, continued to support the economically declining brejo. When road construction was first proposed in 1908 between his home town of Areia and the rail head at Campina Grande, João Machado even pronounced it "the complete solution to our economic problems."[5] Unrealistically, he assumed that brejo centers like Areia would indefinitely facilitate trade between "producing centers" in the backlands and "consuming centers" in the brejos and on the coast.[6] The numerical strength of the cotton lords in the backlands grew, however, as the boom economy gathered momentum and the profits from rising harvests suggested new commercial opportunities. After accumulating a string of tactical victories in município politics during the first decade of the new century, the oligarchy's Neiva–Pessoa challengers rapidly consolidated a statewide coalition under Epitácio's leadership in 1911. Along with partisan conflict in the municípios and dissension within Alvaro's coalitional ranks, Epitácio's ability to deliver infrastructure to the interior of his native state accounted for his leadership victory. By then, the bosses of the backlands, whose harvests were collected in Campina Grande's warehouses, appreciated what Epitácio's leadership could accomplish. It could bring them the roads they needed to transport their cotton production across the Borborema's heights to the gateway to the sertão.

Just as the railroad symbolized the Machado–Leal oligarchy's attachment to a political base in the brejo and on the coast, roads would tie the Neiva–Pessoa oligarchy to its grassroots support in the caatinga-agreste and the backlands. The railroad reached its maximum expansion at about the time the dominance of the Machado–Leal oligarchy ended, although the goal of a trans-Borbo-

[4] State of Paraíba, *Almanach administrativo, mercantil e industrial do Estado da Parahyba para o anno de 1909* (Parahyba: Imprensa Oficial, 1909), p. 236.

[5] Ibid., pp. 405–406.

[6] Ibid.

rema rail line spanning the 600 kilometers from Parahyba to the Ceará border persisted.[7] It remained a visionary dream until the early 1920s, when it was laid aside.[8] Instead of the steam locomotive, Ford trucks became the official means for integrating Paraíba's five zones with a coastal emporium at Parahyba-Cabedêlo. When an automobile first returned to the coast after successfully scaling the rugged ascent to the Borborema Plateau, in 1915, politicians turned to the truck as the means for transforming export infrastructure. Meanwhile, the branch lines of the Great Western Railway in Pernambuco and Rio Grande do Norte continued to advance westward in those states, penetrating the backlands to the southwest and northwest of Campina Grande. Paraíba's politicians expressed alarm that the cotton packtrains from their own backlands were being lured to out-of-state railheads, bypassing Campina Grande altogether. Consequently, the solution appeared to be an east–west highway that would cut straight across the Borborema Plateau and, in the far west, bisect the Piranhas Valley until it reached Cajazeiras, closing the sieve through which cotton found its way to Recife, Mossoró, and Acarí. (See Map II.1.)

With the creation of the IFOCS as a federal drought relief agency in 1909, the resources of the national treasury for the first time offered a limited means for northeastern states to construct interzonal roads. Not until he had been elected president in 1919 could Epitácio secure allocations for roadbuilding that would create a statewide network of highways and feeder roads. Before then, as an official report pointed out, roadbuilding had been undertaken almost entirely at private expense, and even a barely minimal road system still did not exist: "For lack of money, the municípios leave the upkeep of roads in private hands, which means that only

[7] As early as 1917, the Epitacista press advocated a rail route that would pass through the southern portion of Paraíba, siphoning off commerce that would otherwise flow to Pernambuco's Great Western branch lines. Agnello Amorim, "Estradas de ferro," *O Norte* [Capital], 17 May 1917 and 6 June 1918. The projected 88 kilometers connecting Sousa to Baturité, Ceará, were completed in the 1920s. Ministerio da Viação e Obras Publicas, *Relatorio Bernardes 1922*, pp. 95–100; J. A. de Almeida, *Parahyba*, pp. 293–97 and 301. See also Engineer Sylvio Aderne, "Evolução das rodovias no polígono das sêcas," *Boletim do DNOCS* 20 (Nov. 1959):303. The author is very grateful to Albert Hirschman for making available all of the issues of the *Boletim do DNOCS* cited here.

[8] Epitácio's proposed rail route stretched from the western terminus of Ceará's rail network in Baturité eastward across the central plateau of Paraíba to Campina Grande. Irineu Joffily, who proposed the route in the 1880s, said that it possessed the advantage of "cutting through all exists . . . to the neighbor to the south. . . . In this way the secular crisis of Paraíba's commerce would be resolved and its existence in the Union of Brazilian states guaranteed." *Notas*, p. 131.

certain parts on certain properties are maintained. All transport is on the backs of animals."[9]

Ten years later, even after the impressive gains from IFOCS construction became evident, in many sections of the backlands the situation remained unchanged. Arno Pearse, surveying cotton cultivation in the zones of the sertão in 1922, testified to the impossibility of motor car travel in many areas: "The greatest difficulty was encountered when crossing rivers, as bridges did not exist. . . . Finally, we had to abandon the cars and take to horses, a much quicker way of travel than by motor car in muddy country with no roads or only an old, worn-out road, covered with grass, daisies, and even brushwood."[10]

The notion that the State should assume primary responsibility for constructing and maintaining a road system originated with Epitácio Pessoa. As a senator between 1912 and 1919, he had secured several modest appropriations for short stretches of road construction in the caatinga-agreste and backlands, dwarfing the accomplishments of his Machado–Leal predecessors.[11] Then in 1919, in one of his first acts as president, he committed the federal government to regional roadbuilding as part of a broader design to provide the Northeast with an integrated export infrastructure. He brought the full weight of the federal budget to bear on this project: federal expenditure for the IFOCS reached 15 per cent of total national revenues during 1921 and 1922, a proportion never again equaled. Not surprisingly, his native state received the lion's share of the total 378,000 contos spent between 1920 and 1924.[12] In Pa-

[9] Antônio Marques, "A industria da borracha," Monograph no. 8 of the Commissario Geral da Exposição Nacional de Borracha (Rio de Janeiro: n.p., 1913), p. 20. A federal official commented in 1912: "Only one highway (if it is true that it deserves the name) exists in the state, the one beginning in the Capital and ending in . . . Pilar. Its extension is 57 kilometers, more or less." Brazil, Ministerio de Agricultura, Industria e Commercio, *Relatorio apresentado ao Director Geral do Serviço de Inspecção e Defeza Agricolas pelo Inspector Agricolo Interino do Septimo Districto, Diogenes Caldas; exercicio de 1912, anno de 1913—24º da Republica, Estado da Parahyba* (Parahyba do Norte: Jayme Seixas & C., 1913), p. 26.

[10] Pearse, *Brazilian Cotton*, p. 135.

[11] Granted in 1911, these appropriations were funded almost entirely in 1912 and 1913. The drought of 1915 proved instrumental in persuading the national government to appropriate emergency funds for relief projects in the Northeast. Paraíba received 930 contos for the construction of 61 kilometers of road between Campina Grande and Soledade for 1915–1918. Previously, federal support had been given only for the Areia–Alagoa Grande road during 1911–1914. J. A. de Almeida, *Parahyba*, pp. 308–309.

[12] This is Albert Hirschman's figure: "Brazil's Northeast," p. 30. Epitácio's arithmetic yielded 361,000 contos as a gross expenditure for IFOCS from 1920 to 1924,

raíba, over 1,015 kilometers of highway were constructed, more than in any other northeastern state.[13] As a result, the state's roads have been recognized since the 1920s as the best in the region.

Within an incredibly short time, the main highway stretched due west from the Capital for about 450 kilometers, reaching to within 100 kilometers of Sousa in the alto sertão. (See Map II.1.) When Epitácio left office in 1922, all but 200 kilometers linking the alto sertão with Ceará had been completed. By 1926 only the short stretch connecting Sousa and Pombal in the central portion of the far backlands remained to complete, and, by 1929, Gov. João Pessoa had secured funds for its construction. Beginning in 1923, Epitácio's successor, Artur Bernardes, reduced federal support for the IFOCS projects to zero because of his decision to close that agency altogether. But boom harvests of cotton during the 1920s enabled Paraíba's governors to finance completion of the main highway largely from state revenues. As senator for Paraíba again after 1923, Epitácio secured several modest federal loans for the project.[14]

Meanwhile, as early as 1922, trucks began carrying the valuable long-staple cotton of the cariri-sertão and the eastern Piranhas Valley to the gins and rail head at Campina Grande. Arno Pearse summed up the revolutionary impact the new highway system exerted on export production:

> The net of motor roads . . . constructed in the last few years in the States of Paraíba and Rio Grande do Norte . . . [is] already revolutionizing the social and economic life of the vast interior, as the exporters are gradually penetrating into the inte-

---

but eliminated 91,000 contos as not having been expended directly on drought projects. Epitácio Pessôa, *Obras completas*, 25 vols. (Rio de Janeiro: Instituto Nacional do Livro, 1955–1965), Vol. 21:316–17.

[13] Aderne, "Evolução rodovias," p. 215. The second highest recipient of highway appropriations, Ceará, constructed only 521 kilometers of road. Except for Rio Grande do Norte, which built 478 kilometers of road, the other four northeasten states built fewer than 200 kilometers each.

[14] Northeastern intellectuals kept the issue of drought assistance from the federal government alive throughout the twenties, for a number of them were politicians who also contributed scholarly treatments of the problem. See for example, Thomaz Pompeu Sobrinho, "As seccas do nordeste, 1825–1925," in *Livro do nordeste* (commemorative issue of the first centenary of *Diario de Pernambuco*) (Recife: Imprensa do *Diario de Pernambuco*, 1925); Miguel Arrojado Lisbôa and Epitacio Pessôa, *As obras do nordeste (resposta ao Senador Sampaio Corrêa)* (Rio de Janeiro: Imprensa Oficial, 1925); J. A. de Almeida, *Parahyba* (1923); and Octacílio de Albuquerque, *Em prol do nordeste* (n.p., n.p., 1918).

> rior and beginning to have their cotton ginned and baled near to where it has grown. In this way the intermediaries and the farmers are beginning to obtain a price commensurate with their work.[15]

Construction and renovation of the animal trails complementary to the main highway proved equally crucial for infrastructure. They connected isolated estates in the cariri-sertão and alto sertão, via the highway, to Campina Grande. Although over a thousand kilometers of packtrain trails were constructed in Paraíba under IFOCS sponsorship, even that effort was inadequate. Gov. João Suassuna lamented this fact in the mid-1920s, when he pointed out that most planters in the backlands zones still could not avail themselves of truck transport, although the highway reached to Pombal in the alto sertão. They simply did not have access to the highway, for feeder roads remained to be built.[16] As a result, most of the raw cotton still arrived at the ginneries in Campina Grande by the same means as in the 1880s and in the same condition—dirty and in underweight bales that brought inferior prices:

> The crack of the whip announced the approaching packtrains. . . . Soon the lead mule appeared, with jingling bells hanging from her decorated reins. Riding on the last mule came the muleteer, who rested his whip on his shoulder. . . . They were the packtrains descending the [Borborema] mountains and drowning in their huge loads of cotton, poorly baled and tied up only with vines, leaving the waysides of the roads flocked with lint as if it had snowed.[17]

Packtrains also cost more than either the railroad or trucks. They took two to three weeks to reach the coast from the Piranhas Valley, stopping at ranches along an ancient system of trails. The cost of the food and shelter for the muleteers, as well as feed for the animals, was considerable. Consequently, in those areas where feeder roads did "revolutionize" transport, they also lowered costs and increased profits, just as Arno Pearse had pointed out.

[15] Pearse, *Brazilian Cotton*, p. 135. José Américo de Almeida summed up the revolutionary impact of the roads by pointing out that in 1922 he completed an automobile trip from Areia to Sousa, a distance of nearly 400 kilometers, in twenty-four hours. The same trip had taken him nine days on horseback in 1909. *Parahyba*, p. 316.

[16] João Suassuna to Epitácio (Capital), 26 Nov. 1926, AEP/12/268.

[17] I. Joffily, *Notas*, p. 13.

The Port of Cabedêlo

Because Paraíba's economic independence from the Recife emporium demanded a port that would accommodate oceangoing vessels, a deepwater port became the capstone of Epitácio's federally financed infrastructure program. In defending his 1923 budgetary allocations, President Epitácio alluded directly to the crucial role the Port of Cabedêlo promised to play in securing Paraíba's autonomy from Pernambuco:

> Our exports and imports must pass through the Port of Recife [as well as by means of] the railroad that unites the interior of Paraíba with the Pernambuco capital. Now, obviously, in order to liberate ourselves from this tutelage, the first condition is for our Capital to be directly connected by ship to other ports in Brazil and abroad, so that the merchandise we export or receive is not subject to the onerous superiority of the Port of Recife.[18]

As a senator, prior to being elected president, Epitácio had lobbied energetically for a major deepwater port in his native state. Pursuit of that goal, however, became complicated by a practical consideration: due to extensive silting, oceangoing vessels could no longer enter the Paraíba River's delta and proceed directly to the Capital's dock at Varadouro. The fact that all goods had to be transshipped by rail between Cabedêlo and the customs house at Varadouro, a distance of eighteen kilometers, raised freight costs for the Capital's merchants. With backing from the commercial sector of the Capital, Epitácio therefore urged dredging the channel to restore direct access to the sea. Despite the considerable federal expenditure allocated for this project between 1912 and 1918, and particularly during Epitácio's presidency, it proved to be a futile exercise. Epitácio eventually yielded to the recommendations of federal engineers, who concluded that the cost of dredging was prohibitive, and gave his presidential endorsement to an alternative plan for converting Cabedêlo's anchorage into a major deepwater port. Between 1920 and 1923, therefore, Cabedêlo became an important priority in IFOCS expenditures; however, after President Bernardes withdrew budgetary support in 1923, construction proceeded very sporadically. State revenues from a larger volume of cotton exports after 1920 compensated for the loss of federal funds only during 1923–1925 and again in 1928–1929. Se-

[18] E. Pessôa, *Obras completas*, 21:300.

3. A prospective buyer samples cotton in Parahyba's commercial district, 1921. (Arno Pearse, *Brazilian Cotton*, p. 167)

4. Loading cotton onto barges at Varadouro for transshipment to Cabedêlo, 1929. (Alpheu Domingues, *Relatorio do anno de 1929*, p. 28)

vere flooding in 1925–1926 and a limited drought in 1927, coupled with falling cotton prices, reduced revenues to less than one-half their 1920–1925 levels. Thanks again to Epitácio's senatorial leadership, several modest federal appropriations for dredging Cabedêlo's anchorage and building a road connecting it to the Capital were secured.[19] Yet even at João Pessoa's death in 1930 Cabedêlo's docks were still under construction.

The Capital's merchants, always unwilling to surrender their monopoly on the customs house, vociferously defended their obsolete port at Varadouro, even after Cabedêlo had begun to receive major budgetary attention. As long as the customs remained at Varadouro but cargo had to be handled at Cabedêlo, the high cost of exporting goods from Parahyba made the Port of Recife a more economical final destination for the interior's cotton exporters. But because throughout the 1920s construction of Cabedêlo's docks lacked financing, conflict between the Capital's merchants and the interior's producers—who shipped large quantities of cotton to Recife—remained hypothetical. This is why the entrepôt for the interior's production, Campina Grande, continued to function in key respects as "a Pernambucano city, both socially and commercially [set] apart" from coastal Parahyba.[20]

Dams, Reservoirs, and Technology

Reservoirs officially embodied the most direct response to the problem of drought. Although their justification lay in conservation, particularly in years of little or no rain, they contributed much more directly to increasing cotton production than to combating drought. Together, dams and reservoirs absorbed greater federal expenditure than roads, but none of the three massive

[19] On the economic development of Cabedêlo, see Mariz, *Evolução econômica*, pp. 203–207; and J. A. de Almeida, *Parahyba*, pp. 353–71. As senator for Paraíba, Epitácio had secured a federal appropriation of 14,000 contos for dredging the Sanhauá River in order to maintain Varadouro, but those monies were expended by 1918. Mariz, *Evolução econômica*, pp. 205–206. "Trabalhos executados pelo segundo distrito da Inspetoria Federal de Obras contra as Sêcas," *RIHGP* 8 (1934), unnumbered table following p. 169. Município Council of Cabedêlo to Epitácio, 29 Dec. 1927, AEP 9/13. Unfortunately, José Joffily's recent book, *O porto político* (Rio de Janeiro: Civilização Brasileira, 1983), appeared too late to be consulted for this book. Joffily's focus is the IFOCS project to enlarge the Port of Varadouro, one Epitácio backed until 1922, apparently unaware of the scandal of corruption surrounding construction contracts until after he left the presidency.

[20] J. A. de Almeida, *Parahyba*, p. 447.

earthen dams intended to alleviate drought in the Paraíba backlands was finished before 1930. Because the Bernardes administration curtailed federal spending on IFOCS, even the expensive earthmoving equipment reached the government auction block as scrap.[21] In contrast, medium-sized and small earthen dams proved economically and politically much more successful. Between 1911 and 1930, federal monies financed the construction of twenty-six small dams. Although only ten were built during Epitácio's presidency, most of the remaining dams had also received his political sponsorship.[22] Earthen dams provided water for livestock and irrigation for *vazante* agriculture, which referred to the dependence of especially tree cottons on water that seeped underground or reached crops from streams due to periodic flooding. Because of their high cost and the value they added to agro-pastoral production, these dams represented valuable political patronage to the wealthier landowners fortunate enough to have them built on their properties. Rather than offering the panacea for drought that federal planners predicted, the additional water resources directly contributed to the greatly expanded quantity of land planted in cotton during the 1920s. Furthermore, like the roadbuilding projects, reservoir and dam construction provided alternative employment to thousands of agricultural tenants in the interior.[23]

Along with irrigation improvements, technology played an important role in increasing Paraíba's cotton exports after 1919. In 1916 only about 40 per cent of Paraíba's more than five hundred cotton gins were steam-powered, making the animal-driven *bolandeira* still predominant.[24] Prior to that year, only one hydraulic

[21] Inaugural address of Engineer Miguel Arrojado Ribeiro Lisboa (28 Aug. 1913): "O problema das sêcas," *Boletim de DNOCS* 20 (Nov. 1959):49–50 (orig. published in *Annaes da Biblioteca Nacional* [1916]). Hirschman, "Brazil's Northeast," pp. 16–32. For a critique of the reliance on irrigation as a means of combating drought, see Hall, "Irrigation in the Brazilian Northeast,' pp. 157–89. Federal Decree No. 16,403 of 12 March 1924 extinguished the administrative machinery (Caixa Especial das Obras de Irrigação e Terras Cultivaveis do Nordeste Brasileiro) for dispensing federal revenues for drought works. Decree No. 16,769 of 7 Jan. 1923 had already abolished any remaining drought relief projects.

[22] "Trabalhos executados," unnumbered table following p. 169.

[23] "Notas sôbre as sêcas," *Boletim de DNOCS* 20 (Nov. 1959):84–85.

[24] Mariz, *Evolução econômica*, p. 34; Pearse, *Brazilian Cotton*, pp. 56, 171–72, and 176–78; Caldas, "Algodão da Parahyba," *app. 4; State of Paraíba, Repartição de Estatistica e Arquivo Publico, Annuario estatistico do Estado da Parahyba de 1916* (Parahyba: Imprensa Oficial, 1918), pp. 355–87. Pearse's figure of 290 gins in Paraíba in 1916, of which 194 were steam-powered, is a gross undercount, but correctly ranks Paraíba in first place as the state with the largest number of cotton gins in Brazil. *Brazilian Cotton*, p. 56.

5. Animal-driven bolandeiras like this one built in Queimadas in 1856 continued to be used well into the twentieth century. (Celso Mariz, *Evolução econômica da Paraíba*, p. 58)

ginning and baling operation existed in the state—and significantly, its owner was a German immigrant. Furthermore, hydraulic machinery had to be confined to the Capital because the heavy 280-kilo bales it turned out could not be carried by horses or mules, but only by rail. Finally, facilities for processing cotton byproducts were almost nonexistent in 1916, a circumstance that limited state revenues as well as commercial profits.[25]

As early as 1922, the positive changes from improved infrastructure became evident in Paraíba's export economy. For the first time, a majority of cotton gins, which now numbered well over six hundred, were steam-powered. Seven years later, a survey revealed that over one-third of all the cotton gins in the state had already been replaced, indicating widespread willingness to invest in capital equipment. Predictably, the greatest number of steam-pow-

[25] Pearse, *Brazilian Cotton*, pp. 176–78; Matheus d'Oliveira, *Interesses do Estado da Parahyba no Brasil: As industrias* (Parahyba: Imprensa Oficial, 1913), p. 16. In sponsoring the application of Trajano de Medeiros's Rio de Janeiro-based Companhia Industrial de Algodão e Óleos to construct two hydraulic cotton-seed presses in the Capital, Gov. Camilo de Holanda argued that the move would lower export costs and "liberate us from the German monopoly [i.e., the two immigrant owners of high-density presses in the Capital, Guilherme Kröncke and Julius von Söhsten]." Camilo de Holanda to Epitácio (Capital), 13 May 1918, AEP/12/117.

ered gins were concentrated in the caatinga-agreste.[26] The most significant technological change, however, resulted from the new road network and underscored Arno Pearse's insistence that roads "revolutionized social and commercial life." Once businessmen could rely on a highway system in the interior, high-density baling operations could be established beyond the coast because the heavier bales they turned out could be carried by truck directly to Parahyba and Cabedêlo. Altogether, four high-density baling operations opened in the interior between 1920 and 1929. Located in Campina Grande and three other market centers in the intermediate and backlands zones, all used the latest saw-gins capable of turning out 35,000 kilos of seed cotton per day. In 1930 four more high-density baling operations were installed beyond the coast, with two of them in the western Piranhas Valley. Finally, new byproducts industries appeared adjacent to the modern saw ginneries.[27] They produced cottonseed cakes for livestock feed or oil and paste for export. By 1925 at least one-quarter of all cotton revenues collected derived from such byproducts.[28]

The Cotton Boom

Although the entire era of the Old Republic deserves to be considered a boom period for *ouro branco,* cotton's linear expansion reached a spectacular culmination in the 1920s. Even during World War I, when trade with Paraíba's most important customers—Germany and Great Britain—was interrupted, an expanding coastal trade compensated for the loss of foreign markets.[29] After the war, São Paulo's rising demand increasingly

[26] In 1922, 424 of Paraíba's 576 cotton gins were steam-powered. State of Paraíba, *Almanach administrativo, historico e industrial do Estado da Parahyba para o anno de 1922* (Parahyba: Imprensa Oficial, 1922), p. 283. Caldas, "Algodão da Parahyba," app. 4; Juvencio Mariz de Lyra, "Quadro demonstrativo dos descaroçadores, uzinas de beneficiamento e prensas existentes no Brasil, em 1932," in *Aspectos econômicos* (Rio de Janeiro: n.p., 1933), tables 3 and 6; and Alpheu Domingues, *Relatorio da Delegacia do Serviço Federal do Algodão na Parahyba apresentado ao Superintendente F. L. Alves Costa, Anno de 1929* (Parahyba: Imprensa Oficial, 1930), p. 36.

[27] Pearse, *Domingues, Relatorio 1929,* p. 36. *Brazilian Cotton,* pp. 174–76. (See also the sources in note 26.)

[28] Gov. João Suassuna noted that prior to the construction of feeder roads in the backlands, cotton seed had either been used for cattle fodder or burned to create storage space. João Suassuna to Epitácio (Capital), tel. of 31 Jan. 1925, AEP/12/245-E. [Henceforth, telegrams are identified as "tel." Unless otherwise identified, all citations of archival communications are letters.]

[29] Brazil, Ministerio do Trabalho, Industria e Commercio, Departamento Na-

explained cotton's upward export trajectory. During the first decade of this century, annual exports of cotton had averaged 9.8 million kilos, comparing favorably with the boom period of the 1860s and the 1870s. (See Tables I.1 and II.1.) However, the historical significance of high average levels of annual exports lay in the consistency of the upward trend. By 1910, steadily expanding harvests presented a reliable threshold of expectation for planters, exporters, and politicians. For the decade following 1910, average annual exports rose to 13.8 million kilos and during the final decade of the Old Republic they averaged approximately 17.4 million kilos. Since the turnout ratio (of raw to ginned cotton) averaged three to one, annual cultivation of cotton fluctuated around 50 million kilos throughout the 1920s.

The magnitude of Paraíba's cotton boom, which reflected not only the state's geographical advantage but also its more favorable position with respect to federal patronage for infrastructure, is best appreciated by referring to other cotton-producing states in Brazil. Three times during the 1920s, Paraíba ranked first as the largest exporter of cotton among all Brazilian states. (See Table A.2.) During those years the state also accounted for one-quarter of all the cotton exported from Brazil; otherwise it consistently ranked among the top five exporting states in five of the seven remaining years.

Of course, more than merely new infrastructure accounted for Paraíba's boom cycle. Exogenous factors like the boll weevil and the silting of the Nile Valley, which had created a world cotton dearth in the first decade of this century, also explained the long duration of the cotton boom. Nevertheless, recognition that Paraíba produced the finest long-staple cotton available on the world market bore directly on the issue of infrastructure. Because such tree cottons grew only in the two backlands zones, a statewide highway system became indispensable for integrating those zones into the world market. Although they had played only a limited role in export during the nineteenth-century boom, the cariri-sertão and the alto sertão together outproduced all other zones by the first decade of this century. And two-thirds of the cotton exported from Paraíba after 1910 was being cultivated on the Borborema

---

cional de Estatistica, *Commercio exterior do Brasil: Annos de 1920 ate 1925* (Rio de Janeiro: Departamento Nacional de Estatistica, 1931), p. 479; ibid., *Annos de 1926 ate 1930* (1933), pp. 476–77. After 1918, Great Britain remained the only significant foreign buyer of Paraíba's exported cotton, but by the mid-1920s took only 16 per cent, while São Paulo and Rio de Janeiro bought 75 per cent. *A União*, 1 May 1928.

TABLE II.1: Cotton Exported from Paraíba (1893–1929)
(Value in current contos)

Year	Kilos exported[a]	Official value[b]	Year	Kilos exported	Official value
1893	—	456	1912	20,025,000	16,000
1894	—	271	1913	9,829,019	9,052
1895	3,825,000	222	1914	6,873,559	6,377
1896	—	266	1915	14,107,452	13,267
1897	—	305	1916	14,001,723	25,818
1898	—	289	1917	18,330,470	41,276
1899	5,436,875	5,207	1918	12,351,834	38,202
1900	8,124,410	6,578	1919	8,227,276	18,740
1901	5,695,261	4,577	1920	11,716,085	26,952
1902	9,423,090	7,173	1921	15,541,398	22,736
1903	11,693,121	9,822	1922	17,458,996	42,125
1904	8,819,748	6,242	1923	13,633,802	—
1905	8,727,531	5,874	1924	14,045,833	63,379
1906	10,689,317	6,990	1925	18,276,670	64,702
1907	13,451,217	9,109	1926	21,934,142	56,022
1908	9,878,517	7,566	1927	23,138,945	45,045
1909	11,732,524	9,513	1928	22,574,709	72,359
1910	16,914,026	13,531	1929	24,503,378	65,645
1911	17,815,327	13,979			

SOURCES: Lyra Tavares, *A Parahyba*, 2:343–65, 369–77; Brazil, Ministerio da Agricultura, Industria e Commercio, *Relatorio . . . pelo Inspector Agricola Interino do Septimo Distrito, Diogenes Caldas; exercicio de 1912 . . .* (Parahyba: Jaime Seixas & C., 1913), unnumbered chart; João de Lyra Tavares, *Economia e finanças dos estados: Brasil* (Parahyba: Imprensa Oficial, 1914), pp. 72–73; *Diario do Estado*, 27 June 1916; William W. Coelho de Souza, *Impressões da cultura algodoeira no Brasil* (Rio de Janeiro: Imprensa Nacional, 1922), p. 66; *A União*, 29 June 1923; State of Paraíba, Repartição de Estatistica e Arquivo Publico, *Annuario estatistico do Estado da Parahyba de 1916* (Parahyba: Imprensa Oficial, 1918), p. 146; J. A. de Almeida, *Parahyba*, unnumbered chart, pp. 556–57. Domingues, *Relatorio . . . anno de 1929*, p. 45. For 1924–1927, data on official value were taken from the Annual Reports of the Recebedorias e Mesas de Rendas, published in *A União*, 28 April 1925, 13 August 1927, and 19 August 1927, and from Mariz, *Evolução econômica*, pp. 85–86. These figures may be undervalued. Kilos for the same years were taken from the CIFTA sources indicated in Table A.1. Unavoidable discrepancies occur between data in this table and several others in this book, especially

Plateau or in the more humid climate of the Piranhas and Piancó Valleys. (See Table II.2.) Map II.2 graphically illustrates the historic shift toward developing the backlands as the major production zone for export. In the 1860s only five municípios in the backlands zones had produced cotton for export. By 1916 ten additional backlands municípios had entered production on a large scale. In the same year, seven of the nine cotton-producing municípios (of a total twenty-seven) that exported one million kilos or more lay in the backlands.[30]

Cotton's conquest of the economy also transformed the composition of Paraíba's exports during the era of the oligarchies. No longer merely cotton fiber but also oil, paste, and seed cake accounted for over three-quarters of the value of annual exports during the 1920s. Between 1910 and 1920, cotton accounted for nearly two-thirds of total annual exports by value. (See Table A.3.) During the 1920s the greater volume produced for export, more than an upward price trend, increased cotton's share of the total value of exports. Therefore, while cotton had contributed only about one-third of total revenues during the 1890s, by the 1920s the proportion had risen to three-fourths (when revenues from cotton byproducts are included). (See Table A.4, especially note b.)

[30] Between 1916 and 1922, land cultivated in cotton, including intercropped foodstuffs, rose from 68,000 hectares to 104,175 hectares. Rodrigues de Carvalho, "Pequena lavoura," pp. 326–27; Caldas, "Algodão da Parahyba," p. 303; State of Paraíba, *Almanach da Parahyba de 1922*, pp. 296–97. However, wide fluctuation must have been frequent, since estimates for 1927 and 1928 were 70,000 and 84,000 hectares, respectively. *A União*, 1 May 1928. Pearse reported that two-thirds of all cotton exported passed through Campina Grande. *Brazilian Cotton*, pp. 170–71.

SOURCES TO TABLE II.1 (continued)
where statistics collected by the Centro Industrial de Fiação e Tecelagem do Algodão, or CIFTA, were used. In certain years it was not clear whether the annual reports of Paraíba's Recebedoria de Mesas de Renda gave totals reflecting statewide exports or only those from Cabedêlo. Finally, readers should keep in mind the partial picture these statistics offer, since local tax boards withheld statistics together with taxes. In many years, at least one-third of the municípios did not furnish statistics on cotton to state or federal agencies. (Alfeu Domingues, director of the federal Serviço do Algodão, *A União*, 1 May 1928, personal interview.) Where generalizations in this book are comparative, then usually CIFTA data were used.

NOTE: Cotton byproducts excluded.

[a] "Kilos exported" includes both by land and by sea.

[b] Official value referred to value for taxation purposes, but appeared close to market value. (See Table A.5, for a conversion of contos to U.S. dollars by year.)

TABLE II.2: Paraíba Production of Raw Cotton by Geographical Zone in Selected Years (1911–1921)
(In millions of kilos)

Geographical	1911		1912		1913		1914[a]		1916		1921	
Zone	No.	%	No.	%	No.	%	No.	%	No.	%	No.	%
Coast	1,757	9	1,242	5	1,290	8	462	8	1,318	5	224	1
Caatinga-agreste	5,232	27	6,484	28	4,710	29	1,890	35	8,670	30	2,983	13
Brejo	885	4	713	3	203	1	121	2	1,062	4	330	1
Cariri-sertão	5,676	29	7,537	32	4,361	27	2,399	44	6,630	23	4,198	19
Alto Sertão	6,161	31	7,317	32	5,649	35	590	11	11,050	38	14,902	66
Subtotal	19,711	100	23,293	100	16,213	100	5,462	100	28,730	100	22,637	100
Unidentified	6,062		6,523		4,501		—		—		—	
Total	25,773		29,816		20,714		5,462		28,730		22,637	

SOURCES: João de Lyra Tavares, *Cifras e notas (Economia e finanças do Brasil)* (Parahyba: Imprensa Oficial, 1925), p. 61; Diogenes Caldas, "O algodão na Parahyba," *Annaes da Primeira Conferencia Algodoeira*, 2 vols. (São Paulo: Sociedade Nacional de Agricultura, 1916), 2:303; idem, *Estatistica agricola da Parahyba do Norte de 1916* (Parahyba: Imprensa Oficial, 1916), p. 7; José Rodrigues de Carvalho, "Cultura de algodoeiro no Estado da Parahyba—o problema da pequena lavoura," *Annais da Primeira Conferencia Algodoeira*, 2:325–27; and *Almanach . . . do Estado da Parahyba para o anno de 1922* (Parahyba: Imprensa Oficial, 1922), p. 296. Limitations of statistics noted in Table II.1 apply here, too.

NOTE: Original statistics, reported by município, have been reaggregated by the author according to the five geoeconomic zones used in this work. Measurements have been converted to kilos according to Lyra Tavares's designation of 75 kilos to 1 fardo and 1 saca. Lyra Tavares's "unidentified" cotton presumably reported ginned cotton tallied in municípios where the local authorities would not release statistical data, but to which he had unofficial access. The majority of unidentified cotton, however, can be assumed to have come from the cariri-sertão and alto sertão. (See also Table A.1.)

[a] Over one-half of all municípios were not reported in 1914 data.

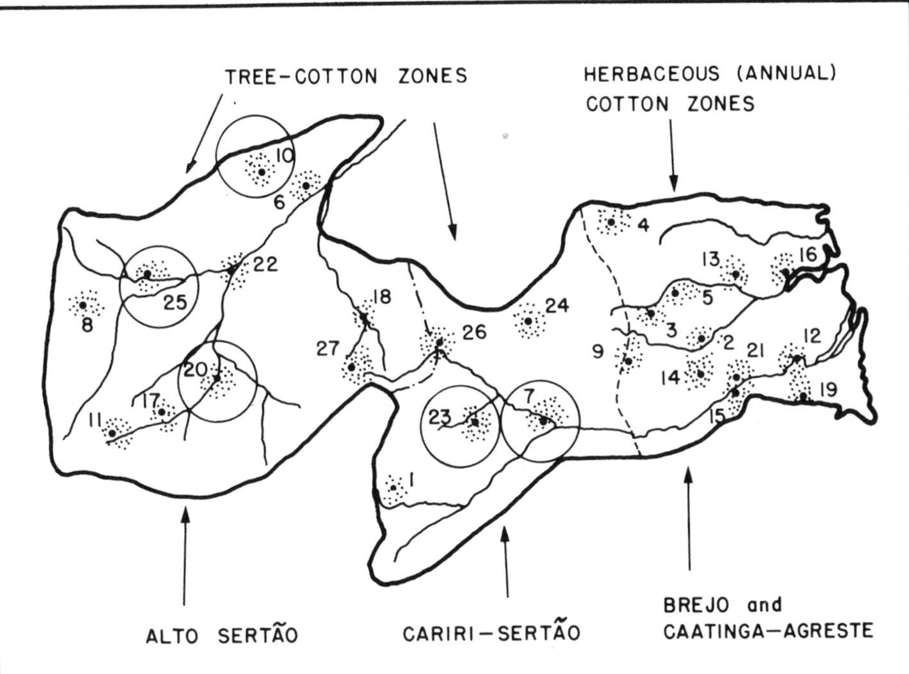

Key

- • Município Capital
- Zone of cotton production
- Zone of backlands cotton production in 1860s

Município Capitals

1. Alagoa do Monteiro	10. Catolé do Rocha	19. Pedras de Fogo
2. Alagoa Grande	11. Conceição	20. Piancó
3. Alagoa Nova	12. Espírito Santo	21. Pilar
4. Araruna	13. Guarabira	22. Pombal
5. Areia	14. Ingá	23. São João do Cariri
3. Brejo do Cruz	15. Itabaiana	24. Soledade
7. Cabaceiras	16. Mamanguape	25. Sousa
8. Cajazeiras	17. Misericórdia	26. Taperoá
9. Campina Grande	18. Patos	27. Teixeira

MAP II.2 Paraíba's Cotton Production Zones by Município (1916) (Scale: 1 inch = 144 km)
SOURCE: Adapted from *Annaes da Primeira Conferencia Algodoeira*, 2 vols. (São Paulo: Sociedade Nacional de Agricultura, 1916), 1:233 (overleaf).

The Political Impact of Export Growth

When viewed from a political perspective, export growth contributed directly to the "anarchy" created by Álvaro Machado and Valfredo Leal or, alternatively, to the "order" imposed by Epitácio Pessoa. The terms "anarchy" and "order" were used by contemporaries to characterize the organizing capacities of those two oligarchies, particularly their respective abilities to impose law and order at the local level and to delineate a clear chain of partisan command in the municípios. Especially under the rule of the Machado–Leal oligarchy, "anarchy" signified the rising incidence of gun battles and assassinations of politicians between 1892 and 1912. But the regularity with which armed confrontations erupted in virtually every market center in Paraíba and the frequency with which ambushes on lonely rural roads claimed political victims transcended the identity of the oligarchy in power.

Although Epitácio's oligarchy curbed violence more effectively, because it addressed the competition that lay behind family feuding, it still could offer no solution to the local warfare inherent in family-based politics. Economic competition historically had nourished internecine feuding at the município level and the commercialization of the export economy made that phenomenon much more pronounced in political life. No mere change in oligarchical styles was adequate to the task of purging violence from local politics. From this município perspective, therefore, "anarchy" did not cease with the Pessoas' assumption of leadership in 1912.

Both family feuding and brigandage deserve assessment in the historical context of economic growth that characterized Paraíba and neighboring states during the Old Republic. The impact economic expansion made on elite family warfare emerged clearly in the 1880s, when the cotton boom first briefly appeared but was then cut short by the great drought of the "triple eights." The railroad's extension into the brejo and then the caatinga-agreste offers ample evidence for the way both growth and infrastructure exacerbated well-established feuding patterns. Ambitious family-based groups, who after 1889 were often new economic challengers even when they bore the names of historically prestigious lineages, fought for the prizes of economic growth against incumbent local elites who not infrequently defended eroding or even anachronistic interest bases. Agricultural land or irrigation rights, new markets, coveted roads, railroad stations, and even the monopoly on local tax collection that yielded the capital for infrastructure investment—these were the most important stakes in local power contests.

Always endemic in the Brazilian Northeast, family warfare rose to epidemic proportions by the end of the Empire. Banditry also reached its historical zenith between 1900 and 1930. The family-based groups who politically controlled a município had always used their monopoly on public office as a means of securing economic resources. And the expansion of the cotton economy introduced unprecedented incentives for the most powerful parentelas to enhance their economic positions. Family control of the local police power, for instance, facilitated the efforts of landowners to acquire more land and labor for cotton production:

> Coronel Alexandrino Cavalcante de Albuquerque, Chief of Police [of Campina Grande], invaded the house of João Pereira, a poor and honorable family man who owned only the small piece of land that he had inherited from his parents. Under threat of imprisonment and a beating with a saber, [Coronel Alexandrino] succeeded in forcing him to sign a document recognizing him as his lessee [foreiro]. Jovino de Barros Brandão, another poor farmer [*lavrador em terras*] whose father built a house and small ranch back in 1846, was also threatened with the imprisonment of his son [as] preliminary to Coronel Alexandrino's conscripting him [into the army].[31]

Land seizures like this, described in Campina's Old Liberal opposition newspaper, *Gazeta do Sertão*, also explain the disappearance of unclaimed land throughout Paraíba by the close of the Empire. The system of subcontracting cotton cultivation implied that the labor of agricultural tenants could be secured more efficiently by those local families in whom the police power had been vested.

However, the bloc of family-based groups who exercised political monopoly in a município frequently had only a precarious grip on their prerogative of rule. Their vulnerability to rapid reversals of political fortune enhanced their propensity toward feuding. For example, six months after denouncing Col. Alexandrino, the *Gazeta do Sertão* prophetically admonished: "Without the command of his police force, [he] will not take more land. And without his party in power, he will vomit what he has swallowed."[32] Thus

[31] *Gazeta do Sertão*, 4 Jan. 1889.

[32] Ibid., 7 June 1889.

when the former Liberal Party opposition deposed the members of Alexandrino's faction from political control in 1891, a decade of extremely violent family warfare began.

The resumption of Cavalcante de Albuquerque control in Campina Grande—which occurred only a decade later, when Coronel Alexandrino's Danish-born son-in-law, Col. Cristiano Lauritzen, was elected prefeito—once again illustrates the close relationship between rising local violence and the rapid expansion of the cotton sector. As the owner of the Casa Inglêsa, the largest import–export establishment in the city, Col. Cristiano used his authority as prefeito and political boss of Campina Grande to insure that his commercial interests, as well as those of his two brothers-in-law who were also cotton buyers, received appropriate political support. When he directed the construction of a new market district and main street for the city, for instance, he used his executive influence with the municipal council to confine Campina's opposition bloc of former Liberal families to their existing commercial houses in the old marketplace. His sale of the land for the site of a railroad station served the same end. Consequently, when the railroad reached Campina Grande in 1907, he and his family-based group controlled both the new market and the environs of the station, while their rivals could only protest in vain that restricted access to the Great Western Railroad's storage facilities placed them in an extremely disadvantageous situation.[33] Between 1902 and 1907, gunfighting became so ferocious in Campina's streets that the lives of many innocent bystanders were endangered. Even the bandit Antônio Silvino found himself caught up in the family warfare that raged throughout the município, for he had opportunistically changed sides too many times. The situation reached a historic nadir when the city's citizens petitioned Gov. Valfredo Leal to end hostilities and then turned to the local vicar in total desperation. Monsig. Luiz Francisco Sales Pessoa, who was also an important politician in the município, responded by suspending—for ten years—all public celebration of Holy Week and the annual

[33] Historically, the respective locations of the cattle and agricultural fairs in Campina Grande had suggested which party was in power: "The change of the fair's location was not a simple act, [but required] the authority of the Municipal Council. If the fair was at the Praça Municipal, in front of the Mercado Velho (i.e., the daily market) . . . [then] without a doubt, the Liberals were in power; if it was on the Rua Seridó, in front of Coronel Alexandrino Cavalcante's Mercado Novo, then the Conservatives had come into power." Elpídio de Almeida, *História de Campina Grande* (Campina Grande: Livraria Pedrosa, 1962), pp. 269–70 (see also pp. 37 and 340); and Câmara, *Datas campinenses*, p. 76.

procession of the city's patron saint.[34] He assumed that depriving the populace of these rituals might be effective in discouraging open warfare. Customarily, armed confrontations—not to mention more subtly disguised attempts to take revenge—occurred where large numbers of revelers mingled with the holiday crowds attracted to the processions. However, appeal to sacred authority proved no more effective than appeal to the secular power. The tinder points of conflict continued to multiply as the growth of the cotton sector enriched some elite families and threatened others with ruin.

The extension of the main highway westward expanded the axis of conflict along geoeconomic lines, especially in the caatinga-agreste. In Campina Grande, for instance, Col. Cristiano's family bloc was opposed by another bloc—led by the intermarried Figueirêdos, Portos, Agras, and Sousa Campos—that had been loyal to the former Liberal Party during the Empire. As loyal Alvaristas and Valfredistas, this opposition bloc had staunchly opposed Epitácio's assumption of oligarchical leadership in 1912. As the losers, however, their economic interests suffered severely due to their partisan alignment. In 1917, when it was announced that a road would be built from Alagoa Grande to Soledade, on the Borborema Plateau, the Old Liberals protested the proposed route. Col. Salvino de Figueirêdo, their boss in Campina Grande and editor of the newspaper *A Razão*, objected that the proposed route would cross very near Fazenda Cabeça de Boi, the property of Campina Grande's prefeito and incumbent party boss, Col. Cristiano Lauritzen, while bypassing his own family's political bailiwick in the market town of Pocinhos. Noting that only one hundred tenants lived at Fazenda Cabeça de Boi, whereas four thousand lived on the estates surrounding Pocinhos, Col. Salvino indignantly concluded that the road's real purpose was to do "irreparable commercial damage" to the market in Pocinhos.[35] As he correctly perceived, the economic losses for those families who found themselves excluded from either the marketplace or new infrastructure could be very high after 1910, a point regularly made by the gun battles that reverberated in the streets of the interior's towns.

Economic growth also meant that the vertical divisions on

[34] The suspension of the public procession of Our Lady of the Vila Rica de Campina Grande by Monsig. Sales Pessoa—who was serving as president of the Municipio Council between 1904 and 1908—remained effective for ten years. Câmara, *Datas Campinenses*. pp. 100 and 108.

[35] *A Razão*, 16 Aug. 1917.

which family-based groups had historically depended no longer operated as successfully to retain the allegiance of the rural tenant population. The initiation of IFOCS construction for drought-relief projects introduced new tensions into landlord–tenant relationships that eventually weakened the control the rural elite had exercised in the rural zones. First, competition for the reservoirs and roads—or for the land on which they were to be constructed—exacerbated old feuding patterns. Second, the demand for wage labor to build the projects had disintegrative consequences. Thousands of day laborers found themselves detached from their traditional clientage relationships as agricultural tenants when they became directly dependent on federal wages. President Bernardes's dismantling of IFOCS, however, left them unemployed and uprooted. The very tempting alternative of banditry attracted a significant proportion of them to take up arms as outlaws and further accelerated the cycle of violence. If not as brigands, then as paid gunmen in the ranks of private family armies, these victims of economic change enlarged a freefloating population that was only marginally integrated in rural society. Their nomadic existence testified to the gradual erosion of landowners' control of the countryside as well as the rising incidence of violence in the political system.[36]

Finally, the expansion of the export sector also contributed to oligarchical cohesion, for the "order of Epitácio Pessoa" drew directly on the benefits of drought relief as valuable patronage. In justifying the massive support his administration was prepared to give IFOCS, President Epitácio emphasized, of course, that the program of drought relief represented "the payment of a debt of honor to [the] impoverished population of the interior" as well as "the revitalization of the region."[37] In spite of his rhetorical insistence that drought was "above all, a moral issue," Epitácio conceived of federal relief policy fundamentally in economic terms. Furthermore, he naively believed that "extinction of the droughts" could be achieved by means of a massive infusion of technology.[38] Paraíba's state party boss declined to raise historical

[36] Amaury de Souza, "The *Cangaço* and the Politics of Violence in Northeast Brazil," in *Protest and Resistance in Angola and Brazil*, ed. Ronald H. Chilcote (Berkeley and Los Angeles: University of California Press, 1972), pp. 109–131. At the São Gonçalo dam site, 12 kilometers from Sousa, José Américo de Almeida found "over 1,000 men working like ants . . . where a year earlier not a living soul could be found." *Parahyba*, p. 337.

[37] E. Pessôa, *Obras Completas*, 21:266.

[38] Ibid. Epitácio and those working in IFOCS had in mind the Nile Valley as a model. Ibid., pp. 270 and 297 (n. 1).

factors, like coronelismo and latifundia, which more accurately explained the region's poverty and underdevelopment, and preferred instead to address narrower questions of infrastructure and technology. Essentially a trickle-down theory of economic amelioration, Epitácio's approach conceived of the railroad, roads, irrigation, dams, and wells as "all of a piece" in combating drought.[39] According to him, each of these elements of drought relief remained inextricably tied to the goal of export expansion—principally cotton—for only the growth of that sector of the economy would justify "the audacity of undertaking the massive public works projects" that he so enthusiastically sponsored.[40] Having incorporated regional export growth within the national IFOCS policy, Brazil's president saw no contradiction between the pursuit of that goal and the distribution of IFOCS benefits among the political bosses in his own oligarchical machine and those of neighboring states.

The Group Basis of Oligarchy

By the late 1880s, a new breed of rural landowner—one who accumulated capital and then invested it in land, steam technology, and new varieties of tree cotton—had already appeared in both the cariri-sertão and the alto sertão. A journalist who traveled throughout the cariri during those years offered an intimate glimpse of the "most progressive" entrepreneurial planters, many of whom also held political office in the provincial oligarchy:

> Fazenda Riachão, [the estate] belonging to Major Saturnino Bezerra dos Santos, had a large and comfortable ranch house with [cotton] planted in an expanse of around one kilometer.

[39] Ibid., p. 306. Epitácio justified the commitment of federal expenditure to the Northeast by drawing a parallel with the federal government's sponsorship of coffee valorization, uniting both policies as *national* issues and dismissing their regional interests. Ibid., p. 281. But he also argued that federal spending between 1920 and 1922 for one railroad to serve only three southern states (the Estrada de Ferro Central) had exceeded the total IFOCS expenditure for 1920–1924. Ibid., p. 317.

[40] "*. . . só a cultura do algodoeiro, além de outras, contribuirá avaliosamente para a economia nacional, com a produção do se intitulado ouro branco, de modo a justificar, até certo ponto, as ousadias do emprendimento.*" Ibid., p. 290. In the interest of stimulating Brazilian cotton exports, Epitácio had personally invited Arno Pearse (general secretary of the International Federation of Master Cotton Spinners & Manufacturers' Association of Manchester, England)—during Epitácio's visit to London in June 1919—to undertake his historic tour of Brazil's cotton production zones in 1920–1921. J. A. de Almeida, *Parahyba*, p. 429.

This field grew with such vigor, that at the end of a period of three years it became a dense wood and remained that way for six or seven years or even longer, always giving an abundant harvest. Besides the [tree cotton] species of *crioulo* and *quebradinho*, Sea Island [Bourbon or Georgia] was also cultivated. I saw the same kind of crop on Dr. Domingos da Costa Ramos's estate, Fazenda Sant'Ana.

Major Saturnino was the most perfect type of planter in the Northeast. On his estate a guest thought himself in a home . . . in a big city, so refined was his distinguished family. He was also a lover of racehorses. A few days earlier, in Pajeú de Flores [Pernambuco], for 600 mil-réis, he had bought a horse known as Earthquake, famous in that region of the sertão . . .[41]

Major Saturnino and "Dr. Mingú" (Domingos da Costa Ramos), who colloquially were recognized as "cotton lords," continued to protect their economic interests—and those of other members of their immediate families—by holding seats in the Paraíba State Assembly during the Old Republic.[42] They represented a new statewide agrarian bourgeoisie whose political influence found confirmation in the state legislature's membership. Of the 204 assemblymen who served between 1889 and 1930, a significant number possessed direct links between land ownership and the ownership of steam-powered gins, commercial establishments, or, less frequently, infant industries. If an analogous group of sugar plantation owners is added to the group of commercialized cotton planters—those who owned the large refineries known as usinas or the smaller scale *engenhos* (mills)—then the proportionate representation of this agrarian bourgeoisie in the State Assembly rises significantly.

Although only 87 of the 204 assemblymen could be positively identified as landowners, all but 16 belonged to the category of the wealthiest property-owners in their municípios. In fact, a much

[41] *Gazeta do Sertão*, 9 Nov. 1888, cited in I. Joffily, *Notas*, p. 29.

[42] Dr. Domingos da Costa Ramos had served as a provincial deputy in the 1880s, as an assemblyman (state deputy) from 1896 to 1903, and then retired as a federal judge. His brother, Padre Ambrósio da Costa Ramos, who was a provincial deputy from the 1860s to the 1880s, also held a seat as an assemblyman from 1896 to 1900. His brother-in-law and cousin, Dr. Elías Eliseu Elíaco da Costa Ramos, also served as a provincial deputy. Finally, Domingos's nephew, Dr. Abdias da Costa Ramos, who was listed as the owner of Fazenda Sant'Ana in 1920 and probably was his son-in-law, had been elected state deputy for 1890–1894. Subsequently, he was appointed a federal judge. The Costa Ramos family ruled the município of São João do Cariri for well over a century, Author's prosopographical file.

higher proportion owned land, but in the absence of a comprehensive census, they cannot be individually identified.[43] In addition, many assemblymen were close kinsmen of those who owned substantial amounts of landed property. Of the 87 individuals who comprised the 43 per cent of landowning assemblymen, 71 could be classified as wealthy men of property; and 66 of them—or one-third of all the assemblymen—belonged to the agrarian bourgeoisie.[44] Their importance for Epitacismo grew after 1915, when a larger proportion of them entered the Assembly, replacing those deputies drawn from either exclusively landed pursuits or the liberal professions.[45]

The Capital's Commercial Sector

In contrast to the agrarian bourgeoisie, the businessmen of the Capital were primarily involved in importing and exporting and, secondarily, in a modest industrial sector. Unlike their peers in interior market centers, they were united by their divorce from landed enterprises. Because the Capital's businessmen had founded the Commercial Association of Parahyba in 1889, at the time the Federal Customs House was moved from Recife to Pa-

[43] Linda Lewin, "Politics and *Parentela* in Paraíba: A Case Study of Oligarchy in Brazil's Old Republic, 1889-1930" (Ph.D. diss., Columbia University, 1975), table 5.24 (p. 295). No comprehensive land census—including the 1920 national census—was completed in Paraíba before 1930. However, the wealthiest landlords can be identified from the following local histories or partial surveys: Lyra Tavares, *A Parahyba*, 2:522–968; Brazil, Ministerio da Agricultura, Industria e Commercio, Serviço da Inspecção e Defesa Agricolas, *Questionnarios sobre as condições da agricultura dos municípios da Parahyba* (Rio de Janeiro: Tipografia do Serviço de Estatistica, 1913); Diogenes Caldas, *Estatistica agricola da Parahyba do Norte de 1916* (Parahyba: Imprensa Oficial, 1916); Domingues, *Relatorio 1929*, pp. 36–41. The names of the most prominent landlords also were listed by município with the names of their properties in a special volume of the 1920 census: *Relação dos proprietários . . . ruraes* (1928). However, the 1920 census excluded all rural property owners with less than 500 mil réis annual income and, in addition, it surveyed only 67 per cent of the rural properties in Paraíba.

[44] The one-third (66 men) included in the agrarian bourgeoisie were wealthy landowners whose assets included the following: 29 owned steam-powered cotton gins, 26 owned steam-powered sugar mills, and 11 owned both types of machinery. These data are drawn from the sources in note 43, and the detailed lists in Lewin, "Politics and *Parentela*," apps. 1 and 2 (pp. 515–26).

[45] Membership lists for each of the eleven Assembly sessions of the Old Republic are found in Luiz Pinto, *Síntese histórica da Paraíba* (Rio de Janeiro: Gráfica Ouvidor, 1960), pp. 101–32. Cf. membership lists for the Provincial Assembly, in Celso Mariz, *Memória da Assembléia Legislativa* (João Pessoa: Impensa Oficial, 1946).

rahyba's Port of Varadouro, they remained unique until the 1920s as the only economic interest group in the state organized formally to exercise political influence.

Although the agrarian bourgeoisie always outnumbered the Capital's commercial sector in the Assembly, after 1900 the members of the Commercial Association steadily gained seats, as the conquest of cotton proceeded in the interior. Unlike the cotton planters in the backlands, however, they gained representation slowly.[46] For the first fifteen years of its existence, the Commercial Association fought with great determination simply to maintain a political voice. During the 1890s all of the Association's most important members were foreigners. But this fact did not prevent the membership from taking the lead to protest the monopoly that certain powerful foreign firms—namely, Lloyd Brasileiro and the Great Western Railway Company of Brazil—exercised over coastal transport, warehouse facilities, and access to the docks.[47] Before 1900 the dozen or so merchants who belonged to the Commercial Association did not represent a native economic elite, although perhaps a majority of them lived in Parahyba as permanent expatriates. By 1910, however, membership had grown to over fifty and become almost entirely native. Foreigners henceforth played no leadership role in the Association's affairs. Furthermore, by the same year ten of the Association's officers had gained seats in the Assembly since 1889.[48]

By 1910 the Commercial Association had clashed repeatedly and bitterly with two of Álvaro Machado's handpicked governors. On one occasion its officers even refused to meet with the governor for deliberations over the state budget and, in retaliation, he boycotted the Association's meetings. Increasingly disaffected from the Machado–Leal oligarchy, the Capital's merchants and businessmen began to look toward the political opposition for support of their efforts to transform Parahyba into a major deep-water port. The turning point came in 1910, when the Association formally petitioned Epitácio Pessoa—who was sitting as a justice of the Supreme Court—to promote the dredging of the Sanhauá River. Only if its channel were widened could Parahyba's

[46] Material regarding both the identity and the conflicts of the Commercial Association was drawn from Renato Ribeiro Coutinho, "História da Associação Comercial da Paraíba," Associação Comercial de João Pessoa, João Pessoa, Paraíba, 1958, typescript. This history is significant for its chronological gaps.

[47] Ibid., pp. 8 and 12. Outrageous freight rates and the failure of the Great Western to maintain a regular schedule were other complaints.

[48] Ibid., pp. 1–14.

businessmen maintain a direct Atlantic connection for their Port of Varadouro. A year later, when Epitácio secured the first of several federal appropriations for the dredging of the channel, and thus offered tangible proof of his political influence in Rio de Janeiro, the Commercial Association's numbers saw that their political future lay with Epitácio.[49] Henceforth, they became his tacit allies in unseating the dominant oligarchy.

The Capital's commercial sector did not acquire a major voice in state politics until the implementation of the export infrastructure in the early 1920s. Nevertheless, its membership shared common goals with the agrarian bourgeoisie of the interior: construction of a statewide road network, expansion of the railroad westward, and conversion of Cabedêlo into a deepwater port (once renovation of Varadouro proved impossible). Consequently, between 1912 and 1922 the political orientation of the Commercial Association posed no seriously divisive issues for Epitácio's oligarchical coalition. In addition, Parahyba's businessmen usually exercised greater political influence than their numbers in the Assembly suggested. Between 1910 and 1920, about a half dozen of the Assembly's thirty deputies represented the commercial sector in the Capital. By 1930, however, one-third of the state assemblymen were recruited from that sector, although several of the ten maintained business outside the Capital. Moreover, archival evidence shows that Epitácio recruited a number of his lieutenants from the ranks of Parahyba's merchants and industrialists. Several of them served long terms as his appointees on the Executive Committee of the Conservative Republican Party of Paraíba.[50]

[49] A complete impasse in the Association's relationship with Gov. José Peregrino de Araújo occurred in 1900–1904. On Epitácio's effective lobbying, see ibid., p. 13.

[50] Businessmen in the Capital who communicated regularly with Epitácio for at least a five-year period as his key political informants included the following: Col. Antônio de Brito Lira (assemblyman from 1908 to 1912 and either deputy prefeito or prefeito of the Capital from 1912 to 1930), a wealthy exporter, retailer, and owner of a sugar refinery; Col. Inácio Evaristo Monteiro (assemblyman from 1896 to 1930 and president of the Assembly from 1919 to 1930), a wealthy landowner and owner of the textile factory, Fábrica Tiburí; Dr. Pedro da Cunha Pedrosa (first Álvaro's lieutenant governor and then an Epitacista senator from 1912 to 1924), a small businessman and professional politician; Dr. Manuel Lira Tavares Cavalcanti (an assemblyman and then a federal deputy in the 1920s), a teacher and a lawyer who owned a sugar refinery in his home município of Alagoa Nova; Col. João (Cavalcanti) de Lira Tavares (an assemblyman, federal deputy, and senator for Paraíba from 1904 to 1915 and then a senator for Rio Grande do Norte after 1915), manager of a Recife firm in Parahyba, owner of a sugar mill and a cotton ginnery, as well as a teacher at the state normal school. Author's prosopographical file.

The Liberal Professions

Another, more heterogeneous, group of officeholders rivaled the agrarian bourgoisie in the number of Assembly seats they commanded—those who practiced the liberal professions. Unlike many of the commercial cotton or sugar planters—who often also possessed university degrees—these men were detached from the land and earned their livelihood as lawyers, physicians, priests, teachers, journalists, or engineers. Since over 50 per cent of the Assembly's members held university degrees, almost always in law or medicine, higher education alone did not reveal the interest orientation of the urban professionals.[51] Because they tended to be men of lesser means, their political influence in the Assembly remained more modest than what either the agrarian bourgeoisie or the commercial sector exercised. Few urban professionals had the financial resources needed to maintain the large retinue of client dependents that advertised the prestige politicians routinely cultivated. Many sought political office as a means to augment otherwise meager personal income or because they possessed a genuine vocation in politics. Frequently, however, they served in the Assembly to represent their families on a rotative basis with other kinsmen, for this category of politician had the highest turnover in office, rarely remaining for more than one four-year term. A number of assemblymen in this group were drawn from the Capital's intellectual elite. Particularly those who were journalists tended to enjoy greater political influence and public recognition because their literary gifts were placed at the service of the oligarchy's official newspaper or the opposition's press organ.[52]

As the *doutôres*, these graduates of law and medical school have been contrasted in the scholarly literature with the supposedly rustic and, above all, more violent coronéis. Yet what distinguished them from the coronéis, more than higher education, was the fact that they lived and worked in an urban environment,

[51] Of the 132 deputies whose education could be determined, 56.5 percent had graduated from an institution of higher education and an additional 6.2 per cent possessed some higher education. Lewin, "Politics and *Parentela*," table 5.14 (p. 264).

[52] The Epitacista intellectuals who served the oligarchy as both journalists and assemblymen included, as the most prominent examples: Carlos Dias Fernandes, director of *A União* for over a decade, Celso Mariz (contributor to *A União* and *O Norte*), José Américo de Almeida (contributor to *A União* and *O Norte*), and Artur Aquiles dos Santos (contributor to *O Commercio* and *A Voz do Povo*). One opposition leader founded his own newspaper: Francisco Alves da Lima Filho (*O Estado da Parahyba*).

alongside the businessmen of the export sector. When doutôres had been financially successful in their professional careers, then they frequently invested in commerce or industry. Occasionally, they owned substantial land in their home municípios, which often meant that they shared more values with commercial planters in the interior, particularly with those whom they had known at law or medical school. Like their rural counterparts, the urban doutôres committed themselves to the expansion of the cotton export sector and sought to promote economic growth through greater federal patronage. They considered urbanization a sign of "progress" and generally supported a larger role for the State in the economy. By the 1920s the social "revolution" that Câmara Cascudo argued had brought cotton planters in the interior to reside in the Capital and other large market centers began to have important consequences. Although most large landowners still resided permanently in the rural zones, they now lived in town during extended business trips, which were also devoted to political caucusing. Consequently, social contact between rural doutôres who were also cotton planters and their urban counterparts became regular and predicated on common political values and goals. Furthermore, both types of doutôres maintained frequent contacts with urban coronéis who shared a similar political outlook.

With the 1915 electoral victory of the Pessoas in the State Assembly, both doutôres and coronéis began to yield ground to deputies who had taken degrees in engineering or agronomy at the newer polytechnical schools, rather than degrees in the liberal professions of law and medicine. Frequently, these newcomers were also successful businessmen in the Capital or Campina Grande. Thus, the dichotomy between doutôres and coronéis so familiar to historians of the Old Republic is perhaps best applied to the decades before 1910. After 1910 the typical coronel in the Paraíba Assembly differed dramatically from his nineteenth-century predecessor, whose activities were much more restricted to the land. Before Epitácio's 1915 electoral victory, more coronéis occupied seats in the State Assembly than after the Pessoas controlled that body. Beginning in 1915, consequently, the coronel-assemblyman began to recede as a figure at the state level of politics, although the rising importance of cotton maintained him as a powerful boss at the local level. Particularly under Epitácio's leadership, the coronéis in the Assembly had strong connections with commerce. Forty per cent of them were businessmen whose activities were completely divorced from the land. An additional 25 per cent of the coronéis in the state legislature engaged in economic activities that combined landed proprietorship and commercial processing, underscoring their membership in the agrarian bourgeoisie. In fact, only 35 per cent of the coronéis managed exclusively landed enterprises.[53] Thus, in most cases their patents in the National Guard advertised their achievements as urban entrepreneurs who, in many cases, had declined to pursue higher education or had left their studies to assume responsibility for family enterprises that were becoming more commercially oriented.

On the other hand, the liberal professions enjoyed much more direct influence as an interest group in federal politics. Virtually all of Paraíba's senators, as well as three-quarters of the federal deputies, had taken higher degrees. As a homogeneous group of doutôres, the national politicians can be contrasted with the cotton-exporting doutôres and coronéis in the interior who belonged to the agrarian bourgeoisie. The national officeholders tended to form a stratum of career politicians. All of the senators and most of the federal deputies expected to be in office as long as the Pessoa oligarchy endured, for they served at Epitácio's pleasure. However, their preference for living in cosmopolitan Rio—particularly in the case of senators—tended to distance them from the political outlook of the state assemblymen. Less concerned with state issues such as infrastructure and export expansion, the national politicians regarded officeholding as a means of maintaining themselves in Rio de Janeiro and pursuing a political vocation. Some even refused to maintain households in Paraíba or make the uncomfortable sea voyage there, remaining in the national capital as permanent residents year-round. Others made very infrequent trips to their native state and confined their visiting to the Capital and its environs. But the national politicians remained dependent on the state assemblymen and the local bosses for reelection, and so geographical isolation in the South did not fully insulate them from the economic interests of their oligarchical counterparts in Paraíba.[54]

[53] This analysis of coronéis and doutôres is drawn from Lewin, "Politics and *Parentela*," table 5.19 (p. 276). Three additional coronéis supported themselves exclusively as a lawyer, a civil servant, and a stock-and-bond dealer. On the multiplicity of occupational roles that coronéis held in the Old Republic, see Pang, "Coronelismo," pp. 66–76; and Maria Isaura Pereira de Queiroz, "O coronelismo numa interpretação sociológica," in idem, *Mandonismo local* (São Paulo: Editôra Alfa-Omega, 1976), pp. 163–212.

[54] Several informants explained Álvaro Machado's partnership with Valfredo Leal to this author in terms of Álvaro's great reluctance to live in Parahyba because

The Group Basis of Conflict

By the 1920s economic growth had reached a point where the group basis of Paraíba's political economy could be meaningfully contrasted with the pre-1910 decades of the Old Republic. Unlike the Machado–Leal oligarchy, the Pessoa oligarchy represented a genuine statewide coalition with roots in all five of Paraíba's geo-economic zones. The Areia clique that had once been dominant in Álvaro's coalition no longer defined the brejo and the coastal zone as the pivot of the oligarchy's organization. Indeed, the few surviving Areiense politicians had long been absorbed by Epitácio's political machine or retired from politics.[55] The fact that after 1910 cotton production had become the basis of the local economy in almost every município in Paraíba imposed a new homogeneity of interest on the oligarchy's factional composition.

State assemblymen reflected a wider range of occupational and economic specialization by the 1920s. The historical distinction between coronéis and doutôres no longer adequately described an important division in that legislative body. Just as the doutor had given way to the coronel in the early years of the Republic, so in the Republic's last decade doutor and coronel both yielded to a new heterogeneity of occupational interest. Most significantly, the businessman who was closely linked to the export sector had replaced the traditional coronel whose economic activities were more narrowly tied to landed enterprise. In addition, after 1915, native-born commercial exporters competed more successfully with the foreigners who had claimed greater attention politically from the Machado—Leal oligarchy. As the tax exemptions awarded by a Pessoa Assembly showed, Paraíbano entrepreneurs gained a small edge over both foreigners and Brazilian outsiders from the South, at least until economic crisis at the close of the decade tipped the balance away from them.[56]

---

his wife, who was "an outsider," insisted that they live in Rio de Janeiro. Such absenteeism was typical. Cf. Pernambuco's Rosa e Silva, Levine, *Pernambuco*, p. 78.

[55] The following Areienses had died: João Coelho Gonçalves Lisboa (d. 1918), Antônio Simeão dos Santos Leal (d. 1921), Álvaro Machado (d. 1912), Ábdon Felinto Milanez (d. 1903), Maximiano Lopes Machado (d. 1895), and João Maximiano de Figueirêdo (d. 1918). After 1912, João Machado lived in "exile" in Rio de Janeiro. Of the original Alvaristas in the Areia clique, only Valfredo Leal survived in to the 1920s. However, several Venancistas from Areia continued to be trusted members of Epitácio's inner circle of federal politicians in the 1920s—most notably, Senators Octacílio de Albuquerque and Venâncio Neiva himself.

[56] Analysis of the tax exemptions voted by the Assembly between 1907 and 1921

Paradoxically, the completion of the road network by 1928 led in the long-run to the domination of Paraíba's cotton export sector by outsiders, since it encouraged out-of-state investors to establish large-scale ginning operations in the interior.[57] As a result, market links were reinforced between the Paraíba backlands and either Recife or Fortaleza, where the owners of the ginneries maintained their warehouses and shipping connections. In Campina Grande the majority of exporting firms nevertheless remained Paraíbano until 1930, though by only a small margin. Not until the 1930s did Campina's cotton exporting sector become absorbed by outsiders, largely foreign corporations that could take advantage of native entrepreneurs' lack of credit or decimation by bankruptcies. In the Capital, Paraíbano exporters more securely dominated exporting, a circumstance, however, that in 1930 would draw them into bitter conflict with their competitors in Campina Grande who were oriented toward Recife. But from the perspective of the final decade of the Old Republic, the Pessoas' oligarchical leadership was associated with gains for Paraíba's native entrepreneurs, both in the Capital and in Campina Grande.

In spite of unprecedented economic growth by 1920, group formation presented a striking limitation to change. To be sure, the commercial cotton planters of the interior became dominant in the Assembly and the Capital's Commercial Association acquired a new political voice in the passage of legislation. Except for the Commercial Association, there were no formally defined economic interest groups in the political arena, and this was perhaps the most salient aspect of several decades of economic growth in Paraíba. Before 1917, not even rural interests in the interior organized formally, as they had in Pernambuco. (An Agrarian Society was founded between 1910 and 1917, but it did not play an active role in political issues until the late 1920s, nor did any of the politicians corresponding with Epitácio ever mention it.) And when exporters finally organized a Commercial Association in Campina Grande around 1920, they did so under threat of a tax assault from the governor as well as from the realization that development of Cabedêlo would cripple their mercantile relationship with southern and international firms based in Recife.

The fact that Campina Grande's commercial sector had been

---

revealed that entrepreneurs took greater advantage of them after 1916 than they had in the earlier Machado–Leal period. Lewin, "Politics and *Parentela*," table 4.3 (pp. 184–85).

[57] Mariz discusses the ascendance foreign monopolies gained in Paraíba's export economy in the 1930s: *Evolução econômica*, pp. 166–69.

able to survive without formal organization for so long says a great deal about the group basis of politics. It suggests that economic interests had been adequately represented by other means. Alternatively, it implies that no strong incentives to create formal organizations dedicated to lobbying had been dictated by the prevailing pattern of economic conflict. In either event, and despite considerable economic growth, the family-based identity of political interest groups in Paraíba remained intact, suggesting that even by 1920 they provided an effective organizational nexus for oligarchical politics.

The Perpetuation of Family-Based Groups

Although political conflict in Paraíba was fueled by economic growth, the clash of competitive interests did not reveal antagonism between clearly opposed sectors of the economy. However tempting it might be to argue that the rivalry between family-based groups proceeded according to conflicting sectoral interests, the fact remains that in most municípios rival blocs competed along identical lines of economic interest. For instance, by the 1890s the political ascendance of the pastoral economy in the caatinga-agreste had passed and ranchers were investing in cotton. In Campina Grande, Col. Cristiano's archrival, Col. Salvino de Figueirêdo, belonged to the same economic elite of cotton exporters as Cristiano. In the backlands zones, where pastoral interests had once been completely dominant, the transition to cotton production nevertheless had proceeded very rapidly—in part, because the cultivation of tree cottons did not threaten the livestock economy's survival to the degree that agriculture devoured pastoral resources in the caatinga-agreste. Tree cottons flourished mostly in pastoral zones, where often transhumance meant that livestock were removed from areas of agricultural production in the dry months preceding the harvest.

One could argue, therefore, that a widely shared interest in expanding the export economy made the emergence of formally organized economic interest groups unnecessary.[58] Certainly, no

[58] On learning that Campina Grande would receive a rail link, Col. Cristiano Lauritzen demonstrated the consensus on infrastructure that his political faction shared with the opposition: "Deliriously happy . . . he went from house to house, indiscriminately inviting everyone, including his most hardened adversaries, to a public celebration at his expense." E. de Almeida, *Históŕia Campina*, p. 361. Hirschman also stressed the high consensus roadworks could create between incumbents and their opposition: "Brazil's Northeast," p. 28.

group formally lobbied to oppose measures for creating infrastructure. Family-based groups fought over the basic issue of who would manage the political economy, not over competing economic endeavors. At both the município and the state level, oligarchical politics dealt largely with one issue: which coalition of factions would exercise management of the export economy. This issue also implied the opportunity to deny economic rivals the resources necessary for their survival as a group. The struggle to control political officeholding therefore remained inseparable from the struggle to control land, markets, tax collection, and any other economic resource.

Those who belonged to the major family-based groups in Paraíba belonged to what more resembled interconnected status groups than a distinct social class. Nowhere is evidence for this assertion stronger than in the claims of entitlement they made on the State. Locally, the explicit recognition they enjoyed from the State strengthened their identity as quasi-corporate groups, for it validated their monopoly on political officeholding, civil service appointments, and the police power. In filling município posts with family members or their friends, the ruling parentelas institutionalized their political representation. In this respect, nepotism should be perceived as preserving the family-based group's local status and political hegemony. But from another perspective nepotism proved equally indispensable for providing the group's members their livelihood and insuring their economic survival on a collective basis.[59]

The Brazilian term for nepotism, "*empreguismo*," suggests how directly the most influential family-based groups depended on close working relations with the State for their economic survival. The term suggests literally the motive impelling individuals to seek political office, namely, *emprego*—employment—and the economic spoils associated with officeholding.[60] More broadly, the term conveys the crucial relationship between a patronage State and a system of family-based oligarchy and provides a clue

[59] Although municipal executives were legally prohibited from holding more than one remunerative public office, they were not restricted in their political appointments of close relatives. Campina Grande's case illustrated perfectly a pattern of interlocking officeholding by men who were close kin: See E. de Almeida, *História Campina*, pp. 229–54 and 357–92: and Câmara, *Datas campinenses*, pp. 72–149.

[60] Empreguismo was so characteristic of Brazilian politics by the late Empire that Sen. Joaquim Nabuco flippantly coined its logical extension—"*empregomania*." Faoro, *Os donos do poder*, 1:227.

for understanding why competition within and between the ruling family-based groups was effectively restrained during a period of economic boom. Empreguismo meant that individuals continued to think in terms of collective strategies for preserving their economic livelihoods. A phenomenon of the Empire, empreguismo's rise coincided with the historical expansion of the Brazilian State and economy. Originally, a response to the historical circumstance that career options no longer remained narrowly confined to the land, empreguismo mushroomed as land itself became scarce. Thus, one could argue that by the era of the Old Republic, empreguismo symbolically projected society's basically segmented organization—with its strong dependence on kinship organization—onto the political plane of the State. Economic growth meant that family interests now had to be guaranteed and maintained by local telegraphers, tax assessors and collectors, clerks, teachers, engineers, and agronomists as much as by the more traditional occupational pursuits on which a purely agrarian society had long relied.

So long as the State remained weakly developed, the elite family would offer the most secure organizational means of individual protection and material security. Empreguismo, consequently, reinforced that group's quasi-corporate identity through the collective entitlement to resources that it conferred on the basis of privilege. By the same token, the *bacharel*'s law or medical degree—whose possession entitled the bearer to privileges sanctioned by law—served as a badge denoting status-group membership, one that also denoted the role the State played in characterizing elite family membership as quasi-corporate. "*Bacharelismo*"—a specific variant of empreguismo—thus developed as the term to describe the intense manipulation of the State for employment resources and related patronage on the part of elite families seeking to place their members in either the higher civil service or elective office. The entitlement they thereby enjoyed also protected some of their members from the downward mobility that otherwise would have been inevitable. Finally, empreguismo limited the potentially destructive effects of competition within the collectivity of the group. Entitlement to employment meant that, among the dominant families at least, all male members—and certain female members—could expect to have a minimal income provided. By the same token, in society at large the appearance of full-blown economic interest groups was retarded, for the dominant family-based groups remained organized as "strategic elites" thanks to their special relationship with the State.

Eventually, however, economic growth and urbanization began to diminish the role that family-based groups played in Paraíba's oligarchical politics. The world crisis of 1929–1930 revealed their limitations as political units and unreliability as a basis for statewide factional coalitions. Although the challenge economic change presented to the way oligarchy had been structured in Paraíba became evident only at the moment the era of the oligarchies came to a close in 1930, the Old Republic demonstrated over its four decades that a period of transition had begun. The adaptation of family-based politics that occurred during the last decades of the Empire testified to its suitability as a system for a decentralized federal republic. And certainly the continuity the political economy reflected from Empire to Republic explained a great deal of the successful adaptation that family-based politics demonstrated after 1889. Yet one structural feature of family-based oligarchy in Paraíba deserves separate attention in that respect: Both the landed economy's segmented organization and the factional basis of the political system remained highly congruent with major social divisions inherently shaped by kinship organization. Only by examining the changing kinship organization of Paraíba's elite extended families, therefore, can the crucial connections between the landed economy and the system of oligarchical power be properly appreciated.

PART TWO

Politics and Parentela

· III ·

The Parentela in Empire and Republic

Marry your daughter to your neighbor's son.
—Nineteenth-century proverb of rural Paraíba

FOR THE POLITICIANS in the Paraíba state oligarchy, membership in a parentela, or extended family, was their most important organizational affiliation. Their private letters confirmed in either language or unspoken assumptions that politics was rooted in a family base. One local boss from the alto sertão, for example, wrote to the governor referring to his struggles with the opposition at the município level as literally *"política de família,"* or family politics.[1] At the national level, politicians also made direct reference to the intimate connections between kinship and politics when delivering rhetorical attacks on their opposition. Thus, Sen. Sílvio Romero condemned "all of the politicking clans who infest our unfortunate Brazil."[2]

Much more than a social organization, the parentela underlay the base of a politician's network of kin and political friends. From it he constructed the core of his personalistic political following, a family-based group that organized and delivered his votes locally, defended his partisan interests in his home município, and served him loyally as officeholders or bureaucratic appointees. Finally, to the extent that a parentela could be considered a quasi-corporate group that endured beyond a politician's life span, it was also an economic organization, by virtue of its members' collective and individual rights in land. In addition, two or more branches of a

The author wishes to acknowledge her appreciation for comments from members of the Family History Seminar of the Shelby Cullom Davis Center for Historical Studies at Princeton University in the fall of 1977, where a preliminary version of this chapter was presented. Parts of this chapter, together with portions of Chapter IV, appeared in revised form as "Some Historical Implications of Kinship Organization for Family-Based Politics in the Brazilian Northeast," *CSSH* 21 (April 1979):262–92. Joyce F. Riegelhaupt deserves special thanks for the valuable critical suggestions she offered for the revised version.

[1] Gov. João Pessoa to Epitácio (Capital), 15 Mar. 1929, AEP/9/13.

[2] Romero, "As oligarchias," p. 401.

parentela usually coordinated their economic activities in ways that enhanced its solidarity as a corporate group.

Paraíba's family-based system of politics depended on characteristics of *Brazilian* kinship organization for the social linkages underlying major elite loyalties or conflicts, however much it represented a regional variety of oligarchy. Consequently, this chapter places the parentela within the Brazilian kinship system. Discussion will focus on the four principal characteristics of Brazilian kinship organization and their significance for Paraíba's oligarchical organization: ambilineal and shallow descent, segmentary organization, endogamous matrimonial preferences, and the quasi-corporate character of the parentela. Evidence has been drawn in particular from several branches of the Pessoa family, in Pernambuco as well as Paraíba, from the Lins family of Pilar, and from a number of parentelas belonging to the Nóbrega family that dominated the Paraíba interior.[3] The special vocabulary of classificatory kinship analysis is used throughout discussion to take advantage of its precision for drawing conclusions based on subtle but important distinctions in kin and family organization. The advantages to historical analysis far outweigh the disadvantage of having to master the complexities of kinship terminology. In addition, classificatory kinship analysis introduces analytical perspectives derived from anthropology that enrich a historical understanding. The classificatory kinship terminology also corresponds to the legal definitions of kin relationships encountered in

[3] Genealogy was elicited in oral interviews and drawn from the following published sources: Liberato Bittencourt, *Homens do Brazil*, Vol. 2: *Parahyba* (Rio de Janeiro: Livraria Gomes Pereira, 1914); Sebastião de Azevêdo Bastos, *No roteiro dos Azevêdo e outras famílias do nordeste* (João Pessoa: Gráfico Comercial, 1954); Trajano Pires da Nóbrega, *A família Nóbrega*, Biblioteca Genealógica Brasileira 8 (São Paulo: Instituto Genealógico Brasileiro, 1956); J. Gabriel Sant'ana, "Biografias paraibanas: Ademar Vitor de Menezes Vidal," *Revista Genealógica Brasileira* (henceforth, *RGB* 6 (1945):47–48; Barão Smith de Vasconcellos, *Arquivo nobiliarchico brasileiro* (Laussane: n.p., 1918); José Leal, "A Família Costa Ramos de São João Cariry," *RIHGP* 16 (Sept. 1968):27–35; Sebastião de Azevêdo Bastos, "O patriarca Caetano Dantas," *RIHGP* 4 (1961):110–12; idem, "Os Arruda da Câmara na Paraíba," *RIHGP* 15 (1964):55–79; idem, "Tópicos para história de Serraria," *RIHGP* 14 (1961):117–29; Alfredo da Rocha Faria, Barão de Nioac, "Appontamentos sôbre a ascendência do Conde de Nioac," *RGB* 2 (1950):45–46; Adauto Miranda Raposo da Câmara, "Câmaras e Miranda Henriques," *RGB* 5 (1944):41–58; Cônego Florentino Barbosa, "A Família Leite no nordeste brasileiro, ramo de Teixeira," *RGB* 3 (1942):414–22; "O Barão de Abiahy," *RGB* 5 (1942):265–68. In addition, a card file on Paraíba families located at the Museo de Açucar, Recife, and another file on individuals enrolled at the Recife Law School were sources consulted. All local histories cited herein contained genealogies.

the Civil Code, facilitating comprehension of its provisions. Finally, the use of classificatory kinship terminology permits greater specificity in drawing key conclusions about male bonding, segmentation, and lineage affiliations as they directly affected political organization.[4]

Group Bases of Affiliation: Family and Parentela

Blood, marriage, and either fictive or ritual ties strongly influenced economic and political associations in Paraíba during the era of the oligarchies. Obviously, the kinship system determined who belonged to the family group by birth and who might be recruited for membership on the basis of marriage or ceremonial inclusion. Because it drew lines between those bonded by ties of blood, marriage, and ritual affiliation on the one hand and the rest of society on the other, the kinship system greatly affected the group basis of oligarchical organization throughout Brazil. Within the family group, kinship determined to a large extent the disparity of access to material rewards, status, and participation in decision-making. From a different perspective, the kinship system reflected how much the family group had to take into account the larger society and how it would interact with that society. Particularly through marriage, the family group selected outsiders and accommodated them to membership according to definite categories of recruitment. Unwritten rules of the kinship system helped the family group select successfully to acquire or maintain the power to defend itself in the wider society. By the same token, the kinship system influenced the extent of mobility in the social structure and, consequently, the capacity of the oligarchical elite to maintain its privileged position in the polity.

Colloquially, the extended family or parentela was simply re-

[4] A Glossary of Brazilian Kinship Terms may be found at the back of this book. See James L. Watson's case for greater rigor and precision in the scholarly usage of key kinship terms, specifically addressed to historians and anthropologists: "Chinese Kinship Reconsidered: Anthropological Perspectives on Historical Research," *The China Quarterly* 92, 4 (1982):589–622. "It is obvious that all who work on Chinese kinship must be precise in their use of key terms. Otherwise it becomes impossible to compare one historical case with another. . . . The effort required to establish a set of definitions upon which we can all agree (or agree to disagree) is the beginning of analysis; it is not an end in itself" (pp. 591–92). The author is grateful to David Keightley for bringing this timely article to her attention.

ferred to as "the family" (*a família*) in Paraíba, as it is everywhere in Brazil today. "Family" at one extreme could embrace only the nuclear family (*família nuclear* or *família conjugal*) of parental couple and offspring, but it most commonly was applied to the enormous extended family (parentela or *família extensa* or *família grande*). The term "parentela" is used here interchangeably with "extended family," although Maria Isaura Pereira de Queiroz has underscored an important nuance of difference between the Brazilian reality and what anthropologists ordinarily mean when they use the latter term. Usually "extended family" is applied to several generations of nuclear families living in a shared household. In Brazil, as she correctly points out, such a situation is the exception rather than the rule. Among the large landowning class as well as the *sitiantes*, or small cultivators, nineteenth-century households were comprised of nuclear families. Unmarried or widowed adult women and men, together with the children of relatives, commonly lived in such households, however. Historical research on family composition in eighteenth- and early nineteenth-century Brazil is confirming the preference for nucleated households over the long run, much as it has been demonstrated in the United States.[5]

Although the extended family included the several generations of lineal and collateral relatives among the Brazilian landowning elite, it customarily was distributed over a number of households situated on separate estates. Maria Isaura has appropriately emphasized this, citing the proverb, "*Quem casa, quer casa*" (Whoever marries wants a house). Consequently, as she notes, "parentela" is less restrictive spatially in Brazil than in most commonly understood contexts.[6] Biographical and anecdotal infor-

[5] On the prevalence of nucleated families in colonial São Paulo and Vila Rica, see the following studies, which emphasize the considerable number of female-headed households: Marcílio, *Cidade São Paulo*, and idem, "Mariage et remariage dans le Brésil traditionnel: Lois, intensité, calendrier," in *Marriage and Remarriage in Past Populations*, ed. J. Dupâquer et al. (New York: Academic Press, 1981), pp. 363–73; Ramos, "Marriage Vila Rica"; and Elizabeth Anne Kusnesof, "An Analysis of the Relationship between Household Composition and Mode of Production: São Paulo, 1765 to 1836," *Comparative Studies in Society and History* (henceforth, *CSSH*) 22 (Jan. 1980), 79–110.

[6] Pereira de Queiroz, "Coronelismo sociológico," pp. 180–81. The analogy often drawn in the scholarly literature between the Roman *gens* and the Brazilian extended family must also be abandoned: ibid. See also Lia Freitas Garcia Fukui's review of the use of the term "family" (família) in the scholarly literature treating Brazilian community studies. She contrasts its meaning with other kinship terms in colloquial usage as well as with terminology in the Civil Code's section on family law: *Sertão e bairro rural* (São Paulo: Editôra Ática, 1979), pp. 25–43.

mation about Paraíba's major parentelas in the Old Republic also confirmed that there were separate households for distinct generations of married couples. A newly married couple might reside temporarily with one set of parents, especially if they married at a young age. More common was the practice of settling married children on estates contiguous with the properties where one set of their parents resided. Those situations, in fact, suggested preferred patterns of either virilocal or uxorilocal residence for at least selected siblings. Because this proximate residence pattern might approach an attenuated form of residentially circumscribed extended family, it is another reason why the term extended family has been retained in this study and is used synonymously with parentela. It has been shortened to "family" for a more practical reason: "family" ("família grande") was the only term encountered in colloquial usage during the Old Republic. "Parentela" was not ordinarily used and even now it remains a technical term for kinship specialists. It also carries a derisive connotation in popular speech today, something like the expression "and all of his tribe." This meaning of parentela was what political bosses in Paraíba intended when they ungrammatically wrote the word "*parentesco*" as an occasional emphatic for a group of someone's relatives, as in the pejorative phrase, "the parentesco[s] of Epitácio Pessoa."[7]

The Brazilian extended family was circumscribed by an individual's bilateral descent group, which embraced both maternal and paternal ascendants and lineal descendants of several generations. Collateral consanguines—aunts and uncles or nephews and nieces—were included. A numerous population of nonconsanguineous kin, however, also belonged to this extended family: affines, or members by marriage, and fictive kin included through ritual (ceremonial *compadresco*) or adoptive (civil or customary *criado*) relationship routinely were incorporated into its folds.[8] Given this

[7] The plural ("*parentescos*") was also occasionally encountered in archival documents for Paraíba as a synonym for "relatives" (*parentes*). Generally, only the word "família" or *parente* was encountered in the correspondence of Paraíba's local bosses.

[8] A distinction is made by Antônio Candido between *compadresco* and *compadrio*. The spiritual relationship of *compadresco* was established between individuals through the religious sacraments of baptism, confirmation, and marriage, but the social relationship that derived from such ritual kinship is referred to as *compadrio*. The comparatively rare usage of the former term, in favor of a nearly universal preference for the latter, signifies the high value Brazilians place on the social dimension of such ritual kin ties. Ties of compadrio bound the ritualistic sponsors as godparents (*padrinhos*) not only vertically to the individual who was the subject of the religious sacrament—the *afilhado* or godchild—but also horizon-

definition, it is worth stressing that the extended family should not be equated with "clan." Unfortunately, both scholarly analyses and popular notions have given credence to the assumption that elite family organization in Brazil was synonymous with that of a patriarchal clan. The image of the patriarchal head of an extended family in Brazil as a "clan chieftain" is so familiar that it needs no elaboration, except to point out that it overlooks a number of key characteristics associated with clan organization. Clans are characterized by a rule or principle of unilineal descent (i.e., traceable through only one parent), by the practice of defining the family group in terms of a common totem, name, and extended household, and by their unambiguously defined corporate organization—one that conserves the group over generations, ordinarily through vesting in it collective rights to property. These were not characteristic of the Brazilian parentela. Furthermore, the archetypical patriarchal clan imposed solidarity on the group to a degree the Brazilian elite family never attained. In fact, the propensity toward fragmentation that Brazil's ruling families demonstrated abundantly over the centuries should be taken as further confirmation that a true clan organization was absent.[9]

Although sometimes equated with the kindred, the parentela is conceptually more meaningful—especially with reference to political organization—if it is distinguished from the kindred. A kindred embraces only cognates, that is, patrilineal and matrilineal consanguines.[10] Consequently, the kindred is narrower than an extended family or parentela when its scope is restricted to living members, because it does not include kin on the basis of affinal

---

tally to each other and to the individual's parents in the much more important relationship that compadrio defined, that of *compadres*, or co-parents. Candido, *Os parceiros*, p. 245; idem, "Brazilian Family," pp. 297–301; Willems, "Structure Brazilian Family," p. 343; Pereira de Queiroz, *Mandonismo local*, pp. 44–46; and Conrad Philip Kottak, "Kinship and Class in Brazil," *Ethnology* 5, no. 2 (1967):428 and 442(n). Due to lack of systematic data on these compadrio relationships for individuals in the Paraíba oligarchy, this relationship is not discussed in this chapter as extensively as its significance deserves.

[9] The naming system also presents a major obstacle to employing the term "clan," although certain similarities exist. The failure to distinguish "clan," which is based on a putative or fictive descent from a historical or mythical figure, from "lineage," which is based on a demonstrated descent from a known ancestor, is integral to its frequent misapplication in discussions of Brazilian kinship. Usually clan is used where lineage is being discussed. Watson, "Chinese Kinship," p. 603.

[10] J. D. Freeman, "On the Concept of the Kindred," *Journal of the Royal Anthropological Society* 91 (1961):195–99. On the kindred in Brazil, see also Wagley, "Luso-Brazilian Kinship," p. 175.

and fictive bonds. Although the consanguineous marriage formerly so widespread in Brazil often blurred the distinction between parentela and kindred, there are still useful reasons for emphasizing the kindred as a separate category. In certain contexts, such as inheritance law, the kindred carried a very precise meaning and application. The parentela was more fluid. Moreover, the kindred inscribed consanguines who might be excluded from the parentela or extended family—because the family's "cutting edge" depended on individual recognition. The range of kinship, the "family" one chose to recognize, in other words, depended in part on a characteristic common to all bilateral descent systems: their capacity for recognizing kinship according to specific behavioral contexts. Certain individuals linked by blood or marriage sometimes did not recognize each other as family, although their consanguinity was evident in the abstract category of a kindred. Others who did belong to the same kindred and had even recognized each other as kinsmen or kinswomen all their lives might choose deliberately to cease doing so.[11]

The subjectivity of membership was evident in political life at a number of levels. For instance, exclusion from the family could follow failure to fulfill obligations of obedience to private family law. Most commonly, offenses stemmed from a refusal to conform to paternal commands to marry, to exact vengeance, or to execute capricious demands by senior members of the group. Paraíba local oral history contained a number of stiking examples of individuals belonging to the oligarchy's major parentelas who were severed from their family nucleus for these infractions. For instance, Geraldo Batista, whose family warred with the Dantas of Teixeira, fled his ancestral home in the far backlands in the 1860s because he was unable to summon either the courage or the armed men to avenge his murdered brother. He failed, in other words, to uphold the concept of family honor that custom demanded. And young women, such as Marcionila Bezerra da Nóbrega, could be pronounced outcasts from the family by stern fathers whose sexual vigilance they had eluded. Preferring to flee with the spouse of her choice, Marcionila lived under a patriarchal death sentence for

[11] Raymond Firth, "Bilateral Descent Groups: An Operational Viewpoint," in *Studies in Kinship and Marriage, Dedicated to Brenda Z. Seligman on her Eightieth Birthday*, ed. I. Schapera (London: Royal Anthropological Institute of Great Britain and Ireland, 1963), pp. 30–31. On subjective recognition, see also Kottak, "Kinship and Class," pp. 432–33; Wagley, "Luso-Brazilian Kinship," pp. 174–77; and Charlotte I. Miller, "Middle-Class Kinship Networks in Belo Horizonte, Minas Gerais" (Ph.D. diss., University of Florida, 1976), pp. 11-12.

more than a decade. Only a brother's unwillingness to carry out their father's deathbed charge that he kill his sister allowed her to return to her family. Others were read out of their families by senior relatives because they had disgraced themselves through acts of disloyalty to a patriarchal figure. A Pessoa Queiroz nephew of Epitácio Pessoa experienced this fate in 1930. When he remained defiantly uncontrite about his involvement in a feud that resulted in the assassination of his cousin, Epitácio pronounced him no longer his nephew.[12] In other instances sons went so far as to adopt new surnames to remove reference to their father's names.[13] Uniquely Brazilian naming customs further refined the subjective criteria for kin recognition that are general to systems of cognatic or bilateral descent. They also testified to the importance of manipulating lineage affiliations for political purposes.

Tracing Descent

Lineages and Names: The Projection of Family Affiliation

Where descent is bilateral or cognitive, as in Brazilian kinship organization, individuals trace it through both parents. An analysis of naming practices associated with the members of the Paraíba oligarchy in the late nineteenth and early twentieth centuries revealed important patterns of tracing descent. Although the details suggest that Paraíba's case conformed with practice throughout Brazil, the evidence made much clearer the connection between Brazilian names and lineage affiliations or segmentation. Brazilian naming patterns cannot quite be equated with tracing descent, but they nevertheless projected socially a politician's lineage affiliation with either one or both of his parents. Moreover, they re-

[12] Pedro Baptista, *Cangaceiros do nordeste* (Parahyba do Norte: Livraria São Paulo, 1929), p. 86. Interview with Irmã Maria Regina do Santo Rosário [Laurita Pessoa], Rio de Janeiro, Oct. 1970; Epitácio to João, Francisco, and José Pessoa de Queiroz (Petrópolis), 27 Mar. 1930, certified (17 June 1965) copy of the original provided by Laurita Pessoa Raja Gabaglia [Irmã Maria Regina do Santo Rosário], AEP/ "Colleção Epitácio Pessoa" (unnumbered group of pastas located at the end of the numbered pastas). Marcionila (b. 1850/1855) was the daughter of Capt. Justino Alves da Nóbrega (d. 1888), the first Conservative Party local boss of Santa Luzia, whose grandsons were officeholders in Epitácio's oligarchy. T. da Nóbrega, *Família Nóbrega*, pp. 578–79.

[13] T. da Nóbrega, *Família Nóbrega*, pp. 578–79.

flected an important element of personal choice, whether individual or familial. Unlike Spanish America, where a fairly fixed formula of nomenclature existed for selecting an individual's names bilaterally—in a standardized combination of both parents' names—Brazil had naming practices that demonstrated greater initial flexibility followed by successive redefinition. Above all, they conveyed idiosyncratic preference in the status system. Names also indicated that very often descent was not bilaterally reckoned at all, since the manipulative projection of family surnames might exclude altogether one of a politician's lineages.

More accurately, the Brazilian system of tracing descent was "ambilineal," that is, reckoned from either one or both parents.[14] Nor was it unusual for naming practices to reflect descent traced from more distant antecedents than parents. Parental names could be overlooked in favor of grandparents' or even great-grandparents'. General practice until the close of the last century favored the tradition of deriving both given names and surnames from the pools of names belonging to an individual's lineal antecedents of the same sex. Thus, female names tended to reflect the given names of older female lineals—mothers, grandmothers, and great-grandmothers. The matrilineal derivation of female names meant that women usually ignored their fathers' surnames, although their sons might include their maternal grandfathers' surnames in their family name. Males derived their given and surnames analogously from paternal antecedents, often excluding their mothers' family names. A daughter, however, often assumed one of the surnames belonging to her paternal grandmother. In addition, a third pool of given names was common to both genders and freely appropriated by everyone in a descent group. It consisted of names such as Custódio/Custódia, Peregrino/Peregrina, Delfim/Delfina, José/Josefa, Joaquim/Joaquina, Augusto/Augusta, and Alexandrino/Alexandrina. Coupled with several variations of a surname combination, these common gender given names often readily distinguished the members of one branch of a parentela from another.

[14] Firth proposed the term "ambilineal," which is perfectly suited to the Brazilian case. "Bilateral Descent," p. 32. The absence of a firm naming rule makes Brazilian family reconstruction very difficult. Maria Luiza Marcílio has noted that it is a problem that still awaits solution or adaptation of technique: *Cidade São Paulo*, p. 74; see also T. da Nóbrega, *Família Nóbrega*, pp. 6–8. She has also suggested that intergenerational patterns in given names within the same descent group might be more useful for family reconstruction than surnames: "Variations des noms et des prénoms au Brésil," *Annales de Demographie Historique* (henceforth, *Annales*) (1972):esp. pp. 347 and 353.

Custom permitted great flexibility of choice, either to parents in bestowing names on their newborn offsping or to individuals who modified their own names in adulthood. Within any set of siblings, there was frequently such a wide variation in names that no two might bear the same surname.[15] In a number of families, even siblings of the same sex employed different surnames. In keeping with the notion of ambilineal descent, in other families, all siblings did bear a uniform surname, usually a combination of the surnames of both parents.

The tendency for given and surnames to reflect the gender of both the bearer and his or her lineal descendants over several generations predominated until at least 1850, but it became much less pronounced by the time of the Old Republic. A purely bilateral paradigm joining the surnames of both parents to form a common name for all siblings, regardless of sex, gradually came to predominate early in this century.[16] After 1930 a patrilineal bias became dominant. As children no longer included their mothers' surnames in their own, they identified themselves solely by names derived from their fathers. However, the politicians in the Paraíba oligarchy, who spanned three generations, made exceptionally creative use of all the opportunities ambilineal descent afforded them with respect to their names. Particularly in their emphasis on maternal lineages, which continued to matter for them in the twentieth century, they manipulated their names very advantageously to project family affiliations on behalf of their career goals.[17] In addition, kinship organization itself oriented them to-

[15] For examples of widely varying sibling names, see Candido, "Brazilian Family," p. 298(n). On Brazilian names before 1850, see Marcílio, *Cidade São Paulo*, pp. 70, 72, and 73; and idem, "Variations noms," pp. 345–53.

[16] In Fig. B.1, the mother of Epitácio—Henriqueta Barbosa de Lucena—exemplified the circa-1850 bilateral name pattern, while Epitácio and his brothers (Fig. B.3) reflected the patrilineal name bias. Only in 1890 were Brazilian wives given the legal right to use their husbands' surnames; however, in 1916 the wording of the new Civil Code suggested that adoption of the husband's surname would automatically follow upon marriage. Brazil, *Decretos do Governo Provisorio . . . Brazil (1890)* (Rio de Janeiro: Typografia Nacional, 1890), Decree No. 181 of 24 Jan. 1890, Art. 56, Par. 4; *Codigo Civil 1916/Alves*, Art. 240. Recently, the Brazilian Civil Code has granted women the right to retain their own surnames—usually paternally or bilaterally derived—at marriage or to reclaim them if they are already married. Law No. 6.515 of 26 Dec. 1977, pertaining to Art. 240 of the Brazilian Civil Code.

[17] In a maternal lineage, ancestors (male and female) can be traced matrilineally, i.e., directly through the nearest female ascendant, to the demonstrated ancestor from whom her lineage is descended. A powerful ancestress per se did *not* define a matriarchy, although informants frequently pointed out in interviews that the

ward a maternal as well as a paternal affiliation. The genealogical existence of a female ancestral figure who had once wielded political or economic power evidently encouraged emphasis on a maternal lineage, either as the paramount one or as co-equal with the paternal lineage. Paraíba's ruling families prided themselves on ancestresses such as Adriana de Oliveira Ledo, who had functioned in their own right as de facto politicians.[18] The daughter of the backlands' conqueror, Teodósio de Oliveira Ledo, Dona Adriana defined what one local historian termed "the oligarchy of the House of Santa Rosa," because she possessed fourteen properties in the Santa Rosa Valley near Campina Grande. Relying on her two sons and her son-in-law as surrogates, Dona Adriana dominated the valley politically and economically until the close of the eighteenth century.[19]

The leaders of the state oligarchy illustrated the flexibility in bilateral descent. Male family heads maximized their political advantage through nomenclature that emphasized bonds with a politician's mother's kinsmen. Alternatively, a politician looked toward influential connections with his wife's kinsmen and selected his name accordingly. Five of the six men who rose to the top of the Paraíba oligarchy between 1890 and 1930 owed their success to ties with either their mothers' or their wives' male kin. One—Venâncio Magalhães Nevia—got his start because his brother had married a sister of the Baron of Lucena. Four of the remaining five, however, gained political influence initially through their maternal uncles: Epitácio through the Baron of Lucena, Gov. Álvaro Machado through Sen. Ábdon Milanez, Gov. Solon de Lucena through Epitácio, and Gov. João Pessoa Cavalcanti de Albu-

---

phrase *"mulher paraibana"* (a woman from Paraíba) in popular speech carried the humorous connotation of a "masculine," i.e., a strong-willed, woman (*uma mulher masculina*). On the misuse of the concept of matriarchy and its irrelevance to matrilineality, see Robin Fox, *Kinship and Marriage: An Anthropological Perspective* (Baltimore: Penguin Books, 1967), pp. 18, 113, 231; and A. I. Richards, "Matrilineal Systems," in *Kinship: Selected Readings*, ed. Jack Goody (Baltimore: Penguin Books, 1971), pp. 277–79.

[18] Generalizations related to matrilineal descent were drawn from E. de Almeida, *História Campina*, Antônio José de Sousa, *Apanhados históricos e genealógicos do grande Pombal* (João Pessoa: Gráfica Comercial, 1971); Câmara, *Datas campinenses*; H. de Almeida, *Brejo de Areia*; and Baptista, *Cônego Bernardo* and *Cangaceiros*. The practice of registering children in official documents under only their fathers' names contributed to the attrition of female names. Azevêdo Bastos, *Roteiro Azevêdo*, p. 21. Costa Pinto, *Lutas de família*, p. 90. Duarte, *Ordem privada*, p. 68.

[19] E. Câmara, *Datas campinenses*, pp. 13, 29(n. 1)–30.

querque through Epitácio.[20] (See Figs. B.1 and B.2.) Gov. Solon (Barbosa) de Lucena's name illustrated the selectivity evident in politicians' names. The son of Virgínio de Melo and Amélia (Barbosa) de Lucena, he preferred to stress the kinship connection with his powerful maternal great-uncle, the Baron of Lucena (Henrique Pereira de Lucena) and not with his patrilineal Melo relations. (See Fig. B.1.) He chose his names from his Barbosa grandparents on both sides and omitted his father's Melo name. His stress of the sole surname of Lucena also emphasized his connection with his cousin-once-removed, the influential Epitácio Pessoa, who enjoyed universal recognition as the baron's favorite nephew. Epitácio's mother was the baron's sister.[21]

In rare cases, a man adopted the names of his wife's male kinsmen. The Baron of Araruna, Commendador Estevão José da Rocha, was a prominent nineteenth-century example. Together with his three brothers, he discarded both parents' names (Ferreira de Macedo and Arruda Camara) in favor of his wife's (Maria Farias da Rocha) surname. The decision obviously followed from the collective alliance the four men formed with the Farias Rocha, since they all married either sisters or cousins in that family. Their children also intermarried, further solidifying the pattern of endogamy.[22]

Finally, it should be noted that individuals who did not bear the family name(s) might still claim affiliation by reciting their genealogical connections to the family, verbally reinforcing the connection where it served them to reveal membership. Because of the extreme flexibility of choice in the naming system, it was inevitable that even closely related individuals would bear different names. In spite of considerable intermarriage, for example, the descendants of Teodósio de Oliveira Ledo bore several dozen important names.[23] What mattered, in other words, was the ambilineal nature of descent; a firm naming rule was absent. As a consequence, the force of kinship in politics acquired optimal flexibility. As projections of individual family honor in society, names ad-

[20] Author's prosopographical file. Only Valfredo Leal was not assisted by an uncle, although his own favoritism for his nephews became proverbial in the critiques leveled against him.

[21] Ibid. Coelho Lisbôa, *Oligarchias*, pp. 11–12.

[22] Maurílio Augusto de Almeida, *O Barão de Araruna e sua prole* (João Pessoa: *A União* Editôra, 1978), pp. 24–26.

[23] Câmara, *Datas campinenses*, p. 71. The major lineages of Teodósio included the Agras, Sousa Campos, Tavares, Figueirêdos, Lunas, Siqueiras, Barretos, Guedes Pereiras, Alcoforados, Arruda Câmaras, Farias Leites, and Araújos.

vertised a collective accumulation of virtue, as one anthropologist has pointed out, that was expressed in a pedigree designed to assert claims to political perquisites on the basis of social status.[24]

The Spatial Dimension of Family Affiliation

Names also served to fix both individuals and branches of a parentela in a specific spatial reference, suggesting for historians a shorthand method of identifying precise family clusters within one large descent group. The preference for settling some siblings on adjacent properties, often contiguous with the estate where the parents resided, suggested that the preferred residence pattern for Paraíba's elite families could best be described as ambilocal, residing with either the husband's or the wife's parents. Like descent, residence admitted no firm rules. In some instances, newlyweds were settled on the bridegroom's inheritance portion, but in others they established themselves on the wife's dotal property. Properties that bore the names "Engenho Novo" (New Sugar Estate) or "Fazenda Nova" (New Estate) testified to the practice of dividing future inheritance portions at the time adult children married. Even today, Col. José (Cavalcanti) de Albuquerque Lins of Engenho Itaipu is remembered in his native município of Pilar for his famous distribution of patrimony among his six daughters. Residents can point out and name the six sugar engenhos on both banks of the Paraíba River flanking his own Engenho Itaipu that he distributed as dowries.[25]

A parentela's geographical distribution, or at least that of several of its branches when it was very large, strongly complemented a group identity derived from descent from the same ancestral cou-

[24] Eric R. Wolf, "Kinship, Friendship, and Patron–Client Relations in Complex Societies in *The Social Anthropology of Complex Societies*, ed. Michael Banton (London: Tavistock Publishers, 1968), p. 9.

[25] Lins genealogy and family history were collected in interviews with the following member of the Lins family: Dona Maria de Lourdes de Toledo Lins, João Pessoa, 22 July 1978; Dona Júlia Lins Vieira de Melo (granddaughter of João Cavalcanti—"Seu Joca"—and great-granddaughter of "O Num"), João Pessoa, 21 July 1978; Dona Montinha (Antónia do Monte) Lins Falcão (daughter of Ana Lins and granddaughter of Col. José (Cavalcanti) de Albuquerque Lins, Engenho Corredor, São Miguel de Taipú (Pilar), 20 July 1978; Dona Clóris Vieira (wife of Henrique Vieira, son of Lourenço Bezerra de Melo—"Lourenço of Oiteiro"), Engenho Oiteiro, São Miguel de Taipú (Pilar), 20 July 1978. The author is sincerely grateful for the gracious hospitality and cooperation extended to her by these and other members of the Lins family of Pilar. Any errors in transcribing names and ascribing kinship are her responsibility.

ple. In practice, family names were popularly identified with specific "home" municípios, where the majority of the members' properties were situated. Usually, a "home" estate also existed that had been the birthplace of at least two generations and where the family group's most prestigious nuclear family resided. A collective identification, with both specific landed properties and a município, was tantamount to the quasi-corporate identity most extended family groups established. In the case mentioned above of Col. José (Cavalcanti) de Albuquerque Lins ("Bubú"), the marriage of his daughter Maria Lins with his sister's son, Henrique Vieira de Melo, rendered part of his extended family a corporate group through joint property ownership. The couple's joint property, two contiguous engenhos, consolidated one-third of Col. José Lins's father's patrimony and united the descendants of two of his six children as a family.[26] (See Fig. C.1.)

The marriage of Henrique Vieira de Melo and Maria Lins also illustrated that endogamy alone did not guarantee the elite family's quasi-corporate identity. Instead, land cemented the most enduring bonds of identification among siblings and their more distant collateral relatives. Above all, land held in close proximity with parents' and siblings' properties insured that the succeeding generation would maintain the corporate nature of the family group. Where siblings' marriages or careers caused them to move away from the home município and to become scattered over a large area, they might retain a position of solidarity by virtue of common propertyholding. The partible inheritance system—one of "forced heirship"—tended to favor a pattern of distributing contiguous estates among siblings.[27] Geographical separation often did determine genealogical attrition in a family, reorganizing it more narrowly so that distant collateral branches dropped from effective recognition. However, the way families maintained their sol-

[26] The most prized dowry, Engenho Massangana, went to the eldest daughter, Luzia, but it became more associated with her husband, Col. Francisco de Paula Cavalcanti, more familiar later as Pilar's colorful local boss, "Coronel Cazuza Trombone"—an important character in the novels of his wife's nephew, José Lins do Rêgo. By the 1920s the Ribeiro Coutinhos, the Lins' more aggressive and entrepreneurial neighbors, had purchased four of the six dotal properties from Col. José (Cavalcanti) de Albuquerque Lins's daughters or their heirs. Ibid. In the 1980s, the Vieira de Melo owners of Engenho Oiteiro purchased adjoining Engenho Corredor and its nineteenth century Big House.

[27] Patterns of contiguous or overlapping (joint) ownership of land by sibling sets, in-laws, and parents (or a widowed parent) could easily be verified in the land surveys cited as sources in Chapter II, n. 43.

idarity through reference to the land—and in the face of long distances—was even more impressive. Then endogamous marriages became almost indispensable elements, for matrimonial alliances with cousins fostered family solidarity over the long run. The ownership of ancestral properties in the rural zones, consequently, fixed the identity of either a parentela or one of its branches in both space and generational time. As the Lins family of Pilar again illustrated, even the nicknames of male kinsmen incorporated the names of their properties. Since family name pools usually remained very small, confusing redundancy was avoided by the vernacular usage of coupling standard nicknames with the owner's estate's name, such as "Joca of Maravalha" for Dr. João Lins Cavalcanti de Albuquerque.[28]

Shallow Descent

The spatial distribution of Paraíba's parentelas reinforced yet another basic characteristic of elite family organization. Because individuals usually ignored their remote ancestors in favor of reference to more immediate ascendants, usually grandparents, descent was defined in extremely shallow terms. Even in the 1760s, the distinguished Pernambuco genealogist, Borges da Fonseca, complained that "individuals of the most noble lineage" were "incapable of giving me information about where their grandparents had been born."[29] His difficulties stemmed from the fact that many had grandparents who had been either Portuguese immigrants or Amerindians—and therefore could not be documented. Trajano Pires da Nóbrega complained nearly two hundred years later about the same vagueness on the part of his informants from the Paraíba backlands when he sought information about their antecedents for his monumental genealogical compendium, *A família Nóbrega*.[30]

Because in practice the correct apical ancestor couple—the original pair from whom a descent group traced its origin—was often ignored, usually in favor of the grandparents, the parentela's effective boundaries were usually restricted to the first-cousin level.

[28] The Lins family nicknames (including Col. José (Cavalcanti) de Albuquerque Lins's nickname "Bubú") were collected during visits to Engenhos Corredor and Oiteiro in Pilar. See n. 25, above.

[29] A. V. Borges da Fonseca, *Nobiliarchia pernambucana*, in *Annaes da Biblioteca Nacional do Rio de Janeiro* (henceforth, the *ABNRJ*) 47 (1925):7.

[30] T. P. da Nóbrega, *Família Nóbrega*, pp. 5–8.

This was especially the case when no matrimonial exchange took place within the family group. Cousins who were geographically separated and did not renew their ties of kinship through marriage eventually became distanced from those who did. Their offspring, as cousins once removed, would refer to each other as "distant relatives" (*parentes de longe*), with the Portuguese term conveying a spatial as well as a kin difference.

Shallow descent affected naming patterns by reducing the size of name pools and necessitating reference to a specific município as a parentela's home base. Collateral branches of cousins could still be identified by placing them spatially. Specific trunk names usually distinguished a parentela's cousin branches. The insertion of a second name in front of or behind the main extended family name identified the parentela's effective boundaries, while pools of given names set off the separate branches even more distinctly, since they were heritable for a number of generations. For instance, the (Cavalcanti) de Albuquerque Lins of Pilar readily distinguished themselves from their distant cousins, the d'Ávila Lins of Areia, although both families knew they were descended from the same apical ancestor, the shipwrecked German sailor, Cibaldo Linz. In the absence of matrimonial exchange, geographical distance had produced an amicable but effective lineage segmentation. The Lins of Pilar therefore referred to the d'Ávila Lins of Areia not only as "the branch of Major Remígio" (i.e., Remígio Veríssimo d'Ávila Lins, Cibaldo's direct descendant), but also as a "different branch" (*outro ramo*), implying a separate family identity.[31]

Segmentation: The Kin Basis for Conflict

Geographical distance and the failure to renew extended family solidarity through consanguineous matrimonial exchange accounted for segmentation from only one perspective. In reality, segmentation regularly occurred within most parentelas because of demographic and historical circumstances. Consequently, shallow descent more correctly was a product of segmentation, not its cause. Ambilineal descent and endogamous matrimonial patterns, coupled with the relatively small size of the local political elite,

[31] Personal interviews with Dona Maria de Lourdes de Toledo Lins, João Pessoa; Dona Montinha Lins Falcão, Engenho Corredor, Pilar; and Dona Júlia Lins Vieira de Melo, João Pessoa, 20–22 July 1978.

posed what might even be termed a familial time bomb. The very nature of kinship organization offered ample opportunity for asserting claims to membership in a range of families, since everyone could claim to belong to at least two parentelas. Individuals potentially could establish kinship with a large number of families. Conflict therefore emerged between those with competing claims to membership in the same family group. How were such claims to be resolved?

Segmentation offered the appropriate resolution, for it insured that the family group did not become too numerous in proportion to the available resources. Behavioral patterns, not unexpectedly, contradicted the legal definition of kinship in the Brazilian Civil Code. Historically, law had established ten collateral degrees as the legal limit of the blood ties inscribing the members of the same family; the number was reduced to six in an important reform in 1907.[32] The more pressing need to maintain an effective size for the family group took precedence in practice, where destructive tendencies frequently arose among a parentela's collateral branches. Even the violence of endemic feuding offered constructive consequences, for it reorganized families according to narrower and more viable units. The "solidarity" of the dominant branch of a parentela survived in its reorganized core, once the more marginal or recalcitrant branches had been pruned through conflict.

Cohesion and fragmentation therefore were opposite sides of the same coin of family survival and perpetuation. As Oliveira Vianna suggests, elite family solidarity was exceedingly tenuous.[33] The intensified parentela-based conflict associated with the Old Republic—conflict that was intrafamilial as well as interfamilial—deserves reconsideration in terms of the kinship system, for it provided a patterned response to the heightened family conflicts associated with an era of rapid growth.[34] The major family wars in Paraíba's backlands usually contained as at least one

[32] Decree No. 1.839 of 31 Dec. 1907.

[33] Oliveira Vianna, *Instituições políticas*, 2:259–60; Firth, "Bilateral Descent," p. 213. On the vulnerability of bilateral descent systems to collateral fragmentation and recombination, see also William Davenport, "Nonunilinear Descent and Descent Groups," in *Kinship*, ed. Goody, p. 209.

[34] A prime example of a major nineteenth-century feud in Paraíba that contained both intrafamilial and interfamilial tension took place in the município of Teixeira between the Dantas and the Batista–Carvalho–Nóbrega families. See Batista, *Cangaceiros do nordeste*, pp. 26–30; idem, *Cônego Bernardo*, pp. 33–65, 104–77; T. P. da Nóbrega, *Família Nóbrega*, pp. 33–38; and Bittencourt, *Parahyba*, pp. 39–75.

dimension a violent schism between first cousins, even when larger units consisted of unrelated families. The circumstance of family warfare best illustrated the strong tendencies toward fragmentation always potentially present in elite family organization; it also posed a limitation to group solidarity beyond the nuclear core.[35]

Brazilian kinship organization did not impose rigid obligations of support on family members *as cousins*. This fact helped to explain why family warfare reached its peak during a period of unprecedented elite prosperity. First, land, which held together a family's intergenerational core, remained finite and therefore an increasingly limited resource in inheritance strategies. Furthermore, law mandated the distribution of land as patrimony according to rules intended to fragment it among heirs. Second, competition for markets and infrastructure improvements at the município level aimed in most cases at a monopolistic control of resources for the winners. Therefore wide distribution of patronage—even among cousins—frequently was not the preferred option. In spite of a period of good times, in other words, elite families still wanted to control mobility at the upper level of society, not to create more "room at the top." Finally, Paraíba's ruling parentelas did not perceive prosperity as long-lasting, although, in fact, the cotton boom persisted for three decades. Instead, they feared that market fluctuations or drought might at any time curtail export expansion. By the same token, they did not perceive the distribution of political power between ins and outs at the município level as static, but calculated that political ascendance—like the economic prosperity it guaranteed—was precariously subject to reversal.[36]

Endogamous Matrimonial Strategies

Aside from dramatic situations of family warfare, individuals daily acknowledged more subtly that family groups needed to

[35] For Oliveira Vianna, who took a skeptical view of the elite family's solidarity, the parentela imposed "no predetermined collective obligations." Nothing except crisis situations obliged its members to a common life; however, both electoral contests and defense of the family group in a feud posed such crises. *Instituicões políticas*, 2:259.

[36] The Dantas family's war with the Batista–Carvalho–Nóbrega families in Teixeira illustrated how domination could be reversed and relegate the losers to a very inferior position. The Carvalho and Batista leaders, Canon Bernardo Andrade de

draw their boundaries closer to home than the theoretical claims of kinship suggested. Otherwise, they risked permitting "family" to become synonymous with society at the município level, where endogamy was highest. Many of the survivors of the Old Republic interviewed for this book confirmed the volitional quality in their kinship recognition when asked how they discriminated family members from outsiders—"*Quem é de família*?" Responses were surprisingly uniform: "Those who are close to me belong to my family" "(*Quem é perto de mim é de família*")[37] This answer did not suggest a paradox, because it emphasized that the respondents themselves decided where to draw the family's "cutting edge"—the line for effective recognition of its members. In almost all cases, they drew it very practically at the first-cousin level. Cousins thus either created a fulcrum for future cohesion through incorporation in the family by marriage, forged an eventual separation through exogamous marriage with outsider stock, or opened a definite cleavage along which a blood feud could develop. However, informants also underscored that cousins frequently bonded in quasi-sibling relationships. In relating genealogies and family histories, their specificity of language for identifying types of cousins suggested that those quasi-sibling relationships formed a key element of kinship organization not only throughout the Old Republic but also during the Empire.

A Plethora of Cousins

The plethora of cousins forming the bulk of any parentela's population was sorted according to three widely recognized categories of kin proximity. Colloquial speech commonly distinguished first cousins as *primos legítimos* (legitimate cousins) or *primos do 1° grau* (first-degree cousins), while in law they were identified as *colaterais do 4° grau* (fourth-degree collaterals).[38] In other in-

---

Carvalho and Padre Antônio Xavier de Farias, permanently migrated from Teixeira and many of their collateral relatives became impoverished. See Linda Lewin, "Oral Tradition and Elite Myth: The Legend of Antônio Silvino in Brazilian Popular Culture," *Journal of Latin American Lore* 5, no. 2 (1979):157–204.

[37] The views expressed by older informants who had grown to adulthood in Paraíba during the Old Republic formed the basis of this conclusion. Denis Twitchett, in commenting on J. L. Watson's examination of Chinese kinship studies (n. 4, above), similarly pointed out that all the key terms in Chinese for kin groupings shared one important meaning: "Those whom we care to consider as part of us" ("Comments," p. 623).

[38] See the explanatory note at the beginning of the Glossary of Brazilian Kinship

stances, however, first cousins were identified as *primos direitos* (parallel cousins) or, only rarely, as *primos germanos* (parallel cousins). In those cases, the category applied only to first cousins of opposite sexes and underscored the potential matrimonial link between cousins whose fathers were brothers or whose mothers were sisters. Although the term *primo cruzado* (cross-cousin) existed, it was not encountered in contemporary documents, letters, or genealogies. Its meaning apparently was also restricted to first cousins of opposite sexes, who were the offspring of siblings of different sexes. (More detailed explanation of this category appears in Table III.1, note b.)

A rich variety of terms described a second category of cousin whose unique kinship proximity derived from multiple matrimonial exchanges between two families and expressed itself in intimate, quasi-sibling designations. The offspring of two sets of siblings who intermarried, double cousins, were designated *primos carnais* (carnal cousins). More frequently, they referred to each other as *primos filhos de irmãos,* that is, cousins who were the children of siblings. Also known as *coirmãos* (co-brothers) or *coirmãs* (co-sisters), they frequently intermarried. Their matrimonial unions as double first cousins (juridically, *colaterais do 4° grau duplo*) proved indispensable for perpetuating a strong family core defined vertically over two or more generations and horizontally between siblings.[39]

Finally, the category *primo do 2° grau* (second-degree cousin) embraced not only first cousins once removed (juridically, *colaterais do 5° grau*) but often more distant cousins. As if underscoring the traditional limits of the family's practical definition at the first-cousin level, *primos do 2° grau* were often colloquially recognized as merely *"parentes"* or *"parentas"* (male or female relatives), even as *"parentes de longe"* (distant relatives). If related also by marriage, the affinal tie received primary recognition and the consanguineous kinship became secondary, underscoring the importance of the "cutting edge" of the family at the first-cousin level.

Terms for the method by which degrees of kinship are reckoned in Brazil. Except for terms in civil law, classificatory kinship terms in this and the following chapter are drawn from family and local histories or the letters of the Paraíba local bosses and thus represent the colloquial usage before 1930.

[39] Colloquial usage confirms the historical weakening of cousin bonds in mid-twentieth-century Brazilian family structure. Today "primos filhos de irmãos" (double cousins) has disintegrated to merely "primos irmãos" and is indiscriminately applied to all first cousins. "Coirmãos" is already archaic in the Northeast.

"Cousin" Marriage

Little systematic longitudinal research has been undertaken about either the incidence or the political and economic implications of endogamy in Brazil, although reliance on family-inscribed marriage pools was a practice going back to colonial times. Historically, it defined a system of preferred cousin marriage.[40] The shortage of white women in the early generations of settlement provided an impetus to consanguineous marriage among the landed elite, for it preserved "purity of the blood" (*limpeza de sangue*) after an initial mingling with indigenous stock during the contact period. Since consanguineous marriage also thrived in Portugal, where it survived until this century, scholarly arguments resting on the Brazilian practice of secluding elite women are insufficient explanations for the practice. Endogamy extended to marriages that in other Christian societies were prohibited by incest taboo; marriages of uncles with nieces or of aunts with nephews were regularly encountered in Brazil.[41]

More powerful motives existed for compounding kinship between individuals and within cognatic descent groups over generations. Elite marriages between cousins and even closer collateral relatives illustrated how the force of kinship consolidated and maintained webs of economic and political power, as well as the social cohesion of the family group. A Brazilian jurist succinctly summed up the economic purpose of consanguineous unions when the new Civil Code of 1916 first prohibited marriage between collateral relatives of the third degree (i.e., between uncles and nieces or aunts and nephews): "The laudable motive of ending marriages between uncles and nieces, a recognized impropriety [that is] psychologically reprehensible," he noted, "almost always was undertaken for the patrimonial interest of the family."[42] In a highly stratified society, kinship itself was a vital resource. The

[40] Societies prescribe marriage within certain categories that are genealogical, although marriage may or may not be genealogically derived. In a preferred marriage system, the categories for wife-giving and wife-taking among males are defined but not mandatory. D. Maybury-Lewis, "Prescriptive Marriage Systems," in *Kinship*, ed. Goody, pp. 205, 119–20. On cousin marriage in Brazil, see Costa Pinto, *Lutas de família*, pp. 90, 152; Oliveira Vianna, *Instituições políticas*, 1:275; Schwartz, *Sovereignty and Society*, p. 343; and Chandler, *The Feitosas*, p. 78.

[41] Pope Pius VI, in his bull of 26 Jan. 1790, granted Brazilian bishops the power to dispense with canonical prohibitions "for all degrees of kinship (except first-degree consanguine lineals) . . ." Mesquita Samara, "Família paulista," p. 48.

[42] *Codigo Civil 1916/Alves*, Art. 183, IV, and p. 158. The quoted opinion belongs to this edition's compiler, João Luiz Alves.

fact that the national political elite favored prohibiting this variant of endogamy, which in Brazil's case had run counter to canon law, indicated the changes in elite family structure evident by the time of the Old Republic.

Endogamous marriage had consolidated landed property in the context of a partible inheritance system that since medieval times had been dedicated to fragmenting property equally among all direct lineal descendants. A British traveler in Brazil during the 1850s summed up the destructive impact of the inheritance system and disparagingly referred to the compensatory strategy of endogamous marriage:

> Upon the death of a rich and influential man with a large family, the division of his property in accordance with the law is disastrous in the extreme. Estates sold to make division, the sons sink into [the group of] the small landed proprietors, the family loses any importance that had accrued to it from its connectedness, and in some instances the very name as a family one disappears, if not in the first, certainly in the second generation. . . . The children have no tie beyond relationship to draw them together or to keep them in one place, and they become dispersed over the Empire, as they are able by means of their fathers' friends to procure for themselves civil or military employment, etc. Brazilians already see [that the resulting] disastrous effects form a bar to improvements [and] withhold a stimulus to exertion. . . . Some adopted the dreadful alternative of intermarriage.[43]

From a perspective that considers marriage as a matrimonial alliance between families, "cousin" marriage is not the most useful term with which to describe the interconnection between consanguinity and affinity over several generations. Because the matrimonial bond extends from parents and grandparents to children and grandchildren, or even further generations, this matrimonial pattern more appropriately connotes the transfer of spouses from one group to another over time. Thus, "kin and affines," not cousins, become the more important categories, for spouses are deliberately chosen by one family group from another family group. Consequently, marriage merely enhances given cousin relationships. What matters most is the identity of the group or groups

[43] James Wetherell, *Brazil, Stray Notes from Bahia*, ed. William Hadfield (Liverpool: Webb and Hunt, 1860), pp. 139–40. The author is indebted to Catherine Lugar for calling this quotation to her attention.

from which a family takes or to which it gives wives. Whether an established pattern of exchange has existed over several generations is even more important. In Paraíba, men bonded as political allies by marrying sisters. If the sisters they exchanged were also their cousins—the ideal situation—then the family core was even more tightly woven. Considered from this political vantage point, cousin marriage as sister exchange between men also reinforced reliance on brother-in-law relationships for coordinating political power locally. That phenomenon will be discussed in Chapter IV.[44]

It is worth asking if there were discernible patterns of preferred cousin marriage that supported certain political relationships in Paraíba. In fact, an examination of the frequency of parallel and cross-cousin categories according to the sexes of those marrying provides several affirmative answers. Examples randomly drawn from the families of Paraíba politicians demonstrate the deliberate weaving of such alliances. However, data collected more systematically from one major Paraíba kindred, the Nóbregas, provide a more reliable basis from which to make generalizations about consanguineous marriages in Empire and Republic.

The quantitative and methodological dimensions of assessing the evidence for cousin marriage in Paraíba, unfortunately, are staggering. Even where complete genealogical records exist, family size rapidly multiplies to over one hundred by the third generation and often exceeds a thousand members by the fifth. Ambiguity in naming patterns poses an additional obstacle. Nevertheless, data extracted from the prestigious Nóbregas' published genealogy provided a useful sample from which to draw conclusions about the relative frequency of both parallel and cross-cousin patterns of marriage. First, it must be pointed out that the generations of Nóbregas whom Trajano Pires da Nóbrega enumerated in *A família Nóbrega* did not define an extended family in the precise sense that the term has been used in this book. Instead, the many generations he listed approximated a kindred, due to the fact that his goal was to include all the identifiable descendants of the Nóbrega family's apical ancestors—Manuel Alves da Nóbrega and Maria José de Medeiros—who were born between the 1760s and the 1940s. (See Table III.1.) Strictly speaking,

[44] The concept of "kin and affines" is drawn from L. Dumont, who argued that it was a more important distinction than cousin types. "The Marriage Alliance," in *Kinship*, ed. Goody, pp. 183–85. This interpretation of cousin marriage draws extensively on Robin Fox, *Kinship and Marriage*, esp. pp. 175–207.

TABLE III.1: Cousin-Spouse Preferences among Four Generations of Nóbregas (b. 1766–1900)

Gender of Nóbrega marrying	Category of Nóbrega cousin-spouse[a]	Generations of identifiable cousin-spouses[b] Second	Third	Fourth	Fifth	All
PATRILATERAL PARALLEL COUSIN						
M marrying	FaBrDa	0	6	11	18	35
F marrying	FaBrSo	0	5	10	19	34
		0	11	21	37	69 (48%)
MATRILATERAL CROSS-COUSIN						
M marrying	MoBrDa	2	6	5	6	19
F marrying	FaSiSo	0	6	2	8	16
		2	12	7	14	35 (24%)
MATRILATERAL PARALLEL COUSIN						
M marrying	MoSiDa	0	3	6	3	12
F marrying	MoSiSo	0	3	3	5	11
		0	6	9	8	23 (16%)
PATRILATERAL CROSS-COUSIN						
M marrying	FaSiDa	0	1	3	2	6
F marrying	MoBrSo	0	3	8	1	12
		0	4	11	3	18 (12%)
Total identifiable cousin-spouses		2	33	48	62	145 (100%)

KEY: Br = Brother; Da = Daughter; F = Female; Fa = Father; M = Male; Mo = Mother; Si = Sister; So = Son

SOURCE: Trajano Pires da Nóbrega, *A família Nóbrega* (São Paulo: Instituto Genealógico Brasileiro, 1956).

NOTE: Figures are tabulated according to the number of individual Nóbregas marrying cousins per generation, so individuals who married more than once were counted more than once. However, frequency of multiple marriages per generation was low, even in the fifth generation, which registered the high of 5 per cent. (See also Table IV.1.) Generational divisions necessarily were arbitrary, as follows: second, born c. 1766–1784; third, born c. 1791–1835; fourth, born c. 1818–1880; fifth, born c. 1860–1900.

[a] In extrapolating specific cousin categories from the Nóbregas' published genealogy, their own family reference became evident from the language the genealogist employed to designate cousins. For instance, parallel cousins tended to be explicitly identified by the kinship term for them—primos direitos—while cross-cousins, particularly patrilateral cross-cousins (i.e., reading from a perspective where EGO* is male), tended to be left implicit, either as a cousin—primo—or unmentioned. Where explicitly described, cross-cousins usually were referred to as "the son of her father's sister" or "the daughter of his father's sister," etc., and never by the classificatory kinship term—

however, he violated the meaning of the term kindred, which is a group defined by ties of blood. By including some of the non-Nóbrega spouses of the Nóbregas in his catalogue of generations, he introduced individuals belonging to other kindreds. This circumstance deserves careful attention when reading the analysis of the data on Nóbrega marriages, because it explains why in Tables III.1 and III.2 the individuals grouped as spouses with the same kinship categories are not symmetrical.

The Nóbregas present an excellent choice from which to sample marriage patterns, for they produced Paraíba senators, congressmen, lieutenant governors, and assemblymen. In addition, their several collateral branches ruled the backlands municípios of Santa Luzia do Sabugi, Soledade, and Patos; they also possessed kin links with a half dozen other ruling families that collectively governed the cariri-sertão zone. Members of the four generations surveyed often lived remarkably long, shared a geographical proximity, and—until the last generation—demonstrated a high fre-

---

NOTES TO TABLE III.1 (continued)

primo cruzado. Thus, the greater specificity of the term used for parallel cousins and the willingness to use it more often suggested, like the frequencies of lost cousins according to the categories described above, that parallel cousins enjoyed a favored status in kinship organization. Similarly, the least favored category, patrilateral cross-cousin, demonstrated the greatest linguistic vagueness, if indeed it was even mentioned.

[b] Of the total 213 Nóbregas marrying their cousins for four generations, 68 had to be eliminated because the genealogist did not identify the category of their spouses as matrilateral or patrilateral. Thus, 145 remained as a population for this table. (See also Table IV.1.) A majority of the 68 who were eliminated belonged to non-Nóbrega families, given that only one parent's sibling had married a Nóbrega. Therefore, the Nóbregas viewed such spouses as cousins from a different family. Because in most cases these outsider cousins were cross-cousins, the data in Table III.1 reflect an exaggerated propensity to conserve parallel cousins and, thus, for parallel patrilateral cousins—i.e., those already *defined as Nóbregas*—to marry.

This circumstance also explains why, although for every given married couple each spouse category theoretically has its gender reciprocal, not all the mates for each individual appear in the data. Only parallel cousins approached numerical balance according to gender, and in both categories the discrepancies of one reflect the genealogist's failure to identify a spouse who was a member of the Nóbrega kindred. By contrast, the cross-cousin categories "lost" more cousin-spouses in the data because the genealogist's approach to resolving the problem of overlapping kindreds methodologically was logical: He did not enumerate the generations of non-Nóbrega spouses; therefore, he did not identify them explicitly as the mates of their cross-cousins—the Nóbregas he did identify. In addition, naming practices contributed to the loss of cross-cousins, for female names often were eroded or even deleted. And by the fourth generation a larger population size also made the precise identification of unnamed or uncategorized cousins more problematic.

* "EGO" refers to the individual—in a genealogical diagram—from whose personal reference all other kin relationships are read. Thus, an individual is an aunt only in relation to another specific individual—EGO—who serves as the reference point for that category.

quency of marriage. Unfortunately, however, age data were not supplied by the genealogist for almost all of the women and for men who were either minor politicians or not well known—the majority of the population catalogued. Consequently, the age at which individuals married could not be determined in order to calculate the average age at marriage by generation or decade.

The data extracted from Trajano Pires da Nóbrega's genealogy for Tables III.1 and III.2, as well as Table IV.1, embraced four generations of Nóbregas descended from the apical ancestor couple. Besides revealing the ambiguous tendencies in Brazilian family organization that have already been noted, the data reflected the genealogist's omission of certain kin categories. For instance, some collateral branches of Nóbregas simply had become lost to the core kindred, to which both the genealogist and many of his informants belonged. On the other hand, in each generation, several collateral branches continued to consider themselves especially close and referred to each other as members of the same (Nóbrega) family, regardless of their family names. Both geographical proximity and regular matrimonial exchange explained this circumstance. In this respect, "family" thus applied to male members who bore the names of paternal ascendants originally outside the Nóbrega descent group—those who traced their descent at some point to a female Nóbrega ancestor who had not married within her family. Consequently, in several branches—and for several generations—men had lost the apical Nóbrega name. This also had occurred much more frequently than among the Nóbrega women, who tended to conserve their apical name of Medeiros over a higher number of generations. Perhaps this circumstance reflects the more conservative character of nineteenth-century female names in Brazil. It may also indicate a pattern of matrilocality.[45]

Table III.1 establishes the preferred categories of cousin marriage within the Nóbrega family for the first four generations of the descendants of Manuel Alves da Nóbrega and Maria José de Medeiros who married between the 1790s and the 1920s.[46] Un-

[45] Kuznesof found considerable evidence for a tendency toward matrilocality in her study of households, which was revealed in the greater survival of female names. Elizabeth Anne Kuznesof, "Clans, the Militia, and Territorial Government: The Articulation of Kinship with Polity in Eighteenth-Century São Paulo," in *Social Fabric and Spatial Structure in Colonial Latin America*, ed. David J. Robinson (Ann Arbor: University Microfilms International, 1979), p. 211. See also n. 49, below. Marcílio demonstrated the much slower rate at which the stock of female names changed in eighteenth-century São Paulo. "Variations," p. 353.

[46] I am grateful to Cheryl Cody for bringing the significance of the actual at-risk

fortunately, the data did not permit computation of the at-risk population for each category of cousin marriage—that is, the number of individuals in each category whom age, geographical accessibility, and social status determined were hypothetical mates. However, it can be assumed that, at least among cousins, the opportunity for choosing from several categories was high by the mid-1850s, because the Nóbregas were concentrated within three contiguous municípios. Nevertheless, the genealogist presented a certain bias that influenced the data, particularly the conclusion that the highest frequency of marriage between cousins occurred between parallel cousins who were patrilateral, the children of brothers. This circumstance derived from the tendency he demonstrated to omit the names or precise cousin categories for individuals who possessed one parent from another kindred than the Nóbregas, those most often found in a cross-cousin category. In Table III.1, consequently, the data within each cousin category are asymmetical for each gender. Table III.2 reflects the same tendency. (See also Table III.1, note b.) Of course, the pattern of omission loaded the conclusion regarding the most preferred category of cousin marriage in favor of the children of brothers, but the genealogist's preference itself is a valuable piece of evidence. His greater unreliability in either recalling or determining the spouses belonging to cross-cousin categories—or his outright rejection of many of them because they were perceived as belonging to a different kindred—confirmed the greater value of the patrilateral parallel cousin category in kinship organization.

The very high frequency of marriages between both categories of parallel cousins demonstrated the importance of sibling bonds—

---

cousin population to my attention and pointing out that the proportion of each category of cousin-spouse in Table III.1 understates the incidence of cousin marriage. This is because those proportions are derived by using the total cousin-spouse population as a denominator: e.g., 69 patrilateral parallel cousin-spouses/145 total cousin-spouses = 48%. In fact, a given individual selects a cousin-spouse from a much smaller population, the one at risk—determined by criteria like marital status, age, geographical accessibility, gender, wealth, etc. at a given point in time. This population is smaller than the total cousin-spouse population, even when those rejected as cousin-spouses (i.e., those who remained unmarried or who married noncousins) are included (as they are not in Table III.1). Therefore, the actual at-risk cousin population would lower the dominator in the above example and raise the proportion of spouses in that category. Unfortunately, an initial effort to quantify the precise incidence of each type of cousin theoretically available for a given individual to marry—the population at risk—had to be abandoned for technical reasons, but in almost every case several types of cousins were available as possible mates.

especially between brothers—for maintaining the family's core over generations. Nearly two-thirds—92 of 145 identifiable cases—of all cousin marriages occurred between patrilateral or matrilateral parallel cousins. It was marriage between the offspring of brothers that emerged as the dominant pattern. In each generation of Nóbregas, more children of brothers (patrilateral parallel cousins) married than any other category. Thus, 69 of the total 145 identifiable cousin marriages—almost 48 per cent—fell into this category. In this case, the discrepancy of 1 between the 35 men and 34 women marrying their patrilateral parallel cousins resulted from the inclusion of a man who was descended from a Nóbrega mother and non-Nóbrega father and the omission of his wife, who was the daughter of his non-Nóbrega father's brother. The genealogist therefore applied a subjective determination of family membership at the very point where two blood kindreds overlapped in order to circumscribe the Nóbregas more narrowly as a family.

The preference for marriages between the children of brothers (primos direitos) bound men together very closely and meant that the family core approximated a segmented patrilineage. Only patrilateral parallel cousin unions were capable of forming a family structure that extended lineally over three generations of males—from a common paternal grandfather to sons who were brothers and then to grandsons who, as cousins, were also collaterally linked by brother-in-law bonds.[47] The significance of marriage between the children of brothers should therefore not be underestimated. In addition to the vertical consolidation it provided within a patrilineage, it also facilitated a horizontal integration between or among collateral branches of the same parentela.[48] Alternatively, sister sets proved secondary to brother sets as the crucial axis that would consolidate the family's core over several generations. Only 23 Nóbrega men and women—12 men and 11 women—married their matrilateral parallel cousins, a mere 16 percent of all cousins marrying.[49] Of the four types of cousin mar-

[47] Peter Dobkin Hall has explored the respective advantages of parallel versus cross-cousin marriage in "Family Structure and Economic Organization: Massachusetts Merchants, 1700–1850," in *Family and Kin in Urban Communities, 1700–1850*, ed. Tamara Harevin (New York: New Viewpoints, 1977), pp. 38–61.

[48] For the role of parallel cousin marriage in an Arabic cultural context, where those boundaries admitted considerable fission, see Robert F. Murphy and Leonard Kasdan, "The Structure of Parallel Cousin Marriage," *American Anthropologist* 61 (1959):17–29.

[49] Maia and Freire-Maia found, in five samplings of twentieth-century cousin

riage, this one ranked next-to-last, slightly ahead of the patrilateral cross-cousin category. (See Table III.1.) Again a discrepancy of 1 exists in the data of paired spouses—for the same reason discussed above—and, similarly, the individual who was "lost" was a woman.

Matrilateral cross-cousin marriage—marriage to mother's brother's daughter—emerged as the category where women played the crucial role in consolidating family bonds. (The EGO perspective is male—to agree with the gender of a politician.) According to this matrimonial strategy, an outsider family would be incorporated through marriage and then continue to provide wives to successive generations of Nóbrega sons. Not surprisingly, it was the second highest category of cousin marriage for Nóbrega men. When they married mother's brother's daughter, they confirmed that Nóbrega sons continued to take wives—a total of 19—from the same family groups from which their fathers had also taken wives. That fewer women fell in this category—16—confirmed not merely the genealogist's bias but also the subtlety of differential status, because for the Nóbregas this type of alliance was first a wife-taking category. In fact, to construe this category as one of cousin marriage detracts from its uniqueness, which lay in the intergenerational pattern of dependence on the same wife-taking pool.[50]

In reality, as an alliance over generations between two intermarried branches of the Nóbregas, the matrilateral cross-cousin bond also suggests a relationship of clientage. For example, the Nóbregas cemented their ties to several generations of Batistas, Carvalhos, and Araújos—who enjoyed a subordinate relationship to them in politics—by means of this matrimonial link. Otherwise, they used the category to maintain a political relationship of near parity with their neighbors in the adjoining município of Al-

marriage outside the Brazilian Northeast, that the parallel cousin matrimonial preference predominated in 70 per cent of all cousin marriages identified: N. Freire Maia and A. Freire Maia, "The Structure of Consanguineous Marriages and Their Genetic Implications," *Annual of Human Genetics* 25 (1961):23–29, cited in Freitas Garcia Fukui, *Bairro Sertão*, p. 59. However, Garcia Fukui found that, where men migrated and women remained geographically fixed, the matrilateral parallel cousin marriage became most common (ibid., p. 60). Her conclusion may explain Kuznesof's generalization about matrilocality in "Clans, Kinship," p. 211.

[50] Dumont, "Marriage Alliance," pp. 183–85 and 187. On the advantages of cross-cousin marriage, see Ernest L. Schusky, *Manual for Kinship Analysis* (New York: Holt, Rinehart and Winston, 1965), p. 60. Epitácio to Toinho [Antônio Pessoa Filho], (Rio de Janeiro), 19 Feb. 1908, ACAP/1/unnumbered.

agoa Grande, the powerful Peregrino de Albuquerques.[51] Conversely, where the Nóbregas maintained a pattern of giving wives to another elite extended family, such as the Peregrino de Albuquerques, mother's brother (a Nóbrega) usually remained an important figure for his sister's sons.

The least common category of cousin marriage for Nóbrega men, the patrilateral cross-cousin union, was contracted with father's sister's children. Its uniqueness lay in the potential intrafamilial conflict it could imply. That only six men from the Nóbrega family married their patrilateral cross-cousins illustrated that this type of marriage tended to be reserved for preserving a client status, for twice as many Nóbrega women as men married their patrilateral cross-cousins. (See Table III.1.) For that reason, father's sister—in contrast to father's brother or mother's brother—became the kin category most likely to be alienated from the core of the family of origin. (Again, the EGO perspective is male.) This was a consequence of local political circumstance. A man's paternal aunt was more likely to be given away to a family with whom tension already existed, particularly where conjugal exchange had not been strongly maintained in the past. The case of the paternal aunt of the famous outlaw Liberato (Cavalcanti de Carvalho) Nóbrega, who was married to the local opposition leader in Teixeira in the 1850s, is one dramatic example where such a union did not diffuse family tensions. In fact, Liberato turned outlaw after being accused of murdering his father's sister's husband. Unlike a paternal uncle, who usually remained within the core of the family of origin, a paternal aunt (father's sister) was the kin category most frequently alienated from the family core because of the political vulnerability it admitted.

Patrilateral cross-cousin marriage best revealed the "hostage" implications of all categories of cousin marriage and the conflict implicit in the family-based political system. (See Fig. III.1.) Fac-

[51] The four marriages of three Peregrino de Albuquerque brothers from Fazenda Rapador in Alagoa Grande illustrated how sister exchange could bind two families in different municípios as allies. Sen. and Federal Deputy Apolônio Zenaide Peregrino de Albuquerque (1857–1908) and his brother Francisco (Peregrino de Albuquerque) Montenegro (1869–1947), a lieutenant governor and then a justice of the State Supreme Court, married Nóbrega women who were close collaterals from Fazenda São Bras in Soledade. Francisco Montenegro married two sisters in a sororate arrangement. A third brother, Maj. Antero Peregrino de Albuquerque, became a local politician in Soledade, when he married a younger sister of the wives of Apolônio (Joaquina da Nóbrega). Apolônio's son, State Deputy Heretiano Zenaide, married his mother's brother's daughter from Fazenda São Braz (Maria Elvídia Nóbrega). T. da Nóbrega, *Família Nóbrega*, pp. 177–82 and 192–207.

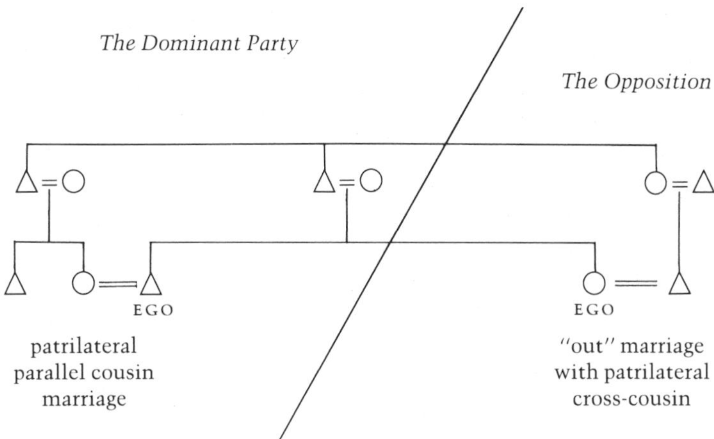

FIGURE III.1: The Political Congruence of Parallel and Cross-Cousin Marriages

tional politics rendered this category more volatile because father's sister was more likely to be married into a family belonging to the local opposition: the outs. More frequently than their brothers, therefore, women could expect to assume the partisan affiliation of the opposition faction at marriage, that is, the affiliation of their family of procreation rather than of their family of origin. Such a hostage wife subsequently watched her children ally against her brothers and sisters and their children. Not surprisingly, relations between such sets of cross-cousins could be cool or openly hostile due to the local factional alignments. A father's sister's children often effected a definite lineage segmentation from the family core in these situations.

In contrast, when men changed political alliances, they usually brought their extended family with them en bloc, as the Costa Ramos of São João do Cariri did. When one of three Costa Ramos brothers married the daughter of the local Liberal Party boss, his two brothers joined him in putting aside their Conservative Party allegiance, and they found brides in the same family. Their case underscored the primacy of the family affiliation and the secondary role of partisan loyalties.[52]

In a family-based system of political networks, family membership could be expected to override partisan loyalties in particular instances. Patrilateral cross-cousin marriage therefore appears to have operated as a deliberate hedge against the day when local par-

[52] Leal, "Família Costa Ramos," pp. 29–30.

tisan fortunes would be reversed and the outs became ins—or vice versa. Anecdotal literature on family conflict and banditry in Paraíba offers a number of accounts of men who received protection from the families of paternal aunts who had married into the opposition faction, especially during periods of open persecution or insurrection.[53] Thus, patrilateral cross-cousin marriage deserves special assessment as a wife-giving category. What may have been greater feuding among such cross-cousins was due not to the cousin category itself but to the potentially explosive situation that had induced a man to have his sister marry into an opposition family in the first place.

Variation on a Theme: Uncles and Nieces/Aunts and Nephews

Marriages between third-degree collaterals (i.e., between uncles and nieces or aunts and nephews) reflected patterns analogous to those between cousin categories, although their lower frequency generally rendered data from the Nóbrega family less indicative for the wider elite population. Table III.2 suggests one such parallel. For example, the absence of marriages between Nóbrega men and either their brother's daughters or their fathers' sisters suggests that both fraternally linked nieces and paternal aunts were less favored choices for the same reason that patrilateral cross-cousins were not the most popular cousin category. In every instance except one, Nóbrega men preferred instead to marry their sisters' daughters. The Nóbregas continued, in other words, to take niece-wives almost exclusively from the same group from which their fathers had taken wives. On the other hand, those seven Nóbrega women who married their paternal uncles invariably were the daughters of fathers who as non-Nóbregas had married into the Nóbrega descent group. For these seven Nóbrega women, marriage to a paternal uncle represented a wife-giving category, one reserved for renewing generational ties with a different descent group and with which the Nóbregas may have enjoyed the status of subordinate clients. Marriage to a fraternal niece was not

[53] T. P. da Nóbrega, *Família Nóbrega*, pp. 30, 34; and Baptista, *Cônego Bernardo*, p. 58. See Nelson Lustosa Cabral, *Paisagens do nordeste* (São Paulo: n.p., 1962), pp. 129–33. For an appraisal of the dangers of cross-cousin marriage, see Jack Goody and Esther N. Goody, "Cross-Cousin Marriage in Northern Ghana," in *Comparative Studies in Kinship*, ed. Jack Goody (Stanford: Stanford University Press, 1969), p. 231.

TABLE III.2: Third-Degree Collateral Spouse Preferences among Four Generations of the Nóbrega family (b. 1766–1900)

Gender of Nóbrega marrying	Category of third-degree collateral spouse	No. of third-degree collateral spouses per generation				
		Second	Third	Fourth	Fifth	All
M	SiDa (sororal niece)	0	6	1	3	10
F	MoBr (maternal uncle)	0	1	4	8	13
M	BrDa (fraternal niece)	0	0	0	0	0
F	FaBr (paternal uncle)	0	0	3	4	7
M	MoSi (maternal aunt)	0	0	0	1	1
F	SiSo (sororal nephew)	0	0	2	0	2
M	FaSi (paternal aunt)	0	0	0	0	0
F	BrSo (fraternal nephew)	0	1	0	0	1
Total		0	8	10	16	34 (100%)

See Table III.1 for key, source, and explanatory notes.

the preferred pattern of uncle–niece unions, for marriages between men and their sisters' daughters was preferred. This category embraced twenty-three (ten men and thirteen women) of the total thirty-four third-degree spouses of both sexes in Table III.2. The higher number of females over males among all thirty-four spouses can be explained by the fact that all seven women who married father's brother did so outside the Nóbrega descent group and half of those who married mother's brother were presumed by the genealogist to have done the same.

Finally, third-degree collateral unions appeared to be common in some families, rare in others, and nonexistent in yet others. The extended family core defined by the marriage of Commendador Luiz Gonzaga de Brito Guerra and Maria Malfada de Oliveira can be singled out to illustrate how much some elite families relied on such marriages. Of course, such unions were intensively complemented by marriages between double cousins and first cousins and extended over a number of generations. (See Fig. C.2.) Even in this exemplary case, endogamous matrimony could not prevent fragmentation of the first generation's patrimony, although it reduced the likelihood of distributing inheritances among a large number of distinct branches. Equally important, this matrimonial strategy merged three families—the Dantas, Gomes de Britos, and Gurgel de Oliveiras—after two generations. In reality, the majority of elite families limited their matrimonial alliances at the double-cousin level, considering a third-degree collateral too close for marriage. They appear to have done so because they feared adverse consequences in genetic endowment, although they were unaware of Mendelian science.[54]

Parentela as Quasi-Corporate Group

Patrimonial Implications of Endogamous Marriage

The complementarity of matrimonial unions between very close collateral relatives and the patrimonial considerations raised earlier deserve further explanation in view of the elite extended family's role as the major property-owning group in Paraíba. Endogamous marriage was practiced for a number of reasons, some of which will be explored in the following chapter, but the most important was to conserve patrimony within the family group. As the authors of Brazil's 1890 Civil Marriage Act were very aware, consanguineous unions represented a social strategy for countermanding the emphasis inheritance law placed on fragmenting patrimony according to "equal shares for all" siblings. Thanks to *pátrio poder* (in Latin, *patria potestas*)—the patriarchal authority of the household head—law denied wives the right to alienate their immovable property or to administer it without their husbands' consent.[55] Men thereby gained de facto control over their wives'

[54] Informants who objected to the practice of third-degree collateral marriages indicated to the author they knew personally that unfavorable traits, particularly (in their view) mental disorders, had been inherited in a given family. However, the scientific findings do not support such an opinion. Others correctly stressed the genetic advantages to be gained from inbreeding.

[55] The 1890 Civil Marriage Act (Decree No. 181 of 24 Jan. 1890, Par. 1–3) prohibited third-degree collaterals and double cousins from marrying under a community property regulation, effectively maintaining each spouse's partrimony under a separate property regulation. Brazil, *Decretos do Governo Provisorio de 1890.*

Until the Republic, pátrio poder was a term reserved for the household head's exercise of patriarchal authority—i.e., over minor children or unmarried adult children living with their parents—and widows also legally exercised it. The male household head's exercise of conjugal authority, which included the right to administer a wife's real property as well as to authorize or forbid its sale, was distin-

inheritances. Thus, the matrimonial strategies just discussed, particularly between third-degree collaterals, conserved wealth within the family core.[56]

The law of succession favored members of the kindred over affines, including spouses.[57] Consequently, when sibling sets married other sibling sets who were also their first cousins, fragmentation could be impressively reduced. An uncle who married his sister's daughter enjoyed a special advantage because he possessed the legal means for acquiring an additional portion of his parents' patrimony. At his sister's death, he stood to succeed to her portion (inherited from his parents) as an uncle-husband, since legally he would administer what his wife inherited from his sister (her mother). Giving away a paternal aunt and keeping sister's daughters within the family core—through marriages with their maternal uncles—thus preserved the most advantageous position on the ladder of inheritance within the family group.[58]

As men took wives from the same family over several generations, property was conserved within a select pool of heirs. Although they did not practice third-degree collateral marriage, the Lins family of Pilar illustrated how dependence on endogamous marriage conserved their patrimony over several generations. Fig-

---

guished in law as *poder marital*. During the Old Republic, however, the two concepts merged as pátrio poder.

[56] Strategies tying matrimonial choices to the inheritance provisions of the Civil Code were not confined to the elite. For a sociological analysis of peasant variations in the state of Minas Gerais, see Margarida Moura, *Os herdeiros da terra* (São Paulo: HUCITEC, 1978).

[57] In the absence of a written agreement to the contrary, under the community property regulation, all goods acquired before or during marriage were held jointly. A surviving spouse received one-half (*a metade*) of the community as his/her original portion, not by virtue of succession (inheritance). The remaining half, known as the *legítima*, represented the deceased's estate that was heritable by succession. Before 1907, two-thirds of it passed directly to the children as the "necessary" or forced heirs and the remaining third could be assigned by will to the surviving spouse. In 1907, the legítima was reduced from two-thirds to one-half and the portion assigned by will increased to one-half, diminishing the significance of matrimonial strategies for retaining patrimony within the family. Decree-Law No. 1839, 31 Dec. 1907.

[58] Darrell Levi has examined the patrimonial considerations in probably the most salient nineteenth-century example of marriage between a niece and her paternal uncle—the marriage of Dona Veridiana Prado (1825–1910), daughter of the wealthy financier-planter, the Baron of Iguape (Antônio Prado) and her father's half brother. However, as Dona Veridiana's 1875 divorce suit (i.e., for a legal separation of property) suggested, even third-degree collateral unions could fail to achieve the family's patrimonial objectives. *Família Prado*, pp. 77–79 and 88–89.

ure C.1 illustrates how the land belonging to the Lins' apical ancestral couple—"Num" (José Lins Calvacanti de Albuquerque) and Antónia do Monte—known as the Sesmaria of Itaipú, was passed to their great-grandchildren. A number of consanguineous unions in several generations and the purchase of inheritance portions among members enabled the Lins to preserve their quasi-corporate identity by retaining their land in greater concentration than the system of forced heirship prescribed.

An Elite Parentela: The Pessoas, 1837–1886

The parentela's identity as a quasi-corporate group is best appreciated in terms of a specific example. Epitácio's own parentela provides an instructive illustration because it reveals both the role of landed patrimony in endowing selected branches of an elite family with an intergenerational identity and the way the central characteristics of Brazilian kinship organization maintained the extended family's identity as a coordinated unit. A reconstruction of his family history over four generations, from Epitácio's grandparents to his nieces and nephews, confirms the importance of endogamous matrimonial strategies, segmentation at the first-cousin level, and ambilineal descent for perpetuating a group interest base among the families of two of Epitácio's four siblings—those who remained most closely associated with his home município of Umbuseiro. When the informal social linkages among several generations of the Pessoas are examined, the rapid crystallization of Epitácio's political network becomes readily comprehensible. (This theme is developed in Chapter IV.)

Epitácio Lindolfo da Silva Pessoa was the youngest of five children born to Col. José da Silva Pessoa and Henriqueta Barbosa de Lucena. As *senhores de engenho*, or titled owners of sugar estates, both of his parents belonged to Pernambuco's landowning elite. (See Fig. B.1.) Their marriage consolidated the elite connections of the Silva Pessoas with the more socially prominent Pereira de Lucenas—or simply Lucenas—across the boundaries of several municípios and two states.[59] Both families were active partisans in

[59] Pessoa family biography is drawn primarily from L. Pessôa, *Epitacio Pessôa* 1:23–24; secondarily from Carlos D. Fernandes, *Epitacio Pessôa* (Rio de Janeiro: Conde Pereira Carneiro, 1919), pp. 7–17; and Flavio Guerra, *Lucena, um estadista de Pernambuco* (Recife: Imprensa Oficial, 1958), p. 50. Epitácio's paternal grandparents, Col. Antônio da Silva Pessoa and Isabel Pessoa, appear to have been related. And his paternal grandfather and his maternal grandmother, who both pos-

Liberal Party conflicts at the local level, an affiliation that in 1848 predisposed the Lucenas to take up arms against the government as rebels. Although all of Epitácio's grandparents were Pernambucanos, his maternal grandparents owned land in southeastern Paraíba as well as in the Pernambuco backlands, where their adjacent home município of Bom Jardim was located. Before marrying Epitácio's mother, around 1856—when both the groom and bride were barely eighteen—Epitácio's father had married her sister. This attempt to align the Lucenas and Silva Pessoas, however, had ended within a year, when Ubaldina Barbosa de Lucena died in childbirth. The second marriage therefore was a sororate arrangement for Epitácio's father.

Col. José da Silva Pessoa and Henriqueta Barbosa de Lucena lived with her parents before they established an independent household in 1861. At the death of Henriqueta's father, Col. Henrique Pereira de Lucena, they migrated to Paraíba to settle permanently as the owners of Fazenda Prosperidade, an estate located in what at that time was the município of Ingá. Subsequently, their hilly Natuba district, which was situated on the Borborema's southern escarpment, became incorporated in the município of Umbuseiro. The Lucena family property, which was valuable for both its land planted in cane and its livestock, had been bequeathed to Henriqueta as her inheritance portion and dowry. Very probably, however, part of it also devolved to Col. José da Silva Pessoa as the sole heir of the infant daughter Henriqueta's sister Ubaldina had borne in 1854, who lived only a few years.[60] By the time they moved to Fazenda Prosperidade, Epitácio's parents

sessed the name "Silva," may have been related. Further evidence for a common matrimonial pool was residential, since his sets of grandparents had lived in adjacent municípios in Pernambuco: the Pessoas' ancestral estate (Engenho Cotunguba) was in Nazaré and the Lucenas' property (Fazenda Fortaleza) was in Bom Jardim. (See Fig. B.2.) L. Pessôa, *Epitacio Pessôa*, 1:23.

[60] Laurita Pessoa refers to the family estate as "Fazenda Marcos de Castro," but letters written as early as the 1870s by Col. José da Silva Pessoa referred to the property as "Fazenda Prosperidade," as did the account book kept by his son, Col. Antônio Pessoa. ACAP/3/14. Dona Maria das Neves Falcão Pessoa (n. 66, below), emphatically confirmed that the ancestral property of her husband's (Osvaldo Pessoa) family had only been known in this century as Fazenda Prosperidade. Laurita Pessoa's assertion that Col. José da Silva Pessoa had "inherited" the land at his father-in-law's death deserves reinterpretation. In-laws did not normally inherit as spouses; daughters and sons—as lineal descendants—did. Therefore, Ubaldina's portion passed to her daughter (Prudência) and then to Col. José da Silva Pessoa as his daughter's (not his wife's) heir, when the child died at age three or four. L. Pessôa, *Epitacio Pessôa*, 1:25.

6. Casa Amarelinha, Epitácio's boyhood home in Umbuseiro, which his father built in 1868. Even the homes of the more prosperous landowners in the backlands tended to be of modest design and simple construction. (Carlos Dias Fernandes, *Epitacio Pessôa*, p. 96)

already had three children—Maria, Miranda (Mirandola), and José da Silva Pessoa. A fourth—Epitácio's favorite brother Antônio da Silva Pessoa—arrived in 1863, and Epitácio completed the sibling set in 1865. (See Fig. B.1.)

In 1874, when Col. José da Silva Pessoa took his family to Recife for a short visit, life changed abruptly for Epitácio and his four siblings. Within weeks of their arrival in the Pernambuco capital, both parents succumbed to smallpox. Relatives quickly decided the destinies of the five orphans. Although he had not yet been ennobled as Baron of Lucena, Epitácio's mother's brother, Henrique Pereira de Lucena, was governor of Pernambuco. Yet he did not take the orphans into his household in Recife.[61] Kinsmen and kinswomen of Epitácio's father took the initiative in finding homes for the children. Marriages were quickly arranged for the two oldest. Maria was married to Cândido Clementino Cavalcanti

[61] Laurita Pessoa explained that Lucena did not take his two youngest nephews into his own household by implying that his office barred him from being named their legal guardian. Ibid., 1:27.

de Albuquerque, a career civil servant in Paraíba. His home município, Pedras de Fogo, was adjacent in Ingá and not distant from the Natuba district. Probably Epitácio's "Aunt Marocas"—Alexandrina Cavalcanti, the widow of his father's brother Joaquim da Silva Pessoa—arranged the match, for the young husband evidently was her relative.[62] Maria's children, who would become the branch of the parentela known as the Pessoa Cavalcanti de Albuquerques, remained very close to Epitácio throughout his life. One, João Pessoa Cavalcanti de Albuquerque, became Epitácio's favorite nephew. In addition, the alliance with the Cavalcanti de Albuquerques linked Epitácio more closely to a major parentela in Paraíba and Pernambuco that enjoyed political influence on the sugar coast and in the caatinga-agreste. (See Fig. B.3.)

Miranda was married to João Vicente Queiroz, the son of a rural neighbor in Umbuseiro and Pernambuco. This marriage produced a second collateral branch of Pessoas, Epitácio's nephews, the Pessoa de Queiroz. (Also referred to as Pessoa Queiroz, particularly by Epitácio, who always omitted the "de" in correspondence.) Although they owned an estate in Umbuseiro, their primary residential identification eventually became Recife, for Miranda's six sons established themselves there in commerce and the liberal professions. The fact that most of the Pessoa de Queiroz were born in Pernambuco, not in Paraíba, would later set them apart politically from their Umbuseiro cousins, the Pessoa Cavalcanti de Albuquerques, as well as the da Silva Pessoas who were the children of Epitácio's brother Antônio da Silva Pessoa. The quasi-sibling rivalry that developed between the Pessoa de Queiroz and the latter two sets of Epitácio's nephews in Umbuseiro, consequently, should also be appreciated in terms of their diverging residential, political, and economic orientations toward Paraíba and Pernambuco. (See Fig. B.3.)[63]

[62] Epitácio's connection by marriage to his Aunt Marocas enabled him to stress more advantageously a distant blood connection with the Cavalcanti de Albuquerques of Paraíba on his father's side—including Pilar's Col. José (Cavalcanti) de Albuquerque Lins. Epitácio provided for Marocas, his mother surrogate, in her old age until the 1920s and he also became the legal guardian of his cousin—and foster brother—Rodolfo's four children, when Rodolfo died at a young age. Ibid., 1:46–47.

[63] Laurita Pessoa was silent regarding the parentage of Mirandola's husband, João Vicente Queiroz, but a biography of their son available in 1986 has revealed for the first time that João Vicente Queiroz was the son of a brother of Mirandola's father: Alcides Lopes, *Francisco Pessoa de Queroz: Vida e ação* (Recife: State of Pernambuco, Secretaria de Turismo, Cultura e Esportes/Fundação do Patrimonio Histórico e Artístico de Pernambuco, 1985), p. 28. Though erroneously described (pp. 27–28),

The children of Antônio da Silva Pessoa comprised the third set of Epitácio's nephews and the second who would reside at Fazenda Prosperidade throughout the Old Republic. Antônio was deemed too frail for the intellectual rigors of school in Recife when his fate as an orphan was decided. He consequently returned to Umbuseiro in 1874 as the one offspring who would remain on the land. From the age of eleven until the late 1880s, therefore, he raised livestock and planted sugar cane and cotton, trying to improve the family patrimony—as his meticulously kept account books still verify. Awarded the family sinecure as an inspector of customs in the Federal Customs House in Recife early in the 1890s—thanks to his influential maternal uncle, the Baron of Lucena—Antônio Pessoa alternated periods of residence in Umbuseiro with briefer ones in Recife. His marriage in 1890 to Margarida de Assunção Santiago provided the Umbuseiro Pessoas with a dual core of male members, for his sons would number ten. Like their Pessoa Cavalcanti de Albuquerque cousins in Umbuseiro, the Silva Pessoas would consolidate the family group through endogamous reweaving with both their matrilateral and patrilateral cousins.[64]

---

as the offspring of José da Silva Pessoa (Mirandola's father), João Vicente Queiroz definitely was identified as the son of a brother of Joaquim da Silva Pessoa (brother of José da Silva Pessoa), the first husband of Maria Alexandrina Cavalcanti, the widowed "Aunt Marocas"—who had remarried Antônio Leonardo(s?) de Menezes Amorim in the early 1870s. Thus, Mirandola and João Vicente Queiroz were patrilateral parallel cousins. (See Fig. B.1.) Except for Joaquim da Silva Pessoa, the names of José da Silva Pessoa's other siblings have not been preserved, but the Pessoa family name pool strongly suggests he had brothers named Antônio and João. (All three branches of the Pessoas included brother sets of José, João, and either Joaquim or Antônio see Fig. B.3.) No information was offered by the biographer of Francisco Pessoa de Queiroz about João Vicente Queiroz's maternal ancestry.

[64] The fact that the wedding of Antônio Pessoa and Margarida de Assunção Santiago took place in Pilar underscored the importance of the Cavalcanti de Albuquerques for Epitácio's later networking. Pilar's political boss, Col. José (Cavacanti) de Albuquerque Lins signed the wedding certificate as a witness ("age fifty-three, of Engenho Itaipu"). Ties between the Pilar and Ingá (Pedras de Fogo) branches (i.e., Epitácio's sister Maria Pessoa Cavalcanti de Albuquerque) later received reinforcement when Col. José de Albuquerque Lins's granddaughter (the child of his daughter Ana), Maria das Neves Falcão, married Osvaldo Pessoa, the son of Epitácio's sister Maria. Interview with Dona Maria das Neves Falcão Pessoa, João Pessoa, 21 July 1978. As Pilar's recent Liberal Party boss, Col. José Lins demonstrated that Epitácio's family retained close ties to families who had been Col. José da Silva Pessoa's Liberal Party allies in the 1870s, even though Epitácio and Antônio assumed the partisan affiliation of their uncle, Baron Lucena, as Conservatives. Marriage Certificate of Antônio da Silva Pessoa and Margarida de Assunção Santiago, 18 Oct. 1890, ACAP/3/unnumbered.

Antônio's marriage to Margarida contained an important dimension of kinship that was ritual or fictive, for Margarida's parents were Epitácio's godparents. In the 1860s and 1870s, they had also been the closest of friends with their *compadres*, Col. José da Silva Pessoa and Henriqueta de Lucena. The ritual kinship was renewed and generationally extended to Antônio da Silva Pessoa and his bride at their wedding when her parents stood as their matrimonial sponsors or godparents (*padrinhos de casamento*). The elderly Manuel de Assunção, Epitácio's godfather, was a hero of the Praieira Revolt who for the next three decades played the key role in Liberal Party politics in southeastern Paraíba. An imperial judge in the 1870s and 1880s, he had also been a provincial assemblyman and later the public prosecutor in his home município of Ingá. For the young Epitácio, however, Manuel de Assunção was an important father surrogate who taught him much about the politics of Paraíba's lawless interior and schooled him in the factional conflicts that locally accounted for the political divisions in his native Umbuseiro.[65]

"The children of Margarida de Assunção"—as Antônio Pessoa's offspring became known in the family—eventually possessed matrimonial bonds with their matrilateral parallel cousins, the Gomes da Silveiras who lived in both Umbuseiro and Ingá. (See Fig. B.3.) By marrying four daughters of Margarida de Assunção Santiago's sisters—their parallel cousins on the matrilateral side—Antônio Pessoa's sons renewed a wife-taking relationship with the family pool from whom their father had taken his wife. In addition, one son married a parallel cousin on his father's side—Ina Pessoa, the daughter of Antônio's older brother José da Silva Pessoa. The Silva Pessoas, however, did not marry their cross-

[65] The bride's mother, Epitácio's godmother, gave her name at the wedding as "Margarida Gomes da Silveira Santiago," although in 1866, in sponsoring Epitácio's baptism, she had given her name as "Margarida Gomes Calafange Santiago." The name "Gomes da Silveira" ("Santiago" belonged to her husband) was more illustrious, but she may also have been prompted in the intervening decades to drop her father's Calafange family name due to a feud with the Calafanges, which by the late 1890s embraced her son-in-law Antônio Pessoa. Her husband, Manuel de Assunção Santiago, was Ingá's Liberal Party boss during the Praieira Revolt and had abducted her as his bride from his prisoner—Margarida's father Manuel Calafange—who was chieftain of the rebels in Ingá. Certified copy of the parish registry entry of Epitácio's birth and baptismal dates (dated 13 May 1919), which originally was entered on 8 January 1866, published in Fernandes, *Epitacio Pessôa*, p. 111. Marriage Certificate of Antônio da Silva Pessoa and Margarida Assunção Santiago, 18 Oct. 1890, ACAP/3/unnumbered.

cousins in Umbuseiro, the children of Maria da Silva Pessoa and Cândido Clementino Cavalcanti de Albuquerque, but the latter sibling set in one case acquired an endogamous tie to their father's brother's (Col. José Bezerra Calvacanti de Albuquerque) son, Celso Cavalcanti, when he married Maria's daughter Priscila Pessoa Cavalcanti de Albuquerque. (See Fig. B.3.)

What matrimonial bonds did not fully accomplish in consolidating patrimony in Umbuseiro, subsequent purchase by Antônio Pessoa from his fellow heirs and siblings did. Both Epitácio and his older brother José da Silva Pessoa sold their inheritance portions to Antônio because their careers led them to settle permanently in Rio de Janeiro. Furthermore, Antônio's eldest son Carlos Pessoa—who in 1978 still lived at Fazenda Prosperidade—did likewise with a number of his eleven siblings.[66] Thus, 110 years after Epitácio's parents had settled on Fazenda Prosperidade, the descendants of their children Maria, Mirandola (perhaps only through her husband's patrimony and independently of her sister and two brothers), José, and Antônio da Silva Pessoa still resided on the family land. Throughout the Old Republic, at least, the children of Epitácio's sisters and his brother Antônio maintained their identity as an extended family by both joint and contiguous patterns of land ownership in Umbuseiro, not to mention their monopoly after 1902 on the political affairs of the município.

In the case of the fourth Pessoa orphan, Epitácio's older brother José da Silva Pessoa, Henrique Pereira de Lucena played a role typical for "mother's brother." As governor of Pernambuco, he arranged for his fourteen-year-old nephew to enter the National Military Academy (Escola Militar) in 1875. In doing so, José Pessoa was following the example of his deceased paternal uncle, Joaquim da Silva Pessoa, and launching a career that half a dozen of his own nephews would emulate. He moved to Rio de Janeiro to begin his

[66] Author's prosopographical file. The author is extremely grateful to Dona Maria das Neves Falcão Pessoa, widow of Osvaldo Pessoa Cavalcanti—Epitácio's nephew and a brother of Gov. João Pessoa Cavalcanti de Albuquerque—and her daughter, Dona Rosário, for providing the names of the Pessoa de Queiroz brothers and either confirming or supplying the names of the siblings comprising the two Umbuseiro lineages, as well as the names of their spouses. Interview, João Pessoa, 21 July 1978. A partial list of Umbuseiro property owners by place or estate name in a volume from the 1920 census shows that Coronel Antônio's sons Carlos Pessoa and Epitácio Pessoa Sobrinho still owned land in the município and that the name pools of property owners also included many Silva, Barbosa, and Pereira descendants of Epitácio's grandparents and collateral relatives. *Relação dos proprietarios ruraes*, pp. 316–36, esp. 323.

studies as a cadet, embarking on a career that separated him geographically from his brothers and sisters and all other close collateral relatives. Yet fourteen years later, when young Epitácio similarly moved to the national capital to advance his career, José Pessoa maintained close ties with his siblings and their families in both Recife and Umbuseiro, although he had married a French woman who was an "outsider"—someone not from Paraíba. Unlike Epitácio, who would also marry an outsider, José Pessoa reinforced his ties with his brother Antônio and with Umbuseiro by having his daughter (Ina Pessoa) marry one of Antônio's sons (his namesake, José Pessoa). (See Fig. B.3.) Although José Pessoa did not father a brood of nephews on whom his brother Epitácio could depend for staffing his oligarchy in Paraíba, he offered Epitácio something better when Epitácio arrived in Rio de Janeiro in 1889: an impressive network in national politics that extended to both civilian and military elites.[67]

As the youngest orphan, eight-year-old Epitácio depended on his paternal relatives as well as his maternal uncle, Lucena, to arrange his future. Although his legal guardian was a Rêgo Barros relative of his father's, Epitácio soon joined the household of his Aunt Marocas, who had recently remarried. He remained in her home even during his days as a law student. Marocas's son, Rodolfo da Silva Pessoa—his first cousin—was the only child with whom he formed a close attachment in Recife, although he continued to return to Fazenda Prosperidade in Umbuseiro and to visit his godparents in Ingá during school holidays. Not until he moved to Rio de Janeiro at age twenty-three would his native cariri-sertão and the rougher society of the Paraíba backlands cease to be part of his cultural ambience. Epitácio completed his education, which had begun in a family setting at Fazenda Prosperidade, by enrolling in Recife's most prestigious elementary and secondary schools. Lucena arranged a public scholarship that paid his tuition—just as he managed to find a sinecure in the Recife Customs House for Epitácio's Rêgo Barros legal guardian.[68]

[67] Epitácio's older brother, Gen. José da Silva Pessoa, retired with the rank of marshal. His Pessoa Cavalcanti de Albuquerque nephews Aristarco and José also pursued military careers, as did Antônio's son Renato and, early in his life, Mirandola's son José. Obituary of Renato da Silva Pessoa, undated and unidentified newspaper clipping (1936) filed in ACAP/3/unnumbered. Interview with Maria da Neves Falcão Pessoa (n. 66, above).

[68] Epitácio's father died in the Recife home of his kinsman Felinto do Rêgo Barros, whom Laurita Pessoa did not precisely identify. Rêgo Barros, as Epitácio's legal guardian, also came from an important coastal sugar family of Pernambuco and

By 1882 Lucena's promising nephew was ready to enter Brazil's most prestigious intellectual institution, the Recife Law School. Declining to experience student life in the Bohemian quarters where his peers found the perfect setting for privileged rebellion in their youth, Epitácio remained a day student and excelled, graduating near the top of an especially distinguished class in 1886. His four years in law school were passed in the superlative company of teachers and fellow students who made Epitácio's "Generation of the Eighties" the most brilliant in the institution's history. Tobias Barreto and Sílvio Romero, for instance, were Epitácio's most renowned professors; his classmates included future novelists Graça Aranha and Lima Barreto, who would soon revolutionize Brazilian literature. In addition, he formed lasting relationships with several other students who later would serve the Pessoas as federal deputies and senators or lead the oligarchy as Paraíba's state governors (for example, João Pereira de Castro Pinto and Francisco Camilo de Holanda).[69]

Although Epitácio moved away from his circle of family and classmates in Recife and Paraíba less than three years after his graduation from law school, he maintained particularly close ties with his brother Antônio and his uncle, the Baron of Lucena, throughout their lives. He married twice during the nineties, but both times he chose women born in the South of Brazil. Consequently, his matrimonial ties did not bind him to a northeastern political network or provide in-laws to staff his oligarchy. Instead, Epitácio relied later on the families of his siblings in Umbuseiro—who maintained a quasi-corporate group identity as a parentela—for political recruits to oligarchical office. In that respect, the lineages of Maria Pessoa Cavalcanti de Albuquerque and Antônio da Silva Pessoa became the most crucial for solidifying the axis of family power on which the Pessoas would depend. Although the children of Maria and Antônio did not establish matrimonial alliances with each other as cross-cousins, they did marry impressively in parallel cousin patterns on the non-Pessoa sides of their families. (See Fig. B.3.) Apparently, the disparities in the ages of their sets of children—who were born fifteen to twenty years apart—accounted for the absence of cross-cousin marriages between them. In addition, the sexual imbalance in their numbers—

Paraíba which had marriage ties with the Cavalcanti de Albuquerques. (Marocas's husband was Antônio Leonardo—or Leonardos—de Amorim.) L. Pessôa, *Epitacio Pessôa*, 1:27.

[69] Ibid., 1:42–43; and Clovis Bevilaqua, *História da Faculdade do Recife*, 2nd ed. (Rio de Janeiro: Institutio Nacional do Livro, 1977), pp. 188–92.

7. Epitácio as a federal deputy to the Constituent Congress in 1890. (Courtesy of the Instituto Histórico e Geográfico Brasileiro)

8. Very much a family man, Epitácio took his three daughters (Laurita, Angela, and Helena, left to right) on the European vacations he and Mary Sayão Pessoa spent in Italy every year and saw that they received instruction in French and English. (Carlos Dias Fernandes, *Epitacio Pessôa*, p. 108)

males out-numbered females three to one—meant that the at-risk cousins were very few. Antônio, for example, had only two daughters, one of whom never married. Maria also had only two daughters and both married their parallel cousins on the non-Pessoa side of the family.[70]

The age and sex distribution of the Pessoa cousin population appears to explain why the Pessoa de Queiroz branch also did not marry with either of the Umbuseiro branches. Like her older sister, Miranda Pessoa de Queiroz had established a family in the 1870s and the 1880s. Unlike the offspring of her three brothers, whose marriages occurred ten to twenty years later, her children began marrying in the nineties.[71] In addition, she too bore mostly sons. (See Fig. B.3.) However, the geographical distancing that reoriented the Pessoa de Queiroz's political and economic interests during the Old Republic seems equally significant in their eventual segmentation from the parentela of Maria, José, Antônio, and Epitácio.

The Pessoas as a parentela demonstrated the survival of kin bases of power in state and national politics throughout the first third of the twentieth century. Like many elite extended families in the Paraíba oligarchy before 1930, they indicated that even new political and economic currents would not destroy the force of kinship in politics for a number of decades. Instead, thanks to the ambiguity inherent in Brazilian kinship organization—the absence of rigid group membership criteria, the blurred lines of shallow or ambilineal descent that made the cutting edge of family boundaries vague, and the wide latitude in matrimonial patterns—the elite extended family was well equipped to adapt to change.

When Epitácio's own generation of national politicians—under

[70] Maria's other daughter, Sebastiana Pessoa Cavalcanti, married her cousin Frederico Neiva, the son of her mother's maternal aunt (and the sister of the Baron of Lucena), Amélia Barbosa de Lucena, and Col. João José Neiva (brother of Venâncio Neiva).

[71] One exception was Miranda's youngest son, Francisco Pessoa de Queiroz, who was born in 1890. Theoretically, he might have married his first cousin Clarice Pessoa Santiago (of the Umbuseiro Silva Pessoas), eight years his junior. But while Francisco was still pursuing his diplomatic career, accompanying his Uncle Epitácio to Versailles as an official member of the Brazilian delegation to the Paris Peace Convention in 1919, Clarice married an older, well-established Recife physician. When Francisco did marry, in 1924, it was with a papal blessing and to a Gaucha, Lotinha Jovim, the goddaughter of the deceased Senator Pinheiro Machado, once Brazil's most powerful politician. Lopes, *F. Pessoa de Queiroz*, p. 115.

his guidance as minister of justice, education, and culture in the late nineties—revolted ideologically against patriarchy and parentally imposed marriage, they formed a new consensus that Brazilian family and inheritance law must be reformed. Yet they did so within a polity where sociopolitical structures still depended crucially on elite family and kinship organization.[72] The reforms they mandated in law in 1915, which produced the first *Brazilian* Civil Code, nevertheless testified to changes that already had occurred in the nineteenth century. Thus, their modifications of family and inheritance law complemented the survival of the elite parentela as an important entity. Its conservative adaptability to change had prevailed in the face of both militant republican ideology and aggressively emerging industrialization. In the absence of an institutional challenge from the central State, the elite parentela withstood, at least initially, the waning of the agrarian society that had historically nourished it. The pliability of Brazilian kinship organization to no small degree explained such an impressive transition. Thus, "the politics of parentela" became perpetuated as an integral feature of oligarchy in Paraíba and in the most underdeveloped states, characterizing the Old Republic as the period when family-based politics reached the height of their influence in Brazilian history.

[72] As minister of justice between 1898 and 1901. Epitácio appointed his fellow northeasterner and the distinguished professor of the Recife Law Faculty, Clovis Bevilaqua, as the architect for drafting a major revision of Brazil's ancient Portuguese civil code, known as the Ordenações do Reino or the Philippine Code. When Clovis's much-amended Draft Code Project came to the Senate for the crucial vote on 31 December 1915, Epitácio brought it to the floor as committee chairman and secured its ratification as the 1916 Civil Code. L. Pessôa, *Epitacio Pessôa,* 2:157–58 and Bevilaqua, *Faculdade Recife,* p. 424.

· IV ·

The Politics of Parentela in the Era of the Oligarchies

There is nothing so similar to a Conservative as a Liberal in power.

—Political adage of the Empire

José Jerônimo was a *concunhado* of Coronel Dario Ramalho, both being married to two sisters of Dario Apolônio and Francisco Montenegro, the second lieutenant governor of the state. . . . Local political boss Dario passed his office to his concunhado, José Jerônimo, also my friend. In Patos Miguel Sátiro bestowed his title of boss on his concunhado Chico Paula, and in Batalhão and elsewhere they are doing the same.

—Inácio Dantas, political boss of Teixeira, to state party boss Epitácio, January 18, 1912

CHANGES in kinship organization that had been transpiring in Paraíba since the mid-Empire can be more easily perceived from the vantage point of the Old Republic. Those changes were by no means confined to Paraíba or even to the Brazilian Northeast. Elite family power was evolving generally throughout Brazil, although regional differences undeniably occurred.[1] However, in smaller, more underdeveloped, and politically subordinate states such as Paraíba, the adaptation to change was more conservative than elsewhere. Brazil's weaker states, consequently, became less dramatically reoriented along the lines of interest group politics than the Center-South, where the states with dynamic economies were experiencing widespread economic change and urbanization.

Three major changes in Paraíba's kinship organization generally reflected similar trends nationally: 1) a trend away from endogamous marriage toward greater reliance on exogamous matrimo-

[1] The broad respects in which changes in Paraíba's kinship organization related to similar changes throughout Brazil can be inferred from the legal changes in family and inheritance law adopted after 1889, particularly in the 1890 Civil Marriage Act, the 1907 Law of Succession, and the relevant sections of the 1916 Civil Code.

nial strategies; 2) a complementary erosion in patriarchal authority as exogamy assumed greater political importance; and 3) a consequent shift in the organization of political networks to incorporate far-reaching horizontal axes defined by sibling or quasi-sibling bonds. This chapter will examine these changes in relation to oligarchical organization and political process from the late Empire to the end of the Old Republic. Together, they signaled the rising importance of outsiders in politics, either as brothers-in-law incorporated in the family group or as so-called political friends (*amigos políticos*) who by the advent of the Old Republic increasingly played key roles in every politician's family-based network. At the conclusion of this analysis of change, examination of the evolution of Epitácio's family-based political network will illustrate how kin-based networks expanded to incorporate outsiders to meet the political needs of their principal members at state and national levels.

The Historical Shift toward Exogamy

Legal Inferences

An appropriate place to begin any analysis of changing patterns of kinship organization in Brazil is with the legal changes that national politicians mandated during the Old Republic. Members of Brazil's Senate and House of Deputies deemed reform sufficiently significant to write many of the changes they advocated into existing family and inheritance law, beginning in 1890, when the first civil marriage law was enacted. Generally, the legal changes coinciding with the arrival of a republic testified to both a restricted patriarchy and declining endogamy. Although family law reduced the authority that fathers as household heads exercised over their children—particularly their sons—patriarchal power persisted with fewer limitations in the legal prerogatives that husbands (and fathers) continued to enjoy over their wives and daughters. This decline of patriarchy bore direct and major implications for a parallel decline in endogamous marriage, whose perpetuation had always depended on the legal subordination of both sons and daughters to paternal command. The fact of declining endogamy received further confirmation in 1907, when a legal reform (incorporated in the 1916 Civil Code) dissolved much of the emphasis that the Philippine Code had placed on the blood kindred by restricting the "family's" size. The new law of succession reduced the kindred's range from ten to six collateral degrees. And, in an unprecedented move, surviving spouses—affines—were permitted to supersede members of the kindred—consanguines—in claiming their inheritance rights where lineal descendants or ascendants were absent.[2]

Belatedly, law was beginning to reflect the elite family's assumption of a more conjugally defined core, although this core was not synonymous with a nuclear family. Instead, the family's organizational pivot became more explicitly defined as a joining of "kin and affines" in nonconsanguineous matrimonial unions. A more exogamously defined family began to relegate the extended family based on the blood kindred and endogamous reinforcement to the historical past.

In the one or two generations that coincided with the Old Republic, the more exogamous character of family organization did not alter perceptibly the parentela's historical identity in Paraíba as a quasi-corporate group. Even at the time national legislators first redefined the kindred and its members' legal inheritance rights more restrictively—in 1907—the parentela could be appraised as having transcended patriarchal decline there. Almost paradoxically, it could be said to have assumed a reinvigorated historical role, for the elite family remained an organizational base for political mobilization statewide. By virtue of its organizational flexibility—its dependence on shallow descent and its lack of a firm rule restricting matrimonial choices to endogamous or exogamous alliances—Brazilian kinship organization facilitated elite families' perpetuation of their control of politics throughout the Old Republic. A rising frequency of exogamous marriage converted a matrimonial strategy that had always been complementary to the preference for endogamous unions to the most favored

[2] Decree No. 1839, Art. 1 (*Codigo Civil 1916/Alves*, Art. 1603). The kindred's legal range in Brazil has continued to contract since 1917 and is now considerably narrower than in the United States, a circumstance testifying to the expansion of the central State: Decree-Law No. 9461 of 15 July 1946 limited inheritance rights for those who died intestate to collaterals within the fourth degree (first cousins or closer), in whose absence the estate of the deceased escheats to the federal government. The 1890 Civil Marriage Act adopted a republican aversion to forced marriage by legally mandating a separate property regulation for marriages where the bride was under fourteen or over fifty and the groom was under sixteen or over sixty. These provisions also applied to matrimonial unions between third-degree collaterals and double cousins. Decree No. 181 of 24 Jan. 1890, Art. 58, pars. 1–3.

9. The marriage of Gov. Solon de Lucena's daughter, Virgínia (Barbosa) de Albuquerque Lucena, and Valdemar Leite de Araújo (second and third figures to the right of Solon, seated) was celebrated in the Governor's Palace on March 10, 1921, and was witnessed by many in Solon's Young Turk faction. Typically, by the 1920s, the bride and bridegroom were not only unrelated by blood but also from families in different political factions (see Figs. B.1 and B.4). (Courtesy of the Acervo Humberto Nóbrega)

strategy. By the Old Republic exogamy prevailed because it best preserved the elite extended family's influence as a political unit.

Genealogical Evidence

Demographic evidence strongly suggests that by the end of the nineteenth century consanguineous marriage within Paraíba's political elite had significantly declined. To what extent, then, had "kin and affines" assumed a different connotation in an increasingly exogamous context? During the Old Republic, only 15 percent of politicians in Paraíba's officeholding elite could be positively identified as marrying their first cousins.[3] The evidence demonstrates that their parents' generation, which had married during the Empire, had contracted over double that proportion of consanguineous marriages—about 35 per cent.[4] The same pattern of intergenerational decline appears in the genealogical evidence for the Nóbrega family's last two generations. (Its fourth and fifth generations correspond to the two generations of the politicians of Empire and Republic just mentioned, for their birth cohorts dated from 1850 to 1889.)[5]

The quantitative evidence presented in Chapter III for categories of consanguineous marriage among four generations of Nóbregas was extracted from a more comprehensive analysis of over one thousand married individuals whose spouses could be identified as having either positive ties of consanguinity or a definite absence of them.[6] Table IV.1 presents those data according to the distribution of endogamous spouse selection in each generation of Nóbregas and according to the degree of consanguinity. The Nó-

[3] Of the 303 members of Paraíba's officeholding elite, the 100 with identifiable wives defined the population for this generalization. In this population 15 per cent could be positively identified as marrying their cousins and 14 per cent definitely did not. The remaining 71 per cent could not be identified in terms of a spousal relationship, so the rate for those marrying close kin was undoubtedly higher. (Often it was more difficult to confirm that a couple were *not* kin than that they were.) Calculated from the author's prosopographical file.

[4] These rates of consanguineous marriage for both generations are considerably underestimated, due to the great difficulty of extrapolating cousin relationships from sources that are not ideal for family reconstruction. In addition, by the time of the Old Republic, naming customs favored a wife's assumption of her husband's name, which complicated cousin identification. About 29 per cent of the 303 officeholders had identifiable sets of parents, and one parent could be identified for another 26 individuals. Of these 89 known cases, 22 (25 per cent) definitely had parents who were first cousins. Another 10 per cent for whom genealogical evidence was ambiguous almost certainly married their first cousins. Since another 35 per cent could be definitely identified as *not* marrying their first cousins, around 30 per cent remained open to question. These data suggest the high rate of cousin marriage in the Empire.

[5] Birth cohorts for the politicians included in this study are explained in Table VII.1.

[6] While 1,110 individuals are categorized in Table IV.1, 387 were excluded from it (and from Tables III.1 and III.2) either because they did not marry or because their spouses were not identified. (The sex distribution of those who never married was nearly even.) The proportion of Nóbregas who did not marry remained low until the fifth generation, when it rose to 19 per cent (or 24 per cent if those without known spouses are included). Only 7.5 per cent of the fourth generation had remained unmarried. The sharp increase suggests that land had become unavailable by the close of the century.

TABLE IV.1: Distribution of Endogamous Spouse Preferences among Descendants of Manuel Alves da Nóbrega and Maria José de Medeiros (m. 1765)

Marriage by category of spouse	Second generation (b. c.1766–1784)		Third generation (b. c.1791–1835)		Fourth generation (b. c.1818–1880)		Fifth generation (b. c.1860–1900)	
	N	%	N	%	N	%	N	%
Marrying third- and fourth-degree kin								
marrying uncle/niece or aunt/nephew	0	(0)	8	(7)	10	(3)	16	(3)
marrying first cousin	2	(13)	38	(32)	59	(17)	80	(12)
Marrying fifth-degree kin (first cousin once removed)	2	(13)	22	(18)	93	(26)	47	(8)
Marrying beyond fifth degree	0	(0)	6	(5)	81	(23)	159	(26)
Marrying nonkin	11	(74)	46	(38)	110	(31)	320	(51)
Total Nóbregas marrying	15	(100)	120	(100)	353	(100)	622	(100)

SOURCE: T. da Nóbrega, *A família Nóbrega*. See Table III.1, Note, for interpretive comments related to the data.

bregas' mating pool moved toward a consanguineous preference by the third generation, peaking around mid-century, when only 43 per cent of them married nonkin. Of those who took consanguineous spouses, 39 per cent married their first cousins and their nieces/aunts or nephews/uncles (i.e., fourth- and third-degree collaterals, respectively). By the fourth generation, however, the preference among those marrying kin had moved toward first cousin once removed—colloquially, a "second cousin" (i.e., a fifth-degree collateral). In the fifth generation, only 15 per cent of the Nóbregas chose first cousin and niece/aunt or nephew/uncle spouses, while 26 per cent married beyond first cousin once removed. Since by the third generation the average consanguinity (the geneticist's coefficient of inbreeding) of all married individuals (for both those marrying kin and those marrying nonkin) approached the fifth degree, or that of a cousin once removed, marriages beyond the fifth degree could be deemed tantamount to marriages with outsiders.[7] Fifth-degree spouses have therefore been grouped with nonkin spouses in Table IV.1.

Besides the trend toward marrying more distant kin or marrying nonkin, by the fifth generation only a low 15 per cent of the Nóbregas chose a first cousin or a niece/aunt or a nephew/uncle as a spouse—the same proportion as among the officeholders who comprised the oligarchy during the Old Republic. In fact, three-fourths of all Nóbrega marriages in the fifth generation were exogamous (i.e., beyond the fifth degree). How can the diluted character of endogamy, as well as the rising incidence of exogamy, be explained?

Endogamy's Sociopolitical Significance

Good elite marriages not only had to reflect overlapping kinship but also consolidate the family group against powerful challengers

[7] Francisco M. Salzano and Newton Freire-Maia have offered a method of computing coefficients of consanguinity that show the probable effect of the distribution of consanguineous marriage displayed in Table IV.1 corresponds to an average value of shared genes in the population for individuals in the third (0.0270) and fourth (0.0260) generations that approaches that of a first cousin once removed (0.03125). (First cousins share a coefficient of consanguinity that is 0.1250.) The fifth generation of Nóbregas shared an average inbreeding coefficient of only 0.0178, which fell closer to a second cousin, i.e., a sixth-degree collateral (0.0156), and therefore just within the legal range of the kindred by 1907. Salzano and Freire-Maia, *Problems in Human Biology: A Study of Brazilian Populations* (Detroit: Wayne State University Press, 1970), pp. 82–83. See their chapter 4 for an extensive

beyond kin bounds. Endogamy traditionally had performed those tasks. It had been fostered by demographic circumstance—the small size of the political elite. In most municípios fewer than a half dozen extended families comprised the ruling faction and usually only two or three dominated politics. Of course, the social elite, which also embraced the opposition faction(s), was larger; however, at the top, society revealed a closed echelon whose membership remained restricted to relatively few families in the município population. As late as 1923, José Américo de Almeida defended the practice of consanguineous marriage on just those demographic grounds. He took to task critics who charged that endogamy posed deleterious genetic consequences:

> In spite of unions between relatives being common, for many small towns are inhabited by only one family [i.e., the population is descended from a common ancestral couple and have intermarried over generations], the offspring of consanguineous unions were not found to be deformed. This offers proof that consanguinity can reproduce in a healthy context. Such a tendency, one transmitting [healthy] characteristics because both parents have [sound] ancestral [genetic] traits and organic constitutions, displays a characteristic uniformity.[8]

Although the small size of the local elite may explain endogamy, that factor is not as useful as it might appear. Research by the geneticists Salzano and Freire-Maia indicates that generalizations about changing rates of inbreeding in Brazil must still be made on a município basis. They found that discrete populations in the interior of São Paulo, for example, experienced extraordinary increases in their rates of consanguineous marriage during the mid-nineteenth century, after a lower frequency at the end of the eighteenth century.[9] Twentieth-century data indicate that the in-

---

treatment of consanguineous marriage in Brazil from a geneticist's (rather than a historian's) perspective.

[8] J. A. de Almeida, *A Parahyba*, p. 485. Of course, this defense of consanguineous matrimony confirms the appearance of a new, critical attitude toward it by the 1920s. On congenital malformations resulting from genetic inbreeding in Brazil, see Salzano and Freire-Maia, *Human Biology*, ch. 6.

[9] Compare these frequencies of consanguineous unions with the scattered, cross-regional findings summarized by Salzano and Freire-Maia: In the first half of the nineteenth century, two towns outside the city of São Paulo registered 8 per cent to 16 per cent of all marriages between first cousins and up to 33 per cent if cousins once removed were included. Unions between uncles and nieces or aunts and nephews registered 3 per cent or 4 per cent during the same period. During 1838–

terior of the Northeast is still the most inbred area in Brazil. The clines—areas of slow changes in the frequency of inbreeding mapped according to large geographical areas—encompassed both the Paraíba capital of João Pessoa and the distant interior município of Cajazeiras. In fact, the latter unit lies within one of the most inbred areas in Brazil, for the interior of Paraíba is overlapped by three major clines.[10] Estimates of the average frequencies of consanguineous marriages calculated by Salzano and Freire-Maia still place Paraíba over the average for the Northeast as a region in marriages between first cousins and equal to the average in unions between uncles and nieces or aunts and nephews.[11] Salzano and

---

1851, in one town (Cotia) unions between uncles and nieces or aunts and nephews reached 3.5 per cent; between first cousins, 8.7 per cent; and between cousins once removed, 6.9 per cent. These categories represented 25.2 per cent of the couples marrying, but a century later (between 1930 and 1944) they represented only 2.2 per cent of the couples marrying (with the respective categories 1.6 per cent, 0.6 per cent, and 0.9 per cent). But in the parish of Ó in the city of São Paulo, where consanguineous marriages had reached a proportion of 23.2 per cent for the period 1804–1850, a century later (1942 to 1950), they maintained almost the same level—22.7 per cent! Finally, in Belo Horizonte (capital of Minas Gerais), a city constructed only in the late 1890s, consanguineous preferences never took hold: the proportion for the period 1924 to 1930 was only 3 per cent and it declined to 0.4 per cent between 1950 and 1952. *Human Biology*, pp. 83–84. Thus, no firm generalizations can be made on the basis of either rural or urban residence, chronological time, or region. Instead, specific population clusters reveal a pattern of persistent endogamy over time that is probably better explained by isolation and the absence of local opportunity for social mobility. During the Old Republic, Paraíba's archbishop, Dom Adauto Aurélio de Miranda Henriques, alluded to such a situation when he singled out the Seridó district (partly in Rio Grande do Norte) as one that had "a new elevated number of marriages where dispensations for marrying within prohibited degrees of consanguinity" had been granted. Azevêdo Bastos, *Roteiro Azevêdo*, p. 21.

[10] Salzano and Freire-Maia, *Human Biology*, p. 89. See p. 87 (Fig. 6) for a map of Brazil's major clines, which are most concentrated in the seven northeastern states. Astoundingly, a study of Petrolina, Pernambuco, revealed that between 1925–1927 and 1950–1951 consanguineous marriage increased. Ibid., pp. 83–84. Citing the well-known ease with which dispensations to marry within degrees of consanguinity prohibited by canon law historically have been granted by the Catholic Church in Brazil, Salzano and Freire-Maia concluded that there was "no reason to suppose that [those] prohibitions have some influence on the inbreeding levels . . ." (p. 17).

[11] The authors omitted mention of the dates to which the following consanguineous marriage frequencies referred, although they implied a contemporary rate and were first published in 1957: Average percentages in the Northeast were 0.08 (uncle/niece or aunt/nephew), 4.35 (first cousins), 1.42 (first cousins once removed), and 2.50 (second cousins), a total of 8.35. Percentages for the same categories in Paraíba were 0.08, 4.50, 1.50, and 2.50, respectively, a total of 8.58. Ibid., p. 88.

Freire-Maia's conclusions confirm that the average size of the population isolates in Paraíba remained very small, for compared with twenty-five other Brazilian states, territories, or large metropolitan areas, Paraíba's ranked seventh-smallest. Although small size was a historical constant underlying the practice of elite endogamy, evidence suggests that the rate of endogamy fluctuated markedly and did not decline linearly in the same clines. Therefore, nondemographic factors must also be considered.[12]

Given the long-term circumstance of a weakly defined State, particularly in the interior where elite families assumed responsibility for maintaining order, it was understandable that individuals would find security in those kinships units. The high level of violence in frontier settlements disposed the population to place its trust and expectations for protection—even survival—in the elite parentelas that dominated society and economy. Thus, the patrimonial considerations raised in the preceding chapter must be placed alongside the political role the elite family played as a securely bounded and closed unit of security. Endogamous matrimonial patterns guaranteed that a fairly rigid dichotomy between the family group's members (*gente de família*) and outsiders (*estranhos*) would be maintained. Colloquial speech clearly revealed the exclusion of outsiders from the family's boundaries, for they were referred to as *forasteiros*—strangers—or even foreigners.[13]

An abundance of anecdotal evidence related to bride abduction—*rapto*—made clear that during the last century the father's preferred candidate for a son-in-law was consistently a blood relative, while often his daughter preferred a nonkinsman for a bridegroom.[14] Even where outsiders could demonstrate equal social and economic standing with the father's candidate, failure to possess the vital blood link usually doomed them to rejection. A sensational court case in Campina Grande in 1869 affirmed the patriarchal prerogative to impose a nephew as a son-in-law. An eighteen-year-old woman's nonkin suitor brought evidence before Judge

[12] A population isolate is a statistical measure of a population's size, which lacks clearly delimited boundaries (geographic, ethnic, socioeconomic, or otherwise), and permits geneticists to estimate at-risk population for given categories of consanguineous kin. Ibid., pp. 96–99. A geneticist's perspective is limited, for it excludes a wide range of sociocultural, economic, and political variables crucial to the incidence of endogamy over the centuries.

[13] These terms were used by informants who answered the questions, "Why (do) did people marry their cousins (uncle, aunt, etc.)?" and "What did your father (mother) want to know about the family of a nonkinsman (woman) before that individual could be permitted to marry someone in your family?"

[14] H. de Almeida, *Brejo de Areia*, pp. 215–25.

Irineu Joffily that documented his socioeconomic standing with the father's candidate—including proof of his "Portuguese" ancestry, that is, his whiteness. Although Joffily found in favor of the woman and her right to the husband of her choice, the appellate judge ruled in favor of her father and marriage to the cousin from the adjacent property, whom her father had insisted she marry, because the woman had not attained her legal majority. But the marriage never took place; the woman and her nonkin suitor disappeared, never to be heard from again.[15]

Consanguineous matrimonial preferences undeniably reflected racial prejudice, particularly after 1870 when gradual emancipation of Brazil's more than two million slaves of African ancestry threatened to increase social mobility. When Col. Segismundo Guedes Pereira permitted three of his ten children to marry nonkin, for instance, his acquiescence depended first on a thorough investigation of each candidate's genealogical antecedents. In the words of his great-great-grandson, Coronel Segismundo "researched" (*pesquisou*) the family trees of potential daughters-in-law, due to his concern for preserving "purity of the blood" (limpeza de sangue) in his sons' children.[16] Genealogy was a separate issue from economic assets and contemporary social position. Oral interviewing in the 1970s suggests that the discrimination in favor of endogamy was intimately connected to the family's self-perception as an almost sacrosanct refuge and select, elite grouping. In the words of Horácio de Almeida: "Consanguineous unions were frequent, above all, between uncles and nieces, not only because of prejudice about white skin but also because of the fear of allowing an outsider to enter the family group."[17] The family's security depended on mutual trust and a deeply shared collective identity that endogamy guaranteed, for it insured continuity between the family of orientation and the family of procreation. A consanguineous recruitment of sons- or daughters-in-law offered greater potential for senior members to control the younger generation and to maintain obedience and loyalty.

Traditionally, parents did not believe that the individual wishes of the marriage partners had to be taken into account. As one scholar summed up the issue, "marriage was too important to be left up to the desires of the parties involved."[18] At least for the

[15] E. Almeida, *História Campina*, pp. 139–46.

[16] Author's interview with Dr. Normando Guedes Pereira, João Pessoa, 28 July 1978.

[17] H. de Almeida, *Brejo de Areia*, p. 217.

[18] Candido, "Brazilian Family," p. 297. The coronel's patriarchal dictation of ca-

most powerful families, marriage was not an emotional arrangement but a matter of economic and political security. Consequently, matrimonial unions were designed to enhance and perpetuate the domination of the family group. Historically, patriarchal authority insured that marriage alliances would be contracted in light of their practical consequences for the family unit and only secondarily, if at all, for the individuals joined in matrimony. Patriarchal power had been legitimated in Brazilian law as pátrio poder or patria potestas in the Roman civil law tradition. For most of the nineteenth century and during the Old Republic, the age of attaining legal majority was twenty-one; however, the legal minimum age for marriage was much lower: twelve for females and fourteen for males in the Empire. These limits were respectively raised by two years in 1890.[19] Minors therefore needed parental consent to be married.

This legal provision fell unequally on women, a majority of whom did marry before twenty-one. Perhaps 50 per cent of men also married while they still were legal minors and needed parental consent.[20] Sons who graduated from law or medical school or who completed a military officer training, however, automatically attained legal majority upon graduation. Thus, privileged access to higher education legally emancipated many men, while their male siblings who remained at home, as well as all of their sisters, remained directly under patriarchal control. The plenary power law conferred on the father as family head to determine the matrimonial unions of his offspring could produce some extreme situations. For instance, one unfortunate young man, forced to marry an aunt he had never met, discovered only after the conclusion of the wedding ceremony that his heavily veiled bride was facially deformed and lacked the capacity for normal speech. Her family had deliberately concealed this fact by refusing him the opportunity to see her—except briefly through a keyhole—on the several occasions when he journeyed a long distance to arrange his mar-

reers for his children is proverbial: "One for the seminary, one for law school, and the daughter to marry her uncle or near relative." Estácio de Lima, *O mundo estranho dos cangaceiros* (Salvador: Editôra Itapoã, 1965), p. 15.

[19] 1890 Civil Marriage Act (Decree No. 181 of 24 Jan. 1890), Art. 18.

[20] Entries in T. P. da Nóbrega's *A família Nóbrega* indicated that from the 1850s until around 1910, the age of marriage (where specified) for women fell between seventeen and twenty-two, which may have reflected postponement due to land scarcity. Few males were described as marrying at sixteen, although a considerable number of females did marry between age twelve to fifteen. Nevertheless, these data cast doubt on the folk wisdom that Brazilian women who remained unwed after twenty (or twenty-five or even thirty) were doomed to spinsterhood.

riage.[21] When bride and bridegroom were unacquainted before marriage, usually a very young girl was being married to a much older man. Sometimes the bride would be returned to her parents after the wedding until she had physically matured for childbearing.[22]

The Decline of Patriarchy

The Revolt against Patriarchy: Elopement

Endogamy nevertheless gave way to greater exogamy even before the era of the Old Republic. It did so either in response to aggressive, direct challenge to patriarchal authority or by conscious, patriarchal decisions prompted by practical necessity. In the latter instance, fathers themselves undermined patriarchy by deferring to their sons' judgment or selecting exogamous unions to promote the family's interest.

Elopement (rapto) posed the most aggressive challenge to traditional patriarchal authority and preferred patterns of consanguineous matrimony. This so-called bride abduction rarely proved genuine, for it usually required the woman's assistance in successfully evading paternal or fraternal vigilance. Rapto was an informal but nearly institutionalized alternative to forced marriage. Its efficacy depended on rendering the woman "unfit" for marriage to her father's candidate through the loss of her virginity. Virtually unmarriagable to any man except the one with whom she had eloped, the rebellious daughter often based her disobedience on the expectation that, after a reasonable period had elapsed, her father would yield, give his blessing to her marriage, and permit her and her husband to be integrated within the family fold. Otherwise, she could marry on the attainment of her legal majority.[23]

[21] H. de Almeida, *Brejo de Areia*, p. 223.

[22] This was the fate of little Miquelina Olindina d'Ávila Lins, who at the tender (and illegal) age of eleven became the bride of her twenty-seven-year-old cousin, Maj. Remígio Veríssimo d'Ávila Lins of Areia. Sent home for a year to play with her dolls, Miquelina returned to become a wife at the legal age of twelve and lived to bear fourteen children, including several state politicians. She and Major Remígio celebrated their fiftieth anniversary in 1925. Ibid., pp. 215–17 and 219; *A União*, 19 April 1929. "Naninha" [Ana Cabral], the wife of Col. Arcanjo [Cabral de Vasconcelos], reported to historian Horácio de Almeida that after her marriage at twelve to her great-uncle, she could think only of her toys. But having subsequently borne eighteen children, she described herself as happily married. Ibid., p. 218.

[23] Clovis Bevilaqua, *Direito da família*, 2nd ed. (Rio de Janeiro: n.p., 1905), pp.

Women who eloped and found the paternal blessing to marry withheld might be loath to do so even when they came of age and had borne children by their partners. Custom served almost as strongly as corporal punishment to enforce patriarchal command. Marcionila de Bezerra Nóbrega, who fled her father's house to elope, felt obliged to wait twelve years before marrying, until her unrelenting father had died. Even then, she secured the blessing of her oldest brother before she would marry the man who had fathered her children.[24] Daughters who failed in an attempted flight with a suitor could fare worse. Cordolina, the niece of the Baron of Araruna (Estevão José da Rocha), fled her father's Bananeiras home with her suitor but was apprehended "sexually intact." The unhappy adolescent was locked up at home for several years by her furious father. Married off later to a husband of his choice, she soon died. Family oral tradition described the cause of death as her inability to overcome the disapproving attitudes of her close relatives, even though she had failed in her escape and retained her virtue. Her attempted flight had brought dishonor to their family name.[25]

Gilberto Freyre has argued that customary elopement rose dramatically during the last century. Although his assertion would be difficult, if not impossible, to substantiate statistically, the anecdotal literature in local histories or genealogies of Paraíba convincingly demonstrated its regular occurrence.[26] References to elopement, which were also made in the descriptions of seventeenth-century settlement, had as a common thread the flight with an outsider—a nonkinsman—or a stranger. Although such evidence remains highly speculative, family law more reliably indicated that the pressure against patriarchy began to build in the last century. The theoretical opportunity for at least sons to chose their own spouses broadened in 1831, when the age of legal majority was lowered from twenty-five to twenty-one.[27] After 1850 so-

82–83. Varena Martínez Alier offers an insightful and well-researched analysis of rapto in a nineteenth-century Cuban context: *Marriage, Class and Color in Nineteenth-Century Cuba* (Cambridge: Cambridge University Press, 1974), pp. 103–19.

[24] T. da Nóbrega, *Família Nóbrega*, pp. 578–80.

[25] M. A. de Almeida, *Barão Araruna*, pp. 165–68.

[26] Freyre, *Sobrados*, 1:129–33; E. de Almeida, *História Campina*, pp. 139–46; H. de Almeida, *Brejo de Areia*, pp. 125–26.

[27] Decree of 31 Oct. 1831, Brazil, *Colleção das leis do Imperio do Brazil de 1831, 1ª Pte.* (Rio de Janeiro: Typographia Nacional, 1875). Playwright Ariano Suassuna, a native of Teixeira, Paraíba, emphasized the survival of popular attitudes supportive of parental matrimonial preferences over those of their offspring during the

cial and economic change rendered that option more a reality for many men from elite families because they postponed marriage until finishing their studies and married at a later age. The raising of the minimum age of marriage to fourteen for girls and sixteen for boys in 1890 permitted wider grounds for contesting imposed marriages. As part of the 1890 Civil Marriage Act, it was coupled with the novel provision that when legal minors were married in private buildings—as was always the case with a civil marriage—the windows and doors had to remain open throughout the ceremony.[28] These changes suggested that the revolt against patriarchy had already taken place by the arrival of the Republic.

Patriarchy Reconsidered

Impressed with the erosion of patriarchal authority in the last century, a handful of writers has popularized its demise. Until recently, scholars accepted the patriarchal complex as a stereotype. The conventional view of the patriarchal elite family had emphasized the absolute and often brutal authority a father wielded over the family group. His virtually unlimited power has been illustrated most graphically by referring to his occasional role as a family executioner. It has been pointed out that his victims could include not only his slaves and tenants but also his wife and daughters, and even his sons. As the legal family head (*chefe de família*), the patriarchal figure dispensed justice against enemies outside the kin group as well as against transgressors within it. Portuguese or Brazilian law, however, never accorded him unlimited power over his wife and offspring under the juridical concept

1950s. He pointed out that audience reactions to performances of *Romeo and Juliet* in the interior of Paraíba and Pernambuco generally disapproved of the young lovers' disobedience of their parents. Bride abduction, he also noted, continued to be a last resort where parents forbade daughters to marry a suitor of whom they did not approve. Interview with Ariano Suassuna, Recife, 27 July 1971. Jason Clay reported a number of court cases in mid-nineteenth century Garanhuns (Pernambuco) where daughters who were legal minors petitioned the local judge to be permitted to marry the suitors with whom they had eloped, while their fathers remained absent from the proceedings. He concluded that the absence was a face-saving measure in view of the *fait accompli* of elopement where paternal opposition had been strong. (Law granted a woman who had eloped as a legal minor and then became pregnant the right to marry without parental consent.) Personal communication, Feb. 1981.

[28] Beginning in 1890, only civil marriage carried legal validity, making it indispensable for preserving the rights of succession and inheritance in law. Decree No. 181 of 24 Jan. 1890, Arts. 17 and 23–46; *Codigo Civil 1916/Alves*, Art. 213.

10. Num (José Cavalcanti de Albuquerque Lins, b. 1786), the family founder of the Lins of Pilar, remained a thoroughly patriarchal figure until his death in 1870. He arranged his children's marriages to their cousins on neighboring estates, preserving the land on which he had built his Engenho Itaipu as a valuable patrimony for his grandchildren. (Courtesy of Maria de Lourdes de Toledo Lins)

of pátrio poder. Usually, the paterfamilias exercised his murderous prerogative as a consuetudinary right, especially in the nineteenth century, when more explicit limits began to be set on his disciplinary exercise of physical force.[29] He often behaved as a bloody ty-

[29] The same set of dramatic examples of patriarchal execution are reiterated in

11. Danish-born Col. Cristiano Lauritzen (1849–1923) represented the talented outsider who was patriarchially recruited into the commercially influential Cavalcanti de Albuquerque family in Campina Grande. Cristiano's business acumen was joined with his father-in-law's political control of the município in 1883, when he married Col. Alexandrino Cavalcanti de Albuquerque's daughter Elvira. By 1892, when this family portrait was taken, Cristiano was a naturalized Brazilian and he had replaced his father-in-law as the family's patriarchal figure. (José Joffily, *Entre a Monarquia e a República*, p. 288)

rant because a weak State could not enforce the law's limitations on patriarchal excess or because he had intimidated those who might testify against him.

The extent to which patriarchal absolutism ever was the exclu-

---

the scholarly literature: Cf. Freyre, *Sobrados*, 1:69–70; Costa Pinto, *Lutas de família*, pp. 56 and 185–91; Candido, "Brazilian Family," p. 295; and Alencar Araripe, "Pater-famílias nos tempos coloniais," *RIHGB* 40, pt. 2 (1893):15–23. The Brazilian Criminal Code of 1831, which superseded the criminal provisions of the Philippine Code, struck out the legal basis for husbands to punish wives physically. Lafayette Rodrigues Pereira, *Direitos de família* (Rio de Janeiro: B. L. Garnier, 1869), p. 133. Fathers were permitted to use "moderate" punishment with minor children. Ibid., pp. 275–76.

sive or even predominant mode of elite family organization and power deserves fundamental reconsideration. Few have inquired whether other models for organizing and exercising power within Brazil's ruling families existed, so it is difficult to assess the degree of "decline" in patriarchal authority that occurred during the last century. Anthropologist Antônio Candido was a rare exception to the uncritical acceptance of a patriarchal stereotype of scholars. He shrewdly noted the blind eye that dominant males, as well as dominated females, could turn to infractions of their ideal code of sexual behavior, for offenders frequently belonged to the intimate core of the family group. Another dissenter was sociologist Costa Pinto, who recognized the importance of female leadership and its frequent converse—male abdication—in the colonial feuding patterns of Brazil's great families.[30]

Because women assumed leadership roles, patriarchal power never was absolute. Strong women who assumed dominant roles in local politics throughout Brazil have been routinely labeled "matriarchs" or dismissed as viragos and "masculinized" women (*machonas*), but, in reality, they always shared power with their male kinsmen. Special circumstances of widowhood or wife abandonment explained their emergence in strong relief and defined them as the exceptions proving the rule that political power was a male prerogative. Rather than appraising such women as challengers to the canons of patriarchy, it might be worth asking if indeed patriarchy was ever as absolute as claimed. Local histories confirm the presence of strong female leadership in Paraíba's município politics in sufficient instances to cast doubt on the notion that patriarchal authority represented an exclusive organizational mode for elite families. Furthermore, widowhood and, more rarely, wife abandonment legally conferred on women the authority of the family head (chefe de família). Epitácio Pessoa's maternal aunt, for instance, exemplified this role. Married at seventeen and widowed at twenty-five, Celecina Barbosa de Lucena managed Engenho Paxois in Vicência (Pernambuco) and, declining to remarry, raised her seven children to adulthood.[31]

[30] Candido, "Brazilian Family," p. 303; and Costa Pinto, *Lutas de família*, pp. 78–89.

[31] Guerra, *Lucena*, p. 42. See also Freyre, *Sobrados*, 1:95–108 and 140 for additional examples of strong and politically influential female figures in nineteenth-century Pernambuco's landed elite. By virtue of their legal status as family heads, widows escaped the restrictions law imposed on married women, not only to submit to their husbands' authority in decisions related to their children's upbringing,

The famous Adriana de Oliveria Ledo of Santa Rosa, the widowed daughter of the conqueror Teodósio de Oliveira Ledo, became legendary because of the political power she exercised in Campina Grande throughout most of the eighteenth century. By virtue of the arrangements she made to place her sons and son-in-law in the local município council, she remained the most powerful politician in the município. Joana Francisca de Oliveira, daughter of the famous Pernambuco elite family of that name and sister of the Empire's well-known Councilor João Alfredo Corrêia de Oliveira, exercised the preponderant influence in the partisan politics of the backlands município of Patos in Paraíba during the 1860s and 1870s—even before she became widowed. A genealogist described her husband as possessing political influence "more because of his wife, who was both strong and decisive, for he was gentle and quiet . . . however capable of energetic action when the necessary moment arose."[32] No doubt, his youthful "abduction" of his bride from her paternal home in Goiana had involved Joana's connivance! For two decades following her husband's death, Joana wielded political authority through her son, José Galdino de Oliveira Nóbrega.

A final illustration of patriarchy's limited distribution as a mode of elite family organization concerns a direct descendant of Dona Adriana of Santa Rosa. Maria das Neves de Araújo Oliveira, known to everyone in the município of Alagoa Nova as "Dona Iaiá," was the epitome of a powerful, politically well-connected woman. In part, she explains why one local historian referred to Alagoa Nova as possessing a tradition of "matriarchy." Several governors during the Old Republic had strong cause to consider her wishes in their partisan decisions related to local appointments and candidates for office statewide. Dona Iaiá's father had been the influential Conservative Party boss of the município at the end of the Empire. Her husband, Dr. João Tavares de Melo Ca-

---

education, and place of residence, but also to alienate property by sale or gift, engage in business, or adminster their own property. Widows could also serve as executrixes of an inventory for dividing property under the law of succession, whereas a married woman had to be represented by her husband.

[32] E. Câmara, *Datas campinenses*, pp. 25–26. Adriana de Oliveira Ledo's political control was exercised formally during the 1790s by her son Paulo de Araújo Soares, a local judge and member of the municipal council (*câmara municipal*) of Campina Grande, and by her son-in-law, Luiz Pereira Pinto, also a councilman. Another son, Manuel Pereira de Araújo, was married to the aunt of yet a third councilman and the possibility could not be excluded that the remaining fourth councilman was also her relative.

valcanti (the Elder) had been a provincial deputy and then served in the Republic as a state deputy and second lieutentant governor in the 1890s, finishing his political career in the House of Deputies as Epitácio's trusted colleague. Dona Iaiá's son, also João Tavares de Melo Cavalcanti, gained a seat as an Epitacista federal deputy in 1922. Her control over the Tavares Cavalcanti family's political fortunes and patronage had been facilitated originally, however, by a *bicunhado* (double brother-in-law) arrangment that had wed her younger sister to her husband's younger brother, Manuel Tavares de Melo Cavalcanti—a state deputy and local politician. In 1929 she was still the owner of Engenho Geraldo, Alagoa Nova's most expensive property, which she had inherited from her parents. After the death of her husband in 1909, she always had the last word in the município's politics.[33]

Gov. João Pessoa complained bitterly to his uncle Epitácio of having to take Dona Iaiá's wishes into consideration when designating local political offices. Referring to her both as a "*coronela*" and "Tavares's mother," he insisted that everyone was afraid of her, including her sons and sons-in-law. Exasperated that no one would "tell her off," he became irate when Dona Iaiá vetoed his preference for a new prefeito in Alagoa Nova. His vexation increased because "she does what she wants with the revenues of the município," he wrote his uncle; "therefore, no one [of his choosing] wants to accept the office [of prefeito]."[34] These illustrations raise the possibility that maternal exercise of political power, when complemented by pátrio poder, was not a deviant variant for the elite family; rather, powerful families may have depended on a greater sharing of authority and leadership than the scholarly literature generally has recognized. If women could suc-

[33] Information on Dona Iaiá was drawn from ibid., pp. 82 and 95; Bittencourt, *Parahyba*, miscellaneous entries; Pinto, *Síntese histórica da Parahiba* (João Pessoa: Imprensa Oficial, 1939), p. 39; and especially Humberto Nóbrega, "Alagoa Nova," *RIHGP* 20 (1975):81. The claim for matriarchy in Alagoa Nova also rested on Maria da Penha de Aquino Mendonça [Dona Penha], "*senhora de engenho*" of Olho d'Agua do Bujari and widow of Tomás de Aquino Mendonça. As the leader of the Liberal Party in Alagoa Nova, she "exercised absolute and ostensible command of the Liberal ranks" through her son-in-law Francisco Inácio de Souza Gouveia. Furthermore, she was a wealthy merchant whose resources enabled her to defeat commercial rivals, for she could buy up all the cereals produced in the município before they reached the lower city's market. E. Câmara, *Datas campinenses*, p. 80.

[34] João Pessoa to Epitácio (Capital), [mid-May] 1929, AEP/9/165–66. The governor complained that Dona Iaiá "even uses [the revenues of the município] to buy gasoline for her car" and "that her son, who is political boss of Alagoa Nova, will not travel to the Capital for a personal interview" [with him].

ceed to these roles in default of a husband—or even a dominant husband—did not the collateral male relatives of the legal family head possess a similar opportunity to exercise collective power? Particularly in the context of violent family feuding, might not men whose natures were more pacific, such as Joana Oliveira's husband—who refused to take revenge for his son's murder—turn to their brothers or brothers-in-law, if not to their uncles and cousins, for a more collective exercise of family leadership?[35]

The scholarly emphasis on patriarchy, it seems reasonable to suggest, may have diverted attention from more enduring cooperative arrangements between male siblings or between them and their in-laws for the management of family affairs as well as local politics. Unfortunately, the extent to which family authority was collectively shared in the colonial period cannot be assessed with sufficient accuracy to make a firm comparison with the nineteenth century. Certain aspects of land tenure patterns in Paraíba during the last century, in conjunction with the inheritance law already mentioned, however, suggest that patrimonial motives traditionally fostered a shared coordination of family authority among male siblings and their brothers-in-law. Political and economic change therefore apparently made existing mutual reliance among siblings more pronounced. Contiguous residential patterns, joint ownership of overlapping property by siblings or other collateral relatives on separate estates, and the accumulation of inheritance portions by a collateral reweaving would all have strongly encouraged mutual cooperation among at least some siblings in a set.[36] It is argued that the 1835 abolition of the entailed estate, or *morgadio*, dealt a powerful blow to both primogeniture

[35] When the men responsible for his son's murder were apprehended and about to be killed, Dona Joana's husband—João Alves da Nóbrega (1777–1862)—arranged for them to escape and paid them a large sum of money not to return to Paraiba. T. P. da Nóbrega, *Família Nóbrega*, p. 26.

[36] Forced heirship imposed "equal shares for all," but parents—or fathers—favored some children over others, particularly by resorting to the *colação*. This provision of the law of succession permitted that prior distribution of portions of the *legítima* (that part of the patrimony divided by forced heirs) during the parents' lifetimes would later be accounted for in the posthumous distribution. *Codigo Civil 1916/Alves*, Art. 1785. See the example of Commendador Felinto Florentino da Rocha, son of the Baron of Araruna, who favored the first six of his eleven children posthumously in the division of the *legítima*. M. de Almeida, *Barão Araruna*. His inventory is published in its entirety on pp. 149–62. On the contemporary distribution of urban real estate as patrimony among siblings, see Miller, "Middle-Class Kinship Networks in Belo Horizonte, Minas Gerais," pp. 176–77. See also Duarte, *Ordem privada*, p. 69.

and patriarchal power by fragmenting family patrimony. If this is so, then an increased reliance on coordinated sibling strategies of rule may have followed.[37]

Sociopolitical Change and the Demise of Patriarchal Power

By the second half of the last century, the paterfamilias had become an archetype on the wane. An heir of a much more autocratically ruled family, he had begun to lose control of his sons. What new set of factors explained the tipping of the scales of domestic authority away from fathers and toward sons? The reasons must be sought in the broader changes confronting the national polity during the Empire and in the relationship between the State and its new administrative elite.

By 1850 new channels of social mobility had opened in Brazil, at least for men. The expansion of opportunities for education preparatory to university studies grew considerably after independence from Portugal in 1822. With the foundation of law and medical faculties in the 1820s, the sons of fazendeiros acquired the formal skills and appetite for professional careers that would free them from the land as well as loosen considerably the bonds of patriarchal control. Historians of the Empire have noted the appearance of the bacharel, or law school graduate, in national politics after mid-century as a product of this social development. However, the implantation of primary and secondary schools in the backlands of the northeastern states, thanks to a handful of dedicated clerics, was a major step in creating opportunity for acquiring the preparation needed to enter professional studies. By the 1860s, recruitment of professional military officers had also expanded, both because of the Paraguayan War and because the national military academy sought larger numbers of candidates. This

[37] Entailed heirs (*morgados*) were prohibited by Law No. 57 of 10 Oct. 1835. John Armitage suggested, however, that the entailed estate (*morgadio*) never took hold as an institution in Brazil: *Historia do Brasil desde o periodo da chegada da familia de Bragança em 1808 ate a abdicação de D. Pedro I° em 1831*, 2 vols., 3rd ed. (Rio de Janeiro: Egas e Garcia Junior, 1933) 1:50–51, and 2:8 and 16. Maria Isaura has argued that endogamy increased as a result of the extinction of the *morgadio*. Pereira de Queiroz, *Mandonismo local*, p. 45, n. 27. Raimundo Faoro reached a similar conclusion, but based on the implementation of the 1850 land law that created legal chaos for families possessing unregistered or dubious land claims. *Donos do poder*, p. 208.

career channel also tempted elite sons to free themselves from patriarchal control.

Many bacharéis left their childhood homes in the Northeast's interior for good and established themselves in coastal centers or the national capital. However, an equally important parallel trend was the return of young doutores to the rural zones. They confronted their fathers with a new filial leverage derived from their specialized training and valuable political contacts acquired at law or medical faculty.[38] Contrary to Gilberto Freyre's contention, the university doutor did not necessarily abandon his autocratic father at graduation, for his newly acquired legal or medical skills proved a political asset to the family.[39] Sons joined their fathers as partners in politics, while their erudition and socially prestigious degrees—not to mention their expertise in transacting politics with the coast's sophisticated networks of power—obliged the fathers to temper their patriarchal absolutism.

Well-educated sons served as crucial links between the município and the national polity and bolstered the family's struggle for local domination, despite their erosion of the paterfamilias's authority.[40] As bacharéis they served as imperial senators, deputies, judges, and public prosecutors, as well as provincial deputies, and filled the key political posts at all levels of government. By mid-century, a new term—bacharelismo—had been coined to capture the flood of law and medical school graduates. Bacharelismo was, in the words of one historian, "both a career pattern and a state of mind," characterizing men who aimed at upward mobility.[41] Their marriages reflected the new mobility derived from the sons' disinclination to accept wives imposed by their fathers, although the trend to marry outside the family's and the município's

[38] The titles, education, and intellectual preparation of the bacharéis who served as the "*mandatarios*" (rulers) of the political parties, were "guarantees of their ability to play the role of *cabeças* [heads] in the Empire." Pereira de Queiroz, *Mandonismo local*, p. 43.

[39] Freyre contended that only sons of inferior intelligence and poor health returned to the patriarchal rural domain. *Sobrados*, 1:18.

[40] By the 1870s and 1880s virtually all provincial deputies in Paraíba were doutôres. Celso Mariz, *Apanhados historicos* (Parahyba: Imprensa Official, 1922), pp. 12–79.

[41] Love, *Rio Grande do Sul*, p. 136. Ron L. Seckinger and Eul-Soo Pang have explored the importance of university training for entry into the national political elite in "The Mandarins of Imperial Brazil," *CSSH* 14 (Mar. 1972):215–44. Faoro, on the other hand, argues that the bacharel-politician often acted against the interests of his own family. *Donos do poder*, p. 226.

boundaries for successful incorporation within the national political elite increasingly gained parental approval.[42]

The surfeit of law school graduates testified to the way elite parentelas were positively responding to major political change by the 1870s. By that decade the gradual abolition of slavery contributed also to a slow undermining of the monarchy which, by the same token, reinforced patriarchy's slow decline. But it was the system of electoral politics introduced after 1835 that most rearranged authority patterns within elite parentelas.[43] With the establishment of provincial legislatures, as well as a Chamber of Deputies and a Senate at the national level, elite families adopted more complex strategies in order to retain their hold on their home municípios and to capture provincial offices. They now had to project their family-based political networks at each tier of officeholding and bureaucracy, particularly the national one. Local bailiwicks of power became more politicized as electoral conflicts regularly punctuated município life. The simultaneous appearance of Conservative and Liberal Parties forced the most powerful parentelas to create coalitions within their electoral districts in order to deliver votes for provincial deputies (assemblymen) representing them.[44] Otherwise, they could not insure that their local interests would be properly represented before either the provincial governor or the national legislature. Consequently, elite

[42] Epitácio's first marriage illustrated the exogamous matrimonial connections with the national elite that many young politicians from the provinces contracted. In 1894 he married Francisca Justiniana das Chagas, the daughter of a prominent imperial politician from Minas Gerais (Commendador Carlos Justiniano das Chagas). (The connection may in part explain Epitácio's good working relations in Congress with a number of Mineiro politicians throughout the Old Republic.) However, his second wife, Mary [born Maria da Conceição] Manso Sayão, whom he married on Nov. 8, 1898, after his first wife died in childbirth (on April 24, 1895), was the daughter of a middle-class physician in Rio de Janeiro (José Francisco Manso Sayão), who was not a politician but a prominent ear, nose, and throat specialist. His mother-in-law Maria Olímpia Brandão was the daughter of landowners in Vassouras (state of Rio de Janeiro). L. Pessôa, *Epitacio Pessôa*, 1:121 and 140; and certified copy of Epitácio's birth registry, Recife Law Faculty (Fichas Biográficas). The death certificate and inheritance (dowry) documents for Francisca das Chagas Pessoa and her stillborn son can be found in the "Colleção Epitacio Pessôa," an unnumbered gray box in the AEP.

[43] Oliveira Vianna, *Instituições políticas*, 1:263 and 295–338.

[44] In the Empire senators—two to ten per province—were selected by the emperor from a list of indirectly nominated candidates and served for life. In the Old Republic they served three-, six-, and nine-year terms and three were elected from each state. Federal deputies served three-year terms.

parentelas had to seek more enduring alliances beyond their home municípios and to mobilize for a political arena that transcended local alliances. University-educated sons, needless to say, possessed the preparation to effect such sophisticated coordination, in which conciliation and the art of compromise were at a premium. As the son, nephew, or brother of the rudimentarily educated coronel, the bacharel became his logical complement in the political process.

The historical decline in endogamous marriage in Paraíba is best appreciated in terms of political changes that encouraged elite parentelas to rearrange their internal organization. Rising exogamy reflected the need to recruit talented "strangers" as brothers-in-law valued for their political utility. The growing influence that sons, and even a few daughters, acquired as a parallel trend was expressed in the insistence on at least a shared decision between parents and offspring on the choice of a mate. Traditionally this had been considered a decision too important to be left to a son. But as he acquired stature through establishing his family's political alliances beyond the município, the selection of his spouse came more under his initiative. In addition, changing values impelled sons to revolt against patriarchal arrangement of their marriages, once the ideological revolt against slavery and monarchy progressed in the 1880s. Of course, arranged marriages continued to be the custom in most elite families in Paraíba into the first decades of the twentieth century. However, even when fathers imposed mates on their children, they recognized the greater necessity for recruiting outsiders. The jeopardy in which an excessive dependence on endogamy could place the family group was evident. The impetus toward exogamy, therefore, received strong paternal sanction even though the right to marry a mate of one's choice may have derived from the revolt against patriarchy.

Since land in the Paraíba backlands zones did not become thoroughly settled until mid-century, population pressure among the elite parentelas living beyond the coast was apparently another factor favoring exogamy. Families such as the Feitosas of the Inhamuns in neighboring Ceará had come to ruin in the nineteenth century precisely because they had relied too heavily on consanguineous unions and on only one economic specialization for guaranteeing their political ascendancy locally. They had failed in the late eighteenth century to cement sufficient alliances with newly arriving outsiders to ensure their control over the newcomers.[45] In Paraíba, the presence of new arrivals in a município added to the inevitable segmentation within already established parentelas and lent an urgency to accelerating exogamous bonding. Older backlands families such as the Nóbregas had sealed their local political fortunes by selecting wisely the parentelas with whom they would intermarry. This strategy explained their matrimonial webs with the eighteenth-century Dantas arrivals, although by the mid-nineteenth century they were choosing endogamous unions.

The advent of the Republic did not so much introduce factors in the political equation of município conflict as it enhanced or aggravated existing ones. Parentela politics continued to accommodate to trends begun in the Empire. For instance, the national Saraiva Law of 1881 had mandated a redistricting for Paraíba that created five electoral districts for elections to the Chamber of Deputies. Since they corresponded to the province's five geoeconomic zones, the law's immediate effect was to fragment the interzonal alliances that previously characterized the province's division into only three districts.[46] Before, dissident wings of both major parties had cooperated with their partisan rivals in delivering votes. These interpartisan coalitions disintegrated as the new districts more clearly and individually delineated local interest. However, no district could be politically effective on its own, so politicans soon felt a greater incentive for extending and maintaining interzonal alliances in electing the five provincial deputies who served in the national delegation. Throughout the Old Republic the Saraiva Law's districts endured as the basic electoral units for Paraíba's representation in the Chamber of Deputies. And the fact that they closely corresponded to geoeconomic divisions encouraged the shift of the political fulcrum inland.

[45] Chandler found that by the end of the eighteenth century only eight of thirty-two Feitosas in the third generation had contracted marriages with nonkin. *The Feitosas*, p. 58.

[46] The Saraiva Law of 9 January 1881 established compulsory electoral districts in all provinces. In Paraíba it eliminated the organization of elections around eight municípios that coincided with eighteenth- and nineteenth-century parish divisions and, by weighing the electorate in favor of coast, brejo, and caatinga-agreste, also favored the Conservative Party. This explained why the two backlands zones fell under Liberal Party leadership. Mariz, *Apanhados historicos*, p. 274. The Saraiva Law had its first impact in the 18th session of the national legislature, when seventy-five Liberals and forty-seven Conservatives were returned to the House of Deputies. See also Introduction (n. 16) and Chapter V.

The major electoral change introduced by the Constitution of 1891 was an alteration of voting requirements. The electorate was enlarged by lowering the minimum property requirement for voter registration. This might have threatened elite control, had not the introduction of a literacy requirement checked that liberalizing tendency. The net result was a rise in both the proportion and the absolute number of voters statewide who had to be mustered to "vote the slate" of the local elite parentelas that commanded their loyalty. The largest proportion of registered voters in any município in Paraíba between 1889 and 1930 was 7 percent of its total population; not surprisingly, those with the most voters lay in the backlands, where bosses were free from coastal surveillance.[47] Usually, however, only 2 to 3 per cent of a município's population was inscribed on its electoral rolls. By 1915 the Capital, with a higher literacy rate, had registered voters equal to about 5 per cent of its population. The backlands, however, not only had a higher proportion of the state's population than the coast but a higher proportion of registered voters; this testified not to a progressive extension of the suffrage due to rising literacy but to the greater competitiveness of politics beyond the coast. An expanded electorate after 1889 placed a premium not only on the use of coercion at election time but also on the need to forge new political alliances on intermunicípio and especially interzonal bases. As the matrimonial patterns reviewed earlier made clear, and primary evidence from the correspondence of Paraíba's local bosses confirmed, greater dependence was placed on bonds forged with outsiders across município lines as each decade of Old Regime unfolded.

The Sibling Axes of Political Organization

Varieties of Brother Bonding

By the time of the Old Republic, the shift away from endogamy and the slow demise of patriarchal authority found logical comple-

[47] The five electoral districts established by the 1881 law redefined voting patterns around the following key municípios and their subordinate neighbors: 1) the Capital (Alhandra [absorbed by the Capital after 1900], Pedras de Fogo, Pilar, and Mamanguape); 2) Campina Grande (Ingá, Alagoa Grande, Guarabira); 3) Areia (Alagoa Nova, Bananeiras, Araruna, Cuité); 4) Pombal (Santa Luzia, Patos, Alagoa do Monteiro, São João de Cariri, Cabeceiras); and 5) Sousa (Cajazeiras, Piancó,

ment in the rising importance of horizontal ties among male politicians. The absence of an endogamous restriction multiplied the possibilities for creative family alliances across município and even zonal lines. The vertically defined power relationships that historically had connected males as father, sons, and grandsons in patriarchally ordered arrangements remained important for transmitting the family group's leadership intergenerationally. However, the principal plane of political coordination had become an extended sibling axis, along which key politicians engaged in electioneering, rotated political office, and mobilized the family group's fighting forces. That this sibling axis was "extended" in kin terms could be verified in the political networks that crucially connected municípios on a zonal or interzonal basis, for ties between brothers-in-law—and especially co–brothers-in-law—provided the means for consolidating alliances within and between electoral districts. The scholarly literature has not sufficiently emphasized how the elasticity of Brazilian kinship organization contributed to such extended networks of power as the national political system opened a larger field for local politicking.

The specificity of the bonds between brothers and brothers-in-law, particularly the varieties of the latter, deserve elaboration before turning to examine their function in oligarchical politics.

A man acquired his wife's brother or his sister's husband as his brother-in-law, or *cunhado*. From the family group's perspective, however, the pivotal relationships were cemented with his wife's sisters' husbands, his 'co–brothers-in-law," or *concunhados*, as Figure IV.1 illustrates.

When sets of siblings married each other, the brother-in-law

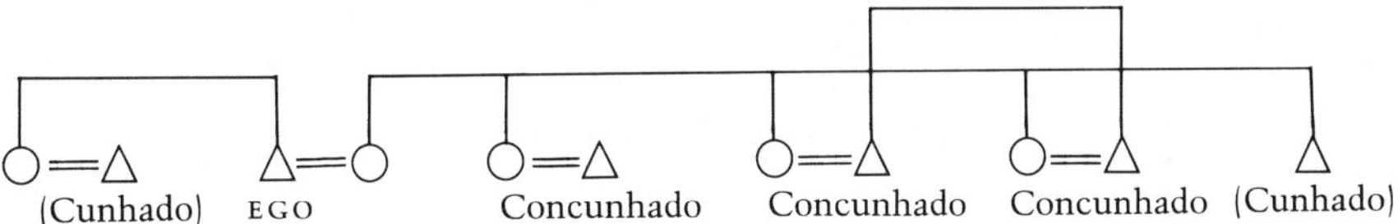

FIGURE IV.1: The Concunhado (Co–Brother-in-Law) Relationship: The Bonds of Sister Marriage

Misericórdia, Teixeira). Ibid. The law still preserved the basic geoeconomic divisions to which the five districts respectively conformed: coast, caatinga-agreste, brejo, cariri-sertão, and alto sertão. Its impact also fragmented Liberals in the two backlands districts and strengthened the Conservatives in the first three zones. Ibid., pp. 274–75 and 277.

bond was naturally doubled. Throughout the Old Republic, colloquial language in Paraíba singled out such relationships as distinct from ordinary concunhado relationships. Double brothers-in-law, whom marriage united as part of two or more sibling sets, were *bicunhados*. This relationship possessed two variants, depending on the genders of a given sibling set. In the first instance, two or more brothers would marry two or more sisters. While compounding their ties affinally as co–brothers-in-law, they also enhanced the solidarity between their two families by virtue of the multiple sets of married couples such alliances created. Figure IV.2 illustrates this common alliance.

The other variant of sibling set marriage occurred when two men exchanged their sisters as wives and defined themselves as brothers-in-law. Figure IV.3 illustrates that relationship, together with those of cunhado and concunhado. This variant often implied of a parity between the bicunhados, while in the other variant (I) the family of the women was likely to have a client status. These interpretations cannot be pushed too rigidly, for sex and age distribution or other subjective criteria also determined which variant could be adopted. In addition, either bicunhado relation-

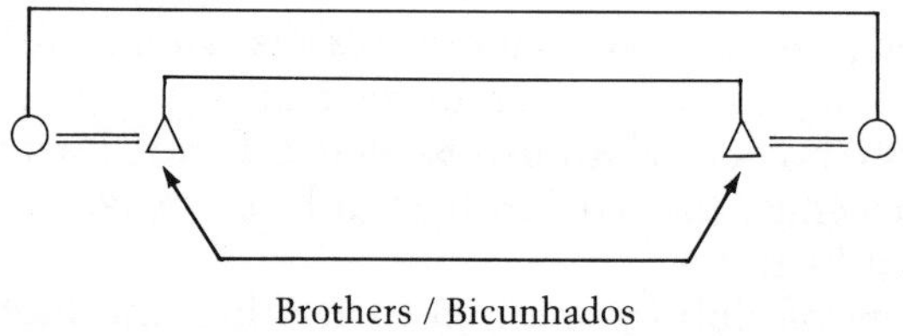

Brothers / Bicunhados

FIGURE IV.2: The Bicunhado Relationship (I): The Bonds of Sibling Set Marriage—Brothers Marry Sisters

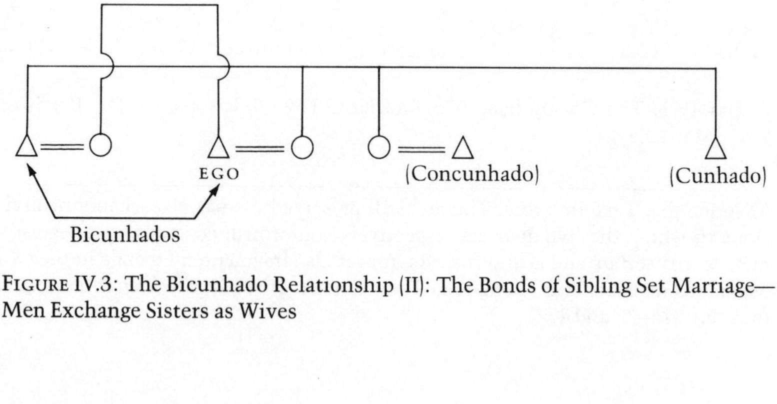

EGO

(Concunhado)

(Cunhado)

Bicunhados

FIGURE IV.3: The Bicunhado Relationship (II): The Bonds of Sibling Set Marriage—Men Exchange Sisters as Wives

ship might also be endogamously overlaid—when sibling sets were also double cousins. In those cases verticality in the relationships of brothers-in-law became more cohesive, since all four spouses shared identical grandparents.

Spatial and Temporal Dimensions of Brother-Bonding in Politics

Men always had bonded as nonconsanguineous brothers-in-law through either marriage to sister sets or marriage in sibling sets.[48] Reliance on brother-in-law or co–brother-in-law bonds therefore hardly represents a nineteenth-century innovation. The difference was the heightened degree to which brother-in-law relationships carried such quasi-brother bonds as primary political connections, both at the oligarchy's leadership level and at the local level. The greater reliance on horizontal linkages between the oligarchy's key factional segments eventually made a qualitative change that directly contrasted with the verticality of a patriarchal pattern of political relationships. In particular, co–brother-in-law relationships—both the concunhado and the bicunhado variants—assumed greater importance than mere brother-in-law (cunhado) relationships for linking ruling families across larger spatial units. The rising significance of exogamously inscribing outsiders rendered the traditional dependence on endogamous bonds more complementary. But the tandem reliance on both consanguine and affinal horizontal linkages was extremely evident in the last decade of the Empire, when each of Paraíba's five electoral districts was controlled by a parentela-based group headed by either pairs, trios, or even a quartet of brothers.[49] The capacity of brother-

[48] Pernambuco's colonial genealogist Borges da Fonseca called one of the families whose genealogies he catalogued from 1686 to 1759 the "Family of the Four Brothers-in-law" (*Título da família que chamam dos Cuatro Cunhados*), due to the marriage of four unrelated Portuguese immigrants to four sisters on the same day. *Nobiliarquia pernambucana*, p. 170. The sixteenth-century partnership between Pernambuco's founding donatary, Duarte Coelho, and his wife's brother, Jeronymo de Albuquerque, is another well-known political alliance of this type.

[49] The Conservative Party was also founded in the 1830s—by three brothers from the Carneiro da Cunha family, which dominated politics on the sugar coast. In the 1880s Silvino Elvídio Carneiro da Cunha (later Baron of Abiaí) and his brother Anísio Salatiel Carneiro da Cunha, with several of their offspring, still led that party. In the caatinga-agreste four brothers headed the Conservatives: Councilors Tertuliano and Antônio José Henriques, respectively a judge and a high officer of the Imperial Treasury; Canon Leonardo Meira, also editor of *O Conservador* (Campina Grande); and Antônio da Trinidade Antunes Meira de Henriques, imperial dis-

in-law relationships to transcend the electoral district as a political unit was indispensable where sets of brothers dominated individual zones.

The trend is perhaps best illustrated by the Leites, a ruling family of the Empire that perpetuated its political influence intergenerationally in the Republic. The Leites relied on the inscription of key outsiders as brothers-in-law, although eventually brother-in-law relationships became consanguineous. Their example also suggests that the frequent emphasis the scholarly literature accords to the "arrival" or political emergence of the *gênro*—the son-in-law—in the late Empire's politics, as well as his greater prominence in the Old Republic, deserves reappraisal from a horizontal perspective that views him as a brother-in-law.

The Leites had been leaders of the Liberal Party since its founding in the late 1830s, by Col. João Leite Ferreira 1º (d. 1848?) and Commendador Felizardo Toscano de Brito (d. 1876).[50] Both men dominated the party as its provincial boss from 1838 to 1876. Their working relationship in politics as nonkinsmen was cemented by uniting João Leite Ferreira's son of the same name with Felizardo's daughter Eugênia Toscano de Brito in marriage. As Figure B.4 illustrates, the succession of leadership in the Liberal Party after the death of Commendador Felizardo Toscano de Brito in 1876 passed first to his son-in-law João Leite Ferreira 2º. With the latter's premature death two years later, his brother-in-law, Dr. Francisco de Paula e Silva Primo, or "Paula Primo," as he was universally known, became Paraíba's new Liberal Party boss. Paula Primo had been the protégé and then the son-in-law of Col. João Leite Ferreira. He married Marcolina Leite after he had followed his three Conservative Party uncles into the Liberal camp in the 1850s and developed close ties with his future father-in-law. Paula Primo, a graduate of the Recife Law School, brought both considerable inherited wealth and powerful political allies to the Leites.

Paula Primo's relationship with João Leite Ferreira 2º meant

---

trict judge in Campina Grande and Ingá. The uncles of the Meira de Henriques brothers—another brother set—originally had founded the party in that zone. In the cariri-sertão three brothers of the Meira de Vasconcelos family—João Florentino, Fausto Nominando, and Roldão—led the Liberals from Pombal, while the Leites represented the other brother/brother-in-law group that headed the Liberal Party in the alto sertão. Mariz, *Apanhados historicos*, pp. 234–304, and author's prosopographical file. The connections between the cariri-sertão and alto sertão (fourth and fifth electoral districts) are further elaborated in n. 53, below.

[50] Sources for this summary of Leite Liberal leadership are listed in Fig. B.4.

that the leadership of the Liberal Party remained affinally structured, for his wife's brother as well as his co–brother-in-law Isidro Leite were provincial deputies. He clearly dominated, however, while another brother of his wife, Col. Tiburcio [Tiburtino] Leite Ferreira, ran political affairs at the local level in the Leites' home município of Piancó. Consequently, the Leites also illustrated another partnership typical for male sibling sets, one where tandems of doutores and coronéis coordinated the interests of their extended family group on all three levels of government. Paula Primo retained the formal leadership of the Liberal Party in Paraíba until its demise at the close of the Empire, surviving the monarchy as the de facto leader of the old Liberals. However, his deep involvement in turbulent município conflicts during the first years of the Old Republic compromised his career, for he was implicated in a political assassination and accused of masterminding it, although the case never came to trial. Illness in 1892 and subsequent confinement in an asylum for the insane effectively retired Paula Primo from state politics.

A third generation of Leites had emerged politically with the Republic, except for Paula Primo's younger brother-in-law, Coronel Tiburcio. (See Fig. B.4.) "Coronel Tiburtino" exemplified the younger brother who belonged more to the generation of his siblings' offspring. He had been too young to join his brother in political leadership in the 1870s. Moreover, he lacked the law degrees that João Leite Ferreira 2° and Paula Primo possessed. Consequently, he saw his ambitions limited to the sphere of the município. Not surprisingly, he had resented his father's, and especially his older brother's, preferential treatment of the more talented Paula Primo.

Coronel Tiburtino eventually engaged in a blood feud with his nephews, the children of his sister Marcolina and Paula Primo, who followed the partisan leadership of their brother-in-law, Dr. Felizardo Toscano Leite Ferreira (1862–1930). Felizardo Leite, as he was known, had married Paula Primo's daughter Joana de Paula Leite Ferreira, his patrilateral cross-cousin. He, of course, was Tiburtino's nephew. Furthermore, Felizardo's father, Dr. João Leite Ferreira (2°), had been Paula Primo's mentor while simultaneously performing as a surrogate father for Tiburtino. In this case, however, close consanguinity and affinal ties led to a blood feud because of the earlier preference accorded to Felizardo's father-in-law, the talented outsider, Paula Primo. Although Coronel Tiburtino had kept him out of politics in the 1890s, Felizardo emerged as the Leites' most influential politician after his paternal uncle's death in 1902.[51] Around 1900, the feud between him and Tiburtino was laid aside by a traditional means, for the Leites' senior rivals married their differences: two of Felizardo's daughters were wedded to two of Tiburtino's sons. As bicunhados, the pairs of cousin-spouses became matrimonial hostages to their parents' mutual hostility.

Once the feud was resolved, Felizardo relied on his brother-in-law bonds more strongly to coordinate politics across município lines among the family-based groups comprising the Old Liberal bloc that still dominated the alto sertão. Paula Primo's two sons worked with him: João Leite Ferreira Primo led the opposition in Pombal and Dr. Francisco de Paula—more familiar as "Chico Paula"—was local party boss in adjacent Patos. Chico Paula rotated his seat in the Assembly during the 1920s briefly with Felizardo's son, his cousin Ademar de Paula Leite Ferreira, who represented a fourth generation of Leites in state politics. Felizardo, however, remained the Leites' driving force. As an old man in the 1920s, he witnessed one protégé, his compadre Padre Aristides Ferreira da Cruz (no relative), wrest control of Piancó from his family-based group following the Valfredistas' defeat in the 1915 assembly election. Although Felizardo had served as a state assemblyman from 1900 to 1912 and then moved to the House of Deputies for 1912–1914, his career in state politics never recovered from the Valfredistas' statewide defeat by the Epitacistas in 1915. His family-based group in Piancó spent most of the 1920s in armed conflict with the new Epitacista boss, Padre Aristides, and then with his successor José Parente, an aggressive entrepreneur allied with Col. José Pereira Lima of Princesa.[52]

In 1912 one local boss of the cariri-sertão outlined the structural reliance of backlands politicians on their networks of co–brothers-in-law relationships, a reliance which now occurred frequently without any parallel dependence on endogamous reinforcement. In a letter to Epitácio, Col. Inácio Dantas, local boss of Teixeira, connected his family's long domination of the município to the Leites and other old Liberal families whose political power spanned three geoeconomic zones:

[51] Between 1840 and 1889, therefore, at least one Leite always sat in the Provincial Assembly. Mariz, *Apanhados historicos*, pp. 234–304.

[52] Padre Aristides Ferreira da Cruz's relationship with the Leites, which included ties of compadrio with Felizardo, is described in Manuel Otaviano, *As mártires de Piancó* (João Pessoa: Editora Theone, 1955), pp. 45–52. (See n. 58.)

> José Jerônimo was a concunhado of Coronel Dario Romalho, each being married to two sisters of Dario Apolônio and Francisco Montenegro, the second lieutenant governor. . . . Local political boss Dario passed his office to his concunhado, José Jerônimo, also my friend. In Patos Miguel Sátiro bestowed his title of boss on his concunhado Chico Paula, and in Batalhão and elsewhere they are doing the same.[53]

In citing his own concunhado network, one that inscribed Chico Paula [Francisco de Paula e Silva Primo], Inácio Dantas revealed that, from the perspective of elite males, their concunhado bonds derived from sister exchange.

By spanning political units larger than one município, cooperating sets of co–brothers-in-law also demonstrated how matrimonial alliances could offset the propensity toward collateral fragmentation that inevitably affected any parentela. Once electoral victories had to be defined according to zonal or interzonal bases, affinal ties with outsiders became superior to endogamous connections. Because they were deliberately selected, affinal bonds carried greater significance than ties of blood in politics. As Figure IV.1 illustrates, brother-in-law and co–brother-in-law relationships, while distinct, almost always worked in tandem to insure a family-based group's political control and representation.

The Emotional Dimensions: Family "Honor" and Machismo

Three psychological factors also made brother-in-law relationships advantageous for perpetuating local family rule. First, the

[53] Inácio Dantas to Epitácio (Teixeira), 18 Jan. 1912, AEP/10/81. As an Epitacista winner, Col. Dario Romalho (de Carvalho Luna) ejected the Dantas from the political leadership of Teixeira in the 1915 federal election. His marriage to a sister of Dario Apolônio (Peregrino de Albuquerque) and Francisco (Peregrino de Albuquerque) Montenegro of Alagoa Grande consolidated his own political ties in his native Teixeira because his mother-in-law (Peregrina Nunes da Costa) had been born and raised in that cariri-sertão município. The Peregrino de Albuquerques had dominated Alagoa Grande (in the adjacent caatinga-agreste) since the Empire. José Jerônimo (Borborema de Albuquerque) came from the cariri-sertão, but belonged to Campina Grande's political elite. Inácio Dantas's references to the Leites' Chico Paula (Francisco de Paula Primo), local boss of Patos, and to Miguel Sátiro, local boss of Pombal, connected those two alto sertão municípios with both the cariri-sertão and caatinga-agreste. Thus, these co–brother-in-law and brother-in-law relationships impressively spanned three geoeconomic zones, extending from the eastern Borborema Plateau to the Piranhas Valley in the far west. Fourteen years later, another native of Teixeira—Gov. João Suassuna—commented that Francisco

age span among siblings was so wide that frequently a man's younger sisters were the age of his daughters when he married them to allies. If the sisters' husbands were also young, the brother-in-law relationship often carried a de facto father-in-law connotation that hierarchically reinforced the brother's control. Second, when established between peers in age, the brother-in-law relationship was politically advantageous because it confirmed an equal status and a significant bond of personal intimacy between the males. To accept an ally's sister as one's wife was preferable to marrying his daughter, in other words. Sister exchange underscored a common plane of respect between two bosses.[54] Finally, and perhaps most important, a man's wife's brother—whether his cunhado or his bicunhado—was the kin category he could most trust with his wife's "honor," which for him was synonymous with the "honor of the family" (*a honra da família*). In other words, a wife bonded her brother and her husband by virtue of the fact that cultural notions of "honor and shame" charged them with preserving and defending her chastity.[55]

Crises over female honor were, of course, fundamentally crises over male honor, since competition among men routinely projected rivalry onto female subjects according to a number of ritualized or customary behaviors.[56] However, the shallowness of the incest prohibition in Brazil and the closed circle of family associ-

---

Montenegro was visiting "with his double brother-in-law" Col. Dario Ramalho in Teixeira and maintaining the important pattern of family visiting across zones. Idem to Epitácio (Capital), 7 Oct. 1926, AEP/12/266.

[54] On family honor and the relations between men and their brothers-in-law, see J. K. Campbell, *Honour, Family and Patronage* (Oxford: Clarendon Press, 1964), pp. 138–39. His study of a Greek mountain village of pastoralists offers comparison with the Northeast's backlands. See pp. 270–72 on seduction as dishonor. See also Fox, *Kinship and Marriage*, pp. 186–87, on "sister exchange" as a loose term.

[55] Similarly, Antônio Candido has stressed that close family members might deliberately ignore adulterous behavior in their midst. "Brazilian Family," p. 303. Chandler, however, described the dire family consequences of adultery when the transgressor was a husband's brother: Pedro Alves de Araújo of the Feitosa family killed both his adulterous wife and brother in 1878 after he discovered them together *in flagrante delicto. The Feitosas*, pp. 91–92.

[56] In other words, a wife's honor belongs to the personal honor of the men culturally charged with defending it—her brothers and her husband. On the difference between "personal" honor and "social" honor, see Peter Schneider, "Honor and Conflict in a Sicilian Town," *Anthropological Quarterly* 42, no. 3 (July 1969):130–54. Eric R. Wolf and Edward C. Hansen discuss the practice of secluding elite women and the related values of honor and masculinity in their analysis of *caudillismo* (the rule of the *caudillo* or chieftain), which examines male alliances within

ation that usually restricted a woman's contact with society to the company of close relatives, also meant that an offense to male honor possessed great capacity for destruction within the family group. A man's own brothers, his father, or his uncles were the likeliest to transgress the chastity of his wife. Consequently, his cunhado—his wife's brother—became worthier of trust than his own blood kinsmen.

Machismo, a behavioral set that demanded and rewarded public demonstration of either the capacity for exercising violence or at least reckless bravado, not to mention the ability to respond aggressively when physical force threatened, placed an additional premium on the quasi-sibling ties between elite males. Men in groups publicly attested to the ability of their dominant member to rule, that is, to command and to punish, as well as to control the electoral process in a município. Powerful local bosses were expected to parade their personal bodyguards and retainers as proof of their might. They frequently needed the assistance of their brothers and brothers-in-law for demonstrating their capacity to react to physical threats with force. When brothers-in-law rode into town on market day, they jointly advertised the presence of several or many elite extended families in alliance.[57] In these situations—as men in groups—brothers and brothers-in-law reminded the local population publicly of the collective capacity of a number of families to retaliate on behalf of any one of their members whose injury or death might demand revenge.

Horizontal Bonding and Elite Family Continuity

A consideration of quasi-sibling axes of organization raised the important issue of the extent to which collateral, as well as vertical, kin ties perpetuated elite family power over time. A related

---

the "regional kindreds" of rural *criollo* gentries in "*Caudillo* Politics: A Structural Analysis," *CSSH* 9 (1967):171–74.

[57] Col. Segismundo Guedes Pereira (1843–1937) of Bananeiras illustrated the male solidarity derived from affinal alliances and how it was publicly exhibited. Seven of his eleven children had been married to eight different siblings (one two times) of Areia's Cabral de Vasconcelos family and then settled by him on dotal estates adjoining his Engenho Gamelas. Every Saturday Coronel Segismundo would ride into Bananeiras for the weekly fair accompanied by his sons and their brothers-in-law, who formed an armed entourage that enabled him to dispense with the *capangas* who otherwise would have been bodyguards. Author's interview with Dr. Normando Guedes Pereira, João Pessoa, 24 July 1978.

Men demonstrated machismo by the readiness to use violence and the capacity

question is the extent to which kin loyalty overrode partisan allegiance in politics. These issues are addressed from another perspective in the following chapters, but the *family* base of power and the related consideration of kinships organization's special features deserve appraisal now in terms of an overarching question: What was the relationship between family affiliation and partisan loyalty over the long run?

Generally speaking, individuals accorded their primary loyalty to the family group itself, with partisan affiliation being a derivative phenomenon. This meant that the main assumption of partisan affiliation was that an elite family would be loyal to a bloc of allied and usually intermarried family segments for associative ends. The long relationship the Leite family of Piancó maintained with the Liberal Party illustrates this fact. As leaders of the Old Liberal bloc during the Old Republic, the Leites gave their allegiance to the Machado–Leal oligarchy from its establishment in 1892 until its downfall between 1912 and 1915. Nevertheless, their membership in the ruling coalition suggested the endurance of a family-based affiliation deriving from a historical association with other Liberal families that dated to the 1840s and 1850s. As Valfredistas, the Leites maintained a high partisan congruence with their imperial affiliation in politics. They were by no means unique. But the defeat of Monsignor Valfredo in the 1915 state and federal elections definitively ended the efforts of Old Liberals to maintain either oligarchical leadership or an effective opposition to the victorious coalition led by Epitácio Pessoa.

As die-hard Valfredistas by 1915, the Leites were typical of many elite extended families in the backlands that locally had been locked in violent struggles for three generations with rival families usually loyal to the Conservative Party. Yet once Valfredo Leal was defeated, they—like Valfredo himself—embraced Epitacismo. Felizardo Leite's reward for a change of partisan allegiance was the opportunity to return to his seat in Congress as a federal deputy—from 1916 to 1930. The Leites' entry into Epitácista ranks, and it was a collective move that brought several branches of the parentela, was dictated by purely pragmatic considerations

---

to dominate females, which implied their ability to deny women to other men. "The theme of sexual competition should also be read against the wider social background in which female seclusion on the part of the gentry symbolizes their hold on property and status." Wolf and Hansen, "*Caudillo* Politics," p. 174. See also Américo Paredes's insightful analysis, "The United States, Mexico, and Machismo," *Journal of the Folklore Institute* 8 (June 1971):17–37.

of family survival: locally, the Epitacista faction led by the parish priest (Padre Aristides Ferreira da Cruz) threatened to eject them altogether from município politics, so the Leites required Epitácio's hegemonic sponsorship. They thus engineered a delicate switch of allegiance and successfully manuevered to be promoted from the status of "compatible adversaries" to "allies." But even as allies they remained suspect, due to their associational ties as Old Liberals and Valfredistas to other family-based groups sharing their history of partisan loyalties.[58]

For a different perspective on the long-run view of kinship and politics in Paraíba, the list of families dominant in the Empire can be compared with those dominant in the Old Republic. Tables D.1 and D.2 reveal this facet of family identity over time in Paraíba's oligarchical organization. The lists were compiled by taking the officeholders in Empire (senators, imperial deputies, provincial deputies, and provincal governors) and those in the Republic (senators, federal deputies, state deputies or assemblymen, and governors) and classifying each politician according to a prevailing family affiliation. This exercise yielded lists of families according to the number of officeholders each had, one set for the Empire and one for the Old Republic. "Leadership families" arbitrarily were defined as having six or more members in office in either the Empire or the Old Republic, while those with one or two representatives in political office were termed "rank-and-file" families. This left an intermediate group having three to five representatives.[59]

Careful perusal of the families listed in Tables D.1 and D.2 reveal an impressive continuity of kin-linked participation in Paraíba's politics. Only at the leadership level did a significant break in the family continuity of oligarchical participation occur. In

[58] Mariz observed that when it served their relatives' interests, rural landowners voted with the rival party. *Apanhados historicos*, pp. 278–79. Faoro also has stressed the family base of conflict at the local level during the Empire. *Donos do poder*, pp. 378–81.

On the Leites' position in Piancó vis-à-vis Padre Aristides and José Parente, see Toinho [Antônio Pessoa Filho] to Epitácio (Capital), 22 Dec. 1916, AEP/12/43; Solon de Lucena to Epitácio (Capital), 3 Nov. 1922, AEP/12/192; and João Suassuna to Epitácio (Capital), 12 May and 7 Oct. 1926, AEP/12/263 and 266.

[59] Names of provincial deputies were derived from Mariz, *Memória Assembléia*, pp. 12–79. For the purpose of counting relatives of politicians, each relative was counted only according to the highest political office he held. (Thus, a politician whose father was a state deputy and then a senator was counted as having a father who was a senator.) Several categories—such as brother who was a senator or federal deputy—were combined. Data on ties of blood and marriage among politicians are from Lewin, "Politics and *Parentela*," pp. 383–85.

most cases, leading families of the Empire remained staunch monarchists after 1889, which largely explains their withdrawal from states politics. Otherwise, the Empire's key politicians belonged to an aging stratum that death removed in the early 1890s. But the pattern that rank-and-file families reflected was survival, for only six of the total thirty-eight represented in the Empire failed to gain representation in the Old Republic.

The converse is worth noting: In the Republic, only eight families were "new"—families that in the Empire had sent no members to either the national or the provincial legislature. (See Tables D.1 and D.2.) Some of these families, however, turned out not to be so new, for usually they had entered republican politics on the coattails of an established family. The Pessoas themselves best illustrate this phenomenon. Epitácio's parents and grandparents had not been active in provincial politics except at the local level, but his consanguine ties to Baron Lucena, as well as his mother's sister's affinal ties to Vanâncio Neiva, gave Epitácio what Brazilians call a "trampoline" for entering politics. In other words, the cutting edge of family membership could be deceiving. This circumstance renders firm conclusions about family continuity from Empire to Republic methodologically arbitrary unless such collateral connections of a politician are taken into account. When they are, connection with a family represented in the Empire's officeholding elite usually emerged, making elite continuity extremely high.[60]

The Pessoas' domination of the Paraíba oligarchy after 1912 could readily be attested by the number of Epitácio's nephews, cousins, and in-laws who held political office during the Old Republic. Among the intermarried family-based bloc of his supporters—Silva Pessoas, Pessoa Cavalcanti de Albuquerques, Lucenas, and Neivas—eighteen individuals held office in the Paraíba Assembly. If the holders of município office had been counted, the number would have been much higher. In contrast, about one dozen politicians who supported the Machado-Leal oligarchy came from its family-based core of supporters—Machados, Milanez, and Santos Leal. This left a crucial swing bloc of politicians

[60] Methodologically, the assignment of a family affiliation opened the classic dilemma posed by all bilateral descent systems—where to draw the line around a given individual's "family." The fact that individuals defined their own affiliation reduced the problem of assigning one; however, since individuals were classified only according to a *primary* loyalty, the ambiguity of dual (at least) membership was avoided. (Politicians born in the Empire but too late to have served in office were also excluded from calculations for Table D.1.)

from the central backlands who were members of the Carvalho and Nóbrega families, for they jointly contributed at least fifteen members to the officeholding elite of the First Republic.[61] (See Table D.2.)

Individual kin links among the oligarchy's officeholders, both vertical and horizontal, deserve final emphasis. First, they help explain the high continuity between officeholding families in Empire and Republic, because a prime criterion of political recruitment in the first decade of republican rule was previous service in the Empire's politics. About 19 per cent of those individuals who held office between 1889 and 1930 had been officeholders in Empire. Eleven per cent of the republican officeholders could also be *identified* as the sons of men who had been imperial or provincial deputies—a gross underestimate. But 43 per cent of the officeholders had fathers who had been either prefeitos or local party bosses—usually both—during the Empire, a statistic that best confirmed elite continuity.[62]

Finally, brother bonds appeared to be extremely significant among the total 303 individuals who held political office in the Old Republic. Not surprisingly, they turned out to be most evident in the Assembly, where 30 per cent of the state deputies had brothers who served either in that body or as state governors. Of the seventy-five sibling sets identified among the officeholders, 18 per cent of the assemblymen had brothers serving in either the House of Deputies or the Senate. Naming customs frustrated considerably positive identification of brother-in-law ties. Although under 20 per cent of the 303 officeholders could be linked as either a brother-in-law or a co–brother-in-law, the actual proportion probably approached 50 per cent.[63]

The Politics of Parentela

Parentela and Panelinha

Although the Introduction drew a distinction between *family-based group* and *family-based network*, kinship made their polit-

[61] The Carvalhos and Nóbregas functioned as a crucial swing bloc between 1904 and 1908 due to the fact that Lieut.-Gov. Francisco Montenegro (Peregrino de Albuquerque) had married two sisters of the Nóbrega family and could rely on those ties to maintain a majority in the Assembly for the Alvaristas.

[62] Lewin, "Politics and *Parentela*," pp. 384–85.

[63] Ibid., pp. 352–53.

ical functions complementary and overlapping. The rising importance of what Sílvio Romero referred to as "friendly groupism" (grupismo amigueiro), or political friendship must be reconciled with the group's greater reliance on a variety of brother-in-law bonds. Basically, the term "politics of parentela" is employed in this study to denote the influential role the extended family group or parentela played in Paraíba as the organizational core for key political groupings. The latter, because they relied heavily on criteria of blood and marriage, were "family-based groups." On a more complex level, however, the politics of parentela refers to how politicking was conducted. It connotes the cohesion that kin connections imparted, not to groups, but to networks. In this respect, as the description from Inácio Dantas's letter revealed, the political utility of brother-in-law ties lay in the way they connected key members of discrete family-based groups to each other, and, particularly, to other networks at higher levels of government. Of course, the closer to the município one looked, the more the family-based group became congruent with the family-based network. However, at a higher level, selected members of a politician's family-based group—either kinsmen or close political friends—served to extend his network beyond the more confined boundaries of the family-based group. Such individuals often served to link the município bailiwick to both state and federal levels.

The fact that both family-based groups and networks admitted affiliations other than those of kinship did not contradict kinship's vital organizing significance. Even though Paraíba's segmentary political organization corresponded to elite family divisions, this did not mean that group loyalty was offered exclusively on the basis of family membership. In a study of Moroccan politics, where a full-blown lineage system of descent was much in evidence, this point emerged as a crucial finding. Its author concluded that rarely did "primordial" considerations—those narrowly confined to ties of blood, family, and ethnicity—exclusively define a political interest group. In the Moroccan case, where agnatic lineages were reinforced by parallel cousin marriage, segmentary factions were organized around "mixed" objectives.[64] In the context of Paraíba's family-based oligarchy, personalism played a growing and important role throughout the Old Republic. However, kinship remained particularly significant for providing a crucial social cement that integrated networks—or selected

[64] John Waterbury, *The Commander of the Faithful* (New York: Columbia University Press, 1970), pp. 68–75.

members of them—at high levels of the political structure. Secondarily, it also enabled individuals to approach each other politically—within either the same group or network—through reference to a common ancestor or even a very distant living relative.

Sociologist Anthony Leeds has stressed the central role networks, or what he refers to as a "*panelinha*"—the common Brazilian term for network—play in political and economic organization in Brazilian society.[65] As a "relatively closed, completely informal primary group held together in common interest by ties of friendship or other personal contact acting for common ends," a panelinha lacks an institutional definition.[66] Its existence, and therefore its key role in economic and political decision-making, in his view, has gone largely unnoticed by scholars:

> The fact that these social structural units [panelinhas] which are so vital in Brazil are known only in *informal discourse* is itself a reflection of the lack of . . . formalization of the social fabric. . . . *One can discover this informal organization only through field work, not through primary sources. But without knowing this organization one cannot understand how Brazil functions, economically or politically.*[67]

Although Leeds viewed panelinhas from a post–World War II perspective that already was witnessing rapid industrialization, most of the behavioral characteristics that he isolated were equally applicable to Paraíba's pre-1930 family-based networks. What differed—as Robert Shirley has suggested—from the panelinhas of southern Brazil that both Shirley and Leeds studied was the composition of these elite networks. In states like São Paulo, single families could not dominate entire municípios.[68] In northeast Bra-

[65] Anthony Leeds, "Brazilian Careers and Social Structure: A Case Study and a Model," *American Anthropologist* 66 (1964):1321.

[66] Ibid.

[67] Ibid., p. 1331. (Italics added.)

[68] The author is grateful to Robert W. Shirley for calling her attention to this difference (letter of 4 Sept. 1984). Shirley's study of Cunha, however, focuses on the post-1932 "functional oligarchy" in a município no longer dominated by "rural fazendeiro clans" but by a "more sophisticated urban-official group" whose members had fewer ties of kinship than the former group: *The End of a Tradition: Culture Change and Development in the Município of Cunha, São Paulo, Brazil* (New York and London: Columbia University Press, 1971). See pp. 82–83. Another anthropologist, Bela Bianco, has addressed the pre-1930 local elite in a different município of São Paulo in her dissertation, now in preparation as a book: "The Petty Supporters of a Stratified Order: The Economic Entrepreneurs of Matriz, São Paulo, Brazil (1877–1974)" (Ph.D. diss., Columbia University, 1980).

zil, on the other hand, single-family domination was almost proverbial; this view appears to be exaggerated, for least in Paraíba domination of a município by one family was the exception, not the rule. Political scientist Jean Blondel characterized coronelismo in Paraíba as "collegial," not monolithic. Family power at the local level almost always was exercised oligarchically, by several intermarried families ruling as allies. Leeds and Shirley note that true panelinhas are composed primarily of nonkin, although they do not exclude kinship ties among members. Thus, one might conclude that they did not really exist in Paraíba at the município level, upholding Shirley's claim that panelinhas are a phenomenon of southern Brazil. But the distinction is by no means so clear-cut.

Even in a family-based oligarchy such as Paraíba's, networks at the local level depended crucially on their nonkin members. The reorganization of the national political system in the 1830s had forced them to become more outward-looking. Brothers-in-law or co–brothers-in-law alone could not represent all of the family-based group's interests beyond the município. Key outsiders therefore were recruited. In Paraíba, and throughout Brazil, probably the most important local political figure who lacked family ties to the município elite was the juíz de direito, or federal district judge (the imperial district judge before 1889). Of course, he often was incorporated through marriage in a local family-based group, for his value lay in his performance as a broker between national and state levels of government. In southern Brazil, the genius of the panelinha lay in its identity as a local group that cross-cut other elite groups at higher levels—zonal, state, regional, and national.[69] Although, as Shirley has pointed out, locally the panelinha in northeast Brazil corresponded closely with a kin grouping, once the perspective shifted beyond the município nonkin members became increasingly significant. When, for example, Sen. Gonçalves Lisboa denounced Paraíba's Neiva–Lucena–Pessoa oligarchy in 1908, he concentrated his ire on individuals related to Venâncio Neiva by blood and marriage, even appending a careful social genealogy of Venâncio's family-based network that spanned several geoeconomic zones as evidence.[70] He might also have identified many in the network who were nonkin, but he declined to do so because he was specifically denouncing nepotism. The difference in the composition of Paraíba's family-based networks and those of pre-1930

[69] Shirley, *End of a Tradition*, pp. 82–83.

[70] Coelho Lisbôa, *Oligarchias*, pp. 11 and 96.

São Paulo may not be as great as the literature on networking assumes. At least the difference was more of degree than kind, for during the Old Republic local elites in São Paulo also relied on chains of kinsmen in the state and national capitals to represent them as brokers. More importantly, the extent to which a network contained kinsmen of the município elite may not have mattered in terms of the functions it performed.

Finally, the stress Leeds laid on the panelinha's heterogeneous membership, which spanned various segments of society to serve a multiplicity of needs, deserves special attention for the politics of parentela. Panelinhas existed to provide "reach" to groups that otherwise would be closed. Consequently, they functioned best when they connected separate levels of government intimately, by facilitating the exchange of news and gossip and serving as conduits of political influence. When Epitácio initiated his political career, between 1886 and 1891, his family-based network already connected him to the political elites of both Pernambuco and Paraíba, as well as the national elite in Rio de Janeiro. Consideration of its membership and political usefulness will illustrate the key roles that both kin and nonkin played in a politician's panelinha. His reliance on his "trampoline," as Brazilians refer to such career networks, was typical of a talented and well-connected young law school graduate of the late Empire.

Epitácio's Family-Based Network: Panelinha as Parentela

After graduation from the Recife Law Faculty in November 1886, Epitácio began his political career the following February as a public prosecutor in the município of Cabo, just south of Recife. This was the typical first rung on a political career ladder. Moreover, Epitácio was following in the footsteps of his distinguished uncle, Baron Lucena, who three decades earlier had also begun as a public prosecutor in a warring backlands município. Like Lucena, Epitácio stayed in his initial post only briefly; he resigned in June 1889, frustrated and defeated by Cabo's local politics. His persistence in prosecuting a defendant in a local murder case had led him into conflict with Cabo's influential imperial district judge, Teixeira de Sá. After their differences were aired in the Recife press, Epitácio earned an admonition from Pernambuco's governor to tread softly. As an earlier experience at eighteen had emphasized to him, when he first argued a murder case in Bom Jardim (Pernambuco) for the accused, the controversy in Cabo forced Epitácio to confront the local family base of state and national politics.[71] Although he eventually submitted his resignation to the governor, he had learned well the lesson that all successful national politicians had to master during both Empire and Old Republic: because coronelismo's family base of political influence reached upward to the governor, it could not be defeated through action taken in the local courts and by an individual acting alone, no matter how courageously.

Four months after quitting Cabo and only two weeks before the fall of the Second Empire, Epitácio arrived in Rio de Janeiro to make his political fortune in the nation's capital. Establishing himself in the household of his older brother, Lieut. José da Silva Pessoa, he immediately came into contact with three powerful individuals who were to set the course of his political career for life. The first, Gen. Deodoro da Fonseca, was introduced to him by his brother José Pessoa, who, until recently, had served as aide-de-camp to Gen. Almeida Barreto, a member of Deodoro's staff. A good friend of Lucena—the two men addressed each other as compadres—Deodoro shortly was to become the principal figure in the fall of the monarchy.[72] As commander-in-chief of the army, he would go to the emperor's first minister, demand the emperor's abdication, insist on the resignation of the first minister and the cabinet, and then assume the responsibilities of the Old Republic's first provisional government as provisional president. After being elected by the Constituent Congress as president in January 1891, Deodoro would serve only eleven months, resigning in November and dying a month later.

The second influential figure in Epitácio's network was Gen. José de Almeida Barreto, Lieut. José Pessoa's senior officer and fellow paraibano. Almeida Barreto had served as Deodoro's aide-de-camp in the Paraguayan War from 1865 to 1870, after beginning his military career as a sixteen-year-old runaway from Sousa, his childhood home in the backlands. At fifty-three he was officer in command of the palace troops when Deodoro executed the republican coup d'état on November 15, Almeida Barreto brought his men to the side of the revolutionaries and won a promotion to marshal. During the war with Paraguay, he had developed a firm

[71] L. Pessôa, *Epitacio Pessôa*, 1:38. Epitácio accepted the defense at the insistence of his godfather, Col. Manuel de Assunção Santiago, whom he assisted in his law practice in Ingá, Bom Jardim, and Limoeiro (the latter two municípios are in Pernambuco) during vacations from law school between 1882 and 1886.

[72] Ibid., p. 55.

and close friendship with three brothers who were compatriots from Paraíba, the Neivas. They in turn served as his aides-de-camp. Two of the brothers, Lieut. João José Soares Neiva and Col. Tude Neiva, pursued military careers, gained promotions to general by 1900, and remained in national politics until their deaths in 1907 and 1908. A third brother, Francisco José Soares Neiva, returned from the front a paraplegic, but made his career in the civil service, first in the Neivas' home município of Areia and then in Parahyba.

It was Lieut. João José Soares Neiva who became the third influential figure in Epitácio's early political network. He had already joined the Silva Pessoas' extended family as Epitácio's uncle by marriage, his *tio afim*, marrying Emília Pereira de Lucena, the younger sister of Epitácio's mother and Baron Lucena. Had Epitácio's father lived, Lieut. João Soares Neiva would have remained the elder Pessoa's co–brother-in-law, by virtue of their marriage to two Lucena sisters. As Baron Lucena's brother-in-law, João Soares Neiva enjoyed strong ties to Brazil's civilian politicians as well as to its military directorate. Thanks to these political connections, he was promoted to marshal on his deathbed.[73]

It was ironic that Epitácio, who would later be remembered as the Old Republic's only president to appoint an all-civilian cabinet, owed his entry into politics to this trio of career army officers—General Deodoro, General Almeida Barreto, and (soon to be promoted) Col. João Soares Neiva. The balance of his political influence, of course, derived from his uncle, Lucena. Firmly connected to the network of conspirators who assumed control of the Brazilian government after they forced the emperor to abdicate, Epitácio enjoyed an insider's view of the monarchy's final two weeks. He accompanied Lucena and his brother José Pessoa to several meetings in Deodoro's house, including the final one that occurred on the eve of the Republic's proclamation. At its conclusion, Deodoro was persuaded by both military and civilian conspirators to act immediately to remove the government.[74]

When Deodoro assumed de facto leadership of the new government, on November 15, 1889, his assignment of political posts clearly benefited the family-based network to which Epitácio belonged. Lucena was named Deodoro's minister of the interior. He in turn insured that his nephew, Lieut. José Pessoa, became Deodoro's new aide-de-camp. Col. João Soares Neiva wanted the Pa-

[73] Ibid., p. 54; Mariz, *Apanhados historicos*, pp. 257–58.

[74] L. Pessôa, *Epitacio Pessôa*, 1:48 and 53.

12. Sen. Venâncio Neiva, on his seventy-fifth birthday in 1924. His marriage to his cousin, Joana Batista Neiva de Figueirêdo (seated) and his sister Deolinda's marriage to Joana's brother Horácio Honório de Figueirêdo linked the men first as bicunhados and later as compadres, according to family ties that cut across partisan affiliations. (Courtesy of the Acervo Humberto Nóbrega)

raíba governorship for yet another of his brothers, Venâncio Augusto de Magalhães Neiva. Venâncio had remained in Paraíba and studied at the Recife Law School while his brothers joined the army. It was, however, General Almeida Barreto who secured the governorship for him. As military commander of Paraíba immediately following the coup d'état, he blocked a rival candidate put forward by Paraíba's Sen. Aristides Liebnitz da Silveira Lobo, who, as a prestigious Old Republican of the 1870s, was named to Deodoro's cabinet. Aristides belonged to the politically influential Miranda Henriques, leaders of the Liberal Party in his home município of Areia. One of Paraíba's two Republicans in national politics before 1889, as Deodoro's minister of justice, he backed Albino Meira, his former Senate colleague and Areiense kinsman for governor. Vanâncio nevertheless received the gubernatorial appointment, suggesting the priority that Deodoro accorded his own political network, particularly Lucena and João Soares Neiva. Finally, Deodoro determined, in consultation with Lucena, that Venâncio's cabinet secretary would be the Baron's newly arrived nephew, Epitácio Pessoa. The young bacharel's impressive command of constitutional law, his membership in the Conservative Party, and his family credentials highly recommended him for the post.[75]

Under such extremely promising circumstances did Epitácio begin his political career in Paraíba. Taking ship immediately for Recife and his new responsibilities in Paraíba as Venâncio's cabinet secretary, Epitácio left Rio de Janeiro only six weeks after his arrival. The name and the reputation of the man under whom he would work from December 1889 until the fall of Deodoro's government in November 1891, Venâncio Neiva, was to be joined with Epitácio's throughout the Old Republic in references to Paraíba's "Neiva–Lucena–Pessoa" oligarchy. Forty years of age in 1889, Venâncio had been serving as an imperial judge in a remote judicial district of Paraíba's backlands, where he established residence in Catolé do Rocha. He had received his appointment as a result of his relationship with Paraíba's last provincial governor, Silvino Elvídio Carneiro da Cunha, who headed the Conservative Party to which Venâncio belonged. Ennobled in 1889 as Baron of Abiaí, the governor was Paraíba's largest landowner and the last representative of the coastal sugar planters to hold that office. His entrepreneurial brother, Anísio Salatiel Carneiro da Cunha, who assisted Abiaí in directing the party, was Venâncio's compadre and friend.[76]

Venâncio illustrated the advantages that incorporation into an influential politician's network could offer a graduate of the Recife Law School when his own social background was nondescript. His brothers experienced similar mobility in the more rapidly advancing context of the career military. The Neivas were descended

[75] Information on the identity of individuals who influenced these appointments was taken from ibid., p. 54; I. Joffily, *Notas*, p. 49; and Mariz, *Apanhados historicos*, p. 189. For a different view, see H. de Almeida, *Brejo de Areia*, p. 70. After Lucena was forced to resign from the cabinet, Epitácio defended him against critics in the first session of the Congress.

[76] Author's prosopographical file. Titles of nobility no longer were granted after November 15, 1889; however, when the author was introduced to the daughter of the Baron of Abiaí in 1970, João Pessoenses still addressed her as "the Baroness."

from a family of modest Portuguese immigrants who had settled in Areia around the turn of the eighteenth century. Three generations of their descendants were career army officers or civil servants, for they owned no substantial assets in either land or commerce. Venâncio's father, a civil servant, had held office briefly as provincial deputy, but the Neivas exemplified talented outsiders who forged advantageous connections with more established families. Venâncio, for example, had managed to marry very well, by creating a bicunhado relationship with the most important imperial district judge in Paraíba, Honório Horácio de Figueirêdo. Venâncio's sister Deolinda Neiva had married Honório Horácio and Honório Horácio's sister Joana de Figueirêdo became Venâncio's wife. Judge Honório Horácio's district was the Capital, although he too was a native of Areia, where elite families maintained a closed matrimonial pool. The Figueirêdos, like the Neivas, included a number of career military officers among their members, but as leaders of Areia's Liberal Party they had not shared the Neivas' partisan loyalty.[77]

The matrimonial tie between Venâncio and Honório Horácio was slightly unusual because bicunhados almost always held the same partisan affiliation. (See Fig. B.1.) In this case, however, intermarriage between Neivas and Figureirêdos had already occurred in the preceding generation, for Venâncio and Honório Horácio were first cousins. So probably the existence of such a kinship bond took precedence over party connections, which may have diverged only following the 1848 Praieira Revolt. And since Honório Horácio had nine siblings, his matrimonial alliance with a member of a Conservative family no doubt represented a strategy of outmarriage: marrying a sister to the opposition as "social insurance" for the day when the ins became the outs, or vice versa.[78] In his case, the arrangement later functioned to protect his family's interests, for the Liberals were thrown out of power in Areia with Deodoro's appointment of Honório's bicunhado Venâncio as governor. But the overriding factor in establishing their matrimonial relationship on divergent party lines appeared to be professional. Both Venâncio and Honório Horácio were members of Brazil's career judiciary, which meant that they were expected to

[77] Genealogical connections of the Neivas and Figueirêdos were taken from Azevêdo Bastos, *Roteiro Azevêdo*, pp. 540–41. Areia historian Horácio de Almeida indicated that Venâncio Neiva and Joana de Figueirêdo were cousins. Oral communication with the author, August 1978.

[78] Bastos, *Roteiro Azevêdo*, pp. 540–41.

maintain good relations with both major parties. As bicunhados they therefore became firmly linked to both partisan camps and could draw directly on family connections in dealing with members of the opposition.

The marriages of Honório Horácio de Figueirêdo's children, who assumed the family name of Neiva de Figueirêdo, reinforced the political network that Venâncio shared with his brother's wife's nephew Epitácio for the first two decades of the Old Republic. (See Fig. B.1.) One of Honório's daughters married Valfredo Guedes Pereira, who became an Epitacista deputy in 1916, when, like the Leites, he converted after the defeat of the Old Liberals under Monsig. Valfredo Leal. Another daughter married Assemblyman Isidro Leite (Ferreira de Araújo), son of Gov. José Peregrino de Araújo (1900–1904) and the grandson of the Liberal Party's cofounder, Col. João Leite Ferreira. (See Fig. B.4.) Isidro also accompanied his Leite relatives into Epitácio's camp as allies after 1915.

The most important Neiva de Figueirêdo, however, was Venâncio's wife's brother, Antônio Batista Neiva de Figueirêdo, who held a seat in the Assembly from 1904 to 1930.[79] In spite of his family's, particularly his brother Honório Horácio's, association with the Old Liberals, Neiva de Figueirêdo joined Venâncio's faction and was the only veteran assemblyman to be a professional career military officer. For this reason, it is worth noting that generally military officers tended to consider themselves a separate "stream" in oligarchical politics, one distinguishable from the currents of both Old Liberals and Old Conservatives with which their families identified. This circumstance may explain Neiva de Figueirêdo's willingness to dissociate himself from his family's partisan affiliation. In addition he also enjoyed, together with several other of his male relatives, ties to Marshal Deodoro, after whom one of his brothers was named.[80] Thus, for a complex set of reasons, Venâncio's cross-cutting matrimonial ties with the Figueirêdos influenced a number of former Liberals from that family to gravitate toward his faction and, eventually, to become allies for Epitacismo.

Epitácio's family-based network illustrated the politics of parentela as it operated on the eve of the Republic in a number of key respects. His political panelinha overlapped several powerful fam-

[79] Ibid. Gen. Antônio Batista Neiva de Figueirêdo (1864–1952) obtained a higher degree in engineering after graduation from the national military academy. See Chapter VI on his proposed candidacy for governor during the 1912 crisis.

[80] Ibid.

ily-based groups in Paraíba beyond his family of orientation (the Silva Pessoas and Barbosa de Lucenas). Marriages with outsiders were key links, such as the ties with Col. João Soares Neiva and Cândido Clementino Cavalcanti de Albuquerque, Epitácio's sister Maria's husband (as noted in Chapter III). Co–brothers-in-law figured even more prominently among the panelinha relationships in his political network at the state and local level. Venâncio's bicunhado relationship is one example; others are found among the Tavares de Melo Cavalcanti of Alagoa Nova, the Guedes Pereiras of Bananeiras, and the Agripino Maias of Catolé do Rocha, all of whom sent Epitacista deputies to the Assembly or Congress. Local politicians in these family-based groups directly depended on co–brother-in-law relationships for solidifying their electoral support and establishing networks across município, zonal, and sometimes state lines.[81]

One striking aspect of Epitácio's political panelinha was its mature development within five years of his graduation from law school. Invariably, politicians formed close working relationships with talented and loyal nonkin during the period of career formation as students or through early professional associations while they were relatively young. Although Epitácio continued to add members throughout his political life, by 1891, he had forged a number of enduring relationships valuable for his later politicking in Paraíba. They were usually still in place in the 1920s, unless death had ended them. The members of this panelinha are identified in the next two chapters. Significantly, their political positions would later reflect spatial linkages vital to Epitácio's state party machine, which encompassed all five of Paraíba's geoeconomic zones.

Where blood or marriage could not offer guarantees of trust and reliability for politics, key friendships based on shared family alignments in partisan politics furnished an alternative. In Epitácio's case, he drew on political friendships with individuals whose families had been affiliated with the Conservative Party. The

[81] The following bicunhado relationships were significant in this respect: 1) those created by the eight siblings in Areia's Cabral de Vasconcelos family with their spouses who were siblings in the Guedes Pereira family in Bananeiras; 2) those created by the marriages of Manuel Tavares Cavalcanti and his brother João Tavares de Melo Cavalcanti (the Younger) to two sisters from the Araújo Oliveira family in Alagoa Nova; 3) those created by the marriages of two of Gov. João Suassuna's sisters to two sons of State Deputy Antônio Gomes in Catolé do Rocha. Author's prosopographical file.

friendships had been formed either in law school, in the Constituent Assembly of 1890–1891, or in the months of political persecution by Alvaristas under Marshal Floriano Peixoto's national government in 1892–1893. Alternatively, men bonded as compadres—as Deodoro and Lucena did. Increasingly, *amizade*—friendship—gained ground as a legitimate bond in political association. As the discussion of the 1915 election in Part Three will point out, the political lexicon of oligarchy in Paraíba included a very rich and refined set of categories ranging from "friends" to "enemies" and ranked according to their willingness to deliver the vote.

Epitácio's panelinha also demonstrated that vertical connections between politicians within their family-based groups and networks continued to be important. In Paraíba the persistence of Conservative and Liberal partisan alignments from the days of imperial politics revealed how vigorously families perpetuated intergenerationally the vertical axes of party organization. By the same token, antagonistic family alignments in oligarchical politics after 1889 usually originated in the Empire. Except at the pinnacle of the state oligarchy's leadership, most of the ruling families in the Old Republic had dominated their municípios during the 1880s. Of course, there were important newcomers after 1900, most of whom appeared in Epitácio's political camp. Vertical bonds also survived most literally among those families that still preferred to rely heavily on consanguineous marriage. In those situations, the politics of parentela operated along stricter family lines and brothers-in-law tended to be double cousins or uncles and nephews. However, except where such families owned substantial amounts of land and firmly exercised local political domination—in only a few municípios—the sphere of family politicking became limited in its "reach" to the state or national levels.

The Old Republic therefore witnessed no sharp break with parentela politics in Paraíba, only a gradual shift that remained imperceptible until the twenties. "Política de família," the foundation for coronelismo in the state, flourished, even marking as its golden years the four decades of the era of the oligarchies. Family-based power endured because socioeconomic change was insufficient for a realignment of group affiliations according to new interests. But Brazilian kinship organization provided an equally significant explanation for the continuity in the group basis of political organization. Its characteristics enabled the family-based group to shift to more horizontal lines of recruitment, mobilization, and economic specialization, while maintaining the deployment of resources that conserved the family's resources as a quasi-corporate entity. The absence of rigid membership criteria, coupled with the shallow tracing of descent, helped perpetuate elite family power over the long run. A wide latitude in matrimonial patterns permitted a range of options that offset many of the devisive propensities in the system of cognitive or bilateral descent and offered maximum opportunity to create advantageous political alliances. Declining patriarchal authority could be countered by greater coordination among male siblings over a wider political territory in an expanding economy. Bonds between "kin and affines" could meet the extended family unit's new priorities. The destructive potential of greater economic specialization within the family group was forestalled by the way kinship organization offered opportunity to coordinate individual economic activities that remained mutually dependent on the agrarian export economy.

As a consequence, the era of the Old Republic in Paraíba witnessed the perpetuation of a system of politics fundamentally organized around family-based groups and their far-flung political networks. The demise of a historical reliance on the blood kindred, with its vertical bonds of solidarity, its patriarchal authority, and its preference for endogamous marriage signaled no immediate deline in family-based power in Paraíba. On the contrary, for ruling families creatively rearranged their organizational features, relying more heavily on co–brothers-in-law and political friends for securing control. They survived both the decline of Brazil's patriarchal order and the fall of the Empire for yet another generation. Encouraged by the Old Republic's constitutional reorganization, the politics of parentela thrived in a decentralized polity that sanctioned and even enhanced the historical role the elite family had played over the centuries.

PART THREE

Oligarchical Politics

· V ·

The Formative Decade: The Republican Nineties

Even when the Republic is firmly established everywhere, Paraíba will be on the side of the throne.

—The Baron of Abiaí to the Count d'Eu, Parahyba, June 20, 1889

For our friends, justice; for our enemies, apply the law.

—Political adage of the Old Republic

ON NOVEMBER 15, 1889, the Second Empire that had been ruled by Dom Pedro II since 1840 collapsed in the face of a republican *coup d'état*. The leaders of the coup were prominent civilian politicians, especially those associated with the Republican Party of São Paulo, and high-ranking military officers with their more positivistically inclined subordinates. The government they imposed, subsequently known as the First or the Old Republic, would endure until 1930. The decade of the nineties witnessed the oscillation of national political power between the civilian and military factions that had created the Republic. The initial civilian–military provisional government headed by Marshal Deodoro da Fonseca became an indirectly elected constitutional administration under President Deodoro. In November 1891, however, Deodoro resigned and Vice-President Floriano Peixoto succeeded him under circumstances that approached a *coup d'état*.

Floriano's administration, which endured until November 1894, represented the zenith of the military's influence in the politics of the Old Republic. Until its last few months, it imposed a virtual dictatorship on the nation.[1] The military failed to unite as a ruling elite, however, and, in 1894, Brazil was restored to civilian rule with the election of a Paulista president, Prudente [José] de Morais e Barros (1894–1898). Civilian politicians battled the military throughout Prudente's term to establish unequivocal control

[1] Floriano used republicanism to appeal to a popular base, urging vigilant defense against monarchical reaction that "works quietly but constantly and relentlessly." Bello, *History Brazil*, p. 138.

of the national government, and, by the close of his administration in 1898, an uninterrupted period of civilian, constitutional government had opened. Partisan fragmentation among the civilian leadership still prevented a strong central government, however. The Empire's two national political parties were replaced by state-based oligarchies that failed to produce partisan organizations capable of the integrating function in national politics that the former Conservative and Liberal Parties had performed. Instead, under two more Paulista presidents—Manuel Ferraz de Campos Sales (1898–1902) and Francisco de Paula Rodrigues Alves (1902–1906)—the oligarchies were institutionalized under an extraconstitutional arrangement known as "the politics of the governors."

The generation that launched the Old Republic was a product of the late Empire. Despite their republican ideology, a remarkable elite continuity determined that the political outlook of Brazil's national politicians would reflect their formation in the Empire. As members of "the Conservative classes," they remained highly elitist and dependent on the hierarchical patterns of social and political organization inherited from the preceding slavocratic society. In Paraíba, where the news of the Republic's proclamation was received with considerable disbelief, the nineties reflected continuity with the late Empire even more strongly than at the national level.[2] Both the Conservative and the Liberal Parties had been constituted along fairly consistent family lines of affiliation for several generations. On the eve of the Republic, a Republican Party had not existed, "only those dispersed Republicans existing in the Conservative and Liberal Parties."[3] The family blocs who had controlled provincial government since the 1830s had taken the labels of the national parties, without subscribing to their economic or ideological outlook. Thus, as in a majority of Brazil's states, in Paraíba family alignments determined partisan alignments, for "the Azevêdo e Cunhas were always Conservatives and the Dantas always Liberals."[4]

Even party labels did not provide clear—if arbitrary—guides to

[2] Mariz, *Apanhados historicos*, pp. 290–91.

[3] Ibid., p. 289.

[4] Azevêdo Bastos, *Roteiro Azevêdo*, p. 21. Table D.1 lists the names of Paraíba's ruling families during the Empire and indicates their party affiliations. Tables D.2 and D.3 demonstrate the continuity of partisan alliances over the long run. See José Murillo de Carvalho, "A composição social dos partidos políticos imperiais," *Cadernos de Departamento de Ciência Política* [Universidade Federal de Minas Gerais, Faculdade de Filosofia e Ciências Humanas, Belo Horizonte] 2 (Dec. 1974): 1–34.

Paraíba's political alignments along family lines. Family affiliations were more complex because each party tolerated one dominant and at least one dissident "current" or "stream." This fragmented circumstance of political life derived from national Conservative and Liberal alignments during the War with Paraguay in the 1860s. Voting patterns in the Senate and House of Deputies had shifted to sanction the dissident stream of one party voting with the dominant stream of the other. In Paraíba, cross-voting was even more pronounced and overladen with local hostilities than at the national level. The factional alignments of the 1880s, consequently, could still be perceived in the third decade of the Old Republic. Their significance persisted because each of the Empire's four partisan streams possessed a personalistic loyalty to a factional leader as well as a definite zonal base of geoeconomic and political interest. The dissident Conservatives of the 1880s, for instance, followed Antônio Trinidade Antunes da Meira Henriques and were concentrated in the caatinga-agreste. As "Meiristas," they voted with the Liberal Party's dominant stream based in the two backlands zones and loyal to Paula Primo (Francisco de Paula e Silva Primo). The label "Meirista"—or "Felizardista"after Felizardo Leite succeeded Paula Primo—mattered more than "Conservative" or "Liberal." Personal and family loyalty, not partisan fealty, was the hallmark of the political system.

Except for the religious question, ideology did not account for significant conflict in Paraíba's politics. The Republic's adoption of compulsory civil marriage divided politicians and the public over the 1891 Constitution's separation of church and state. This issue briefly explained the appeal of a monarchist party in the early 1890s, but not subsequent partisan divisions, for individuals within the same faction more frequently disagreed over the church–state question.[5] During the Empire, partisan orientation had reflected a geoeconomic emphasis according to coast and backlands that persisted less significantly in the Republic. The Conservatives were stronger in the coastal sugar zone, while the

[5] The church–state issue centered on the strong resistance to the introduction of civil marriage, because those who opposed it lost legal protection for their patrimony if they married only in the Church. As late as 1928–1929, Dom Adauto da Câmara Meira Henriques, whose tenure as archbishop of Paraíba had begun in 1894, still successfully blocked the adoption of a revised state constitution that conformed to the federal constitution's secular state. He objected to the absence of religion and God in the school curriculum: "Many say to us, 'The Government does not want to know God, so why should we?' " Dom Adauto to Epitácio (Capital), 13 Apr. 1929, AEP/9/43.

Liberals' strongest support lay in the two backlands zones and the brejo. The fact that the Conservatives represented the party of the sugar planters also had made them the party of infrastructure, a distinction carrying some significance in the early Republic. The wealthiest senhores de engenho had been the first to sponsor the construction of the railroad and to call—unsuccessfully—for Cabedêlo's development as a port. However, at the município level, the members of each party pursued economic interests that often were identical.

The partisan affiliations of Paraíba's politicians reflected not ideological divisions but a widely shared consensus about how the political system should function and the basic ends toward which political activity should be directed. The close similarity of social backgrounds among the oligarchy's members explained this consensus. The principal factor was education, for most politicians had studied first at the Capital's elite secondary school—the Parahyba Lyceum (Liceu Paraibano)—and then at the Recife Law Faculty.[6] A shared consciousness as members of "the Conservative classes" also reinforced the homogeneity in outlook about political values, goals, and behavior. The central horizontal division between mass and elite—between *"o povo"* (the people) and *"os poderosos"* (the powerful)—so detectable in political oratory lay at the heart of all social distinctions. Thus, a firm political consensus drew directly on the goal of maintaining the social order.

Paraíba's Oligarchical Politics

For both the Neiva–Pessoa and the Machado–Leal oligarchies, the nineties and even the decade that followed demonstrated strong continuity with the closing decade of the Empire, rather than ushering in a new era of politics. After 1889, an ideological emphasis on the values of republicanism was rhetorically detectable—in many official pronouncements, in the verbal clashes between prominent members of the former imperial political elite and their younger successors, and in frequent symbolic attempts to introduce republican laws or impose republican political institutions.

[6] Of the 160 identifiable university graduates (of a total of 203 state politicians), 91—57 per cent—held degrees from the Recife Law Faculty. Eighty-two per cent of Paraíba's senators, 66 per cent of the federal deputies, 75 per cent of the governors, and 62 per cent of the assemblymen were Recife Law Faculty graduates. Lewin, "Politics and *Parentela*," table 5.15 (p. 266).

The political milieu, nevertheless, remained basically conservative, fiercely Roman Catholic, and staunchly hierarchical and familial in its personal relationships. Nor did it reform its historical dependence on electoral fraud, violent intimidation, and private family warfare as the principal means for achieving and maintaining political hegemony. Especially before a "generation of 1910" replaced the senior "generation of the mature Empire"—those who had entered politics in the 1850s and 1860s—as the primary partners of Epitácio's intermediate "generation of the eighties," oligarchical politics in Paraíba closely resembled the Empire's factions and political consensus.[7]

The contrasts in oligarchical style and organization among Paraíba's competing factional coalitions throughout the first two decades of the Old Republic should not obscure the fundamental identity of their political goals. Depending on whether they were of the dominant coalition or its opposition, oligarchical politicians strove either to maintain an existing statewide monopoly over officeholding or to capture control of the electoral machine that would confer such a monopoly. The political and economic patronage to be derived from domination of officeholding and the strategic denial of appointive positions to the rival coalition were the primary goals of political activity. These objectives dictated politicians' continued reliance on their informal, family-based groups. The group's allegiance to a personalistically defined factional leader was the most reasonable means for achieving and maintaining a winning electoral majority.[8]

[7] For this study, politicians were grouped according to four generational divisions correlating with their entry into politics: generation of the mature Empire (1855–1880), generation of the 1880s (1876–1900), generation of 1910 (1896–1920), and generation of the late Republic (1916–). The largest proportion of federal politicians who attended Recife Law School did so in the eighties. (See table VII.1.)

[8] Part Three's discussion of factions draws on Ralph W. Nicholas's "sociological definition." He offers five characteristics of factional groupings: 1) they emerge from conflict situations; 2) they organize conflict around the use of public power; 3) they lack permanence, i.e., they are not corporate; 4) they recruit deliberately and by virtue of the personalistic appeal to a leader; 5) they recruit according to diverse criteria. "Factions: A Comparative Analysis," in *Political Systems and the Distribution of Power*, ed. Michael Banton (London: Tavistock Publications, Ltd., 1968), pp. 27–29. Nicholas stresses Raymond Firth's view that factions "are usually structurally diverse—they may rest upon kin ties, patron–client relations, religious or politico-economic ties or any combination of these; they are mobilized and made effective through an authority structure of leader and henchman whose roles are broadly defined and whose rewards in many cases depend upon the leader's discretion" ("Introduction to Factions in Indian and Overseas Societies," *British Journal of Sociology* 8 [1957]:292, cited in ibid., p. 29).

A great deal of political activity, consequently, was directed toward creating and consolidating electoral majorities that reflected alliances across Paraíba's five geoeconomic divisions. In addition to securing a successful local base, the oligarchical leadership at the state level had to insure that its connections at the federal level remained politically dependable. Since the state governor might need federal intervention from the executive branch to maintain his ruling coalition in power—in the event of an armed threat to its hegemony—a good relationship with the president of Brazil became indispensable. These tactical considerations consumed enormous quantities of time and political energy, as the private correspondence of the local bosses and state and federal politicians testified.[9] And a constant jockeying for power characterized political behavior at all levels of government.

In the first decade of the Old Republic, when national consolidation was extremely fragile, and material resources in Paraíba and from the federal government were nearly nonexistent, the key issue in Paraíba politics was who would rule. Consequently, intraelite competition dominated the political stage when the drama of oligarchical politics was enacted publicly, as daily newspaper accounts demonstrated. The same issue pervaded political communications for private eyes or ears, as Epitácio's political lieutenants in Paraíba verified in their regularly dispatched factional intelligence to Rio de Janeiro. Astute analysis of political gossip, for instance, became a sophisticated art, strategically indispensable for gaining and maintaining a political position. Dramatic public postures, ranging from real or contrived petty affronts to public outrage over an attempted assassination, contained important symbolic meaning readily comprehensible to every oligarchical politician.

Spurred to compete by the issue of who would lead the oligarchy, the factional contenders were organized essentially around strong, family-based groups or segments, loyal to a personal leader. These factions informally defined the major political actors in the system, representing the building blocks of an oligarchical coali-

[9] In correspondence, Paraíba's politicians reflected a preoccupation with winning the next election and "personal intrigues." The time consumed in those activities, however, is significant for a factional system of politics, as Daniel R. Gross concluded from his anthropological study of a small town in the State of Bahia in the 1960s: "Since factions are not ideologically oriented and tend to crosscut socioeconomic strata, they reduce the possibility of class-based struggle by dissipating energy in petty strife serving private interests." "Factionalism and Local Level Politics in Rural Brazil," *Journal of Anthropological Research* 29, 2 (1973):141.

tion regularly in flux between 1892 and 1912. The Pessoas' competition with the Machado–Leal oligarchy during the formative period reflected systemic continuity with the preceding Empire and left a very lively political legacy of personalistic rivalries after 1912. In fact, the personal rivalries and grievances Paraíba's major extended family groups experienced in that formative period survived to collide eventually with national currents of change that culminated in the so-called Revolution of 1930.

The Turbulent Nineties

The Neiva–Lucena Oligarchy, 1889–1891

The first oligarchy to come in power in republican Paraíba, the one directed by Venâncio Augusto de Magalhães Neiva, was short-lived, lasting barely two years. Its significance cannot be underestimated, however, for it provided the basic support for bringing the Pessoas to power, initiating their political patriarch, Epitácio, into his oligarchical career in Paraíba politics. Venâncio Neiva's installation as governor in December 1889 also illustrated the integration of Paraíba's family-based oligarchy at both national and local levels. Finally, the brief Neiva–Lucena oligarchical interregnum illustrated the pattern of factional competition and persecution in the republican nineties that would mark key political alignments in Paraíba throughout the Old Republic.

Paraíba's first republican governor came to power thanks to the influence that his military brothers, Cols. João José and Tude José Soares Neiva, exercised nationally, through Gen. Almeida Barreto and the Baron of Lucena. He was also selected because he had belonged to the former Conservative Party's dominant wing in Paraíba's provincial politics.[10] However, unlike that party's former head, the Baron of Abiaí, Venâncio conspicuously lacked a political base centered in the sugar coast and the brejo; he had been an

[10] Although Venâncio had been a "Conservative-Silvinista"—a member of that party's dominant Silvinista stream loyal to the Baron of Abiaí—his political mentor had been the baron's brother, Anísio Salatiel Carneiro da Cunha. Abiaí's influence enabled Venâncio to climb in the imperial judiciary: first, as public prosecutor in Teixeira in the 1870s, then as an assistant judge in São Paulo state during the early 1880s, and finally as an imperial judge in a Paraíba backlands judicial district (Pombal, Catolé do Rocha, and Brejo do Cruz), where he was serving when he became governor of Paraíba. Apolônio Nóbrega, *História republicana da Paraíba* (João Pessoa: Imprensa Oficial, 1950), p. 58.

imperial judge in the backlands. Initially, Venâncio's situation as governor was complicated by his worsening position with the former Conservative Party's prestigious leader, the province's ex-governor. His conflict with Abiaí came to a head during the first six months of 1890, as preparations got under way for the election of Brazil's Constituent Congress. Venâncio's candidates for Paraíba's five seats in the House of Deputies and three in the Senate were noteworthy because they neither included former officeholders from the Empire nor represented the baron's political base in his native sugar coast.

Abiaí presented a rival slate that drew on former Conservative Party politicians as well as members of the former dissident wing of the Liberal Party who had voted with the dominant wing of the Conservatives in the eighties. As Paraíba's ranking imperial politician, the baron firmly declared himself still a monarchist. He fervently proclaimed his Catholic principles, refusing to accommodate to the new Republic especially because of its separation of church and state. With Irineu Joffily, Campina Grande's leading journalist and a respected imperial judge who had belonged to the Liberal Party, Abiaí founded a short-lived Catholic Party for the purpose of winning the September 1890 election. This partisan challenge was no more than a die-hard effort by a defunct personalistic faction largely representing the moribund sugar coast. Adroitly overcome by Venâncio's superior political networking and dramatic electoral eve appeal for votes, Paraíba's last baron of the Empire was literally forced to withdraw into exile, embarking for Rio de Janeiro and ending any possibility of a monarchist resurgence.[11]

Venâncio's choices for Paraíba's five federal deputy seats underscored his strong political connections to both the Paraíba backlands zones and the national military, although he himself was a native of Areia. Venâncio's older brother, Col. João José Soares Neiva, was responsible for the selection of the delegation's lone military deputy, João da Silva Retumba. Both João Neiva and Retumba had been comrades-in-arms with Gen. Almeida Barreto on the fifteenth of November when the general, commanding the loy-

[11] Abiaí's death in 1892 removed the strongest champion of antirepublicanism in Paraíba. Irineu Joffily, the other important opponent of the Republic, died in 1902, but illness removed him by 1895. Diogo Velho Cavalcanti de Albuquerque (Viscount of Calvalcanti), Paraíba's other major imperial politician, withdrew from state politics in the early nineties and became a senator in Rio Grande do Norte. Author's prosopographical file.

alist forces, had placed his men in support of the *coup d'etat*.[12] The remaining four seats in the delegation went to: a dissident Liberal lawyer, Antônio Joaquim do Couto Cartaxo, who owned a cotton ginnery in his native Cajazeiras in the far backlands; João Batista de Sá Andrade, a young Republican medical doctor from Sousa's ruling Sá family whose father had been a distinguished provincial deputy; Areia's famous painter, Pedro Américo de (Figueirêdo) Almeda, Venâncio's very distant kinsman (partly an honorific nomination and partly a nativistic token of recognition to the former Liberals in Areia); and Venâncio's young and talented secretary of government, Epitácio Pessoa, nephew of his brother's wife and a native of the backlands.[13] Conspicuously absent from this slate were candidates from the former imperial elite in Paraíba.

Venâncio's candidates for the more prestigious Senate suggested why his name would be so associated with "oligarchy" during the Old Republic. Like Abiaí, he designated his own brother for one of the three seats: Col. João José Soares Neiva was named for a six-year term. The senior position as head of the Paraíba federal delegation, conferring a nine-year term, went to Gen. Almeida Barreto, João Neiva's career mentor and Paraíba's ranking general in the new Republic. The junior (three-year) seat went to Firmino Gomes da Silveira, a member of a prestigious family from the cariri-sertão zone who had served contemporaneously with Venâncio as an imperial judge in the backlands of Paraíba.[14] Lacking ties to the sugar coast, and instead representing family connections with the interior of the state, Venâncio's senatorial slate indirectly symbolized the new governor's political dependence on the military, especially the incumbent camarilla loyal to Almeida Barreto.

Venâncio's candidates easily defeated their opposition in the election of September 1890, with the twenty-six-year-old Epitácio

[12] Almeida Barreto, commander at Army General Headquarters on November 16, 1889, insured a republican victory when he denied the emperor military support. Mariz, *Apanhados historicos*, p. 294; Belo, *History Brazil*, p. 99.

[13] Almeida Barreto claimed personal credit for placing only Pedro Américo's name on Paraíba's congressional slate, but João Batista de Sá Andrade came from his home município of Sousa. Almeida Barreto to Epitácio (Rio de Janeiro), 9 Aug. 1890, AEP/10/1.

[14] As Paraíba's military commander in 1890, Almeida Barreto delivered backlands votes because he toured the interior with his troops and visited his native Sousa after an absence of forty years. E. de Almeida, *História Campina*, p. 337. Firmino Gomes da Silveira had also been an imperial judge in Almeida Barreto's home town of Sousa, where the general's family apparently was related to the ruling Conservatives, the Gomes de Sá. Author's prosopographical file.

Pessoa drawing the largest number of votes.[15] It was extremely significant that the slate carried the two backlands zones, except for the município of Teixeira. Teixeira was the stronghold of the powerful Dantas family, who, with Leite allies, had led the Liberal Party in the Assembly in the 1880s.[16] On the eve of the election, Venâncio masterfully engineered a leadership confrontation with the Baron of Abiaí that sharply defined his own following. He "broke" with the baron in a semi-ritualized manner that was characteristic of factional conflict throughout the Old Republic. Even though their differences were directly political, an incident of personal insult supplied a pretext for the break. An opportune context was provided by a gala dinner dance that had assembled the Capital's society to celebrate Venâncio's slate of candidates. Venâncio had an antagonistic exchange of words with the baron that led Abiaí to stalk out of the assemblage of guests in indignation.[17] Venâncio then communicated to the assembled guests, who included the Capital's former Conservative Party elite, that in the future he would have nothing to do with the exceedingly resentful baron. His announcement forced those still undecided in their factional allegiance to choose sides once and for all. Most of the Old Conservatives recognized that Abiaí's political values had become anachronistic and that Venâncio was extremely well connected in national politics; therefore, the incident of personal affront solidified the governor's support and relieved him of any future obligation to accept Abiaí in his coalition following the election. A redefinition of political allegiance could be more readily transacted on personalistic than on ideological grounds.

Although Venâncio's administration completed the major task of drafting a state constitution in Paraíba's Constituent Assembly, the governor's central attention was directed toward consolidating his political machine. Throughout his remaining year in office, he was confronted with local opposition. In Areia, armed rebellion broke out because he replaced the Empire's Liberal Party elite

[15] Mariz reported that Epitácio received 9,975 votes, while the favorite candidate of the opposition earned only 2,730. *Apanhados historicos*, p. 296.

[16] The antagonism between the Dantas of Teixeira and Epitácio that emerged in 1911–1912 may have originated in an earlier confrontation between them and Venâncio, who served as a public prosecutor in Teixeira in the late 1870s, or even with Baron Lucena who also had served in that capacity in the 1860s. A. Nóbrega, *História republicana*, p. 58.

[17] The precise content of the hostile exchange between Venâncio and the baron was never revealed in the written sources. Mariz, *Apanhados historicos*, pp. 292–93.

with their former Conservative Party opponents.[18] If Emperor Dom Pedro II had remained in power, Paraíba's provincial and local government would have become Liberal, since that party had carried the elections only weeks prior to the fall of the monarchy. Families such as the Dantas of Teixeira were frustrated by their loss of political "prestige" locally, a circumstance indirectly due to the ascendance of Marshal Deodoro in the national executive. Consequently, Manuel Dantas Correia de Góis, the powerful patriarchal head of the Dantas family in Teixeira and an ex-governor of Paraíba, could no longer claim his elected position as president of Paraíba's unicameral Assembly.[19]

Where partisan strife ran strongest, rival family-based groups in a number of municípios resorted to open warfare to contest local leadership. The Old Liberals usually expected, in vain, that they might be designated by Venâncio for at least some local offices. However, the most serious threat occurred in Venâncio's birthplace of Areia, the stronghold of Paraíba's ruling clique of provincial politicians during the Empire. In particular, it was a município known for its Liberal Party militants or republican-leaning activists. When Venâncio installed an Old Conservative as Areia's local boss and then placed the members of his own family-based network in an impressive number of its elective or appointive offices, he created a *casus belli*.[20] In the spring of 1890, he had to send the Paraíba State Police and a detachment of federal troops to put down the Old Liberal opposition in Areia. Although Venâncio overcame the resistance, he and his successors, Álvaro and Val-

[18] Opposition to Venâncio in Areia derived from the patronage gains his family members made there. State Chief of Police João Coelho Gonçalves Lisboa was dismissed by Venâncio after he opened an official inquiry into alleged crimes of fraud committed by Venâncio's father and other Neiva relatives as employees of the national postal service. Minister of Justice Campos Sales upheld his dismissal. Coelho Lisboa, *Oligarchias*, pp. 72-80.

[19] The Liberal winners of the November 1889 elections were disgruntled at having to return to the *status quo ante* after being out of office for most of the 1880s. In addition, the great drought of 1888–1890 had exacerbated local family warfare, since the imperial government's relief supplies had been distributed to the interior's population via Conservative politicians.

[20] Venâncio's "family oligarchy" in Areia and the Capital included his Arruda da Camara son-in-law, whom he named public prosecutor in the Capital, the latter's brother, named public prosecutor in Areia, and a second brother, named a captain in the state police. His father-in-law had received the contract to transport all mail shipped from the Capital's port, while his double brother-in-law Honório Horácio de Figueirêdo assumed Venâncio's old position as a federal district judge in Catolé do Rocha and Brejo do Cruz. (See Fig. B.1.) Coelho Lisbôa, *Oligarchias*, pp. 73–75.

fredo, would confront the imperial legacy of Areia's intraelite partisan conflict throughout their administrations. If only because of their intellectual or professional talent, as well as their professional ambition, Areia's numerous politicians never proved tractable for either oligarchy to rule.

When he designated his candidates for the Senate and the Assembly's thirty seats in 1890, Venâncio also determined the composition of Paraíba's own Constituent Assembly, because one of the Assembly's first tasks was to write a state constitution. He thereby created what became the loyal core of the Autonomist Party that he and Epitácio would found in 1892 as the opposition to Álvaro Machado. Essentially a legislature of Old Conservatives, with a number of prominent and powerful Old Liberals included either as a token opposition or because their families had voted with the Conservatives in the eighties, the first four-year session of the Paraíba State Assembly antagonistically overlapped Álvaro Machado's appointment as governor in 1892. Its Venancista majority experienced "persecution" once an Alvarista Assembly had been installed to replace it in 1894. What became significant about the first session's membership was Venâncio's political debt to it over the long run. The local political vendettas against Venancistas that followed Álvaro's elevation of former Liberals to political power in 1892 fell heaviest on a core of Old Conservative assemblymen. Usually the opposition bosses whose families had ruled their municípios during 1890–1891, they remained loyal to Venâncio throughout the nineties and provided the political base locally for "Venancismo's" comeback under Epitácio's leadership after 1900. Even in 1920, the survivors of the nineties were a privileged echelon of veterans in Epitácio's machine, politicians who had remained supporters of Venâncio after the Machado–Leal oligarchy had come to power and who had suffered considerably as a loyal opposition.[21]

Hardly in office long enough to establish his oligarchical machine on a firm electoral base, Venâncio Neiva found that his 1890

[21] The Old Conservative majority in the First Session of the Assembly (1891–1894) contained the late Empire's most important local bosses from that party and a smaller core of young Venancista politicians who later became Epitácio's key lieutenants in the Pessoa oligarchy: Antônio Massa (Espírito Santo and the Capital), Pedro da Cunha Pedrosa (Umbuseiro and the Capital), Cristiano Lauritzen (Campina Grande), Flávio Maroja (Pilar and the Capital), João Gualberto Gomes de Sá (Sousa), João Pereira de Castro Pinto (Mamanguape), and Francisco Alves de Lima Filho (Catolé do Rocha and the Capital). Pedro da Cunha Pedrosa, *Minhas próprias memórias*, Vol. 2: *Vida privada* (Rio de Janeiro: Tipografia *Jornal do Comércio*, 1973), p. 62.

electoral victory marked the apogee of his gubernatorial administration, not its effective inauguration. Paraíba's first republican governor did not survive in office long enough even to witness the state's federal delegation finish its first session in Congress, once the Constituent Congress drafted and passed Brazil's 1891 Constitution. Soon after Paraíba's federal delegation returned to Rio de Janeiro to complete the first session of Congress in mid-1891, Vice-President Marshal Floriano Peixoto began his efforts to force the President Deodoro to resign from office. Floriano's silent *coup d'état* removed the chief executive in November 1891 and simultaneously replaced the state governors designated in 1889 with loyal appointees. Venâncio Neiva soon received a summary order to resign. Refusing to turn over the state administration to an interim military junta designated by Floriano and composed of native sons of the Old Liberal factions, Venâncio had to be forcibly removed by the federal officers. He always insisted that his administration had been overthrown by "four *capangas*," or thugs.[22] His oligarchy was replaced by one similarly founded on family-based groups, but this time politically centered in the brejo zone. Paraíba's Old Liberals, returned to power by the national executive, now formed a ruling clique drawn largely from the município of Areia. The Areienses would seek to keep their zone's interests paramount for the next twenty years.

The Machado–Leal Oligarchy, 1892–1902

The man Floriano Peixoto chose to succeed Venâncio Neiva as Paraíba's second governor, Álvaro Lopes Machado, was even less well known as a politician than his predecessor. Like Venâncio, he owed his appointment to his family-based network and its military connections in Rio de Janeiro. After removing Venâncio from power, Marshal Floriano had sought the advice of a former senator from Paraíba, Ábdon Felinto Milanez, concerning the designation of a governor. Ábdon, who had become friendly with Floriano when he visited Paraíba for three months in 1886, had suggested his own nephew—Álvaro Lopes Machado—for the post.[23] Álvaro was also chosen by Floriano, however, because he had pursued a

[22] Mariz, *Apanhados historicos*, p. 299.

[23] Celso Mariz, *Cidades e homens* (João Pessoa: *A União* Editôra, 1945), pp. 156–57 (n. 11). Prior to appointing Álvaro Machado governor of Paraíba, Marshal Floriano—who admired Epitácio's courage and political skill—twice offered the position to him. Epitácio firmly turned down the offer both times. L. Pessôa, *Epitacio Pessôa*, 1:99.

military career. In 1891 he was an instructor of engineering at the Military Academy and the Polytechnic School in Salvador, Bahia. Finally, since he came from a Liberal family in Areia, the only place in Paraíba that had sent Republican Party politicians to national office during the Empire, Álvaro could be expected to work well with Floriano's supporters in both Paraíba and the Congress.[24] Former Liberals were more likely to be sincere republicans in the 1890s than their Conservative counterparts, who frequently had endorsed the Republic on the purely pragmatic ground of political survival.

As the senior partner in the political team that would lead the Paraíba oligarchy until 1912, Álvaro was acknowledged by contemporaries as extremely intelligent; he subsequently enjoyed a reputation as a capable administrator. In addition, he possessed—according to a younger contemporary who studied him well—"a gift for dissimulation."[25] He personified the talented man of intellect, often a professor, historically associated with Areia's political elite during the second half of the nineteenth century, when that city gloried in its reputation as Paraíba's intellectual capital. As an adolescent, Álvaro had been termed a mathematical genius and was sent to Recife for his secondary education at age thirteen. The move ended his residence in the interior of Paraíba, and, for that matter, in the state, except for brief residences in the Capital in 1892–1895 and 1905. Completing his higher studies at the national military academy, the Escola Militar in Rio de Janeiro, he graduated in 1887, receiving a degree in military engineering. Simultaneously, he became a bacharel of mathematics and the physical sciences.

Although he had not lived in Paraíba for twenty years, when Álvaro returned in February 1892 to assume his gubernatorial responsibilities he immediately attracted a talented group of former Liberals. Largely drawn from Areia's elite families, his political re-

[24] Areia's most prominent Republican politician in the Empire was Aristides Liebnitz da Silveira Lobo (born in Mamanguape), a Miranda Henriques. His maternal grandfather had been a martyred hero of the 1817 Republican Revolt in Pernambuco and his father, Manuel Lobo de Miranda Henriques, had also fought in that movement for independence from Portugal. Aristides, who died a senator for the Federal District in 1896, had served as an imperial deputy to the Constituent Congress in 1890–1891. Albino Meira was Areia's other Historical Republican who had served as a senator in the Empire. Pro-Praieira in 1848, he withdrew from Areia to the Recife Law Faculty in the 1850s, where he became a distinguished professor. Sen. João Coelho Gonçalves Lisboa, Areia's last genuine Republican, was much more ambivalent in his political affiliations.

[25] Mariz, *Cidades*, p. 154.

cruits included the controversial João Coelho Gonçalves Lisboa, who had acted as the go-between for Ábdon Felinto Milanez with Floriano when he proposed Álvaro's appointment.[26] For most of the decade, Álvaro relied on João Tavares de Melo Cavalcanti as his key representative in the Assembly, because he was a loyal partisan of former Judge Antônio Trinidade Antunes da Meira Henriques. The judge was one of Paraíba's few Conservative politicians of the Empire to survive at the federal level in the Old Republic. His Meirista faction, drawn from family-based groups in the caatinga-agreste and cariri-sertão, was crucial to Álvaro's oligarchical dominance during most of the nineties.

More fundamentally, however, Álvaro relied on close relatives in his family-based group in Areia to consolidate his relationship with the national government in the first decade of the Old Republic. His first slate of candidates for the 1892 federal elections clearly reflected this dependence on close kin and explained why he was soon publicly criticized for founding an "oligarchy."[27] (See Fig. B.2.) For instance, Álvaro's mother's brother, former imperial senator Ábdon Felinto Milanez, served a nine-year term beginning in 1894 as the senior member for Paraíba in Álvaro's first federal delegation. One of Ábdon's sons, Álvaro's cousin Prudêncio Cotegipe Milanez, joined his father as a junior senator the same year. Another son, who bore his father's name, Ábdon Filho, served one term in the State Assembly and then joined his father and brother as federal deputy in the delegation in Rio de Janeiro. Álvaro's father's brother, the aging Maximiano Machado, also served as a federal deputy until his death in 1895. One of Álvaro's brothers, Afonso Lopes Machado, became Paraíba's second lieutenant-governor during the same decade. Ten years later, another brother, João Lopes Machado, developed a fraternal political relationship with Álvaro similar to the one that Epitácio Pessoa's brother, Col. Antônio da Silva Pessoa, was developing with Epitácio.[28] A state deputy in 1904, João Lopes Machado was elected governor only four years later, much as Col. Antônio Pessoa would move from the Assembly to the governorship in 1912. Oligarchy's family base

[26] Ibid., pp. 156–57 (n. 11).

[27] Ibid., p. 155.

[28] Álvaro's family was typical of Areia's political elite for its career associations in politics, imperial administration, and the military, rather than landed enterprises. Usually the grandsons of Portuguese immigrants who had settled in Areia in the late eighteenth century, the município's ruling families derived cohesion from their comparatively recent immigrant origins as well as their predominantly commercial economic activities.

in the nineties, while readily evident, was largely taken for granted by those in the political elite.

A tightly knit group of formerly Liberal families from Areia comprised much of Alvaro's support in the State Assembly. This network also included the Leites of Piancó and the intermarried Agras, Portos, and Sousa Campos of Campina Grande, who commanded political prestige in the backlands. The principal families from Areia who supported Álvaro included his own relatives in the intermarried Machado, Milanez, and Cotegipe families. For half a century this family alliance had been the município's political leadership in partnership with the Santos Leal, Almeidas, and Ávila Lins. In the 1840s, Paraíba's Provincial Assembly had been dominated by Álvaro's paternal uncle, Maximiano Machado. Together with Areia's Liberal Party boss, Joaquim José dos Santos Leal, and an Areiense provincial deputy, Luíz Vicente Borges, Maximiano had formed a triumvirate representing these extended families. They shared a humiliating defeat as republican rebels in a regional revolt of 1824, known as the Confederation of Equador. Its objective had been the establishment of a republic in Northeast Brazil. A similar but much more violent revolt in 1848–1849, known as the Praieira, involved the same families. Hence, Areia's Liberals were regarded in the nineties as more seriously republican than their Conservative peers. The fathers of many Conservatives had been associated with the punishment or imprisonment meted out to the Liberals by the Conservative Party leadership after the Praieira Revolt was quelled.[29] When Epitácio Pessoa referred directly to "the Liberals of Álvaro Machado" in his private comments, he had in mind their historical association with either republicanism or rebellion and bellicose defense of those positions

[29] On Areia's pro-Praieira families, see H. de Almeida, *Brejo de Areia*, pp. 77–91; Mariz, *Cidades*, pp. 130, 132. Antônio Borges da Fonseca (1808–1872), the principal architect and propagandist of the Praia faction during the 1840s, was born and raised in Areia but received his higher education in Germany. Once the revolt collapsed—in February 1849—he accompanied a thousand of his remaining troops in a retreat from Pernambuco to Areia, where the leaders were hidden by Liberal sympathizers, including Provincial Deputy Maximiano Machado. When Areia was attacked and occupied by the provincial governor's militia, those forces sacked and razed the houses of prominent Liberal supporters of the Praia cause, such as Joaquim dos Santos Leal. The government troops whipped and physically abused many Liberals as pro-Praieira prisoners, for their officers tended to be Conservatives. Ibid. As Naro has recently emphasized, the political divisions in the Praieira conflict eventually reflected "family solidarity rather than partisanry." Nancy Priscilla Naro, "Brazil's 1848: The Praieira Revolt" (Ph.D. diss., University of Chicago, 1982), pp. 132, 180, and 206.

in nineteenth-century Areia.[30] More recently the município had been associated with abolitionism, since it was the Liberals of Areia who had led the campaign in the province in the late eighties, making their município council the first to abolish slavery.

Given the long alliance between the Machado and the Santos Leal families in Areia, it was not surprising that, when Álvaro ran for election as Paraíba's governor in March 1892, his running mate as first lieutenant governor, Valfredo Soares dos Santos Leal, was another scion of an important Old Liberal family from his home town. Already enjoying an immensely popular reputation as "the Curate of Guarabira," Valfredo Leal had served first as that município's parish priest and then as its monsignor for ten years. He was the nephew of Joaquim dos Santos Leal, Areia's former Liberal political boss in the 1840s and 1850s, who had been politically ruined by his involvement, with three of his brothers, in a notorious assassination.[31] When Valfredo and Álvaro joined their talents as an oligarchical team in 1892, consequently, they were drawing on a mutual family alliance that was already intergenerational and political. In addition, Valfredo was related to other first families of Areia—the Freires, Soares, and Almeidas. His expanding flock of nephews soon became ubiquitous in elective and appointive office in Paraíba. (See Fig. B.2.) These nephews, like Álvaro's relatives, contributed to the creation of "oligarchy" in Paraíba, as critics in the press regularly reminded readers.[32]

Several of Valfredo's kinsmen played leading roles in his oligarchy. His cousin once removed, Antônio Simeão dos Santos Leal, known simply as Simeão Leal, had become his most influential kinsman ally in state politics by 1900. (See Fig. B.2.) Simeão was routinely lumped with Valfredo's nephews when the opposition press charged Valfredo with "filhotismo," or nepotism. An Areia businessman until 1894, Simeão gave up commerce to work as a state assemblyman and eventually became a federal deputy. An-

[30] Mariz, *Cidades*, p. 155.

[31] In 1852, Joaquim José dos Santos Leal and his three brothers (Valfredo's maternal uncles) had been convicted for their complicity in the 1849 assassination of a prestigious imperial judge in Areia—Trajano Alípio Holanda Chacon—the município's Conservative Party boss. The crime's notorious instigator (*mandante*), Carlota Lúcia de Brito, was the mistress of Joaquim dos Santos Leal; she received a life sentence on the island penal colony of Fernão Naronha, together with her lover and his brothers. The fate of the Santos Leal brothers, however, was as much a result of the earlier involvement of two of them in the Praieira as it was of Carlota's scheming. H. de Almeida, *Brejo de Areia*, pp. 113–17; Mariz, *Cidades*, pp. 131–34.

[32] Mariz, *Cidades*, p. 155.

other one of Valfredo's nephews, Padre Matias Freire, a young parish priest in the Capital, enjoyed tenure as a state assemblyman from 1908 to 1915, serving as the Valfredista president of the Assembly during 1911–1914. After he lost the crucial 1915 election for the State Assembly,[33] Padre Matias did not ally himself as a Valfredista with Epitácio. Valfredo's most famous kinsman, José Américo de Almeida, did associate himself, however, with the Pessoa oligarchy. He had graduated from the Recife Law School and entered Paraíba politics in 1909, too late to participate in the ascendant years of the Machado–Leal oligarchy, which was just then being swallowed by its Neiva–Pessoa opposition.

The dual oligarchical leadership Álvaro and Valfredo exercised in Paraíba endured into the second decade of this century. Officially the senior member of Paraíba's oligarchy, Álvaro always acknowledged Valfredo as his friend and "right arm," for Valfredo was "as loyal as his name [Leal] suggested."[34] When Álvaro acceded to the leadership of his native state, at only thirty-nine, he was still a novice in politics. He needed the electoral support that the boss of Guarabira could muster, for the curate enjoyed wide popularity throughout the brejo zone. Monsignor Valfredo had proved even more zealous in political affairs than in his clerical calling; he typified the priest whose real vocation was politics and during an era when a significant number served as bosses and assemblymen. Even in the Empire, the priest who functioned as a coronel had been a common political figure throughout the Northeast.[35]

Valfredo's superior talents enabled him to rise higher in politics than most clerics, however. He enjoyed a long tenure in national office, even associating himself in the Brazilian Senate with Pinheiro Machado. Valfredo maintained a personal and a professional friendship with Pinheiro, who dominated Brazilian politics as president of the Senate from 1909 until his assassination in 1915. In 1910, when he undertook the only significant attempt during the Old Republic to build a national political party, Pinheiro

[33] Padre Matias Freire was also a brother-in-law of the Baron of Mamanguape (Flávio Clementino da Silva Freire) and had been a provincial deputy in the late Empire. He was president of the Paraíba Assembly from 1911 to 1915. (See Fig. B.2.) Demócrito de Almeida, another nephew of Valfredo, also entered politics, eventually becoming an important Epitacista after his uncle's 1915 defeat. Author's prosopographical file.

[34] Mariz, *Cidades*, p. 155.

[35] Eul-Soo Pang, "The Changing Role of Priests in the Backlands of Northeast Brazil, 1889–1964," *The Americas* 20 (Jan. 1974):341–72.

placed Valfredo Leal on the Executive Board of his Conservative Republican Party, or PRC (Partido Republicano Conservador). "The Padre," as Epitácio called him, was selected "not only because [Valfredo] was Epitácio's rival" but also because "the Monsignor was tough and had much support in Paraíba."[36] Pinheiro and Valfredo enjoyed good working rapport, and the priest's political skill, not to mention his obvious relish for the cabalistic machinations of factional politics, probably highly recommended him to Brazil's most powerful senator.

Coalition-Building and Electoral "Rules of the Game"

The dependence of the ruling oligarchy on a coalition constructed from multiple personalistic factions—a minimum of three that allied the Alvaristas, Valfredistas, and one or more others—meant that major attention was directed toward rewarding the head of each faction. The incumbent oligarchy's factional base could be identified in the list of individuals who held a federal office or a slot in the gubernatorial executive. Álvaro and Valfredo spent the largest proportion of time distributing and redistributing the coveted offices of senator, federal deputy, governor, and lieutenant governor.[37] They resorted to a standard formula for rewriting the electoral "rules of the game" that was used during the Old Republic—either amending the state constitution or, more normally, "reforming" existing electoral law and regulations. "Reform" permitted them to rotate Paraíba's governorship, first and second lieutenant governorships, and legislative offices in the federal delegation among the major factional leaders.

Except briefly during the 1905 crisis, Álvaro served as a senator from the time he left the governorship—during the mid-term in 1895—until his death in January 1912. Valfredo, who had been first lieutenant governor until 1895, relieved Álvaro as governor and finished the four-year term in 1896. He then moved to the House of Deputies or the Senate until 1912, except for one term in

[36] Mariz, *Cidades*, p. 155.

[37] Title III, Chapter 1, of the Paraíba State Constitution defined the qualifications for governor and lieutenant governors (Art. 27, Sec. 3, Para. 1). Art. 32 defined a significant prohibition against consanguineous or affinal kinship between the governor and his lieutenant governors or between him and his immediate predecessor. However, candidates beyond the third degree of consanguinity (i.e., first cousins or more distant) were considered simultaneously eligible for these executive offices. *Regimento interno da Assembléa Legislativa; Constituição do Estado da Parahyba do Norte* (Parahyba: Imprensa Oficial, 1924).

1904–1908 as governor. In many states, especially those with simply organized oligarchies dependent on either a kin or highly personalistic base, candidates for lieutenant governorships were consciously selected for their potential rotation to federal office or the governorship. Usually, advancement came through a strategic resignation followed by a special election. Resigning executive office in favor of his first vice-governor, a state governor would be eligible to run for the Senate or the House of Deputies in a special election. On occasion the succeeding first lieutenant governor might also resign the governorship in favor of the second lieutenant governor. Alternatively, a senator who headed an oligarchy might assume the governorship briefly—as Álvaro did during the 1904–1905 crisis—by first resigning from the Senate, then being appointed first lieutenant governor by the incumbent governor, and soon succeeding to the office when the governor resigned. These changes were almost always deliberately calculated and frequently arranged years in advance.

In the early 1890s, the ruling Machado–Leal oligarchy established its partisan organization, one devoted almost exclusively to the narrow aim of winning elections and delivering the vote to the candidates it officially designated at the local, state, and federal levels. In April 1892, Álvaro and Valfredo had founded the Republican Party of Paraíba, or PRP (Partido Republicano Paraibano). It underwent a number of nominal metamorphoses but never became a true political party in more than a superficial sense. Intended as a state branch of Marshal Floriano Peixoto's national party organization, the PRP outlived the Iron Marshal. It survived into the first decade of this century, in Paraíba as in most other states, but performed merely an organizational task: It delivered the vote for the quadriennial contests for Assembly, governorship, and presidency, as well as the triennial elections for both the House of Deputies and Senate. It failed, however, to adopt clearly identifiable political goals or programs in Paraíba.

Since the PRP was synonymous with the ruling oligarchy's leadership stratum, it also sponsored official candidates for the key positions at the grass-roots level: the local offices of municipal judge, prefeito, deputy prefeito (sub-prefeito), and municipal council (the latter referred to as *intendências* until 1900 and then as *câmaras municipais*). Álvaro made one important procedural change during the mid-1890s, which endured until 1930 and eventually strengthened the governor's authority over the municípios. Through an amendment to the state constitution in 1895, the local offices of prefeito and deputy prefeito became appointive, to be filled by the governor, instead of elective.[38] However, since those who directed the politics of a município largely determined whether the governor's official slates of candidates would receive a favorable vote, his appointments for these offices were still largely determined by the performance or preferences of the most powerful family-based groups who supported him in each município.

As a rule, the governor designated individuals from the family-based group that dominated a given município's politics, usually in alliance (through matrimonial ties) with one or two other family-based groups. In a majority of the state's thirty-nine municípios, the same individual was both prefeito and chefe político or party boss. The governor appointed the chefe político, also called the "*chefe local*," who was charged with delivering the vote to the state party machine. Ideally, both the prefeito and the chefe político might "advise" the governor regarding local factional maneuverings, periodically supplying the political intelligence essential for a successful electoral strategy. The local boss usually enjoyed the rank of a coronel, a captain, or a major in the National Guard, when he was not a university graduate. His patent in the Guard usually had been conferred as patronage by the ruling oligarchy.[39] The linchpin of the political system, the local party boss, as coronel or doutor, organized and financed delivery of the so-called "herd vote" (*voto de cabresto*), one cast largely by his family allies and their kinsmen, clients, and tenants. His demonstrated ability to deliver the vote to the PRP legitimated his family-based group's hold over local partisan and political offices as well as distribution

[38] A state law of 22 May 1895 had created a gubernatorially appointed prefeito and deputy prefeito, as well as the locally elected municipal council (*câmara municipal*). It abolished the former imperial municipal organization, which had depended on an elected council (*intendência*) whose president (*intendente*) was the municipal executive. But immediately following José Peregrino's inauguration as governor in October 1900, the 1895 law was rescinded and the former arrangement, renamed a municipal council (conselho municipal) with its president, restored until 1904. E. de Almeida, *História Campina*, pp. 361–62.

[39] In 1897 Epitácio indicated that he had already spoken with Almeida Barreto concerning National Guard patents for those in the directory of the Autonomist Party. Almeida Barreto, in his varied capacity as senator, retired marshal, and former senior commander of the National Guard, was an ideal patronage broker for local bosses such as Cristiano Lauritzen, who sought the prestigious patents: "Barreto wants Cristiano to receive a patent and has given assurances that it will soon arrive in Campina [Grande]." Epitácio to Venâncio (Rio de Janeiro), 16 Dec. 1897; AEP/10/5.

of patronage locally. Without the vote, he risked being replaced by either his local allies or the opposition and losing the monopoly he enjoyed with his close collateral kinsmen over the key local offices. Commonly, a boss coordinated município politics, often in tandem with a brother, brothers-in-law, or cousins, while a third brother or nephew served the family-based group's interests in the State Assembly.

Prior to 1912, the fact that Paraíba's governors lacked significant state and federal revenues restricted the material resources they could offer to bosses as patronage. Consequently, their political territory was very circumscribed and their opportunity to impose central authority virtually nonexistent. The governor's control of local officeholding afforded him some leverage, but even that was a two-edged sword, since the coronel had what the governor fundamentally needed even more: the vote. The State Police Force offered the governor a limited opportunity to impose certain decisions, but only near the Capital, where it could be concentrated. In the interior, budgetary limitations prevented the governor from deploying the Police Force in great numbers for any significant length of time. Elite family-based groups in the municípios usually had armed men superior in number to the police reinforcements the governor might send. During the nineties, the entire State Police Force fell short of four hundred men.[40] Consequently, local autonomy remained the rule in almost all the municípios. The Machado–Leal oligarchy governed very minimally.

Because local and state offices were the most coveted grants of patronage that the governor could offer the family-based groups who supported his party in the municípios, state politics revolved around elections. Frequently and reliably, elections punctuated factional competition at every level of government, according to both a fixed and a movable calendar. March, the month of federal elections, originally hosted the gubernatorial contest, which was later moved to June. Assembly elections usually fell on the last day of December or the last day of January, as did the local contests for município councils. Senatorial elections, however, were staggered in three-year intervals for terms of three, six, and nine years. Resignations or deaths instigated the special elections that breathed combative zest into the factional and personalistic rival-

[40] State of Paraíba, *Almanach do Estado da Parahyba para o anno de 1900* (Parahyba: Imprensa Oficial, 1900), n.p.; Linda Lewin, "The Oligarchical Limitations of Social Banditry in Brazil: The Case of the 'Good' Thief Antônio Silvino," *Past & Present* 82 (Feb. 1979):129.

ries ubiquitous in the system, since the governor had the prerogative to fix or postpone their dates. Given the intricate prearranged shuffle between congressional chairs and gubernatorial offices, vacancies due to death often presented unexpected defections. Rarely were all factional leaders satisfied by the triennial and quadriennial redistribution of the top offices: the eight federal and three gubernatorial posts. The small number of offices automatically limited admission to the most prestigious rungs of the ladder of oligarchy.

Elections were always crisis points, since politicians who had been promised or otherwise expected the rewards of high office and did not receive them frequently withdrew their factional support and usually pledged it to the opposition. Their reaffiliation could threaten the incumbent oligarchy in two respects. First, it might jeopardize the governor's majority in the thirty-member Assembly, where he usually needed three factions to maintain it. Álvaro and Valfredo, for example, depended on an alliance with the Meiristas for their legislative majority. Second, if a defector controlled the votes in enough municípios, he could jeopardize the oligarchy's ability to deliver federal elections. Successful oligarchical leadership, therefore, had to be both shrewd and skillful in its distribution of federal and gubernatorial offices. Otherwise, it courted desertion and risked being toppled by the opposition.

Planning the Revanche: The Neiva–Pessoa Opposition, 1892–1900

The rise of the Pessoas' political machine in Paraíba is best appreciated in terms of three aspects of the political system: First, the continuous, personalistic jockeying for power that characterizes group rivalry in any system of factional politics; second, recognition of the family-based group as the essential unit of political mobilization; and third, the ability of the family-based network to connect the key actors in the political process at local, state, and federal levels. Although Venâncio and Epitácio were ejected from their political positions within the dominant oligarchy in 1891 and 1893, respectively, throughout the nineties they both worked toward an eventual revanche that would reintegrate their factional followings into the incumbent Machado–Leal oligarchy. Possessing no personalistic faction of his own in 1893, Epitácio nevertheless gained many admirers—some, powerful national politicians—for his courage in denouncing Marshal Floriano's dictatorship. By the close of the decade, many Paraibanos, usually Old Conservatives, had begun to think of themselves as "Epitacistas."

The "Years of Persecution"

Following the close of the Constituent Congress, Epitácio Pessoa returned to his seat as a federal deputy in the first regular session of the Brazilian Congress in January 1892. The appointment of Álvaro Machado as Paraíba's new governor a month later rendered the congressional delegation highly anomalous, since most of its members were loyal to former Governor Venâncio Neiva. In November 1891, Floriano had succeeded to the presidency, but the constitutional legality of his move remained highly dubious. As he began to assume the prerogatives of dictatorial power, but significantly retained the title vice-president, the mood of the nation became extremely tense. Epitácio won his national political spurs in this critical context. Displaying a courage that bordered on recklessness, he assumed a position in the forefront of the verbal attack against Floriano on the floor of Congress, challenging the vice-president as a dictator who had already begun to ignore the new Constitution of 1891. On four separate occasions over a period of fourteen months, he delivered speeches denouncing Floriano's usurpation of power, gaining for himself rousing cheers, respectful applause, and the open admiration of many older and more seasoned national politicians. One admirer was São Paulo's Sen. Manuel Ferraz Campos Sales, head of the committee to reform civil marriage, on which Epitácio had served during the Constituent Convention.[41]

Epitácio's maiden speech was a long-remembered denunciation of Floriano's illegitimate tenure in office and his trampling of civil liberties. Subsequently, Paraíba's Sen. Almeida Barreto, recently advanced to the rank of marshal by Deodoro, joined Epitácio and attacked Floriano. In March 1892, Almeida Barreto's name was first on a list of thirteen generals, commanders, and admirals of

[41] L. Pessôa, *Epitacio Pessôa*, 1:61–63. Excerpts of Epitácio's speeches denouncing Floriano appear in ibid., pp. 75–112, while full texts appear in E. Pessoa, *Obras completas*, Vol. 1: *Discursos parlementares (1890–1893)* (1955), pp. 54, 71–92, 99–106. Meeting Epitácio in 1890, when they both served on the same congressional committee, Campos Sales immediately admired his "great juridical competence." Campos Sales, *Propaganda a presidencia*, p. 208.

the army and navy signing a public manifesto that urged Floriano to order a presidential election to "take place at once as provided in the Federal Constitution and electoral law, and to be held freely and without pressure."[42] The signers were deprived of their commissions and retired from the military by Floriano. Within a year, Almeida Barreto and the twelve other officers, as well as a contingent of civilian opponents to Floriano's rule that included the great abolitionist José do Patrocínio, found themselves under arrest and on a ship bound for the Amazon. They spent the remainder of the dictatorship in exile in Manaus.

Faring better than Almeida Barreto, Epitácio escaped the Iron Marshal's dragnet. In mid-April 1893, he fled north to Salvador, Recife, and Paraíba, eventually finding refuge in the interior of his native state. This was the last time he would pay more than a token visit to Paraíba, or, for that matter, to the untamed and underdeveloped backlands of the Northeast. Local opposition bosses, particularly Cristiano Lauritzen in Campina Grande, offered the young opposition deputy sanctuary in their homes or on their properties.[43] So did friends and colleagues of Venâncio, who apparently had also sought protection in the same zone. The most important consequence of this exciting but brief period in Epitácio's life was the personal bond he formed with Cristiano, or "the Gringo," as he always preferred to call himself. Cristiano, an even closer friend of Epitácio's brother, Antônio da Silva Pessoa, was already a firm Venancista. He had just begun to experience local Alvarista persecution of his Cavalcanti de Albuquerque family-based group. The period of "political exile" in the nineties, as the Danish-born merchant of Campina Grande always referred to it, forged extremely close personal ties among the Venancista outs in Paraíba. They never forgot their persecution at the hand of the lo-

[42] Bello, *History Brazil*, pp. 98–99; L. Pessôa, *Epitacio Pessôa*, 1:80.

[43] Laurita Pessoa has denied that her father, Epitácio, had to seek refuge from Floriano's police, asserting that the Iron Marshal intentionally spared him out of admiration. L. Pessôa, *Epitacio Pessôa*, 1:119–20. However, she notes that Epitácio spent perhaps eight months (September? 1893 to April? 1894) in Paraíba and Pernambuco and returned to Rio de Janeiro only when Floriano's rule collapsed. Her father may well have been in greater danger from Paraíba's Old Liberal-dominated state government than from Brazil's dictator. Although he had first denounced Floriano on January 8, 1892, according to Laurita Pessoa, he was still in Rio de Janeiro in March. But she adds that on May 27, he delivered another speech, "having just returned from the Northeast" (p. 80). E. Câmara suggested why he had been absent and why he escaped persecution the following year: "Dr. Epitácio suffered such serious persecution from Floriano Peixoto [in 1892] that he was forced to seek refuge on Cristiano Lauritzen's estate, 'Cabeça de Boi.' " *Datas campinenses*, p. 63.

cal Alvarista or Valfredista opposition, especially in Campina Grande. Despite the return of civilian government to Brazil in 1894, they remained out of politics locally for another eight years. Working with Venâncio and, increasingly, Epitácio, they plotted for a political revanche that would reintegrate them in the incumbent coalition. Although no firm evidence exists, apparently Epitácio also met a number of the most influential former Venancista (Old Conservative) bosses from municípios further west in the backlands zones during this period. Very likely he did so through Cristiano, since a number of them were Cristiano's customers; or possibly Venâncio was an intermediary, since the latter had resided in three important backlands centers as an imperial judge: Catolé do Rocha, Pombal, and Teixeira.[44]

Floriano's dictatorship opened a round of political persecution in Paraíba that escalated during the nineties, apparently due to the confidence of Alvarista and Valfredista factions that they would remain in power. Previously, imperial politics had injected a rotational quality to family-based control in Paraíba's municípios, producing expectations on both sides that in a reasonably short time the ins would inevitably become the outs again and vice versa. This phenomenon appears to have mitigated the local persecution of out factions; implicitly, it also recognized the inevitability of factional reintegration in many situations.[45] In any case, what began as the usual settling of old scores between feuding families was transformed, with the advent of Alvarista rule in 1892, into the greatest escalation of local violence in Paraíba's history. Cristiano and his Cavalcanti de Albuquerque in-laws were singled out for negative attention by the Agras and Portos who controlled Campina Grande's police, town council, executive branch, and judiciary, but they were more fortunate than others who were killed in ambushes.[46] As merchants, Cristiano, Lindolfo

[44] For Venâncio's political friendships in Catolé do Rocha, see Celso Mariz, *Notícia histórica de Catolé do Rocha* (Mossoró: Editôra Comercial, 1956), pp. 15–16; in Sousa, see Cunha Pedrosa, *Minhas memórias*, Vol. 1: *Vida pública*, pp. 57–60.

[45] During the Empire, provincial governors (presidents) had been appointed by the emperor from career bureaucracy and were drawn from other states and frequently rotated. Their partisan affiliations agreed with whichever party possessed a majority in the national legislature and since the national government alternated rather regularly between the two parties, it was difficult for one party to be entrenched for long periods in local politics. There were, of course, numerous exceptions. See Pang and Seckinger, "Mandarins of Brazil," pp. 215–44.

[46] Two salient murder cases of politicians during the decade of the nineties were those of Lieut. Col. José André Pereira de Albuquerque, president of the Intendên-

Montenegro, and Alfredo Espínola had issued their own scrip, known as *valés*, redeemable in kind from their commercial establishments in Campina Grande, an already well established practice in the 1880s. This was the pretext for their rivals to "apply the law," for they were arrested, tried, sentenced to prison, and confined in the Capital's jail. However, when the defendants appealed their case to Rio de Janeiro in 1895, their sentences were reversed and all charges dropped. It seems that "military figures connected to the Neiva brothers" had intervened on behalf of Cristiano and his fellow Old Conservative merchants, to set them free.[47]

During the final year of Floriano's dictatorship, Epitácio regained the liberty to return to Rio de Janeiro, where he first began a private law practice. His marriage to the daughter of a Mineiro politician soon took him and his bride to Europe for a year of travel. This year, from mid-1894 to mid-1895, appears to have been the only time he was truly "out of politics," although his foremost biographer extended that generalization to all of the years between 1894 and 1898, when he joined Campos Sales's Cabinet as minister of justice, education, and culture.[48] Since Epitácio's wife died in childbirth in Paris barely a year after their

---

cia (Municipal Council) of Campina Grande, on December 24, 1892, and Assemblyman Tomaz de Araújo Aquino, local party boss of Misericórdia, on July 15, 1897. José Leal, *Itinerário da história (Imágem da Paraíba entre 1518 e 1965)* (João Pessoa: Gráfica Comercial, 1965), pp. 325–26. It was widely asserted that the murder of Pereira de Albuquerque had been ordered by Col. Eufrásio da Camara, an Epitacista whose son married a daughter of Venâncio Neiva. Former Assemblyman Eufrásio was himself gunned down in 1923 by the son of José André Pereira de Albuquerque. E. Câmara, *Datas campinenses*, pp. 77, 129.

[47] All of the accused were absolved on appeal to the Federal Supreme Court on June 25, 1896. E. de Almeida, *História Campina*, p. 258; E. Câmara, *Datas campinenses*, p. 81.

[48] Epitácio's actual post was minister of the interior, which included the responsibilities for justice, education, and culture. However, in this book the latter terms of his official title are used, since this was the conventional designation. Epitácio was nominated by Campos Sales to his ministerial post in October 1898. His biographer implied more than that he had been out of office when she stated that he had remained "outside all political activity, even in Paraíba," and that "he watched congressional politics as a spectator, from a distance," until late November 1898. L. Pessôa, *Epitacio Pessôa*, 1:145. Although Epitácio was out of political office from 1893 to 1898, his correspondence confirmed his intimate involvement in Paraíba politics, except during his year in Europe. His political correspondence with his uncle, Baron Lucena, verifies his close attention to political appointments and developments at the federal level: Arquivo Público Estadual, *Arquivo do Barão de Lucena: Catálogo* (Recife: Imprensa Oficial, 1956), pp. 137–85, lists the relevant correspondence.

marriage, just as his father's first wife had died, he returned to Rio de Janeiro in April 1895. Subsequently practicing law, he kept informed of the maneuvers of the Machado–Leal oligarchy and, especially, the affairs of its opposition. In 1892 he and Venâncio had founded the Autonomist Party of Paraíba as the official organization of their factional opposition, only one month after Álvaro and Valfredo had founded the PRP. Epitácio remained in touch, through either letters or personal meetings in the national capital, with several important Autonomistas and Sen. Almeida Barreto, as well as his uncle by marriage, João José Neiva. Patiently pursuing a strategy of quietly building support in Paraíba, especially in the backlands, neither he nor Venâncio could tip the scales against the incumbent oligarchy until the situation at the federal level of politics changed.

The "Case of Paraíba" and the "Politics of the Governors"

Tensions during the Florianista period receded very gradually in the nineties, even after the Iron Marshal had departed from politics in late 1894, and Brazil's first directly elected civilian president, Prudente de Morais, was installed in November. Prudente's administration, which lasted until 1898, proved the most tumultuous of any Brazilian president's until Epitácio's own government came to a close in 1922. Conflict between military and civilians, or among civilians, especially those adhering to Floriano's civilian counterpart and heir, Sen. Francisco Glicério and his Federal Republican Party, or PRF (Partido Republicano Federal), continued at a high level. A naval revolt launched by a monarchist reaction during Floriano's last year of rule became more explosive in 1894, mounting yet another military challenge to civilian rule. The national economy was still reeling from the financial disaster of 1891, known as the "Encilhamento," when rash overborrowing and floods of unsecured paper currency had bankrupted commerce and individuals of all social classes, eventually denying Brazil its international credit.[49] The foreign debt was suspended, the gold standard abandoned, and inflation impeded the tasks of stimulating exports and encouraging industrialization when Prudente assumed power.

[49] As his first task as president-elect, Campos Sales secured from the House of Rothschild in London the 1898 "funding loan" that fully restored Brazil's international credit. He discussed its negotiation and significance, which he saw as complementary to his "politics of the states," in *Propaganda a presidencia*, pp. 179–98, esp. p. 195.

In 1895, Sen. Álvaro Machado also permanently established himself in Rio de Janeiro as the leader of the Paraíba delegation in Congress. Partisan competition in Paraíba was nearly nonexistent, and state revenues remained so meager that they engendered no competition within the ruling coalition. Álvaro now had to make his oligarchy useful in congressional politics, where the most powerful state, São Paulo, dominated, and only a few others truly mattered. Imprudently allying himself with Sen. Francisco Glicério's PRF voting bloc, he created the opening that the Autonomistas needed to gain a foothold on the ladder of oligarchical power in Paraíba. His management of the factional alliances he had constructed within Paraíba proved to be his Achilles' heel; Álvaro failed to distribute the rewards of officeholding so as to consolidate his factional support.

Between 1892 and 1897, Álvaro's coalition rested on three personalistic factions: 1) his own Alvaristas, centered in the brejo and overlapping the caatinga-agreste (the backlands Old Liberal bloc); 2) the Valfredistas, whose geographical links were congruent with those zones but also reached to the Leite and the Dantas family groupings of Old Liberals in the cariri-sertão and alto sertão; and 3) the Meiristas, loyal supporters of the former imperial judge, now a federal deputy, Antônio Trinidade Antunes da Meira Henriques. Still an extremely prestigious leader, Trinidade led what had been the dissident Conservative stream in his bailiwick of the caatinga-agreste and the environs of Campina Grande. His key follower in Paraíba was a politician who had served in the Provincial Assembly, João Tavares de Melo Cavalcanti, a wealthy cotton and sugar planter from Alagoa Nova, who was one of the most successful agrarian entrepreneurs in the state. Trinidade was also Almeida Barreto's acknowledged personalistic factional leader, since he and Trinidade, who were contemporaries in age, had formed a close political bond long before Venâncio had begun to make his mark on state politics.[50] Epitácio, who could not help admiring Trinidade, candidly summed up the tremendous personal effect his rival's aristocratic bearing and personal appearance had on the

[50] Almeida Barreto's position in federal politics deserves more attention, due to the extent of his enormous panelinha, which included Trinidade. But little of his personal or political connections could be documented. Trinidade had first served as a local judge in Ingá in 1874, where Epitácio's godfather Manuel da Assunção Santiago undoubtedly argued cases before him. He then sat as a provincial deputy for two terms in the Assembly (1872–1878); for the remainder of the Empire, he was an imperial judge whose district included Campina Grande and Ingá. Author's prosopographical file.

younger generation, even those who, like himself, resented Trinidade's influence in state politics: "I never saw a man so disinterested, self-abnegating, so loyal, so patriotic, and even so handsome."[51] Almeida Barreto, who remained in the Brazilian Senate until his death in 1905, and Trinidade were the only prominent Old Conservatives to hold federal office in Paraíba between 1893 and 1900. At his death in 1911, Trinidade held the same federal deputy seat he had occupied since the Constituent Congress, and his political following of Meiristas remained committed to him, not to Álvaro.

Álvaro's failure to accord Trinidade "representation" commensurate with the latter's significance in the dominant oligarchy's majority in the Assembly provided Epitácio and Venâncio with a useful wedge to drive into the ruling coalition's monolithic control of state and local politics. In exchange for delivering their votes to elect President Prudente de Morais in 1894, the Meiristas had expected to gain seats from Álvaro in the Paraíba Assembly. By 1896, however, they had become disenchanted with Álvaro, who did not concede them. João Tavares de Melo Cavalcanti, instead of being advanced to federal office, became second lieutenant governor. Except for "Dr. Meira," as Trinidade was affectionately known, the four other federal deputies in the Paraíba delegation were either Valfredistas or Alvaristas. In 1897, Trinidade secretly defected from the alliance with Álvaro and Valfredo and made a private pact with Epitácio and Venâncio.

Marshal Almeida Barreto served as the go-between for a formal agreement between the Meiristas and the Autonomistas, achieved in mid-December 1897, three months before the presidential election. It is worth underscoring that Epitácio had calculated that the Autonomistas enjoyed a numerical superiority over Trinidade's factional followers in the Paraíba interior. However, since the federal government still backed Álvaro and Valfredo in the leadership of the Paraíba oligarchy, he wisely concluded that to challenge Trinidade's position would be foolish. Instead, he "aimed for an alliance."[52] The Autonomistas' position was complicated by Almeida Barreto's primary loyalty to Trinidade, which overrode his ties of friendship with Epitácio and the Neiva brothers. At the

[51] Epitácio to Venâncio (Rio de Janeiro), 16 Dec. 1897, AEP/10/5. The letter is published in E. Pessôa, *Obras completas*, 1:251–52.

[52] Ibid. "It [our following] has to be victorious regarding the organization of the local Autonomistista Party directorates, and with the course of time we will be assured of the effective leadership of the Party throughout the state."

time the agreement was drawn up, Almeida Barreto had declared he would not "return to our [Epitácio and Venâncio's] group detached from Trinidade, since [Almeida Barreto] was publicly allied to him and [he] had pledged so to the federal government [i.e., the president]."[53] Epitácio correctly perceived that if Almeida Barreto "abandoned" the Autonomistas, the latter would be "placed in a precarious position for lack of an intermediary with the federal government":

> I met here [Rio de Janeiro] today with [Minister of Justice and the Interior] Amaro Cavalcanti [Pernambuco], [Vice-President] Rosa e Silva [Pernambuco], João Neiva, [Almeida] Barreto, and Trinidade. . . . The [Federal] Government [Prudente de Morais] continues to disparage our group and favors the other side. [If we challenge Trinidade,] the final result would be our exclusion in theory and fact [from the presidential political machine]. More than ever, the Government is going to need deputies and senators, who soon will have to certify the [1898] presidential election [returns of the states]. . . . We should aim for an alliance. If later there is a break, we will be on the right side. We can bend to the Government's wishes. According to the precise terms of the agreement, the nine-member directorate of the new alliance would include "four representatives named by Trinidade and four by us [Venâncio and Epitácio], and one as a representative of the Marshal [Almeida Barreto]." After being selected, this directorate will be elected in a meeting of those [i.e., the followers] allied; each of the partisan [i.e., factional] groups will publish a small manifesto in suitable language not provoking insults, announcing to the State [of Paraíba], that the fusion [of Meiristas and Autonomistas] is about to begin operating, a fusion that will take the title of Republican Party (Partido Republicano). This will be published following the publication of the circular about the presidential elections.[54]

Epitácio counseled Venâncio to support Trinidade's anticipated break with Álvaro and Valfredo, but he also looked to the day when Trinidade himself would become more marginal.[55] National politics largely determined this strategy, because Prudente's government was making a determined effort to consolidate its sup-

[53] Ibid.
[54] Ibid.
[55] Ibid.

port among the more stubborn states, Paraíba included, for the coming presidential election. Minister Amaro Cavalcanti warned during the meeting that if the Autonomistas directly challenged Trinidade's followers in Paraíba for the leadership in the municípios, just "when the federal government was attempting to form strong nuclei of resistance to local governments" [like Álvaro's] that favored Prudente's enemy, Senator Glicério, then Prudente's government "would never forget that we [the Autonomistas] betrayed them."[56] Epitácio concurred. The fear was that, once a challenge by the Autonomistas was issued to the Meiristas, defections from the Autonomista faction would appear on a small but nevertheless threatening scale and would weaken Autonomista support for the federal government in the forthcoming election. Vice-President Rosa e Silva advised the same course to Epitácio, correctly predicting that in time the Autonomistas would control Paraíba. To make an issue with Trinidade now over leadership of the opposition to Álvaro would be unwise, he argued, since Prudente would not recognize the Autonomistas as the dominant faction.[57]

In this manner, an opposition alliance to Álvaro formed in late 1897, with Almeida Barreto at the head of its directorate and designated as sole authorized intermediary with the federal government. Venâncio, however, acted as the directorate's intermediary, or spokesman, in Paraíba, a point Epitácio had insisted upon with Trinidade, since the former governor was still the official leader of the Autonomist Party. Because, for reasons never disclosed in the documents, Almeida Barreto enjoyed Prudente's support, he had distanced himself from Venâncio and Epitácio by late 1897. Epitácio was therefore advised by Vice-President Rosa e Silva, the leader of a northeastern bloc in Congress, to cooperate with him and Trinidade, for unless the Autonomistas remained "neutral" and left Trinidade unchallenged, they would lose presidential support later.[58]

The nomination of Campos Sales to the presidency in a national convention, held in October 1897, guaranteed that the next president of Brazil would be, like his predecessor, a strong opponent of

[56] Ibid. According to the letter, two meetings had been held. Appended to the letter was a copy of Epitácio's telegram to Trinidade, dated "January 1898," and stating that Epitácio was willing to put into practice the accord with Almeida Barreto. Epitácio also included himself among those who had felt resentment toward Trinidade but acknowledged that the December 16 meeting had persuaded him that such an attitude was "without foundation." Ibid.

[57] Ibid.

[58] Ibid.

Sen. Francisco Glicério. He was elected in March 1898. Since Álvaro Machado's followers in Paraíba had delivered their votes to Francisco Glicério's candidate, Lauro Sodré, Campos Sales had motives for assisting Epitácio's faction in Paraíba, apart from his personal liking for his minister of justice and education. The bonds between Epitácio and the new president, from their days together as federal deputies writing Brazil's 1891 Constitution, were strengthened during the latter's presidency from 1898 to 1902. Epitácio immediately used his new direct access to the Brazilian president to intercede on behalf of Venâncio and the Autonomistas for an eventual return to power in Paraíba.

Although Álvaro Machado had already set the stage for Campos Sales's articulation of the policy that came to be known as "the politics of the governors," it was Epitácio's specific effort to place a Meirista in the governorship, effectively ousting Machado–Leal leadership of Paraíba's oligarchy, that set the policy in motion.[59] Epitácio and Venâncio backed the Meirista, João Tavares de Melo Cavalcanti, for governor in 1900. He had been plucked from the Assembly and made second lieutenant governor in 1896, rather than being granted a greater reward. More irksome to Trinidade, Álvaro had recently preempted a coveted Senate seat for himself, anticipating his eventual resignation from the governorship and move to Rio de Janeiro. Trinidade had been particularly irritated that he had not been able to move from the House of Deputies to the Senate, when retiring Governor Valfredo succeeded to João Neiva's seat after the latter's six-year term expired in 1896.[60] The conflict between Campos Sales and Álvaro, however, first escalated when the president, acting on Epitácio's request, indirectly warned Álvaro, by sending a telegram to Paraíba's outgoing Governor Antônio Gama e Melo. He offered his personal "suggestion"

[59] Epitácio to João Tavares de Melo Cavalcanti (Rio de Janeiro), tel. of [Jan.? 1900], AEP/10/32. João Tavares de Melo Cavalcanti (Filho) was "Tavares" in Epitácio's political correspondence. He is not to be confused with João de Lyra Tavares, whom Epitácio addressed as "Lyra" in his letters. Epitácio's telegram, attached to a copy of President Campos Sales's telegram to Paraíba Governor Gama e Melo bearing the same date (see n. 61), informed João Tavares that it was at Epitácio's personal request that Campos Sales was intervening to communicate his "suggestions," i.e., that João Tavares should be nominated and elected governor in 1900. This telegram offers direct evidence for Epitácio's intervention with President Campos Sales on behalf of an Autonomista government in Paraíba. What is more important, it connects the outcome of the 1900 congressional election, as well as the 1899 Assembly contest, to the earlier struggle over the governorship, a circumstance the scholarly literature has ignored. Cf. Carone, *República Velha*, pp. 307–308.

[60] Mariz, *Apanhados historicos*, pp. 307–308.

that the next governor of Paraíba should be João Tavares de Melo Cavalcanti.[61] In an extremely understated and cautionary tone, Campos Sales indicated that the Paraíba oligarchy would find itself in serious trouble if his suggestion was not heeded: "Without wanting to intervene in the private affairs of the state, but having in view the possibility that state politics in Paraíba could become more impassioned and create problems, I would ask you to concur patriotically to a solution which will conciliate state interests."[62]

Campos Sales's oblique phrasing pointed to the federal congressional elections, which had already been held on December 30, 1899. They were still susceptible to reversal if the appropriate committees of both houses did not certify Governor Gama e Melo's official slates as the winners. The five seats in the House of Deputies, as well as the lone Senate seat, potentially could be awarded to the Autonomista losers. Campos Sales was indicating his tremendous influence in this respect when he warned Governor Gama e Melo: "The nomination of this candidate [João Tavares de Melo Cavalcanti] would also bring the advantage of removing great embarrassments that are predictable in the verification of the [respective voting] strengths in the federal election of [your] state."[63]

Defiantly, Gama e Melo ignored the president's threat and placed his preferred candidate, another Old Liberal, in the governorship for 1900–1904. He selected the grandson of that party's Ferreira Leite and Toscano de Brito founders, Federal Judge José Peregrino de Araújo. In so doing, he initiated a tempestuous period of open conflict between the Autonomistas and the partisans of the incumbent oligarchy. He also challenged Campos Sales to deliver what soon would be known colloquially as a presidential *degola* or "beheading." The president did so in 1900; thus, a federal degola was first used to punish a disobedient state oligarchy in Paraíba. Campos Sales's action implied that in the future official slates of state oligarchies had to be cleared with the president of Brazil before they were officially announced and circulated. Otherwise, a state governor would risk presidential disciplining. By making alterations in the parliamentary procedures of both

[61] President Campos Sales to Dr. Gama e Melo, Governor (Rio de Janeiro), tel. of [Jan.? 1900], AEP/10/32. (See n. 59 for Epitácio's telegram to João Tavares.) Laurita Pessoa is silent about the "Case of Paraíba" in 1900 in spite of the considerable press attention it received.

[62] Ibid.

[63] Ibid.

houses of congress, Campos Sales also insured that thereafter the president would have the last say about which slate of candidates—or which individual candidates from both slates—would be officially recognized as the winners of federal elections and be seated as legitimate members of their state's delegation.[64] Such a policy, subsequently known as "the politics of the governors," rendered secondary the official electoral returns presented to the congressional credentials committees. When a governor attempted to have his slate of winning congressional candidates seated without having secured a presidential assent, he ran the risk of a degola.[65] In such instances, he would witness the rival slate's candidates being seated and his own excluded.

In 1900, Governor Gama e Melo faced a dilemma. If he deferred to the presidential suggestion and named Second Lieutenant Governor João Tavares de Melo Cavalcanti as the official gubernatorial candidate, he would be turning over the state government not to an Old Liberal (a Valfredista or Alvarista) but to an Old Conservative, one with strong ambitions and a powerful family-based group behind him. João Tavares was personally loyal to Trinidade as his factional chief, and Trinidade was cooperating secretly with the Automistas after 1897. In short, as governor, João Tavares would open the door of state politics to Autonomista control. Especially if several deaths were to occur among the aging members of the federal delegation, the new governor could fill the vacancies with Autonomistas.[66]

[64] Although Campos Sales defended his "politics of the states" [i.e., "governors"] on the ground that it countermanded the centrifugal force of factional politics in Brazil, others argued that it was responsible for the oligarchies' tremendous power during the Old Republic. José Maria Bello even asserted that it had created the oligarchies: "Campos Sales' federalism and presidentialism resulted in the formation of state oligarchies and the crushing of Congress, and rendered it impossible to control republican politics by means of large national parties." *History Brazil*, p. 164.

[65] Campos Sales used the term "faction" (*facão*) in defending his politics of the states, implicitly divorcing the word from the notion of a true political party, just as he did the term "fraction" (*fração*). *Propaganda à presidencia*, pp. 153, 227–34.

[66] Documentation in Epitácio's archive was too meager for 1898–1899 to discern exactly what transpired between the time the Autonomistas and Meiristas negotiated an accord, in December 1897, and the time Campos Sales intervened in the Paraíba gubernatorial race in January 1900. However, the Meiristas and Autonomistas ran a combined slate for the Assembly in the December (1899) elections. By 1901, Epitácio and Trinidade appeared to be on antagonistic terms because Epitácio was willing to follow Vice-President Rosa e Silva's orientation and Trinidade was not. M. T. Cavalcanti, Preface to A. Nóbrega, *História republicana*, p. 18. See also Epitácio to [Francisco Alves de] Lima Filho (Rio de Janeiro), Aug. or Sept. 1901, in E. Pessoa, *Obras completas*, 2:257–58; and n. 69, below.

The Old Liberal candidate, José Peregrino, had officially carried the gubernatorial election of June 1900. However, since he would not be inaugurated until October 22, incumbent Governor Gama e Melo could still set him aside in favor of João Tavares de Melo Cavalcanti. The governor, in other words, might have complied with President Campos Sales's "suggestion" by having João Tavares certified the winner in a recount. His refusal created a political impasse in Paraíba throughout 1900. Countless incidents of violent confrontation arose between opposing factions in Paraíba. The entire nation became spectators to a burlesque competition, as *two* congressional delegations from Paraíba descended on the national capital, each determined to be officially recognized and claiming to have been rightfully elected. Both delegations issued their demands from the floor of Congress, hurling accusations and counteraccusations of electoral fraud or presidential influence at their opponents.

At the state level, two rival slates of Assembly candidates also contested the December 1899 election. The dominant oligarchy's partisans fought with their Autonomista rivals in the streets of the Capital throughout the year. Because elections to the Assembly were also subject to a federal review that certified the winners, the political fortunes of state legislature candidates were tied to the outcome of the federal contest. The dispute implied an influential role for President Campos Sales. In Congress, Epitácio was singled out for verbal attack because it was believed that his political influence with the Brazilian president would determine the electoral outcome in Paraíba.[67]

In June 1900, the "Case of Paraíba" became immortal when Campos Sales executed his famous degola. Both in Congress and in the Paraíba Assembly, the Autonomista slates were declared the official winners of the elections. In spite of the historic precedent it set, the "Case of Paraíba" proved a short-run victory for the

[67] Epitácio was accused of offering a "deal" to Gama e Melo, whereby Gama would move to the House of Deputies and, eventually, acquire a Senate seat, if he first enabled João Tavares to become his successor. Gama e Melo was expected to resign the governorship in favor of the first lieutenant governor (Joaquim Fernandes) who would, in turn, resign in favor of the second lieutenant governor, João Tavares. Epitácio to [Francisco Alves de] Lima Filho (Rio de Janeiro) Aug. or Sept. 1901, in E. Pessoa, *Obras completas*, 2:258. Lima Filho, whom Epitácio had earlier indicated as a go-between with Gama e Melo, accused Epitácio of making this deal, as did Trinidade. The charge appears accurate. Indeed, Epitácio had pointed to Gama e Melo's precarious financial situation after he left the governorship as a factor that would tempt him to negotiate a deal. Epitácio to Venâncio (Rio de Janeiro), 15 Aug. 1900; *Obras completas*, 2:258.

13. Flanked by troops from the state police, Gov. Álvaro Machado's 1905 inaugural parade approaches the Paraíba State Assembly. (José de Nazareth Rodriguez, ed., *2 séculos da cidade; passeio retrospectivo—1870–1930,* n.p.)

14. President Campos Sales's first cabinet: (standing, from left to right) Epitácio Pessoa (Justice, Education, and Culture), Olinto de Magalhães (Foreign Affairs), and Severino Vieira (Transportation); Adm. Balthazar da Silveira (Navy), General Mallet (War), and Joaquim Murtinho (Interior) are seated, left to right. (Courtesy of the Instituto Histórico e Geográfico Brasileiro)

Autonomistas. The determining factor in the 1900 electoral crisis turned out to be not the minister of justice's widely acknowledged influence with Campos Sales but what Epitácio himself would describe as "the police and thugs (*capangada*) of Peregrino."[68] The Autonomistas' factional followers simply were not strong enough to maintain themselves in Paraíba against the pro-Peregrino coalition. In Paraíba, the Peregrino government still commanded. Following their declaration as the official winners of the election, the Autonomistas invaded the Assembly, assumed their seats, and elected João Tavares de Melo Cavalcanti the president of that body. Taking advantage of President Campos Sales's absence in Argentina, Governor Peregrino ordered his police to surround the Assembly and clear it of its last protesting Autonomista. Throughout the state, but especially in the Capital, Peregrino controlled the police power on behalf of the Old Liberals. After six months of intermittent street fighting in the environs of the Assembly, Epitácio acknowledged that the Autonomistas were not the stronger faction. He was, however, hard pressed to convince Venâncio and key Autonomista lieutenants in Paraíba not to seek presidential intervention to remedy the situation.[69] Epitácio argued instead that the Autonomistas should sue for peace, acknowledge their weaker position, and negotiate with the new governor-elect.

To persuade Venâncio that they should "study" reaching a precise agreement with José Peregrino, Epitácio candidly assessed the hopelessness of holding out for federal recognition of João Tavares de Melo Cavalcanti as the officially elected governor:

> On October 22, Gama [e Melo], the legitimate governor, will transmit the government [to] José Peregrino, supported by the State Police Force and by the Assembly [i.e., the governor's favored slate] with whose Executive Power [i.e., the gubernatorially indicated president of the Assembly] he maintains [good] relations [so] that it votes for the laws [that he executes] without protest. What can we do? Have recourse to civil elements [i.e., their factional followings] in order to place Tavares in power? We are not capable of confronting the police and the thugs of Peregrino; this is the truth; we would be left looking very rash and presumptuous. Resort to federal [armed]

[68] Epitácio to Venâncio (Rio de Janeiro), Aug. 1900, in E. Pessoa, *Obras completas*, 2:254.

[69] Ibid., p. 255.

> intervention? Do you not realize that this would not redound to the good of the [Autonomist] Party? [Or] that I, with responsibilities in the federal government and solidly behind the Constitution's ends, cannot propose or suggest to the President a move of that magnitude . . . ? It is out of the question, for it would sacrifice all of our principles, our prestige, and our credit.[70]

Even if Tavares were placed in the governorship and enjoyed the support of the State Police—a crucial determinant of the outcome—Epitácio argued to Venâncio, "Peregrino would not remain quietly at home" or "forget that he has friends, a strong party, a press ready to advocate his cause, municipal councils working for him . . . and deputies and senators who would soon give articulation to his protest."[71] Peregrino's "inevitable" protests to the federal government, Epitácio assured Venâncio, would lead Congress eventually to award him the victory. Epitácio counseled that the Autonomistas should instead count on the inevitability of schismatic divisions within the Alvarista–Valfredista coalition. Explicitly recognizing that factional politics depended on fluid alliances, he predicted a splintering within the dominant coalition because "power is power," and advised cooperation:

> I propose an agreement with Peregrino that, if still possible, would enable us to get a governor from our side. Things are on such a footing and embarrassments so large, that I dare to say we should accept conciliation. . . . The change of governors offers the opportunity for a rapprochement with the state government. I, continuing as I expect in the Ministry [of Justice] will, little by little, move to assume an influential position in the affairs of state so as to guarantee and maintain our party's rights.[72]

The documentation in Epitácio's archive revealed no evidence directly connecting his influence to Campos Sales's decision to seat the Autonomistas.[73] It did establish, however, that the presi-

[70] Ibid., p. 254.

[71] Ibid.

[72] Ibid., pp. 255–56. "Power is power" is a literal translation of "*O poder é o poder.*"

[73] The swing vote on the divided five-member Credentials Committee was cast by a Mineiro deputy in favor of recognizing Epitácio's slate—after Epitácio had written the governor of Minas to ask for his support vis-à-vis the Minas congressional delegate on the committee. Epitácio to [Governor] Silviano Brandão (Rio de

dent had attempted a compromise slate prior to the 1900 congressional election that would have included Meiristas and Autonomistas in the Machado–Leal oligarchy's official slate. In 1899, Epitácio had met for that purpose with President Campos Sales and Sen. Pinheiro Machado, who represented Sen. Álvaro Machado and his governor, but a mixed slate failed to appear.[74] The archival evidence of Campos Sales's earlier insistence on João Tavares de Melo Cavalcanti's gubernatorial candidacy, however, also confirmed Epitácio's role on behalf of the Autonomista congressional candidates. Quite plainly, Campos Sales had delivered on the threat in his telegram to Governor Gama e Melo in early 1900. Public opinion and the subsequent judgment of historians also concurred that the president was acting directly on Epitácio's behalf by recognizing the Autonomista slates.

Undoubtedly, Campos Sales also had acted for what he believed to be reasons of state, although they coincided with Epitácio's aims in Paraíba politics.[75] He knew that disciplining the Paraíba oligarchy, which had been affiliated with his opponent, Sen. Francisco Glicério, since the early nineties, would strengthen the presidency. His degola served as a warning to any other state governor contemplating an independent course of action. His "politics of the governors" also enhanced the congressional influence of the more powerful states on which the national executive directly depended, by making it more likely they could rely on a majority for

---

Janeiro), n.d. [1900, before 23 Apr.], AEP/10/23. The Credentials Committee's official report ruling in favor of seating the combined Autonomista–Meirista opposition slate is Parecer No. 69-1900, published in Brazil, Congresso Nacional, *Annaes da Camara dos Deputados, Terceira Sessão da Terceira Legislatura,* Vol. 1: *(Sessões de 18 de abril a 31 de maio de 1900)* (Rio de Janeiro: Imprensa Oficial, 1900), pp. 102–22. Seated on June 11, 1900, the official delegation included João Soares Neiva, Francisco Alves de Lima Filho, and Francisco Camilo de Holanda (Autonomistas), and Antônio Trinidade da Meira Henriques and Antônio Marques da Silva Mariz (Meiristas). Ibid., Vol. 2: *(Sessões de 1 a 30 de junho de 1900),* p. 168.

[74] Epitácio's telegrams to Venâncio (Rio de Janeiro), n.d. [1899–1900], in AEP/10/79, contain details of an aborted compromise Campos Sales tried to effect between Epitácio and Álvaro.

[75] In describing the procedural changes he imposed on the national legislature in 1900 instituting his "politics of the states," Campos Sales indirectly related their introduction to the dilemma presented by the "Case of Paraíba," citing the "terrifying thought that a *dual legislature* might exist" composed of "Republicans" (the official slate) and "Concentrados" (the Autonomist–Meirista slate) (italics added). Campos Sales, *Propaganda a presidencia,* p. 236. On Campos Sales's formulation of the politics of the governors, which preceded the "Case of Paraíba," see Rosa Maria Godoy Silveira, *Republicanismo e federalismo, 1889–1902* (João Pessoa: Editôra Universitária, 1978), pp. 143–82.

their legislative initiatives. A secondary consideration in Campos Sales's decision had been the popularity and immense prestige of Sen. Almeida Barreto. As the military officer who had opposed the emperor at a critical moment in 1889, Almeida Barreto enjoyed the status of "a venerated reliquary" of the Republic.[76] Recognition of the official slate would have removed Almeida Barreto from his seat in the Senate, silencing his voice in Congress for the first time since 1890. Consequently, Paraíba's senior senator also retained his seat by virtue of the degola.

The victory Campos Sales handed the Autonomistas in 1900 was so compromised by the political situation in their home state that both the incumbent oligarchy and local historians subsequently judged it a failure. Epitácio's judgment proved correct: The Autonomistas were no match for Peregrino's forces, who even controlled the federal battalion in the Capital. Sympathizers with the incumbent oligarchy later wrote that the Autonomistas were so disgusted and dejected by their forcible removal from the Assembly that they formally dissolved their party the following day.[77] For the remainder of the Fourth Session of the Assembly, Peregrino's slate legislated and ignored the powerless Autonomistas.

Yet Campos Sales's degola was not as empty a victory as many tried to make it. Epitácio argued to Venâncio that real progress had been made. Did they not have a minister (himself) in the president's cabinet and had not the degola given them a senator and three federal deputies?[78] For the first time, Álvaro and Valfredo would have to take their rivals into account, if only because their own coalition was now more vulnerable to internal splits, due to Epitácio's influence with the president. In addition, civil strife in

[76] "In the Senate, Marshal Almeida Barreto was very much loved, as if he were a venerated reliquary of the fifteenth of November." M. T. Cavalcanti, Preface, *História republicana*, p. 18. Almeida Barreto was recognized and officially seated in the Senate on May 23, 1900. Brazil, Congresso Nacional, *Annaes do Senado Federal, Primeira Sessão da Quarta Legislatura, Sessões de 18 de abril a 31 de julho de 1900* (Rio de Janeiro: Imprensa Nacional, 1900), 1:120. See pp. 92–119 for the full debate, esp. Álvaro Machado's rebuttal of Parecer 121, containing a review of all of Paraíba's contested elections since 1894 (pp. 102–19).

[77] E. Câmara, *Datas campinenses*, p. 37 (n. 20); Mariz, *Apanhados historicos*, pp. 309–10. On the dissolution of the Autonomista Party, see A. Nóbrega, *História republicana*, pp. 89–90; E. de Almeida, *História Campina*, pp. 253–54.

[78] Epitácio to João Tavares [de Melo Cavalcanti] (Rio de Janeiro), 27 Nov. 1900, in E. Pessoa, *Obras completas*, 2:257. Campos Sales's degola also awarded João Tavares the first lieutenant governorship on May 24, 1900. *Annaes Camara, Terceira Sessão, Terceira Legislatura*, 1:210.

the Capital continued to characterize Peregrino's administration, for the weaker Autonomistas could still disrupt civil order and fight back. Above all, the incumbent oligarchy had to consider that Epitácio's growing federal influence might again threaten their representation in Congress.

Epitácio's patient strategy for revanche had obviously produced results. After ten long years he and Venâncio could seriously contemplate a reintegration of their partisans within the dominant oligarchy that had preserved the Empire's major family-based groups. During the next decade, earlier divisions continued to preoccupy the incumbent oligarchy with intraelite conflict, as well as challenges by a more aggressive opposition. The political and economic fluctuations of the nineties had left little opportunity to contemplate the tremendous growth coming after 1900 from a cotton boom. "White gold" soon produced new spoils for factional competition. The internal splintering that Epitácio predicted soon appeared, offering the Autonomistas an opening to return to power. Henceforth, however, revanche would be pursued not as Autonomistas but as Epitacistas. After the 1900 degola, "Dr. Epitácio began to have a national political trajectory. . . . From this time forth, the Venancistas took new blood and demoted Alvaristas in various contests."[79]

[79] Mariz, *Apanhados historicos*, p. 308.

· VI ·

From "Anarchy" to "Order," 1900–1912

> My insistence in favor of [my brother] Antônio could appear to be a family matter and conceal the motive of implanting one oligarchy in Paraíba under the pretext of bringing down another.
>
> —Epitácio Pessoa to Pedro da Cunha Pedrosa, December 21, 1911

> They [the Salvationists] talk about oligarchy in Paraíba, but this is a pretext for a campaign they intend to mount against those in power [the Machado–Pessoa–Leal oligarchy]. Oligarchy does not exist among us; we are entering a new and promising phase.
>
> —Valfredo Leal to Epitácio Pessoa, February 24, 1912

THE SECOND DECADE of Machado–Leal rule in Paraíba coincided with a period of republican consolidation in the nation. Thanks to "the politics of the governors," the presidential succession did not engender the domestic conflict that had characterized national politics in the nineties, nor did secessionist movements wrack the nation. Under the political entente defined between São Paulo and Minas, colloquially christened "the politics of café com leite," federal policy favored the expansion of the export sector, guaranteeing the preeminence of the coffee elite in the polity. The federalism embodied in the 1891 Constitution ensured São Paulo's unrivaled position in the nation and militated against a more equitable distribution of national revenues to the poorer states of the Northeast, North, and Far West. "King Coffee" determined Brazil's new economic well-being, but the Constitution provided that the export taxes levied on coffee would accrue to the treasuries of the states whose planters cultivated and sold it. The states of the Northeast confronted a widening of the gap in political influence and economic growth between them and the wealthier states. Another drought in 1899–1900 only intensified their appreciation of growing regional inequality. Subordinated to the president of Brazil by "the politics of the governors," the northeastern states, even as a regional voting bloc, could obtain only minimal federal resources.

A divisive presidential election in 1910, however, hinted at the changes the 1920s would witness, beginning in Epitácio Pessoa's own presidential administration. The 1910 campaign carried important implications for family-based oligarchy in Paraíba as well. Nationally, it reflected the new ascendance of Riograndense Sen. Pinheiro Machado, president of the Senate. His candidate, Gen. Hermes [Rodrigues] da Fonseca, was pitted against a civilian, Bahia's Sen. Rui Barbosa, Brazil's knight errant of liberalism. When Hermes emerged the victor, Rio Grande do Sul irrevocably influenced the partnership between São Paulo and Minas Gerais and secured a decisive voice in determining the presidential succession. For the first time since the nineties, the role of the military in politics again became an issue; however, it was the oligarchies that emerged in the aftermath of the campaign as the fundamental issue, for the presidential candidates had appealed to the urban middle and working classes for votes. Identified with the old agrarian order and smacking of a retrograde association with the Empire's "aristocratic" base, Rui could not escape his oligarchical backing. Nor could Hermes's supporters be described as free of the taint of oligarchy, due to Pinheiro's backing. The significance of the campaign lay in the political awakening of Brazil's tens of thousands of new urban voters, who began to become consciously antiagrarian as they perceived how national political organization was weighted in favor of rural interests.

In Paraíba, where the 1910 presidential vote was loyally delivered to Hermes, "oligarchy" was raised more as a pseudo-issue than a real one. The national mood, however, found some sincere resonance. Certain characteristics associated locally with oligarchy—family-based warfare, banditry, and the region's inferior position in the nation—came under closer scrutiny and more vocal attack. Given another decade of national political developments, this critique would gain greater significance, obliging Paraíba's more powerful family-based groups to defend their mode of political organization. Meanwhile, by virtue of the assistance offered in 1912 by President Hermes himself, oligarchy endured for two more decades in Paraíba—under the direct leadership of Epitácio Pessoa and his family-based network.

Factional Politics, 1900–1908

The "Anarchy of the Municípios"

The presidential disciplining meted out by Campos Sales to the Machado–Leal oligarchy in 1900 inaugurated a period of local factional disarray within Paraíba's ruling coalition. The oligarchy's twelve remaining years in power became known as "years of anarchy," specifically "the anarchy of Álvaro Machado." By 1915, when Epitácio gained hegemonic control of the state, the years of anarchy would be deliberately contrasted with "the order of Epitácio Pessoa." Anarchy and order connoted divergent styles of oligarchical organization in Paraíba, although oligarchy's foundation in a family-based system of factional politics endured throughout Epitácio's leadership. Anarchy and order signified the implicit expectations Paraíba's politicians held, precisely in terms of how their factional divisions continued to be grounded in family-based affiliations. Incumbent local bosses expected congruence between the state and município levels of government, so that, as Alvaristas and Valfredistas, the distribution of local offices would guarantee their family-based groups firm control and deny the Autonomista opposition political representation. Instead, "anarchy" began to overtake them in 1902, when the Old Liberal families of the backlands, who had loyally supported the Machado–Leal oligarchy for a decade, were forced to share power with their adversaries, the Autonomistas. Furthermore, they found themselves even replaced by those Old Conservatives, who, as Venancistas and Epitacistas—in alliance with the Meiristas—sought to control a majority of Paraíba's thirty-nine municípios.

Largely thanks to Epitácio's growing national political role, his formerly Autonomista followers first gained representation in município councils and the local offices of prefeito, deputy prefeito, resident police officer, and justice of the peace. Consequently, as the appointees of Álvaro and Valfredo, they received recognition from the dominant oligarchy as official local bosses of the PRP. Then, in 1908, thanks to a formal pact between Álvaro and Epitácio, they gained one-half the seats in the Assembly. Forced to cede a dominant position at all levels of government, the Old Liberal wing of the Machado–Leal oligarchy in the backlands resorted to violence at the local level to check the rising political gains of their adversaries, the Venancistas and Epitacistas. The latter, emboldened by their statewide revanche at the local level, challenged their Alvarista or Valfredista rivals openly in armed conflicts, believing their improving political position would help them to defend themselves.

"Anarchy," consequently, referred to two connected phenomena. First, the term connoted not a true state of anarchy, but the disappearance of the oligarchy's near-hegemony in Paraíba's municípios. No longer did the ruling oligarchy consist exclusively of Alvaristas or Valfredistas. In more and more municípios, the rapprochement between Álvaro and Epitácio forced the Alvaristas to divide the municipal council seats evenly with the Venancistas. In many cases, they suffered the governor's humiliating appointment of a prefeito chosen from among their adversaries. The second phenomenon was the escalation of local violence, most dramatically an epidemic of banditry that characterized Paraíba after 1900. Fundamentally, however, local violence perpetuated the historical pattern of family warfare, with a spectacular recrudescence of feuding in every geoeconomic zone of Paraíba except the coast. Exacerbating traditional rivalries, the drought of 1899–1900 was followed by a cotton boom for the next three decades, which exerted a powerful influence in factional competition at the município level. The unprecedented economic gains brought new urgency to the local struggles to control political officeholding. As a result, family warfare in the municípios spiraled upward.

The explanation for the "anarchy" that characterized the last decade of the Machado–Leal rule lay paradoxically in the success of Epitácio Pessoa's political challenge. The presidential decision favoring the Autonomistas in the election of 1900 brought them considerable political advantage for the long run. Even Venâncio's formal dissolution of the Autonomist Party in 1900 signaled not a factional defeat but a victory. It removed the only obstacle to affiliation with the Machado–Leal oligarchy. During the last two years of José Peregrino's governorship, between 1902 and 1904, the course of Autonomista revanche was clear-cut: The Machado–Leal oligarchy was obliged to adopt the policy of reintegrating its rivals, first at the local and then the state level of government. Primarily, Epitácio's potential influence at the federal level in future elections dictated this course of action. Although he was obliged to leave the Ministry of Justice in August of 1901, after student demonstrations directed against his educational reforms threatened Campos Sales's efforts to maintain public order in the nation's capital, Epitácio moved to a more influential position of public responsibility less than five months later. In January 1902, the president appointed him a justice of the Supreme Court. Five months later, on June 7, he was appointed concurrent attorney general, a position he would hold until 1905.

The willingness of Álvaro and Valfredo to incorporate a proportion of Venancistas and Epitacistas in their ruling coalition merely reflected one organizational verity of a factional system of politics. Any faction that gained sufficient political influence to threaten the incumbent oligarchy's political majority would find itself becoming an official ally.[1] Consequently, the Venancistas, who represented a preponderance of Epitácio's "elements," or supporters, continued to be identified by that personalistic label because they became only the allies of Álvaro and Valfredo, not their personal supporters. Col. Cristiano Lauritzen made this point emphatically to Álvaro Machado in a conversation between them in 1903. As Campina Grande's prospective new political boss, Cristiano visited Rio de Janeiro to lobby for extending the railroad from Itabaiana to Campina Grande. Accompanied by his old political friend, Sen. Almeida Barreto, Cristiano was received by President Rodrigues Alves in a special audience convened to announce the federal authorization of funds for the long-sought rail connection.[2] Before Cristiano left Rio de Janeiro, he was assured he would soon be appointed Campina Grande's local party boss on behalf of the incumbent oligarchy, displacing his Old Liberal adversaries, the Portos, Agras, and Sousa Campos, in the partisan leadership of the município. Furthermore, Álvaro pledged that in the following year he would appoint Cristiano and his brother-in-law Campina's prefeito and deputy prefeito, respectively, for 1904–1908. With a majority of the municipal council seats awarded to his formerly Autonomista bloc of family-based groups, the Gringo's "years of exile" had ended.[3]

The arrangement between Cristiano and Álvaro, one of around ten negotiated between 1902 and 1905, signified that Epitácio had become a silent partner in the Machado–Leal oligarchy, for his consent was a condition of Cristiano's acceptance of Alvaro's of-

[1] Waterbury's "segmental faction," as the principal instrument for competition for the control and allocation of resources, is germane. The segmental faction is "bound at once by affective links and common material interests and engaged in both ritualistic and objective conflict." *Commander of the Faithful*, p. 68. Thus, factional recombination is in the self-interest (material and affective) of the participants for long-run survival.

[2] E. de Almeida, *História Campina*, p. 347.

[3] Ibid., p. 361.

fer. Indeed, the offer was part of Epitácio's grand design. In bargaining with Álvaro for a gradual restoration of Old Conservatives to leadership positions within the oligarchy, however, Epitácio took a calculated risk. Armed force still decided local contests for domination. Even as the officially designated representatives of Álvaro's party and electoral machine—not to mention as the group controlling local political office—Epitácio's and Venâncio's followers would have to fight. They would be expected to back up their appointments by dominating elections. Cristiano Lauritzen's appointment offered a crucial test, since in Campina Grande former Conservatives and Liberals were almost evenly matched in their capacities to react violently.

No one understood the power considerations better than Col. Cristiano Lauritzen himself. His acceptance of Álvaro's invitation to become PRP party boss of Campina Grande specified certain "guarantees" vis-à-vis his local adversaries designed to insulate his own following. A decade later, he reminisced in a candid letter to Epitácio about the latter's role in his rapprochement with the incumbent oligarchy, referring to the subordinate position he and his Cavalcanti de Albuquerque family-based group had still occupied in Campina even after he became the local party boss and prefeito:

> During the ten years of fights necessary for us to reconquer our lost positions [i.e., local political offices], from which we were violently ejected [in 1892 when Álvaro was installed as governor], no one suffered as much as I and my friends did, and because of the element that here in Campina had been called Liberal in the Empire and today is called [the] Democratic [Party]. It is the most pernicious and unscrupulous element that exists in the state, directed as it is by the Agras [i.e., the family of João da Costa Agra].[4] That family, in spite of enjoying a recognized position, is the most crapulous and undignified that ever existed. In order not to continue indefinitely

[4] Until 1904, Campina Grande's Old Liberals were still headed by aging Col. João Lourenço Porto (1831–1928), their party boss in the Empire. His young nephew, Dr. Afonso (Rodrigues) de Sousa Campos, succeeded him after 1905. The Sousa Campos and Agras were virtually one family after three generations of matrimonial exchange. Three Agra sisters had married three Sousa Campos brothers who were also their first cousins; a fourth Sousa Campos sister had married another cousin, Col. Salvino [Gonçalves] de Figueirêdo, who succeeded to the leadership of the Porto–Sousa Campos/Agra–Figueirêdo bloc on the death of Afonso de Sousa Campos in 1915. Author's prosopographical file.

> with my friends in being the victims of people such as these, I accepted, in agreement with Drs. Epitácio and Venâncio, the invitation of Álvaro Machado [in 1903] to enter his party. He distinguished me with his good will and personal trust.
>
> We entered the ranks of the [Alvarista] Party and were well treated by its chief. But you understand, Dr. Epitácio, we were *agregados* [dependents; literally, squatters] and we entered only after enormous concessions.[5]

Cristiano's penchant for underrating his own strengths when reciting the injustices done him by the Agras extended in this case to omitting reference to the concession he had extracted from Álvaro: Cristiano would not be required "to enter agreements with his local adversaries," the Old Liberals.[6] Moreover, Cristiano's stipulation that his followers "would not become allies of the Alvaristas" was met.[7] In effect, he became a working ally of Álvaro and Valfredo at the state level for the purpose of delivering the votes of his family-based group and its allies, but he uncharacteristically was exempted from local political cooperation with the Old Liberals. Sensing that a formal alliance with the Portos and intermarried Agras and Sousa Campos, who previously had dominated Campina Grande, would render his already precarious situation more vulnerable, Coronel Cristiano maintained his faction's distance. A decade of bitter feuding had made it unrealistic for Campina Grande's competing family blocs to cooperate as allies. Consequently, throughout the twenties, Old Liberals and Old Conservatives continued to mount competing slates of candidates in local elections. On those occasions, their armed confrontations rose to peak levels. In many other localities too, reintegration of the former Autonomistas progressively "anarchized" the municípios; eventually, Álvaro's Old Liberal base of support eroded.

Although no record survived of Epitácio's criteria for selecting municípios that were to have their Old Conservative family leadership restored, by 1905 it was evident that the Old Liberals in the backlands zones were the hardest hurt by his strategy of revanche. Álvaro apparently deemed those zones more expendable, perhaps because an older generation of imperial local bosses had been more firmly entrenched there before 1900. Gov. José Peregrino evidently concurred, even though he belonged to the same backlands age co-

[5] Cristiano Lauritzen to Epitácio (Campina Grande), 15 May 1912, AEP/10/169.

[6] E. de Almeida, *História Campina*, p. 176.

[7] Ibid., p. 361.

hort. In 1904, he had the Assembly revoke a 1900 law that opportunistically had extinguished the offices of prefeito and deputy prefeito. New legislation conferred on the governor the appointive power for filling those offices as well as the right to intervene in município affairs and remove a prefeito.[8] Implicitly, Álvaro calculated that he could rely on his core support from the brejo zone, especially his own Areia clique of politicians, and substitute cooperative Venancistas from the backlands for most of the Old Liberal bosses there.

A major impetus for the demotion of Old Liberals in the backlands zones came in 1902 from Pedro da Cunha Pedrosa, a key Venancista in Gov. José Peregrino's cabinet. A loyal veteran of 1890–1891, when Venâncio had placed him in the Constituent Assembly, Pedrosa was appointed to Epitácio's former cabinet post as secretary of government. His strategic task was the reintegration of his fellow Venancistas in the politics of Paraíba's municípios. As his memoirs later made clear, Old Conservatives soon took control of those interior municípios where the Liberal Party had been the stronger element in the 1880s.[9] Epitácio's home município of Umbuseiro, which in the 1880s had been under the Liberal leadership of his godfather, Manuel de Assunção Santiago, was one of the first to experience a partisan reversal. Pedrosa later explained how he had assisted Epitácio's brother, Col. Antônio Pessoa, to become that município's party boss in 1903:

> Coronel Antônio Pessoa was invited to assume the political leadership of Umbuseiro by Simeão [dos Santos] Leal, State Chief of Police for [Gov.] José Peregrino. He replaced Coronel Sindulfo Calafate Calafange who until that time had the job. However, since I had affiliated with Alvaro's government in 1902, Coronel Pessoa wanted me to represent him to the powers [government] of the state, and from then on, whatever he wanted for Umbuseiro was obtained through my intervention. I represented him in all political affairs treated in the Ex-

[8] Three weeks after his gubernatorial inauguration, Álvaro reestablished Law No. 27 of 2 May 1895, on 14 Nov. 1904 (as Law No. 221). Ibid.

[9] In addition to Coronel Cristiano of Campina Grande and Umbuseiro's José Fabio de Costa Lira, the following Old Conservative political bosses were allied with Álvaro in 1909: Col., Marcolino Pereira in Princesa, Col. João Tavares de Melo Cavalcanti in Alagoa Nova, Felix Daltro in Taperoá, Antônio Gomes de Arruda Barreto in Brejo do Cruz, Col. Pedro Bezerra da Silveira Leal in Alagoa do Monteiro, and Col. Benvenuto Gonçalves da Costa in Catolé do Rocha. State of Paraíba, *Almanach administrativo, 1909*, p. 335.

ecutive Committee [of Álvaro's PRP] or in Party Conventions. This occurred until he assumed the governorship [in 1915].[10]

Reintegration and Epitácio's Family-Based Network

Pedrosa's account revealed the extent to which key intermediaries in Epitácio's family-based network, such as Pedrosa, were architects of factional reintegration for the former Autonomistas. Epitácio's revanche, set in motion by his demonstrated influence in federal electoral politics during 1900, depended equally on the less visible contributions of the members of his family-based network. Pedrosa, who had received his first significant career appointment from Gov. Venâncio Neiva in 1890, when he was designated federal district judge for the backlands município of Sousa, was its most able member.[11] He had been born in the Barra de Natuba district of Umbuseiro where both Epitácio and Col. Antônio Pessoa had been born. Only two years older than Epitácio, with whom he had attended the Recife Law School, Pedrosa had also been a neighbor of Col. Antônio Pessoa between 1892 and 1902, when he withdrew from state politics to manage his family estate in Natuba. Like Epitácio, he had a large extended family in Umbuseiro, some of whom were intermarried with the Pessoas' Pereira, Lucena, and Barbosa cousins. In interceding on Col. Antônio Pessoa's behalf with Gov. José Peregrino, Pedrosa had acted also to favor his own family faction in that município.[12]

[10] Cunha Pedrosa, *Minhas memórias*, 1:173. As early as 1901, Epitácio had advised his brother Antônio to accept the political leadership of Umbuseiro. Epitácio to Col. Antônio Pessoa (Rio de Janeiro), 10 Nov. 1901, ACAP/1.

[11] Pedrosa's massive, family-based network in Paraíba started to grow politically when Abiaí named him municipal judge for Pilar in 1887 and he became a friend of Col. José Lins de Albuquerque. In Sousa, Pedrosa favored the Old Conservative family bloc led by Col. José Gomes de Sá, but he also cultivated the good will of the opposition boss, Dr. Antônio Marques da Silva Mariz. When asked to nominate a Sousa politician to the Constituent Assembly, he diplomatically indicated both bosses' names. Forty-three years later, he remained in touch with the Gomes de Sá; and Pilar's Col. José Lins sent congratulatory telegrams on Pedrosa's saint's day for over thirty years. *Minhas memórias*, 1:56–58 and 60; E. de Almeida, *História Campina*, p. 334.

[12] Biographical material on Pedro Pedrosa is taken from his memoirs: *Minhas memórias*, 1:9–42. Pedrosa's mother (and probably his father; apparently, they were double cousins) was a Pereira de Araújo on both sides of her family. Azevêdo Bastos, *Roteiro Azevêdo*, p. 388. His daughter Stella Pedrosa married Joaquim Gomes Hardmann, a relative of Col. Antônio Pessoa's wife's Gomes da Silveira family. Ibid., p. 384.

Col. Antônio Pessoa's nomination as Umbuseiro's party boss in 1903 illustrated several dimensions of local parentela politics in Epitácio's strategy for a revanche. First, Antônio Pessoa's appointment was of some assistance in extricating him from a precarious position in a local feud with Umbuseiro's previous party boss, Col. Sindulfo Calafange, his wife's kinsman.[13] Second, the appointment placed him advantageously to move to the more influential position of deputy in the State Assembly in 1908. Finally, as Epitácio's brother, Antônio was the one individual whom Paraíba's future political patriarch trusted unreservedly. Inseparable as children, Antônio and Epitácio had remained the closest among the five Silva Pessoa siblings. While Epitácio always played the protective role of older brother with Antônio, he viewed him as a partner when politics in Paraíba were reorganized as a Pessoa "family business" in 1912–1915. By late 1911, when Epitácio contemplated moving to the Senate, Col. Antônio Pessoa emerged as the logical partner to oversee Paraíba's local politics as governor, while Epitácio concentrated his attention on the federal level.

In 1902, however, Epitácio possessed no immediate ambition to head Paraíba's oligarchy personally in the federal legislature. His responsibilities on the Supreme Court and as attorney general were perfectly tailored to his intellectual gifts in the fields of constitutional law and jurisprudence. They also afforded him a more prestigious position than could a senatorship from a small, northeastern state. His life appointment to the Court meant not only that his position was secure but also that he could choose the most advantageous time to resign to advance his political career. Epitácio understood that, to pursue a successful career in the Senate, he would have to secure undisputed leadership of the oligarchy that governed his native state.

[13] Ibid., p. 173. Epitácio to Toinho [Col. Antônio Pessoa] (Rio de Janeiro), 8 Feb. 1907, AEP/1. Col. Antônio Pessoa's feud with Col. Sindulfo Calafate Calafange may have derived from the Praieira conflict in Umbuseiro (then Ingá) fifty years earlier, when Barra de Natuba was the only theater of warfare in Paraíba. Col. Antônio Pessoa's father-in-law, Col. Manuel de Assunção Santiago, as Ingá's Liberal Party boss, had been sent to arrest Col. Manuel Calafange (presumably, Coronel Sindulfo's father), Natuba's Liberal Party boss and commander of its pro-Praieira forces, but he also abducted his daughter (Margarida Gomes Calafange) and married her. By 1890, Margarida, together with her daughter Margarida Assunção Santiago Gomes da Silveira—who married Antônio Pessoa—had dropped the Calafange name and called herself Margarida Gomes da Silveira. L. Pessôa, *Epitacio Pessôa,* 1:47; Naro, "Praieira," pp. 149, 180. The 1920 Census listed a "Creomacio Calafange da Silveira," presumably Coronel Sindulfo's heir, as an Umbuseiro property holder. *Relação dos proprietarios . . . ruraes,* pp. 319–20 (estate nos. 75 and 141).

Yet it would be simplistic to evaluate Epitácio's years of effort to reintegrate the former Autonomistas, and, in particular, his own family-based group, within the Machado–Leal oligarchy as a goal dictated merely by his personal career ambition. His political career equally exemplified the relationship his family-based group enjoyed with him; from their perspective, Epitácio was, in important respects, their political creation. For instance, in an attempt to recruit a prestigious opposition politician for Epitacismo in 1913, Gov. Castro Pinto argued that Epitácio possessed "a great family, the friends and relatives of Venâncio." The opposition, Valfredo's nephews, on the other hand, Castro Pinto argued "were unconditional and absolute oligarchs who created all kinds of difficulties for the government."[14] Although by this date Venâncio was more dependent on Epitácio's family and friends than vice versa, the comment revealed the significance of their joint family-based network in building factional alignments. It also attested implicitly to the network's statewide, not to mention federal, presence. As minister of justice, between 1898 and 1901, Epitácio had brought his federal influence to bear. But as chief justice from 1902 until 1911, he remained on good terms with all of Campos Sales's presidential successors, especially Gen. Hermes da Fonseca.

In a fundamental sense, Epitácio's family-based network in Paraíba was responsible for his eventual attractiveness as a candidate for senator and state party boss in 1912–1913. The network also accounted for the 1915 victory of the Epitacista slate that gave his oligarchical machine hegemony until 1930. The groundwork for winning the 1912 and 1915 elections, however, was laid in the decade beginning in 1902, drawing on networks from the nineties. Hence, Epitácio's later identity as Paraíba's patronage boss par excellence was conditioned by the expectations of those in the network, who felt he owed reciprocal obligations to them.

Venâncio Neiva was crucial to Epitacio's network after 1900, due to the position he occupied in the local politics of the far backlands zone. During the 1900 "Case of Paraíba," Epitácio—as minister of justice—had enhanced his family-based following in the interior by appointing Venâncio federal district judge for the municípios of Catolé do Rocha and Brejo do Cruz. This was political

[14] Remark quoted in Ascendino (Carneiro) da Cunha to Epitácio (Parahyba), 24 Sept. 1913, AEP/11/77. Ascendino reported Castro Pinto's comments, including his view that Valfredo's nephew Matias Freire, president of the Assembly, was a man "full of antagonism in spite of his having been designated for Christ."

territory familiar to Venâncio, who had served as an imperial district judge in the same municípios in the late 1880s. In his new post he replaced his retiring double brother-in-law, Judge Honório Horácio de Figueirêdo, whom Venâncio had appointed in 1889, when he left the judgeship to become Paraíba's first republican governor.[15] With more than a decade of Neiva–Figueirêdo networking in those municípios, the extended family bloc of Col. Francisco Hermenegildo Vasconcelos Maia again regained political ascendance after 1902, and on behalf of the Old Conservatives. Epitácio's faction immediately received widespread support in both Catolé do Rocha and Brejo do Cruz.

Epitácio drew directly on the generation of Col. Francisco Maia's sons, especially his son-in-law Col. Antônio Gomes de Arruda Barreto. A close friend of Col. Antônio Pessoa, Antônio Gomes exchanged electoral support in Catolé for a position in the incumbent oligarchy after 1900. A third generation of Maias, intermarried with Agripinos and Suassunas, contributed young recruits to the "generation of 1910" that emerged politically just as Epitácio made his bid for direct leadership of the Paraíba oligarchy in late 1911.[16] Future Governor João Suassuna was its outstanding member. As Col. Antônio Gomes's brother-in-law and foster son, he had been commended to Col. Antônio Pessoa for a political apprenticeship as a local judge in the Pessoas' home município of Umbuseiro. By 1910, consequently, Suassuna became "like a member of the Pessoa family."[17]

The family-based political networking Epitácio both encouraged and depended upon with families such as the Maias was duplicated throughout every geoeconomic zone in Paraíba by 1910. At all three levels of government, key mediating figures, either kin or political friends, coordinated the revanche as members of his

[15] Mariz, *Apanhados historicos*, p. 310.

[16] Col. Antônio Gomes de Arruda Barreto had married two daughters of Col. Francisco Maia in succession. Around 1899, after being widowed a second time, he married the older sister of João Suassuna, who brought her three brothers—including João Suassuna—to live with her. A younger sister of Suassuna later married Col. Antônio Gomes's son by Júlia Maia, Chateaubriand Arruda Barreto. The latter, together with Suassuna and Col. Francisco Maia's adopted son, the younger João Agripino (Maia), belonged to the same extended family classroom in Catolé, where Col. Antônio Gomes established a school. The author is extremely grateful to Ariano Suassuna, son of João Suassuna, for offering the details of this complex household and political relationship. Personal interview, Recife, 25 and 27 July 1971. Azevêdo Bastos, *Roteiro Azevêdo*, pp. 216–27, contains complementary Maia, Agripino, and Suassuna genealogy.

[17] Cunha Pedrosa, *Minhas memórias*, 2:210.

network. Although nonkin appeared in very prominent positions in the network, an impressive number of Epitácio's close relatives forged the key linkages on a zonal basis throughout Paraíba. This broad geographical distribution of Epitácio's network proved crucial in 1915, when he defeated Senator Valfredo for control of the State Assembly.

In November 1911, Epitácio acquired a final advantage for his network when the aging Trinidade da Meira Henriques, who still represented Paraíba in the House of Deputies, died. This removed one serious obstacle to Epitácio's exclusive leadership of the oligarchy. Trinidade's loyal Meirista following was now free to adhere directly to Epitácio. Col. José Bezerra Cavalcanti de Albuquerque, whose brother Cândido Clementino had married Epitácio's sister Maria, summed up this affiliation in a matrimonial metaphor. As a Meirista, he wrote to Epitácio several weeks after Trinidade's death, describing himself as "now a widower in politics." In formally petitioning to adhere directly to Epitácio's personal faction, José Bezerra added that he had "never been acceptable to the Republicans [the Alvaristas] of the state."[18] Accepting José Bezerra's adherence "with great pleasure," Epitácio could now contemplate assuming direct leadership of the Paraíba oligarchy.[19] With Trinidade gone and Álvaro Machado mortally ill in Rio de Janeiro by December, his rivals were reduced to Sen. Valfredo Leal and Álvaro's brother, Gov. João Machado.

Gubernatorial Crises

The gubernatorial succession always provided a major issue in Paraíba's factional politics. Characteristically, it divided the ruling coalition. At the least, it produced important defections that usually redounded to the advantage of the opposition. In both 1904 and 1908 the issue of the gubernatorial succession irrevocably fragmented the Machado–Leal oligarchy at its Old Liberal base. The two backlands zones were progressively alienated when their candidates were set aside in favor of Areienses from Álvaro's family-based clique. This intrafactional dissension helped Epitácio and Venâncio gain footholds in the oligarchy. Their reintegration developed until, by 1908, Álvaro and Valfredo depended on the for-

[18] Col. José Bezerra (Cavalcanti) de Albuquerque to Epitácio (Capital), 12 Nov. 1911, AEP/10/71. Trinidade's loyal supporters, Generals Tude Neiva and João Soares Neiva, had died in 1902 and 1903.

[19] Ibid. (verso).

mer Autonomistas' support to maintain their majority in the State Assembly. The Old Liberals of the backlands had gradually withdrawn their votes.

The gubernatorial candidate was, of course, the key to continuation of a local faction's rule. At the state level, conflict over who would be the candidate held a slightly different implication. The choice of a governor was directly connected to the choice of members of the federal delegation and therefore connoted a reward for faithful years of service. Those senior politicians passed over normally felt betrayed. More fundamentally, however, the choice of a governor identified which personalistic faction and supporting family-based groups would control officeholding and the appointive power in civil service statewide. In 1904, for instance, outgoing Governor José Peregrino tried to name Valfredo's cousin once removed, State Police Chief Simeão Leal, as his successor. First, however, he tried to "reform" the Constitution, lowering the minimum age for the governorship to thirty, so that his extremely youthful candidate could qualify. Pandemonium broke loose in the Capital while the Assembly was in session, for a substantial bloc of Old Liberals from the backlands refused to approve Simeão's candidacy and revolted against the constitutional "reform." Eventually, Álvaro was obliged to return to Paraíba to take charge personally of the crisis, while Simeão Leal had to be content with a seat in the House of Deputies for 1904–1908.[20] Álvaro quelled revolt in his own party only by proposing himself as an alternative. He served as Paraíba's governor for a year and returned to Rio de Janeiro as a senator in October 1905, turning his administration over to his first lieutenant governor, Valfredo Leal. These maneuvers were possible only because they were supported by the former Autonomistas, who were included in Álvaro's PRP and voted his official slate. Meanwhile, Valfredo remained in Paraíba to serve out the remainder of Álvaro's term.

By 1908 a power struggle within Álvaro's ruling coalition erupted over the gubernatorial candidacy of João Lopes Machado, Álvaro's younger brother. Several important politicians, under the leadership of ex-Governor Gama e Melo, permanently withdrew their support from the incumbent oligarchy.[21] They justified their

[20] Mariz, *Assembléia Legislativa*, pp. 66–90; idem. *Apanhados historicos*, pp. 313–16; Cunha Pedrosa, *Minhas memórias*, 2:87.

[21] Gama e Melo was assisted by Sen. João Coelho Gonçalves Lisboa, who had sought the nomination for himself. Mariz, *Apanhados historicos*, pp. 315–16; Luíz Pinto, *Octacílio de Albuquerque* (Rio de Janeiro: Editôra Minerva, 1966), p. 44; Cunha Pedrosa, *Minhas memórias*, 2:80–91.

revolt in highly personalistic language that charged "betrayal" or disloyalty of his cronies when he attained by Álvaro the pinnacle of oligarchical power. More than the simple personal disgruntlement of several gubernatorial hopefuls, the schism could be plotted along zonal lines delineating key family blocs in the interior. It demonstrated the escalating grievances of the family-based groups primarily in the backlands zones and, secondarily, in parts of the caatinga-agreste. The former Liberals who since 1902 had been progressively deprived of their local "prestige"—their monopoly over município officeholding—now openly declared their refusal to back the ruling oligarchy.[22] They understood that, unless the next governor was committed to reversing the process, their losses locally would be irreversible.

Although one defeated gubernatorial hopeful, João Coelho Gonçalves Lisboa, took his denunciation of Álvaro to the floor of the Senate, where he flayed a newly fused "Neiva–Lucena" and "Machado–Leal" oligarchy for its nepotism, João Machado was nevertheless elected Paraíba's new governor. He won only because Álvaro and Epitácio had come to a written agreement defining the latter's participation as a co-equal factional partner. Epitácio extracted a commitment for future factional representation in the Senate, as well as in the lower house and the State Assembly.[23] Following Almeida Barreto's death in 1905, the former Autonomistas had possessed no representation in the Senate, so Epitácio obliged Álvaro to designate Pedro da Cunha Pedrosa for a future senate seat. This pledge became the issue that determined the final fight for Epitacista control of the Assembly in 1914–1915. Meanwhile, Pedrosa was elected first lieutenant governor and assigned the task of coordinating voting support for João Machado in the realigned Assembly.[24]

João Machado's 1908 election marked an important division in both the political base and the outlook of the incumbent oligarchy. He won the election because Venancistas controlled enough

[22] "The political orientation of Álvaro Machado soon annoyed a good portion of his former co-religionists [i.e., the Old Liberals], who did not agree with the preeminence of [the Venancistas] among their adversaries . . . to whom he gave the key positions in the gubernatorial administration." Leal, *Itinerário*, p. 335.

[23] Pedro da Cunha Pedrosa to Epitácio (Capital), 2 Aug. 1911, AEP/10/70; idem, *Minhas memórias*, 2:88–89.

[24] João Machado's candidacy was put forward by Valfredo—not by his brother Álvaro Machado—so that Cunha Pedrosa could assert that Álvaro was not creating an oligarchy in Paraíba. *Minhas memórias*, 2:90. Similarly, Gov. José Peregrino advanced the gubernatorial candidacy of Valfredo's cousin, Simeão Leal, while Valfredo remained aloof.

votes in the state legislature to nullify the defection of Old Liberals from Álvaro's faction. Since Epitácio endorsed and supported João Machado, his followers' votes for Álvaro's brother also signified that in the next election Epitacista votes would figure more crucially than those of Venancistas. Those Old Liberals most opposed to João Machado represented an old guard more associated with the Empire. As senior politicians, they had witnessed their supporters in the interior being supplanted by their former rivals, now Epitacistas. Many of these Epitacistas were fostering greater integration of the backlands' cotton production with the transatlantic market. Often a generation younger, they looked to Epitácio's political talent at the federal level to bring financial support for creating infrastructure in the backlands zones. By 1912, Epitácio had emerged as the figure whose "ideas were those of the majority" in Paraíba, while Valfredo was perceived as a politician "who had no reputation in Rio de Janeiro," for he was "without the ability even to obtain entry to the ministries there."[25] According to Governor-Elect Castro Pinto, Valfredo had maintained himself in state politics by virtue of his "unconditional surrender" to the president of the Senate, Pinheiro Machado, but "tomorrow Pinheiro would need Epitácio more than Valfredo."[26]

Political Issues in a Family-Based Oligarchy

The issue of "who would lead the oligarchy"—in the words of one of Epitácio's younger recruits—dominated Paraíba politics in 1912.[27] In a political system where participation was based on competition for the patronage of officeholding, it was only logical that the issue of who should rule consumed nearly all political activity. Although a decade of unprecedented economic growth had already unfolded, it was still difficult to discern change in the informally defined political system, founded on family-based groups whose paramount goal was access to patronage. Significant issues were emerging, however. Either explicitly or implicitly, Epitácio Pessoa was identified by his followers as progressive in his political thinking because of his positions on these issues. When, in

[25] The observation was made by Gov. Castro Pinto, as reported in Ascendino Carneiro da Cunha to Epitácio (Capital), 14 Sept. 1912, AEP/11/77.

[26] Ibid.

[27] This phrase is taken from a letter to Epitácio six years later: Demócrito de Almeida to Epitácio (Capital), 10 Sept. 1918, AEP/12/135. It summed up, however, the implicit focus of most of Epitácio's correspondents in Paraíba during 1912.

1912, Col. Cristiano Lauritzen contrasted Epitácio as a politician "whose ideas are those of the majority" to his rival Valfredo, whose "docility in the hands of Senator Pinheiro Machado" had rendered him a political liability, he had in mind Epitácio's demonstrated influence in federal politics and future ability to extract patronage for Paraíba.[28]

A cursory reading of the Capital's major newspapers—*A União*, *O Norte*, and *O Commercio*—reveals that federal patronage was becoming a more pressing political issue by 1910, precisely because of the cotton boom. As politicians in both state and local government recognized the special opportunities cotton presented for economic growth, dissatisfaction with a number of characteristics inherent in Brazilian oligarchy emerged. One source of dissatisfaction concerned the paucity of resources the federal government allocated to Paraíba. The first two decades of the Old Republic demonstrated that the national government's patronage was distributed to favor the wealthier and more populous states. The federal government itself, however, determined that expectations would change when it established the drought relief agency known as the IFOCS (originally, the DNOCS), which received a budget for construction projects in the six northeastern states. Thus, expanding infrastructure on or near the coast to the backlands zones also became a possibility.

The unfavorable national attention the oligarchies had received during the 1910 presidential campaign and its aftermath made northeastern politicians more outspoken in Congress regarding their inferior position in the nation. They resented their oligarchical subordination in Congress, as part of the regional bloc led by Pernambuco, and their clientistic role in the political design of Sen. Pinheiro Machado. Epitácio Pessoa became an appealing candidate, in the critical mood of 1912, when he made his bid for the oligarchical leadership of Paraíba. No latecomer to championing the Northeast's regional needs vis-à-vis the federal government, he had first presented a project for drought assistance to Congress in 1891, condemning some his peers' characterization of federal assistance as "alms" and insisting instead that it was a right.[29] In 1896, he had embarrassed the Machado–Leal oligarchy by accusing its leadership of obstructing federal drought assistance to Pa-

[28] Col. Cristiano Lauritzen to Epitácio (Campina Grande), 15 May 1912, AEP/10/69.

[29] E. Pessoa, speech in the House of Deputies, 20 Aug. 1891, in *Obras completas*, 1:49–53, esp. p. 52; ibid., 2:113.

raíba. He filed a formal complaint with the federal government that Paraíba's governor had misappropriated federal funds for drought assistance.[30] Particularly in the backlands, therefore, Epitácio could claim to be an old critic of the coastal politicians surrounding Álvaro and Valfredo. Increasingly their political orbit was narrowed to the interests of the Capital or matters of national politics in Rio de Janeiro.

A second issue, still nascent in 1912, also derived from the insufficiency of revenue in the State Treasury. Tax collection was beginning to attract more attention at the oligarchy's apex, although public rhetoric made only oblique reference to this most delicate question in a family-based oligarchy. Due to the de facto autonomy the municípios enjoyed, it would have been premature for any governor to raise it openly. In the nineties, the paucity of Paraíba's revenues had been proverbial, due primarily to the severe droughts that had opened and closed the decade: "Scarcity of rain . . . created an agonizing situation for the public coffers through the diminution of revenues that followed as a result of lowered rural production."[31] The new century dawned with greater promise, for the boom in cotton exports augured better times for the Treasury.

Although its major source of revenues was a tax on exports, the state government had limited ability to collect taxes. Several structural factors inherent in the family base of oligarchy accounted for the low volume of revenues. First, antiquated methods, particularly tax farming, remained in force, testifying to the patrimonial character of the State. Even in more progressive and bustling Campina Grande, município revenue collection was auctioned off to the highest bidder in 1920.[32] A federal inspector of agriculture complained about the difficulty of obtaining statistics on the local collection of revenues during 1911–1913 in his official report. And an expert on fiscal practices in Brazil, who was also a federal deputy for Paraíba, noted that the share of revenues tax collectors retained in his native state as remuneration for their collection of taxes was shockingly high relative to other Brazilian states.[33] In addition, revenue collection was very arbitrary; fre-

[30] Epitácio to Antônio Olinto (Minister of Industry) (n.p.), undated letter of 1896, published in ibid., 2:249–50.

[31] Leal, *Itinerário*, p. 324.

[32] E. de Almeida, *História Campina*, p. 381.

[33] Diogenes Caldas, inspector of agriculture, noted the reluctance of federal collection agents and "state and local authorities" to respond to his questionnaire. Six

quently the local opposition bore the brunt of paying tax levies. Finally, since the most important source of revenue was the export tax levied on cotton or livestock, evasion was widespread. Rural producers circumvented collection posts by choosing remote backlands routes for sending their products to market. Before 1912, perhaps as much as one-half, certainly one-third, of all cotton exported from Paraíba left the state untaxed.[34]

These obstacles notwithstanding, state revenues began to rise after 1909. (See Table A.4.) Because both the volume and the assessed value of cotton exports—on which an 8 per cent ad valorum tax was levied—ascended so stupendously, revenues dramatically increased. Although the rate of taxation remained constant, state revenues for 1908–1912 rose by 48 per cent over the 1903–1907 period. The prior increase over the late nineties had been a negligible 6 per cent. Because cotton taxes constituted 80 per cent of the total revenues from exports and export taxes accounted for 50 per cent of all state revenues, token and arbitrary compliance with revenue collection could continue largely unabated while revenues still expanded. However, the implication for future revenues was impossible to ignore: If collection methods were more rigorously imposed, the resources of the state government would be considerably expanded.[35] The governor's limited power in this respect, however, was tied to the third issue, law and order. By 1912, it

municípios—five from the backlands zones—never answered (São João do Rio de Peixe, Teixeira, Campina Grande, Soledade, Areia, and Pombal). Caldas, *Estatistica agricola*, pp. 5–6.

According to João de Lyra Tavares, "Not only is the revenue collection for the period [1900–1912] in the interior very expensive, and perhaps without parallel in . . . the Republic, but also the proportion [18 per cent–19 per cent on the average] established as the collectors' [commission] is manifestly unjust. Obviously, this percentage cannot be permitted to continue, due to the State's greater responsibilities and the inequality of remuneration [between state and federal tax collectors]." (The federal collectors received only 2 per cent to 5 per cent of the gross collected for their expenses.) Lyra Tavares, *Economia e finanças dos estados; Brasil* (Parahyba: Impensa Oficial, 1914), p. 60.

[34] Although a minority of Paraíba's cotton exports passed through the Capital, the 1912 breakdown of export taxes collected at thirty-three revenue posts revealed that the interior was a "sieve" for revenues: The Capital alone collected 1,679 contos. The remaining twenty-eight interior posts remitted smaller amounts. Lyra Tavares, *Economia e finanças*, p. 58. Of the 363 contos collected in Campina Grande, 51 were retained for collection expenses, i.e., personal commissions. Ibid., p. 60.

[35] Ibid., pp. 58, 71, and 74. The 50 per cent figure excludes revenue from the additional tax, a surcharge on exports levied at 20 per cent of the export tax collected. (Ibid., pp. 58, 71.)

overshadowed both federal patronage and tax collection as an issue of rising public concern.

More accurately, the problem of law and order was the problem of the State's inability to curb private violence, whether the agents were members of feuding elite family groups or the bandits known in the Northeast as *cangaceiros*. Intimately intertwined, these two sources of disorder had attracted increased attention in the Paraíba press by the close of the nineties. Rising public outrage imparted a new significance to an endemic situation. Urbanization in the interior had produced an incipient middle class in the market centers of the caatinga-agreste and brejo. Merchants, journalists, and professionals vociferously protested the indifference of public authorities to rising levels of private violence.

Banditry acquired a new significance by the turn of the century. It became the first long-term issue to produce concerted interest-group action in Paraíba's oligarchical politics. In the Capital and other important market centers, retailers and merchants in the import–export sector uttered the loudest outcries against the scores of brigands who roamed the interior. *O Commercio*, a major daily in Parahyba, complained in August 1900 that "a virtual economic depression" had resulted from the recent rise in bandit attacks, noting that "business has almost stopped between the Capital and the interior."[36] Protesting that brigandage was "threatening the Conservative classes," the newspaper pointed to the "complete disorganization" of the weekly market in Alagoa Nova following the appearance of the cangaceiro Antônio Silvino at its Sunday fair on August 19. With a small band of men, he had extorted money "from merchants under threat of death."[37] Two weeks earlier, the Capital's mercantile sector had closed its doors at midday to attend a protest meeting called by the Commercial Association. Both "members and nonmembers" were invited "to discuss the serious events in the backlands and to deliberate the complaints that would be lodged with the authorities, due to the infestation of the entire interior by thieves and murderers."[38]

The petition to the governor that was drawn up and signed at the meeting indignantly complained of the impunity with which Sil-

[36] *O Commercio* (Capital), 4 Aug. 1900.

[37] Ibid., 4 and 23 Aug. 1900.

[38] Ibid., 4 Aug. 1900. Lieut. Antônio de Brito Lira, future president of the Commercial Association and Epitácio's prefeito in the Capital after 1915, was one of the dozen signatories, all of whom were wealthier merchants, whether foreign or native-born.

vino and others robbed and extorted. First implicitly, and then more openly, petitions and denunciations published in the press over the next decade drew a direct connection between the "infestation" of bandits and the figures known as "*coiteiros*" (protectors) who held influential political positions.[39]

Beginning in 1897, the bandit career of Paraíba's most famous outlaw, Antônio Silvino (Manuel Batista de Morais), coincided with the duration of the Machado–Leal oligarchy. His celebrated robberies and running war with the Paraíba State Police Force did more than anything else to crystallize public opinion in favor of a tougher state government stance against banditry.[40] Silvino's exploits, moreover, won him instant immortality in regional poetry and song. The *folhetos*, or chapbooks, that around the turn of the century began to acquire a mass circulation in the Northeast converted him into a respected antihero. In Paraíba they redefined banditry as a political issue.[41]

To make matters worse for the incumbent oligarchy, Silvino took a hand in politicizing the issue of brigandage. Beginning around 1904, he publicized his personal grievances with the gubernatorial administration of Monsig. Valfredo Leal and Valfredo's state chief of police, Antônio Massa. Silvino also accused the British-owned Great Western Railway Company of expropriating his patrimonial land in the município of Campina Grande.[42] An accomplished extemporaneous bard in his own right, Silvino sent

[39] *O Commercio* implied that the cangaceiros possessed privileged information regarding movements of the interstate police squads known as the Flying Squads (Forças Volantes): "It appears that the bandits operate in well-defined groups and that the attacks take place in distinct locations at the same time in order to disorient the efforts of the Flying Squads" (5 Aug. 1900).

[40] The turning point in rousing public opinion was the fierce battle of Surrão (Campina Grande), on June 17, 1901. The combined State Police Forces of Paraíba and Pernambuco confronted over fifty bandits and suffered large casualties. Silvino's alleged revenge murder of the Paraíba police commander, Capt. Paulino Pinto de Carvalho, stirred public outrage to new levels several months later. The public subscription to a fund for the disabled survivors and the families of the slain policemen was unprecedented. *Diario de Pernambuco*, 29 Mar. 1906 and 17 Apr. 1910; E. Câmara, *Datas campinenses*, pp. 96–97; Carlos D. Fernandes, *Os cangaceiros: Romance de costumes sertanejos* (Parahyba: Imprensa Oficial, 1914), p. 100.

[41] For extensive treatment of Silvino's connections to elite family warfare in Paraíba and Pernambuco, see Lewin, "Social Banditry in Brazil," pp. 116–36.

[42] Fernandes, *Cangaceiros*, pp. 100, 107; Francisco das Chagas Batista, *A historia de Antonio Silvino* (Recife: Imprensa Industrial, 1907), pp. 27 (stanzas 1, 5) and 28 (stanza 1).

politically derisive and threatening verses to Valfredo and Massa in a "telegraph war" that popular poets kept before their audiences in growing installments. Silvino revealed what no single local boss was ever capable of demonstrating: that the political authority of the state government ended outside the Capital. To the delight of the poets, his soubriquet "Governor of the Sertão"—frequently appended to his threatening telegrams—testified to his territorial mobility in the interior of four states.[43] Occasionally Silvino even stumped for political candidates at election time. His choices were always the individuals with whom he enjoyed relationships of protection and for whom he was performing a "service."[44]

An explicit critique that banditry coexisted with coronelismo developed in sophistication and intensity between 1900 and 1912. During that period, Epitácio and his brother in Umbuseiro became personally involved in the issue of the protection that Silvino and other cangaceiros derived from influential figures in the dominant oligarchy. The situation illustrated the close connection between rising banditry and rising internecine local feuds. In 1907 the 27th Federal Battalion was ordered to the Paraíba backlands by Gen. Hermes da Fonseca, then minister of war to President Afonso [Augusto Moreira] Pena. However, the order came at the personal request of Justice Epitácio Pessoa. Epitácio had persuaded Hermes that the epidemic of banditry in his native state required the drastic measure of federal assistance.[45] The truth was slightly

[43] Francisco das Chagas Batista, "A história de Antônio Silvino; novos crimes," in *Literatura popular em verso; antologia*, Vol. 4: *Francisco das Chagas Batista* (Rio de Janeiro: Fundação Casa de Rui Barbosa/MEC, 1971), p. 109. A refrain in many poems about Silvino expressly referred to his "governorship" of the interior: "I sent him [Valfredo] this order: Doctor / Look after what is yours there. / The Capital belongs to you, / But the state is mine." [*Mandei-lhe dizer: Doutor, / Cuide lá no que for seu, / A Capital lhe pertence / Porém o estado é meu.*] Leandro Gomes de Barros, "Antônio Silvino; o Rei dos Cangaceiros," in *Literatura popular em verso; antologia*, Vol. 2: [*Leandro Gomes de Barros*] (Rio de Janeiro: Fundação Casa de Rui Barbosa/MEC, 1976), p. 102 (stanza 1).

The historical evolution of the Brazilian (northeastern) chapbook literature and its connection with Teixeira's poets and family wars is analyzed in Linda Lewin, "Oral Tradition and Elite Myth," pp. 157–204.

[44] Gustavo Barroso, *Almas de lama e de aço (Lampião e outros cangaceiros)* (São Paulo: Editora Proprietaria Melhoramentos, 1930), p. 250; José Rodrigues de Carvalho, *Serrote Prêto; Lampião e seus sequazes* (Rio de Janeiro: Sociedade Editôra Gráfica Ltda., 1961), pp. 360–67.

[45] In 1900, Col. Antônio Pessoa had written Epitácio, asking him to take up with the federal government the question of the capture of Silvino, who was very active in the Umbuseiro borderlands. Epitácio to Toinho [Antônio Pessoa], 6 Jan. 1905(?), ACAP/1. Later arrangements related to the transfer of the 27th Federal Battalion to the Paraíba backlands are discussed in Epitácio to Toinho [Antônio Pessoa] (Rio de

different. For over five years, the name of Epitácio's brother, Col. Antônio Pessoa, had been on an impressively long list of intended victims whom Antônio Silvino had vowed he would kill on sight.[46] Since the late 1890s, Umbuseiro had been one of Silvino's favorite refuges, besides serving as a theater for his gun battles and extortion visits. He enjoyed powerful protection there from Col. Antônio Pessoa's enemy, Umbuseiro's opposition boss, Col. Sindulfo Calafate Calafange.[47]

The 27th Battalion failed to snare Silvino despite over a year of concerted effort. Simultaneously, Col. Cristiano Lauritzen coordinated an impressive manhunt, but Silvino eluded that too. Silvino boldly derided his pursuers' clumsy efforts and bragged he knew the soldiers' marching orders before their officers received them.[48] Criticism rose as the months passed and Silvino remained at large. Eventually, the federal battalion was withdrawn in 1908 because it had come to threaten the civilian population more than Paraíba's famous outlaw. Yet the battalion's ineffectual pursuit of Silvino and the reprisals it meted out to the rural population aroused the public to a new level of outrage.[49] In 1908, a sensational indictment appeared in an interior newspaper suggesting why Silvino could not be apprehended. Addressed "To the People of Campina Grande," it pointed an accusatory finger at Gov. Valfredo Leal and half a dozen influential party bosses living in or near that município—including Campina Grande's Cristiano Lauritzen—and denounced them as Silvino's protectors:

Janeiro), 8 Feb. 1907, ACAP/1. Idem, 14 June 1907 and idem, tel. of 5 July 1907, ACAP/1.

[46] "I have been anxious to see you out of Umbuseiro, having been frightened by the news . . . according to which Antônio Silvino and his people intend to take your life." Epitácio to Toinho [Antônio Pessoa] (Rio de Janeiro), 31 Mar. 1903, ACAP/1. Four years later, Silvino had not abandoned his effort: "Copy of the Inquiry [Auto de Perguntas] Administered to Manuel Joaquim da Moura ["Manuel Diga"] on 29 April 1907 in . . . Umbuseiro . . . by the Town Clerk," ACAP/2/209.

[47] Mariano Rodrigues Laureano to the Editor of *A Provincia* [Recife], 6 Apr. 1906; republished in *A União*, 12 Apr. 1906. Calafange's protection of Silvino is noted in Epitácio to Toinho [Antônio Pessoa] (Rio de Janeiro), 8 Feb. and 9 Mar. 1903 and 6 Jan. 1905, ACAP/1. Calafange's ally, Col. Augusto Rezende of Ingá, publicly presented Antônio Silvino with a rifle after the bandit made a political speech on Rezende's behalf. *O Município* [Itabaiana], 28 June 1908.

[48] José Fabio de Costa Lira to Compadre Toinho [Antônio Pessoa] (Umbuseiro), 24 Feb. 1907, ACAP/2/88.

[49] Several members of Coronel Antônio's faction in Umbuseiro were murdered by soldiers from the battalion, allegedly on orders from one of its officers. José Fabio de Costa Lira to Compadre Antônio Pessoa (Umbuseiro), 27 July 1907, ACAP/2.

To Your Excellency [Valfredo Leal], First Magistrate of the State and the principal individual responsible for order and tranquillity, we, the inhabitants of Campina Grande, address [this appeal]:

Certainly, you are not unaware that Campina Grande is the only município in the state where the cangaceiro Antônio Silvino camps freely and with impunity.

There does not exist any well-intentioned effort to capture that bandit that does not find its hands tied, due to the serious obstacles placed [before it] by the protectors of Silvino, who exist in an escalating number. Your Excellency—who are yourself a political prisoner of those protectors—already should have realized that it is time to cease praising the concealed motives of these big politicians with the French, Hungarian, or Polish names, whose LOYALTY [*LEALDADE*] to Your Excellency's government is explained only by the fear that they will come to be discovered.[50]

Although Silvino remained free and the federal intervention failed, the "Governor of the Sertão" was denied the gubernatorial pardon he had sought prior to 1908, probably because of a changing climate of public opinion.[51] Banditry continued unchecked until 1912, but, once Gov. Castro Pinto inaugurated Epitacista rule in October of that year, more determined measures were adopted to combat it. Since his lieutenant governor was Col. Antônio Pessoa, whose own denunciation of Silvino's protectors had appeared in the newspapers of two states, an aggressive campaign was immediately implemented. Even under the Pessoas, the task of extirpat-

[50] Unidentified newspaper clipping, dated March 1908 and filed in ACAP/2/205. (The typeface indicates the most likely source is *O Município*, published in adjacent Itabaiana.) The article named four political bosses who paid money to Silvino or protected him and singled out Col. Cristiano Lauritzen and Col. Eufrásio (de Arruda) Camara, co-leaders of the civilian manhunt working with the Federal Battalion, as complicit parties in Silvino's evasion of capture. Eufrásio was the largest landowner in the caatinga-agreste. His Fazenda Cabeças, spanning Ingá and Campina Grande, was described as "a paradise of bandits" because "the police themselves would not cross one stone over the boundaries in pursuit of anyone." Rodrigues de Carvalho, *Serrote Prêto*, pp. 366–67. The article also charged that Eufrásio kept two "good and loyal friends of Silvino" on his property, adding sarcastically, "Did you not know that Coronel Eufrásio presented each officer of the federal force with a good horse to more easily press after the cangaceiros?" The reference to "LOYALTY" was a pun on Valfredo Leal.

[51] *Diario de Pernambuco*, 1 Mar. 1907; Rodrigues de Carvalho, *Serrote Prêto*, pp. 376–77; Mario Souto Maior, *Antônio Silvino, Capitão de trabuco* (Rio de Janeiro: n.p., 1971), pp. 65–66.

ing banditry proved difficult because of the protection extended to brigands by the incumbent oligarchy's local bosses. By 1913, budgetary appropriations reflected greater political emphasis on this issue. Expenditure on the State Police Force and security personnel rose proportionately after 1910. Finally, a backlands insurrection in March 1912 brought home the lesson that the large pool of bandits plaguing the interior also posed a political threat to the incumbent oligarchy.

Oligarchical Crisis

Family-Based Revolt in the Backlands

In early 1912, the Machado–Leal oligarchy faced an insurrection of Old Liberals in the backlands, led by two powerful family-based groups. A privately raised army numbering well over a thousand men threatened to dislodge Gov. João Machado from office as the last resort for redressing local grievances. Both the Dantas and Santa Cruz de Oliveira families took up arms after losing political control of their respective municípios to local Epitacista rivals between 1904 and 1908. Each Old Liberal family-based group experienced local persecution at the hands of its rivals, assisted by the State Police Force. Each had suffered armed attacks and the destruction of valuable property, including crops and livestock.[52] Franklin Dantas Correia de Góis commanded the most politically powerful group, composed of the members of his very large Dantas extended family at Fazenda Imaculada, in Teixeira. Their patriarchal figure was his uncle, aging Inácio Dantas Correia de Góis, who once had been in business in Campina Grande. Franklin's father, Manuel Dantas Correia de Góis, had been a provincial assemblyman and, with several of the Leites, one of the most important leaders of the Liberal Party in the 1880s. Governor-Elect of Paraíba when the advent of the Republic prevented his installation, Manuel Dantas continued to play a central role in the Assembly for the dominant oligarchy between 1892 and 1904. As an Alvarista assemblyman, he had maintained his family's position in Teixeira's município politics against the rising challenge of the Carvalhos and Batistas, the Dantas' rivals for over half a century. However,

[52] The Dantas' grievances are detailed in an unidentified newspaper clipping [*O Estado da Parahyba*(?) (Capital)], n.d. [April? 1912], filed in ACAP/3. A comprehensive description appears in *O Estado da Parahyba*, 28 Aug. 1912.

in 1904, Gov. Álvaro Machado named as Teixeira's party boss and prefeito Col. Dario Romalho de Carvalho Luna, leader of the opposition faction and a successful entrepreneur loyal to the former Autonomistas. In 1908 Álvaro gave Dario a seat in the State Assembly. The Dantas thereby lost the leadership of Teixeira's politics that they had held since the late 1860s.[53]

Like Franklin Dantas, who held a medical degree, Augusto Santa Cruz de Oliveira, his fellow rebel chieftain, was a bacharel with a law degree from the Recife Law Faculty. The Santa Cruz had ruled their native município of Alagoa do Monteiro and were represented in the State Assembly by Augusto's brother Miguel Santa Cruz, who served two terms as a deputy prior to 1904. However, in that year, Gov. Álvaro Machado replaced him with the leader of the local opposition faction, Col. Pedro Bezerra da Silveira Leal, an Epitacista businessman. Persecuted by the faction led by Pedro Bezerra, Augusto Santa Cruz was jailed and convicted of murder four years later, as his adversaries attempted to remove him from politics by "applying the law." He was freed after a judicial appeal, but the violent police attacks he and his extended family had experienced earlier at the hands of Pedro Bezerra's faction escalated. Consequently, the Santa Cruz family, together with their agricultural tenants and armed retainers—135 individuals—left Monteiro in 1909 and sought refuge with Padre Cícero in Joaseiro. After over a year in neighboring Ceará, they returned to Monteiro in 1911 determined to regain their forfeited local position.[54]

Prior to instigating their insurrection, the Dantas and Santa Cruz had each sought restitution from João Machado. Failing to extract concessions, they turned to Epitácio in early 1912, seeking his intervention to gain common demands: the right to political representation locally and "guarantees," that is, the governor's

[53] Inácio Dantas had served as an assemblyman with his brother Manuel in the Fourth Session (1900–1904). Successfully established in Patos as a businessman, he owned a large dam in Teixeira as well as a sugar mill. Col. Dario Romalho, who was even wealthier, owned four large dams and a cotton ginnery in Teixeira. In addition, he was the concunhado of José Jerônimo Borborema Filho, an important figure in Epitácio's network in the cariri-sertão. Santa Cruz, on the other hand, apparently possessed more limited economic interests in stockraising, while his rival Pedro Bezerra was a successful merchant-entrepreneur who owned a cotton ginnery. Author's prosopographical file.

[54] Della Cava, *Miracle Joaseiro*, pp. 143–44. Santa Cruz was accompanied by two dozen cangaceiros, but Padre Cícero insisted that his entire retinue be disarmed in Joaseiro.

word, that they would be spared future attacks on their persons and property by the State Police. Santa Cruz also insisted on monetary indemnity for sizable losses of livestock and real property incurred when the State Police burned his estate.[55] Inácio Dantas, as senior spokesman for the Dantas of Imaculada, threatened Epitácio implicitly with revolt and warned that the dominant oligarchy needed the Dantas' votes to carry the fourth electoral district in the federal and gubernatorial election scheduled for March.[56] Despite the advice of his lieutenants in Parahyba, Epitácio refused any conciliatory gesture, making the insurrection inevitable. It was a dangerous gamble, for he had been apprised of the backlands army being organized by Franklin Dantas and Augusto Santa Cruz to depose João Machado and install a new governor. He was also well aware, since November 1911, when the Salvationists' *coup d'état* had succeeded in Alagoas in November, that national politics offered a very favorable context for the rebels to succeed.

The "Redemption" of the Paraíba Oligarchy

In 1911, the movement of young officers in the Brazilian Army called the Salvationists or the Redeemers (Salvacionistas) acted on its claim that the oligarchies should be overthrown as unprogressive political structures and replaced with a political elite more

[55] "Santa Cruz is hiding in Ceará, still threatening to disturb the interior [of Paraíba], promising to invade cities and towns and sack them in case the [state] government does not give him the 329 contos he demands for his property in Alagoa do Monteiro. João Machado brought this to the attention of [President] Hermes, charging that Santa Cruz is serving the political interests of [Coelho] Lisboa and Lima Filho." Pedro da Cunha Pedrosa to Epitácio (Capital), 7 Nov. 1911, AEP/10/71.

[56] Inácio Dantas told Epitácio that it was unacceptable for the Dantas of Teixeira to cooperate with Col. Dario Romalho's family bloc as allies. But he promised Epitácio Teixeira's 700 votes in the 22 March federal election of 1912 "which you . . . won't have to worry about," if the Dantas would be recognized as the município's sole Machadista faction. Thus, he implicitly threatened realignment with the opposition in Paraíba, which in late 1911 began allying nationally with the Salvationists, by tying Teixeira's votes to the statewide majority that the incumbent oligarchy was expected to deliver. Inácio Dantas to Epitácio (Teixeira), 18 Jan. 1912, AEP/10/81. In a final attempt to extract from Epitácio a pledge to restore the Dantas' political representation in Teixeira, Franklin Dantas used the veiled threat of a backlands insurrection, together with its implicit connection to the Salvationists. He warned that since the Dantas and their friends "could even write [fix] the election," they were "the majority" in Teixeira and that to compromise with them "would perhaps avoid a calamity." Franklin Dantas to Epitácio Pessoa (Teixeira), 14 Mar. 1912, AEP/10/126.

cognizant of the national interest. As fervent republicans, they objected to the great influence that reactionary agrarian interests exercised in national politics, mainly through the oligarchies of northeastern states. In particular they opposed powerful Sen. Pinheiro Machado's successful efforts since 1910 to reorganize the state oligarchies in that region under his Conservative Republican Party or PRC (Partido Republicano Conservador), as a compact voting bloc susceptible to his manipulation in Congress.[57] They sought to "redeem" (*salvacionar*) the Republic from politically retrograde state oligarchies, as well as the growing political influence of Pinheiro Machado.

At least rhetorically, the Salvationists challenged the national political system's "backward" dependence on agrarian-based oligarchies, appealing considerably to urban voters. Initially, they had received some backing from President Hermes da Fonseca when, in November and December 1911, they organized military revolts in the federal garrisons in Recife and Maceió. After toppling the oligarchies in Pernambuco and Alagoas, they placed Gen. Emígdio Dantas Barreto and Col. Clodoaldo da Fonseca in the governorships of those states. They were encouraged to attempt similar *coups d'état* elsewhere in the Northeast. In January 1912, when the Salvationists installed Sen. J. J. Seabra as Bahia's new governor, however, President Hermes did not decree a federal intervention on their behalf.[58]

Major opposition to the Salvationists came from Brazil's "kingmaker," Sen. Pinheiro Machado of Rio Grande do Sul. Since 1910, when he had established the PRC as his national party, Pinheiro's political influence had grown until he rivaled President Hermes. Erroneously assuming that he could manipulate Hermes, whom he personally had groomed for the presidency in 1909–1910, Pinheiro initially obtained crucial support from the higher officer corps. By 1911, however, the latter were less solidly behind him. The movement of younger officers known as the Salvationists looked directly to Hermes, and even more to Hermes's military son and nephews, for support in their campaign to "redeem" certain states for the Republic. Eventually, however, the Salvationists became enmeshed in the internecine factional struggles of the

[57] As a result of Pinheiro's reorganization, the Partido Republicano Paraibano (PRP) was renamed the Partido Republicano Conservador Paraibano (PRCP).

[58] On the Salvationist revolts, see Bello, *History Brazil*, pp. 218–25; Levine, *Pernambuco*, pp. 81–83; Pang, *Bahia*, pp. 83–93; Della Cava, *Miracle Joaseiro*, pp. 128–36; and Love, *Rio Grande do Sul*, pp. 156–63.

states where they militarily intervened and were subordinated to the ends of the oligarchical outs they placed in power.[59]

In late 1911, the Salvationists turned to Paraíba as the next target. Eying the federal election scheduled for March as an advantageous context for ejecting the oligarchy, they plotted to replace the Machado–Pessoa–Leal candidate with their military candidate, Col. José Joaquim do Rêgo Barros. Although Rêgo Barros was a native son whose military duty had included a stay in Teixeira and a term in the Assembly in the nineties, he had spent little time in Paraíba since 1900. Nevertheless, his candidacy immediately catalyzed the resentment toward Álvaro held by many Old Liberal backlands families. The Salvationists' movement to unseat the incumbent oligarchy, consequently, became a means for the Dantas and Santa Cruz families, along with other former Alvaristas deposed from local politics, to redress their grievances over political representation.[60]

By late 1911, Álvaro was gravely ill. The realization that his illness would complicate the gubernatorial succession led to a crisis. A struggle for the control of the PRCP emerged between Epitácio on the one hand and Valfredo and João Machado on the other. In December, Álvaro placed the contest in Hermes's hands, asking him to resolve it.[61] Initially, Epitácio underestimated Senator Valfredo's gubernatorial ambitions, believing the latter would not "presume to be elected by the same governor [i.e., João Machado] whom he [Valfredo] had elected."[62] Valfredo, as acting state party boss for the incapacitated Álvaro, soon revealed that he did indeed desire to become governor again. As a senator in Rio de Janeiro, he schemed to convince President Hermes of his suitability, while Epitácio maneuvered to persuade Hermes not to endorse Valfredo officially. Epitácio even offered Valfredo a personal pledge not to back his brother, Antônio Pessoa, as a gubernatorial candidate. In exchange, he asked that Valfredo desist from seeking the nomination.[63] Meanwhile, Epitácio wrote Hermes asking him to dissuade

[59] Levine, *Pernambuco*, p. 81; Love, *Rio Grande do Sul*, p. 163.

[60] Local historians referred to Rêgo Barros as an "outsider" and a military man "without influence" in Paraíba, universally ignoring that he was a native of Mamanguape and had served in the Assembly under Álvaro Machado during the Second Session (1894–1896). A. da Nóbrega, *História republicana*, p. 67; José Lins do Rêgo, *Fogo Morto*, 10th ed. (Rio de Janeiro: José Olýmpio Editôra, 1970), p. 23.

[61] Epitácio to Hermes da Fonseca (Rio de Janeiro), 30 Nov. 1911, AEP/10/72. Pedrosa to Epitácio (Capital), 11 Nov. 1911, AEP/10/71 and 74.

[62] Epitácio to Hermes da Fonseca (Rio de Janeiro), 30 Nov. 1911, AEP/10/72.

[63] Ibid.

Valfredo from his reelection plan and to intercede with Pinheiro Machado, who still backed Valfredo.[64]

The contest over who would lead the oligarchy in Paraíba, consequently, became a struggle for national domination between President Hermes and Pinheiro Machado. The first round was decided in a historic meeting in the presidential Catete Palace on the evening of December 9, 1911. In the presence of the two rival contenders, Hermes pronounced that Paraíba's next governor would be an Epitacista, João Pereira de Castro Pinto, recently indicated by Álvaro Machado for reelection as senator.[65] As Epitácio's old law school chum, Castro Pinto was a candidate who signified the end of the Machado–Leal oligarchy, especially because Antônio Pessoa was named his running mate for first lieutenant governor. Antônio's nomination later gave credence to the suspicion that Castro Pinto's selection was deliberately calculated to place Col. Antônio Pessoa in the governorship by means of a resignation. Epitácio had confessed privately to Pedrosa that he entertained no such motive.[66] Although Epitácio did not hold political office in Paraíba, Hermes took the unusual step of placing him on the Executive Committee of the PRCP as its co-director with Valfredo. The Senate seat Castro Pinto would occupy from January until his October inauguration would then be given to Epitácio for a nine-year term.[67]

With the announcement the following day that Valfredo Leal had been eliminated by Hermes, the Old Liberals of the backlands saw their last hope for redress within the oligarchy slip from their grasp. As if to seal the president's pronouncement, Álvaro Machado died the following month—on the day of the federal elec-

[64] Ibid.

[65] Pedrosa recruited João Castro Pinto, a Venancista from the Constituent Assembly, for the House of Deputies in 1904 as a key figure in the integration of the former Autonomistas. A native of Mamanguape, Castro Pinto was related to Antônio Massa on his mother's (Cavalcanti de Albuquerque) side. Author's prosopographical file.

[66] Epitácio to Pedro da Cunha Pedrosa (Rio de Janeiro), 21 Dec. 1912, republished in Cunha Pedrosa, *Minhas memórias*, 1:112. Epitácio denied that "my insistence in favor of Antônio could appear to be a family matter and conceal the motive of implanting one oligarchy in Paraíba with the pretext of bringing down another." No archival evidence suggested such a motive and Castro Pinto's resignation did not appear to be part of a prearranged strategy. However, Epitácio probably intended Antônio to succeed him in the 1916 election.

[67] Epitácio to Hermes da Fonseca (Rio de Janeiro), 30 Nov. 1911, AEP/10/72.

tions, January 31. An opposition Democratic Party had already been established by Francisco Alves de Lima Filho, a disgruntled federal deputy and Old Liberal from Catolé do Rocha. Its sole purpose was to legitimate the candidacy of Col. Rêgo Barros. Ex-Senator Coelho Lisboa, who had broken with Álvaro and Valfredo in 1908 over the selection of João Machado as governor, coordinated Salvationist support for Rêgo Barros in Rio de Janeiro, while Lima Filho campaigned among the Old Liberals of the backlands for his Democratic Party's candidate. He also approached Pernambuco's new governor, Dantas Barreto, whom the Salvationists had recently installed, allegedly enlisting his support for an invasion of Paraíba.[68]

O Estado da Parahyba, Lima Filho's opposition newspaper in the Capital, aired the grievances of the Dantas of Teixeira and the Santa Cruz in Monteiro, while publicizing the pro-Salvationist aims of the Democratic Party by endorsing Rêgo Barros's candidacy. However, the real party of the insurrectionists was their menacing army, which was organized by March. Franklin Dantas and Augusto Santa Cruz headed a private army of heavily armed kinsmen, capangas, and rural tenants recruited from their family estates, reinforced by scores of bandits, cutthroats, and prominent gunslingers from half a dozen states. Numbering around one thousand, it coalesced in the eastern alto sertão throughout March and April. In either late April or early May, it moved eastward, striking first at the city of Patos around May 21. An eyewitness reported that Patos was "reduced to one vast cemetery."[69] The frightened residents were forced to submit to the humiliating abuse of the attackers, who sacked commercial establishments and robbed the homes of more prosperous citizens. Over the next week, Santa Luzia do Sabugi, Soledade, and Batalhão were also pillaged, as the army moved eastward toward Campina Grande.[70] Finally, at the

[68] Pedrosa to Epitácio (Capital), 7 Nov. 1911, AEP/10/71. Pedrosa alleged that Lima Filho had told Hermes that Epitácio was "interfering in state politics" and would "make an oligarchy worse than what now exists." Ibid. See also Pedrosa's memorandum of 10 Nov. 1911, published in Cunha Pedrosa, *Minhas memórias*, 1:99–103.

[69] João Machado to Epitácio, tel. of 24 May 1912, AEP/10/71. Santa Cruz had first attacked Alagoa do Monteiro with 200 men on 6 May. He surrounded and bombarded the county seat, released his local followers from jail, and locked up the prefeito, his enemy Col. Pedro Bezerra, together with other town officials and eighteen policemen. *A União*, 12 May 1912.

[70] "Conditions in the sertão are bad. Besides sacking Patos, Santa Luzia, Sole-

end of May and in early June, the rebels were definitively repulsed on the outskirts of Campina Grande. Federal troops commanded by Capt. Adolfo Massa arrived just in time to reinforce the outnumbered State Police.[71]

The Dantas-Santa Cruz insurrection was a powerful reminder to the Paraíba oligarchy not only of the de facto independence of many municípios in the interior but also of its own dependence on the federal government. The rebel chieftains had been counting on support from the federal soldiers garrisoned in Paraíba's Capital, who had backed Rêgo Barros earlier in the year. Contrary to official references to the insurrection issued after its defeat, Epitácio, Pedrosa, Venâncio, Valfredo, and João Machado had all privately expressed great apprehension that Rêgo Barros would succeed.[72]

Epitácio managed to save the oligarchy in which he recently had gained an official leadership role. He rescued it by virtue of his skill in factional maneuvering and his personal relationship with President Hermes. In February, Pedrosa outlined the course Epitácio had already begun to pursue:

> It is necessary that you reach an agreement with [Senator] Pinheiro [Machado], through the intermediary of [Senator Antônio] Azeredo, his friend, in order to avoid any failure in the Senator. The Marshal [Hermes] can be of influence here also. Coronel João Pessoa [de Queiroz] and Mena Barreto [minister of war] should be confidentially apprised of the measures which should be taken here [in Paraíba, i.e., chang-

---

dade, and Batalhão, small isolated bands of cangaceiros are marauding individual fazendas and settlements. The celebrated Antônio Silvino is on the road again—this time on horseback—and he is no longer content with the loot that formerly was sufficient. . . . The attack he made on Santa Luzia fifteen days ago was unbelievable. The local boss . . . was barbarously and insultingly beaten and robbed of ten contos and his friends lost over forty contos. There were also 'unspeakable outrages' to the most respectable ladies in society." Federal District Judge Antônio Marques da Silva Mariz to Epitácio (Sousa), 20 June 1912, AEP/10/186.

[71] Two months earlier, the state chief of police had advised: "What is happening in the interior [the recuitment of a private army] is a consequence of the inaction of Governor João Machado. The reestablishment of order in the affected municípios will be difficult without federal troops." Antônio Massa to Epitácio (Capital), 26 Mar. 1912, AEP/10/130. Gov. João Machado reported that 900 policemen were not sufficient to repel the insurgents, who, by the end of March, had begun "to strike in a number of places at once under Santa Cruz' leadership." João Machado to Epitácio (Capital), 26 Mar. 1912, AEP/10/128.

[72] Pedrosa to Epitácio (Capital), 7 Feb. 1912, AEP/10/87.

ing the Fourth Company's officers] so that the orders of the Marshal are not weakened by others in the Ministry of War in favor of [Col.] Rêgo Barros or any other military candidate. Coronel João Pessoa should not favor Rêgo Barros or the plans of Lima Filho. The latter, they say, is disposed to join João Machado against you and therefore accepts the candidacy of Rêgo Barros. The same motives are shared by [State] Supreme Court Judge Heráclito [Cavalcanti Carneiro Monteiro], [Federal Deputy] Felizardo [Leite Ferreira], and [Federal Deputy José Francisco de Lima] Mindêlo, who prefer Rêgo Barros to you.[73]

As Pedrosa suggested, the division in the federal government pitted President Hermes against Minister of War Mena Barreto, who was considered to be pro-Salvationist. Pedrosa was so alarmed by the high odds favoring the Salvationists that he actually proposed to Epitácio breaking with the president and fielding a second military candidate on behalf of their faction! Desperate, he suggested Venâncio's brother-in-law, who had been a military deputy in the State Assembly since 1908, Capt. João Batista de Figueirêdo Neiva.[74]

Valfredo Leal offered an analysis that more clearly revealed the relationship of the political lineup at the federal level to the factions struggling for control of Paraíba. Suggesting that the oligarchy he had led with Álvaro no longer existed, he attempted a clumsy reapproximation with Epitácio:

> The examples of Bahia, Ceará, etc. [where Salvationist *coups d'état* had occurred in 1911] have raised the hopes of the Rêgo Barros faction. Therefore, our intriguing to take revenge on their candidate could get dangerous, because the majority of the officers of the Fourth [Federal] Company [assigned to the Capital] are with Coronel Rêgo Barros. The majority of the state is with us and, except for a [federal, pro-Rêgo Barros] military intervention, we would have no doubt that the [Salvationist] opposition would be smashed. If the people [of Pa-

[73] Ibid. The proinsurrection Heraclista faction that Pedrosa identified represented Epitácio's most important opposition from 1915 to 1930. As a family-based group of Old Liberals, it included Heráclito Cavalcanti (Monteiro), a state supreme court justice; Felizardo Leite, a state assemblyman; and Lima Mindêlo, a former assemblyman who was Heráclito's brother-in-law. Azevêdo Bastos, *Roteiro Azevêdo*, pp. 592, 594, and 672. (See Fig. B.4.)

[74] Pedrosa to Epitácio, 7 Feb. 1912, AEP/10/87.

raíba] are convinced that the government of the Union is not behind him [Rêgo Barros] and furnishing him support, [then] our victory is certain. They [the Salvationists] talk about "oligarchy" in Paraíba, but this is a pretext for a campaign they intend to mount against those in power. If Álvaro Machado represented that, he is now dead after eighteen years of power here. . . . Oligarchy does not exist among us; we are entering a new and promising phase in accordance with the intentions of Marshal Hermes. However, Lima [Filho] exploits militarism very much, saying there are two politics: that of Catete [the presidential palace] and that of General Headquarters directed by the Ministry of War. It has reached the point where they are saying that, although there is no oligarchy, there is going to be a fight between Dr. Epitácio and the military. [Lima Filho and partisans of the Salvationist candidate] know the Marshal [President Hermes] is both his [Epitácio's] and Coronel José Pessoa's real friend, [and they argue that Hermes] desires to please them. [Consequently,] in the appropriate moment before the gubernatorial election, [they argue that] the orders of the Marshal are going to be countermanded by General Headquarters [i.e., by order of War Minister Mena Barreto, not Hermes]. So [by] these means, Rêgo Barros hopes to knock out João Machado or whatever candidate is offered. They say also that [Pernambuco Governor] Dantas Barreto is behind them. His and [Augusto] Santa Cruz' participation would create anarchy. Santa Cruz . . . is hiding in Pernambuco.[75]

Valfredo's lengthy and essentially correct assessment suggested the nature of the strategic checkmate that Epitácio already had begun to implement in Rio de Janeiro. First, he aimed to countermand the orders assigning four new military officers to the Federal Fourth Company, which already was en route to the Northeast at Epitácio's request. Family-based networking on the part of the rebel Old Liberals had determined that the company's commander would be sympathetic to their cause, for he was Lieut. Adolfo Dantas Correia de Góis, a first cousin of Franklin Dantas. Consequently, Epitácio asked President Hermes to replace Lieut. Adolfo Dantas with Capt. Adolfo Massa, brother of Paraíba's state chief of police, Antônio Massa.[76] His intervention went even further, for

[75] Valfredo Leal to Epitácio (Capital), 24 Feb. 1912, AEP/10/105.

[76] Epitácio to Gov. João Machado (Rio de Janeiro), tel. of 22 April 1912, AEP/10/140.

Hermes's orders to the regional commander indicated that when the company arrived in the Northeast, the commander in Natal was to "recall Alfredo Dantas Correia de Góis from Paraíba. No officers may visit Paraíba. Rêgo Barros [in Parahyba] is to return to Rio de Janeiro by ship. Captain Massa is in charge of the Fourth Company and authorized to operate in the interior. Reinforce him with 100 to 200 troops."[77]

Thanks to Epitácio's quick action, the planned uprising of federal troops in Paraíba designed to coordinate military support for Rêgo Barros in the Capital with the backlands rebellion never took place. Earlier, President Hermes had dismissed Mena Barreto and named a new minister of war, while all four of the Federal Fourth Company's officers were replaced by the individuals Epitácio designated. Gov. João Machado could then employ the Fourth Company in the backlands to disperse the rebels, relying on several hundred additional federal soldiers sent from the garrison in Recife.[78] The crisis of law and order was resolved by mid-June, and a postponed gubernatorial election was held on the twenty-second. Castro Pinto and Col. Antônio Pessoa won and were inaugurated in October as Paraíba's governor and first lieutenant governor. However, the Assembly elected the preceding December still reflected the dominance of the Valfredistas and Machadistas (the followers of ex-Governor João Machado). Epitacistas throughout the state were elated over their victory, none more than Col. Cristiano Lauritzen. Only a month earlier, as the rebels were preparing to advance on Campina Grande, he had anxiously written to Epitácio of the "fears that assault me when I realize that, with one turn of the wheel of fortune, Marshal Hermes could disappear and, with him, our most important support."[79] Three weeks later, he sent Epitácio a telegram containing "the appreciation of forty-six commercial firms in Campina Grande" for quelling the revolt, and asked that President Hermes be advised of their gratitude.[80]

For Epitácio, the backlands insurrection that nearly toppled the

[77] Ibid. Antônio Massa to Epitácio (Capital), 20 Feb. 1912, AEP/10/102.

[78] Epitácio to João Machado (Rio de Janeiro), tel. of 22 April 1912, AEP/10/140. Epitácio to Hermes, 27 Mar. 1912, AEP/10/137. Epitácio also arranged for ammunition to be sent from Recife. Ibid. Hermes's new minister of war, Vespasiano Gonçalves de Albuquerque e Silva, was appointed on 29 March 1912. Max Fleius, *História administrativa do Brasil*, 2nd ed. (São Paulo: Cia. Melhoramentos de São Paulo, [1922]), p. 650.

[79] Col. Cristiano Lauritzen to Epitácio (Campina Grande), 15 May 1912, AEP/10/169.

[80] Idem, 3 June 1912, AEP/10/122–23.

oligarchy offered the opportunity to secure it more firmly for himself and his family-based network in Paraíba. His career as a national politician also looked much more promising than a year earlier, when he had to be relieved of his duties on the Supreme Court because a severe medical crisis had threatened his life. Assuming formal command of the Paraíba oligarchy between June and December, Epitácio took definitive leave of the Court in August.[81] However, by late October he had agreed to run in November for Castro Pinto's vacated Senate seat. Because the offer of this seat had been formally extended by the PRCP's Executive Committee—and its only Epitacistas were Castro Pinto and Col. Antônio Pessoa—this implied a presidential dictate. Two weeks earlier, Valfredo had assented to Hermes's suggestion that Epitácio be the PRCP's sole director and agreed to step down as co-director. Finally, on December 28, Epitácio was formally recognized as the senior senator for Paraíba.[82] At the PRCP's convention in Parahyba the following February, a vote by acclamation confirmed him as state party boss.[83]

As the new head of Paraíba's congressional delegation, Sen. Epitácio Pessoa assumed his place in the upper house together with Pedro da Cunha Pedrosa, newly appointed to the vacancy left

[81] By March 1911, Epitácio was bedridden with an acute gall bladder ailment. His doctors told him to seek surgery in Europe or he would not live much longer. After removal of his gall bladder in Paris, on 4 September, he left for Brazil on October 27, arriving only days before President Hermes offered him the leadership of Paraíba's oligarchy. Meanwhile, Epitácio resumed his position on the Supreme Court in time to support Hermes's controversial nonintervention in the Salvationist seizure of power in the State of Bahia in January 1912. Prior to his resignation on 17 August 1912, ostensibly for reasons of health, this was his last major case. L. Pessôa, *Epitacio Pessôa*, 1:198–203.

[82] Executive Committee of the PRCP (Capital) to Epitácio, tel. of 25 Oct. 1912, AEP/10/218. The Committee's non-Epitacista members included five of a total of seven: Federal Deputy Valfredo Leal, Assembly President Inácio Evaristo Monteiro, Federal Deputy Seráfico Nóbrega, State Supreme Court Justice Heráclito Cavalcanti, and Federal Deputy Felizardo Leite. When Pinheiro Machado had twice offered him a seat in the Senate in 1912, Epitácio had refused. L. Pessôa, *Epitacio Pessôa*, 1:205.

[83] The following confirms the groundswell of popular support for Epitácio's candidacy as state party boss and senator for Paraíba: Pedro da Cunha Pedrosa to Epitácio (Capital), 4 Feb. 1912, AEP/10/85; Cristiano Lauritzen to Epitácio (Campina Grande), 7 Feb., 19 Mar., and 15 July 1912, AEP/10/121–23 and 192, respectively; José Jerónimo de Albuquerque Borborema to Epitácio (Campina Grande), 31 Jan. 1912, AEP/10/84; Pedro da Cunha Pedrosa to Epitácio (Capital), tel. of 7 Feb. 1912, AEP/10/287; Venâncio, Pedrosa, and Antônio Massa (Capital), tel. of 9 Feb. 1912, AEP/10/96.

by Álvaro, and Valfredo Leal, who had been reelected. Epitácio's next task would be to eliminate Valfredo and ex-Governor João Machado as factional challengers to his leadership of the Paraíba oligarchy. With Hermes's manifest backing, Epitácio would succeed. Even "Pinheiro [Machado] would need Epitácio," as Castro Pinto had observed.[84] "The years of anarchy," Pedrosa noted, were drawing to a close; the "order of Epitácio Pessoa" had begun.[85] In Paraíba, family-based oligarchy would enjoy its most secure political direction during the next eighteen years of direct Pessoa rule.

[84] Castro Pinto, cited in Ascendino Carneiro da Cunha to Epitácio (Capital), 24 Sept. 1913, AEP/11/77.

[85] Pedro da Cunha Pedrosa to Epitácio (Capital), 13 Oct. 1912, AEP/10/218.

· VII ·

The Pessoas in Power: The Years of "Order," 1912–1924

I prefer Paraíba's tamed oligarchy to the wild and shameless ones that hereabouts still run free.

—State Deputy Artur Aquiles dos Santos, c. 1912

Gentlemen, Ladies,
There is a special charm for me in being in Paraíba—*minha terra pequena e boa*—for I have never . . . dissociated myself from her. I have shared with Paraíba, and I will always continue to share, the distinctions and honors paid to me.

—President-Elect Epitácio Pessoa, July 12, 1919

THE INAUGURATION of Governor Castro Pinto on October 22, 1912 opened a new era of direct domination by the Pessoa oligarchy in Paraíba. Epitácio's assumption of a seat in the Senate two months later, followed by his election as state party boss in February 1913, initiated a decade of superbly coordinated factional cohesion that endured unchallenged until 1924. Between 1912 and 1915, Epitácio secured undisputed control of the state oligarchy through electoral victories that awarded his faction control of the Congressional delegation and Assembly and reduced his opposition's political representation to the legal minimum.

At the federal level, Epitácio maintained a good working relationship with President Hermes and his successor, Venceslau Brás. Thus, in the six years he served in the Senate before assuming the presidency, Epitácio continued to anchor his oligarchical order firmly in the national capital. In the Senate, he made his most lasting legislative contribution to Brazil when he crafted the successful compromise that brought the Civil Code Project to the floor for a favorable vote on December 31, 1915. In Paraíba, however, Epitácio contributed most significantly only after his election to the presidency. The program of drought relief that he sponsored while in executive office confirmed his public pledge as president-elect not to forget the debt he owed to his native state. He is still remembered there and throughout the Northeast not only as the author of an invigorated IFOCS program but also as the man who set the precedent for massive federal expenditure on antidrought projects for both the Vargas dictatorship and the populist governments that followed. However, his efforts on behalf of drought relief also contained long-term significance for Paraíba's system of family-based rule: The patronage that Epitácio channeled to his governors enabled them to initiate the transformation of the relationship between the State and the município that historically testified to the strength of elite family power throughout the region.

Oligarchical Consolidation

Defeating the Opposition

As soon as he was elected state party boss, in February 1913, Epitácio pursued a political strategy that would enable him to control all nominations to state and federal office in Paraíba. First, he eliminated his weaker and less popular rival, former Governor João Machado, who expected Pedro da Cunha Pedrosa to resign a Senate seat in his favor.[1] Epitácio vetoed such a move in an announcement before a large audience of friends, relatives, and national politicians gathered at his ship as he was embarking on his annual European vacation. After reaffirming his new leadership of the PRCP, he insisted that Pedrosa would not yield his seat to João Machado.[2] João Machado, who was standing nearby, then engaged Epitácio in a heated exchange and stalked off. Writing immediately to President Hermes, Epitácio pointed out that "a severe shock to Paraíba politics could be avoided" if Hermes would up-

[1] In 1908, the pact Epitácio sealed with Álvaro stipulated that Pedrosa should move to the Senate: "I believe that the President would not refuse his [Pedrosa's] nomination, since his name comes from the [official] list [of candidates], above all because these are the wishes of those directing the state's politics. I certainly have good relations with the current President [Afonso Pena]. I also have them with the future one [Hermes da Fonseca], and I think in this respect that the favorable circumstances will not change." Epitácio to Venâncio (Rio de Janeiro), 27 Dec. 1909, AEP/12/64. Cunha Pedrosa, *Minhas memórias*, 1:108 and 115–23; idem to Epitácio (Capital), 2 Aug. 1911, AEP/10/70. Valfredo Leal, Epitácio, and Pedrosa were senators in 1913.

[2] Epitácio to President Hermes da Fonseca (Rio de Janeiro), 16 May 1913, AEP/11/34.

hold Pedrosa's right to his Senate seat by standing aloof from Epitácio's quarrel with João Machado.[3] Maintaining that he had been insulted by João Machado when they argued on the dock, Epitácio termed his rival's behavior "not bad manners" but "an act of indiscipline threatening to split the Party." Supporting João Machado, consequently, was impossible, because "he could not elect an enemy," for that would be "completely impolitic."[4] Hermes remained neutral, and Pedrosa kept his Senate seat. Two years later, in March 1915, when Pedrosa faced João Machado in a race for reelection—still without Hermes's support—he retained his seat. For João Machado, any hope of remaining in state politics vanished.

The "Padre," Monsig. Valfredo Leal, was a more formidable obstacle to Epitácio's total control of the state of oligarchy. Valfredo still enjoyed immense popularity among many Old Liberal bosses in the interior. Unlike João Machado's reputation, Valfredo's had not suffered from the 1911–1912 insurrection, because he had counseled compromise with Augusto Santa Cruz. Epitácio therefore adopted a different strategy for overcoming Valfredo's opposition. Ostensibly pursuing a compromise position with the Valfredistas throughout 1914, Epitácio suddenly declared a formal political break with the Padre in early January 1915. The issue that provoked their split was the slate for the federal election in March. Epitácio thus imposed a crisis of choice on Paraíba's local bosses prior to the January 31 Assembly election. This move enabled him to direct his partisans to vote only for Epitacista candidates, withdrawing support from the Valfredistas and thereby revoking the pact President Venceslau Brás had sealed between him and Valfredo. He and Valfredo had divided the state legislature's thirty seats evenly between their factions in 1911. In December 1914, however, with less than justifiable provocation, Epitácio charged that the Padre would not similarly compromise on the distribution of congressional seats between their factions. In reality, his overriding concern was Valfredo's willingness to compromise.[5] In

[3] Ibid.

[4] Ibid.

[5] During December 1914, Epitácio and Valfredo met six times with President Venceslau Brás and federal politicians such as Senators Urbino Santos and Antônio Azerêdo to try to achieve a compromise. Epitácio always insisted that he and Pedrosa retain two seats in the Senate, leaving Valfredo the intolerable option of ceding his Senate seat to João Machado. Hence, the deadlock: "My greatest desire is to break [with Valfredo], convinced [as I am] of the impossibility of reestablishing the agreement [with Valfredo] which is really undone. But how to break if Valfredo sub-

what amounted to a ritualized behavior, Paraíba's new state party boss dramatically broke with Valfredo. He thus gained the tactical advantage of speed, sending separate circular telegrams on January 2 announcing his break to his "friends" and "allies" among the local bosses. Calling upon them "to vote my slate," he released their votes for an all Epitacista and Venancista ticket.[6] Four weeks later, on January 31, Valfredo's last hope of independent political survival evaporated when his faction obtained only the legally required minority of six seats in the Assembly. His defeat in the March federal election was a foregone conclusion.

Now controlling the governorship and the Assembly, Epitácio went on to win the congressional election in what subsequently was proclaimed "the freest" election held in Paraíba until that time. A spirited press campaign witnessed the most zealous of his younger supporters engaging in a journalistic war of lampoons with the Valfredistas, whom they dubbed the "Bacuraus"—after a bird known for its short flight.[7] The Epitacista propaganda of these self-styled "Condors"—so-called because "Epitácio soared like an eagle"—contributed significantly to Epitácio's victory. Not only was Pedrosa reelected but also four of the five seats in the lower house went to the Epitacista candidates.[8] In Pinheiro Machado's estimation, Epitácio now had replaced Valfredo in federal political power. A preelection letter from Pedrosa to his party boss confirmed this opinion. It established why Pedrosa was not worried about losing the contest:

> [Pinheiro] was satisfied with your going [to Paraíba to campaign] in [January 1915], and your position regarding the "Case of Rio," in view of your personal relationship with [Rio de Janeiro's Governor] Nilo [Peçanha]. He praised you and said

---

mits himself to Castro Pinto's [compromise] formula?" Epitácio to Antônio Massa (Rio de Janeiro), 19 Dec. 1914, AEP/11/23.

[6] Epitácio's circular telegram to "all friends" [thirty-one local bosses of the PRCP] (Rio de Janeiro), 2 Jan. 1915, AEP/11/243. "Valfredo having made an issue of the slate, taking three deputies and leaving me one, the [1911 Catete] agreement [specifying their shared direction of the PRCP] has become impossible." Ibid. The telegram correctly informed the bosses that both President Brás and national PRC head, Sen. Pinheiro Machado, had declared "complete neutrality," so that the election would determine which faction would dominate the oligarchy.

[7] Cunha Pedrosa, *Minhas memórias*, 1:155. The Bacuraus controlled *O Estado da Parahyba* and were lampooned by the Epitacistas controlling *O Norte*.

[8] Three of the other four Venancista deputies elected were Areienses: Maximiano de Figueirêdo, Octacílio de Albuquerque, and José Maria da Cunha Lima; Camilo de Hollanda was from the Capital.

he was your sincere friend. . . . He said that in the event of a "slip-up against me at the polls," I could count on him in every way. We are more in Pinheiro's favor [now] than is Valfredo.[9]

The "banner of Epitacismo" now was hoisted statewide and at each level of government. Next, Epitácio turned to the task of reorganizing his party.

The Resolution of Gubernatorial Crises

After the accession of Castro Pinto to the governorship in 1912, the colloquialism, "the order of Epitácio Pessoa," gained popularity. It suggested that the schismatic crises over the gubernatorial succession characteristic of Álvaro Machado's last twelve years of leadership would no longer arise. Epitácio's success in this respect rested on the fact that, following Castro Pinto's resignation, first Epitácio's brother and then their distant cousin and loyal friend, Solon de Lucena, occupied the governorship. Contrary to popular assumption, Castro Pinto's surprise resignation in 1915 did not appear to be a calculated move on Epitácio's part to enable his brother to become governor. Instead, Castro Pinto appeared to have resigned out of sheer personal frustration—to the great relief of all of Epitácio's lieutenants in Paraíba. In personality, he was unsuited to the executive responsibilities a state governor undertook vis-à-vis the local bosses. He idealistically opposed the chicanery and violence on which coronelista politics was grounded, so much so that he found himself a public laughing stock when he attempted to carry out Epitácio's instructions for a "free" election in 1915. After resigning the governorship, he abandoned Paraíba politics and moved permanently to Rio de Janeiro.[10]

First Lieutenant Governor Antônio Pessoa, who succeeded Cas-

[9] Pedro da Cunha Pedrosa to Epitácio (Rio de Janeiro), 17 Jan. 1915, AEP/11/253. Pedrosa referred to Epitácio's visit as having occurred in December, but the month has been corrected to January in this translation. The "Case of Rio" referred to Epitácio's role in drafting a Senate report accusing the Supreme Court of an unconstitutional decision in upholding Nilo Peçanha's election as governor of Rio de Janeiro in 1914, implying, consequently, that Pinheiro's quid pro quo would be to guarantee Pedrosa's seat, even if João Machado carried the vote. See also Cunha Pedrosa, *Minhas memórias*, 1:158–64. In spite of a "maximum effort" to have Congress verify *their* majority (7,473 votes for João Machado and only 6,439 for Pedrosa), the opposition lost. Fenelon Nóbrega and Valfredo Leal to Antônio Marques da Silva Mariz and Zé Vicente (n.p.), tel. of (Mar.?) 1915, AEP/11/260.

[10] Earlier, Epitácio and Pinheiro Machado had prevailed on Castro Pinto to re-

tro Pinto in June 1915, was ideally suited for the governorship. His worsening heart condition, however, led to his resignation in August 1916 and upset the advantageous oligarchical partnership that Epitácio had maintained with him. His death, on October 31—at age fifty-two—also robbed Epitácio of his closest and most trusted relative.[11] Nevertheless, the choice of a gubernatorial successor raised the specter of schism only briefly, between 1915 and 1916. Conflict erupted over who the candidate would be, as the young Epitacista Condors who had just defeated the Valfredista Bacuraus turned their rhetorical attack on Epitácio's senior supporters, the veteran Venancistas. Calling themselves "Young Turks," the younger generation sarcastically lampooned the Venancistas in the press, carrying their antagonism so far that Epitácio personally intervened in the rivalry when he visited Paraíba in January 1915. Assisted by Col. Cristiano Lauritzen, he smoothed the political transition by designating a Venancista as the new governor, Camilo de Holanda. A compromise choice for the 1916–1920 term, Camilo only temporarily placated the Young Turks.[12]

Epitácio's tight control of PRCP organization largely explained the absence of divisive crises over the gubernatorial succession until mid-1924. Unlike Álvaro Machado, Epitácio retained the title of state party boss during his tenure in the Senate. But in 1920 presidential responsibilities prompted him to transfer the office to the aging Venâncio. Once Solon de Lucena was inaugurated governor—in October—the title devolved to him.[13] Irrespective of who held this office, Epitácio retained primary authority, reserving for himself not only the power of a final veto in oligarchical decision-making but also the crucial prerogative to choose Paraíba's congressional delegation. His choices for governor between

---

main in the governorship. Cunha Pedrosa, *Minhas memórias*, 1:153. Pinto, *Octacílio de Albuquerque*, pp. 51, 60–65.

[11] Antônio Pessoa wrote Epitácio a last letter voicing grave reservations about Camilo de Holanda's loyalty and deploring "the rabble represented by Camilo's relatives." Antônio Pessoa to Epitácio (Umbuseiro), 19 Oct. 1916, AEP/12/24.

[12] In 1916, the Young Turks controlled the newly founded *A Notícia* (Capital) and editorially opposed the Guelas, who monopolized editorial policy on *A União*, the official PRCP organ.

[13] Unless Epitácio continued to "advise" him, Solon threatened to resign the governorship at the time Epitácio was leaving the presidency, obliging him to accept the office of state party boss. Solon de Lucena to Epitácio (Capital), 3 Nov. 1922, AEP/12/192; Epitácio to Solon de Lucena (Rio de Janeiro), 12 Dec. 1922, AEP/12/194. See also Epitácio to Inácio Evaristo Monteiro (Rio de Janeiro), 18 Nov. 1922, AEP/12/156.

1912 and 1924—Castro Pinto, Antônio Pessoa, Camilo de Holanda, and Solon de Lucena—reflected his strong preference for candidates who were loyal and tractable. Although he erred in these respects when he selected Camilo, his choice of two of his kinsmen, Antônio and Solon, best assured him reliable governors who would faithfully execute his policies as obedient surrogates. Besides his own, very commanding, personal style, Epitácio also depended on a reorganization of the PRCP to insure that his power as state party boss would remain paramount. The organizational changes he made, which he undertook between 1914 and 1916, were of great concern to Paraíba's local party bosses. They best suggested what the so-called order of Epitácio Pessoa meant.

Disciplining the PRCP

Even prior to the 1915 election, Epitácio started to reorganize the PRCP along lines that eventually reduced the opposition's factions to token representation. First, he stopped his predecessors' practice of permitting party members to run as independent candidates (*candidatos avulsos*) against the official PRCP slate of candidates. Thus, potential fission within his coalition was held to a minimum. Any local boss who wished to contest an election with an official candidate faced expulsion from the PRCP.

Epitácio's second reform aimed at co-opting a portion of the opposition, by virtue of his enforcement of the Rosa e Silva Electoral Law (1901). It guaranteed the opposition a minimum legal representation of 20 per cent of all legislative seats—in Congress, the Assembly, and the município councils—although in many states enforcement was at best sporadic.[14] Consequently, one of Paraíba's five federal deputies and six of the thirty state deputies were always elected from the opposition. In the Senate, compliance was suspended between 1918 and 1921 only after Valfredo lost the election because in some municípios the number of votes he received exceeded registered voters. Otherwise, Valfredo or Simeão Leal—Valfredo's cousin—represented the opposition. Epitácio drew more advantage from observing the law than did the opposition, because it enabled him to decide which family-based network in the opposition would hold office and, more significantly, which would be excluded. He thus denied to his more dangerous adversaries—the group led by State Supreme Court Justice Herá-

[14] L. Pessôa, *Epitacio Pessôa*, 1:220. On electoral reform, see *A União*, 15 Oct. 1919.

clito Cavalcanti—any chance of holding office and consigned them to what politicians in the Old Republic called "exile." After 1922, when Epitácio permitted Valfredo to name all six opposition assemblymen, Heráclito's faction failed to gain representation. The Padre then ceased to be regarded as Epitácio's opposition, although he did not declare himself to be an Epitacista until 1927.[15]

The third factor that explained the cohesion of Epitácio's machine was his personalistic style. His two visits to Paraíba—first in January 1915, shortly after his break with Valfredo before the Assembly elections, and then in the summer of 1916, when he returned after Antônio Pessoa's election as governor, firmly established his oligarchical leadership on a face-to-face basis. With his brother Antônio at his side, Epitácio personally acknowledged the "friends and allies of 1915" by reconfirming or appointing them anew as the local party bosses. These bosses would be the backbone of his electoral machine until 1930. His correspondence with them attained voluminous proportions throughout the 1920s, and even while he was president he remained accessible, granting their special petitions or adjudicating their local quarrels. At the pinnacle of his national political career, Epitácio's correspondence with Gov. Solon de Lucena, giving advice and instructions regarding the local bosses, indicated his awareness that loyalty was a reciprocal relationship. His organizational success could be traced in no small measure to the patient and careful attention his letters paid to município politics and the personal elements of Paraíba's política de família.

Epitácio used a standard oligarchical vocabulary recognizing gradations of loyalty among the local politicians in his 1915 coalition. For instance, the bosses who had delivered his vote were "the friends and allies of 1915"; however, "friends" received the prefeituras and local chefias because their long years of loyalty before 1915 distinguished them as senior claimants, while "allies" had pragmatically voted for Epitácio, but owed personal allegiance to a politician other than Epitácio. Following Valfredo's 1915 defeat, allies also tended to be deserters from the Padre's ranks who were eager to reintegrate with the ruling coalition as inferior latecomers. "Dissident friends" posed a thornier issue. Although they

[15] Valfredo's earlier political subservience to Epitácio is manifest in Valfredo Leal to Epitácio (Capital), 5 Dec. 1923, AEP/12/210. But in asking for reelection as a federal deputy in 1924, the eighty-four year-old Valfredo declared that he had "no other political chief than [Epitácio]." Valfredo Leal to Epitácio (Rio de Janeiro), tel. of 10 Dec. 1926, AEP/9/62.

had voted for Epitácio and declared themselves Epitacistas even before 1915, the local "friends" insisted that they be denied full integration, and refused to accept them in any ruling family-based faction.[16] Finally, there were two categories of "adversaries"—"compatible" and "incompatible"—depending on how they comported themselves during elections. Where their use of violence was judged excessive, they might be granted only a fragile truce.

These factional distinctions were crucial for assessing município politics. Local bosses were expected to write either to Epitácio or to the governor, reporting their projections for coming elections, providing precise, arithmetical estimates of their own and the opposition's strengths, and providing an assessment of the degree of violence anticipated on election day. Upsets were expected where adversaries made themselves "incompatible" or allies defected. Beginning in the 1915 federal election, Epitácio became famous for his insistence on "free and honest" elections. The instructions he sent to all of his local bosses—including the toughest coronéis—employed the phrase "according to the law" to stress his personal opposition to the violent intimidation and fraud that routinely accompanied elections during the Old Republic. He could not have been unaware, however, that the local bosses preferred to deliver their votes as winners, not losers. They might occasionally commend Epitácio's "respect for the law," but they relied on time-honored violent means to control elections.[17]

Epitácio took the extreme step of forbidding Gov. Castro Pinto to send the State Police Force to some municípios until the very day of the 1915 election. In reducing the level of preelection coercion by his supporters, he appeared to be sponsoring an electoral contest that would test which of two local factions competing for his recognition as the ruling group was stronger.[18] An examination

[16] The category "dissident friends" implied that there were more claimants to Epitácio's patronage than offices at his disposal. Valfredo acknowledged that it was impossible to confer "advantage" (political office) on all the party's friends, "either by virtue of service or intrinsic capacity. . . . Instead, we ought to combine the criterion of the effectiveness of their influence with that of [the] family tradition of the names [they bear]." Ibid. Thus, family affiliation was one criterion of political influence.

[17] Cunha Pedrosa, *Minhas memórias*, 1:147; Pinto, *Octacílio de Albuquerque*, p. 65. In Campina Grande, "there were shots . . . in this election as in others. . . . Even the dead voted, which still happens today in spite of the secret ballot." Cristino Pimentel, *Abrindo o livro do passado* (João Pessoa: Editôra Theone, 1956), p. 60. *O Norte* carried reports on April 18 and June 10, 1915, regarding the kidnapping of municipal council presidents preparatory to the March 1 election. See also H. de Almeida, quoted in Pinto, *Octacílio de Albuquerque*, p. 67.

[18] One governor explicitly stated this motive in 1916: "The liberty that you or-

of voter registration statistics by município in the five years preceding 1915 confirmed the impression that the Epitacistas usually needed less recourse to violence because they already had enlisted an impressive majority of the registered voters. Between 1910 and 1915, the number of registered voters in Paraíba had increased by 38 per cent, much in excess of population growth.[19] The median number of registered voters in backlands municípios, for instance, rose from about 550 in 1910 to 700 in 1915.[20] A rapid rise in registered voters thus preceded the landslide victories the Epitacistas enjoyed in both the Assembly and Congressional elections, particularly in the backlands zones. Judging from newspaper accusations, however, the Epitacistas took no chances where the outcome of a município's vote was in doubt and resorted to intimidation and violence when a local boss believed them warranted.

The cohort of bosses who formed the base of Epitácio's electoral machine in 1915 enjoyed a reciprocal arrangement with him: They delivered votes, he awarded patronage. By 1915, Epitácio had already established, as a senator, that he could better lead the oligarchy by virtue of his effectiveness in federal politics. His accession to the presidency in 1919 brought his ability to dispense local patronage to its zenith. His presidency witnessed an important shift in the relationship between the state government and the local elites, due to the increased patronage the IFOCS projects placed at the governor's disposal.

The Patronage State

President Epitácio, 1919–1922

When Epitácio left Brazil, on December 29, 1918, as the head of the delegation to the Paris Peace Conference, he did so on the eve of a crisis over the presidential succession. The national political sys-

dered, which was observed during the election of the 20th [of December 1916], has the advantage of letting us know the condition in which the Party stands and also the weak points which need strengthening for the big federal election scheduled for March 1, 1917. We undertook a strategic reconnoitering. . . . In the federal elections, we will eat by other means." Camilo de Holanda to Epitácio (Capital), 18 Dec. 1916, AEP/12/44.

[19] State of Paraíba, *Annuario estatistico 1916*, pp. 61–70. In 1910, 23,471 voters were registered statewide, a figure that rose to 32,485 in 1915, although there were no statistics on voters in the município of Campina Grande for any of the six years.

[20] Ibid.

tem had become vulnerable to the politics of café com leite, for the three most powerful states increasingly failed to concur over the choice of a president. Epitácio's election to his nation's highest office, barely three months later—on April 13, 1919—resolved temporarily a political impasse that would return in 1922 and 1930. In 1919, however, the succession crisis was precipitated by the death of the president-elect, [Francisco de Paula] Rodrigues Alves, who succumbed shortly after the Brazilian delegation reached Paris in February. During the four months of his illness, São Paulo, Minas Gerais, and Rio Grande do Sul had not reached agreement over a successor. But when Bahia's Sen. Rui Barbosa made clear his intention to obtain official nomination, they realized that their failure to agree on a candidate would hand the election to Rui by default. This circumstance explained Sen. Raul Soares's nomination of Epitácio, on behalf of the state of Minas Gerais.

Epitácio's election was insured because he was backed by the states of Minas, São Paulo, and Rio Grande do Sul. They found him an appealing compromise candidate, whereas his aging opponent, the indominable Rui—who was again running for the presidency—was at the end of his career. Rui's running mate, Gov. Nilo Peçanha of Rio de Janeiro, presented a stronger challenge. He would make a direct bid for the presidency in 1922, with Bahia's Sen. J. J. Seabra as his vice-presidential choice. Epitácio's 1919 election victory signaled a new era in national politics. (249,342 votes were cast for Epitácio; Rui polled 118,303.) Although his election took place without significant political conflict, his administration would witness the important split between Brazil's military and civilian elites that opened the door to the Revolution of 1930. Because Epitácio proved that he was no passive creature of the three most powerful states, his decisions would contribute to the fragmentation of Brazil's national political elite, regardless of whether he intended such a consequence.

Although Epitácio could never expect to attain the independence of action that a candidate from São Paulo, Minas, or Rio Grande do Sul could command as his political birthright, he exhibited surprising independence. For instance, he began his term of office by appointing Brazil's first all-civilian cabinet, instantly earning antagonism from the higher officer corps of both the army and the navy.[21] He also wasted no time in announcing and implement-

[21] Hélio da Silva, *1922—Sangue na areia de Copacabana* (Rio de Janeiro: Editôra Civilização Brasileira, 1964), p. 51.

15. In 1925 Epitácio published *Pela verdade* (For Truth's Sake), a rebuttal and vindication of his conduct as president in the face of a press campaign alleging graft and malfeasance of office during his administration. In this political cartoon, Truth asks, "Why are they shouting?" and Epitácio replies, "Plagiarists! Each one of them has his own bunch of truths to publish!" (J. Carlos, in *O Malho*, 7 April 1925)

ing his long-cherished goal of an ambitious program of federal assistance for the drought-ridden Northeast. In that respect, Epitácio's identity as a northeasterner and a politician who lacked compromising commitments to Brazil's most powerful states afforded him the initiative to implement a federal policy to benefit an otherwise neglected region. His renovation of the federal government's drought-relief agency, which he renamed the IFOCS, became the price the coffee interests of the South were prepared to pay—albeit only for the duration of his administration—for maintaining their precarious policy of café com leite by means of Epitácio's nomination.

From the perspective of Epitácio's oligarchical control of Paraíba, the IFOCS carried a special significance. The federal patronage that it placed in his hands—and by delegation in the hands of his governor—insured the PRCP's survival as a cohesive electoral machine. This patronage also enlarged the role of the state government in município affairs. While Epitácio's public addresses related to the IFOCS public works projects stressed the importance of technology and infrastructure for overcoming the region's underdevelopment, in distributing the IFOCS patronage he was behaving as a classic state party boss. The unprecedented quantity of this federal patronage nevertheless contributed to the erosion of município autonomy by strengthening the governor's political role.

Patrimonialism, Order, and Change

In 1919, Paraíba politics still reflected many aspects of what the scholarly literature has analyzed in Weberian terms as the patrimonial or quasi-patrimonial State of the late Empire. The impact of economic change after 1900 was shaped in several crucial respects by the patrimonialistic nature of the State.[22] On the one hand, *what* the political system managed changed in both kind and degree. On the other hand, as political power came to be exercised over new or enlarged areas of economic endeavor—the road network, urban public works, commercial franchises, and tax exemptions—these endeavors were incorporated within spheres of local control monopolized by the dominant family-based groups. Paraíba's local ruling families exercised political authority in the municípios according to clearly recognized economic domains and for the purpose of furthering and protecting their private interests. Their essentially patrimonial relationship with the State enjoyed broad customary support and the legitimacy of historical sanction, so that a conservative check was imposed on a potential tendency toward more significant economic and social change. In acting as an archetypical state party boss, Epitácio confirmed the

[22] The patrimonial legacy represented a compromise between the State and the social groups on which the power of the State was built because neither the local elites nor the State was self-sufficient. Uricoechea, *Patrimonial Foundations*, p. 52.

patrimonialistic character of the State, reinforcing the clientistic relationship Paraíba's local bosses enjoyed with his surrogate governors. But in doing so after 1919, he acted within a historical ambience where the accumulating impact of growth was introducing significant change.

As in most states in Brazil, patrimonialism referred to the political legitimation by the State of personalistic and family-based groups—their exercise of political power and their disposition of resources. When Epitácio or his governors indicated which family-based groups would monopolize local political authority and dispose of patronage, they exercised a *personal* discretion that was the hallmark of a patrimonial system.[23] When he recognized his own family-based group's right to elective office, Epitácio exercised this prerogative most legitimately. Between 1916 and 1930, he placed five of his nephews in the Assembly and two more in the national congress and the governorship.[24] Nevertheless, by the 1920s the State could no longer be so closely equated with the patrimonial model of the Brazilian Empire. Since the 1870s, a growing complexity of interest groups, aggressively competing at each level of government, had begun to alter that model. Thus, although nepotism and clientism—the hallmarks of a patrimonial order—still prevailed in the 1920s, a new range of interest groups,

[23] Greenfield, quoting Talcott Parsons, emphasized the survival of patrimonialism in Brazil in the post–World War II period: "The position of authority . . . is still traditionally legitimized, but not the detailed structure of carrying it out, which is . . . a 'right' of the chief to do what he will within his sphere of personal prerogative." Quoted in Sidney Greenfield, "Charwomen, Cesspools, and Roadbuilding: An Examination of Patronage, Clientage, and Political Power in South-Eastern Minas Gerais," in *Structure and Process in Latin America*, ed. Arnold Stricken and Sidney Greenfield (Albuquerque: University of New Mexico Press, 1972), pp. 71–100. The survival of a patrimonialistic order in twentieth-century Brazil has been examined in a wide range of contexts: Emílio Willems, "Bureaucracia e patrimonialismo," *Administração pública* 3 (Sept. 1945):12–17; Shirley, "Patronage in São Paulo," pp. 239–40; and Greenfield, ibid. Nunes Leal underscored the aspect of personal prerogative enjoyed by local bosses in the Old Republic when he offered an "incomplete list" of over two dozen "personal favors" a boss was expected to undertake for his client voters. *Coronelismo*, p. 38 (n. 34).

[24] Epitácio's nephew João Pessoa served as governor from 1928 to 1930, while João Pessoa's brother Joaquim Pessoa served in the 10th Assembly (1924–1927). (Their brothers Cândido and Osvaldo Pessoa also served as federal deputies after 1930.) Four sons of Col. Antônio Pessoa served in the Assembly as Epitácio's designates: Antônio Pessoa Filho in the 8th Assembly (1916–1919), Carlos Pessoa and José Pessoa in the 10th Assembly, and Fernando Pessoa in the 11th Assembly (1928–1930). Carlos Pessoa also moved from the Assembly to House of Deputies in 1924, where he remained until 1930.

together with a civil administration and an electoral system, deprived the congeries of elite family groups ruling in the municípios of the exclusivity they had once enjoyed in asserting claims before the State. Despite the Old Republic's weak institutionalization, new ideological values associated with the emergence of a middle class increasingly militated against the persistence of a frankly patrimonial order.

Patronage and the Política de Família

The decade of the 1920s witnessed conflicting currents of change and continuity in Paraíba. As early as 1912, Epitácio's leadership of the state oligarchy confronted a rising tension between de facto local autonomy—reinforced by policies at the national level—and the centralizing efforts of the governors. Although Epitácio chose to accept the prevailing system of coronelismo, including the patrimonialistic prerogatives so embedded in local politics, he appreciated how patronage bestowed on local bosses could also serve gradual centralization. The substantial patronage that he channeled to Paraíba by means of the IFOCS shored up and intensified a clientistic relationship between him—or his governors—and the local bosses. Particularly in the two backlands zones, which by 1920 possessed double the number of votes of the coast, brejo, and caatinga-agreste combined, the prospect of federal reservoirs, dams, and wells cemented this relationship until the end of the decade.[25] Even certain privileged opposition bosses—those "compatible" with their local adversaries—received his largesse.[26]

[25] Benno Galjart offered a similar observation about IFOCS patronage in the 1950s: "The aims of such projects, even if realized, do not in any clear way upset the local balance of power." "Old Patrons and New: Some Notes on the Consequences of Patronage for Local Development Projects," *Sociologia Ruralis* 7, no. 4 (1967):336. Registered voters statewide averaged around 3.5 per cent of the total population during the 1920s, whereas in some backlands zones the proportion rose to 5 or 6 per cent. *Annuario estatistico 1931*, pp. 54–55; *A União*, 8 June 1929. In the presidential election of 1930, with 1.3 million inhabitants, Paraíba cast slightly under 37,000 votes.

[26] For instance, the São Gonçalo dam in Sousa benefited the Mariz family, Epitácio's erstwhile allies who turned Valfredista after 1905. But he tried, in vain, to help them when Bernardes ordered that all IFOCS construction equipment be auctioned as scrap. Antônio Marques da Silva Mariz to Epitácio (Sousa), tel. of Oct. 1923, AEP/12/260. Glum assessments on the curtailing of IFOCS appropriations can be found in Ascendino Carneiro da Cunha to Epitácio (Capital), 25 Apr. 1923, AEP/12/196–205; and Solon de Lucena to Epitácio (Capital), 14 June 1923, AEP/12/206.

The most vital patronage remained elective and appointive offices. Epitácio exercised superb political judgment in distributing those offices to foster the cohesion of his electoral machine. He gave daily personal attention to balancing the claims for his patronage with skill and sensitivity. This attention went far to explain Epitácio's order for most of the 1920s. Although governors might deny that they were obliged to recognize política de família, and in private correspondence disparaged it, a large part of their role was dedicated to balancing the intense competition among family-based groups for political control of a município. In addition, the patronage of employment was tenaciously sought by a legion of petitioners, particularly during Epitácio's presidency. Gov. Camilo de Holanda, in exasperation, openly complained to Paraíba's oligarchical chief of "the weeping and the wailing" he was forced to endure from job-seekers and petitioners for "lands, houses, handouts, and even libraries"—on behalf of their relatives.[27] Although he justified turning them away because "the Party should shut its ears to those who are out for their relatives," he himself was busily depriving Epitácio's nephews and friends of their appointments so that he might favor his own group of nephews and friends.[28]

Because the política de família consumed the largest portion of a governor's attention, casting him in the role of perpetual arbiter, Epitácio forged ad hoc policies to guide his gubernatorial surrogates in sorting out the claims of family affiliation laid before him. Except during Camilo de Holanda's administration—between 1916 and 1920—Epitácio personally vetted every appointment to state and federal office and also made the final selection of prefeitos in Paraíba. His criteria of "loyalty" and "worthiness" measured a boss's capacity to deliver the local vote over a number of years. The boss's future capacity to do so was signaled by his appointment or reappointment. In 1927, even when Epitácio was absorbed in the affairs of the Permanent International Court of Justice, he vetoed Gov. João Suassuna's preference for removing the Pereira da Costa family from the leadership of their home município of Araruna. Instead, he insisted that Col. Targino Pereira da

[27] Camilo de Holanda to Epitácio (Capital), 13 May 1918, AEP/12/117.

[28] Camilo de Holanda to Epitácio (Capital), 13 Jan. 1918, AEP/12/106. Camilo had also written Epitácio about his determination to find a position for a young bacharel, "the son of Luiz Pontes, the tax auditor, and the fiancé of Heráclito [Cavalcanti's] daughter, so that he can have the means to marry her." Idem, 14 Dec. 1916, AEP/12/42.

Costa be retained on the 1928 Assembly slate because his uncle had been an "old friend," one loyal even before 1908, when Epitácio had placed him in the Assembly:

> We should adopt reelection as a rule but enlarge a little the exception. . . . We should not pass over old friends and exclude Targino. Do this in consideration of his uncle, a strong friend whose [local] adversaries are trying to undermine him by [resorting to] measures against his property. [Our] excluding the nephew will be taken as [a sign] confirming [that] their intentions [receive our support].[29]

In backing "reelection as a rule," Epitácio was affirming that a permanent core of elite families would be maintained in the Assembly as his oligarchical foundation of support, although the rotation of individuals from those families was also the rule. Exclusions from the electoral slate—of incumbent assemblymen—preserved what Epitácio viewed as the "political character" of the slate because then officeholding was rotated among different members of the same family-based group. That the importance of the group overrode the individual was what his advice to Suassuna suggested: "The fewer exclusions, the greater the chance the slate will lose its *political* character and assume the nature of a *personal* one," he advised.[30] Making a number of substitutions himself, Epitácio justified each as preserving a family position. Thus, Gentil Lins was a "deserving" choice and Severino Lucena's name was placed on the slate as "necessary to undo intrigues inherited from his father," former Gov. Solon de Lucena, while Epitácio's own nephew Fernando Pessoa would "replace his brother José [Pessoa]."[31]

Epitácio not only was willing to reward loyalty but also tolerated deviations from loyalty, and this perhaps better indicates the importance of claims based on kinship in Paraíba's oligarchical politics. When he instructed Col. Cristiano Lauritzen about the approaching federal congressional election in 1918, he stipulated, "Friends should together vote the [official] slate. Only special cases of kinship [parentesco], friendship, and gratitude owed the local opposition boss will permit a defection of votes to an outside candidate."[32] In 1925, Gentil Lins offered Epitácio just such a rea-

[29] Epitácio to João Suassuna (Rio de Janeiro), 24 Nov. 1927, AEP/12/284.

[30] Ibid. (italics added).

[31] Ibid.

[32] Epitácio to Cristiano Lauritzen (Rio de Janeiro), 23 Feb. 1918, AEP/12/108.

son for delivering the votes of the município of Espírito Santo to the opposition instead of the PRCP. Epitácio overlooked his breach of loyalty because the local opposition boss had arranged medical care for Gentil's wife when she was dangerously ill. He had also facilitated delivery of expensive refining equipment for Gentil's sugar usina.[33] Gentil's name was placed on the 1928 Assembly slate, for he was still "deserving."

In most instances, however, política de família increased Epitácio's votes. An important politician in the Peregrino de Albuquerque family, and the first to abandon its collective commitment to Valfredismo in their home município of Alagoa Grande, proudly explained how family politicking could be expected to work from "the top down":

> I have the honor of communicating to Your Excellency that in the gubernatorial election occurring here today I visited the polls and voted, along with my friends, who in this município obey the leadership of Dr. Heretiano Zenaide. This action, consequently, signifies not only my sincere and loyal support for Your Excellency's political leadership [but also] that my frank and impartial services will be at your disposal. Such behavior, I hope, will be adopted by my friends and relatives who still are not to be found at Your Excellency's side. I will only be satisfied in this respect when I achieve the most complete unity of viewpoint in the bosom of my [own] family.[34]

Family-based networks even recruited votes for Epitácio across state lines. Col. José Pereira Lima's offer to assist Epitácio through his family-based network's connections in the Pernambuco legislature provided the most striking example:

> All the many relatives of [Pernambuco Assemblyman Antônio] Medeiros [Siqueira Campos] in the município of Princesa are members of our Party, and Medeiros . . . continues to be your follower. When, for instance, the Pernambuco Assembly voted to censure the Government of the Republic [i.e., Epitácio's administration's military intervention in Pernambuco in 1922], Medeiros stayed with you. . . . He was first an Epitacista. In Flores [the Pernambuco município adjoining Princesa], where his brother José Medeiros is local party boss, An-

[33] Gentil Lins to Epitácio (Engenho Pacatuba, Espírito Santo), 1 Feb. 1925, AEP/12/245.

[34] Francisco Montenegro to Epitácio (Alagoa Grande), 22 June 1915, AEP/12/1.

tônio [Medeiros] has made an extension of Paraíba throughout family ties and cordiality. I believe that in the Pernambuco Assembly he would be first a Paraíba candidate.[35]

This frank political confidence revealed one of several dimensions of Col. José Pereira's political reputation as Paraíba's most powerful coronel. His nexus of power in the backlands subtly interwove kinship ties, commercial supremacy, and local and state officeholding into a common strand.

Epitácio's discretionary power was reflected also in his distribution of appointive offices as patronage. With the growth of both federal and state civil service during the 1920s, Paraíba's elite families looked to the State to provide additional employment opportunities. As agricultural and pastoral producers or as businessmen they recognized the need to protect their economic positions politically by bureaucratic linkages to the state and national governments. Extension of the federal telegraph system throughout the interior—which occurred very slowly between the 1890s and the 1920s—was a mundane example of the vital role a new technical bureaucracy played in local politics. Because telegraphers were privy to all political communications entering a município, they had to be drawn from the incumbent coalition, if those in power were to defend their position effectively. The notion of a neutral civil service selection system contradicted the factional basis of local politics, whereas nepotism—empreguismo—was its logical extension.

Technological change dictated wider economic specialization among the generation of 1910, a pattern evident in the changing occupational composition of the State Assembly. Even elite daughters were moving into the closed labor market that empreguismo connoted, as local schoolteachers, librarians, or low-level civil servants. A rare few returned from Recife with law degrees. The new demand for expertise overrode personal discretion to some extent where technological competence was indispensable; however, engineers and agronomists could be found in every personalistic faction, so discretionary power continued to be exercised in the face of rising demands for technical competence.[36]

The burgeoning patronage deriving from civil service expansion

[35] José Pereira Lima to Epitácio (Princesa), 8 Nov. 1928, AEP/9/37.

[36] For example, Epitácio reprimanded Camilo de Holanda for hiring "a dentist-agronomist" as the Capital's city engineer, instead of an engineer. Epitácio to Camilo (Rio de Janeiro), 11(?) Apr. 1917, AEP/12/63–64.

validated the corporatistic nature of the State. Elite family-based groups looked to the State as a source of enfranchisement for a plethora of privileges that were accessible only by virtue of group membership. Rather than perceiving the State as a guarantor of individual rights, the members of Paraíba's elite parentelas sought privileges from the State vis-à-vis each other, advancing their claims on the basis of possessing a bacharel's university degree, a coronel's patent in the National Guard, or an officer's commission in the armed forces. The pervasive clientism characteristic of the relationship such groups enjoyed with the State conveyed the strong contrast between the State's corporatistic nature in Brazil, and Latin America, and the State's liberal underpinnings in North Atlantic countries. Clientism also explained why generally "most of the administrative resources of the State were devoted to maintaining the system rather than doing the work," as one anthropologist recently commented.[37]

Clientistic networking thrived on the expansion of federal and state government patronage during the 1920s, but erosion appeared where politicians relied on the force of kinship for binding the key elite groups together in the polity. They could no longer count so securely on their kinship ties to insulate and defend them against the encroachment of a central State. While Epitácio recognized the significance of elite family-based groups for his oligarchy's political cohesion, and preserved a patronage relationship with them, he also contributed to centralization of the State. However much family-based groups still relied on horizontal bonding among sibling sets and pursued kin networking, socioeconomic change introduced alternative organizational strategies after 1920. The oligarchical participants probably did not see the contradictions inherent in the new modes of organizing, but the force of kinship in politics was becoming less reliable.

Oligarchical Issues and Political Change

The Federal Dimension: 1922

Epitácio's final year in the presidency—1922—was a watershed in twentieth-century Brazilian politics. The new cultural militancy of nationalism colored São Paulo's centennial celebration of

[37] Shirley, "Patronage in São Paulo," p. 145. These corporatistic elements are elaborated in Schwartzmann, "Back to Weber," pp. 89–106, esp. p. 100.

"Modern Art Week" in April and shots were fired in the July Copacabana Revolt. The abortive attempt by fewer than seventy-five military cadets and officers from the Copacabana Fort to depose Epitácio by force of arms alerted the nation to the split between Brazil's civilian and military elites, which the March presidential election had opened. By 1930, it would grow into Getúlio Vargas's opposition Aliança Liberal, directed against São Paulo's domination of national politics. The Copacabana Revolt underscored that in the March election former Governor Artur Bernardes of Minas Gerais—the official candidate—had failed to gain a decisive victory over his opponent, ex-Governor Nilo Peçanha of Rio de Janeiro. The Nilistas had organized an opposition "Republican Reaction" (Reação Republicana), led by Rio Grande do Sul and a cluster of lesser states, to defeat Minas and São Paulo, but the contest was thrown into the hands of Congress for a final count of the vote.[38] Bernardes was proclaimed the victor at the cost of national unity and Epitácio stepped down from the presidency with his commitment to constitutionalism maintained.

Nilo's campaign introduced into national politics a critique of the politics of café com leite, backed, for the first time, by a formidable opposition. Although its prime mover, Gov. Borges de Medeiros of Rio Grande do Sul, attempted to influence Epitácio to support the Republican Reaction ticket, the pressure of São Paulo and especially of Minas Gerais, whose Sen. Raúl Soares had nominated Epitácio, was more successful.[39] During a notorious "Affair of Honor" that impugned the army's reputation and questioned the military's constitutional role in politics, Epitácio reprimanded higher officers—including Hermes da Fonseca—for their unconstitutional intervention in national politics. He ordered Hermes, who was the president of the Military Club, into European exile for his destructive role as the army's spokesman. This crystallized the division between civilians and military. Bernardes assumed office, as Epitácio publicly pledged he would. But Epitácio believed privately that the nation would have been better served if Bernardes had withdrawn.[40] When Bernardes was made privy to this view, it cost Epitácio his successor's good will.

[38] Love, *Rio Grande do Sul*, pp. 190–92.

[39] Ibid., p. 192. The Paraíba congressional delegation had closely cooperated with Minas Gerais for a decade.

[40] The Military Club held Bernardes responsible for insulting the honor of the army because a letter critical of the army was allegedly written in Bernardes's handwriting; it was proved a patent forgery. In another famous meeting at the pres-

In Paraíba, the 1922 presidential campaign held a different significance. The Republican Reaction found much more fertile soil for its critique of the oligarchies than in the 1910 presidential campaign. This was the result of urban growth. Urban middle-class—and, to a lesser extent, working-class—organizational activity emerged in the 1920s to assume significant political influence for the first time. As in the Salvationist campaign of 1911–1912, the opposition in Paraíba sided with the national opposition ticket headed by Nilo Peçanha. As the outs, the Nilistas were led by State Supreme Court Justice Heráclito Cavalcanti Monteiro, who marshaled votes in the cities and towns of the coast and the interior.[41] "Heraclismo," however, represented an urban protest vote rather than mere affirmation of personalistic loyalty. Campaign rhetoric also confirmed that the "social question"—which President Bernardes would soon define in his notorious pronouncement as "a matter for the police"—was becoming an issue in Paraíba politics. General strikes in 1917 and 1919, coupled with the dislocation produced by IFOCS construction in the interior, had increased public awareness of a growing working class and a larger, more marginalized, underclass accompanying its historical emergence. For that matter, President Epitácio Pessoa's repressive policy toward labor in the Center-South—one that did not distinguish him from his successor Bernardes—had also contributed to a new awareness of the social and political implications of Brazil's industrialization.[42] The protest vote of "Heraclismo" thus presaged the emergence of class consciousness in Paraíba's politics. By the next decade, that factor would significantly color partisan orientations and introduce a competing element to the personalism characteristic of Paraíba's factional allegiances.

The 1922 presidential campaign and its aftermath illustrated

---

idential Catete Palace, on May 1, 1922, Epitácio upheld Bernardes as the official winner. Earlier, he had supported him as the official candidate. Epitácio to José Bezerra (Rio de Janeiro), 16 June 1921, in L. Pessôa, *Epitacio Pessôa*, 2:488, 520–22.

[41] The Reação Republicana carried the election in the Capital (led by Isidro Gomes da Silva), Campina Grande (led by Col. Salvino de Figueirêdo), Sousa (led by the Mariz), and Bananeiras (led by Antônio Rocha). Luiz de Oliveira, *Minhas campanhas* (Recife: Oficina Gráfica do *Jornal do Comércio*, 1943), pp. 9–14. L. Pessôa, *Epitacio Pessôa*, 1:479. Most Valfredistas, however, voted for Bernardes. Mariz, *Assembléia Legislativa*, p. 74.

[42] During the general strike of 1919, Epitácio pioneered in a federal policy of working-class repression when he issued orders to the chief of police of Rio de Janeiro to deport foreign labor leaders or to prevent them from disembarking when they arrived. AEP/43 (Anarchistas).

that socioeconomic change had made Paraíba and the Northeast more receptive to national political change. The same year brought to a close Epitácio's efforts to transform the region through the IFOCS program. Economic change had introduced new factors in Paraíba's political system, most significantly, class-based political conflict. Beginning in 1917, the year of Brazil's first great general strike, widespread social unrest appeared in the state's urban centers. Dock and transport workers organized to seek the unattainable goals of an eight-hour day, a minimum wage, and the right to unionize. They were supported by factory workers in the Capital's two textile mills, albeit weakly. Nationwide, workers in transport, manufacturing, and commerce also had been seeking since the end of the war to form associations dedicated to securing rights for labor. Workers in Paraíba, working in concert with those in Recife, where the industrial proletariat was better organized, failed to gain either better working conditions or a shorter working day.[43]

The demand for higher wages, however, gained a new urgency in the early 1920s, as federal spending on drought-relief projects rose and the prosperity of the cotton export sector became evident. Change in the countryside directly fueled urban demands for higher wages, because the agricultural population acquired unprecedented mobility due to the massive construction projects IFOCS undertook between 1919 and 1923. Thousands of workers were lured from subsistence agriculture and the urban export sector to assume federal employment as the diggers of irrigation ditches and dams or the builders of roads and reservoirs.[44]

The IFOCS projects also caused new concern among the landed elite about the growing marginalization of the rural population. A

[43] In 1933, there were only two officially recognized labor unions in Paraíba, while sixteen existed in Pernambuco. Minas Gerais, Rio de Janeiro, São Paulo, and Rio Grande do Sul had sixteen, forty-seven, forty-four, and forty-eight, respectively. *Correio da Manhã* (Recife), 7 July 1933, cited in J. Joffily, *Revolta*, p. 133.

[44] Rural wages in Paraíba remained fairly stagnant for three decades prior to 1919 and lower than in Pernambuco—ranging from $700 to 1$000 per day. *Questionnarios agricultura Parahyba*, pp. 9–23. By comparison, in 1916, industrial workers in the Capital's tile factory were paid 2$500 per day; an estate manager in Araruna received 50$000 per day. *Annuario estatistico 1916*, p. 333. Between 1919 and 1923, however, agricultural wages rose to an all-time high level as landowners competed with IFOCS construction for labor. José Américo stated that agricultural laborers were receiving an average of 2$000 to 2$500 per day, but other observers listed 4$000 to 5$000 per day. *Parahyba*, p. 481; Gouveia, "Algodão no Parahyba," p. 3; Fleury Monteiro, *Margem Carirys*, p. 74. By 1919, wages had fallen to almost a pre-1919 level, ranging from 1$500 to 3$000 per day. J. Joffily, *Revolta*, p. 126.

16. During the 1920s, the automobile transformed political and social life. Drought victims who were employed to build IFOCS roads and did not return to agriculture enlarged the urban proletariat. (Courtesy of the Arquivo Fundação Casa de José Américo)

larger, permanently uprooted labor force—one that contributed thousands of vagrants to the pool of seasonal migrants who moved between coast and interior during harvests—became a new fact of social and political life. President Bernardes's abrupt suspension of all IFOCS projects in 1923 produced a labor crisis in Paraíba's interior and underscored the local elites' inability to control such a large and nomadic population. One direct consequence was the upward trajectory of banditry throughout the twenties. Young men rejected reintegration in the landed economy's onerous sujeição arrangements and instead turned to the life of a cangaceiro, which offered them a better standard of living and freedom from detested subordination to a landlord.[45]

Thus, the 1922 presidential campaign offered a small window

[45] Lewin, "Social Banditry in Brazil," p. 139; de Souza "The *Cangaço*," pp. 124–27.

through which to glimpse the erosion of Paraíba's agrarian world and an increasing middle-class interest in social and economic change. In addition to law and order, other political issues began to claim the attention of newspaper readers in the state. Taxation, tax collection, electoral representation, and popular mobilization, for instance, were discussed in front-page articles and, for the first time, juxtaposed with the more cosmopolitan issues of socialism, feminism, and the postwar internationalism of the League of Nations. As the road network penetrated the backlands and modified ancient patterns of communication, political awareness about the implications of such issues for the survival of the oligarchies increased. The closer integration of the backlands' cotton economy with a world market, while producing social disintegration in the rural order, nevertheless caused politicians and the urban middle-class groups to evaluate their political system more intelligently and critically. The Young Turk group that emerged in Epitácio's camp during 1915–1916 appeared to be a precursor of the more complex group formation of the 1920s. Not coincidentally, the priority the Young Turks assigned to economic development produced the first important clash in the oligarchy's leadership since Epitácio had assumed control. This altercation presaged the changing nature of group conflict in the final decade of the Old Republic.

The Young Turks

Between 1905 and 1915, a successor generation to Epitácio's generation of the 1880s appeared in his political camp. By 1920, as Table VII.1 indicates, this generation of 1910 became the preponderant one in Paraíba politics. In 1915, it was already gaining recruits from an even younger generation of the late Republic, while death and political retirement were taking a greater toll from the generation of the 1880s. Although still heavily recruited from the Recife Law Faculty, the generation of 1910 had more varied occupational and intellectual pursuits than its predecessors. Due to its generational challenge, moreover, economic growth became an explicit issue. Encouraged by a rapid expansion of newpapers, in both the Capital and the interior cities, some of its more militant members placed their journalistic talents at the service of Epitacismo in the 1915 election campaigns. They were attracted by Epitácio's goals of integrating the interior's cotton-producing zones with coastal markets to develop a statewide economy, and

TABLE VII.1: Oligarchy's Political Generations

Political generation	Birth cohort	Entry into politics	No.	%
Mature Empire	Before 1850	1855–1880	36	18.2
The eighties	1850–1869	1876–1900	80	40.4
Nineteen ten	1870–1889	1896–1920	63	31.8
Late Republic	After 1890	1916–	19	9.6
Total			198	100.0

SOURCE: Lewin, "Politics and *Parentela*," table 5.6 (p. 243).
NOTE: Data for an additional 105 politicians were incomplete.

they openly admired his influence in federal politics. This new generation was a purely Epitacista faction. It viewed antagonistically the older cohort of Venancistas who dominated the PRCP's leadership and monopolized federal officeholding. Drawing political momentum from their press war with the Valfredista "Bacuraus," a core group from this generation organized themselves formally in 1916 as the "Young Turkey" under the leadership of Solon de Lucena.[46] Their older mentor, Col. Antônio Pessoa—as governor—endorsed their eagerness for political change. Even by the end of 1915, they had deliberately dissociated themselves from the Venancistas, derisively referring to them as "Guelas," after a local shorebird known for its raucous cry.[47] The Young Turks came predominantly from the backlands and, secondarily, like Solon, from the brejo. Antônio Pessoa's oldest son, Antônio Pessoa Filho, his protégé João Suassuna, and Celso Mariz—another backlander—were among the most important Young Turks. One Areiense, Demócrito de Almeida, represented the brejo and rounded out their leadership.

It was no accident that José Américo de Almeida, cousin of Demócrito de Almeida, benefited greatly from the research assist-

[46] The Young Turks first organized in Solon de Lucena's house at Fazenda Roma, Bananeiras, in mid-1916. Cunha Pedrosa, *Minhas memórias*, 1:177. Besides borrowing their name from Mustafa Kemal Ataturk's 1909 Revolution, they may have been inspired by the "Young Turk" officers in the Brazilian Army who edited a nationalistic magazine, *A defesa nacional*.

[47] Ibid., 1:173–204.

ance of another Young Turk, his close friend Celso Mariz, in undertaking a pathbreaking historical study of his native state, *A Parahyba e seus problemas*. A scholarly work of the first order, it offered many clues about the political orientation of the Young Turks with whom José Américo associated, not to mention his parallel evolution in Brazilian letters as one of the early Modernists. Published in 1923, just when the IFOCS projects were extinguished, *A Parahyba e seus problemas* was woven around the theme of underdevelopment. In praising the IFOCS projects and endorsing policies that would direct economic growth and federal spending to improve export infrastructure connecting the Paraíba interior to coastal markets, the book projected a statewide vision of beneficial development that coincided with the Young Turks' aspirations.[48]

The Young Turks also offered the Venancistas a generational challenge, as Sen. Pedro da Cunha Pedrosa, the senior Venancista, was in a position to emphasize. But the grounds on which they challenged their elders went beyond merely differences of age.[49] Their critique demonstrated that factional politics was acquiring an explicit emphasis on economic issues, which previously had been undetectable in the excessive emphasis on personalistic rivalry. The Young Turks aggressively repudiated the anachronistic political orientation they associated with Venancistas. Epitácio even reprimanded them in 1915 for using *A Notícia* to call upon the Venancistas in Congress to sever their ties with Sen. Pinheiro Machado. The Young Turks, consequently, regarded the PRCP's Old Guard as "tainted" because of the subservient relationship Álvaro and Valfredo enjoyed with Pinheiro between 1910 and 1915, and thus unfit to direct the oligarchy.[50] No doubt the Young Turks' attitude influenced Epitácio in 1917 to modify the PRCP label to PRC do P—Partido Republicano Conservador *do* Paraíba—in recognition of his total victory over Álvaro and Valfredo. Far from

[48] José Américo joined the Young Turks around 1917, having earlier supported his uncle, Monsig. Valfredo Leal. Celso Mariz's research contribution to José Américo's book is acknowledged in Solon de Lucena to Epitácio (Capital), 23 Jan, 1924, AEP/12/220; and by José Américo in *Parahyba*, p. ii. José Américo's famous novel, *A bagaceira* (1928)—the first northeastern contribution to Brazilian Modernism—drew directly on *A Parahyba e seus problemas*. See pp. 480–96, esp. p. 482.

[49] In 1916, both the average and the median ages of assemblymen had risen by five years over 1890 figures. The maximum age of an assemblyman was also twelve years older, and the minimum age five years older than in 1890. Lewin, "Politics and *Parentela*," table 4.1 (p. 176).

[50] Cunha Pedrosa, *Minhas memórias*, 1:184.

17. The Young Turks (ca. 1924): José Américo de Almeida, Demócrito de Almeida, and Celso Mariz (seated, left to right); Walfredo Guedes Pereira and Álvaro de Carvalho (standing, left to right). (Courtesy of the Arquivo Fundação Casa de José Américo)

being a clique of coastal bacharéis—as sometimes has been assumed—the Young Turks condemned the coastal focus of the Venancistas. Correctly, they perceived Epitácio's Old Guard to be motivated by cronyism and mutual ties drawing on a common birthplace in Areia. Above all, the Venancistas in the federal delegation remained confined to Rio de Janeiro or, at best, the Capital. As men born and brought up in the Paraíba interior, the Young Turks defined their base of support beyond the Borborema—as well as on the coast. They demanded greater budgetary allocations for export infrastructure and militantly opposed the capture of Paraíba's cotton exports by out-of-state markets. Unlike the urbane Guelas, they saw their political future lying within the state, not in the national capital. In referring to their mission as "the regeneration of Paraíba's political customs," they underscored a patriotic devotion to their native state and repudiated the Venancista politicians who looked to federal office as a means of fleeing Paraíba.[51]

Camilo de Holanda, who succeeded to the governorship in October 1916, only two weeks after the death of Col. Antônio Pessoa, immediately defied the expectations of those who had recommended him as a candidate. Col. Cristiano Lauritzen, now in the twilight of his power as the central backlands' political broker, had proposed him to Epitácio as an individual capable of steering a neutral course between Turks and Guelas. Because the Pessoas were identified with the Young Turks, Epitácio, in accordance with Cristiano's counsel, designated his old law school classmate who was a native of the coastal zone. However, to counterbalance the Venancistas, he saddled Camilo with a cabinet composed entirely of Young Turks, a combination that proved disastrous.[52]

Naturally, Camilo preferred his own nephews and family-based group to Epitácio's, which reopened a volatile issue about his treatment of Col. Antônio Pessoa's old following—including Antônio Filho. But when Camilo immediately embarked on a grandiose renovation of the Capital, he drew much wider condemnation upon himself. His construction projects absorbed nearly the entire state budget for three years, eventually alienating the Capital's Commercial Association and Col. Cristiano Lauritzen. In particular, his zealous use of the right of eminent domain to confiscate urban property irked Epitácio. The costly acquisition of the State Normal School—for refurbishing as a governor's palace—

[51] For a "coast/doutôres versus backlands/coronéis interpretation of the Young Turks, see Eul-Soo Pang, "Coronelismo," p. 75. Gov. Camilo de Holanda identified the Young Turks as Celso Mariz, Matheus Ribeiro, João Suassuna, Demócrito de Almeida, Antônio Pessoa Filho, João Espínola, Dias Junior, Álvaro de Carvalho and Carvalinho [Rodrigues de Carvalho?]. Camilo to Epitácio (Capital) 6 Apr. 1917, AEP/12/63–64. Fernando Nóbrega, who began his political career in 1924 as João Suassuna's secretary of government, confirmed the interpretation of the Young Turks offered here. He identified the following local bosses in the interior zones as Young Turks: José Parente the Elder (Piancó), Col. José Pereira Lima (Princesa), Col. Targino Pereira da Costa (Araruna), and Benedito de Quiroga (Pombal)—in addition to Solon de Lucena for the coast and brejo and João Suassuna and Celso Mariz for coast and backlands. Interview with Fernando Nóbrega, Rio de Janeiro, 1 Aug. 1978. A complaint on the growing strength of the Young Turk faction in the backlands is contained in Sen. Rebaldo d'Oliviera to Camilo de Holanda (São João de Piranhas, Paraíba), 30 May 1917, AEP/12/74.

[52] Cristiano Lauritzen to Antônio Pessoa (Itabaiana, Paraíba), 19 July 1915, AEP/2/56. Cunha Pedrosa, *Minhas memórias*, 1:190-91. Epitácio's designees for Camilo's cabinet included Solon de Lucena as secretary of government, Demócrito de Almeida as state chief of police, and Antônio Pessoa Filho as prefeito of the Capital.

demonstrated Camilo's dissimulation and outright duplicity in parrying his party boss's concerned inquiries related to spending and appointments.[53] Eventually, Camilo's transformation of the Capital, which produced a central avenue modeled after the Champs Elysées and named the Avenida Epitácio Pessoa, contributed to his fall from political grace. His efforts to favor his relatives—some of whom were related to the opposition leader, Heráclito Cavalcanti—also exacerbated interfactional strife in the Capital and compounded the negative attitude which the commercial sector eventually held toward him.

Camilo illustrated Epitácio's forbearance with ineptitude and rumored disloyalty. The governor disparaged the Young Turks as "Epitácio's kin" [parentesco] and harrassed them into resigning from his cabinet.[54] His really unforgivable transgression, however, was committed against the Young Turks' idol, Col. Antônio Pessoa. The incident was concealed from Epitácio until their persecution by Camilo became intolerable, since it had occurred after his inauguration. On the day news of Antônio Pessoa's death had reached Camilo, a number of Epitácio's loyal followers reported, the governor was heard exulting noisily over it.[55] When Epitácio was apprised of this circumstance, he had already nominated Camilo for a federal deputy seat in the March 1921 election. Camilo's name never appeared on the ballot, however. As Epitácio explained, once the affront became public knowledge, "[Camilo's]

[53] Complaints about Camilo are contained in a series of letters between Young Turks or Camilo and Epitácio, written between 16 Mar. and 10 Sept. 1917, filed in AEP/12/59–74. Epitácio confessed he was "depressed" to see "Camilo and Paraíba, both under my political direction," accused of "certain dishonesties practiced in the shadow of my administration." Would not it have been better to spend revenues on road and dams or other capital improvements, he remonstrated? "Why 1,000 contos on a Normal School when a [gubernatorial] residence already existed?" Epitácio to Camilo (Rio de Janeiro), 23 Jan. 1920, AEP/12/155.

[54] Camilo de Holanda to Epitácio (Capital) 8 Feb. 1917, AEP/12/63–64. Epitácio had sharply rebuked Camilo for persecuting his nephew and other members of his family-based network in the Capital: "In spite of our old friendship, you are behaving as an adversary. It is enough to say that your government only considers as its adversaries my family and the most intimate friends of my family. Valfredo [Leal], Simeão [dos Santos Leal], José Rodrigues [de Carvalho?], Heráclito [Cavalcanti Carneiro Monteiro], to cite a few adversaries, are showered with favors and deference, while Solon, [Antônio] Pessoa Filho, and Carlos Espínola—friends—are forgotten." Epitácio to Camilo de Holanda (Rio de Janeiro), 6(?) Apr. 1917, AEP/12/63–64.

[55] This charge is confirmed in the following exchange of letters: [See Solon de Lucena to Epitácio (Capital), 8 Feb. 1921, AEP/12/163]; Epitácio to Caldas Brandão (Rio de Janeiro), 9 Feb. 1921, AEP/12/164; Caldas Brandão to Epitácio (Capital), 9 Feb. 1921, AEP/12/164. See also Cunha Pedrosa, *Minhas memórias*, 1:203.

name could not appear on a slate drawn up by Antônio Pessoa's brother."[56] Thus, in driving Camilo into what colloquially was known as "ostracism," the Young Turks also placed the Venancistas on the defensive.

Camilo's ejection from the state oligarchy—he retired to Rio de Janeiro permanently—signaled a change in the gubernatorial guard. Henceforth the Venancistas, who had dominated the cabinets of Governors Castro Pinto and Antônio Pessoa, were confined to the federal delegation. The two governors who followed Camilo—Solon de Lucena and João Suassuna—were both Young Turks. Consequently, the Young Turk faction had maximum influence during the years of increased state resources, first from the IFOCS and then from rising revenues in the Treasury.[57] Solon delivered on Epitácio's basic commitment to his electorate by channeling resources to a road network for interior producers and by rewarding the Capital's businessmen with lucrative government contracts and tax exemptions. He also initiated construction of a deepwater port at Cabedêlo. By furthering infrastructure, a widely appealing goal, he maintained a political balance of zonal interests in a manner never again to be witnessed. Although by Suassuna's inauguration, in October 1924, construction at Cabedêlo had tapered off—as federal money no longer was routinely appropriated—the new governor's commitment to its completion maintained Epitácio's carefully crafted coalition.

Taxation and Revenue Collection

Starting with Camilo's administration, the trend toward expansion of the State's authority in the hinterland became detectable. Although rising revenues reflected the growth in cotton production, as early as Castro Pinto's administration (1912–1915), the state government adopted a more determined policy of tax collection.[58] Camilo's administration was the first to report that all

[56] Epitácio to Camilo de Holanda (Rio de Janeiro), 10 Feb. 1921, AEP/12/165.

[57] Revenues averaged just under 6,000 contos annually during Camilo's administration (1917–1920), but during Solon's second year in office (1922), they rose to over 7,700. In 1923, a windfall of 14,269 contos was collected, with nearly 10,000 contos deriving from cotton export taxes. Lyra Tavares, *Cifras e notas*, p. 270. See also Table A.4.

[58] Lyra Tavares, *Economia e finanças*, p. 56. Gov. Camilo de Holanda alluded to Castro Pinto's introduction of such "severe measures," when he referred to the "more advantageous" substitution of "military officers" for civilian revenue officials because the former "command more respect from our adversaries [i.e., local

thirty-nine of Paraíba's municípios had remanded taxes to the State Treasury.[59] Still dissatisfied, Camilo fulminated over the obstacles he confronted vis-à-vis revenue collection. He identified the major impediment as survival of a patrimonialistic practice, condemning "all the prefeitos who divide among the members of their families the revenues . . . as, unfortunately, happens in the majority of the municípios."[60] This propensity of elite families to withhold locally collected revenues vexed him, because, as he acknowledged to Epitácio, "The same prefeitos are good political colleagues" and the PRCP needed their votes.[61] But the deficit he left to this successor—Solon—was attributable more to his extravagant renovation of the Capital than to the local bosses' self-aggrandizement.[62]

During Solon de Lucena's administration, both the telegraph system and the road network network were developed, so the State drew on those technological achievements for more efficient revenue collection. Local party bosses and prefeitos in many municípios could now drive to the Capital in a day or two, or even hours. As a result, the governor caucused with them more regularly and found the opportunity to apply more effective pressure for insuring that revenues would be remanded. With the telegraph established, and the telephone making a steady conquest of the interior, local bosses found it more difficult to evade a governor's summons to travel to the Capital for a consultation. Solon's efforts to collect revenues were reinforced by the impressive patronage he controlled in the form of IFOCS spending. And, because many local bosses were reaping greater profits from the export sector, as cotton production increased, they were less likely to begrudge the Treasury a share of revenues.[63]

opposition factions], whereas, civilian officials are almost always the business friends and relatives of the local bosses who name them." Camilo de Holanda to Epitácio (Capital), 30 Mar. 1917, AEP/12/61.

[59] Camilo de Holanda to Epitácio (Capital), 8 Feb. 1917, AEP/12/52.

[60] Camilo de Holanda to Epitácio (Capital), 27 Jan. 1918, AEP/12/106.

[61] Ibid.

[62] In his 1921 Annual Message, Gov. Solon de Lucena identified the causes of the deficit (1,000 contos of long-term debt and another 1,000 contos of short-term debt) inherited from Camilo de Holanda as due to "the expense of damages to urban property demolished without appropriate [legal] expropriation and the revocation of contracts in the hundreds of contos." Lyra Tavares, *Cifras e notas*, p. 272.

[63] After only two years in office, Solon acknowledged that Paraíba was indebted to Epitácio for "one thousand kilometers of roads." Lyra Tavares, *Cifras e Notas*, p. 270.

The issue of who would be taxed was squarely confronted first in Camilo's administration. Proud that "all of the interior [had] begun to pay taxes," Camilo attributed this to "budget revisions" and the use of police officers as tax collection agents.[64] All the local bosses, he elaborated, "have been made to see that the changing of the revenue officials [to police personnel] is not a partisan [i.e., political] move, but that it has [only] fiscal [economic] ends."[65] Camilo's success was stubbornly opposed by the interior's largest cotton buyer, however; the governor was obliged to admit that "everyone except Cristiano Lauritzen agrees with me."[66] In fact, Campina Grande's political boss was so angry that Camilo had to confess, "Cristiano no longer writes to me."[67] Cristiano had strong reason to break off communication with Paraíba's new governor, for Camilo was attempting to enforce what Cristiano and other buyers in the backlands considered a punitive tax on Campina Grande's cotton exports. New legislation passed by the Assembly attempted to force Campina Grande's buyers to export their cotton via the Capital instead of via Recife.[68] In addition, however, the governor was trying to favor the economic interests of his own family-based network in the Capital. Some of its members would soon receive preferential tax exemptions on their importation of new capital equipment to improve their cotton-processing establishments. (Law No. 464 of October 19, 1917, exempted from the industrial and professional taxes any individual or firm importing cotton-processing equipment as the first of its kind.) Opposition to the higher tax from exporters in Campina Grande therefore remained adamant.

This struggle between Camilo and Col. Cristiano Lauritzen marked a turning point in Paraíba's family-based politics, for it illustrated that the more complex issues of economic growth could not be addressed by resorting to family-based networks operating

[64] Camilo de Holanda to Epitácio (Capital), 8 Feb. 1917, AEP/12/52.

[65] Ibid.

[66] Ibid.

[67] Ibid.

[68] E. de Almeida, *História Campina*, pp. 378, 381. In the Capital, an 8 per cent ad valorum tax was levied on cotton exports. But, beginning in 1915, an adjustable table was adopted for markets in the interior from which cotton was exported to other states by pack train. Consequently, in centers such as Campina Grande, Itabaiana, and Alagoa Grande, the ad valorum tax was raised to 10 per cent or 12 per cent. As a freshman congressman. Epitácio had lobbied for such a differential in order to encourage producers and middlemen to send their cotton to the Capital for ginning and export. E. Pessôa, *Obras completas*, 2:178–79ff.

behind the scenes. Instead, formally organized groups gained a new role and Coronel Cristiano found himself isolated and less effective. As early as 1915, he had privately voiced objection in principle to imposition of a higher tax on Campina Grande's cotton exports than in the Capital. For several years, the law enacting the tax was ignored. However, Camilo's efforts to enforce it and extract the taxes from Cristiano's home territory sounded the cry to battle. On December 16, 1916, newly installed Governor Camilo had drawn up the state budget at a meeting in the Capital attended by its most important businessmen.[69] Initially, thirty-two owners of large commercial firms in Campina Grande refused to pay their state taxes in protest over the budget, which was largely devoted to construction in the Capital. By March 1917, only eight firms were still holding out.[70] In this atmosphere of protest against the commercial tax, Cristiano determined to react against the export tax. However, apparently due to Epitácio's intervention, Cristiano reversed his position—to the dissatisfaction of many of his peers in Campina Grande's commerce—and capitulated.[71]

Lino Gomes da Silva, one of Cristiano's strongest backers, resigned his seat in the município's council—one he owed to Cristiano—to demonstrate angry protest against Cristiano's oligarchical obedience. Organizing his opposition, he founded the Campina Grande Commercial Association, the first of a number of commercial associations to be established outside the Capital and among the market centers of the brejo and caatinga-agreste in the 1920s. Members of the Commercial Association vigorously opposed imposition of the export tax schedule for cotton and brought suits related to issues of local tax collection in the município; nevertheless, the governor's fiscal assault was successful by 1920.[72]

[69] Camilo de Holanda to Epitácio (Capital) 13 Dec. 1916, AEP/12/41.

[70] Camilo de Holanda to Epitácio (Capital), 30 Mar. 1917, AEP/12/61. E. da Câmara, *Datas campinenses*, pp. 111–12.

[71] Cristiano Lauritzen to Epitácio (Campina Grande), 24 Nov. 1915 (1916?) ACAP/2/62–65. E. de Almeida, *História Campina*, pp. 381–82. Evidence is indeterminate, but Cristiano's influence appeared to decline after the death of his friend and patron, Col. Antônio Pessoa. Epitácio confined his communication with Cristiano to expressing concern over revenue collection during 1917. He coupled congratulations for Cristiano's "brilliant election results" to a request that Cristiano fire two revenue agents in Campina Grande after an audit turned up "serious problems." Epitácio to Cristiano Lauritzen (Rio de Janeiro), early June 1917, AEP/12/72.

[72] E. de Almeida, *História Campina*, p. 382; E. Câmara, *Datas campinenses*, p. 112.

The conflict over taxation set the stage for a larger clash at the end of the decade, when Cabedêlo's cargo capacity was expected to increase and the main road to the Ceará border was complete. Between 1915 and 1916, Campina Grande's local revenues had tripled, indirectly suggesting the gains the State Treasury would make by taxing its commerce.[73] Diverting its commerce to the Capital, however, was a prerequisite.

Law and Order

The progress achieved in revenue collection could be traced to a parallel offensive by governors to impose law and order in the hinterland. Annual expenditure on police and security rose steadily after 1912 and comprised the single largest item in the annual budgets of the 1920s. Although greater interstate cooperation after 1920 meant that brigandage was better addressed as a police matter, its political dimension was not as effectively addressed. What Governor Castro Pinto had written confidentially to Epitácio in 1912 still summed up the basic problem a decade later:

> I agree with those who want to extinguish banditry. We should, in this case, begin in our own house, with our fellow party members and friends who live by *cangaceirismo* . . . with the estates . . . which are filled with criminals and which have understandings with Antônio Silvino or others they help. . . .
>
> You know better than I the very true causes for which repression of banditry in the interior of the state was and will be ineffective. . . . It is the local bosses who protect it . . . and politics originates from these bosses by virtue of their [control of] their voters.[74]

A 1912 agreement by Paraíba and her neighbors Ceará, Pernambuco, and Rio Grande do Norte facilitating "hot pursuit" merely put the State Police more frequently in confrontation with land-

[73] E. de Almeida, *História Campina*, pp. 378-83.

[74] João Castro Pinto to Epitácio (Capital), 28 July 1912, AEP/10/198 (Castro Pinto's italics). Castro Pinto was described as engaged in a "fight without a truce against bandits and their protectors." Pinto, *Octacílio de Albuquerque*, p. 48. Castro Pinto "attack[ed the bandits] and penetrat[ed] areas never before entered by the police . . . breaking with the scruples or fears of previous administrations over the power exercised by the local bosses who sheltered them." Mariz, *Apanhados historicos*, p. 321.

owners exercising their ancient prerogative of *homísio* (the customary right of powerful landlords to extend personal protection and hospitality to any individual seeking it within the boundaries of their rural properties). The sanctuary that wealthy landlords granted to fugitive criminals was the most striking illustration of the discretionary power they enjoyed in a quasi-patrimonial political system.[75] In 1922, the same states signed another agreement that somewhat liberalized the rules of the chase. Its impact, however, was tempered by the increasing threat of banditry.

In 1921, Virgulino Ferreira da Silva, more commonly known as "Lampião," started his career as a professional bandit, embarking on the path that would make him the acknowledged "King of the Cangaceiros." His cruelties produced nostalgia for "the Good Thief," Antônio Silvino, confined in the Pernambuco State Penetentiary since his capture in November 1914. One of thousands of bandits who plagued the Northeast during the next two decades, Lampião was feared primarily because of the large band under his command—forty to fifty men on routine raids. In spite of a greater expenditure on the State Security Forces, particularly for the Flying Squads (Volantes) who were specialized in "hot pursuit," the police were no match for the bandits.[76] Better armed and supplied with intelligence about their pursuers, the latter usually knew the local territory more thoroughly. Where former brigands such as Antônio Silvino had attacked only isolated rural estates and small settlements, Lampião expanded to larger properties, towns, and even interior cities.[77] The residents of the interior in the seven-state region of the Northeast knew no respite until his

[75] José Américo, noting in 1922 that "until a few years ago [this] inviolability [of homísio] was respected," observed that only the landowner "had the right to hand over criminals to justice—if he did not prefer [to grant] the impunity [from justice that] homísio [represented]." *A Parahyba*, p. 480. See Oliveira Vianna, *Instituições políticas*, 1:244–45, on the historical evolution of homísio in Brazil.

[76] Expenditure on public security, police, and the local guards usually consumed over 25 per cent of the annual state budgets by the 1920s: Spending rose from 265 contos in 1916 to 937 contos in 1920 to 1,112 contos in 1923. By 1926, it doubled to 2,884 contos. Lewin, "Politics and *Parentela*," appendix 6 (pp. 533–35), and Lyra Tavares, *Cifras e Notas*, p. 271. After 1915, revenues often exceeded the official appropriations budgeted in the preceding year, making the budgetary breakdowns an inaccurate guide to total expenditures. Police and security personnel expanded from 796 in 1916 to 829 in 1920 to 1,247 in 1925 (the highpoint for the period 1889–1930). Lewin, ibid.

[77] Lampião's career is carefully detailed by Billy Jaynes Chandler in *The Bandit King: Lampião of Brazil* (College Station, Texas: Texas A & M University Press, 1978).

death in 1938. On July 27, 1924, the armed attack by his brother, Levino Ferreira, on Sousa, Paraíba, awakened the nation to the new magnitude of the threat. About one hundred cangaceiros captured the city in a predawn attack. They robbed and humiliated prestigious members of the Paraíba backlands' first families, including its ruling Mariz. Federal District Judge Arquimedes Souto Maior was singled out for special, revengeful abuse, bringing public outrage to a new level.[78]

One of the few coronéis in Paraíba strong enough to resist Lampião, Princesa's José Pereira Lima had intermittently protected him since 1921—apparently because of family connections.[79] The attack on Sousa changed his mind. Three months later, Paraíba's new governor, João Suassuna, appointed Princesa's political chief the head of a massive civilian effort, coordinated with the State Police, to drive Lampião and other bandits operating in his wake from Paraíba. As a result, Princesa became the repository of the largest arsenal of weaponry in the backlands. A Second Battalion of State Police was also created solely for the pursuit of bandits, with regular patrols in a half dozen municípios of the backlands. Within sixty days, Lampião's force was expelled from Paraíba, returning briefly to Piancó in early 1925, but only en route to Alagoas.[80] Lampião attacked settlements in Princesa in August, as retaliation for his brother Levino's murder by the Pernambuco and Paraíba Flying Squads; however, the Paraíba Police pursued him to Ceará through October, accompanied by Zé Pereira's privately re-

[78] Sixty-five warrants were issued for the arrest of the attackers of Sousa, including Chico Pereira. *A União*, 5 Oct. 1924. See also "Os acontecimentos de Sousa," *A União*, 12 and 14 Aug. 1924. Souto Maior, dressed in only his undershorts, was forced to crawl down the main street on his hands and knees before Sousa's terrified population. His wife paid a ransom for his release. *A União*, 7 Sept. and 3 Oct. 1924; Chandler, *Bandit King*, pp. 52–53; Padre Pereira Nóbrega, *Vingança não!* (Rio de Janeiro: Livraria Freitas Bastos, S.A., 1960), pp. 222–24.

[79] Lampião was a good friend of the wealthy rancher, Col. Marçal Diniz, Zé Pereira's uncle and father-in-law, but a better friend of Marçal's son Marcelino Diniz, who obtained the bandit's release from jail in 1923 after he had murdered a federal district judge. The Diniz's Fazenda Abóboras—in Triunfo, Pernambuco—was contiguous with the município of Princesa and had provided shelter for Lampião since 1921. Chandler, *Bandit King*, pp. 48–49.

[80] Humberto Nóbrega, "João Suassuna—O estadista," *RIHGP* 18 (1972):13–14; Chandler, *Bandit King*, pp. 58–59. Five hundred thousand rifle cartridges were purchased for use in the campaign against Lampião: Rio de Janeiro, Arquivo Histórico do Itamaraty [Foreign Ministry], Governos, Repartições e Authoridades Regionais e Locais, Telegramas Expedidas, Parahyba, 1900–1930 (henceforth, AHI/AR/PB): [Foreign Minister] Felix Pacheco to João Suassuna, tel. of 3 Mar. 1926, and João Suassuna to Felix Pacheco, tel. of 20 Mar. 1926.

cruited forces.[81] Lampião's subsequent avoidance of Paraíba marked an achievement that the backlands' popular poets celebrated in song, citing as the reason Zé Pereira's reputation as the state's powerful coronel.[82]

The government's more aggressive stance against banditry, and its limited success in repelling Lampião, challenged local family-based power. Although rural magnates continued jealously to guard their prerogative to maintain their private security forces, and to offer protection on their rural properties to whomever they chose, their offers of sanctuary encountered stronger urban condemnation and, in some cases, violation by the police. Greater pressure for the State's assumption of a more aggressive role emanated from residents of the cities and towns in the interior, as well as on the coast, for the entire backlands were now very vulnerable to attack.

Urban critics did not rest at calling for an end to banditry in demanding greater law and order. They also indicted family-based politics. For instance, in November 1924, following Suassuna's installation as governor, the Municipal Council of Itabaiana, a market center in the caatinga-agreste, took the unusual step of sending a "Manifesto of the People of Itabaiana" directly to Epitácio. The councilmen withdrew their support of the Ribeiro Coutinho family's control of the município specifically on the grounds of its "*mandonismo*," or iron-fisted rule, because they "could no longer stand the oppression, the public funds disappearing into private pockets, the attacks which used to be made outside of town on the rural properties [that] are now done right in the main streets . . . and most of all, public officials and government workers . . . living in splendor while the people toil."[83] The manifesto, signed by several dozen influential citizens, also foreshadowed a trend, by the end of the decade, for the wealthier middle class in large urban centers to ally with the working class to oppose the "mando-

[81] Chandler, *Bandit King*, p. 60.

[82] The relevant stanza explained: "*Lampião acovarde-se / Com a sua cabroeira / Não entra na Paraíba / Com mêdo de Zé Pereira / O doutor João Suassuna / Mandou dar-lhe uma carreira.*" [Lampião has turned coward / With his gang of henchmen. / He doesn't set foot in Paraíba / For fear of Zé Pereira. / Doctor João Suassuna / Gave orders to give him a thrashing.] H. Nóbrega, "João Suassuna," p. 15.

[83] Manifesto of the People of Itabaiana, from the *Livro de actas das seções do Conselho Municipal de Itabaiana*, sent to Epitácio, 5 Nov. 1924, AEP/12/255. Petitioners wanted to replace the local boss, Flávio Ribeiro Coutinho, who governed in partnership with his brother, Odilon Maroja, with Epitácio's nephew Fernando Pessoa.

nismo" that coronelista politics ordained, even in the cities and towns.

Beginning in Solon's administration and continuing under Suassuna, the government undertook a more vigorous prosecution of prominently connected men implicated in murders deriving from local family warfare. Previously, even if brought to trial, which rarely happened, such cases were handled by the local authorities and the families involved. Under Brazilian law, individuals could be indicted for murder by either a judge or police officials. Consequently, around 1920, the state chief of police took an active role in bringing several of the most erring members of local elite families to trial.[84] Trial by a locally empaneled jury, however, remained the insurmountable obstacle to effective legal prosecution. When packing juries with relatives did not bring acquittals, murder threats against jurors who would bring a verdict of guilty did. Otherwise, a reversal in the State Supreme Court offered another alternative, in addition to the fact that state and federal elected officials were legally immune from criminal prosecution.

In the long run, although this family prerogative of jury-packing has survived in parts of the Northeast until the present, the State assumed a more active posture in local prosecution proceedings. Significantly, those indicted belonged not only to the opposition but also to the incumbent PR do P. Publicity given to murder charges and trials became divisive of family solidarity, particularly the horizontal ties between brothers and brothers-in-law. Even where aquitted, individuals risked their family's loss of local political power. Governor Suassuna, for example, relieved his own foster brother of the political leadership of Brejo do Cruz, which hastened the violent fragmentation of his own Agripino–Maia family-based group both there and in neighboring Catolé do Rocha. Nor were the Pessoas immune from the family fragmentation as the State began to exercise a greater role in local political affairs.

[84] The most sensational case, that of Sousa's Francisco ["Chico"] Pereira Nóbrega, is discussed in the next chapter. In 1918, the son of Areia's federal deputy, José Antônio Maria da Cunha Lima, was shot to death while resisting arrest by the state chief of police (Democrito de Almeida), immediately after murder charges against him had been dismissed by the judge. Camilo de Holanda to Epitácio (Capital), 27 Feb. 1918, AEP/12/111. In 1927, Suassuna refused to appoint another son of Cunha Lima, then Areia's political boss, after the father broke his pledge to confine his son to the family property in Areia. The son's involvement in physical assaults and allegations of murder against him led to the measure of confinement, as a compromise, rather than bringing him to trial. Suassuna to Epitácio (Capital), 20 Apr. 1927, AEP/12/278.

Change and Epitácio's Declining Order

At the close of Solon de Lucena's gubernatorial term, in 1924, the order of Epitácio Pessoa began to lose its impressive political cohesion. When Epitácio's presidency ended, the IFOCS appropriations evaporated; rising revenues from the State Treasury still sustained the patronage State—although more modestly—maintaining the Pessoas as Paraíba's family-based oligarchical rulers until 1930. Epitácio had administered his patronage to uphold the political prerogatives of "the friends and allies of 1915," who were the family-based powerholders in the municípios. He never directly challenged their entitlement to political office or claims to empreguismo within their local bailiwicks of power, as long as they loyally delivered the vote for his slate. From the narrow perspective of his electoral machine, his distribution of IFOCS patronage largely reinforced existing political arrangements along more organized and cohesive lines, militating against any drastic reform of the entrenched prerogatives elite families exercised.

In spite of Epitácio's conservative distribution of political and economic patronage, his performance as a classic oligarchical boss contributed to several important changes in the role the governor played. Greater patronage resources, both a cause and a result of economic growth and commercialization, enabled governors to chip away at the semi-autonomy of Paraíba's municípios. Greater demand for revenue and public peace, goals with which Epitácio identified, led the governors to adopt policies increasing centralization. As banditry reached its maximum intensity in the Northeast between 1920 and 1938, the State aggressively assumed the offensive to protect its revenues and commerce, not to mention its citizens' lives.

Elaboration of infrastructure caused economic interests to become more complex. Representation based merely on membership in a family-based group no longer served local interests adequately, as the establishment of commercial associations in the interior's largest cities suggested after 1920. In many instances, the State and the local elites became interdependent, as they jointly undertook physical improvements, mutually fostered export growth, and cooperated to create a public peace on which prosperity could rest more securely. The backlands bosses became accustomed to frequent visits to the Capital, if not part-time residence there. This in turn obliged them to heed gubernatorial admonitions to remit state revenues and to cooperate with the Flying Squads in their pursuit of bandits.

Broader political change was also at work beyond Paraíba. After 1915, increased federal spending expanded the size of the civil service, as the national government fostered agricultural production, commercial export, public works, and infrastructure.[85] Curtailment of the IFOCS projects still left intact a more conspicuous federal bureaucracy, staffed largely by Paraibanos. As an important politico-bureaucratic elite in Paraíba, the civil service was a force for greater centralization of the State. Bureaucratic officials readily conceived of the State as an agent of reform that could rationalize resources, increase rural production, and expand transportation and communications networks. Elected politicians and civil service personnel alike saw a stronger State as the only alternative to counter the local prerogatives ruling families exercised at their personal discretion. Increasingly, política de família was deemed a retrograde system. Rising currents of nationalism reinforced the view of the semi-autonomous coronel—or his "mandonismo"—as a relic of the past. The old structure impeded positive change and was a political embarrassment.

In the 1922 presidential campaign, votes for the Republican Reaction had challenged national politics based on the oligarchies. In Paraíba, however, those votes often indicated rejection of coronelismo. Many who voted for Nilismo supported neither Nilo Peçanha nor his opposition leader in Paraíba, Heráclito Cavalcanti. Instead, they were signaling their distaste for the national political system founded on coronelismo and a rurally controlled electorate. New currents of political dissent were gaining ground in Paraíba. Many who felt in 1915 that Epitácio Pessoa's "tamed oligarchy" was preferable to those in other northeastern states began to reexamine that judgment. As the decade unfolded, the old issue of which personalistic faction would lead the oligarchy had become secondary; throughout Brazil—and in Paraíba—the national political system and oligarchy itself were called into question.

[85] One example of the growing federal presence was the federal government's cotton agency (Serviço de Defesa do Algodão), reorganized on March 10, 1924 (Decree No. 1246), as a state agency (Serviço Estadual do Algodão). *A União*, 30 Mar. 1924. Unfortunately, José Otávio's *A Revolução estatizada um estudo sobre a formação do centralismo em 30* (Mossoró, Rio Grande do Norte: Edições Escola Superior de Agricultura de Mossoró/Fundação Guimaraes Duque, 1984) appeared too late to be taken into account in this study. Its author addresses considerable attention to the expansion of the federal government's role in Paraíba both in the 1920s and following the Revolution of 1930. See Steven Topik, "The State's Contribution to the Development of Brazil's Internal Economy: 1850–1930," *HAHR* 65, no. 2 (1985): 203–28.

· VIII ·

The Oligarchy Moves toward Crisis, 1924–1930

> If it were not for Uncle Epitácio, I, my brothers, and my cousins would never have gone beyond being lowly stevedores [*reles carregadores*] in the Recife Customs House.
>
> —Gov. João Pessoa, June 1928

> We of the North have only the right to receive the candidates' names and to order the slate to be printed.
>
> —Gov. João Pessoa to Epitácio, May 1929

As THE DECADE of the twenties rolled toward the Revolution of 1930, national events carried greater significance for oligarchy's survival in Paraíba. The 1922 presidential crisis had revealed that the politics of café com leite was nearly exhausted as a basis for oligarchical consensus among the most powerful states. In its aftermath, divisions among the elite grew. Career officers in the military, both senior and junior, continued to be disaffected with the priority their civilian counterparts in government accorded to the regional interests of state oligarchies with rural power bases. The expanding urban middle class and working class voiced increasing dissatisfaction with their underrepresentation in government. Although a populist period had not yet opened, the stage was being set for the emergence of mass politics during the 1930s. In the aftermath of World War I, Brazil's industrial base deepened and import substitution and exports resumed prewar levels. Despite greater vulnerability to fluctuations in the international market, coffee remained king and paid for Brazil's rising list of imports, facilitating the steady emergence of the Industrial Triangle of São Paulo, Rio de Janeiro, and Belo Horizonte.

The most dramatic condemnation of the national political system was articulated by the Tenentes—or Lieutenants—the young survivors of the 1922 Copacabana Revolt.[1] In August 1924, on the

[1] "Tenentismo" refers to both the Tenentes' critique and their authoritarian orientation, particularly after the October (1930) Revolution. See John D. Wirth, "Tenentismo in the Brazilian Revolution of 1930," *HAHR* 44 (May 1964):161–79; Ed-

second anniversary of the Copacabana Revolt, an uprising aimed at overthrowing the federal government erupted in the city of São Paulo. Although the revolt was crushed by federal troops after a month of fighting, several hundred rebels, led by Lieutenants Luis Carlos Prestes, Miguel Costa, and Eduardo Gomes—veterans of Copacabana—formed a military column and retreated south from the city. Eventually turning northward, the Prestes Column trekked over 30,000 kilometers through the interior—mostly in the states of the Northeast—denouncing the retrograde organization of national politics and calling for revolution. Small, poorly defended towns and settlements in the Northeast's backlands became the victims of the column's military attacks, as the Tenentes sought to make object lessons of local bosses and foment a revolutionary mood.

In Paraíba, the Prestes Column delivered one of its most notorious attacks in 1926, when some of its units captured the City of Piancó. As part of the strategy of provoking the tenant population to revolt against the rural landlords, they executed the município's controversial Epitacista boss, Padre Aristides Ferreira da Cruz, along with several other local officials. In Paraíba, as elsewhere, however, the backlands client population loyally supported their landlords when the column attacked. (Juarez Távora, a native of Paraíba and a Tenente of the Copacabana Revolt, was one of the Column's commanders.) The Tenentes' revolutionary exhortations may have gone unheeded in the backlands, but their message was heard in the burgeoning cities and towns near the coast. Although a decade of impressive economic growth had allowed Paraíba's governors to make their presence felt beyond the coast, there was little gubernatorial control of the hinterland. The modest military challenge by the Prestes Column revealed the federal government's impotence to all. The Tenentes' critique struck sympathetic chords in Paraíba's cities and towns because it linked latifundia and coronelismo to the electoral fraud on which the politics of the governors rested. Its condemnation of the nation's rural-based politics fueled growing discontent with the Northeast's inferior position at the federal level. Thus, as the national debate matured between 1924 and 1930, it found participants as well as listeners in Paraíba. Greater politicization, cou-

---

gard Carone, *O tenentismo* (São Paulo: Difel, 1975); and Michael Conniff, "The Tenentes in Power: A New Perspective on the Brazilian Revolution of 1930," *Journal of Latin American Studies* 10, no. 1 (1978):61–82.

pled with the impact of phenomenal growth in the backlands cotton zones, gradually eroded the cohesion in Epitácio's 1915 coalition. The interests of the ruling family-based groups were becoming more complex. As tension grew between urban groups in the Capital and a core of family-based groups in the rural hinterland, a similar polarization on the national level between urban and rural interests contributed to the fragmentation overtaking Epitácio's oligarchy in 1930.

The Ruling Coalition Fragments

Factional Rivalry among "the Family and Friends of Epitácio Pessoa"

In 1924, for the first time since Epitácio had assumed direct control of the Paraíba oligarchy, a serious division opened within the ranks of his key lieutenants. His endorsement of João Suassuna, outgoing Governor Solon de Lucena's handpicked successor, touched off a controversy that exploded like "a real atomic bomb in the midst of the former Guelas."[2] The negative reaction to Suassuna's candidacy was so strong that three Venancistas—Senators Octacílio de Albuquerque and Venâncio Neiva and Federal Deputy Antônio Massa–broke formally with their state party boss after nearly thirty-five years of loyal support. Epitácio was at The Hague, sitting on the Permanent International Court of Justice, when Suassuna's rumored nomination was revealed as Solon's decision in March. His rebellious old guard thus had an initial tactical advantage, and they wasted no time in taking their protest directly to President Bernardes. Although they couched their objections to Suassuna's candidacy in terms of his alleged involvement in "shady deals" connected to IFOCS projects when he had been Solon's inspector of the treasury, their opposition turned more basically on his identity as a Young Turk and a backlander who was related to parentelas that rose in revolt in 1912.[3] Ber-

[2] A. Nóbrega, *História republicana*, p. 162. By nominating Suassuna, Solon believed that he could exercise authority over him and that "as a friend of Antônio Pessoa," Suassuna would "be popular among the Young Turks," who did not predominate in the federal delegation. Solon de Lucena to Epitácio (Capital), 15 Feb. 1924, AEP/12/221.

[3] Bernardes voiced his objection to Suassuna's candidacy simply by alluding to "the suspicions" in Paraíba that Suassuna was "a businessman." The Venancistas,

nardes's involvement confronted Epitácio with a crisis, particularly in view of the president's recent hostile dismantling of the IFOCS projects. Epitácio's control of the Paraíba oligarchy would be shaken if Solon were forced to withdraw Suassuna's candidacy. For this reason, Epitácio returned to Brazil from The Hague in early May and set aside his retirement from national politics. During the summer, he resumed his seat in the Senate—as Solon's appointee prior to being elected to a nine-year term—and commanded Paraíba's federal delegation. His determination to defend Suassuna's candidacy from the floor of the upper house was a direct response to President Bernardes's carefully worded threat of May 19 that a presidential degola was in the offing if Suassuna's name was placed on the ballot:

> In politics, as Your Excellency well knows, the identity of interests is what determines alliance. If there is a fight, we must expect a fusion of the two currents opposed to the dominant administration in Paraíba [i.e., the Venancistas and the Heraclistas].[4]

Only a national crisis prevented Bernardes from acting on his word—and Epitácio's superb talent for personal diplomacy. On July 5, the São Paulo Revolt erupted, absorbing President Bernardes's attention for several months. Meanwhile, Epitácio succeeded in convincing both Venâncio and Antônio Massa to withdraw their objections to Suassuna, at the same time using the Senate as a national forum to defend Suassuna's candidacy and condemn his critics.[5] Suassuna, therefore, was elected governor and Bernardes did not apply the sanction of a degola.[6] Although Epitácio once again weathered a gubernatorial crisis, the break with his old Venancista lieutenants—particularly with Sen. Octacílio de Albuquerque, who remained unreconciled—would haunt him in 1930.

---

however, referred to Suassuna's record in spending federal monies. Artur Bernardes to Epitácio (Rio de Janeiro), 29 May 1924, AEP/12/250. Suassuna defended himself in a press interview in *O Jornal* (Parahyba), 17 May 1924. See also Solon de Lucena to Epitácio (Capital), tel. of 8 May 1924, AEP/12/233.

[4] Artur Bernardes to Epitácio (Rio de Janeiro), 20 May 1924, AEP/12/250.

[5] Epitácio to Artur Bernardes (Rio de Janeiro), 20 May 1924, ibid.

[6] In 1930 evidence was discovered of a Heraclista plot to place Gen. Ivo Soares in the governorship in 1924—instead of Suassuna—presumably with Bernardes's sponsorship. Ivo Soares, Bernardes's personal physician, was the uncle of Oscar and Orris Soares, nephews of ex-Governor Camilo de Holanda. Joaquim Pessoa, brother of João Pessoa, was one of the plotters. Joaquim Pessoa to Gen. Ivo Soares (Capital), tels. of 27–28 May 1924, AEP/12/245A. A. Nóbrega, *História republicana*, p. 162.

Suassuna's administration heightened and made overt the latent tensions between the Capital's commercial sector and agricultural producers in the interior. In a fiscal assault, one of his first acts was to cancel most of the tax exemptions granted to owners of the largest firms in Parahyba, including South America's textile giant, the Lundgrens of Recife.[7] Correctly, Suassuna evaluated those privileges—mostly granted during Camilo's and Solon's administrations—as depriving the State Treasury of desperately needed revenues. He singled out Solon's "generosity" for particular criticism, condemning his predecessor's commitment of state revenues for the construction of the Capital's first sewage system as needless debt. Privately, he complained to Epitácio, "Look at this harvest [i.e., by those firms holding tax exemptions] of the revenues made during Solon's administration that I now face."[8] Publicly, however, he charged that such firms, particularly the Lundgrens' textile factory, had not fulfilled the reciprocal clauses in their contracts to provide schools and job training for their employees. The Lundgrens' failure to prepare proper annual reports containing the appropriate statistics related to the value of their annual production and exports—a condition for their exemption from taxes for twenty-five years—also provided Suassuna with a major argument in his special memorandum on the cancellation of their exemption.[9]

Suassuna's aggressive attack on Parahyba's most highly capitalized firms was launched to offset the federal government's suspension of funds for the IFOCS highway and port projects. He was extremely eager to complete the remaining stretch of the main highway west, for only about one hundred kilometers were left to be constructed between Patos and Sousa in the alto sertão. In addition, although the port at Cabedêlo was being deepened, neither the wharves nor the road connecting the port to the Capital had been built. Severe floods in the winter of 1925 destroyed crops in the backlands and lowered cotton exports, reducing state revenues. The backlands dominated Suassuna's attention and his letters to Epitácio were filled with routine references to the rains, crops, harvests, and roads. Nevertheless, he remained very much

[7] The contract between the State of Paraíba and the Lundgrens' Fábrica de Tecidos Paraibanos, signed in 1920, granted "an exemption on any fees, contributions or taxes whatsoever, be they already existent or still to be created, for a period of twenty-five years." Memorandum of José Américo de Almeida, forwarded by Gov. João Suassuna to Epitácio (Capital) 8 Oct. 1924, AEP/12/254.

[8] João Suassuna to Epitácio (Capital) 21 Dec. 1924, AEP/12/252.

[9] Ibid.; Memorandum of José Américo, 8 Oct. 1924.

a Young Turk regarding Paraíba's export infrastructure. In other words, he supported development of the Capital as a major terminus for the exports of the interior. His words to Epitácio—on whom he was depending for several modest federal loans or appropriations—make clear that orientation:

> What we can do depends on the federal government. Rio Grande do Norte, Ceará, and Pernambuco['s] [markets] encroach on us more every day. Our own penetration [of the far backlands] is going rapidly forward between Patos and Sousa. It is a great shame to see the land unused. Fortaleza will lose out when it is completed. . . . I think that with 5,000 contos I can finish that stretch of highway.
>
> On the other hand, the Port of Cabedêlo is now at a depth of nine meters and needs only the docks in order to begin using it for export. Five thousand contos will do it.[10]

Yet the highway west was still uncompleted when Suassuna left office and the docks were finished only during Getúlio Vargas's presidency, when the federal government again made the IFOCS a major priority in spending.

Suassuna's last two years in office further divided Epitácio's winning coalition of 1915. By 1927 Suassuna himself spent less time in the Capital, withdrawing to his family estate in the município of Taperoá in the cariri-sertão. He was embittered by his deteriorating personal relationships with key Epitacistas, particularly the sons of his old mentor, Col. Antônio Pessoa, and, more fundamentally, by the growing differences in outlook and interests between the backlands zones and the coastal capital. The fact that weather conditions considerably reduced revenues for Suassuna's administration determined that Cabedêlo's development had to be suspended, a circumstance that meant the Capital's interests received significantly less attention than under his predecessor. Given his identity as a *sertanejo*—a backlander—one in which Suassuna evidently took great pride, and the obviously superior representation of those zones in the Assembly, the governor's growing unpopularity among coastal politicians is not surprising.

[10] João Suassuna to Epitácio (Capital), 26 Nov. 1926, AEP/12/268. In cooperation with the federal government, Suassuna established the state agency known as the Service for Agricultural and Pastoral Industries (Serviço de Agricultura e Industria Pastoril). In the interior, his most ambitious project was the completion of the Puxinanã Reservoir and Dam, which serves Campina Grande and today bears his name.

On one level Suassuna's growing estrangement from the Umbuseiro Pessoas could be directly traced to his personal affiliation with the Dantas of Teixeira, the leaders of the 1912 rebellion that had been coordinated with the Salvationist attempt at a *coup d'état*. His marriage to Rita Dantas Vilar and his establishment of a household near his Dantas in-laws in Taperoá—and not far from his birthplace in Teixeira—connected him to a powerful family-based group in the backlands who, at best, were highly suspect among Epitácio's closest lieutenants. On another level, the Pessoas' growing antagonism toward Suassuna expressed a social and cultural split between elite families in the backlands and those on the coast. Economic growth and diverging geoeconomic interests caused rifts in widely shared elite values, styles, and customs deriving historically from a rural culture. Urbanization altered elite fashions, speech, and identity during the 1920s, frequently reinforcing differing perceptions of geoeconomic interest between coast and interior. "Modernity" in a capital of provincial outlook such as Parahyba still meant dancing to European music—waltzes and polkas—although in Rio de Janeiro the samba already had begun its twentieth-century conquest of the nation's social elite as Brazil's national dance. Politicians in Parahyba relied on cosmopolitan tastes—even when out-of-date—to distinguish themselves from country cousins in the interior who still preferred to sing the *desafio*[11]—like Suassuna—or to dance to the traditional folk melodies of their nineteenth-century forebears.

On a third level, Suassuna's estrangement from the Umbuseiro Pessoas and other veteran Epitacistas was no more than family-based competition characteristic of Paraíba's factional politics. His withdrawal to his estate in Taperoá by 1927 and the infrequency of his communication with his Party Chief Epitácio by that year signaled growing hostility between him and Carlos Pessoa, the second eldest of Col. Antônio Pessoa's ten sons. Their mutual antagonism catalyzed grievances connected to the issue of which family-based groups would control the governorship and specific municípios in the alto sertão and cariri-sertão. A veteran of fifteen years of service, Suassuna had been obliged to vacate his seat in the House of Deputies to become governor in 1924. More

[11] The desafio is a poetic duel, sung by two competing poets for hours, or even days, and according to strict rules of rhyme and meter. The winner "trips" his opponent into stumbling on the rules or stumps him with his superior stock of facts and memorized book learning. Teixeira was the place in the Northeast from which the desafio was disseminated by a school of poets resident there between the 1850s and the 1880s.

prestigious than the governorship, his membership in the lower house had been achieved in 1920 as a reward for service to Epitácio. Suassuna renounced the seat so that Epitácio could advance Carlos Pessoa to the House of Deputies. Carlos, on the other hand, resented Suassuna because Carlos had wanted to be governor in 1924, but his birth in Pernambuco made him ineligible. Initially, he even sought to pursuade his Uncle Epitácio to revise the state constitution so that he might qualify to run for that office. At the same time, he was said to have attempted to dissuade Solon from nominating Suassuna to succeed. These efforts were in vain, but in compensation, Carlos was placed in the House of Deputies. Since he had been in politics for not quite eight years, his rise was quite exceptional—a mark of Epitácio's preference for one of his nephews. Carlos had received another such mark in 1920, after he was elected to represent Umbuseiro in the State Assembly: he was named speaker, a position that had always been held by a seasoned politician. Thus, Suassuna not only had grounds for feeling slighted but also perceived a realignment in the oligarchy's leadership: As the sons of Col. Antônio Pessoa reached adulthood and could be entrusted with the management of the oligarchy's affairs, political friends such as Suassuna would increasingly play supporting roles.[12]

In an attempt to restore the *status quo ante*, Suassuna provoked considerable conflict when he backed as *his* successor Júlio Nascimento Lira, his own godson. Lira, the state chief of police in Suassuna's cabinet, proved acceptable only to certain backlands families that already supported Suassuna, not to either the Pessoas or Epitácio's other lieutenants, such as Pedrosa or José Américo de Almeida. Epitácio returned from The Hague in 1928 to find another serious gubernatorial succession crisis, this one without any clear alternative to Lira's candidacy. He resolved to break the impasse over Suassuna's successor by naming his favorite nephew, João Pessoa Cavalcanti de Albuquerque, as the next governor. Suassuna could not object to this choice; nor could Epitácio's followers, who opposed Lira. But Paraíba's outgoing governor did indicate his displeasure over the arrangement by initially refusing to accept the seat in the lower house that Epitácio offered him, stating that he would not continue to "serve a party which had raised me only to humiliate me."[13]

[12] Author's interviews with Ariano Suassuna, Recife, 25 and 27 July 1971, and Fernando Nóbrega, Rio de Janeiro, 1 Aug. 1978.

[13] João Suassuna to Epitácio (Capital), 31 July 1928, AEP/12/292.

Although Suassuna finally accepted the seat in the House of Deputies (the third time Epitácio offered it), his extensive political network in both zones of the backlands viewed the leadership realignment with disfavor. João Pessoa was virtually an outsider and not likely to advocate their political and economic interests. For their part, Epitácio's nephews, who now were closely associated with the Capital, viewed Suassuna's intimacy with the Dantas of Teixeira—especially his long friendship with João Duarte Dantas, son of the 1912 insurrectionary leader, Franklin Dantas—with distrust. A more serious objection, Suassuna's friendship with Paraíba's most powerful local boss, Col. José Pereira Lima of Princesa, eventually led Gov. João Pessoa to regard his precedessor as *persona non grata*. In 1930 João Pessoa would refuse to draw on Suassuna's political services, even to save Epitácio's disintegrating coalition.

The Kin Dimensions of Factional Schism

In 1922, relations between the Umbuseiro Pessoas and their Pessoa de Queiroz cousins in Pernambuco erupted into open hostility because of an intrafamilial quarrel that resulted in murder. The incident engendered considerable antagonism among Epitácio's three sets of nephews and spilled over family boundaries to involve Coronel José Pereira as the protector of the Recife-based Pessoa de Queiroz. Both Gov. João Pessoa's tenacity in pursuing his Tributary War with the Recife entrepôt in 1929–1930 and Coronel José Pereira's equally stubborn determination in launching his "Revolution of Princesa" deserve to be assessed in terms of the bitter divisions that the murder had instilled among Epitácio's sets of nephews. The war José Pereira and João Pessoa waged to the death in 1930 drew on the animosity of 1922. Similarly, Epitácio's break with his Recife nephews shortly before João Pessoa's death also reflected the earlier deterioration of his relationship with the Pessoa de Queiroz. At least until João Pessoa was assassinated, Epitácio's relationship with his Recife nephews was never lower than in the months following his retirement from the presidency.

On November 5, 1922, one of the six Pessoa de Queiroz brothers—Epitácio's namesake, Epitácio Sobrinho Pessoa de Queiroz—killed the husband of his cousin Clarice Pessoa Santiago. (See Fig. B.3.) Clarice was Col. Antônio Pessoa's daughter, the sister of Antônio Pessoa Filho—who was then serving as Epitácio's personal secretary in Catete Palace—and the sister of Carlos Pessoa,

Speaker of the Paraíba State Assembly. She had been married only three years. At twenty-four, she was expecting her second child. The victim, Dr. [José] Bandeira [de Melo] Filho, aged thirty-nine and a well-known Recife gynecologist, was the son of a prominent Rio de Janeiro lawyer who was also a member of the Recife Law Faculty. The murder, which appeared to be motivated by strictly personal reasons, occurred while Bandeira Filho and Epitácio Sobrinho were alone, shooting birds following their Sunday dinner, together with their wives, at Epitácio's house in Casa Amarela, an outlying neighborhood of Recife. A crime of passion, the murder's precise cause remained bitterly disputed. No one, however, including Epitácio Sobrinho, disputed that the victim died from several gunshot wounds delivered by his wife's cousin after a furious fistfight. And although there were no witnesses to Epitácio's confrontation with Bandeira Filho, both his wife—Laura Mattos—and her close friend Clarice later contradicted his own testimony regarding what had taken place on the Sunday afternoon and the preceding day.[14]

Initially fleeing the murder scene, a wooded area near a stream at the edge of the city that belonged to Epitácio Sobrinho's neighbor, the murderer surrendered himself to Recife's chief of police a full day after he had killed Dr. Bandeira. And he did so in the mansion of his older and very wealthy brother, the prominent Recife businessman, Col. João Pessoa de Queiroz. Surrounded by his family members and helped by three lawyers, a visibly distraught Epitácio Sobrinho assumed full responsibility for the crime. In the weeks that followed, his detailed testimony that he had killed Bandeira Filho after denouncing him as a "traitor"—for having betrayed him with his wife—was corroborated by his and Laura's household servants. Nevertheless, on November 10, Epitácio Sobrinho was remanded to the Pernambuco State Penitentiary, since, as the judge emphasized, the law was clear that in such cases the

[14] Epitácio Sobrinho [Pessoa de Queiroz] to Tio Epitácio (Recife), 10 Nov. 1922, AEP/73. Correspondence related to this case and cited below is filed in Pasta 73 of the AEP (where usually it was unnumbered), unless otherwise noted. Where references are consecutive, therefore, the standard AEP designation has been omitted. This description of the crime draws also on accounts published in *Diario de Pernambuco* (Recife), 7 and 9 Nov. 1922 and on Clarice's statement given to the Recife police, which was partly published on 20 and 21 Nov. 1922 in the same newspaper. According to a portion of Bandeira Filho's autopsy published in *Diario de Pernambuco* on November 7, he received two mortal wounds in the back, one in the lumbar region and the other behind his left lung. Each wound contained over twenty-five pieces of buckshot and was fired at very close range, for clothing around the wounds was badly burned.

murderer was not only a potential threat to public safety but he himself might be in need of protection from the relatives of the victim, if they sought revenge.[15]

Together with her Cavalcanti de Albuquerque cousins in Umbuseiro, Clarice's brothers supported her when she contended that her husband's murder had been unprovoked and that there was no foundation to the charge he had maintained an adulterous relationship with Laura. Margarida Assunção Santiago, Clarice's mother and the strong matriarchal figure among the Umbuseiro Pessoas since her husband's death seven years earlier, even insisted that the crime had been premeditated. For her part, Laura Mattos remained with Clarice and under the protection of the murdered man's brothers-in-law, refusing to return to her husband of fourteen years.[16]

In a letter addressed to Mary Sayão Pessoa, wife of ex-President Epitácio, in which she pleaded her innocence of adultery, Laura Mattos revealed the strong undercurrents of antagonism and rivalry that existed between Epitácio's sister Mirandola and his sister-in-law Margarida da Assunção and their respective children. In discussing Bandeira Filho's murder during the police investigation, she characterized her husband as "an instrument of his mother [Mirandola] and his brothers, most notably, João Pessoa de Queiroz." Margarida da Assunção and Antônio Filho, not to mention João and Francisco Pessoa de Queiroz, also revealed in their letters to Epitácio the extent to which profits from the federal drought relief works had so recently fanned the competition among Epitácio's sets of nephews.[17]

[15] Epitácio Sobrinho to Tio Epitácio (Recife), 10 Nov. 1922. *Diario de Pernambuco*, 7 and 11 Nov. 1922. The local judge (juíz municipal of the Fifth District of Recife) who originally ruled for preventive detention (under Art. 13, Par. 2 of Law No. 2.033 of 1871 and No. 2.110 of 1909) stated that, when his indictment went to the State Supreme Court (a mandatory provision) for review, his ruling would be sustained. *Diario de Pernambuco*, 11 Nov. 1922.

[16] Toinho [Antônio Pessoa Filho] to Epitácio (Recife), 26 Dec. 1922. "There is not one shred of evidence in the documents [presented in court] to support the criminal's actions [i.e., his defense that he acted for reasons of "family honor"]," Antônio Filho wrote his uncle. Margarida da Assunção concluded that "Bandeira was condemned some time ago," and based her charge that the murder had been premeditated on the confession of a seamstress who had worked for the wife of one of Epitácio Sobrinho's brothers. The woman, Margarida alleged, had told her that she and her mistress had heard the brothers plotting to kill Bandeira Filho, but feared that if they warned him they, too, would be killed. Sinhá Pessoa [Margarida da Assunção Santiago] to Epitácio (Rio de Janeiro), 4 Jan. 1923.

[17] Portions of Laura's statement to the police, published in *Diario de Pernambuco*, 10 Nov. 1922. In the statement she was quoted as saying she believed her

The murder of Bandeira Filho acquired important significance beyond the Pessoa extended family, once Epitácio Sobrinho became a fugitive and received homísio, or effective sanctuary, from Col. José Pereira of Princesa. Although Epitácio Sobrinho had been indicted for murder when he was remanded to preventive detention, in late December his indictment was reversed on appeal and he was freed. Margarida da Assunção and Antônio Filho assumed that the presiding judge acted in favor of the defendant because he had been suborned by Epitácio Sobrinho's powerful brothers. Determined that he should stand trial, they were initially frustrated by the unwillingness of judges to serve in a capacity that would antagonize the Pessoa de Queiroz. Nevertheless, in late February the case was again brought and the original indictment for murder reinstated.[18] Once again, Epitácio was to be remanded to custody

---

husband had committed the murder "not only because of the anonymous letters [charging her with infidelity, which Epitácio Sobrinho claimed he had received but never produced] and his flight from the scene of the crime but also because her husband is a victim and an instrument of his mother and his brothers, notably João Pessoa de Queiroz." To Mary Sayão Pessoa, she wrote, ". . . if his family had wanted, [Epitácio Sobrinho] would not have done this [i.e., murdered Bandeira Filho], especially my mother-in-law, who has an enormous influence on her sons. They carry out her orders." Laura Mattos to Mary [Sayão] Pessoa (n.p., Recife?), 17 Dec. 1922. Margarida da Assunção reminded her brother-in-law how quickly the Pessoa de Queiroz had become wealthy during his presidency: "Remember the nominations [appointments] of inspectors and employees in the customs house which they obtained from you, and the efforts they went to in obtaining them? Already, you can see today that it is not possible for someone who has neither an inheritance or a great stroke of luck to become a millionaire so fast and so many times over." Sinhá Pessoa [Margarida da Assunção Santiago] to Epitácio (Rio de Janeiro), 4 Jan. 1923. See also J. Joffily, *O porto politico*. João Pessoa de Queiroz, who until the murder had invested some of Margarida da Assunção's money in his enterprises, also cast doubt on how his Umbuseiro cousins had acquired their assets: "Many times you have told us, 'In my family there are violent individuals, even murderers; however, there are no thieves.' What do you think now?" João Pessoa de Queiroz to Meu Caro Tio e Padrinho [Epitácio Pessoa] (Recife), 11 Feb. 1923. He also blamed Epitácio's policies as president for the loss of 5,000 contos he suffered in the drop in the sugar market. But, like his brother Epitácio Sobrinho, he had disapproved of Clarice's marriage to Bandeira Filho and said that if Clarice's father had been alive, it would not have taken place. Idem to idem, (Recife), 30 Mar. 1924; Epitácio Sobrinho to Sinhàzinha [Margarida da Assunção Santiago] (Recife), 10 Dec. 1922 (a handcopied letter which Antônio Pessoa Filho made of the original and sent to Epitácio).

[18] Sinhá Pessoa [Margarida da Assunção Santiago] to Epitácio (Rio de Janeiro), 4 Jan. 1923. Toinho [Antônio Pessoa Filho] to Epitácio (Rio de Janeiro), 26 Dec. 1922. Probably on December 24, Epitácio Sobrinho's indictment was set aside on the ground that he had committed the murder "while acting in a state of being totally deprived of his reason." On February 27, 1923, Federal District Judge José Ulisses

in the Pernambuco Penitentiary. But before he could be placed under arrest, he fled Recife for the backlands of Pernambuco, Ceará, Rio Grande do Norte, and Paraíba.

Gubernatorial efforts to curb the local privilege of homísio had become more determined since 1912, although they enjoyed only marginal success. In Epitácio Sobrinho's case, Gov. Solon de Lucena had to face a challenge delivered by a backlands boss recently acknowledged as one of Lampião's protectors and a local powerholder capable of fielding his own army of retainers and henchmen—Col. José Pereira Lima. A loyal Epitacista since 1909, when he succeeded to his father's mandate to rule the município of Princesa, Zé Pereira had also served for over a decade as a state assemblyman. Furthermore, he was tied to the Pessoa de Queiroz by ritual kinship, for he was compadre to both Epitácio Sobrinho and João Pessoa de Queiroz, who was also his major business partner. Together with Col. José Pessoa de Queiroz, Col. Zé Pereira was a partner in the import-export trade that tied the southern alto sertão of Paraíba to Recife. Most of Zé Pereira's merchandise, which he sold wholesale to distributors in southern Paraíba, proceeded from the Companhia de Tecelagem de Seda e de Algodão, the cotton and silk factories owned by the Pessoa de Queiroz. And Zé Pereira's exports of cotton and hides found their way from his local suppliers in Paraíba to the warehouses of the Pessoa de Queiroz on the Rua da Imperatriz and the Avenida Marquês de Olinda in Recife.

By June 1923, Epitácio Sobrinho had settled down to a comfortable life in Princesa, at the invitation of Col. José Pereira, beyond the reach of the Pernambuco State Police. Despite the efforts of his powerful uncle to persuade him to return to Recife for trial, Epitácio Sobrinho remained in Princesa for nearly two years, building a home that was considered the best in town. But he was an embarrassment to Gov. Solon de Lucena, who owed his election to ex-President Epitácio, due to the continued demands of Clarice's brothers that Solon either send the Paraíba State Police to arrest their cousin or expel him to Pernambuco where he would be imprisoned. Solon, who was distantly related to all the cousins, pro-

de Luna reinstated the indictment for murder, offering a long and erudite legal opinion to the effect that Epitácio Sobrinho was in possession of his reason on the day of the murder. It is published in *Diario de Pernambuco*, 31 Mar. 1923. See also "O processo Epitácio Pessoa de Queiroz: Os deploráveis incidentes," in *Diário de Pernambuco*, 9 Feb. 1923, which discusses "the strange proceedings of Judge Aquino Ribeiro in the trial of Epitácio Pessoa de Queiroz, which placed the arrested prisoner in liberty. . . ."

tested that he wanted to remain neutral in what he delicately termed "an intimate family matter" and "a moral crime"—since adultery was the presumed motive.[19]

More menacingly, the Pessoa de Queiroz in Recife objected to what they saw as Solon's condemnation of their brother's extended residence in Princesa as well as to Zé Pereira's offer of homísio. But they were more furious over their uncle's direct interference in what they regarded as a family matter, for Epitácio had written to remonstrate that they "did not have the right to demand of this friend [Solon de Lucena] such a sacrifice [i.e., that Epitácio Sobrinho remain in Princesa] when he is governor of the state [and] responsible for the legal [administration] of justice in the territory he governs."[20] In this respect, their uncle's position was very revealing of the evolution of family-based politics in Paraíba, for rather than attempting to assist the sons of Col. Antônio Pessoa, he appeared to be more genuinely annoyed that his oligarchy was being used to harbor a fugitive and that homísio still counted more than the obligation to stand trial when indicted. This stance, which broke the "neutrality" that the Pessoa de Queiroz expected him to maintain, cost Epitácio dearly in terms of the balance of good will he had maintained between his sets of nephews in Recife and Umbuseiro. With the expiration of Solon's term as governor, in October 1924, his successor—João Suassuna—virtually guaranteed Epitácio Sobrinho immunity from arrest or eviction from Paraíba. The fact that Suassuna would not satisfy Carlos Pessoa and Antônio Filho, by placing pressure on his old friend Col. José Pereira to deny refuge to the fugitive and oblige him to stand trial, appears to have been an important factor in Suassuna's growing alienation from the sons of his mentor, Col.

[19] Solon de Lucena to Epitácio (Capital), 14 June 1923, AEP/12/206. Solon referred to Epitácio Sobrinho as "indicted." Details on Epitácio Sobrinho's residence in Princesa were provided by Dr. Fernando Nóbrega, personal interview (Rio de Janeiro), 1 Aug. 1978. Copies of the letters Epitácio sent to his Pessoa de Queiroz nephews in 1923 and 1924 about these events could not be located. But João Pessoa de Queiroz quoted his uncle's own words to him: "Your Excellency said [to us] 'You ["Vocês"—Francisco placed the familiar form of you in quotes] do not have the right to reduce Paraíba to the homísio of an indicted escapee from Pernambuco.' This is very harsh language for us." Idem to Epitácio (Recife), 30 Mar. 1924.

[20] Francisco Pessoa de Queiroz to Epitácio (Recife), 17 Feb. 1924. João Pessoa de Queiroz also telegraphed Epitácio in protest over the criticism he received from his uncle: "Epitácio [Sobrinho] has been visiting all over Pernambuco, Paraíba, and Rio Grande do Norte [and] the only person to be attacked for offering him hospitality was José Pereira Lima. . . . The sons of Margarida Assunção did that." Telegram of 30 March 1924. See also idem to idem, letter of 30 Mar. 1924 (Recife).

Antônio Pessoa. The competition which flared openly between Suassuna and Carlos Pessoa over Suassuna's seat in Congress drew directly on the animosity engendered by Suassuna's personal loyalty to Col. Zé Pereira in the matter of the homísio he had extended to Epitácio Sobrinho.[21]

The murder of Bandeira Filho profoundly affected Epitácio's relationship with his Pessoa de Queiroz nephews, but already it had been severely tried during his presidency. A number of his nephews had moved to Rio de Janeiro after his election to work either in the presidential office or—as with Col. José Pessoa de Queiroz—to be attached to the Ministry of War.[22] (For this reason, the national press had dubbed Epitácio "Tio"—Uncle.) The Pessoa de Queiroz, however, acquired the reputation for seeking to expand their business opportunities through the influence of their uncle. Although as a young man Epitácio had enjoyed good, even warm, relations with the two oldest Pessoa de Queiroz brothers—João and José—by the time he became president his special relationship with João Pessoa Cavalcanti de Albuquerque, the son of his sister Maria, was obvious to everyone. Only thirteen years older than João Pessoa, Epitácio—who was without sons—behaved liked a surrogate father toward his favorite nephew. He had taken the boy to Rio de Janeiro at age ten, and placed him in the national military school in 1889, intending—with the help of Col. José Pessoa—to make an army officer of him. Although João Pessoa proved too rebellious—he eventually had to resign from the Military Academy and returned to Recife in 1899—Epitácio continued to advise him

[21] Antônio Pessoa Filho, in his letter to Epitácio of 26 December 1922, already had referred to the interference of João Pessoa de Queiroz in Solon's anticipated nomination of Carlos Pessoa to the Chamber of Deputies, alleging that his cousin had traveled to Parahyba for the express purpose of dissuading Solon from naming him.

[22] Epitácio's brother, Gen. José da Silva Pessoa, served as commander of Military Police in the Federal District during his presidency. He therefore commanded the troops that quelled the demonstrators during the Copacabana Revolt on July 5, 1922. Venâncio's brother-in-law, Gen. Antônio Neiva de Figueirêdo, was also attached to the General Staff during the same years, and Epitácio's nephew, Col. José Pessoa de Queiroz, was attached to the Ministry of War. (Although like his older brother João he was a coronel, José held regular military rank, not that of the National Guard.) The opposition in Paraíba had several military figures in the high command in Rio de Janeiro during Epitácio's presidency, the most prominent of whom were Gen. Ivo Soares and Gen. Inácio Cavalcanti Monteiro (brother of the opposition's leader, Judge Heráclito Cavalcanti Monteiro). And one of the young cadets who instigated the Copacabana Revolt was the son of either Heráclito or Gen. Cavalcanti Monteiro.

in adulthood. The special guidance he gave João Pessoa fueled competition between the older Pessoa de Queiroz brothers and their cousin.

In Recife, João Pessoa lived with Col. Antônio Pessoa and his family, who had abandoned living in Umbuseiro in the first years of this century, because of death threats from the bandit Antônio Silvino.[23] Two years after taking his degree from the Recife Law Faculty, in 1905, João Pessoa married Maria Luisa de Sousa Leão, the daughter of Pernambuco's former governor, Segismundo Gonçalves. He established his law practice in Recife and taught at the Normal School. In 1909, he left the Northeast for Rio de Janeiro, where presumably with Epitácio's intervention, he began his bureaucratic career in the federal government as an official auditor for the Navy in the Interior Ministry's Division of Ports. Like his uncle, Col. Antônio Pessoa, João Pessoa had a talent for accounting, which similarly would be used to bring greater fiscal accountability to Paraíba's State Treasury. He would later serve as the official auditor of the Paraíba State Treasury in the administration of Camilo de Holanda and João Suassuna. By 1914, during the presidency of Hermes da Fonseca, João Pessoa had risen to become auditor general of the Navy. That same year, he served as an interim justice on Brazil's Supreme Military Tribunal, but returned to his former post in 1915. With Epitácio's accession to the presidency in 1919, João Pessoa's career took a new direction. He was chosen from three candidates proposed by Epitácio to become justice of the Supreme Military Tribunal, Brazil's highest military court. He was still serving in this capacity in 1928, when Epitácio recruited him for the governorship of Paraíba.

These details of João Pessoa's career suggest how Epitácio's patronage role in the family, especially as president of Brazil, led to the hostility of the Recife cousins, particularly João and Francisco Pessoa de Queiroz. The Pessoa de Queiroz brothers' high political ambitions ultimately could not be realized. They felt shortchanged by Epitácio in comparison with João Pessoa, although their uncle's denials of political support to them were based on his own ethical judgments or common sense. Shortly before his death, João Pessoa explicitly acknowledged his cousins' competitive strivings on a personal, quasi-sibling level. He wrote Epitácio that Francisco Pessoa de Queiroz "always wanted to be Governor of

[23] Biographical details on João Pessoa are from Ademar Vidal, *João Pessoa e a Revolução de 30* (Rio de Janeiro: Edições GRAAL, 1978), pp. 18–19; and from "Há quarenta anos morria João Pessoa," *O Globo* [Rio de Janeiro], 27 July 1970.

Paraíba instead of me. . . . In Pernambuco he is out of politics, for he cannot rise higher than federal deputy."[24]

The jockeying for position by the Pessoa de Queiroz had another dimension that dated from Epitácio's years as a senator. The Pessoa de Queiroz had sought political office in Pernambuco—as members of the opposition to Gov. Manuel Borba—and their determination had embarrassed Epitácio in the national press by leading to a story associating him erroneously with "cangaceiros" and his old adversaries in the 1912 insurrection. In January 1918, Epitácio flatly declined to help Francisco Pessoa de Queiroz obtain nomination for federal deputy from Pernambuco's oligarchical boss, Borba. João Pessoa de Queiroz asked Epitácio to intercede directly with President Venceslau Brás on behalf of his younger brother's candidacy and obtain a "guarantee" of "free" elections.[25] In other words, since Borba opposed the Pessoa de Queiroz, they wanted the president to apply pressure to prevent the governor from sending in the Pernambuco State Police to insure that votes in the 3rd Congressional District would be cast for his official candidate. Since Borba already had ordered the local bosses in the 3rd district to deliver their votes to his candidate, the Pessoa de Queiroz knew that without presidential influence they never would carry the election. Epitácio categorically refused, declining to create an issue at the federal level and believing that Francisco's ambition was causing him to act imprudently.[26]

Having failed to obtain Epitácio's intercession, but not abandoning an expectation that it would be forthcoming, Francisco and João Pessoa de Queiroz resorted to a military alternative. Detachments of capangas, or thugs, were marshaled from Col. José Pereira's forces in Princesa as well as from Dr. Augusto de Santa Cruz's retainers in Alagoa do Monteiro, for an attack on Triunfo, in adjacent Pernambuco.[27] On 22 January 1918, the *Estado de São Paulo* reported that "the partisans of Senator Epitácio Pessoa" were organizing "armed groups in the border cities of both Paraíba and Ceará for the purpose of invading the Pernambuco backlands under the command of the famous cangaceiro Santa Cruz." Gov-

[24] João Pessoa to Epitácio (Capital), 26 Aug. 1929, AEP/9/142.

[25] João Pessoa de Queiroz to Epitácio (Recife), 4 Jan. 1918, AEP/73; João Pessoa de Queiroz to Epitácio, 22 Jan. 1918, AEP/73.

[26] Francisco Pessoa de Queiroz to Epitácio (Recife), tel. of 25 Jan. 1918, AEP/73/unnumbered; and Epitácio to Francisco Pessoa de Queiroz (Rio de Janeiro), 25 Jan. 1918, attached to preceding.

[27] Augusto Santa Cruz to Epitácio (Alagoa do Monteiro), 2 Mar. 1918, AEP/12/112.

ernor Borba sent a large contingent of State Police to repel the invaders from Triunfo, which forced them to abandon the capture of the 3rd District. Only when the Commercial Association of Recife—which had sponsored Francisco's candidacy—withdrew its support, did he finally concede the defeat Epitácio had predicted.[28]

During Epitácio's final months in the presidency, the Pessoa de Queiroz thoroughly angered him when they attempted again to use his influence to thwart Pernambuco's oligarchical boss. Epitácio's controversial and much-censured federal intervention in Pernambuco in November 1922, weeks before he left office, appears to have been due to his Recife nephews' manipulation of his presidential authority.[29] The officer posted to command the federal garrison in Recife, Col. Jaime Pessoa da Silveira, was assigned by Col. José Pessoa de Queiroz, the youngest of the three brothers, because he was attached officially to the Ministry of War during his uncle's administration.[30] This time, the Pessoa de Queiroz were seeking to expel Borba from oligarchical leadership and to secure Francisco's recently won seat in Congress. And thanks to the fall of Borba, Francisco remained in the Pernambuco delegation in the Chamber of Deputies for most of the 1920s. Two months after the Pernambuco intervention, Epitácio refused a gift of an expensive automobile from Francisco, the second of the three brothers. He attached to it a cold denial of his kinship with his nephew and pointed out how inappropriate it would be to accept such an expensive present.[31] Thus, even without the murder of Bandeira

[28] Firms belonging to Recife's Commercial Association feared a "conflagration in the interior" if the Pessoa de Queiroz pressed Francisco's candidacy further. Francisco Pessoa de Queiroz to Epitácio (Recife), 30 Jan. 1918, AEP/73. A year later and days before Epitácio's election to the presidency, Epitácio again had to restrain the Pessoa de Queiroz' political ambitions and warn them not "to get involved in partisan fights." Epitácio to Pessoa [de] Queiroz (Paris), tels. of 5 and 9 Apr. 1919, AEP/73/unnumbered.

[29] L. Pessôa, *Epitacio Pessôa*, 2:562–63. Author's interview with Irmã Maria Regina do Santo Rosário [Laurita Pessoa], Rio de Janeiro, Oct. 1970. Many of Borba's partisans were killed when the federal garrison in Recife used force to depose him. The commander, Jaime Pessoa da Silveira, gave orders to shell the city.

[30] Silva, *1922 Copacabana*, pp. 48–50 and 106. [João] Jaime Pessoa da Silveira (b. 1865) was a Paraibano and bore both the names of Epitácio's family and that of Col. Antônio Pessoa's in-laws, but Laurita Pessoa denied in the 1970s that he was a relative of her father.

[31] "It is not possible for me to accept your present of an automobile. . . . If it were from an old personal friend, *a relative*, it would be understood . . . but from a citizen who never was known as my particular friend and who is director of a firm receiving favors directly from the Government, you can imagine the bad stories . . ." (ital-

Filho, Epitácio's relationship with the sons of his sister Miranda had seriously deteriorated. This is why by early 1923 he could do little to improve the worsening situation between them and his other two sets of nephews in Umbuseiro, where—according to both Antônio Pessoa Filho and João Pessoa de Queiroz—armed clashes between the retainers of the cousin sets were resulting in beatings and injuries on both sides.[32]

The Parentela and Socioeconomic Change

The quasi-sibling rivalry among Epitácio's sets of nephews can be seen merely as an illustration of the parentela's tendency toward fragmentation at the first-cousin level. Epitácio's sister Miranda had been given in marriage to a family whose economic interests were centered in another state, although they possessed some property in Umbuseiro. Hence, from the perspective of Brazilian kinship organization, the growing alienation of the Pessoa de Queiroz from the other two collateral branches of Pessoas did not represent an unusual development. However, this antagonistic segmentation deserves closer scrutiny, for it also illustrates socioeconomic and political changes that had been overtaking elite extended families in the Northeast during the second half of the Old Republic.

Several factors suggested that the Pessoas' elite family solidarity—like that of many parentelas—was more susceptible to disintegration by the 1920s. Since Epitácio had once enjoyed a close relationship with his older Pessoa de Queiroz nephews, which dated to his vacations from the Recife Law School, the timing of the relationship's disintegration deserves notice. In the first place, it was directly affected by Epitácio's increasing access to federal pa-

ics added). Epitácio to Francisco Pessoa de Queiroz (Rio de Janeiro), 8 Jan. 1923, AEP/73. An effective denial of his kinship with his nephew, this repudiation by Epitácio may have more reflected his anger over the murder of Bandeira Filho than the proffered gift. Antônio Filho's letter raising the possibility of premeditation was written only four days earlier (Dec. 26, 1922). Epitácio may also have already learned what his nephew João Pessoa divulged in 1929, that Francisco Pessoa de Queiroz, who had access to his presidential office, allegedly had unethically used official stationery to write recommendations on behalf of his friends seeking to do business with United States firms. João Pessoa to Epitácio (Capital), 16 Aug. 1929, AEP/9/142.

[32] João Pessoa de Queiroz to Epitácio (Recife), 11 Feb. 1924, AEP/73. Toinho [Antônio Pessoa Filho] to Epitácio, 16 Dec. 1922. Solon de Lucena to Epitácio (Capital), 3 Nov. 1923, AEP/12/21.

tronage and influence, which culminated during his presidency.[33] In the second place, Brazil's federal system of government, adopted in 1891, profoundly constrained the political boundaries of the relationship. Finally, the political context of an expanding State, during Epitácio's leadership of the Paraíba oligarchy, further eroded family solidarity. This dimension became most obvious in the attempt to bring Epitácio Sobrinho Pessoa de Queiroz to trial for murder. The State's encroachment on local prerogatives complicated and conflicted with the Pessoas' ties of family loyalty, bringing to a crisis point divisions that had been deepening for years. The implications of a federal structure in the context of these extended family differences deserve elaboration.

During the Empire, a parentela's distribution across provincial boundaries usually had worked to strengthen its political influence and to cushion its economic losses. While this still could be the case during the Republic, a parentela's spatial distribution generally brought mixed negative and positive effects in terms of political utility and group cohesion. The 1891 Constitution gave the states authority previously granted to the central government.

[33] IFOCS patronage widened the divisions between the Pessoa de Queiroz and the Umbuseiro Pessoas. João Pessoa de Queiroz accused "the sons of Margarida Assunção" of enriching themselves at the expense of IFOCS, pointing to the "houses of the nabobs built from the money for the droughts in Umbuseiro's Natuba district" as well as "properties bought there with federal funds during Epitácio's presidency." João Pessoa de Queiroz to Epitácio (Recife), 2 Feb. 1924, AEP/73. See also idem to idem, 15 Apr. 1930.

The Pessoa de Queiroz apparently became prosperous only after 1900, when Col. José Pessoa de Queiroz's importing business grew. His youngest brother, Francisco, was sent to Recife in 1894 to be raised in the home of his godparents, Maria Alexandrina Cavalcanti (Marocas, his great-aunt by marriage) and Antônio Leonardo(s) de Menezes Amorim, because his parents "depended on agriculture and small-scale stockraising for a living" and Francisco "could have a better chance in life." A. Lopes, *F. Pessoa de Queiroz*, p. 28. From age four, therefore, Francisco's upbringing in the Recife household of his Aunt Marocas as a foster son duplicated the pattern of his Uncle Epitácio's childhood twenty years earlier. (See Fig. B.1.) Undoubtedly, this was also the reason Francisco became the only Pessoa de Queiroz brother to become a *doutor*. As a graduate of the Recife Law Faculty in 1911, he had studied with both Col. José Pereira and João Suassuna. There is some evidence to suggest that Francisco's greater anger toward Epitácio Pessoa after 1922—in comparison with that of either João or José Pessoa de Queiroz—was connected to a direct rivalry with Epitácio as Marocas's foster son, rather than to rivalry of a quasi-sibling type with his cousin João Pessoa Cavalcanti de Albuquerque. After his death at age ninety, in 1980, and his reburial in 1982 in the Igreja da Conceição dos Militares, Recife, the remains of Marocas and Antônio Leonardo(s) were reburied with him. Ibid., pp. 29 and 153.

Most states also adopted a new electoral qualification that governors be natives of the states where they were elected. Hence, the recruitment pool for state executives narrowed, and men such as Carlos Pessoa or Francisco Pessoa de Queiroz, who yearned to govern Paraíba oligarchically on behalf of their uncle, were prohibited by the adoption in the Republic of new rules appropriate for a decentralized political system.

The Pessoa de Queiroz sought political influence in Paraíba because their varied and complex economic interests needed protection in that state. Their principal market in the Paraíba backlands was jeopardized because the Federal Constitution had vested the power to tax exports in the states. Their commerce became highly vulnerable to the Paraíba State Assembly's revision of the export tax schedule. Thus, three Pessoa de Queiroz brothers—João, José, and Francisco—sought political influence within Epitácio's oligarchy to counter the inevitable proposals to use fiscal incentives to channel backlands production toward the Capital and Cabedêlo.

The antagonistic segmentation of the Pessoa de Queiroz also has to be assessed in the context of the economic boom of the 1920s, which nourished the hostility between them and their Umbuseiro cousins. First, horizontal solidarity within elite extended families, always a limited phenomenon, was weakening, as economic specialization, coupled with residential distancing, made inroads on the collectivity of family interest associated with an agrarian society. New opportunities for urban employment, for instance, attracted a number of the sons of Col. Antônio Pessoa and several of João Pessoa's brothers from Umbuseiro to the Capital. Second, the opportunity for rapid and unparalleled prosperity encouraged splintering within large and influential elite extended families, for it fueled competition and underscored differential status positions among and within cousin branches. The Pessoa de Queiroz, for instance, amassed considerably greater wealth than either of the Umbuseiro cousin sets, some of whom still farmed or ranched a modest landed patrimony there. The success of the risk-taking entrepreneurial Recife branch inevitably made many cousins in the Umbuseiro sets envious of their achievements.

Finally, as a boom economy brought stresses and strains to elite family solidarity, the state governments of the Northeast were beginning to take a more aggressive stance vis-à-vis local issues. This trend introduced greater conflict and division within both nuclear and extended families, as they sought strategies to counter

State encroachment.[34] Thus, the struggle that exploded among Epitácio's nephews in 1930 could be traced directly to the state government's internal offensive against local prerogatives that protected fugitives as well as its growing ability to challenge Pernambuco's domination of its backlands economy. Although it is possible to view the "Tributary War" that ensued as indicative of the familiar process of antagonistic kinship segmentation, such a perspective overlooks the conflict's deeper roots in socio-economic and political changes that transpired during the two decades after 1910.

João Pessoa and the Tributary War

João Pessoa, Governor

Epitácio's decision to place João Pessoa in Paraíba's governorship in the June 1928 election enabled him to reject diplomatically Suassuna's preference for his godson and protégé, State Chief of Police Júlio Lira. But, by imposing a favorite relative and close friend, Epitácio intended to do more than preempt internal dissent over the succession issue. He was also considering the national political context. After leaving the presidency, Epitácio lacked an advantageous relationship with the president of Brazil for the first time since the dictatorship of Floriano Peixoto. In trying to convince Suassuna to accept João Pessoa, Epitácio cautioned that the choice of a governor should not facilitate "southern imperialist action," and stressed that dissension within Paraíba's political elite over Lira's candidacy "would whet the appetite of southern politics, which is always inclined to intervene in the choice of northeastern governors."[35] Maintaining that he had been approached by members of Congress and the executive branch, who were unanimous in advising him that an "unknown candidate" such as Lira would be unacceptable at the federal level, Epitácio then insisted

[34] As a case in point, Joaquim Pessoa, brother of Gov. João Pessoa, sided against his brothers and their Umbuseiro cousins and in favor of the Dantas of Teixeira as early as 1924, and then in 1930 supported the Pessoa de Queiroz. Solon de Lucena to Epitácio (Capital), 3 Nov. 1922, AEP/12/192.

[35] Epitácio to João Suassuna (Rio de Janeiro), 3 Jan. 1928, AEP/12/285. Suassuna was reported to be retaliating for the rejection of Júlio Lira by "organizing a personal political movement in the backlands" and was said to have given a speech in which he "frankly retracted his solidarity with Epitácio." José Américo de Almeida to Epitácio (Capital), 30 Mar. 1928, AEP/12/219.

that his designation of João Pessoa as Suassuna's successor was dictated by his abilities as "a Paraíbano, not a relative."[36] This assertion failed to carry conviction. Nor did the declaration that the new governor should be "one who is outside state politics, not directly involved, so he cannot have personal preferences" quite describe João Pessoa.[37]

Since 1923, Epitácio had been spending at least six months every year in Europe, largely in connection with his seat on the Permanent International Court of Justice. His personal direction of Paraíba's oligarchy, consequently, lost some of the regular contact he had formerly maintained through trusted emissaries who traveled between Parahyba and Rio de Janeiro. With João Pessoa as governor, he must have concluded, he could retain a more secure control on the oligarchy's leadership echelon, while it would be managed directly on behalf of his family-based group. On his part, João Pessoa averred that he accepted the nomination as a family obligation that he owed to Epitácio Pessoa.[38] Yet he may also have intended to use executive office in Paraíba as a stepping stone to a new career in the national legislature.

João Pessoa is remembered in Paraíba as a reformer with many progressive goals for his native state. He was, however, poorly equipped by both experience and temperament to undertake them. His career preparation had shaped him as an auditor and a judge, meaning that he was used to pronouncing rather than to negotiating decisions. In the give-and-take politics of Paraíba's local bosses, he was at a decided disadvantage. By personality, he was extremely impatient and given to the outbursts of Pessoa temper that had inspired the British consul in Recife to characterize his younger brothers and cousins from Umbuseiro as "a band of well-known hotheads."[39] While such characterizations deserve to be treated cautiously, certainly João Pessoa lacked the reserve that had enabled his uncle—who also possessed a formidable temper—to remain in control of his anger. Thus, while João Pessoa possessed compelling gifts as a public orator and an informal conversationalist, and displayed even a charming personal style in win-

[36] Epitácio to João Suassuna (Rio de Janeiro), 3 Jan. 1928, AEP/12/285.

[37] Ibid.

[38] L. Pessôa, *Epitacio Pessôa*, 2:789.

[39] William Seeds to A. Henderson (Recife), 12 Aug. 1930, Public Record Office, London, Foreign Office General Correspondence, Political, FO 371/14200, file no, A 5839/106/6. Transcripts of Crown-copyright records in the Public Record Office appear by permission of the Controller of H.M. Stationery Office.

ning over followers to his political views, he could just as easily antagonize. In treating with the local bosses, the latter tendency often became uppermost, for it was also wedded to a zealous belief in the correctness of his policies. José Américo de Almeida, a great admirer and personal friend of the new governor, who served him as secretary of the interior and justice, observed that "nothing could assuage the rigidity of João Pessoa's convictions, which were part of his blood and embedded in his very nature."[40] A less friendly observation, however, placed him in "that class of people for whom the best remedy for a headache is the guillotine."[41]

João Pessoa, Reformer

Zealous for change, João Pessoa began his administration by addressing his predecessor's gubernatorial record antagonistically, and with reason. Boosting his own "new broom" sweep in government, he authorized an official audit of the State Treasury. Civil servants had not been paid for six months and the Treasury was bare. After the audit's results were revealed, even the Rio de Janeiro papers proclaimed that Suassuna had emptied if for personal gain—and absconded with the silverware that belonged in the governor's palace.[42] Whatever the facts of the scandal, João Pessoa's investigation and denunciation of Manuel Madruga, Suassuna's treasurer, accelerated the polarization within the leadership echelon of Paraíba's oligarchy. In the backlands, many of the "friends of 1915" read the action as further evidence of their rapid decline in "prestige."

If João Pessoa's political identity as a family oligarch can be overlooked—and what that implied for his role as governor—it is possible to evaluate his twenty-one months in office as a "protopopulist" phase in Paraíba's historical periodization. He introduced a new rhetoric and a new strategy of political mobilization which, though failing to fulfill his goals, signaled an important new direction for Paraíba's politics. From the moment he was in-

[40] Quoted in Ademar Vidal, *1930; história de João Pessoa e da Revolução na Paraíba* (São Paulo: Cia. Editôra Nacional, 1933), p. 23.

[41] Barbosa Lima Sobrinho, *A verdade sôbre a Revolução de Outubro* (São Paulo: n.p., 1933), p. 176. See also Vidal, *1930; história*, pp. 8–9.

[42] Suassuna's inspector of the treasury, Manuel Madruga, was found guilty of malfeasance of office and stealing government documents. "Copy of the Administrative Inquiry Conducted by the Inspector of the Treasury to Examine the Appropriation of Copies of State Treasury Documents by Former Inspector of the Treasury, Dr. Manuel Madruga," 28 Feb. 1929, AEP/9/64–78.

augurated, the governor announced his determination to eradicate the abuses classically associated with coronelismo—privately monopolized violence, fiscal irresponsibility, banditry, and the lack of due process in criminal proceedings. Styling himself a crusader for reform, João Pessoa brought to Paraíba some of the political impact of urbanization and industrialization that he had experienced in Rio de Janeiro. As a justice of the Supreme Military Tribunal, he had been part of the national capital's political elite. His brother Cândido Pessoa had just finished a term as a city councilman in Rio de Janeiro and another brother, Ivan Pessoa, would be recruited in the mid-1930s by the Federal District's first populist mayor—Pedro Ernesto—to be his secretary of finance.[43] João Pessoa's strategy in Paraíba appears to have been influenced by his own firsthand experience and observations in Brazil's largest city, where, undeniably, the social order derived from an agrarian and plantation society no longer could be maintained in the face of steady industrial expansion.

The "social question" emerged as a national issue in the 1920s. Ironically, as Boris Fausto notes, it had first been raised as a major campaign issue in the 1919 presidential race—by Epitácio's opponent, who carried the Federal District, Sen. Rui Barbosa. A growing industrial proletariat, drawing on hundreds of thousands of immigrants, had produced a militant anarcho-syndicalist movement by World War I. Thereafter, an organized body of strikers would be capable of forcing the government of the national capital to contend with Brazil's changing class structure. João Pessoa's adoption of what could be termed a multiclass appeal to catalyze support for his reforms appears to have borrowed from his understanding of social change in Rio de Janeiro, in spite of the enormous differences between the political milieux of his native state and that of a cosmopolitan city. Although Paraíba was by no means Rio de Janeiro, the impact of economic growth, technological change, and even marginal gains in industrialization affected social organization in similar respects. By 1928 the landed elite no longer exercised a tight control over the rural population, as the epidemic of brigandage revealed. Since 1923, when the IFOCS projects were abandoned by the federal government, the "nomadism" characteristic of part of the interior's labor force had increased. As a consequence, governors had confronted the eruption of violent clashes between landlords and tenants as well as urban

[43] Conniff, *Urban Politics*, pp. 98–107; and personal communication with the author, 30 Apr. 1984.

strikes and labor protests coordinated with Recife's better organized labor movement.[44]

Greater social differentiation in Paraíba's urban centers explained more directly João Pessoa's adoption of a proto-populist stance. Class consciousness among both the middle- and lower middle-class sectors emerged in their denunciations of the most unsavory practices commonly associated with coronelismo. These sectors lacked adequate representation in state and município government, where the most powerful agrarian entrepreneurs tended to dominate officeholding as a higher bourgeoisie or only the largest import–export concerns enjoyed an influential voice. João Pessoa therefore appealed to both these sectors, particularly to what could be called an awakening lower middle class and an emerging urban proletariat that sought certain guarantees, like an eight-hour day, from the State. He tried to build an alliance that included these urban elements to oppose a sector of the agrarian elite that popular rhetoric often condemned as "seigneurial" or, in Portuguese, as *"os mandatários,"* those who ruled arbitrarily in their own interests, and without accountability. Not surprisingly, such individuals could be encountered where tendencies toward latifundia were stronger and, usually, agrarian pursuits had remained less diversified—in the sugar zone and in the far backlands, where certain families with agro-pastoral interests also monopolized landowning. In these instances, the commitment to coronelismo—to local autonomy—was also strongest where family-based rule had been more tightly consolidated among only a few families and, frequently, where isolation also enhanced relative independence. João Pessoa, however, did not think in terms of mobilizing urban sectors against the agrarian order but of constructing a coalition that also drew on a sector in the countryside that recently had experienced downward mobility, namely small farmers, both freeholders and tenants. In this respect, he was competing openly for the allegiance of the rural oligarchy's electorate and counting on the antipathy toward individual landlords known for their exploitation and cruelty to gain him support. Yet it was in the urban centers that his rhetoric fell on fertile ground.

During the 1920s, for the first time in Paraíba's history, formally organized groups based on occupational status and proclaiming a class identity began to appear in significant numbers. Most of the

[44] Boris Fausto, *Trabalho urbano e conflito social, 1890–1920* (São Paulo: DIFEL/DIFUSÃO, 1979), p. 219. Solon de Lucena to Epitácio (Capital), 14 June 1923, AEP/12/206.

new organizations reflected occupational affiliation and possessed what the sociological literature describes as "top–down" organization, for they functioned in most cases to control the threatening consequences that derived from the emergence of an urban-industrial society, one gradually acquiring consciousness of class. Perhaps the best example of group formation after 1917 was the appearance in Campina Grande in 1920 of an Association of Employees in Commerce. This body proclaimed itself "instituted for the defense of class and seeking to foster among its members a love for the great principles of modern Socialism," but quickly disavowed any "enthusiasm for the sound of Lenin's trumpet."[45] The organization attracted the upper level of retail clerks and a white-collar managerial stratum. Not surprisingly, it emerged as the clientistic offspring of the higher bourgeoisie in the city's commerce and industry, for the parent organization, the Commercial Association of Campina Grande, had been founded only the year before to combat Gov. Camilo de Holanda's fiscal assault. By 1928, both commercial associations and associations of employees in commerce had been founded in Itabaiana, Pilar, Guarabira, and in distant Cajazeiras. Meanwhile, for the first time, a statewide Agrarian Society, founded in 1917, began to organize the more prosperous landowners after a decade of dormancy.

The associations of employees in commerce were direct responses by the higher bourgeoisie to the first significant strike actions in Paraíba, which occurred in 1917 and 1919. Working on behalf of the largest commercial firms and industrial plants, the associations were dedicated to teaching "man a just concept of his position . . . and his rights and duties, immunizing him against the revolutionary virus in contemporary society so profusely propagated by destructive demogoguery."[46] Because trade unions did not acquire full legal status until the 1930s, parallel associations were organized among workers in the artisanal trades, such as cobblers and tailors, and in the informal economy, such as street vendors and chauffeurs.[47] Alternatively, the more militant anarcho-syndicalists had made progress among some of the artisanal trades, but particularly attracted support from dock workers and railroad employees.

[45] *Almanach de Campina Grande para o anno de 1926* (Recife: Oficina Gráfica do *Jornal do Commercio*, 1925), pp. 73–74. Lino Gomes da Silva, founder of the Association of Employees in Commerce (fifty members), also founded Campina's Commercial Association. See also J. Joffily, *Revolta*, p. 131 (n. 2).

[46] *Almanach Campina 1926*, p. 73.

[47] A list of these associations appears in J. Joffily, *Revolta*, p. 132.

These formally organized groups enabled João Pessoa to embark on a strategy aimed at subordinating the entrenched coronelista bosses to the governor's centralizing authority by appealing to class interests broadly in the population. He created several financial institutions that furthered this goal and expanded the rural workers' only credit agency, the Caixa Rural Operária, founded in 1927, to eight statewide branches. Since many small farmers were no better off than foreiros—lessees—of the larger landlords, their factional loyalty was influenced by their status as dependent clients who sought credit annually for planting. The offer of an alternative source for credit, however limited in this case, was an innovative political tactic. But the fact that João Pessoa's public appeals to small farmers addressed their grievances against larger, extremely exploitative landlords made him even more popular. Not content to rely solely on rhetoric, the governor coupled his denunciations of "mandonismo" to well-publicized clashes with several influential coronéis known for their brutality. Thus the campaign against the patrimonial prerogatives of a certain wing of the bosses in his own coalition—and some in the opposition—gained him genuine support and explain why as recently as the 1970s oral interviewing revealed he was still recalled as a champion of the rights of small farmers.

The main thrust of financial and credit reform—or proposed reform, since the governor's conflict with the federal government aborted these innovations—nevertheless favored the commercial and industrial bourgeoisie of the larger cities, particularly the Capital. In 1924, Gov. Solon de Lucena had founded the State Bank of Paraíba (Banco do Estado da Paraíba).[48] Advocated as far back as the 1850s, this bank was completely reorganized as soon as João Pessoa took office. But when he found that the bank was inadequate for the credit needs of commerce and industry, he created the Commercial Bank of the State of Paraíba (Banco Comercial do Estado da Paraíba) in 1929. A land or mortgage bank was also founded, but eruption of the war with the Recife emporium in March 1930 left its existence on paper. These institutions served a dual purpose. First, they strengthened the governor's ties to the influential commercial sector in every major city. Second, they aimed at freeing Paraíba's commerce from financial dependence on the Recife capital market. As the cotton economy prospered

[48] The State Bank of Paraíba was actually founded over a decade earlier, but until João Pessoa's governorship it had existed only on paper. A commercial bank, by March 1929, 973 contos' worth of shares had been sold.

throughout the 1920s, the limited lending resources of a few affluent local capitalists—usually foreigners—or even the collective savings of elite families that historically functioned as limited sources of credit proved inadequate for the greater demand native entrepreneurs now demonstrated. João Pessoa's crackdown on the local bosses who withheld taxes from the State Treasury or even the federal government, while depriving them of the most important source of local capital, served his goal to enable the State to play a larger role in Paraíba's credit market. At the same time, in bypassing Recife's financial market, he intended to diminish Pernambuco's commercial penetration of Paraíba.

The main thrust of João Pessoa's reform program was political and reflective of the national mood. Even before July 1930, when he accepted the vice-presidential nomination to run with Getúlio Vargas on the Aliança Liberal (Liberal Alliance) ticket, he was campaigning in Paraíba for many of the goals that subsequently the Aliança adopted.[49] In the first phase of João Pessoa's centralizing campaign, he denounced the "seigneurial" practices associated with coronelismo: the exploitative land tenure structure, the theft of state revenues by local officials, and the exercise of private violence as a prerogative of local political power—singling out in particular cangaceiros and the coiteiros who, often as politicians, protected them. These were the hallmarks of so-called mandonismo, practices associated in widely varying degrees with the majority of the local bosses who ruled Paraíba's municípios and delivered votes to Epitácio's oligarchical machine. The new governor appointed José Américo de Almeida his secretary of interior and justice and enlisted him as a partner in curbing private violence. They adopted a two-pronged approach. First, examples were made of certain more retrograde bosses to demonstrate the governor's legitimate commitment to eradicate privately exercised violence and the corruption of the judicial system. Second, a determined campaign against banditry was initiated.

João Pessoa benefited from his predecessor's record of declining prosecutions of either alleged murderers or the rumored protectors of bandits. In Areia—José Américo's home town—he demoted the political boss, the brother of a federal deputy and the former boss,

[49] The following points in João Pessoa's advocated reforms for Paraíba coincided with the Aliança's platform: 1) the secret ballot; 2) economic redress for the Northeast; 3) fiscal reorganization; 4) tax reform; and 5) creation of new financial institutions—mortgage banks, rural credit angencies, and state banks. Vidal, *1930; história*, pp. 19 and 26.

because of the criminal indictments brought against him and his brother and the numerous complaints João Pessoa had received alleging their violent attacks against local residents.[50] João Pessoa's demotion of Antônio Suassuna, brother of his predecessor, from both the chefia and prefeitura of Brejo do Cruz, which the Suassunas had ruled for twenty years, gained him considerable admiration from many in the urban middle-class sectors. Antônio Suassuna had extended protection and hospitality to the outlaw Chico Pereira [Francisco Pereira Nóbrega], one of the assailants in the notorious attack on Sousa by a group of cangaceiros led by Lampião's brother Levino in 1924. He had even flaunted his protection of the fugitive, who was his brother's Dantas kinsman by marriage, by driving Chico Pereira around in his personal automobile.[51] Several years earlier, Governor Suassuna had had to endure strong public criticism for his own preferential treatment of Chico Pereira, when first he failed to prosecute him aggressively after Chico was apprehended in connection with the Sousa attack, and then when a jury acquitted him. Evidence exists to confirm the widespread belief at the time that the acquittal resulted from direct pressure exerted by the governor. Suassuna thereby became severely compromised in the eyes not only of the urban sectors but also of many in the political elite who had relatives in Sousa on the day of the attack. By the same token, some in the political elite who supported Chico Pereira held Suassuna responsible for the young man's death at the hands of the Rio Grande State Police, since Suassuna authorized his extradition after Chico Pereira committed a robbery there.[52]

Outside the cities, reactions to João Pessoa's removal of local bosses were ambivalent. For instance, in Brejo do Cruz—one of the virtually autonomous municípios—Antônio Suassuna's removal was deemed an antagonistic act. Angered elite families in that part of the far backlands had expected the governor to maintain neutrality, even indifference, to the conduct of local bosses in their

[50] João Pessoa to Epitácio (Capital), 5 Dec. 1929, AEP/9/188; and Ademar Vidal, *João Pessoa e a Revolução de 30* (Rio de Janeiro: Edições GRAAL, 1978), pp. 77–78. João Pessoa also opposed the local boss of nearby Barra de Santa Rosa, whose district he referred to as "the fief of Souza Lima." Idem to idem, 29 Nov. 1929, AEP/9/198–99.

[51] João Pessoa to Epitácio (Capital), 22 Nov. 1929, AEP/9/196.

[52] Regarding Suassuna's role in Chico Pereira's acquittal, see Fernando Pessoa to Epitácio (Capital), 12 Nov. 1928, AEP/9/38; and Pereira Nóbrega, *Vingança, não!*, pp. 199 and 222–24. Author's interview with Ariano Suassuna, Recife, 27 July 1971.

municípios. To make matters worse, a feud had erupted in 1926 between the Suassunas and their old family allies, the Maias of neighboring Catolé do Rocha. Antônio Suassuna's loss of prestige therefore deserved interpretation as a sign of favor for the family of Col. Sérgio Maia. Fundamentally, however, João Pessoa's intervention directly upset local assumptions connected to the arrangement known as the politics of the governors. Since its tacit assumption was the free hand governors enjoyed from presidential interference, as long as they loyally delivered their states' votes to the presidential candidate, this principle carried analogous effect further down the ladder of rule. Local bosses expected that the governor would not inquire too closely as to the means they used to maintain their power as long as they could deliver their municípios' votes on election day.

João Pessoa's actions ran against the grain of an understanding that had been in place for decades, but to some extent, Epitácio himself had set the tone for a higher standard of accountability. Earlier in 1928, he had intervened on behalf of one of his stalwarts in Areia, who had written to complain about the conduct of public officials in an inquiry he had requested over the circumstances of an attack on him and his son. The victim charged that the officials had shown partiality and applied pressure to their tenants and employees—presumably the witnesses—leaving "the criminals" who were identified as the attackers undisturbed. Epitácio recommended Suassuna appoint an outsider, a police officer, to conduct an independent inquiry and concluded by asking Suassuna to pay careful attention, "because we must give public opinion a proof that, in our state citizens who are upright, substantial, and well-intentioned may find in the public authorities effective guarantees of life and labor."[53] Suassuna had also been obliged to remove the name of his own foster brother, João Agripino (Maia), from the political direction of Brejo do Cruz in 1926, after Agripino had been found responsible for the murder of its local judge and another individual in April. Although he retained his Assembly seat—and even was placed on the ballot for reelection in 1928, after the State Supreme Court set aside a lower judge's verdict of guilty—the leadership of Brejo do Cruz was not restored to him.[54]

[53] Epitácio to João Suassuna (Rio de Janeiro), 27 June 1928, AEP/12/290. See also idem to idem, 18 Feb. 1928, AEP/12/287.

[54] Suassuna relieved Agripino of the chefia of Brejo do Cruz after he was indicted as the "intellectual author" of the "horrible crime of April 25, 1926"—the murder of a local judge and one other man. A year later, however, he expressed his intention

João Pessoa moved more aggressively after 1928. Gubernatorial intervention was directed not only at families loyal to Epitácio for twenty or thirty years but also at key figures, such as judges and prosecutors, who were essential for a ruling family's control of a município. In Alagoa Nova, for instance, João Pessoa objected strongly that bandits were being sheltered while the local judge, a loyal instrument of the município's dominant family, took no action; he lived, the governor alleged, "like a true seigneur" and his sons went around "beating up people." João Pessoa determined to call the judge to the Capital for a consultation and insisted that "if he does not talk, we will replace him."[55] After only six months in office, he had removed local or federal district judges in three municípios.

It was João Pessoa's determined campaign to rid the interior of bandits that most angered the Epitacista bosses in the backlands. He took office during a resurgence of banditry. According to a front-page interview in *A União* in October 1929, former Governor João Suassuna blamed the "general crisis" created by "the plague of cangaceirismo" that had begun at the end of his administration on the failure of both Pernambuco and Ceará authorities to take appropriate action.[56] However, Pernambuco had been dissuaded from more aggressive action when it appealed to President Washington Luis for federal assistance to combat bandits. Earlier, the presence of the Prestes Column in the backlands of all the northeastern states meant that its aggressions offered new opportunities to bandits like Lampião. An attempt had been made to en-

---

"to reelect Agripino" to the Assembly on the condition he would stay out of politics in Brejo do Cruz, the Suassunas' home município, and despite the still pending appeal of his indictment. Suassuna to Epitácio (Capital), 19 May 1926, 7 Oct. 1926, and 3 Oct. 1927, AEP/12/263, 266, and 278 (second letter of that date), respectively. In April 1928 Agripino "succeeded in proving [his] innocence before the [State Supreme] Court," that is, his indictment was overturned. So his name remained on the ballot. João Agripino to Epitácio (Catolé do Rocha), tel. of 15 Apr. 1928, AEP/9/33. See also Epitácio to Agripino, tel. of 17 Apr. 1928, attached to preceding.

[55] João Pessoa to Epitácio (Capital), mid-May 1929, AEP/9/65–66. The judge's sons sent telegrams of complaint to President Washington Luis, under the name of the deputy prefeito—according to the governor—voicing criticism of his policies. Ibid. João Pessoa voiced his belief that there "were no good judges" and noted that "every day complaints reach me about judges from Patos, Pombal, and Alagoa Grande." Ibid. In Alagoa Grande, the ruling Zenaides, Epitacistas since 1912–1915, defected to the Perrepista opposition.

[56] *A União*, 20 Oct. 1929. Privately, however, Suassuna had made the same charge about Pernambuco and Ceará two years earlier: idem to Epitácio (Capital), 20 July 1927, AEP/12/278.

list Lampião and his band to fight the Prestes Column. Dr. Floro Bartolomeu, political boss of Joaseiro (Ceará) officially deputized the bandit to this end, but Lampião appeared to be interested only in gaining arms and ammunition. He made one halfhearted pass at confronting the column, which intimidated him, and then went on his own way, better armed. Yet Washington Luis refused to reinforce the state police with federal troops, a Paraíba senator reported, because he was assumed "to be of the opinion that the states must request federal intervention if they want assistance with banditry."[57] Federal intervention would not be requested because it deprived a state governor of his executive authority.

Left to his own devices, therefore, João Pessoa embarked on a new approach to an old problem. As part of his annual message of 1929, he announced a tough policy toward banditry, striking at the source of the cangaço's survival, the landowners who protected bandits:

> It is an obligation to cleanse the society of the habit of protecting banditry, whose principal cause has been the small arsenals with which . . . landowners protect those loyal to them. Henceforth, my obligation to promote general disarmament will be put into practice without distinction between friends and enemies, or weak and powerful—already this has reached some incumbent local bosses.[58]

No governor had ever proposed transgressing on the local elite families' prerogative of maintaining their own armed forces. João Pessoa was particularly concerned about the hundreds of thousands of rounds of ammunition distributed by Governor Suassuna in 1926 to combat the Prestes Column, which had found their way into local arsenals in the backlands. Much of the ammunition was in the possession of bosses allied with Col. José Pereira because, as the head of the government's effort to repulse Prestes, he had overseen its distribution.

Reaction to the new policy varied widely. In the backlands, many urban residents and the subjugated majority of the rural population applauded João Pessoa's effort, although whether it could succeed remained doubtful. The governor's logic promised a diminution of the mauraders who were drawn to Paraíba from outside the state:

[57] At least this was the conclusion of Sen. Antônio Massa: Massa to Epitácio (Capital), 15 Oct. 1927, AEP/9/1.

[58] *A União*, 6 Aug. 1929.

If not all come to the point of freely supplying arms and ammunition, many are still dispossessed of them through violence, supplying the bandits and serving as involuntary resources. . . . This measure [disarmament], thus generalized, would reduce the incidence of criminality. And certainly no group will look to enter our territory knowing it cannot count any more on the arsenals at our disposal.[59]

The backlands local elite, already antagonized by the governor's demotions of local bosses, prefeitos, judges, and prosecutors, greeted this proposal with alarm and opposition. Without their private retainers and sufficient arms, they would be at the mercy of João Pessoa's State Police. Coupled with this direct assault on their autonomy, the governor was also proposing a crucial juridicial reform that would remove from local control the empanelling of juries in murder cases.[60] The implication of this change was very clear.

Even Epitácio became concerned about his nephew's reformist zeal, knowing that the backlands bosses were capable of revolting and manipulating the governor to provide a federal intervention:

I have already told you more than once, no one can in a moment extirpate vices ingrained for years and years. You should act skillfully, [going] little by little, in order to avoid colliding violently with the [coronelista] ambience. It is necessary to remember that these vices have become, through habit, normal occurrences; that fact mitigates considerably the culpability of those who practice them.[61]

Epitácio's warning, which summed up his own working relationship with Paraíba's local bosses as well as his philosophical attitude toward the political milieu that had provided his base of support since 1912, went unheeded. In fact, João Pessoa increased the pressure on many local bosses, apparently on the mistaken assumption that his own State Police Force was adequate to address local rebellion. Incredibly, he reduced the annual budgetary ex-

[59] Ibid.

[60] Inês Caminha Lopes Rodrigues, "A Revolta de Princesa: Uma contribuição ao estudo de mandonismo local (Paraíba, 1930)" (Master's thesis, University of São Paulo, 1976), p. 14. On the mass support that João Pessoa gained in the backlands for denouncing landlords who supported bandits, see Barbosa Lima Sobrinho, *Revolução Outubro*, p. 172.

[61] Epitácio to João Pessoa (on board the *Dulio*), 5 May 1929; in *Obras completas*, vol. 24, *João Pessoa-Aliança Liberal-Princesa* (1963), p. 19.

penditure for the police—after Suassuna had increased it—cutting the force by 200 men.

The Tributary War

Although political reforms weakening the local bosses' powers earned João Pessoa the animosity of many chefes, his fiscal offensive channeled that sentiment along broader and more organized lines. The governor's first tax reform merely extended the efforts of his predecessors to enforce revenue collection in the municípios. No doubt he was moved by the situation of the State Treasury when he was inaugurated, for civil servants had not been paid for six months. To meet the government's obligations, he contracted the so-called Popular Loan with the federal government. But his campaign to oblige local bosses, mostly those in the backlands, to remand the state government's revenues basically reflected his design to impose executive authority on the Paraíba hinterland. Local bosses were even less inclined to remit taxes to the Treasury because of the governor's campaign to curb their local prerogatives. João Pessoa approached the issue with the determination of a zealot. Taking advantage of his control of *A União*, he used the front page to embarrass or antagonize the recalcitrant bosses whose municípios were negligent in remanding revenues. Their names, together with the names of the tax collection agents, were published in conspicuous lists for the public to read. Previously, the only complaints in this respect had come from several federal officials who alluded to the tendency of many prefeitos to withhold statistics they had been requested to supply because the data would reveal a município's potential tax base. However, individual names had not been released.[62]

The governor's major fiscal offensive, however, was designed to address Paraíba's commercial dependence on Pernambuco. As part of his budgetary package for 1929, passed by the Assembly in November 1928, Paraíba adopted a new schedule of export taxes. In the months ahead, itemized lists of all the state's imports and exports supplemented the original document. The purpose of the new schedule was to seal Paraíba behind a "Chinese Wall" of tariff protection and to insulate the state from its neighbors' commercial domination. Export taxes were raised to discourage the flow of cotton to out-of-state markets and to diminish Recife's role in the

[62] *A União*, 20 July 1929.

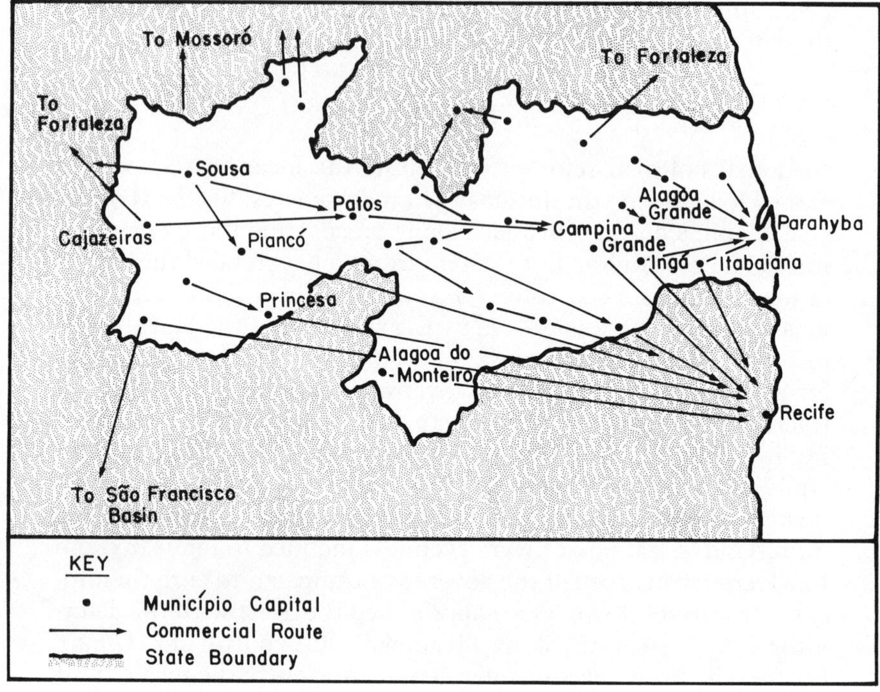

MAP VIII.1: Market Orientation of Major Municípios in Paraíba (c. 1928)
(Scale: 1 inch = 174 km)

SOURCES: Celso Mariz, *Evolução econômica da Parahiba* (João Pessoa: *A União* Editôra, 1939), pp. 35–46; *A União*, 1919–1930; Brazil, Ministerio da Agricultura, Industria e Commercio, Serviço de Inspeção e Defesa Agricolas, Inspectoria Agricola do 7° Districto, *Questionnarios sobre as condições da agricultura . . . Parahyba* (Rio de Janeiro: Tipografia do Serviço de Estatística, 1913), pp. 1–144.

state's economy. Above all, the new export tax schedule was intended to redirect cotton leaving Campina Grande and the backlands to the Capital and Cabedêlo. (See Map VIII.1.) This policy represented a *casus belli* for the Recife emporium. By February 1929, with the Pessoa de Queiroz brothers at the forefront of the attack, a Tributary War had begun. Pernambuco retaliated by adopting its own schedule of taxes designed to reward cotton producers in the Paraíba backlands and to encourage retailers in that state to remain dependent on Recife's wholesalers.

João Pessoa's Tributary War represented an aggressive response to the accelerated penetration of the Paraíba backlands by Recife firms in the mid-1920s. After 1923, when the main highway system neared completion, the Capital and Cabedêlo (which remained without docks to accommodate oceangoing vessels) did not gain an appreciably larger share of the caatinga-agreste's cotton harvests that were channeled from Campina Grande to either Parahyba or Recife. Cabedêlo's exports had remained fairly stable between 1923 and 1927, at around 15 to 16 million kilos, and then rose to over 19 million in the record harvest of 1929. The fragmentary statistics available for Campina Grande's cotton exports by destination, however, suggest Recife's position as Campina Grande's preferred market remained unchanged.[63]

While Paraíba had been investing in a deepwater port since 1921, Pernambuco's state government had been more heavily investing in railroads, extending lines far into the backlands of its own territory. After 1923, Recife businessmen, taking advantage of the IFOCS road network that linked the two states, began establishing profitable, high-density ginning and baling equipment in the Paraíba backlands. Even for the many cotton producers who could not avail themselves of these establishments, the comparatively cheaper transport costs to Recife decided the destination of their harvests. Col. José Pereira's município of Princesa, located in the remote southern alto sertão bordering Pernambuco, illustrated why Recife remained the principal outlet for Paraíba's cotton west of Campina Grande. (See Map VIII.1 and Map II.1.) In order to send cotton to Cabedêlo, 428 kilometers away, producers in Princesa first had to ship by mule and truck to the railhead at Campina Grande, a distance of about 327 kilometers. Only the final 100 kilometers was by rail, so cost was lowered very little. They preferred to send their cotton by mule to Rio Branco, Pernambuco, 130 kilometers to the southeast, from which the final 300 kilometers to Recife could be completed by rail, at a considerably lowered transport cost. In addition, Pernambuco's taxes were several percentage points lower than those levied in Paraíba.[64] This situation explains why, when Gov. João Pessoa waged the Tributary War, he set the export tax levied on Paraíba's backlands cotton routed to Cabedêlo at one-third the rate (per fardo or sixty-five-

[63] *A União*, 1 May 1928. Campina Grande's cotton exports to Recife were roughly double what they were to the Capital during 1919–1924. Cotton shipped to the Capital in those years totaled (in sacks of 65 pounds) 28,022 (1919), 53,807 (1920), 60,935 (1921), 41,300 (1922), 19,457 (1923), and 94,371 (1924). Recife received the following quantities from Campina Grande: 53,400 (1919), 107,399 (1920), 79,330 (1921), 123,219 (1922), 200,130 (1923), and 47,900 (1924). These figures, however, are only partial quantities. *Almanach Campina 1926*, unnumbered table, n.p. Tax schedules were authorized under Laws No. 67–73 of 17 Nov. 1928.

[64] Caminha Lopes Rodrigues, "Revolta Princesa," p. 3.

pound sack) levied on cotton shipped overland to out-of-state markets, primarily Recife.[65]

Imports represented a second field of competition between Paraíba and Pernambuco, especially because, in the backlands, sales of cotton exports usually were tied to purchases of imports. A new schedule of taxes made many imports from Pernambuco or other neighboring states prohibitively expensive in Paraíba. For instance, a liter of kerosene that was imported via Cabedêlo carried a 3 per cent tax. If it arrived overland from Pernambuco, the tax was increased to 40 per cent.[66] Unlike the export tax, the import tax aimed to force Recife firms with branches in Paraíba to incorporate legally as bona fide businesses in Paraíba. Then they could be more closely regulated by the state government, which could levy either an industrial or a commercial tax on them. The modest textile industry in Paraíba particularly struggled against Recife competition, for most of the lowest quality cloths sold in the backlands were manufactured in the Pernambuco emporium. This circumstance also explained the fierce opposition of the Pessoa de Queiroz to João Pessoa's fiscal assault, since their mills supplied the bulk of the textiles sold in the Paraíba backlands.[67] So great was Governor Pessoa's determination to tax these firms that many were reclassified as retailers, forcing them to lose their more favorable status as wholesalers.[68]

Governor Pessoa justified his fiscal discrimination against out-

[65] *A União*, 12 Apr. 1929.

[66] *A União*, 17 Apr. 1929. Barbosa Lima Sobrinho, *Revolução Outubro*, p. 171. Silk from the Pessoa de Queiroz' factory carried a tax four times higher than that levied on silk imported via Parahyba. *Jornal do Commercio*, 29 Apr. 1929.

[67] The Pessoa de Queiroz owned a number of importing firms, the most important of which were J. Pessoa de Queiroz e Cia.; Lopes, Pessoa de Queiroz e Cia.; and Queiroz e Cia. As purveyors of luxury and manufactured goods from North America, Europe, and Rio de Janeiro, they sold petroleum products, automobiles, refrigerators, clocks, barbed wire, plows, matches, and fine fabrics. J. Joffily, *Revolta*, pp. 231–32. During 1925–1926, both João and José Pessoa de Queiroz served as presidents of the Bank of Pernambuco, for they were politically allied with Gov. Estácio Coimbra, Pernambuco's oligarch. Levine, *Pernambuco*, p. 184. Evidence suggests that their commercial empire in the backlands was strengthened by concessions they obtained as consuls in Pernambuco with jurisdiction in Paraíba. See, for example, the request for confirmation of João Pessoa de Queiroz' appointment as consul of China to the minister of foreign affairs by Gov. Solon de Lucena, in AI, Avisos recebidos, 1900–1930, Paraíba 309–1–14.

[68] Merchants who protested tax increases from 30 per cent to 300 per cent were advised to relocate in Pernambuco because their "unpatriotic behavior" branded them "enemies of the people." *A União*, 11 Mar. 1929.

of-state markets on the ground of the Capital's declining textile exports, citing the fact that firms were going out of business—and disregarding the worsening condition of the international economy.[69] Initially, the Commercial Association endorsed his campaign enthusiastically, although by early 1929 the *Jornal do Comércio* of Recife, founded in 1919 to serve his Pessoa de Queiroz cousins' ambitions for political office, was leading the attack against him.[70] Unconcerned about the 60,000 contos in trade the Recife emporium claimed it was losing as a result of his policies, João Pessoa pointed out that Parahyba would gain 100,000 contos of new trade—all of it from the state's internal market.[71] Parahyba's recently founded *Correio da Manhã* supported Governor Pessoa and placed the issue in a national context, suggesting that Paraíba's demand for commercial autonomy from the regional emporium was far from unique and duplicated the efforts of a number of Brazil's smaller states since 1910.[72]

Paraíba's new tax schedule initially levied a 13 per cent tax on cotton ginned in the interior's markets—whether its final destination was Parahyba or Recife—while in the Capital the rate was an advantageous 11 per cent.[73] Sen. João de Lira Tavares, then representing Rio Grande do Norte, had warned in 1924 about creating such "sensitive differences" between markets in the interior and the Capital.[74] He urged caution because the Recife emporium possessed such a strong investment in the commerce of Paraíba's backlands, but he also understood the interzonal conflict such a fiscal policy could create in Paraíba.

Reaction to the higher tax for markets in the interior soon followed. Cotton-buying firms in Campina Grande, led by its export giant, Abílio Dantas & Co., loudly protested against the discrimination that favored the Capital. A number of firms in Campina Grande were branches of firms in the Capital established since 1920, and their owners resented competing against themselves. This group of cotton buyers petitioned the governor for equalization of the export tax on cotton, and added a plea that he rescind

[69] *A União*, 12 Apr. 1929. By 1928, a national slump in textiles had arisen due to international market conditions. Annual Report of the Cia. Paraibana de Tecidos, *A União*, 25 Jan. 1929.

[70] Ibid.

[71] Ibid.

[72] Reprinted in A União, 12 Apr. 1929, without original publication date.

[73] *A União*, 12 and 17 Apr. 1929.

[74] Lyra Tavares, *Cifras e notas*, p. 271.

his suspension of local credit, which normally was financed through the local tax collection boards of the State Treasury. Their petition warned that to deny them vital capital just before the agreste's cotton crop was to be harvested would dangerously restrict liquidity in Campina Grande's—and the caatinga-agreste's—economy.[75]

João Pessoa did not heed their demands until distant Cajazeiras's cotton exporters, who shipped via Fortaleza, Ceará, and Mossoró, Rio Grande do Norte, took their case to Mossoró's powerful Commercial Association and the national press.[76] Objection to the governor's intermunicípio tax differentials reached such a high level that he reversed himself and equalized the export tax at 11 per cent, placing all of Paraíba's markets on a par with the Capital. In addition, he cut the freight rate schedules of the Great Western Railway Company by 30 per cent to make Paraíba "less dependent on the English firm for the distribution of its products."[77] This measure appeared to be an olive branch, but the damage to his ruling coalition had already been done. Only six months after the Capital's Commercial Association had applauded his Tributary War with "delirious" satisfaction, the protective wall of tariffs had alienated the support many local bosses had given his government.

The winter of 1928/1929 produced a bumper crop in the tree cotton zones of the backlands, which brought in the largest quantity of revenues ever collected in Paraíba.[78] (See Table A.4.) Although this eased João Pessoa's concern about the Treasury's low level, landowners and cotton buyers noting the market situation foresaw that their commodity was headed for a slump. This realization fed their dissatisfaction with the governor's fiscal policies. The purchase of Paraíba's economic liberty was at their expense, they concluded. When the world price took a downturn, after three years of marked decline, they saw the specter of a glutted market approaching.

[75] *A União*, 19 Apr. and 18 May 1929.

[76] *A União*, 27–29 Mar. 1929.

[77] Freight rates were only lowered on the two major runs to the Capital from Campina Grande and Guarabira. *A União*, 13 Oct. 1929.

[78] From February to December 1929, 43,203 sacks (2,817,030 kilos) of ginned cotton went by rail from Campina Grande to the Capital, while trucks carried another 1,830,097 kilos by rail from Campina to the Capital between August and December. Domingues, *Relatorio 1929*, n.p., and "Quadro demonstrativo do transporte de saccas de algodão em rama, por caminhão de Campina Grande a Capital do Estado, no período de agôsto a dezembro de 1929" (ibid.) n.p. Cf. 1919–1924, n. 63.

The Pessoas Fall from Power

The Aliança Liberal Campaign

When João Pessoa accepted the vice-presidential nomination on the Aliança Liberal ticket headed by Getúlio Vargas, in July 1929, a period of crisis began in Paraíba. As the question of the presidential succession again dominated the nation, Rio Grande do Sul and Minas Gerais determined to challenge the outgoing president's official candidate. As a Paulista, President Washington Luis was expected to indicate a successor from a state other than São Paulo, most probably a Mineiro or a Gaúcho (a native of Rio Grande do Sul). In refusing to do so, he shattered the consensus of the politics of café com leite and insured the birth of the opposition Aliança Liberal coalition. Amorphous and ill-defined, the Aliança incorporated a heterogeneous group of factional followings loyal to personal leaders who often had little in common. Although the Aliança attracted most of the urban middle-class vote, it also drew on the oligarchical outs in a number of states who represented rural interests. Politicians in the Aliança ranged from older conservatives reminiscent of nineteenth-century liberals, such as Epitácio Pessoa, to more radical authoritarian military elements, including several Tenentes. The movement's strength lay in its leadership, which drew on the powerful Republican Parties of Minas and Rio Grande do Sul, whose governors had been denied presidential nomination.[79]

João Pessoa's political outlook illustrated the diversity of the Aliança's ideological orientations on questions as fundamental to its role as seizing the national government by force of arms. As a justice of the Supreme Military Tribunal, he had passed sentence on the young rebels of the Copacabana Fort in 1922 and then later denied their appeals for amnesty. As late as June 1930, he stated that he was not a revolutionary and would remain opposed to a movement plotting a *coup d'état*.[80] João Pessoa's strong personal sense of justice explained much of his anger at the inferior position of Paraíba and the Northeast in the national political system. His indignation over the power exercised by the ruling triumvirate of states explains much of the reckless enthusiasm with

[79] Correspondence between João Pessoa and Gov. Antônio Carlos, at whose suggestion João Pessoa was nominated, can be found in AEP/9/169–78.

[80] On João Pessoa's reluctance to espouse revolution, see José Américo de Almeida, *O ano do négo*, p. 59.

which he, like a David, embraced a battle with the Goliath of the national presidential machine, for he viewed the northeastern states as the machine's rubber stamp.[81] On the other hand, he maintained that he had accepted the vice-presidential slot only on Epitácio's counsel, insisting that his first reaction had been to refuse because he had "no love for politics" and wished to return to private life.[82] His courageous reply to Washington Luis's preliminary poll of state governors prior to the nomination convention, in which the president solicited their support of São Paulo's Gov. Júlio Prestes as the official candidate, should not be evaluated as serving João Pessoa's candidacy for the vice-presidency, for it was not yet a possibility. The refusal João Pessoa telegraphed to the president—his famous "*Négo*" incorporated since 1930 into Paraíba's flag—created enormous sympathy and support for his subsequent candidacy and for the Tributary War that he was waging with Recife.[83] Nevertheless, Paraíba's situation as a small and poor state, without political influence, made its economy and its civil administration totally vulnerable to presidential reprisal.

João Pessoa's decision to run on the Aliança ticket was also a consequence of his gubernatorial policies, particularly the Tributary War. Viewing his candidacy as a "simple accident of my political life," João Pessoa was eager to extricate himself from an increasingly hostile atmosphere, where he was discouraged by his growing isolation in politics and the "desertion of friends."[84] To Epitácio he expressed incredulity that his "actions in defense of states' rights" would create such dissension within the dominant oligarchical elite, and he complained that even his children were bullied in school.[85] Whatever the outcome of the presidential election—and a victory for Vargas was unlikely—he wrote Epitácio at the end of August 1929, he intended to resign as governor in six months, around the time of the federal election.[86]

João Pessoa's vice-presidential candidacy marked a turning

[81] Voicing his displeasure about Antônio Carlos's rumored nomination for the vice-presidency, João Pessoa told his uncle that it seemed "sufficient to give our approval [for the ticket] and not show up for a pantomime at the National [Nominating] Convention to make a choice which is already made." João Pessoa to Epitácio (Capital), (?) May 1929, AEP/9/142.

[82] João Pessoa to Armando Alencar (Capital), 17 Aug. 1929, AEP/9/168. João Pessoa to Artur Victor (Capital), tel. of 21 July 1929, ibid.

[83] In fact, João Pessoa's telegraphed reply was "*Veto*"—I veto the candidacy.

[84] João Pessoa to Epitácio (Capital), 26 Aug. 1929, AEP/9/142.

[85] Ibid.

[86] Ibid.

point in his Tributary War. By accepting the nomination, he handed the political advantage to his enemies in Paraíba, who longed for a pretext for presidential intervention. The governor's decision to ally with the national opposition to the presidential machine considerably increased opposition to him in the Capital. The commercial sector correctly feared that inevitable reprisals by Washington Luis would tip the scales away from João Pessoa's cause of commercial liberation from Recife and reinforce decisively his backlands opposition. Naturally, Washington Luis was determined to make an example of "tiny Paraíba" to discourage other weaker states that might contemplate breaking with the presidential machine—as some of them had done in 1922—and joining the Aliança Liberal. In addition, he wanted to deny Minas and Rio Grande do Sul a foothold in the Northeast for any seditious scheme to stage a *coup d'état*. Notwithstanding his assurances on August 9 to Governor Pessoa that "the law will be respected," Brazil's president had already taken the first steps a week before to discipline both João Pessoa and the State of Paraíba.[87] He arranged with Federal Deputy Artur dos Anjos, leader of the opposition in Paraíba's congressional delegation, to dismiss all federal employees in the state who had not joined the "Perrepistas"—as the supporters of Júlio Prestes and his PRP (Partido Republicano Paulista) were popularly known. Dos Anjos, a businessman whose warehouse operations were integrated with the Capital's largest import–export firm, Vergara & Co., coordinated a strategy relying on Washington Luis's alliance with Isidro Gomes, president of the Commercial Association.[88] In seeking to destroy João Pessoa's government, Isidro Gomes began by resigning his presidency and reproving the governor for assuming a role in national politics that would ruin Paraíba's economy. The Commercial Association, he objected, had been converted into "a political committee of the state government."[89]

Isidro Gomes joined forces with the opposition faction aligned against Epitácio since his decisive 1915 electoral victories and led by State Supreme Court chief justice, Heráclito Cavalcanti. Former Valfredistas and Old Liberals, the core group around Heráclito

[87] João Pessoa to Washington Luis (Capital), tel. of 9 Aug. 1929, AEP/9/178. João Pessoa to Manuel Tavares Cavalcanti (Capital), tel. of 29 Aug. 1929, AEP/9/179.

[88] Artur dos Anjos to Isidro Gomes (Rio de Janeiro), tel. of 29 Aug. 1929, AEP/9/178.

[89] *A União*, 25 Aug. 1929. Isidro Gomes also resigned his seat in the Assembly in protest, after accusing João Pessoa of "intriguing with commerce." Ibid.

was loosely family-based and included a significant number of wealthy merchants and industrialists of the Capital. Although Heráclito's opposition to Epitácio had been consistent and firm, some of his relatives by marriage in this group, such as Col. Inácio Evaristo Monteiro—probably the Capital's most successful entrepreneur and businessman—had steadfastly supported Epitácio and João Pessoa. Others who had ties of blood and marriage to Heráclito, such as ex-Governor Camilo de Holanda—who had granted generous contracts and tax exemptions to individuals in this group—became Epitácio's adversaries. Earlier, the firms of a number of men in this group also had become targets for Gov. Solon de Lucena's condemnation of their offices and warehouses, under the eminent domain authority he exercised vis-à-vis IFOCS construction projects, which permitted demolition of buildings in the Capital. Although Solon's attempt to take their properties as sites for urban improvements had antagonized a number of these businessmen in 1921–1924, the fact that they had also been determined, as former Valfredistas, to maintain good relations with Epitácio assisted them in protecting their property. João Vergara, who owned Vergara & Co., for instance, had always been close to Heráclito, but his loud cries of protest over the loss of his main building—and the paltry indemnification Solon offered—reached Epitácio. Solon was forced to adjust the compensation and some of his other targets of demolition were questioned by his party chief.[90] In 1929–1930, this group perceived the threat to their economic assets to be more serious, one that would lead to bankruptcy. Despite their good relations with Epitácio, João Pessoa's open challenge to Washington Luis led them to break with the dominant oligarchy and throw in their lot with Heráclito Cavalcanti and the national cause of Perrepismo.

João Pessoa's goals for Paraíba are hard to fathom, for, as a candidate of the national opposition, he must have known that he was endangering his political control of Paraíba on both the federal government and state oligarchy levels.[91] His blind determination

[90] Isidro Gomes to Epitácio (Capital), tel. of 1 Sept. 1922, AEP/64/unnumbered. Epitácio to Solon de Lucena (Rio de Janeiro), 22 Oct. 1922, ibid. A portion of the core of Heráclito's family-based group is identified in Chapter 6, note 73. See also Fig. B.4.

[91] João Pessoa's direct investment in the Capital's commerce appeared modest, although his brother Osvaldo Pessoa had business interests there. Because of a conflict of interest while he was a justice of the supreme Military Tribunal in 1925, João Pessoa had conceded power of attorney to Osvaldo and transferred 500 shares of stock that he owned in the Cia. de Beneficiamento e Prensagem de Algodão

to pursue the Tributary War without quarter—and his mistaken assumption that he could win—locked him into an irreversible situation, given the passionate animosity between him and the Pessoa de Queiroz. In taking on the president of Brazil, he may have placed excessive confidence in the improved situation of the State Treasury and calculated that the 1929–1930 cotton crop would be record-breaking (which it was). On the other hand, he could have saved face and, more important, acquired the leverage to defeat the Recife emporium had he been elected Getúlio Vargas's vice-president. Whatever his reasoning, by committing Paraíba's recently replenished revenues to a new, military struggle with his cousins in Recife, he indirectly changed the course of Brazilian history.

Washington Luis lost no time unleashing a presidential disciplining of Paraíba. In September 1929, all federal employees in Paraíba who were not Perrepistas lost their jobs and were replaced by partisans of Júlio Prestes. Such an action severely hampered Governor Pessoa's communication with the rest of Brazil, since it removed trusted postal, telegraph, and telephone workers and substituted them with members of the opposition who then relayed useful intelligence to Heráclito and Washington Luis. Perrepista customs officials later denied precious shipments of arms and ammunition to João Pessoa's government, effectively weakening the military response to the rebel forces. And all federal appropriations were suspended for the duration of João Pessoa's administration. However, thanks to a swift warning from Antônio Filho in Rio de Janeiro, the governor evaded Washington Luis's order to freeze the accounts of the Bank of Paraíba in the Bank of Brazil, and the money was withdrawn hours before it was to be frozen. The same warning advised João Pessoa that the federal government would foreclose on the Popular Loan before it was due—in thirty days—in order to force the state government to declare bankruptcy.[92] By withdrawing the State of Paraíba's accounts, João Pessoa foiled such a strategy. A campaign immediately launched

to the firm's owner, Heronides de Holanda. "Um documento de honradez e desinteresse pessoal," *A União*, 1 May 1929. Nevertheless, João Pessoa de Queiroz accused him of receiving "fat tips" from Heronides. João Pessoa de Queiroz to Epitácio (Rio de Janeiro), tel. of 17 June 1929, AEP/73/unnumbered.

[92] Toinho [Antônio Pessoa Filho] to João Pessoa (Rio de Janeiro), tel. 29 Aug. 1929, AEP/9/179. The balance due on the Popular Loan was paid in advance of the thirty-day call Washington Luis placed on it, thanks to public subscriptions. João Pessoa to Epitácio (Capital), 26 Aug. 1929, AEP/9/142.

in the national press attempted to condemn both Paraíba and João Pessoa's candidacy in the approaching federal election. A growing chorus of oligarchical outs living in exile in Rio de Janeiro emerged from political obscurity to contribute editorials and interviews denouncing João Pessoa: Former governors such as João Machado and Camilo de Holanda and former congressmen such as Octacílio de Albuquerque received prominent journalistic attention.

As Epitácio warned, "Heraclito and his bunch" were seeking a presidential degola for Paraíba as well as the election of Júlio Prestes.[93] True to the prediction, João Pessoa's government lost its political voice in the national Congress with the 1 March election, while Júlio Prestes and his running mate, Vital Soares, carried the official vote and defeated Vargas and João Pessoa.[94] The congressional election returns revealed that all four of the Paraíba deputies, as well as the delegation's leader, Sen. Manual Tavares Cavalcanti, lost their seats. Only Federal Deputy João Suassuna, together with Sen. Octacílio de Albuquerque—who again defected—were reelected, and as Perrepistas.

The Princesa Revolt

Fifteen months after assuming office, João Pessoa confronted the situation that Epitácio had cautioned him to avoid—a revolt by his own local bosses in the backlands. Although evidence confirms that Col. José Pereira began to plan for war as soon as João Pessoa's vice-presidential nomination became a fact, the Princesa boss did not openly break with the governor until later February 1930.[95] José Pereira may have been waiting for the March federal elections to bring a presidential intervention from outgoing President Washington Luis and to put Perrepistas in the Congress, denying João Pessoa a public forum. Or he may have been waiting to see if the composition of the federal slate, as well as the approaching As-

[93] Epitácio to João Pessoa (Montecatini, Italy), 22 Sept. 1929, in E. Pessoa, *Obras completas*, 24:29–31.

[94] The official returns for the State of Paraíba gave 26,095 votes to Getúlio, with 10,579 going to Prestes. But Epitácio's private computations corrected them to 32,106 and 11,277, respectively, with the remark, "But we will not make an issue of these corrections." Undated notes forwarded to João Pessoa, AEP/9/249.

[95] "Coronel Zé Pereira is understood to be arming men. . . . Several rumors have it that he's got 100 men. . . . According to the way I see it, Coronel José Pereira is intending to find a way to break with . . . the governor." Manuel Arruda [local police officer] to João Franca (Princesa), 4 Sept. 1930, cited in Vidal, *1930; história*, pp. 77–78.

18. Vice-presidential candidate João Pessoa campaigns for the Aliança Liberal ticket in Goiana, Pernambuco (with Commander Elísio Sobreira, in uniform, to his right), 1929. Vargas and João Pessoa undertook the first real grassroots presidential campaign in Brazil, one that relied heavily on the automobile for appearances throughout the northeastern states. (Courtesy of the Acervo Humberto Nóbrega)

sembly elections, would include candidates representing incumbent bosses in the backlands. But the timing of his so-called Revolution of Princesa suggested that the immediate cause—João Pessoa's congressional slate—was merely the last of several reasons for resorting to the extreme of armed insurrection.

The slate mandated by Gov. João Pessoa deprived half a dozen backlands municípios of their family-based representation at the federal level. Coupled with the governor's previous dismissals of local judges and prosecutors, it signaled their waning "prestige" at the oligarchy's leadership level and presaged further loss of economic control in their home municípios. When the Executive Committee of the PR do P met on February 16, 1930, to discuss the federal slate, the members learned that the governor had drawn up the list of candidates two days earlier, solely on his own initiative. João Pessoa justified his disregard of the customary mutual consultation that normally preceded the announcement of the slate on the ground that he was implementing a new policy of "no reelection." Yet the slate belied this: Although four incumbent deputies were denied their seats, the governor's cousin Carlos Pessoa was on the ballot for a second term. When the Assembly's president, Col. Inácio Evaristo Monteiro, learned that his son-in-law,

Oscar Soares (the nephew of former governor Camilo de Holanda) had been dropped from the slate, he refused to approve it in his capacity as a member of the Committee. The omission of João Suassuna's name also provoked strong dissent. For failing to consult with the Executive Committee and consider its preferences, the governor received a powerful lesson in the veto power the backlands bosses exercised.

On February 18, accompanied by his secretary of interior and justice, José Américo de Almeida, João Pessoa drove to Princesa to receive Col. José Pereira's customary endorsement of the federal slate. Typically this event became a festive celebration, but the signs of disaffection and hostility were unmistakable. As José Américo has recounted, the ominous silence of the fifty "cangaceiros" with whom they dined that evening reflected the level of tension, one that may also have evidenced a plot to assassinate João Pessoa. Nevertheless, João Pessoa subsequently denied seeing any sign of trouble and he received Zé Pereira's pledge of support for the slate without perceiving even a hint of resentment.[96] The bomb exploded on their return to the Capital. In a telegram condemning the federal slate as a "palpable insult to the respective members of the Executive Committee," Princesa's party boss and assemblyman of twenty years declared that João Pessoa's conduct "had inspired a lack of confidence [on his part] in the breast of Epitacismo."[97] Furious, he broke with the governor and denied him the votes he commanded in his and neighboring municípios:

> Your departure [from Epitácio's policy] puts an end to the agreements of the veteran stalwarts of the 1915 victory, for Your Excellency has just falsified their principles. I have, therefore, decided not to endorse the federal slate, and to concede to my friends freedom to vote in accordance with the dictates of their opinions, pledging myself to defend them against whatever act of violence the state government might try against their right to vote as insured by the Constitution.[98]

[96] José Américo also recounted that an assassination attempt on João Pessoa had been abandoned at the last moment. *O ano do négo*, p. 63. To João Pessoa's query about the presence of the cangaceiros, José Pereira responded that they were "the electors of your uncle, Epitácio." José Gastão Cardoso, *A heróica resistência de Princesa* (Recife: Artes Gráficas da Escola Industrial Governador Agamemnon Magalhães, 1954), p. 33.

[97] José Pereira Lima to João Pessoa (Princesa), tel. of 22 Feb. 1930, AEP/9/205. (The full text appears in Vidal, *1930; história*, pp. 88–89.)

[98] Ibid.

19. Tavares, a small town near Princesa heavily bombarded in 1930 by the state police during Col. Zé Pereira's insurrection. Isolated by the vastness of the alto sertão, Tavares was typically vulnerable to attackers, whether they were police, bandits, or private henchmen. (Courtesy of the Acervo Humberto Nóbrega)

20. Princesa's Col. José Pereira Lima (front row, center, indicated by an "x"), posing with the officers and some of the men who served in his private army from March to October 1930. The elderly Col. Marçal Florentino Diniz (no. 8) and Joaquim Florentino Diniz (no. 5), Zé Pereira's relatives from Flores and São José de Egíto (Pernambuco), also appear. (Courtesy of the Acervo Humberto Nóbrega)

The story of Zé Pereira's armed revolt, which began in early March, remains vivid oral history in Paraíba and, at least in the backlands, assumes epic proportion. Although João Pessoa never conceded the fact, the backlands rebels held the military advantage from March through July, when he was assassinated. The rebels were repulsed and the insurrection quelled only when João Pessoa had been killed and a federal intervention imposed. When the last insurgent forces had been driven back to Princesa, where they surrendered to the federal army in October, Col. Zé Pereira, like his compadre João Pessoa de Queiroz and his two brothers, already had fled and was in hiding. And, although they lived in disguise as fugitives for several years, the rebel chieftains fared better than the unlucky Suassuna. A paid assassin stabbed him to death in the national capital—on the orders, so it has always been conjectured, of one of João Pessoa's brothers—only a few days after the triumph of the Revolution of 1930.

Written details of the rebellion's course are not only conflicting but also plagued by considerable omission. An army of around five hundred apparently held the field on behalf of Princesa's secession from the State of Paraíba, an act that produced both a flag and a newspaper dedicated to the new "republic's" status as *terra livre*. This rebel force was recruited from Princesa's *"filhos de terra,"* the sons of its native families, together with their dependents and retainers. But a perhaps larger contingent of bandoleiros drawn from surrounding states and the Paraíba backlands, which had been recruited probably since the preceding August, rounded out the private army. Throughout their eight months of armed rebellion, the insurgents regularly received material assistance from the Pessoa de Queiroz brothers in Recife, although the armaments they delivered to Princesa were placed at their disposal by President Washington Luis.[99] Vital radio and telephone contact could be maintained beween Recife or Rio de Janeiro without interruption because Col. José Pereira established his military headquarters in Pernambuco, on the estate of his Diniz relatives and neighbors in adjacent São José de Egíto.[100]

[99] João Pessoa de Queiroz' son-in-law, former Assemblyman Joaquim Inojosa, identified Zé Pereira's source of arms as the Pessoa de Queiroz. Interview with the author, Rio de Janeiro, May 1971. Vidal identified the arms as manufactured at the federal munitions factory in Realengo (Rio de Janeiro). *1930; história*, p. 143. Documentation on Washington Luis's supplying arms can be found in AEP/Pasta 63, (Governo W. Luis, violências, falcatrucas).

[100] A more detailed account of the military campaign appears in Lewin, "Politics and *Parentela*," pp. 469–96.

In contrast, Gov. João Pessoa was unprepared for war. He commanded only 800 men in the State Police for all of Paraíba. The "Provisional Battalion" that he raised for the campaign, which he claimed amounted to 1,500 recruits, was, in any case, no match for the rebels. Supplies were woefully short; the federal government sealed the coastline from arms smugglers and patrolled the beaches, as well as the borders with neighboring states, to deny João Pessoa war matériel. During the first few months of the insurgency, from February to April, the state government's forces were rumored to have had only 1,600 rounds of ammunition—five shells for every man—and they were "rusted and moldy."[101] Consequently, the State Police Force and patriot fighters scavenged for cartridge shells; in desperation they resorted to simulating the sound of gunfire by banging together gasoline cans.[102] In May, Epitácio, who was at The Hague, began attempting to smuggle ammunition to João Pessoa by concealing it in shipments of tinned fruit.[103] João Pessoa's cousins in Rio de Janeiro attempted to use rolled up newspapers for the same end, but their ruse was detected and the ammunition intercepted.[104] The State Police Force and the Provisional Battalion, which had occupied the key backlands cities of Pombal, Sousa, and Cajazeiras, managed to hold a tenuous line of defense due west along the main highway. They were, however, confined to those cities just as João Pessoa was a prisoner on the coast. A stalemate was reached in June that persisted until the governor's assassination on July 26. Instead of declaring a federal intervention, President Washington Luis simply waited. Time would drain Paraíba's State Treasury and João Pessoa would suffer more ignominious defeat than any federal intervention could effect.[105] Meanwhile, the federal army would not be diverted in the Northeast's backlands unless needed to repel more serious threats, such as a *coup d'état* directed against the national government.

[101] Vidal, *1930; história*, p. 104.

[102] Ibid., p. 208.

[103] Author's interview with Irmã Maria Regina do Santo Rosário [Laurita Pessoa], Rio de Janeiro, October 1970.

[104] Ibid.

[105] By the end of July, the Treasury was totally depleted and the state government in debt. Because João Pessoa had demanded early payment of taxes—in December 1929—credit was severely constricted. Some 2,000 people were unemployed by that time and all public works projects stopped. William Seeds to A. Henderson (Recife), 25 Aug. 1930, Public Record Office, London, Foreign Office General Correspondence, Political, FO 371/14200, file no. A 6072/106/6. Vidal, *1930; história*, p. 259.

João Pessoa immediately struck at enemies who were within reach in Paraíba. Following Zé Pereira's declaration of secession, the Dantas family of Teixeira became the governor's first object of retaliation. As friends of the Princesa boss, they could be expected to deliver their votes in the March 1 federal election to the Perrepistas. Consequently, on election eve, João Pessoa sent a contingent of the State Police to Teixeira with instructions to guarantee a fair election. Privately, however, he admitted that "the takeover of the town is preferable to losing Teixeira's vote."[106] Since João Suassuna, who had been born in Teixeira, was running as a Perrepista, this was an accurate assessment of the electoral outcome. In occupying Teixeira—which they succeeded in holding only twenty-four hours before the local population led by the Dantas retook the município seat—the State Police seized the voter registries, making it impossible for the Perrepistas to cast their ballots. They also insulted and locked up the Dantas women, including the mother, sisters, and sisters-in-law of João Pessoa's future assassin, João Duarte Dantas. These women were also relatives of João Suassuna's wife, the concunhadas of Rita Dantas Vilar. In late April, in a drive on Piancó, the police arrested and imprisoned Joaquim Duarte Dantas—brother of João Duarte—who was the husband of Rita Dantas Vilar's sister. By then, they had also burned the Dantas' ancestral home in Imaculada, which belonged to Franklin Dantas—leader of the 1912 insurrection—and Fazenda Santo Agostinho, the family home of his son, João Duarte Dantas. Later, in July, the Capital's police would search João Duarte Dantas's law office, which was across the street from João Pessoa's office in the Governor's Palace, and confiscate the contents of his safe. This violation of his private papers would provide the final provocation for João Pessoa's assassination.[107]

By June 1930, João Pessoa's situation had become extremely bleak. Although João Suassuna helped Epitácio initiate mediation

[106] João Pessoa to Epitácio (Capital), 17 Mar. 1930, AEP/9/113.

[107] João Duarte Dantas to João Pessoa (Recife), tel. of 1 June 1930, AEP/9/223. In a letter to the editor published in *Veja*, 22 Feb. 1978, José Alves Nóbrega, a resident of Patos, Paraíba, confirmed "what [the newsmagazine previously] had said in part," that two unmarried sisters of João Duarte Dantas were raped by members of the Paraíba State Police while in their custody in Teixeira, providing additional motivation for the governor's assassination. The federal government's minister of justice wired João Pessoa, seeking guarantees for four relatives of João Suassuna "under arrest as hostages" by the State Police—"two of them respectable women." Viana do Castelo to the Governor of Paraíba, tel. of 1 Mar. 1930, AEP/9/208. J. Joffily, *Revolta*, p. 266.

between his friend Col. José Pereira and Gov. João Pessoa, those efforts came to nothing since João Pessoa would not tolerate Suassuna's playing a role.[108] Epitácio, who remained in Europe at The Hague, could do little to improve the situation. Once the Brazilian Congress had certified Júlio Prestes and Vital Soares as the official winners of the presidential election, the national following of the Aliança predictably faded. In Paraíba, political alignments became completely polarized. João Pessoa still commanded considerable support on a mass level: crowds thronged to his speeches denouncing Perrepismo from the balcony of the Governor's Palace. Privately, however, politicians close to him saw his cause as doomed. José Café Filho, who had toured the backlands with him in May and early June, later wrote that João Pessoa's friends kept the truth from him.[109] Yet the governor himself was determined not to recognize the odds against him. The British consul in Recife, who claimed to have heard all of João Pessoa's speeches, noted a new tone in their rhetoric: they now "preached revolution, on one occasion even defying President Washington Luis and neighboring states to conquer Paraíba by arms."[110] Those Perrepistas still living in the Capital, he noted, now had guards stationed at their doors for their safety. Their Republican Party was "not tolerated by Governor Pessoa," who, the consul charged, was "despotic in character."[111]

Indeed, João Pessoa's increasingly hostile rhetorical attacks on the opposition eventually contributed to his death. The British consul was unfavorably impressed by the governor's "violent" language and the fact that he "displayed a fondness for washing his opponent's dirty linen" in public, a circumstance that "made him

[108] Epitácio and Antônio [Pessoa] Filho to João Pessoa (Rio de Janeiro), tel. of 20(?) Mar. 1930, AEP/9/209. João Pessoa replied, "The traitorous word of a Suassuna does not deserve to be trusted." João Pessoa to Epitácio (Capital), tel. of 20(?) Mar. 1930, AEP/9/213.

[109] "We told João Pessoa the true situation, which . . . was one of panic, exhaustion, and rout. The troops fought scared and, as much as possible, avoided combat, abandoning their positions and refusing to face the enemy. . . . João Pessoa, who had been ignorant of all this, because his friends did not dare to give him a true statement, choked with anger. . . ." João Café Filho, *Do sindicato ao Catete*, 2 vols., Coleção Documentos Brasileiros, no. 125 (Rio de Janeiro; Livraria José Olýmpio Editôra, 1966), Vol. 1, *Memórias políticas e confissões humanas*, p. 57.

[110] Seeds to Henderson, 25 Aug. 1930, PRO/A 6072/106/6. "On the contrary, João Pessoa, by habit, would not tolerate speaking of revolution. He would only admit it in the desperation of the cause." José Américo de Almeida, *O ano do négo*, p. 59.

[111] Seeds to Henderson, 25 Aug. 1930, PRO/A 6072/106/6.

enemies, even of those previously his friends."[112] This vein of attack led the governor to condone, if not to authorize personally, the publication on the front page of *A União* of much of the contents of the papers found in João Duarte Dantas's safe. On July 26, a brooding and introspective poem by João Duarte was featured in order to reveal the author's belief that the "blood of a butcher" and the "evil blood of a cangaceiro" flowed in his veins.[113] In addition, the paper referred more sensationally to notes he had authored that were "a narrative of the amoral acts he had practiced . . . but could not be published because they would offend public decency." "Whoever wants to see them," *A União* invited, "could do so at the police station."[114] Thus, in spite of the newspaper's front-page focus on João Duarte's alleged identity as a co-conspirator with Col. José Pereira and the federal government against Governor João Pessoa, emphasis shifted to a more intimate level.

In seeking to dishonor as well as to incriminate a Dantas insurgent whom otherwise he could not reach, João Pessoa depended on a tactic that Epitácio had always avoided and one deemed unethical by many in his own social class. For several years, João Duarte, a bachelor, had maintained a clandestine liaison with Anayde Beiriz, a young and unmarried teacher in Cabedêlo's elementary school. *A União* never published their love letters, as often has been maintained. But in issuing an open invitation to read João Duarte's personal notes about his intimate relationship with Anayde, the newspaper assumed responsibility for the rapid circulation of gossip about the couple that inevitably ensued from its innuendo. The public intimation *A União* made of their relationship, and the immediate advantage a number of men prominent in

[112] Ibid.

[113] The byline read "Blood of a cangaceiro" and the poem was entitled *My Blood [Meu sangue]*. Only one verse, which observed, "*Em minhas veias circula um sangue de carniceiro . . . Sangue mau, de cangaceiro!*" was published. The front pages of *A União* for 22 through 26 July (with page two) have been reproduced and placed at the rear of José Otávio's *A Revolução estatizada*. Each day, *A União*'s headline read, "Revealing the Tortured Souls of the Conspirators against the Order and Dignity of Our Land," with the byline referring to "The sensational documents seized by the police from the residence of Dr. João Dantas." The nature of these documents, however, was largely political.

[114] The full text of the invitation, which frequently has been presumed to have been attached to extracts of "love letters" written by João Duarte, read as follows: "*No cofre marca 'Torpedo' encontrado no quarto do bacharel João Dantas, a polícia achou notas redigidas pelo próprio espião com a narrative de atos amorais pelo mesmo praticados. Tais notas não podem ser publicadas porque offendem ao decoro comum. Mas quem quizer vel-as o pode fazer na polícia.*"

the Capital's elite took of the invitation to visit the police station, ruined Anayde's reputation and tainted her respectable middle-class family with humiliating scandal. Her father disowned her and, driven from her family home, she fled Parahyba for Recife, where she spent the few remaining months of her life trying to hide from journalists. In titilating its readers, *A União* also reinforced the interpretation the police were insinuating, that João Duarte engaged in sexual perversions. He, too, was to be dishonored for what in a different context probably would have earned him at most an informal and private reproach, since only the social class of his female companion would have come under censure.[115] In view of the quite unrestricted freedom of the press prevailing in the Old Republic, and the fact that the Capital's chief of police was both João Pessoa's appointee and personal friend, João Duarte's only sanctioned retaliation was an act of personal revenge. The same issue of *A União* carrying the vicious revelation of his intimacy with Anayde suggested such an opportunity, for a small item on page one called attention to Governor João Pessoa's presence in the Pernambuco capital on that very day.

On July 26, João Pessoa made a fateful trip to Recife. He had received the news that ammunition from the state governors of Rio Grande do Sul and Minas Gerais would soon become available, and he wished to make arrangements for receiving the contraband.[116] He anticipated using it for a final military advance against Princesa. In spite of strong urging by friends to avoid Recife—because of recent death threats—Governor Pessoa remained undeterred and stressed only his wish to visit a sick friend. In a gesture of bravado that seemed to court death, he refused friends' counsel to take his bodyguards with him. That afternoon, while seated

[115] Anayde Beiriz committed suicide shortly after assisting João Duarte Dantas to take his own life and that of his brother-in-law (by consent), while they were imprisoned in the Pernambuco State Penitentiary. These events, as well as Anayde's liaison, are the subject of a recent, very popular feature film, *Paraíba, mulher macha* (1982), directed by Tizuka Yamasake, although they are very freely interpreted. For two divergent views on the notes' contents, see Vidal (chief of police in 1930), *João Pessoa*, pp. 248–49, 365, and J. Joffily, *Revolta*, pp. 267–68. *A União*'s byline for João Duarte's poem insinuated perversion by describing him as "A perfect type of degenerate" (p. 2).

[116] Antônio Carlos to João Pessoa (Belo Horizonte), 21(?) July 1930, AEP/9/212. This strategic motive was, of course, kept secret and *A União* referred only to João Pessoa's purpose as a visit to a sick friend. That circumstance has recently lent support to the view popularized by the film *Paraíba, mulher macha* that João Pessoa's concealed motive for the visit to Recife was to keep an amorous tryst. No archival evidence supports this conclusion.

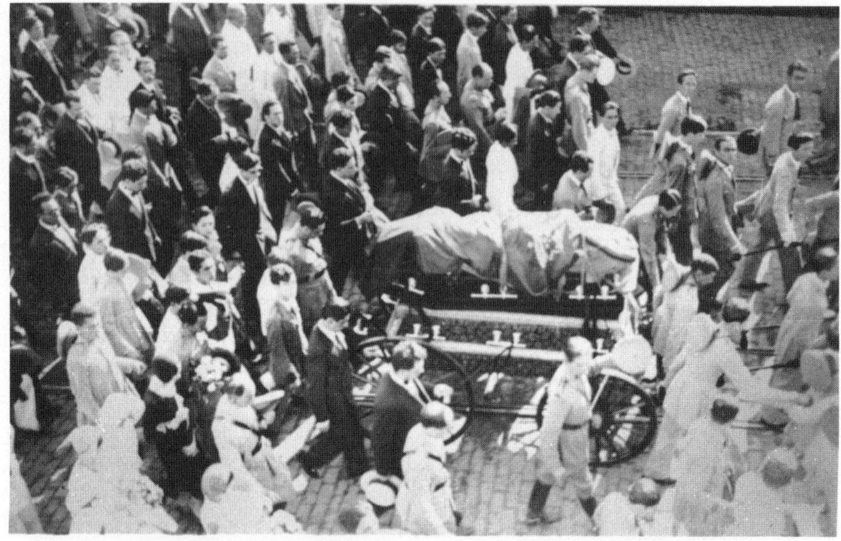

21. The return of João Pessoa's body from Recife to Parahyba on the night of July 26, 1930 (prior to being taken to Rio de Janeiro for burial) ignited public anger against his opposition in the Capital. Unchecked for five nights, Aliancista mobs attacked Perrepistas and burned and looted their homes and businesses. (Courtesy of the Acervo Humberto Nóbrega)

with only his driver in the Confeitaria Glória in downtown Recife, and minutes before he was to return to Parahyba, João Pessoa was accosted by João Duarte Dantas, who fired several shots that instantly killed him.

In Paraíba, the news of João Pessoa's death provoked a full week of mass hysteria and violent rampage. Pro-Aliança mobs looted and burned the homes and commercial properties of all the businessmen who had supported President Washington Luis as Perrepistas, including the influential Casa Vergara. Similar attacks occurred against Perrepistas in the market centers of the caatinga-agreste and the brejo. Perrepista politicians in the Capital sought refuge at the federal garrison or fled to Recife because, as the British consul who witnessed the week's events reported, "the Aliancista leaders went home and closed their doors, leaving the mob to do its work."[117] On the night of August 8–9, President

[117] Seeds to Henderson, 25 Aug. 1930, PRO/A 6072/106/6. Acting Governor Álvaro de Carvalho's assertion that he relied on the 22nd Federal Company to "pacify the town" and avoid burning the best properties of our adversaries" ignored the fact

22. The Casa Vergara, a leading import-export house in Parahyba, on July 30, 1930, after an angry mob sacked and burned it. (Courtesy of the Acervo Humberto Nóbrega)

Washington Luis finally decreed the federal intervention so long anticipated.

In death, João Pessoa provided Getúlio Vargas and the leading Aliancista politicians with the catalyst they needed to revive their waning political appeal. The arrival of João Pessoa's body in Rio de Janeiro for burial and a national funeral during the first week in August evoked a martyr's farewell from thousands in the Aliança Liberal. Those who knew otherwise did not publicize the motive behind João Pessoa's assassination, which rendered his death an act of personal revenge.[118] Instead, his murder was laid at the feet of Washington Luis, not João Duarte Dantas, who was dismissed as a mere instrument of presidential policy.[119] The funeral procession to the Church of Candelária, in the center of the city, reawakened the nation and galvanized into action the forces opposing the president and his officially elected successor.

While Governors Getúlio Vargas and Antônio Carlos plotted the *coup d'état* that would remove Washington Luis, Paraíba continued to play a supporting role in the revolutionary drama unfolding between August and October. Ironically, the man whom João Pessoa had sentenced to prison in the 1922 Copacabana Revolt, his fellow Paraibano Juarez Távora, coordinated the revolutionary offensive in the Capital. In hiding in Parahyba as a fugitive for several months before the assassination, Juarez served as the liaison between sympathetic young lieutenants in the federal garrison

---

that they had already been burned. Álvaro de Carvalho to Epitácio (Capital), 26 July 1930, AEP/9/107. See also two widely read fictional accounts of the events of July 26 to August 1, 1930—Virgínius da Gama e Melo, *Tempo de vingança* (Rio de Janeiro: Civilização Brasileira, 1970) and José Bezerra Filho, *Fogo!* (João Pessoa: n.p., 1970).

[118] A facsimile page (without number) from *Time* magazine (Chicago), dated 11 Aug. 1930, appearing in J. Joffily's *Revolta* (p. 340), referred to the official news blackout regarding the circumstances of João Pessoa's murder: "Rio de Janeiro officials did their best to hush this up too. A Federal censorship was established. [Aliança] Liberal-owned radio stations were closed. Chief of Police Oliveira Sobrinho called editors of opposition papers into his office, and pointed out how unfortunate it would be if they should publish 'false and misleading' accounts of the assassination of the unfortunate little affair of the 'independent state' [Princesa] in Paraíba." Thus, fearing it would be linked by the Aliança Liberal press to the assassination and identified as the possible mandante, the administration of President Washington Luis imposed a strict censorship—unwittingly playing into the hands of the Vargas opposition.

[119] Ann Quiggins Tiller, "The Igniting Spark—Brazil 1930," *HAHR* 45, no. 3 (1965):385–92; and J. Joffily, *Revolta*, p. 277. These authors also point out that post-1930 historiography has followed the trend of the pro-Aliança interpretation.

there and a core of civilian politicians led by José Américo de Almeida and Ademar Vidal.[120] Their goal was to seize the Northeast on behalf of Vargas and the Aliança, in coordination with parallel efforts in Rio Grande do Sul and Minas Gerais. On the night of October 3–4, led by Juarez and three civilian politicians, the federal garrison of the Capital mutinied and declared the State of Paraíba in support of Getúlio Vargas's revolution. Marching to Recife, they quelled Perrepista resistance and, together with Pernambuco conspirators, raised the banner of the triumphant Aliança Liberal.

[120] Earlier, when João Pessoa had been informed of Juarez's presence in the Capital, he refused to meet with Juarez because he was a fugitive. The governor treated with him only indirectly, through Antenor Navarro. Vidal, *João Pessoa*, p. 383. Additional conspirators, all of whom (except the last) became politically prominent in the 1930s, included Lieutenants Juracy Magalhães, Agildo Barata, Jurandir Mamede, Paulo Cordeiro, and Col. José Ávila Lins (brother of the Capital's prefeito João Ávila Lins).

Conclusion: The Demise of Family-Based Politics

THE ERA of the oligarchies had ended, and the Pessoas had been swept away in its wake. But what of the role that family-based politics had played in Paraíba? Had the developments of the 1920s modified those powerful, informal groups? Did the decade mark a significant transformation in the political alignments historically reflecting affiliations of kinship and friendship?

On the most obvious level, the conclusion could be drawn that little had changed. José Pereira's Princesa Revolt appeared to represent a cyclical phenomenon in Paraíba's oligarchical politics, one common in the Northeast: the attempt of powerful backlands parentelas to redress their grievances following exclusion en bloc from the dominant coalition. Many families who had adopted such a course of action in 1912, such as the Dantas of Teixeira, joined Col. José Pereira in revolt in 1930. As in 1912, they seized an opportunity presented by events at the national level of politics. A breach between the federal government and the oligarchy's leadership offered the opening they needed. However, in 1912 the president had sided with the ruling oligarchy against the rebels, whereas in 1930 Paraíba's governor was abandoned by the president of Brazil and left to be devoured by the forces of his own intracoalitional schism. If the October Revolution had not intervened, no doubt the rebels would have weathered the final stalemate and toppled the state government. And it could still be argued that they achieved their literal goal: by assassinating João Pessoa, the Princesa rebels defeated him.

Yet the Princesa Revolt was also a manifestation of political and economic change. It therefore signifies how the Old Republic was an era of transition in Paraíba's system of family-based rule. Unlike the 1912 insurrection, Col. Zé Pereira's 1930 rebellion pushed the issue of the backlands economy—and the commercial empire of the Pessoa de Queiroz—to the forefront of the crisis. The mere loss of political representation that a group of backlands families suffered, while a strong motive, might not have led such a large bloc of them to join the rebellion. In 1912, for instance, the politically motivated Dantas–Santa Cruz insurrection occurred only after those families had spent a decade trying to redress their loss of political prestige by other means. The Princesa Revolt, on the other hand, was a reaction to a decade of economic growth. Epitácio's oligarchy had furthered a widely shared economic goal, the creation of a statewide export infrastructure mutually advantageous to coast and backlands. The consensus implied in the commitment to infrastructure was not contingent on the sacrifice of any zone. Similarly, under the Machado–Leal oligarchy, even when preferences had been granted on the basis of geoeconomic zone—to the coastal Capital and the brejo—they did not spell economic ruin for the oligarchy's incumbent blocs in the backlands. João Pessoa's policies ended the consensus so carefully constructed by his uncle. By 1929, therefore, family blocs in the southern Paraíba backlands were locked in conflict with the state government over an economic issue vital to their survival.

At the beginning of the 1920s, the gradual demise of family-based politics in Paraíba was most evident in the political structure, although economic change best explained how an older, patrimonial set of relationships had ceased to characterize all political behavior. In the nineties, a still strongly patrimonialistic State cast a long shadow across the factions comprising the ruling oligarchy, complementing the familialism and personalism on which they depended. Factional alignments reflected the Empire's principal parentela divisions, subsuming them as Conservatives and Liberals; however, family affiliations took precedence over partisan or ideological allegiances while incorporating collective material interests. Although parentela divisions continued to reflect the antagonistic alignments of the nineties for several decades, by the 1920s strong currents of both zonal and individual economic interest had come to the forefront. The two backlands zones, for instance, had been buttresses of the Liberal Party until the 1880s and continued informally to express that alignment even after 1912. But they answered Col. Zé Pereira's call for secession from the State of Paraíba when an economic issue became paramount. The family affiliations of the late Empire, in other words, gave way to ones directly reflecting the investment in export agriculture that elite families in the backlands had acquired since the 1880s.

João Pessoa catalyzed the conflict implicit in rapid socioeconomic growth by converting accepted quasi-patrimonial relationships into political issues. His challenge called into question the historical reliance of elite families in the municípios upon a patronage State. In attempting to expand the state government's role at the expense of local prerogatives, João Pessoa broke important new ground. Although his efforts failed in the short run, his stance presaged eventual change for family-based politics. His determination to expand the authority of the State in the Paraíba hinterland simply extended the efforts of his predecessors since 1912, although the ability of all of them to effect reforms depended on the pace of socioeconomic change.[1] In challenging mandonismo, João Pessoa attempted to draw on the most important socioeconomic change of the 1920s, the emergence of a class-based society. He turned to popular mobilization as a means of undercutting the strong vertical alignments on which both clientism and family-based politics depended. Despite the absence of a political context in which such a strategy could be successful, he thus foreshadowed the populism that would flourish in the decades after 1930.

The governor's strategy depended on mobilizing public opinion, which had first found a political voice by denouncing banditry at the turn of the century. The success of his appeal drew directly on the erosion of social control that rural landlords in particular exercised. In the cities and towns of both coast and interior, strikes bore witness to a parallel challenging of the bonds of clientism between workers and employers that also contributed to João Pessoa's mass popularity. Thus, by the end of the 1920s, public opinion had evolved beyond a limited class base in the Capital's commercial and professional sectors, reaching to both town and countryside in the interior. The governor found support for his anti-coronelista reforms among small freeholders, agricultural tenants, and rural wage laborers as well as the expanding urban lower middle class and working class.

In reality João Pessoa's target was never oligarchy per se but oligarchy's retrograde wing—a sector of the agrarian bourgeoisie that continued to be unaccountable to the governor, the courts, their client dependents, or public opinion. This wing survived by virtue

[1] See Conniff, *Urban Brazil*, pp. 152–59. The first genuinely populist campaign for the presidency would have taken place in 1938, had not Getúlio Vargas proclaimed a dictatorship. Its momentum was evident in the presidential candidacy of Paraíba's José Américo de Almeida, whose position on the ticket of the National Liberating Alliance (Aliança Nacional Libertadora) in 1937 gained sufficient popular support to split the vote between him and Vargas, opening the possibility that the oligarchies would return to power by default.

of its rural political entrenchment, a closed social milieu, and relatively great economic power at the município level. Not surprisingly, it embraced the bosses most given to peculation, violence, and the exploitation of tenants, those whom João Pessoa and his coterie regarded as "seigneurial." Although the governor mobilized a multiclass base against this retrograde sector of the oligarchy, he himself represented a different sector, that of the urban professionals and civil servants who were middle class. He spoke effectively on behalf of the commercial-agrarian bourgeoisie, especially in and around the Capital, which sought a larger role for the State. By imposing both fiscal responsibility and law and order, this exporting bourgeoisie expected to further economic growth. João Pessoa's campaign for "clean" government and his effort to enlarge the State's resources, as well as to expand its role in the economy, coincided with this sector's notion of the "public interest." The governor's campaign to make local bosses more accountable to his central authority, they expected, would extend their influence in the interior by rationalizing the basis on which commerce was transacted.

At the leadership level, the polarization in 1929–1930 between Aliancista "Liberals" and Perrepista "Republicans" in Paraíba revealed a new dimension of the political alignments inherited from the nineteenth century. On the one hand, those Perrepistas most strongly opposed to João Pessoa—a majority of the Capital's Commercial Association—belonged to mostly Old Liberal families who had been Valfredistas; and many traced their social origins to Valfredo's home town of Areia and its early nineteenth-century Portuguese immigrant families. Even during the 1920s, among the Capital's Soares, Holandas, and Cavalcanti Monteiros, as well as between them and the Lima Mindêlos and Leites, several generations of intermarriage and close ties of friendship had coalesced to produce an influential family bloc. Under Governors Camilo de Holanda and Solon de Lucena (1916–1924), their patronage status had oscillated between lucrative favoritism and punitive confiscation. These polar positions merely mirrored the pattern of ins versus outs characteristic of factions in a family-based oligarchy.

On the other hand, this wealthy commercial bloc which dominated the Commercial Association endorsed João Pessoa, offering enthusiastic initial support for his policies of "liberation" from the Recife emporium. The family-based groups belonging to the bloc set aside their partisan preferences deriving from a pattern of historical affiliation because their commercial interests would be well served by the new governor's commitment to the development of a deepwater port and the erection of a wall of protective tariffs. But even before 1928, this large and influential bloc of merchants and entrepreneurs with strong ties of loyalty to Heráclito Cavalcanti Monteiro—a member of one of its families—could hardly be called an opposition. Its cooperative relationship with Epitácio and several of his governors was too pragmatically successful. And, reciprocally, João Pessoa courted its support. The new economic role this bloc had acquired in the Capital since about 1910 had eroded older lines of alignment according to either the partisan label of Old Liberal or the family-based affiliation implicit in its composition since the late Empire.

Gradually, the organizational raison d'être of economic interest assumed a primary claim on the affiliative motives of the Heraclista bloc, although superficially they appeared to be bound primarily by ties of blood and kinship. Thus their break with Governor Pessoa resembled a closing of ranks as die-hard Valfredistas or Old Liberals. But they were reacting on the basis of the anticipated damage to their economic interests that João Pessoa's national candidacy with Getúlio Vargas augured. This is why Isidro Gomes, president of the Capital's Commercial Association, denounced João Pessoa for attempting to "intrigue with commerce"—to enlist his economic interest group on behalf of the governor's *personal* ambition in national politics. The new national implications of João Pessoa's domestic politics implied, like the taxation of the Capital's branch firms in Campina Grande, that further political support would be prejudicial to their interests as businessmen.[2] Just as in the backlands, where families had been investing heavily in the production of cotton for export, by 1930 economic interest had acquired new importance for political alignments in the Capital.

Long-term patterns of family allegiance in politics cannot be ignored. Although after 1930 family-based groups and networks became decisively weakened in their organizing capacity, they persisted as primary units of political mobilization for more than a

[2] Whether kinship links connected Isidro Gomes to exporters in Campina Grande could not be established, but the Holandas and Borges had business establishments in both cities, suggesting that their interests in Campina probably were hurt by the Tributary War. The extent to which João Pessoa's own followers repudiated him on the basis of either his national candidacy or the deadlock in the Tributary War also could not be assessed. His status as a political martyr for fifty years meant that no direct criticism of him—with the exception of a few items published in Pernambuco by those in the Dantas opposition—appeared in print until 1980.

decade. "The force of kinship does not suddenly drop dead," Morton Fried once reminded students of kinship organization in postrevolutionary China.[3] Although the major causes of their demise were evident during the 1920s, the political system had yet to undergo transformation to an organizational dependence on interest groups more directly derived from ties of income, occupation, social class, or ideology. Recent revision of Brazil's political periodization has meant that historians now recognize the years from 1922 to 1937 as the crucial years of transition in the country's modern political evolution. Since the events of 1930 no longer are regarded as constituting a revolution, the absence of greater change in Paraíba's informal political system before that year is not surprising.

Careful scrutiny of the changes that did emerge during the 1920s nevertheless reveal evidence of the transformation of family-based politics in Paraíba that became more apparent later in the century. For instance, ideological appeal as the basis for a mass political appeal first achieved significance in Paraíba during the 1920s, although (until the Estado Nôvo banned political parties in 1937) such appeals are more appropriately associated with the post-1930 political context. But with the initiation of the Aliança Liberal campaign in 1929, ideological divisions gained momentum against the ties of family-based loyalties. João Pessoa's call for reform within Paraíba, prior to his candidacy, had evidenced the new role of ideological issues in both national and state politics after 1930, especially questions of constitutionalism, the Tenentes' authoritarian nationalism, legal rights for labor, and the role of the State in the national economy. Increasingly, these issues would involve individuals from all social classes in a new national debate.[4] The growing significance of ideology in Paraíba's intraelite divisions could be deduced from provisions in the Aliança Liberal's platform. Because Perrepismo—in Paraíba as well as the nation—stood for the defense of the status quo, it was directly defensive of coronelismo and localism. When the Aliança's platform enlarged the role of the State in national politics, a new ideological element was injected in Paraíba's politics, one heightening intra-

[3] Morton Fried, "Some Aspects of Clanship in a Modern Chinese City," in *Political Anthropology*, ed. Marc J. Swartz, Victor W. Turner, and Arthur Tuden (Chicago: Aldine Publishing Co., 1966), p. 285.

[4] Epitácio's effective retirement from national politics reflected a withdrawal in the face of new ideological currents in the national debate, in addition to his distaste for the authoritarian direction of Vargas and the Tenentes, about which he had "doctrinal reservations." L. Pessôa, *Epitacio Pessôa*, 2:822.

elite divisions both among and within the principal family-based groups.

In the long run, the key element missing in the 1920s was a strong, centralized State. The demise of family-based politics in Paraíba is best explained, therefore, in terms of the imposition of a central State during the 1930s, when the Vargas Revolution restructured political and economic institutions at the national level. Although a strong State emerged only in 1937, when the Vargas dictatorship imposed the Estado Novo, incremental change at the federal level had already pointed in a statist direction. In hindsight, the 1920s also reflected the larger role the federal government had begun to play in Brazil's national economy and, indirectly, in the economies of the states, as historical scholarship has recently stressed.[5] In that respect, political developments in Paraíba during the final decade of the Old Republic suggested that the trend toward centralization had begun to accelerate. Again, socioeconomic change at the national level was important. Demand for greater state revenues also led Paraíba's governors to attempt to impose their authority on the hinterland. Despite the absence of decisive victories, definite incremental progress had been made since 1912. Thus, the centralization imposed by Vargas after 1930, which expanded a federal presence at the expense of the state governor, drew on gubernatorial initiatives in the late 1920s to enlarge the sphere of the State. In this respect, between 1930 and 1932, Vargas picked two Paraibanos to govern the Northeast—Juarez Távora, "the Vice-Roy of the North," and José Américo de Almeida, his successor as the federal government's regional interventor. Both implemented centralization on behalf of the national government.[6]

The most important federal policy to strike at family-based politics' survival in the Northeast after 1930 built directly on the campaign of João Pessoa and his predecessors to curb private violence. It relied on the Brazilian army to disarm the backlands. The federal government's unprecedented offensive against banditry received wide publicity; the confiscation of arsenals belonging to many backlands bosses—and even their arrest—transformed the relationship between the central State and the elite families who had ruled the region's interior. After Lampião's death in 1938, the

[5] Steven Topik's *The Political Economy of the Brazilian State, 1889–1930* (Austin: University of Texas Press, in press), explores this trend as a major theme.

[6] Conniff offers a succinct analysis of the Tenentes' reforms in this respect in "Tenentes in Power," pp. 72-82.

23. José Américo de Almeida succeeded Juarez Távora as regional governor of Northeast Brazil in 1931, following the latter's tragic death. José Américo is shown here (center) with fellow revolutionary conspirators Antenor Navarro and Odon Bezerra in João Pessoa in 1932. A stronger federal presence throughout the 1930s dramatically reduced family warfare and extinguished banditry by 1940. (Courtesy of the Acervo Humberto Nóbrega)

demise of banditry was rapid. Unlike the experience in 1907, when a federal battalion failed to capture the bandit Antônio Silvino, this effort adopted an interstate approach and struck at the vital protection bandits received as part of the pattern of family warfare characteristic of the political milieu. The federal government thus played the paramount role in delivering the final blow both to the cangaço and to family warfare.[7] The historical distribution of power that had made the hinterland of the Northeast semi-autonomous now shifted not toward the coastal capitals of the state governors but to Rio de Janeiro and the president of Brazil. The reversal was permanent. The new role of the federal government in state politics significantly hastened the demise of the family-based groups and networks on which oligarchy in Paraíba rested. And the suspension of electoral politics by Vargas from 1937 to 1945 robbed coronelismo of its raison d'être in the national political system.

[7] See Chandler, *Bandit King*, pp. 234–37.

The national government's centralizing offensive is a development of only the last forty years. In appraising the survival of family-based politics in Paraíba, therefore, change should be evaluated in terms of generations, not decades. The Old Republic lasted little more than a generation. Change can be measured more meaningfully by assessing the 1920s from the hindsight of the 1970s—a span of two generations. The gradual trend toward reducing elite family prerogatives at the local level can perhaps best be evaluated in terms of one issue that Gov. João Pessoa confronted in the 1920s, namely, the influence local elites exercised over juries, particularly in murder trials related to family vendettas. In 1971, Brazil's major pictorial weekly, *O Cruzeiro,* featured a prominent article on the "new mentality" evident in northeastern states in these cases. Where formerly acquittals for murder had been *pro forma* in vendettas, the magazine noted that now circumstances and issues inherent in individual cases were receiving attention. And, it reported, convictions were being handed down. No longer was it easier, the article pointed out, to obtain an acquittal than to obtain a writ of *habeas corpus* for the original indictment. Family affiliations, implicit in partisan interest, could be overridden to bring a murderer to justice, it concluded, for a new breed of juror (often residing outside the venue of the trial) was having an impact.[8]

Family-based power still survives at the local level in Paraíba and Northeast Brazil in its most familiar form, coronelismo. Given the parallel survival of latifundia, exploitative labor relations in rural zones, poverty, illiteracy, and disease in many parts of the northeastern states, this is not a startling revelation. One of coronelismo's hallmarks, family feuding, also endures on a greatly reduced scale, reminding students of political and social behavior that where the historically supportive milieu has remained largely unchanged the política de família can still be studied. Between April and August 1981, the national press reported a recrudescence of a well-known feud between the Alencars and Sampaios of Pernambuco. Originating in the backlands município of Exu, this feud began in 1947. Its latest cycle erupted in downtown Recife during the noon hour. While waiting for a traffic light to change, two Alencar cousins were gunned down in their car by assassins

[8] Tobias Granja, "O vingador absolvido," *O Cruzeiro* [Rio de Janeiro], 21 Apr. 1971, pp. 95–98.

acting on behalf of the Sampaios.[9] The number of victims sacrificed since the feud began reached well over thirty by August 1981. The Sampaios and Alencars have been fighting over which of their family-based groups would control their home município of Exu.[10] Needless to say, in the forty-four years of their conflict, each had periodically wrested a precarious hold on local officeholding from the other.

Catolé do Rocha, in Paraíba, also can be cited for the well-publicized feud there between the Suassunas and Maias. Its origins can be traced to the mid-1920s, as Chapter VIII implies, when the brothers of João Suassuna and the sons of Col. Francisco Hermenegildo Maia went to war over the control of local offices in Catolé.[11] A century after Col. Francisco Maia greeted Venâncio Neiva as the município's new imperial district judge in the 1880s, his grandson, "Doutor" Zé Sergio Maia, met with a reporter from the newsweekly ISTOÉ, and in the company of Romero Suassuna—patriarchal head of his family—discussed the history and causes of their feud. Their interview offered confirmation that many municípios today are ruled by descendants of the same families who controlled them in the late Empire. And, in a surprising number of cases, family alignments still reflect a nineteenth-century pattern, although the Suassunas and Maias ceased to be allies sixty years ago. Romero Suassuna pointed out that, as a result of his family's feud with the Maias, the Suassunas became Perrepistas in 1929–1930, while the Maias embraced João Pessoa's Aliança Liberal. His explanation of the Suassunas' repudiation of Epitacismo ignored the reasons at the state level of oligarchy that had prompted his kinsman João Suassuna to run as a Perrepista. Understandably, his concern was with the local elite struggle for Catolé. But his point is well taken, for, as he stressed, the two families have consistently affiliated with opposing parties at the national struggle due

[9] "A luta de Exu chega a Recife e faz dois mortos," *Folha de São Paulo*), (?) July 1980, p. 1; "Mais duas vítimas na sangrenta Exu," ibid.

[10] Ernesto Neves, "Exu, o medo domina uma cidade," *O Estado de São Paulo*, 31 July 1981; Marvine Howe, "Violent Life-Style Seems to Revive in Rural Brazil," *New York Times*, 29 Nov. 1972, p. 12. Warren Hoge, "In Brazil's Wild Northeast, No End to Bloodletting," ibid., 20 Aug. 1982.

[11] Antonio Carlos Fon, "A morte como professão," ISTOÉ [São Paulo], 12 July 1983. (The author is indebted to Richard Parker for bringing this article to her attention.) Like ISTOÉ, popular accounts of this feud focus on a "Romeo and Juliet" dimension, when the Suassunas vetoed Francisco Sergio Maia's courtship of Noêmia Suassuna and shot and killed her rejected suitor's father. Ibid.

to their rivalry over officeholding. After enumerating the successive affiliations of Suassunas and Maias at the national level since 1945, Romero clinched his point by adding, "It could just as well have been the other way around. Whatever party we belong to, they will join the opposing one, or vice versa."[12]

Nevertheless, it would be misleading to conclude this analysis by overly emphasizing either the continuity of post-1930 political alignments with those dating to the Empire or the persistence of feuding. Instead, some of the findings of the French political scientist Jean Blondel deserve concluding remark. Blondel studied Paraíba's partisan politics during the early populist period in 1950–1951 and identified factors that in this book were shown to have emerged during the 1920s, although he ascribed them to the post-1945 era.[13] Basing his conclusions on field work in Paraíba and an analysis of the elections held during 1945–1950 (the first since the collapse of the Estado Novo after World War II), Blondel found that the political machine so indispensable to the Pessoa oligarchy no longer existed: "Studying the political machine means nothing," he emphasized, "because it does not exist."[14] Competitive party politics, a phenomenon introduced in Brazil in the post-1945 era, coupled with greatly expanded suffrage, he argued, had freed a number of the most powerful local party bosses from traditional machine politics.[15] These new bosses tended to be professionals who lacked ties to the landed economy and were therefore frequently opposed to "the aristocracy," that is, oligar-

[12] Ibid. The author has reversed the partisan affiliations that Fon, the reporter, ascribed to the Suassunas (Aliança Liberal) and the Maias (Perrepista). As if to validate Romero's point, the reporter confused the association of family names and party labels. Romero stated that in 1945 the Perrepistas joined UDN (União Democrática Nacional) and in the 1970s entered the PMDB (Partido do Movimento Democrático Brasileiro), while, simultaneously, the Aliancistas first belonged to the PSD (Partido Social Democrático) and then shifted to the PSD (Partido Democrático Social). Ibid.

[13] Blondel, *Vida política Paraíba*. For instance, he assumed that coronelismo's "collegial" character was a feature of the post-1930 period and claimed that the "monarchical" coronel was a relic of Paraíba's past. Ibid., pp. 60–62.

[14] Ibid., p. 132.

[15] On the other hand, Blondel confirmed the wide divergences in Paraíba's local political organization, particularly between urban and isolated rural contexts. Without mentioning either Maias or Suassunas by name, he described their political dominions in Catolé do Rocha and Brejo do Cruz, as well as that of the intermarried Ribeiro Coutinhos and Veloso Borges on the coast, singling out latifundia, family size, and family cohesion to explain their control of those municípios. Ibid., pp. 61–62.

chy's surviving vestiges. Even in rural areas, they no longer controlled elections.[16]

However, Blondel singled out one factor which Sílvio Romero had stressed as a key basis for political bonding during the Old Republic: *"amizade,"* friendship or regard. Parties, he observed, remained subordinated to personalities.[17] And competition between parties occurred along factional lines that remained personalistic. Thus, as kinship bonds have come into greater conflict with socioeconomic change since the 1920s, political friendship has increasingly taken up the slack and filled analogous demands for trust and loyalty. This trend could be clearly discerned in Gov. João Pessoa's administration, in contrast to his predecessors. Although he relied on a number of his brothers and cousins for mobilizing support at all levels for his policies, in his cabinet appointments he drew disproportionately on political friends, not relatives. The most prominent choices for those posts—José Américo, Antenor Navarro, Ademar Vidal, and Álvaro de Carvalho—did not have even a remote degree of kinship to him. Nor had they formerly been intimate friends in the affective sense. Instead, they were bound to him by shared political values, a common opposition to local family-based prerogatives, and their ties to Epitácio.[18]

Peter McDonough has recently analyzed Brazil's national elites and drawn several conclusions about "upwardly mobile elite linkages" which touch on the role of kinship at the national pinnacles of power. He found that among the smaller and wealthier elites in the worlds of business and politics kin ties tend to be denser than among the elites representing the poorer strata in the population—labor unions and the civil service. In the latter instance, ties based on friendship tended to be denser.[19] This distinction confirms what has been argued here regarding the broad role of elite kinship organization in Empire and Republic: it served to restrict the resources of officeholding and material patronage to the highest echelons of society. Although there were dramatic exceptions, Paraíba's cotton boom produced only a small increase in upward social

[16] In both João Pessoa and Campina Grande, "the political boss had virtually disappeared." Ibid., p. 116.

[17] Ibid., pp. 116–19.

[18] Blondel, for instance, pointed to Antenor Navarro as illustrative of a new type of political boss, one whose power originates in the central authority. Ibid., pp. 68–69.

[19] Peter McDonough, *Power and Ideology in Brazil* (Princeton: Princeton University Press, 1981), p. 96.

mobility, if any at all. While Epitácio's archive contains some impressive testimonials to how individuals of humble origin had been raised in his oligarchy—in the capacity of political friend—such examples usually attached importance to affiliation with a politically influential family.[20]

There are two points to be made in this respect. First, because social structure in Brazil remains extremely hierarchical, it is not surprising that many of the same families who enjoyed political office in the Old Republic continued to do so in the populist era beginning in 1945—as Jean Blondel found.[21] For that matter, the family continuity of recruitment in politics, despite many exceptions, could still be observed in the post-1964 authoritarian era during the 1970s and the 1980s. Given that in Paraíba economic power continues to be highly concentrated among a small number of elite families, this circumstance is not surprising. With the imposition of military rule, moreover, the mass politicization characteristic of the populist era came to a close in 1964. In Paraíba's case, a decade of rural militancy, which had witnessed the regional emergence of the peasant leagues, ended in a brutal repression of hundreds of peasant leaders in the coastal sugar zone and adjacent caatinga-agreste. And for yet another two decades, the tightly interwoven elite families controlling both land and sugar refineries in those zones remained free from any challenge on a class basis that aimed to open the political system to either peasants or rural wage labor. The so-called Várzea Group (Grupo da Várzea) that still continued to represent the sugar latifundia interests in Paraíba in the 1980s—the same whose presumed agents were indicted for the 1962 murder of Brazil's most famous peasant leader,

[20] Álvaro de Carvalho, for example, expressed his gratitude on being nominated João Pessoa's first lieut. governor: "Poor, without family of any standing, at first unprotected and alone, I came out of a barbershop where the common sense of my alert father had placed me at age ten. I never thought that this . . . would be the [goal] of my career. . . ." Álvaro de Carvalho to Epitácio (Capital), 4 Feb. 1927, AEP/9/2.

[21] Blondel saw in the major parties—the UDN and PSD—"some of the *panelinhas*" common to the political generation of the Old Republic and its "aristocratic circles." *Vida política Paraíba*, p. 31. Former Senator Octacílio de Albuquerque observed in the 1930s: "Even today, he who studies, examines, and observes the dominant family groupings can verify and point out that the names of the families are always the same: The Araújos, Medeiros, Galvãos, Figueirêdos, Lucenas, Gondins, Vasconcelos, Ribeiros, Dantas, Coutinhos, Albuquerques, Barbosas, Gomes, Portos, Maias, and I do not know how many more." Quoted in L. Pinto, *Síntese histórica*, p. 216.

João Pedro Teixeira—illustrates how the survival of such influential clusters of elite family power derives directly from the conservative evolution of class structure.[22] Unfortunately, especially the reliance on violence and assassination to exclude substantial segments of the state's population from meaningful participation in politics continues into the present, postauthoritarian era, as the generation succeeding Pedro Teixeira's attempts to resume the fight to gain legal protection and representation for those in the rural work force.[23] Thus, in this extremely significant instance, one that today can be apprised again on the front pages of *A União* and *Correio da Paraíba*, family-based power remains inextricably tied to both the post-1945 pattern of officeholding and an impressive concentration of economic power grounded in a modern latifundia. Any attempt to assess class structure in Paraíba since World War II must confront such an obstacle to change.

The second point worth emphasizing is that the shift away from a reliance on kinship and toward a greater dependence on political friendship may not have altered fundamentally the informal group basis of politics in Paraíba. This is so even though over the last decade a remarkable number of newcomers—outsiders to the Capital's closed social elite—have risen to prominence in state politics. Although the basic units of mobilization no longer are characterized by a pervasive reliance on kinship bonds, those groupings rely heavily on political friendship in the context of a national society that enjoys distinction in Latin America as one whose elites have impressively resisted the forces of social mobility since World War II. Thus the shift toward political friendship

[22] João Pedro Teixeira was the president of the peasant league in Sapé, Paraíba, until his murder on April 2, 1962. With the imposition of military rule soon afterward, his widow went into hiding under an assumed name in Rio Grande do Norte for eighteen years. Recently, her story during those years, coupled with parts of a film begun on the peasant leagues in 1961, has been the subject of a highly acclaimed film directed by Eduardo Coutinho, *Uma cabra marcado para morrer* (1984). The "Várzea Group" refers to the agroindustrial bloc of Ribeiro Coutinhos, Veloso Borges, Lundgrens, and Gadelhas, whose landed enterprises embrace the production of other commodities than merely sugar. César Benevides's *Camponeses em marcha* (Rio de Janeiro: Paz e Terra, 1985) is an excellent new analysis of the peasant leagues in Paraíba. See pp. 30–31 on the officeholding patterns of certain members of the Várzea Group by family, as well as pp. 27–31 on its history.

[23] The notorious assassination of Margarida Maria Alves, president of the Sindicato dos Trabalhadores Rurais de Alagoa Grande, on August 12, 1983, is a case in point. The official investigation of her death concluded that she had been shot by an agent of landowners, but no indictment could be brought. Fernando Antônio Azevêdo, in Benevides, *Camponeses*, p. 17–18.

and away from kinship, rather than evidencing basic change, may even belie it.

This is why, at the level of the central State, patrimonialistic features have persisted, albeit unevenly, to limit change and to preserve a still fairly closed pool for political recruitment. In this respect assessment of recent change in Paraíba again raises the relevant factor of change at the national level. Of course, a strong countertrend began in the late 1920s, with an anti-oligarchical critique that condemned the political system's reliance on personal discretion and entitlements based on status. This countertrend led eventually to the statist revolution that began in the 1930s and introduced merit principles of bureaucratic recruitment, opening considerably the political system to new groups. Then the populist era in politics during the 1940s, 1950s, and early 1960s continued to challenge Brazil's patrimonial legacy by stressing political participation and goals derived from egalitarian values. Yet, as the scholarly literature makes very clear, this countertrend is recent and it has not rid the State of many attributes associated with patrimonialism.

Finally, two closing points can be offered in connection with the fading role of the elite family in politics. First, socioeconomic change in Paraíba, which has been considerable in the last two decades, has caused the elite family to surrender irrevocably a preponderant political influence. But that influence has not altogether ceased. The adaptation inherent in the shift over a century ago to exogamous and horizontal bonding, which has received central attention in this book, continues to account for the influential survival of political influence exercised by a number of elite parentelas. Nor has kinship organization displayed dramatic modification as a result of rapid socioeconomic change over the last quarter century. As anthropologist Jack Goody recently cautioned students of Europe's evolving kinship organization, evidence of historical change in family structure should not be sought in a search for new forms. The evolution of family organization is fairly conservative: "It is not a matter of replacement," he cautioned, for shifts in family structure associated with the emergence of a modern society "still leave a bilateral core as the dominant form."[24] His point that "what remains is . . . a more restricted core of the former kin grouping" can easily be appreciated in Pa-

[24] Jack Goody, *The Development of the Family and Marriage in Europe* (Cambridge: Cambridge University Press, 1983), p. 233.

24. Revolutionary President Getúlio Vargas (seated left) and his wife Darcy (seated right) stood as *padrinhos de casamento* for the Northeast's Governor General Juarez Távora when he married his first cousin, Nair B. Távora, on January 14, 1931. In the decades since 1930, cousin marriage has declined markedly, but for many it continues to be a matter of choice, perpetuating that option as a distinctive feature of Brazilian kinship organization down to the present. (Courtesy of the Arquivo Fundação Casa de José Américo)

raíba and Brazil.[25] What Goody stressed for nineteenth-century Europe was also true for Northeast Brazil, where the same system of cognatic descent holds, because "the bilateral reckoning of [descent] and the bilateral balance [in organization] remain."[26] In other words, kinship organization reflects an evolution of its own that will find expression in the family's endurance over generations according to remarkably familiar organization features, even if today the role that family plays is much stronger as a unit of social and economic security than as a political actor.

The second point, consequently, concerns the erosion of the role

[25] Ibid.

[26] Ibid., p. 210.

that the elite extended family has played in this century. Although future research will undoubtedly establish distinctly regional patterns in the historical demise of family power in Brazil, the evidence presented in this study for Paraíba's case can still be taken as broadly suggestive for Brazil. What stands out clearly is the loss of a quasi-corporate identity that accompanied the decline in the elite family's reliance on a landed base. As the 1920s indicated, once commerce, industry, and the professions provided the majority of a parentela's membership with their livelihoods, then the dependence on a pattern of joint and contiguous land ownership by members of the same family declined. The strategy for maintaining an impressive collective and intergenerational identity no longer remained viable—or it did so among very few members. By the same token, spatial mobility no longer could be as effectively offset because the notion of a home município—however symbolically maintained—ceased to bind generations together. The parallel reform of inheritance law, one that granted new impetus to individualism at the expense of a family collectivity, accelerated the demise of the elite family's quasi-corporate identity by rendering patrimony more varied and disposable. More recently, declining elite family size also has generationally confined solidarity.

Hence, today elite family solidarity, which at best was always precarious over generations, is infinitely more restricted. Confined to a conjugal core and not expected to endure much beyond a generation, this solidarity remains but a pale image of what for centuries the great families in Brazil perpetuated—or sought to perpetuate—among two or three generations of descendants. Yet the disappearance of the elite family's influential role, one that implied the aggregation of an extremely broad set of social, economic, and political functions, may not hold great significance in Paraíba or Brazil. The survival of an impressive degree of social hierarchy still offers, on the basis of rank, many of the entitlements that formerly were claimed by virtue of membership in "a traditional family." But this blurring of distinction between class and kinship does not diminish the historical role that the elite extended family has played for centuries as a pivotal political and economic unit. Brazil's elite parentela, with its "política de família," will continue to offer one of the most fascinating keys for unlocking the rural history of the nation, particularly at a regional level.

Appendix A: Cotton Production and Export, 1889–1930

TABLE A.1: Annual Production of Raw and Ginned Cotton in Paraíba (1911/12 to 1930/31)

Year	Raw cotton in kilos	Ginned cotton in kilos
1911/12	35,167,054	11,605,158
1912/13	31,088,185	10,569,983
1913/14	38,789,273	13,188,353
1914/15	39,926,327	13,175,688
1915/16	27,283,017	9,278,480
1916/17	27,283,017	9,276,226
1917/18	31,555,088	10,727,370
1918/19	33,428,182	11,365,585
1919/20	37,089,154	12,239,421
1920/21	36,644,453	11,726,225
1921/22	38,276,018	12,248,326
1922/23	36,691,357	13,098,069
1923/24	40,099,417	13,633,864
1924/25	56,158,980	18,717,176
1925/26	—	20,600,062
1926/27	—	19,999,955
1927/28	—	19,899,792
1928/29	—	17,999,959
1929/30	—	28,999,825
1930/31	—	17,999,959

SOURCES: Centro Industrial de Fiação e Tecelagem do Algodão [CIFTA], "Produção e manufactura do algodão no Brasil e exportados" (Rio de Janeiro: CIFTA, n.d.), unnumbered tables; Juvencio Mariz de Lyra, *Aspectos economicos da exploração algodoeira no Brasil* (Rio de Janeiro: n.p., 1933), chart 2.

NOTE: Annual production figures for raw and ginned cotton have been drawn from official state and local sources for the State of Paraíba, rather than from CIFTA's federal government statistics used to compile comparative statistics on cotton for all Brazilian states. Although in given years discrepancies occurred, the Paraíba sources appeared to be more reliable not only because they directly reflected local reporting but also because they could be confirmed or indirectly reflected in other sources. (CIFTA's statistics appeared to be underreported.)

TABLE A.2: Paraíba's Rank Order in Maritime Exports of Raw Cotton by State (1920–1930)

Year	Kilos exported	Rank order	Value (in rounded contos)	Rank order	Total Brazilian exports (in kilos)
1920	(1,802,359)	5	(5,106)	5	(24,696,079)
1921	(3,035,264)	4	(5,473)	4	(19,060,566)
1922	(4,554,144)	4	(12,883)	4	(33,947,395)
1923	(3,040,839)	4	(20,133)	3	(19,169,584)
1924	(1,261,638)	3	(6,049)	3	(6,464,382)
1925	(6,326,188)	5	(22,940)	3	(30,635,260)
1926	(4,861,902)	1	(11,672)	1	(16,689,017)
1927	(3,357,514)	1	(11,455)	1	(11,916,356)
1928	(3,868,800)	2	(9,060)	2	(10,009,909)
1929	(15,945,720)	1	(48,288)	1	(48,727,852)
1930	(6,218,976)	3	(17,855)	3	(30,415,842)

SOURCES: "Exportação do algodão brasileiro," in Centro Industrial de Fiação e Tecelagem de Algodão [CIFTA], *Relatorio de 1927 e 1928* (Rio de Janeiro: Tipografia *Jornal do Comércio*, 1939), unnumbered chart; Juvencio Mariz de Lyra, *Aspectos economicos da exploração algodoeira no Brasil* (Rio de Janeiro: n.p., 1933), table 8.

NOTE: CIFTA's export figures for Paraíba are considerably lower than the official figures (cf. Table II.1). Note that the above figures include only cotton taxed and shipped directly from the customs office in the port of Cabedêlo.

TABLE A.3: Major Exports of Paraíba as Percentages of Total Value of Exports (1900–1929)
(Money amounts in rounded contos)

Year	Value of total exports	Cotton: Official value	Cotton: % of total	Cattle and leather: Official value	Cattle and leather: % of total	Sugar: Official value	Sugar: % of total	Cotton, cattle, and sugar combined as % of total
1900	10,051	6,883	68	1,891	19	917	9	96
1905	9,574	6,151	64	2,118	22	665	7	93
1910	17,890	13,531	76	2,988	17	387	2	95
1915	23,499	13,777	59	7,602	32	540	2	93
1920	44,715	27,319	61	6,739	15	2,502	6	82
1925	87,935	69,428	79	8,458	10	2,961	3	92
1929	99,555	73,557	74	4,376	4	1,653	2	80

SOURCES: Lyra Tavares, *A Parahyba*, 1:343–451; J. A. de Almeida, *Parahyba* ("Exportação geral do Estado pelas mercadorias," unnumbered chart); Lyra, *Aspectos exploração algodoeira*, tables 7, 9, 11–12; Diogenes Caldas, "Sínopse histórica do açucar," *Annuario Açucareiro* 1 (1935):107–108; *Exportação de 1929*, pp. 125–55; State of Paraíba, *Almanach do Estado da Parahyba do Norte de 1913* (Parahyba: [Imprensa Oficial], 1913), pp. 319, 322; *A União* (Capital), 13 Aug. 1927.

TABLE A.4: Revenue and Expenditure of the State of Paraíba: Export Taxes on Cotton as a Component (1891–1929) (Money amounts in contos)

Year	Total revenue	Expenditure	Surplus or deficit	Revenue from cotton[a]	
				Amount	Per cent[b]
1891	512	463	49	—	—
1892	725	619	106	—	—
1893	1,067	950	117	466	43.7
1894	1,033	1,235	−202	279	27.0
1895	1,325	1,163	162	163	12.3
1896	1,410	1,312	98	274	19.4
1897	1,108	1,322	−214	317	28.6
1898	999	1,177	−178	309	30.9
1899	1,006	1,241	−235	329	32.7
1900	1,143	1,181	−38	425	37.2
1901	1,271	1,314	−43	295	23.2
1902	1,265	1,549	−284	462	36.5
1903	1,608	1,539	69	644	40.0
1904	1,309	1,612	−303	397	30.3
1905	1,306	1,574	−268	498	38.1
1906	1,670	1,658	12	583	34.9
1907	1,840	1,754	86	803	43.6
1908	1,533	1,840	−307	629	41.0
1909	2,244	2,096	148	786	35.0
1910	2,751	2,526	225	1,084	39.4
1911	2,886	2,891	−5	1,058	36.7
1912	3,144	3,172	−28	1,284	40.8
1913	3,798	4,035	−237	3,391	89.3
1914	3,116	3,380	−264	898	28.8
1915	3,313	3,299	14	1,093	33.0
1916	4,769	3,749	1,020	2,063	43.3
1917	6,923	6,108	815	3,401	49.1
1918	6,522	7,618	−1,096	3,015	46.2
1919	5,240	6,167	−927	1,908	36.4
1920	5,720	5,961	−241	2,390	41.8
1921	5,521	5,755	−234	2,367	42.9
1922	7,729	6,866	863	4,179	54.1
1923	14,269	10,786	3,483	9,823	68.8
1924	11,679	14,515	−2,836	6,024	51.6
1925	11,486	12,458	−972	5,344	46.5
1926	9,684	10,379	−695	3,333	34.4
1927	12,790	12,039	751	3,933	30.8
1928	13,383	11,394	1,989	6,622	49.5
1929	13,063	13,744	−681	9,639	73.8

SOURCES: J. Santos Coelho Filho, *Impostos na Paraíba* (João Pessoa: *A União* Editôra, 1946), pp. 41–42; State of Paraíba, Secretaria da Fazenda, Agricultura e Obras Públicas, *Exportacão de 1929* (João Pessoa: Imprensa Oficial, 1932), pp. 44–45; J. A. de Almeida, *Parahyba*, p. 559; Lyra Tavares, *A Parahyba*, 1:343–451.

NOTE: See Table A.5 for the value of contos in U.S. dollars in given years. Arithmetic errors in the originals have been corrected.

[a] Revenues pertain only to those derived from ginned cotton, not from byproducts, such as seed cakes, oil, paste, and linter, which after 1920 raised the proportion of total revenues from all cotton products to at least 75 percent of the annual average for the decade.

[b] The statistics for 1923–1927 demonstated how falling world prices reduced Paraíba's revenues from cotton, even though exports rose to a record high, remaining between 14,703,771 and 16,709,801 million kilos annually. The official value (in contos) of cotton exports and the total taxes collected on cotton exports, as reported by Alfeu Domingues, federal director of the Serviço do Algodão do Paraíba, were as follows for each of the five years: 97,331 (9,823); 70,885 (6,577); 54,245 (4,704); 25,028 (2,221); and 45,045 (3,933). Annual report to the Ministry of Agriculture, quoted in *A União*, 1 May 1928. Where these figures for annual revenues from cotton exports disagree with those in this table (1924 to 1926), Domingues's information is probably accurate.

TABLE A.5: Value of Brazilian Contos in U.S. Dollars

Year	1 conto in U.S. dollars	Year	1 conto in U.S. dollars
1892	$ 244.4	1911	$ 321.0
1893	$ 230.3	1912	$ 331.8
1894	$ 207.0	1913	$ 321.3
1895	$ 198.5	1914	$ 318.0
1896	$ 177.6	1915	$ 292.7
1897	$ 143.9	1916	$ 230.6
1898	$ 136.4	1917	$ 247.5
1899	$ 146.1	1918	$ 245.7
1900	$ 186.2	1919	$ 267.4
1901	$ 223.0	1920	$ 225.1
1902	$ 234.9	1921	$ 131.2
1903	$ 239.9	1922	$ 129.5
1904	$ 251.8	1923	$ 102.3
1905	$ 309.6	1924	$ 109.4
1906	$ 317.5	1925	$ 122.0
1907	$ 301.3	1926	$ 144.4
1908	$ 301.8	1927	$ 118.4
1909	$ 303.5	1928	$ 119.7
1910	$ 302.7	1929	$ 111.1
		1930	$ 107.1

SOURCE: John Wirth, *Minas Gerais in the Brazilian Federation* (Stanford: Stanford University Press, 1977), pp. 262–63 (taken from the *Retrospecto Commercial do 'Jornal do Commercio,'* calculated from the mean of the highest and lowest quotation for the U.S. dollar in Rio). From 1919 on, the rates from New York as cited in the U.S. Department of Commerce, *Statistical Abstract of the United States*, various years.

NOTE: The largest monetary unit, one conto (1:000$000, or 1:000$), was equivalent to one thousand mil-réis. One mil-réis was written 1$000.

Appendix B: Elite Family Genealogies

Abbreviations Used in Appendix B

Political, Juridical, and Bureaucratic Offices

CCS	career civil servant
CM	career military
FD	federal deputy
FDJ	federal district judge (*juíz de direito*)
GC	gubernatorial cabinet
Gov.	governor
ID	imperial deputy
IDJ	imperial district judge (*juíz de direito*)
LG	lieutenant governor
ME	imperial minister (cabinet member)
MR	republican minister (cabinet member)
MSCJ	military supreme court justice
PD	provincial deputy (assemblyman)
S	senator
SCJ	supreme court justice
SD	state deputy (assemblyman)

Given and Family Names

Alb[que]	Albuquerque
Cav[ti]	Cavalcanti
Fran[ca]	Francisca
Fran[co]	Francisco
M.	Maria

NOTE: Since the compilation of the genealogies in this appendix sometimes obliged the author to choose between conflicting sources, errors may exist. The author would appreciate corrections and the evidence for them.

Figure B.1 Lucenas, Neivas, and Pessoas

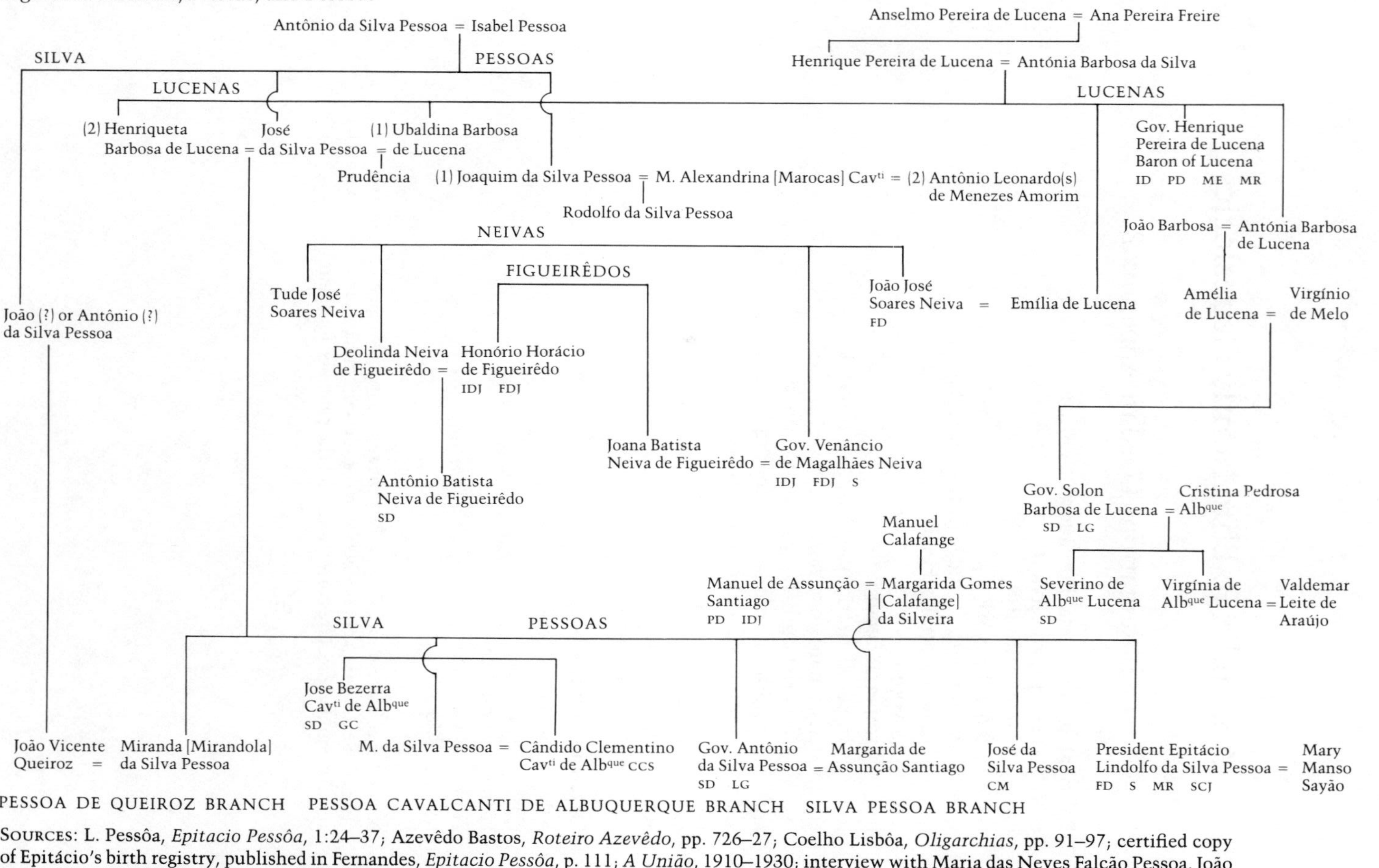

SOURCES: L. Pessôa, *Epitacio Pessôa*, 1:24–37; Azevêdo Bastos, *Roteiro Azevêdo*, pp. 726–27; Coelho Lisbôa, *Oligarchias*, pp. 91–97; certified copy of Epitácio's birth registry, published in Fernandes, *Epitacio Pessôa*, p. 111; *A União*, 1910–1930; interview with Maria das Neves Falcão Pessoa, João Pessoa, 21 July 1978; Lopes, *F. Pessoa de Queiroz*, pp. 27–29; certification of Epitácio's birth registry, Recife Law Faculty (Fichas Biográficas); interview with Paulo de Lucena, João Pessoa, 12 Aug. 1986.

Figure B.2 The Machado–Leal Oligarchy Intermarried with Milanez and Almeidas

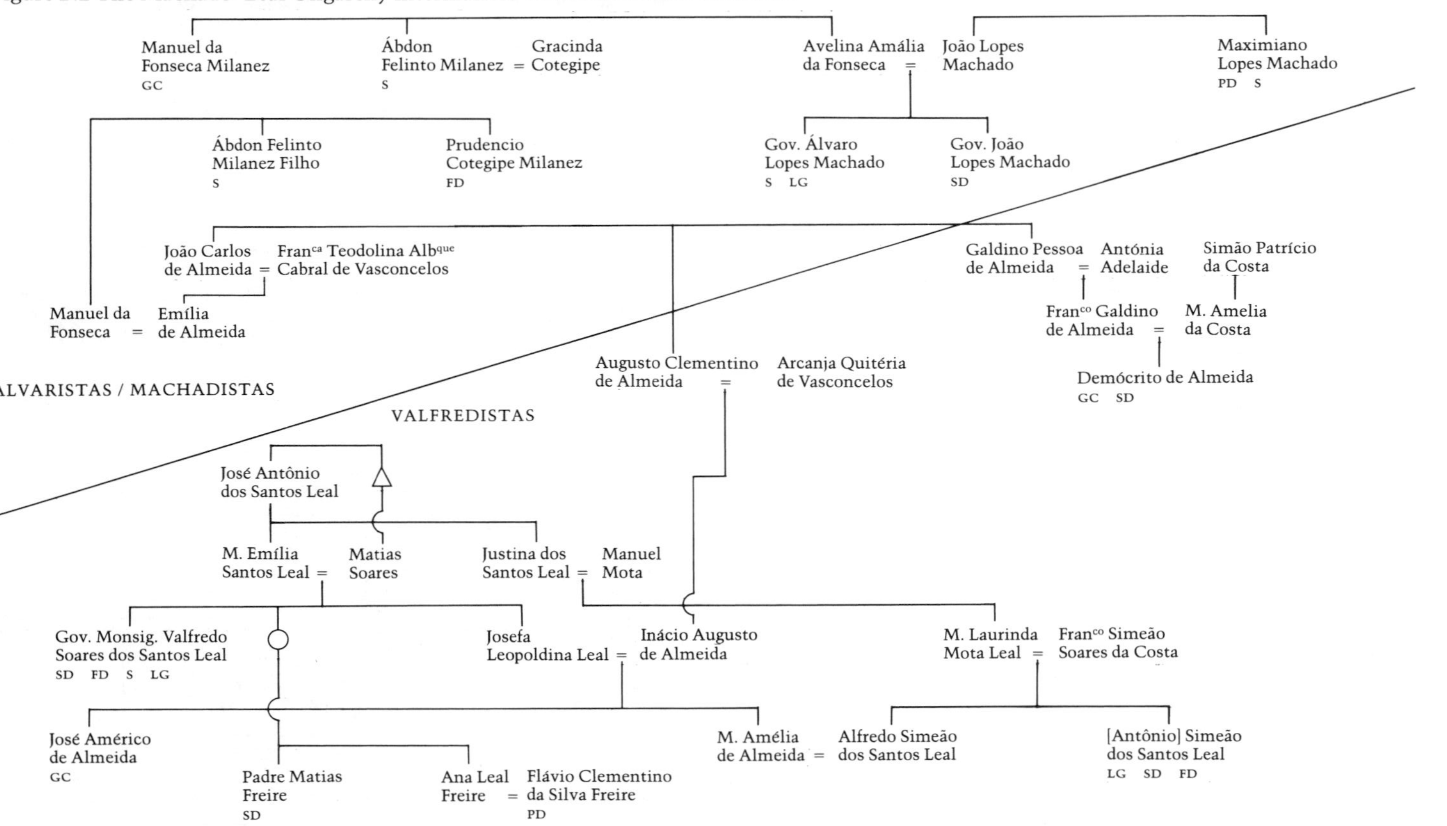

SOURCES: Azevêdo Bastos, *Roteiro Azevêdo*, pp. 633–36; José Américo de Almeida, *Memórias; antes que me esqueça* (Rio de Janeiro: Livraria Francisco Alves Editôra, 1976), pp. 11, 39, 58, 71–75.

Figure B.3 The Pessoa Lineages: Silva Pessoa, Pessoa Cavalcanti de Albuquerque, and Pessoa de Queiroz

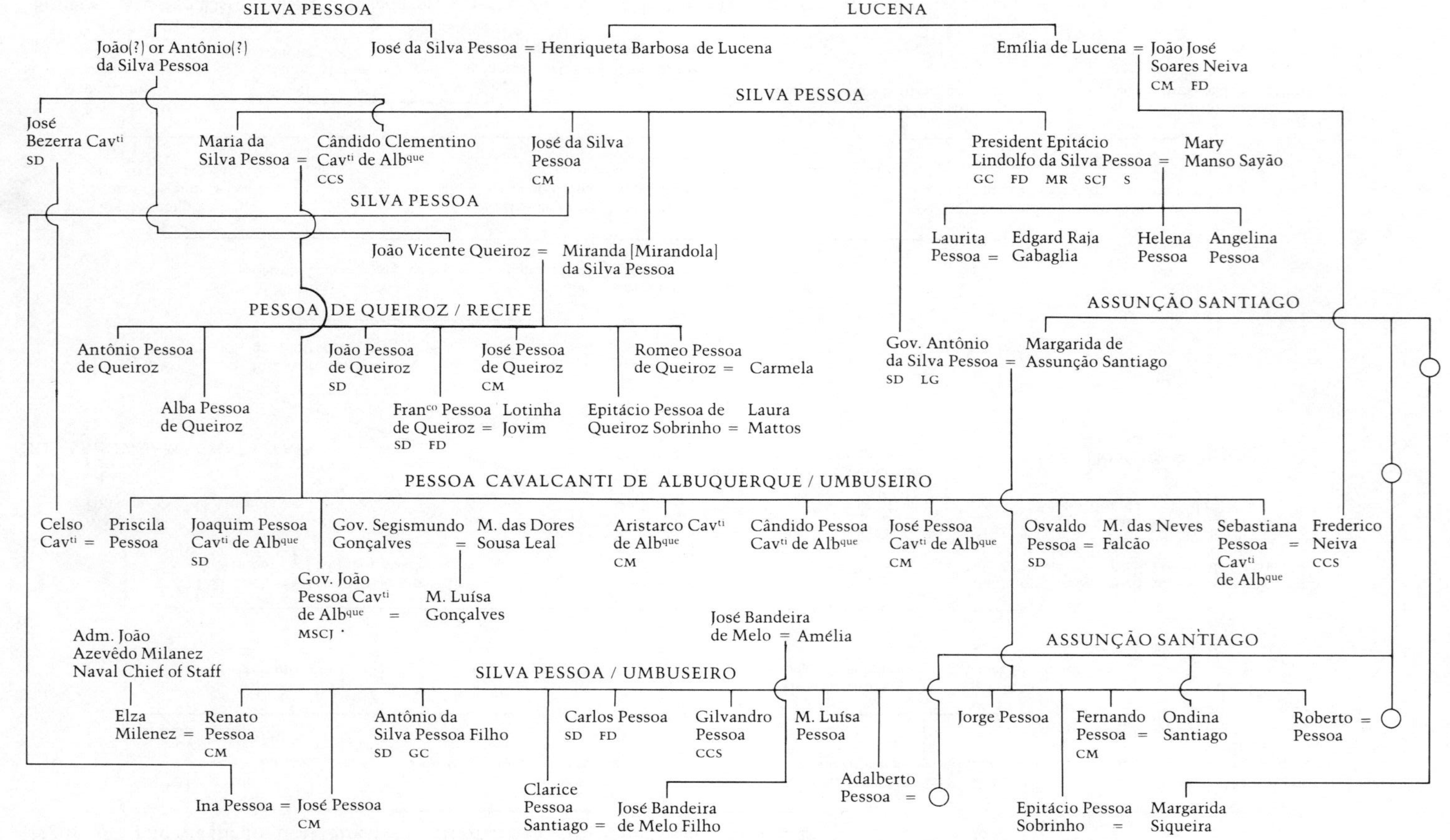

SOURCES: See Fig. B.1; obituary of Renato Pessoa, undated newspaper clipping (1936), ACAP/3/unnumbered; *Diario de Pernambuco*, 7–10 Nov. 1922; Epitácio Pessoa de Queiroz Sobrinho to Epitácio (Recife), 10 Nov. 1922, AEP/73/unnumbered.

Figure B.4 Brother-in-Law Bonds in the Leite Family's Leadership of the Liberal Party (1839–1889) and the Old Liberal Bloc (1889–1930)

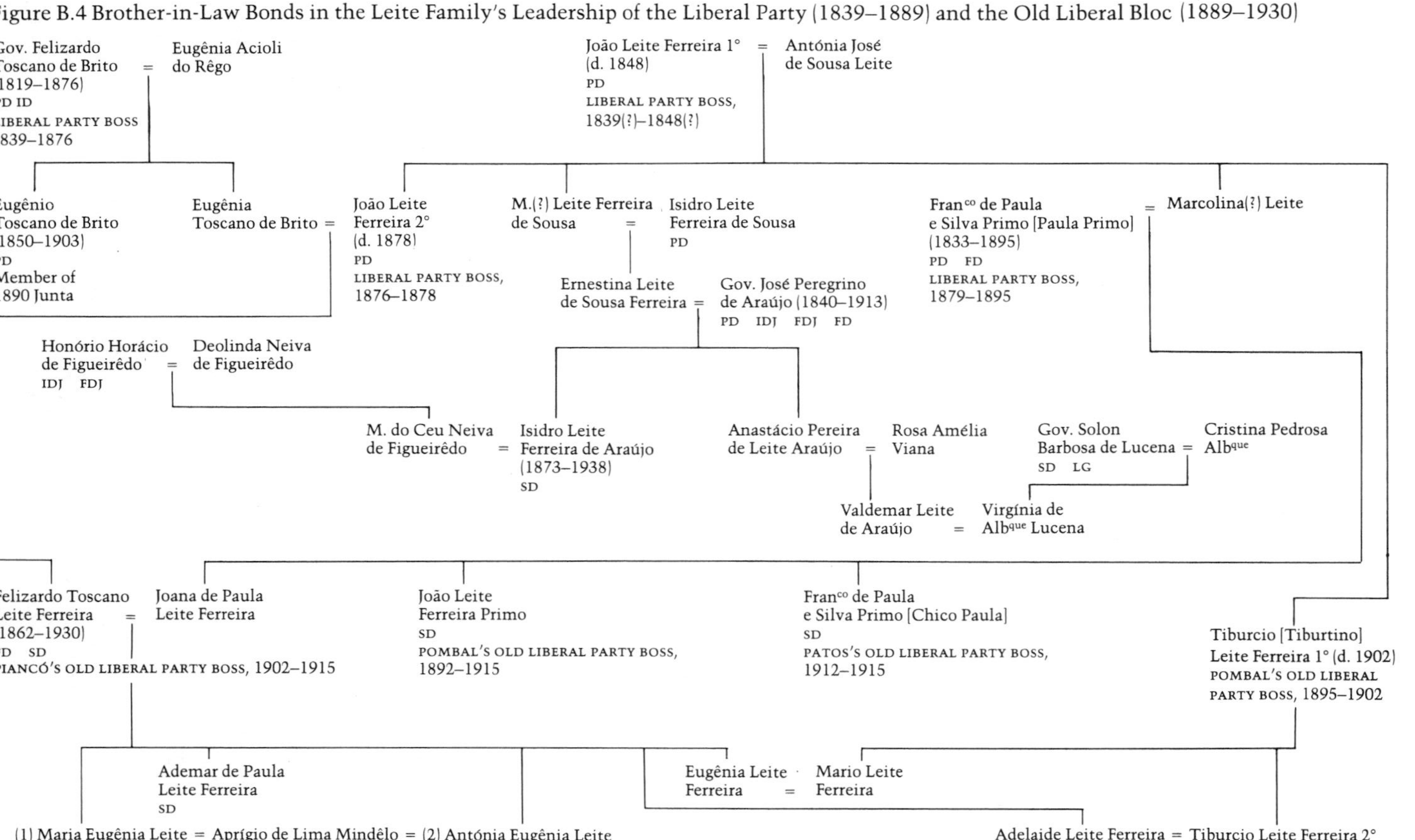

Sources: Mariz, *Apanhados historicos*, pp. 234–35, 244, 267, 276, 305; António José de Sousa, *O grande Pombal* (João Pessoa: Gráfica Comercial, 1971), p. 68; Otaviano, *Mártires Piancó*, pp. 11–12, 45–52; Azevêdo, *Roteiro Azevêdo*, pp. 541, 599–603; obituary of José Peregrino de Araújo, *A União*, 7 Oct. 1913; interview with Paulo de Lucena, João Pessoa, 12 Aug. 1986.

Note: After 1889, leadership of the Old Liberals fragmented along município lines.

Appendix C: Patrimonial Implications of Endogamous Matrimonial Strategies

Figure C.1 The Sesmaria of Itaipu: Nineteenth-Century Distribution among Selected Descendants of Num of Taipu (José Lins Cavalcanti de Albuquerque) and Antónia do Monte

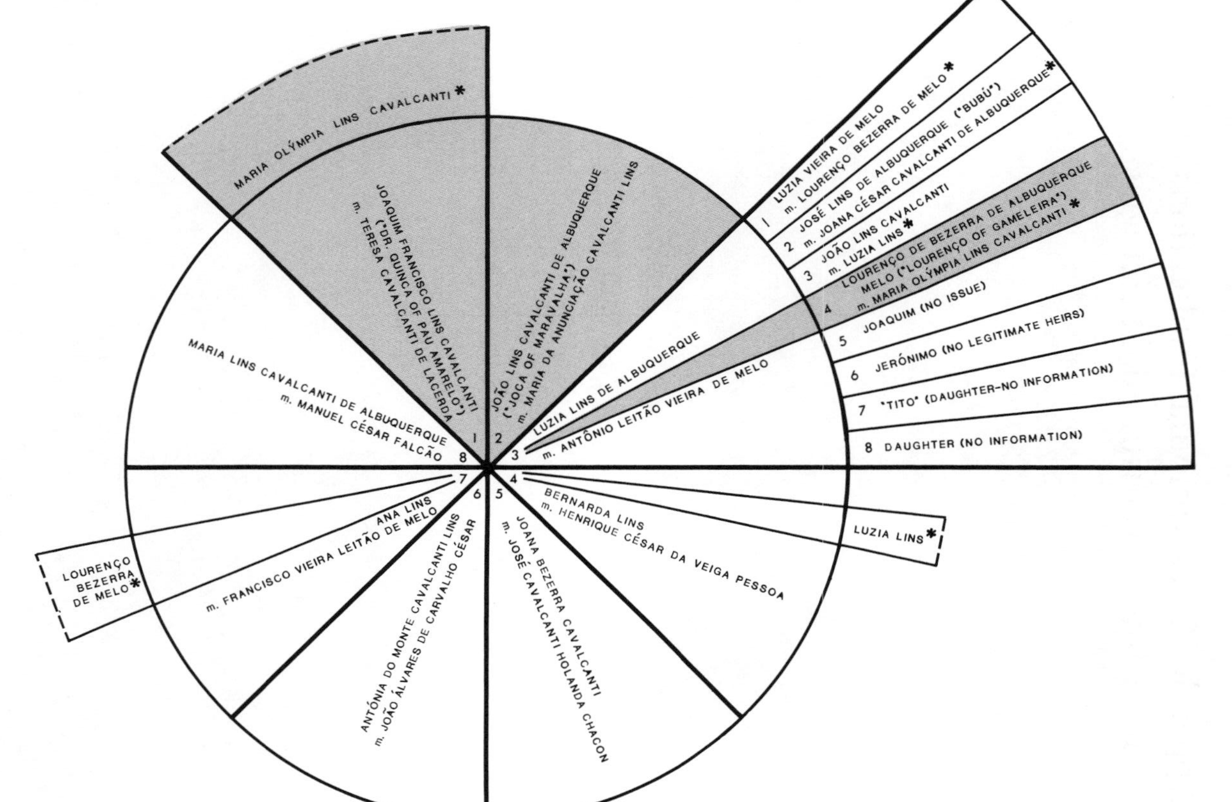

SOURCE: Figure C.1 reproduces a small portion of D. Maria de Lourdes de Toledo Lins's family genealogy for the ten generations of Num of Taipu and Antónia do Monte, according to an original design she created to illustrate the transmission of land in her family. I am extremely grateful to D. Lourdes for permission to reproduce it and to use her valuable oral history, given in interviews in July 1978 and January 1986 and in her letters of March 21 and June 12, 1986, to illustrate important aspects of Brazilian elite family history in this book. (Any inaccuracy is my responsibility.)

NOTE: Joana César Cavalcanti de Albuquerque (m. Col. José Lins de Albuquerque) was either the daughter of Bernarda Lins, Antónia do Monte Cavalcanti Lins, or Maria Lins de Albuquerque.

KEY: [shaded box] Portion of Sesmaria of Itaipu inherited by "Lourenço of Gameleira" (Lourenço de Bezerra de Albuquerque Melo) and Maria Olýmpia Lins Cavalcanti.

* Cousin-spouses of children of Luzia Lins de Albuquerque and Antônio Leitão Vieira de Melo.

The landed patrimony distributed among the descendants of Num of Taipu (Col. José Lins Cavalcanti de Albuquerque) and Antónia do Monte, the great-great grandparents of the novelist José Lins do Rêgo, illustrated how consanguineous marriage retained property within the family and thereby imparted to the group a quasi-corporate identity. Figure C.1 is a partial reconstruction of the original Sesmaria (grant) of Itaipu, purchased (and possibly inherited) by Num from his brother, Padre João Marinho Falcão, probably between 1810 and 1820. Originally, the land had belonged to the Jesuits in Pilar, from whom it was confiscated and sold by the Portuguese Crown, probably in the 1760s or 1770s. Num, who was born in 1786 at Engenho Pasmado in Pernambuco, arrived in Pilar as a very small boy around 1792. He was apparently raised by his brother, for he served him as sacristan in the parish church of São Miguel de Itaipu. He and his brother were the sons of Francisco Berenguer d'Andrade and Maria Lins de Albuquerque, who had ten other children. This diagram represents the property as Num divided and distributed it in eight equal shares for each of his children, probably during the several decades before his death in 1870.

Num's grandson Lourenço de Bezerra de Albuquerque Melo—distinguished from his cousin of nearly the same name as "Lourenço of Gameleira"—was the fourth of eight children born to Num's daughter Luzia Lins de Albuquerque and Antônio Leitão Vieira de Melo. Lourenço of Gameleira therefore inherited one-eighth of his mother's land, which was one-sixty-fourth of his grandfather Num's sesmaria. However, he bought his uncle's inheritance portion—the land belonging to his mother's brother, known in the family as "Joca of Maravalha" (Dr. João Lins Cavalcanti de Albuquerque)—thereby increasing his own holdings eightfold. Lourenço of Gameleira married his matrilateral cross-cousin, Maria Olýmpia Lins Cavalcanti. Because she was an only child, he added another one-eighth of Num's sesmaria to the patrimony he already possessed from Num—that which had been inherited by Maria Olýmpia's father, "Dr. Quinca of Pau Amarelo" (Dr. Joaquim Francisco Lins Cavalcanti). Thus marriage to Maria Olýmpia accomplished for Lourenço of Gameleira the same consolidation of land that marriage to an aunt would have achieved.

Similarly, Dr. Gentil Lins, the son of Lourenço of Gameleira and Maria Olýmpia, maintained the family preference for marriage with a first cousin. He married Alice Vieira de Melo, a daughter of Dr. Quinca, of Engenho Novo (Joaquim Bezerra de Melo). On the other hand, even though in 1923 their daughter Nanita Lins (Ana Vieira) married a cousin once removed—Dr. José d'Ávila Lins, the son of Maj. Remígio and Miquelina Olindina d'Ávila Lins—her marriage was tantamount to an exogamous union, because the bridegroom belonged to the Areia Lins. (See Ch. IV, n. 22.) Segmentation had overtaken the Pilar and Areia cousin branches in the nineteenth century due to the failure to maintain matrimonial exchanges over considerable distance. However, the couple's establishment of a household in the Capital, not far from the bride's home at Engenho Pacatuba in Pilar, renewed contact between these branches of the Lins according to a residential pattern—migration to Parahyba—that had become increasingly common after 1910. Even as land more typically fragmented due to rising exogamy, certain families, like the Lins, rewove remote cousin branches matrimonially, thanks to a recently heightened spatial mobility. And purchase, as the Vieira de Melos recently illustrated while this book was being written, continues to achieve what formerly endogamous marriage routinely accomplished, the reuniting and preservation of the pieces of Num's Sesmaria of Itaipu for at least some of his late twentieth-century descendants.

Figure C.2 Marriages between Uncles and Nieces or Aunts and Nephews over Four Generations in the Family of Councilor Luís Gonzaga de Brito Guerra

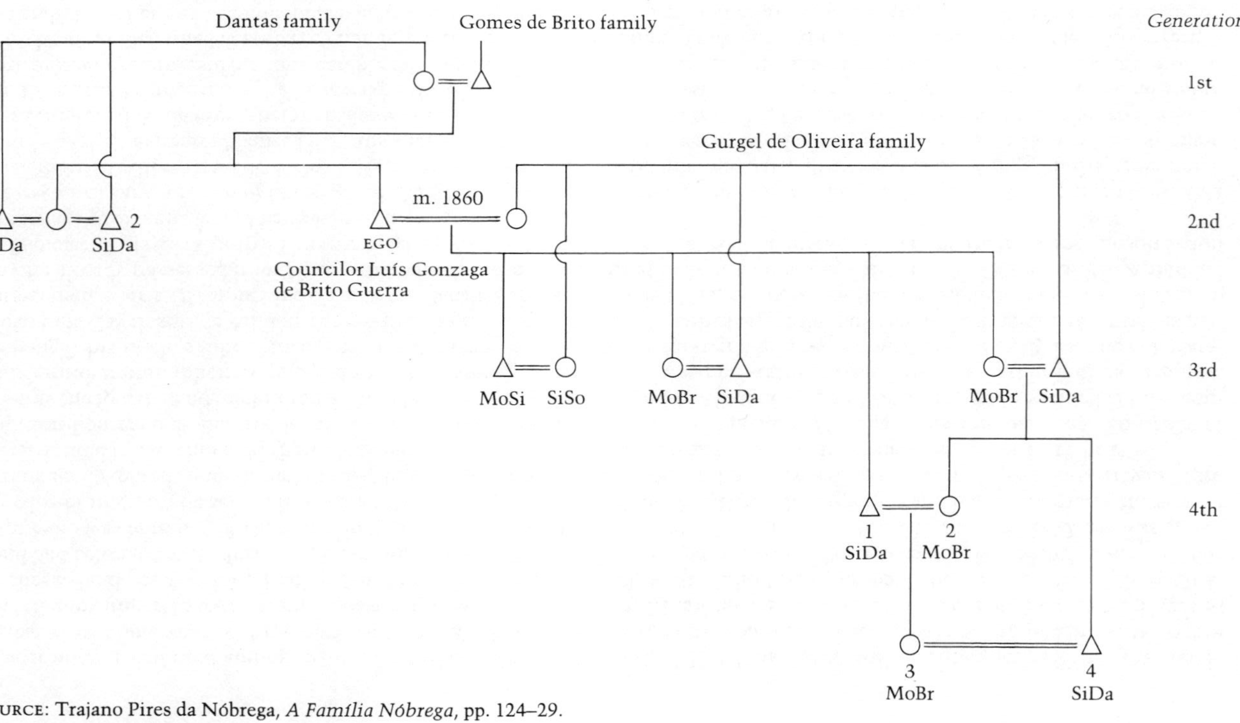

SOURCE: Trajano Pires da Nóbrega, *A Família Nóbrega*, pp. 124–29.

NOTE: Relationships diagrammed refer to the councilor's children by his first wife, Maria Malfada de Oliveira. Reading from EGO, the councilor's sister married two maternal uncles in succession; his two sons married a maternal aunt and a maternal niece, respectively; his two daughters married two maternal uncles; and, among the sets of his grandchildren who intermarried, two were marriages of nieces to maternal uncles (number 2 with 1 and 3 with 4). Each kinship reference identified in the chart refers to the spouse in terms of the EGO under which that referent kinship term appears (e.g., the councilor's first son married his mother's sister, etc.).

Appendix D: The Family Base of Oligarchy in Paraíba

TABLE D.1: Principal Families in Politics in Paraíba during the Empire (1835–1889)

Conservative Party	Liberal Party
LEADERSHIP FAMILIES	
Carneiro da Cunha (6)[a]	Leite Ferreira (6)
Meira/Meira de Henriques (6)	Dantas (3)
Cavalcanti de Albuquerque (8)	Lôbo Miranda Henriques (4)
	Meira/Meira de Vasconcelos (4)
MAJOR RANK-AND-FILE FAMILIES	
Sousa Rangel	Limeira
Holanda Chacon	Ramos
Lima Filho	Dinoá
Gomes de Sá	Borges
Lins Cavalcanti de Albuquerque	Milanez
Tavares de Melo Cavalcanti	Cruz Cordeiro
Espínola	Costa Machado
Pessoa de Lacerda	Rêgo Barros
Gouveia Monteiro	Nóbrega
Correia Lima	Alves Pequeno
Costa Pereira	Pereira da Costa
Rêgo Vasconcelos	Alves Viana
Chaves Sales Pessoa	Fernandes de Carvalho
Montenegro	Teixeira de Brito Lira
Barros Brandão	Pereira Luna
Farias Leite	Santos Leal
Souto Maior	Costa Agra
Arruda Câmara	Figueirêdo
Oliveira Azevedo	Rolim
Costa Cirne	Araújo
Carvalho Nóbrega	Porto
DISSIDENT LIBERALS	
Galvão	Cartaxo
Sousa Carvalho	Mariz
Aragão e Melo	Coelho Lisboa
Bernardino dos Santos	Cordeiro Senior

SOURCES: Mariz, *Apanhados historicos*, pp. 216–96; and idem, *Assembléia Legislativa*, pp. 80–88.

NOTE: Descent being ambilineal, each politician really represented at least two families. For methodological purposes this ambiguity was resolved rather arbitrarily by assuming each to have had only one family of political affiliation. This was usually decided by reference to the name the individual bore. In a few cases where an individual identified with a family whose name he had omitted from his own, he was placed with the family he publicly claimed as his political affiliation.

[a] Numbers in parentheses denote how many individuals from each respective family served in the Provincial Assembly, 1836–1889. Otherwise, the number was two.

Table D.2: Principal Families in Politics in Paraíba during the Old Republic (1889–1930)

LEADERSHIP FAMILIES[a]

Pessoas: Silva Pessoa, Pessoa Cavalcanti de Albuquerque, Lucena (9)
Neiva/Figueirêdos (9)
Carvalhos (8)
Nóbrega (with Carneiro da Cunha) (7)
Machado/Milanez (8)
Peregrino de Albuquerque (5)

INTERMEDIATE STRATUM FAMILIES[b]

Almeida/Santos Leal	Cartaxo
Santos	Medeiros Paes
Silva Mariz	Peregrino de Araújo
Carneiro da Cunha	Rolim
Cavalcanti de Albuquerque/Lauritzen	

RANK-AND-FILE FAMILIES[c]

Albuquerque	Joffilly
(Andrade) Espínola	Lima Botelho
Arruda Câmara	Lima Mindêlo
Ávila Lins	Limeira Dinoá
Barbedo	Lira Tavares
Botto de Menezes	Lordão
Brito Lyra	(Luna) Freire
Cabral de Vasconcelos	Maroja
Costa	Meira Henriques
Costa Cirne	Oliveira Cruz
Cunha Lima	Pereira Lima
Dantas	Pinto Pessoa
Evaristo Monteiro	Rego Barros
Faria Leite	Rodrigues Pinho
Ferreira Leite	Sá
Gomes de Sá	Silveira
Gomes Gambara	Soares
Holanda	Sousa Lemos

Source: Mariz, *Assembléia Legislativa*, pp. 60–82.
Note: See Table D.3 for factional alignments according to family.
[a] More than four members in the Assembly.
[b] Three or four members in the Assembly.
[c] Two members in the Assembly.

Table D.3: Partisan Alignments of Major Family-Based Groups in Paraíba (1900–1915)

Circa 1900

The dominant coalition Partido Republicano da Paraíba/PRP (Alvaristas and Valfredistas)	The opposition Autonomistas (Venancistas)
Machado/Milanez/Santos Leal	Neiva/Figueirêdo/Silva Pessoa/Lucena
Almeida	Cavalcanti de Albuquerque/Lauritzen
Agra/Porto/Sousa Campos/Figueirêdo	Melo Cavalcanti
Santa Cruz de Oliveira	Bezerra Cavalcanti
Ferreira Leite	Arruda da Câmara/Cavalcanti de Albuquerque
Costa Ramos	Cunha Lima
Nóbrega	Vasconcelos Maia
Dantas Corréia de Góis	Gomes de Sá
Lobo Maia de Vasconcelos	Meira Henriques
Lima Mindêlo	Carvalho Nóbrega

Circa 1908–1912

The dominant coalition Partido Republicano Conservador da Paraíba/PRCP (Alvaristas, Valfredistas, Venancistas)	The opposition Old Liberals or Democratic Party (Rêgo Barros and Lima Filho)
Machado/Milanez/Santos Leal/Almeida	Dantas Corréia de Góis/Dantas Vilar/Saldanha
Neiva/Figueirêdo/Silva Pessoa/Lucena/Barbosa	Porto/Sousa Campos/Figueirêdo
Cavalcanti de Albuquerque/Lauritzen	Lobo Maia de Vasconcelos/Saldanha/Alves Lima
Silva Mariz	Ferreira Leite
Montenegro/Albuquerque	Santa Cruz de Oliveira
Agripino Maia/Suassuna	Queiroga
Arruda da Câmara/Cavalcanti de Albuquerque	Lima Mindêlo
Carvalho Nóbrega	

Circa 1915

The dominant coalition Partido Republicano Conservador Paraibano (Epitacistas)	The opposition Partido Republicano Conservador da Paraíba (Valfredistas)
Neiva/Figueirêdo/Silva Pessoa/Lucena	Santos Leal/Machado/Almeida
Cavalcanti de Albuquerque/Lauritzen	Porto/Sousa Campos/Figueirêdo
Pessoa Cavalcanti de Albuquerque/ Bezerra Cavalcanti	Ferreira Leite
Agripino Maia/Suassuna	Lobo Maia de Vasconcelos/Saldanha
Carvalho Nóbrega/Carvalho	Dantas Corréia de Góis
Pereira Lima/Diniz	Cavalcanti Lins
Cunha Lima	Santa Cruz de Oliveira
Holanda Soares/Evaristo Monteiro	Cavalcanti Monteiro
Arruda da Câmara/Cavalcanti de Albuquerque	Nóbrega
Melo Cavalcanti	Silva Mariz/Mariz Nóbrega
Gomes de Sá	Ribeiro Coutinho

SOURCES: Mariz, *Assembléia Legislativa*, pp. 58–69; idem, *Apanhados historicos*, pp. 205–325; *A União*, 1912–1915; *O Norte*, 1912–1915.

GLOSSARY OF PORTUGUESE TERMS

Aforamento: The annual leasing of land to lessees known as *foreiros*; the most common system of subcontracting land and labor in the Brazilian Northeast.

Agregado: An agricultural tenant whose situation in the Northeast of the Old Republic ranged widely from that of a relatively well-off squatter to an impoverished tenant-at-will, but always implied a critical degree of subordination to a more powerful landowner.

Agreste: Very fertile strip of land surrounded by much drier, intermediate zone of the *caatinga*.

Agreste acaatingada: A transitional geographic zone which is characterized by polyculture. Also *caatinga-agreste*.

Aldeia: A village.

Alto sertão: The far backlands zone of the Brazilian Northeast, beyond Borborema Plateau.

Amigo político: Political friend, or individual incorporated into a political network whose friendship is instrumentally defined, although it may also be affectively overladen, with or without ties of kinship.

Amizade: Friendship.

Arroba: An old Portuguese measure of weight used in Brazil; equivalent in the nineteenth century to thirty-two pounds or fifteen kilograms.

Bacharel (pl. *bacharéis*): A graduate of law or medical school.

Bacharelismo: The predominance of law school graduates (*bacharel de direito*) in political office and civil service posts characteristic of the late Empire and the Old Republic.

Bandeira: One of the armed bands of adventurers or explorers who opened up the interior during the seventeenth and eighteenth centuries; their purpose was to hunt for Indian slaves or to search for gold. Also *entrada*.

Bandeirante: Member of a *bandeira*.

Bandoleiro: Bandit; often one who is a hired gunman.

Barracão: A company store.

Bolandeira: Animal-driven cotton gin or mill for grinding sugar cane, manoic, etc.

Brejo: An elevated geographical zone in the Brazilian Northeast characterized by polyculture.

Caatinga: A semi-arid, intermediate zone suitable for stockraising or dry farming; the xerophytic vegetation or "bush" found in this zone.

Caatinga-agreste: A transitional geographic zone of the Brazilian Northeast, characterized by polyculture. Also *agreste acaatingada*.

Caatingueira: A low-lying, xerophytic creeper.

Cabra do coronel: A landlord's favorite henchman.

"Café com leite": *See* Politics of *café com leite.*

Câmara municipal: Municipal council (also *intendência*), the legislative body at the município level, usually five men who were elected every four years.

Cambão: An oppressive sharecropping or quasi-rental arrangement (similar to feudal corvée) which constitutes the tenant labor system in the Northeast. Previously referred to as *a sujeição.*

Cangaceirismo: Banditry, coupled with the protective network afforded bandits by rural landlords implying a sociopolitical system so defined.

Cangaceiro: A bandit historically associated with the region of the Northeast.

Capanga: Bodyguard or thug who during the Old Republic usually possessed ties of clientship and personal loyalty to his boss; otherwise, a hired gunman.

Capangada: Political vernacular of the Old Republic for a group of *capangas*, or thugs.

Cariri-sertão: The more elevated, dryer part of the Paraíba backlands, situated on the Borborema Plateau and closer to the coast. See *sertão.*

Catete: In the political vernacular of the Old Republic, the president of Brazil, after the presidential Catete Palace.

Chefe do partido: Party boss of the party in power; at the município level, also *chefe local, chefe político.*

Chefia: Office of local boss, either of the incumbent or opposition party/faction.

Cidade: City; implies a politico-legal identity superior to a *vila*, or town.

Coiteiro (*couteiro*): Protector of a bandit who offers food, shelter, and protection from police, usually on his rural estate.

Conto: In the monetary system of the Old Republic, 1,000 *mil-réis. See* Table A.5.

Coronel (pl. *coronéis*): Possessor of a patent of colonel in the National Guard, or one to whom that rank is honorifically ascribed; colloquially, any powerful boss, rural or urban.

Coronela: A woman who behaves as a *coronel.*

Coronelismo: The system of local boss rule, based on fraudulent elections and violence, associated with the Empire and Old Republic.

Crioulo: A long-staple tree cotton; probably a hybrid derived from *inteiro* (*Gossypium brasiliense*), the so-called Persian cotton introduced in Brazil in 1796 and otherwise known as "ox kidney" (*rim de boi*) cotton.

Degola: Political vernacular in the Old Republic for a "beheading," i.e., punitively denying or removing elected politicians from office, usually in connection with the so-called "politics of the governors," by denying recognition through a credentials committee.

Dona de engenho: Female owner of a sugar estate. Also *senhora de engenho.*

Doutor (pl. *doutôres*): The holder of a law or medical degree.

Emprego: Employment.

Empreguismo: Pejorative term for the nepotistic control of public office.

Engenho: Small-scale mill for grinding sugar and cereals or for ginning cotton; driven by water, oxen, or steam. Attached to the name of a property, it signifies an estate (e.g., Engenho Cotunguba, the Silva Pessoas' family estate in Nazaré, Pernambuco).

Entrada: Expedition of frontiersmen seeking slaves, gold, or cattle ranches in the interior. Also *bandeira*.

Época da alta: The era of the boom.

Fação: Faction.

Fardo: An old Portuguese weight which, in the case of cotton, was equivalent to approximately seventy-five pounds.

Fazenda: A rural property, either a ranch or a plantation; title of an estate, as in the Pessoas' Fazenda Prosperidade.

Filho da terra: Member of the landed elite.

Filhotismo: Patronage; a pejorative term for nepotism.

Folheto: Chapbook, i.e., a penny booklet of popular poetry usually printed on a private press that attained mass circulation in the Northeast of Brazil during the first decade of this century.

Foreiro: Agricultural lessee under an oral contract called *foramento*.

Gaúcho (fem. *gaúcha*): A native of Rio Grande do Sul.

Homísio: Hospitality and protection offered by a landlord to a visitor or a fugitive, customarily implying immunity from police pursuit.

Juíz de Direito: A judge appointed at the national level by the minister of justice who in both Empire and Republic performed a key mediating role between national and município levels of government by virtue of his jurisdiction over elections and all serious crimes; his district, a *comarca*, usually encompassed several municípios, except when the state capital. In this text he is identified as an imperial judge until 1889 and as a federal district judge after 1889.

Lavrador em terras: Poor farmer in nineteenth-century Brazilian Northeast.

Legítima: The legitimate portion of the deceased's estate legally designated for the forced heirs; until 1907, two-thirds of the estate; afterward, one-half.

Machismo: The cult of virility in which a male exercises power over women as well as other men.

Machona: A "masculine" woman; i.e., a woman who exercises power.

Mameluco: In the colonial period, an individual of mixed Portuguese and Amerindian ancestry.

Mandate: The person who gives the orders for someone to be killed either by a retainer or a paid assassin; "intellectual author" of a crime.

Mandonismo: Iron-fisted, personalistic rule at the local level; see also *coronelismo*.

Mata: Lit., the forest or "bush" that originally covered the coast and intermediate zones; those zones, once cleared of forest and associated with fertile, agricultural land; the type of cottons (herbaceous) associated with the brejo and caatinga-agreste that were intercropped in those zones of polyculture.

Matuto (Colloq. northeast Brazil): Any rural agriculturalist of humble social status, but most frequently from the *mata* (i.e., *caatinga-agreste*), the zone of polyculture.

Meeiro (fem. *meeira*): Sharecropper; in law, the surviving spouse under a community property regulation.

Meiação: A system of sharecropping in which the tenant generally gives 50 per cent of the crop to the landlord.

Mil-réis: See *conto*.

Mocó (*Gossypium vitifolium*): A long-staple tree cotton indigenous to Rio Grande do Norte and Paraíba's Seridó district; valuable for the length (up to 38 mm.), fineness, and silkiness of its staple.

Morador: Specially favored squatter or small holder.

Morgadio: In law, rights of primogeniture and entail.

Morgado: In law, the firstborn or eldest male son; the heir to an entailed estate; the estate itself.

Município: "County" in Anglo-Saxon political terminology is the closest approximation, but the município is legally invested with great autonomy and its executive, the *prefeito*, possesses broader powers over both urban and rural territory under Brazilian law.

Négo: A refusal or denial; lit., "I refuse"; attributed to Paraíbo's Gov. João Pessoa as an important symbolic slogan in the Revolution of 1930, deriving from his negative vote cast for Paraíba in the 1929 nomination of Júlio Prestes as the official presidential candidate in the 1930 election.

Panelinha: Network, or "informally defined primary group held together in common interest through ties of friendship or other personal contact acting from common ends." Anthony Leeds, "Brazilian Careers and Social Structure: A Case Study and Model," *American Anthropologist* 66 (1964):1321.

Parnaíba: Long knife used in the Brazilian Northeast.

Pátrio poder (Lat., *patria potestas*): In law, in the Empire, a husband or a widow's parental authority over minor or unemancipated children; in the Republic, his conjugal authority over his wife (formerly, *poder marital*) as well as parental authority.

Perrepista: Member or supporter of the Republican Party of São Paulo's (PRR, hence "perripista") 1930 presidential candidate, Gov. Júlio Prestes.

Poder marital: In law, until 1916, a husband's conjugal authority; subsumed, after 1916, as part of *pátrio poder* (i.e., *patria potestas*).

Podorosos: The powerful or the powerholders.

Política de família: Undercurrent of family-based rivalry at the município level that is strongly and usually violently competitive regarding political officeholding.

Política dos governadores: A contemporary expression used to denote the president's power over the states in the national political system before 1930.

Politics of *café com leite*: Refers to the domination of national politics by São Paulo (a coffee state) and Minas Gerais (a dairy state), particularly their control of the presidential succession.

Prefeito: Lit., prefect; mayor, but unlike the North American context, political jurisdiction over the município (county) is broader and more centralized.

Prefeitura: The political office held by a *prefeito*.

Queibradinho (*Gossypium puperescens*): A long-staple tree cotton, silky and glossy like *mocó* but somewhat shorter and with smaller seeds; probably introduced in Brazil in the 1830s.

Rapadoura: Unrefined sugar.

Rapto: Elopement; bride abduction.

Real (pl. *réis*): In the monetary system of the Old Republic, 1/1,000 of a *mil réis*. See Table A.5.

Saca: A sack weighing approximately seventy-five pounds when filled with cotton.

Sêca: Drought.

Senhor de engenho: Titled (heritable with land) owner of a sugar estate.

Senhora de engenho: Female owner of a sugar estate. Also *dona de engenho*.

Sertanejo: Inhabitant of the backlands (*sertão*); adjectival form of *sertão*.

Sertão (pl. *sertões*): The backlands of the Brazilian Northeast; also used in the plural, especially when referring to both the *alto sertão* and the *cariri-sertão* collectively.

Sesmaria: Land grant given by Portuguese Crown up to 1822.

Sitiante: Small cultivator.

Sítio: In the backlands of the Brazilian Northeast, an estate usually devoted to stockraising as its primary economic activity.

Sujeição: An oppressive sharecropping or quasi-rental arrangement (similar to feudal corvée) which constituted the tenant labor system in the Northeast. Referred to today as *cambão*.

Tenente: Lit., lieutenant; the younger army officers who as cadets participated in the 1922 Copacabana Revolt and subsequently played an important role in national politics, before and after the Revolution of 1930.

Terça: In law, until 1907, the one-third of his/her estate that a testator could dispose of freely under either a separate or a community property regulation; after 1907, it was increased to one-half.

Travessão: A man-made barrier for preventing livestock from entering the agricultural agreste.

Usina: Machinery for milling sugar or ginning cotton; most commonly, a modern sugar refinery.

Vazante: A type of agriculture dependent on water seepage underground or from streams due to periodic flooding; therefore practiced along riverbanks and beside reservoirs, ponds, and seasonal water holes (*cacimbas*).

Vila: Town; implies a politico-legal status inferior to a *cidade*, or city, but one superior to an *aldeia*, or village.

Voto de cabresto: "Herd vote," under the control of a *coronel* and composed of his relatives, tenants, and clients.

Zona da mata: The coastal sugar zone; originally, heavily forested.

GLOSSARY OF BRAZILIAN KINSHIP TERMS

Brazilian civil law has always reckoned degrees of consanguinity according to Roman, not canon, law. Lineal degrees are counted by generation. Collateral degrees are reckoned by counting the generations back to a common ancestor and then down to the individual to whom kinship is being reckoned. Thus, reckoning one's uncle or aunt is two generations back to a common ancestor (grandparent) and then one more down in direct descent to the aunt or uncle, the offspring of the grandparent, a third-degree collateral.

Afilhado (fem. *afilhada*): Godson (goddaughter).

Bicunhado: Double brother-in-law (resulting from the marriage of two or more sibling sets); a *concunhado* who is a brother or a double *conhado*.

Chefe de família: Family head.

Chefe do clã: Clan chieftan, i.e., family head (a colloquial usage).

Coirmãos (fem. *coirmãs*): Double cousins, i.e., literally, co-brothers or co-sisters. Also *primos filhos de irmãos* (*primos irmãos*); *primos carnais*.

Colaterais do 3° grau: In law, third-degree collaterals: uncle to nephew or aunt to niece.

Colaterais do 4° grau: In law, fourth-degree collaterals; first-degree cousins.

Colaterias do 4° grau duplo: In law, double fourth-degree collaterals; double cousins. Also *primo carnal* or *co-irmão*.

Colaterais do 5° grau: In law, fifth-degree collaterals; second-degree cousins.

Compadre (fem. *comadre*): The referential term of fictive or ritual kinship established by *compadrio*, i.e., between two men (women) who are godparent and father (mother) of the child whose baptism, confirmation, or marriage sacramentally establishes this bond between them. The term is also used without such a ritualistic bond between men who are close and life-long friends. See also *afilhado, compadresco, compadrio, padrinhos de casamento*.

Compadresco: Ritual co-parenthood (its religious, spiritual aspect), i.e., the relationship formed between individuals through their participation in the rituals of baptism, confirmation, or marriage. See also *compadrio*.

Compadrio: Ritual co-parenthood, the social relationship growing out of the ritual bonds of compadresco. See also *compadresco*.

Concunhado: Co-brother-in-law; i.e, a man's wife's sister's husband (or *concunhada*: a woman's husband's brother's wife).

Criado: Foster child, not legally adopted.

Cunhado (fem. *cunhada*): Brother-in-law or sister-in-law (either a man's wife's brother or his sister's husband; either a woman's husband's sister or her brother's wife).

Estranho: Stranger, outsider; i.e., nonkin.

Família: Family; used either to embrace only the nuclear family, or the large, extended family.

Família conjugal: Conjugal or nuclear family, i.e., a parental couple and offspring. Also *família nuclear*.

Família extensa: Extended family, i.e., a composite group of two or more nuclear families usually living in separate households. Also *família, família grande*. See also *parentela*.

Família grande: Extended family, i.e., a composite group of two or more nuclear families usually living in separate households. Also *família extensa*. See also *família, parentela*.

Família nuclear: Nuclear family, i.e., a parental couple and offspring. Also *família conjugal*.

Forasteiro: Foreigner, stranger; i.e., nonkin.

Gênro (fem. *nora*): Son-in-law (daughter-in-law).

Gente de família: Family members, including nonkin who are on very intimate terms with a family.

Limpeza de sangue: Purity of blood (i.e., of exclusively European, Christian descent).

Meeiro (fem. *meeira*): In law, the surviving spouse under a community property regulation (from *meia*, a half of the community).

Padrinhos de casamento: Matrimonial sponsors linked through ritual kinship to the bride and groom (and often the parents of one, or the aunt and uncle of one) by the religious ceremony; although the *padrinhos* do not have to be a married couple, it appeared that they almost always were. Fictive parenthood is thus established by the ritual. Also *paraninfos*.

Parente (fem. *parenta*): Relative.

Parente de longe: Distant relative.

Parentela: Extended family, including relatives by blood, marriage, and ritual (usually distributed over a number of households). Colloquially, a derisive term for a plethora of kin. Also, kindred. Also *parentalha*.

Parentesco: Kinship; bothersome group of relatives (colloq. northeastern).

Primo carnal (pl. *primos carnais*): Double (carnal) cousin; i.e., a cousin relationship defined by the offspring from the marriages of two sibling sets. Also *primos filhos de irmãos, coirmãos*, and *coirmãs*.

Primo cruzado: Cross-cousin; i.e., a cousin relationship between the offspring of two siblings of different sexes. (Not used colloquially but implied when someone is identified as *not* a *primo direto*, i.e., a parallel cousin).

Primo direto: Parallel cousin; i.e., a cousin relationship between the offspring of two siblings of the same sex.

Primos germanos: Parallel cousins; *primos filhos* [*de irmãos*]; in law, *primos do 4° grau*.

Primo legítimo: Legitimate or first-degree cousin. Also *primo do 1° grau*. In law, *colaterais do 4° grau*.

Primo do 1° grau: First-degree cousin. Also *primo legítimo*. In law, *colaterais do 4° grau*.

Primo do 2° grau: Second-degree cousin (often used colloquially to include not only first cousins once removed but even more distant relatives). In law, *colaterais do 5° grau*.

Primos irmãos: Cousins (a contraction of *primos filhos de irmãos*); originally, cousins who were the offspring of married sibling sets. Also *primos carnais, coirmãos*, and *coirmãs*. Today, any first cousins.

Tio-afim (*tia-afim*): Uncle (aunt) by marriage.

SELECTED BIBLIOGRAPHY

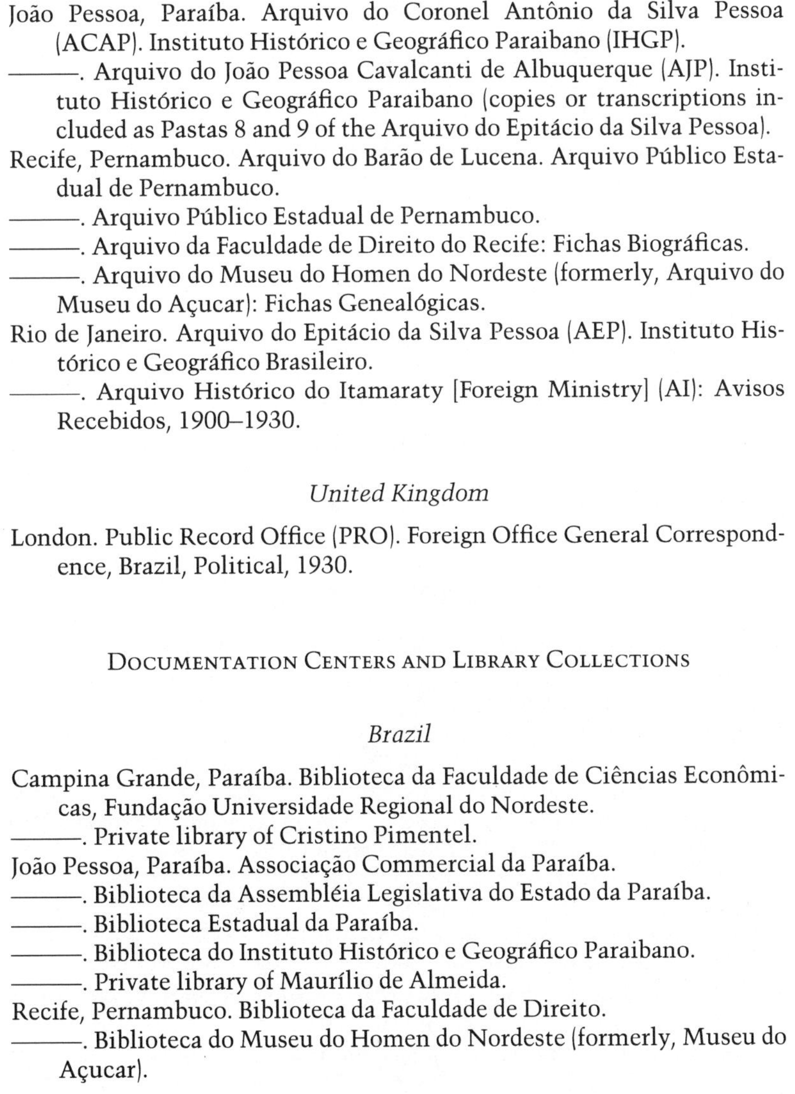

Archives

Brazil

João Pessoa, Paraíba. Arquivo do Coronel Antônio da Silva Pessoa (ACAP). Instituto Histórico e Geográfico Paraibano (IHGP).

———. Arquivo do João Pessoa Cavalcanti de Albuquerque (AJP). Instituto Histórico e Geográfico Paraibano (copies or transcriptions included as Pastas 8 and 9 of the Arquivo do Epitácio da Silva Pessoa).

Recife, Pernambuco. Arquivo do Barão de Lucena. Arquivo Público Estadual de Pernambuco.

———. Arquivo Público Estadual de Pernambuco.

———. Arquivo da Faculdade de Direito do Recife: Fichas Biográficas.

———. Arquivo do Museu do Homen do Nordeste (formerly, Arquivo do Museu do Açucar): Fichas Genealógicas.

Rio de Janeiro. Arquivo do Epitácio da Silva Pessoa (AEP). Instituto Histórico e Geográfico Brasileiro.

———. Arquivo Histórico do Itamaraty [Foreign Ministry] (AI): Avisos Recebidos, 1900–1930.

United Kingdom

London. Public Record Office (PRO). Foreign Office General Correspondence, Brazil, Political, 1930.

Documentation Centers and Library Collections

Brazil

Campina Grande, Paraíba. Biblioteca da Faculdade de Ciências Econômicas, Fundação Universidade Regional do Nordeste.

———. Private library of Cristino Pimentel.

João Pessoa, Paraíba. Associação Commercial da Paraíba.

———. Biblioteca da Assembléia Legislativa do Estado da Paraíba.

———. Biblioteca Estadual da Paraíba.

———. Biblioteca do Instituto Histórico e Geográfico Paraibano.

———. Private library of Maurílio de Almeida.

Recife, Pernambuco. Biblioteca da Faculdade de Direito.

———. Biblioteca do Museu do Homen do Nordeste (formerly, Museu do Açucar).

Recife, Pernambuco. Biblioteca Pública.
Rio de Janeiro. Biblioteca do Arquivo Histórico do Itamaraty.
———. Biblioteca do Arquivo Nacional.
———. Biblioteca da Casa da Agricultura (Sociedade Nacional de Agricultura).
———. Biblioteca da Casa da Paraíba.
———. Biblioteca da Fundação Getúlio Vargas.
———. Biblioteca do Instituto Brasileiro de Bibliografia e Documentação.
———. Biblioteca do Instituto Histórico e Geográfico Brasileiro.
———. Biblioteca Nacional.
———. Instituto Brasileiro Geográfico e Estatístico, Centro de Documentaçaõ e Informação.
———. Private library of Horácio de Almeida.
———. Sindicato das Indústrias de Fiação e Tecelagem do Rio de Janeiro (formerly, CIFTA).
São Paulo. Instituto Genealógico Brasileiro.

United Kingdom

London. Public Record Office.

United States

Bethesda, Maryland. Library of the United States Department of Agriculture.
Washington, D.C. The Library of Congress.

Personal Interviews

Almeida, Horácio de. Rio de Janeiro, October–November 1970 and April–May 1971.
Guedes Pereira, Normando. João Pessoa, 24 July 1978.
Inojosa, Joaquim. Rio de Janeiro, May 1971.
Leal, José. João Pessoa, December 1970.
Leitão, Deusdedet. João Pessoa, July 1971.
Lins Falcão, Montinha [Antônia do Monte]. Engenho Corredor, São Miguel de Taipú (Pilar), Paraíba, 20 July 1978.
Lins Vieira de Melo, Júlia. João Pessoa, 21 July 1978.
Mariz, Celso. João Pessoa, July 1971.
Nóbrega, Fernando. Rio de Janeiro, 1 August 1978.
Nóbrega, Humberto Carneiro da Cunha. João Pessoa, July 1971.
Pessoa, Laurita Raja Gabaglia [Irmã Maria Regina do Santo Rosário]. Rio de Janeiro, August and October 1970.
Pessoa, Maria das Neves Falcão. João Pessoa, 21 July 1978.

Pimentel, Cristino. Campina Grande, Paraíba, December 1970 and July 1971.
Seixas, Wilson Nóbrega. João Pessoa, December 1970.
Suassuna, Ariano. Recife, 25 and 27 July 1971.
Toledo Lins, Maria de Lourdes de. João Pessoa, Paraíba, 22 July 1978.
Vieira, Clóris. Engenho Oiteiro, São Miguel de Taipú (Pilar), Paraíba, 20 July 1978.

Newspapers

O Academico Parahybano [Recife]. 1886.
O Commercio [Parahyba]. 1900.
Correio de Campina [Campina Grande, Paraíba]. 1912–1928.
Diario do Estado [Parahyba]. 1915–1919.
Diario de Pernambuco [Recife]. 1906–1907.
O Estado da Parahyba [Parahyba]. 1892 and 1912.
Gazeta da Parahyba [Parahyba]. 1889–1890.
Gazeta do Sertão [Campina Grande, Paraíba]. 1888–1890.
Jornal do Brasil [Rio de Janeiro]. 1971.
Jornal do Commercio [Recife]. 1928–1930.
Jornal de Princesa [Princesa, Paraíba]. 1930.
O Municipio [Itabaiana, Paraíba]. 1908.
New York Times. 1919.
O Norte [Parahyba]. 1908–1919.
A Provincia [Recife]. 1906.
A Razão [Campina Grande]. 1908 and 1917.
A União [Parahyba]. 1911–1930.

Official Government Publications

Brazil. *Collecção das leis do Imperio do Brazil do 1831., 1ª Pte.* Rio de Janeiro: Typografia Nacional, 1875.
———. Congresso Nacional. *Annaes da Câmara dos Deputados, Terceira Sessão da Terceira Legislatura,* Vol. 1: *Sessões de 18 de abril a 31 de maio de 1900*; Vol. 2: *Sessões de 1 a 30 de junho de 1900.* Rio de Janeiro: Imprensa Oficial, 1900.
———. Congresso Nacional. Camara dos Deputados. *Diário do Congresso Nacional.* Vol. 41, nos. 2 and 8 (1930). Rio de Janeiro: n.p., 1931.
———. Congresso Nacional. Senado. *Annaes do Senado Federal, Primeira Sessão da Quarta Legislatura, Sessões de 18 de abril a 31 de julho de 1900.* Rio de Janeiro: Imprensa Nacional, 1900.
———. Coordenação do Aperfeiçoamento de Pessoal Nível Superior. *Es-*

tudos de desenvolvimento regional (Paraíba). Rio de Janeiro: Campanha Nacional de Aperfeiçoamento de Pessoal de Nível Superior (CAPES), 1959.

———. *Decretos do Governo Provisorio da Republica dos Estados Unidos do Brazil (jan.-abril de 1890)*. Rio de Janeiro: Typografia Nacional, 1890.

———. Inspectoria de Obras Contra as Seccas. *Mappa do Estado da Parahyba organizado sob a direcção do Engenheiro Guilherme Lane, Chefe Topographia*. Rio de Janeiro and São Paulo: Hartmann-Reischenbach, 1913.

———. Inspectoria de Obras Contra as Seccas. Quarta Secção (Topografia e Cartografia). Guilherme Lane, Chefe. *Mapa do Estado da Parahyba organizado pelo Engenheiro Robert Miller*. São Paulo and Rio de Janeiro: Secção Cartografica da Companhia Litografica Ipiranga, 1926.

———. Ministerio da Agricultura, Industria e Commercio. *Relatorio apresentado ao Diretor Geral do Serviço de Inspecção e Defeza Agricolas pelo Inspector Agricola Interino do Septimo Distrito, Diogenes Caldas; exercicio de 1912, anno de 1913–24º da Republica, Estado da Parahyba*. Parahyba do Norte: Jaime Seixas & C., 1913.

———. Ministerio da Agricultura e Commercio. Directoria Geral de Estatistica. *Recenseamento de população do Imperio de Brazil a que se procedeu no dia 1º de agosto de 1872*, 21 vols. Rio de Janeiro: Leuzinger & Filhos, 1873–1876.

———. Ministerio da Agricultura, Industria e Commercio. Directoria Geral de Estatistica. *Recenseamento do Brazil realizado em 1 de setembro de 1920*. Vols. 1–5 in 17 vols. Rio de Janeiro: Typografia da Estatistica, 1922–1930.

———. Ministerio da Agricultura, Industria e Commercio. Directoria Geral de Estatistica. *Recenseamento do Brazil realizado em 1 de setembro de 1920. Relação dos proprietarios dos estabelecimentos ruraes recenseados no Estado da Parahyba*. Rio de Janeiro: Typografia da Estatistica, 1928.

———. Ministerio da Agricultura, Industria e Commercio. Directoria Geral de Estatistica. *Sexo, raça e estado civil, nacionalidade, filiação culto e analphabetismo da população recenseada em 31 de dezembro de 1890*. Rio de Janeiro: Oficina da Estatistica, 1898.

———. Ministerio da Agricultura, Industria e Commercio. Directoria do Serviço de Estatistica. *Divisão administrativa em 1911 da Republica dos Estados Unidos do Brazil*. Rio de Janeiro: Tipografia annexa a Directoria do Serviço de Estatistica, 1913.

———. Ministerio da Agricultura, Industria e Commercio. Serviço de Inspeção e Defesa Agrícolas. Inspetoria Agrícola do 7º Distrito. *Questionnarios sobre as condições da agricultura dos municipios da Parahyba*. Rio de Janeiro: Tipografia do Serviço de Estatistica, 1913.

———. Ministerio do Trabalho, Industria e Commercio. Departamento Nacional de Estatística. *Commercio exterior do Brasil: Annos de*

1920 ate 1925. Rio de Janeiro: Departamento Nacional de Estatistica, 1931.

———. Ministerio do Trabalho, Industria e Commercio. Departamento Nacional de Estatistica. *Commercio exterior do Brasil: Annos de 1926 ate 1930*. Rio de Janeiro: Departamento Nacional de Estatistica, 1933.

———. Ministerio da Viação e Obras Publicas. *Relatorio apresentado ao Presidente Artur da Silva Bernardes . . . anno de 1922*. Rio de Janeiro: Imprensa Nacional, 1924.

Caldas, Diogenes. *Estatistica agricola da Parahyba do Norte de 1916*. Parahyba: Imprensa Oficial, 1916.

———. *Relatorio apresentado à Directoria Geral de Inspecção e Defeza Agricolas pelo Inspector Agricola Interino do 7º Districto: Exercicio de 1912 (1913), Estado da Parahyba*. Parahyba: Typographia de Jayme Seixas e Cia., 1913.

Domingues, Alpheu. *Relatorio da Delegacia do Serviço Federal do Algodão na Parahyba apresentado ao Superintendente F. L. Alves Costa, Anno de 1929*. Parahyba: Imprensa Oficial, 1930.

Paraíba, State of. *Almanach administrativo, historico e industrial do Estado da Parahyba para o anno de 1922*. Parahyba: Imprensa Oficial, 1922.

———. *Almanach administrativo, mercantil e industrial do Estado da Parahyba para o anno de 1909*. Parahyba: Imprensa Oficial, 1909.

———. *Almanach do Estado da Parahyba do Norte de 1913*. Parahyba: [Imprensa Oficial], 1913.

———. *Collecção de leis e decretos do Estado da Parahyba de 1920 e 1921*. Parahyba: Imprensa Oficial, 1922.

———. *Colleccão dos actos dos poderes legislativo e executivo do Estado da Parahyba em 1906 e 1908*. Parahyba: Imprensa Oficial, 1913.

———. Departamento de Estradas e Rodagem. *Mapa rodoviário 1950 (Based on the work of Engineer L.F.H. Clerot)*. João Pessoa: Imprensa Oficial, n.d.

———. *Regimento interno da Assembléia Legislativa; Constituição do Estado da Parahyba do Norte*. Parahyba: Imprensa Oficial, 1924.

———. *Repartição de Estatistica e Arquivo Publico. Annuario estatistico do Estado da Parahyba de 1916*. Parahyba: Imprensa Oficial, 1918.

———. Secção de Estatística do Estado. *Annuario estatistico do Estado da Parahyba de 1931*. Anno 2. João Pessoa: Imprensa Oficial, 1934.

———. Secretaria da Fazenda, Agricultura e Obras Publicas. *Exportação de 1929*. João Pessoa: Imprensa Oficial, 1932.

Books and Articles

Alcântara Machado, [José de]. *Vida e morte do bandeirante*. São Paulo: Editôra Itatiaia, 1980.

Alencar Araripe, [Tristão de]. "Pater-famílias nos tempos coloniais." *Revista do Instituto Histórico e Geográfico Brasileiro* 40, pt. 2 (1893):15–23.

Almeida, Elpídio de. *História de Campina Grande*. Campina Grande: Livraria Pedrosa, 1962.

Almeida, Horácio de. *Brejo de Areia; memória de um município*. Rio de Janeiro: Ministério da Educação e Cultura, Serviço de Documentação, 1958.

———. *Contribuição para uma bibliografia paraibana*. Rio de Janeiro: Apex Gráfica e Editôra, 1972.

———. *História da Paraíba*. 2 vols. João Pessoa: Editôra Universitária/UFPB, 1978.

Almeida, José Américo de. *O ano do négo: Memórias do José Américo*. Rio de Janeiro: Gráfica Record Editôra, 1968.

———. *A Parahyba e seus problemas*. Parahyba: Imprensa Oficial, 1923.

Almeida, Maurício Augusto de. *O Barão de Araruna e sua prole*. João Pessoa: *A União* Editôra, 1978.

Almeida e Silva, Josefa Gomes de. "Considerações sôbre a Revolução de 1930." Master's thesis, Instituto de Ciências Humanas, Fundação Universidade Regional do Nordeste, Campina Grande, Paraíba, 1971.

Alves, João Luiz, ed. *Codigo Civil da Republica dos Estados Unidos do Brasil (promulgado pela Lei No. 3071, 1 jan. 1916)*. Rio de Janeiro: F. Briguet e Cia., 1917.

Andrade, Delmiro Pereira de. *Evolução histórica da Paraíba do Norte*. Rio de Janeiro: Editôra Minerva, 1946.

Armitage, John. *História do Brasil desde o período da chegada da família de Bragança em 1808 até a abdicação de D. Pedro I° em 1831*. 2 vols. 3rd ed. Rio de Janeiro: Egas e Garcia Junior, 1933.

Arrojada Lisboa, Miguel, and Epitacio Pessôa. *As obras do nordeste (resposta ao Senador Sampaio Corrêa)*. Rio de Janeiro: Imprensa Oficial, 1925.

Arruda da Camara, Manoel de. *Memoria sobre a cultura dos algodoeiros, e sobre o metodo de o escolher, e ensacar, etc. em que se propoem algumas planos novos, para o seu amelhoramento . . . offerecida S. A. Real, o Principe Regente Nosso Senhor por M. A. da Camara, formado em Medicina e Filosofia e Socio de varias Academicas, etc. Impressa de Ordem do Mesmo Senhor por Fr. José Mariano da Conceição Velloso*. Lisbon: Casa Litteraria do Arco do Cego, 1799.

Associação Commercial Beneficiente de Pernambuco. *Relatorio da Associação Commercial Beneficiente de Pernambuco*. Recife: n.p., 1903.

Atlas geográfico da Paraíba. João Pessoa: Universidade Federal da Paraíba, 1965.

Azevêdo Bastos, Sebastião de. *No roteiro dos Azevêdo e outras famílias do nordeste*. João Pessoa: Gráfica Comercial, 1954.

Baptista, Pedro. *Cangaceiros do nordeste*. Parahyba do Norte: Livraria São Paulo, 1929.

———. *Cônego Bernardo*. Rio de Janeiro: Civilização Brasileira, [1933].

Barbosa Lima Sobrinho, Alexandre José. *A verdade sôbre a Revolução de Outubro*. São Paulo: n.p., 1933.

Barman, Roderick J. "The Brazilian Peasantry Reexamined: The Implications of the Quebra-Quilo Revolt, 1874–75." *Hispanic American Historical Review* 57, no. 3 (1977):401–24.

Barnes, J. A. "Networks and Political Process." In *Local-Level Politics*, edited by Marc J. Swartz, pp. 107–30. Chicago: Aldine Publishing Co., 1968.

Barroso, Gustavo, *Almas de lama e de aço (Lampião e outros cangaceiros)*. São Paulo: Editôra Proprietario Melhoramentos de São Paulo, 1930.

Bello, José Maria. *História da República*. 3rd ed., rev. and exp. São Paulo: Cia. Editôra Nacional, 1956.

Benevedes, César. *Camponeses em marcha*. Rio de Janeiro: Paz e Terra, 1985.

Berlinck, Manuel Tosta. *The Structure of the Brazilian Family in São Paulo*. Ithaca: Cornell University Press, 1969.

Bevilaqua, Clovis. *Direito da família*. 2nd ed. Rio de Janeiro: n.p., 1905.

Bianco, Bela Feldman. "The Petty Supporters of a Stratified Order: The Economic Entrepreneurs of Matriz, São Paulo, Brazil (1877–1974)." Ph.D. diss., Columbia University, 1980.

Bittencourt, Liberato. *Homens do Brasil*, Vol. 2: *Parahyba*. Rio de Janeiro: Livraria Gomes Pereira, 1914.

Blondel, Jean. *As condições da vida política no Estado da Paraíba*. Rio de Janeiro: Fundação Getúlio Vargas, 1957.

Borges da Fonseca, A. V. *Nobilarchia pernambucana*. In *Annaes da Biblioteca Nacional do Rio de Janeiro*, vols. 47 and 48. Rio de Janeiro: Biblioteca Nacional, 1925.

Branner, John C. *Cotton in the Empire of Brazil*. Department of Agriculture Miscellaneous Report, no. 8. Washington, D.C.: U.S. Government Printing Office, 1885.

Câmara, Epaminondas. *Datas campinenses*. João Pessoa: Departamento de Publicidade, 1947.

Câmara Cascudo, Luis da. *Vaqueiros e cantadores*. Porto Alegre: Editôra Globo, 1939.

Caminha Lopes Rodrigues, Inês. "A Revolta de Princesa: Uma contribuição ao estudo de mandonismo local (Paraíba, 1930)." Master's thesis, University of São Paulo, 1976.

Cammack, Paul. "O 'coronelismo' e o 'compromisso coronelista': Uma crítica." *Cadernos DCP* [Universidade Federal de Minas Gerais, Faculdade de Filosofia e Ciências Humanas] 5 (Mar. 1979):1–20.

Campbell, J. K. *Honour, Family and Patronage*. Oxford: Clarendon Press, 1964.

Campos Salles, [Manoel Ferraz de]. *Da propaganda a presidencia*. São Paulo: n.p., 1908.

Candido, Antônio. "The Brazilian Family." In *Brazil: Portrait of Half a Continent*, edited by T. Lynn Smith and Alexander Marchant, pp. 291–312. New York: The Dryden Press, 1951.

———. *Os parceiros do Rio Bonito*. Rio de Janeiro: José Olýmpio Editôra, 1964.

Cardoso, José Gastão. *A heróica resistência de Princeza*. Recife: Artes Gráficas da Escola Industrial Governador Agámemnon Magalhães, 1954.

Carone, Edgard. *A Primeira República (1889–1930): Texto e contexto*. São Paulo: Difusão Européia, 1969.

———. *A República Velha (Instituições e classes sociais)*. São Paulo: Difusão Européia, 1970.

Carvalho, Álvaro de. *Nas vesperas da Revolução: 70 dias na presidencia do Estado da Parahyba de 26 de julho a 4 de outubro de 1930*. São Paulo: Emprêsa Grafica, 1932.

Chandler, Billy Jaynes. *The Bandit King: Lampião of Brazil*. College Station, Texas: Texas A & M University Press, 1978.

———. *The Feitosas and the Sertão dos Inhamuns*. Gainesville: University Presses of Florida, 1972.

———. "The Role of Negroes in the Ethnic Formation of Ceará: The Need for a Reappraisal." *Revista de Ciências Sociais* 4, no. 1 (1973):31–43.

Cintra, Antônio Olavo. "Traditional Brazilian Politics: An Interpretation of Relations between Center and Periphery." In *The Structure of Brazilian Development*, edited by Neuma Aguiar, pp. 127–66. New Brunswick, N.J.: Transaction Books, 1979.

Clay, Jason. "The Articulation of Non-Capitalist Systems of Exchange with Capitalist Systems of Exchange: The Case of Garanhuns, 1845–1917." Ph.D. diss., Cornell University, 1977.

Coelho Gonçalves Lisbôa, João. *Oligarchias, seccas do norte e clericalismo*. Rio de Janeiro: Imprensa Nacional, 1909.

Conniff, Michael. *Urban Politics in Brazil*. Pittsburgh: University of Pittsburgh Press, 1981.

Correia de Andrade, Manoel. "História Regional: Nordeste." Paper presented at the XI° Simpósio Nacional de História de ANPUH, João Pessoa, 19–24 July 1981. Paraíba.

———. *A terra e o homem no nordeste*. 2nd ed. São Paulo: Editôra Brasiliense, 1969.

Costa Pinto, Luís de Aguiar. *Lutas de família no Brasil (Introdução ao seu estudo)*. Biblioteca Pedagógica Brasileira, ser. 5, Brasiliana, v. 263. São Paulo: Cia. Editôra Nacional, 1949.

Costa e Silva, Genny da. *Sesmeiros da Paraíba*. João Pessoa: Universidade Federal da Paraíba, 1965.

Cunha, Euclides da. *Rebellion in the Backlands (Os Sertões)*. Translated by Samuel Putnam. Chicago: University of Chicago Press, 1944.

Cunha Pedrosa, Pedro da. *Minhas próprias memórias*, Vol. 1: *Vida pública*. Rio de Janeiro: Tipografia *Jornal do Comércio*, 1963. Vol. 2: *Vida privada*. Rio de Janeiro: Tipografia *Jornal do Comércio*, 1937.

Della Cava, Ralph. *Miracle at Joaseiro*. New York: Columbia University Press, 1970.

Dillon Soares, Gláucio Ary. *Sociedade e política no Brasil*. São Paulo: Difusão Européia do Livro, 1973.

Duarte, Nestor. *A ordem privada e a organização política nacional*. 2nd ed. Brasiliana 172. São Paulo: Cia. Editôra Nacional, 1939.

Dumont, L. "The Marriage Alliance." In *Kinship: Selected Readings*. edited by Jack Goody, pp. 183–98. Baltimore: Penguin Books, 1971.

Dunshee de Abranches, [João]. *Governos e Congressos da República, (1889–1917)*. 2 vols. São Paulo: n.p., 1918.

Erickson, Kenneth Paul. *The Brazilian Corporative State and Working-Class Politics*. Berkeley and Los Angeles: University of California Press, 1977.

Estudos de desenvolvimento regional (Paraíba). Rio de Janeiro: Campanha Nacional de Aperfeiçoamento de Pessoal de Nível Superior, 1959.

Faoro, Raimundo. *Os donos do poder*. 2 vols. São Paulo: Editôra Globo/ Editôra da USP, 1975.

Fausto, Boris. *Trabalho urbano e conflito social, 1890–1920*. Rio de Janeiro and São Paulo: DIFEL/DIFUSÃO Editorial, 1979.

Fernandes, Carlos D. *Os cangaceiros: Romance de costumes sertanejos*. Parahyba: Imprensa Oficial, 1914.

———. *Epitacio Pessôa*. Rio de Janeiro: Conde Pereira Carneiro, 1919.

Firth, Raymond. "Bilateral Descent Groups: An Operational Viewpoint." In *Studies in Kinship and Marriage, Dedicated to Brenda Z. Seligman on Her Eightieth Birthday*, edited by I. Schapera, pp. 22–37. London: Royal Anthropological Institute of Great Britain and Ireland, 1963.

Fishlow, Albert. "Origins and Consequences of Import Substitution in Brazil." In *International Economics and Development: Essays in Honor of Raúl Prebisch*, edited by Luis Eugenio di Marco, pp. 318–22. New York: Academic Press, 1972.

Fleius, Max. *História administrativa do Brasil*. 2nd ed. São Paulo: Cia. Melhoramentos, [1922].

Fleury Monteiro, Zenon. *A margem dos Carirys*. São Paulo: Editôra Helios, 1926.

Flory, Thomas. *Judge and Jury in Imperial Brazil, 1808–1871*. Austin: University of Texas Press, 1981.

Forman, Shepard, and Joyce F. Riegelhaupt. "The Political Economy of Patron–Clientship: Brazil and Portugal Compared." In *Brazil: Anthropological Perspectives*, edited by Maxine Margolis and William E. Carter, pp. 379–400. New York: Columbia University Press, 1979.

Fox, Robin. *Kinship and Marriage: An Anthropological Perspective.* Baltimore: Penguin Books, 1967.

Freeman, J. D. "On the Concept of the Kindred." *Journal of the Royal Anthropological Society* 91 (1961):195–99.

Freyre, Gilberto. "The Patriarchal Basis of Brazilian Society." In *The Politics of Change in Latin America,* edited by Joseph Maier and Richard W. Weatherhead, pp. 153–73. New York: Praeger, 1964.

Fukui, Lia Freitas Garcia. *Sertão e bairro rural.* São Paulo: Editôra Ática, 1979.

Furtado, Celso. *The Economic Growth of Brazil.* Translated by Ricardo W. Aguiar and Eric Charles Drysdale. Berkeley and Los Angeles: University of California Press, 1968.

Galjart, Benno. "Old Patrons and New: Some Notes on the Consequences of Patronage for Local Development Projects." *Sociologia Ruralis* 7, no. 4 (1967):335–46.

Godoy, Rosa Maria Silveira. *Republicanismo e federalismo, 1888–1902.* João Pessoa: Editôra Universitária, 1978.

Goody, Jack, and Esther N. Goody. "Cross-Cousin Marriage in Northern Ghana." In *Comparative Studies in Kinship,* ed. Jack Goody, pp. 216–34. Stanford: Stanford University Press, 1969.

———. *The Development of the Family and Marriage in Europe.* Cambridge: Cambridge University Press, 1983.

Granja, Tobias. "O vingador absolvido." *O Cruzeiro,* 21 Apr. 1971, pp. 95–98.

Great Western of Brasil Railway Co., Ltd. *Rio Grande do Norte, Parahyba, Pernambuco, Alagoas.* London: Waterlow & Sons, 1903.

Greenfield, Sidney. "Charwomen, Cesspools, and Roadbuilding: An Examination of Patronage, Clientage, and Political Power in South-Eastern Minas Gerais." In *Structure and Process in Latin America,* edited by Arnold Stricken and Sidney Greenfield, pp. 71–100. Albuquerque: University of New Mexico Press, 1972.

Gross, Daniel R. "Factionalism and Local Level Politics in Rural Brazil." *Journal of Anthropological Research* 29, no. 2 (1973):123–44.

Hall, Peter Dobkin. "Family Structure and Economic Organization: Massachusetts Merchants, 1700–1850." In *Family and Kin in Urban Communities, 1700–1850,* edited by Tamara Harevin, pp. 38–61. New York: New Viewpoints, 1977.

Harevin, Tamara. *Family and Kin in Urban Communities, 1700–1850.* New York: New Viewpoints, 1977.

Hirschman, Albert. *Journeys Through Progress.* New York: W. W. Norton & Co., Inc., 1973.

Hoge, Warren. "In Brazil's Wild Northeast, No End to Bloodletting." *New York Times,* 20 Aug. 1982, p. 2.

Howe, Marvine. "Violent Life-Style Seems to Revive in Rural Brazil." *New York Times,* 29 Nov. 1972, p. 12.

Inojosa, Joaquim. "Princesa: Nós aqui estamos livres," *O Cruzeiro*, 13 Oct. 1970, pp. 38–43.

Instituto Brasileiro de Geografia e Estatística. *Divisão territorial dos Estados Unidos do Brasil.* Rio de Janeiro: Serviço Gráfico do Instituto Brasileiro de Geografia e Estatística, 1940.

Instituto Histórico e Geográfico Brasileiro. *Diccionario historico, geografico e ethnografico do Brasil.* 2 vols. Centennial ed. Rio de Janeiro: Imprensa Oficial, 1922.

Joffily, Irinêo. *Notas sobre a Parahyba.* 2nd ed. Brasília: Thesaurus Editôra, 1977.

———. *Sinopse das sesmarias da Capitania da Parahyba.* Vol. 1. Parahyba: Typografia M. Henriques, 1894.

Joffily, José. *O porto político.* Rio de Janeiro: Civilização Brasileira, 1983.

———. *Revolta e revolução: Cinqüenta anos depois.* São Paulo: Paz e Terra, 1979.

Julião, Francisco. *Cambão—The Yoke.* Baltimore and Middlesex: Penguin Books, 1972.

"O júri no nordeste: Nova mentalidade." *O Cruzeiro*, 21 Apr. 1971, p. 98.

Koster, Henry. *Travels in Brazil.* 2 vols. Philadelphia: M. Carey & Son, 1817.

Kottak, Conrad Philip. "Kinship and Class in Brazil." *Ethnology* 5, no. 2 (1967):427–48.

Kuznesof, Elizabeth Anne. "An Analysis of the Relationship between Household Composition and Mode of Production: São Paulo, 1765 to 1836." *Comparative Studies in Society and History* 22 (Jan. 1980):79–110.

———. "Clans, the Militia, and Territorial Government: The Articulation of Kinship with Polity in Eighteenth-Century São Paulo." In *Social Fabric and Spatial Structure in Colonial Latin America*, edited by David J. Robinson, pp. 207–31. Ann Arbor: University Microfilms International, 1979.

Leal, José. *Itinerário da história (Imágem da Paraíba entre 1518 e 1965).* João Pessoa: Gráfica Comercial, 1965.

Leeds, Anthony. "Brazilian Careers and Social Structure: A Case Study and Model." *American Anthropologist* 66 (1964):1321–47.

Leff, Nathaniel H. "Economic Development and Regional Inequality: Origins of the Brazilian Case." *Quarterly Journal of Economics* 86 (May 1972):243–62.

Lelis, João. *A campanha de Princesa (1930).* João Pessoa: A União Editôra, 1944.

Levi, Darrell E. *A família Prado.* São Paulo: Livraria Editôra, 1977.

Levine, Robert M. *Pernambuco in the Brazilian Federation, 1889–1937.* Stanford: Stanford University Press, 1978.

Lewin, Linda. "The Oligarchical Limitations of Social Banditry in Brazil: The Case of the 'Good' Thief Antônio Silvino." *Past & Present* 82 (Feb. 1979):116–36.

Lewin, Linda. "Oral Tradition and Elite Myth: The Legend of Antônio Silvino in Brazilian Popular Culture." *Journal of Latin American Lore* 5, no. 2 (1979):157–204.

———. "Politics and *Parentela* in Paraíba: A Case Study of Oligarchy in Brazil's Old Republic, 1889–1930." Ph.D. diss., Columbia University, 1975.

———. "Property as Patrimony: Changing Notions of Family, Kinship, and Wealth in Brazilian Inheritance Law." Paper presented at the Symposium on Latin American Kinship Structure, sponsored by Social Science Research Council, Ixtápan de la Sal, Mexico, September 1981.

———. "Some Historical Implications of Kinship Organization for Family-Based Politics in the Brazilian Northeast." *Comparative Studies in Society and History* 21, no. 2 (1979):262–92.

Literatura popular em verso; antologia, Vol. 2: [*Leandro Gomes de Barros*]. Rio de Janeiro: Fundação Casa de Rui Barbosa/MEC, 1976. Vol. 4: *Francisco das Chagas Batista*. Rio de Janeiro: Fundação Casa de Rui Barbosa/MEC, 1977.

Lopes, Alcides. *F. Pessoa de Queiroz: Vida e ação*. Recife: State of Pernambuco, Secretaria de Turismo, Cultura e Esportes/Fundação do Patrimonio Histórico e Artístico de Pernambuco, 1985.

Love, Joseph L. *Rio Grande do Sul and Brazilian Regionalism*. Stanford: Stanford University Press, 1971.

———. *São Paulo in the Brazilian Federation, 1889–1937*. Stanford: Stanford University Press, 1980.

"A luta de Exu chega a Recife e faz dois mortos." *Folha de São Paulo*, 25 July 1981, p. 1.

Lyra Tavares, João de. *Cifras e notes (Economia e finanças do Brasil)*. Rio de Janeiro: Typografia da "Revista do Supremo Tribunal," 1925.

———. *Economia e finanças dos estados: Brasil*. Parahyba: Imprensa Oficial, 1914.

———. *Historia territorial da Parahyba*. 2 vols. Parahyba: Imprensa Oficial, 1909–1911.

———. *A Parahyba*. 2 vols. Parahyba: Imprensa Oficial, 1910.

Machado, Maximiano Lopes. *História da Província da Paraíba (Reprodução da edição de 1912 . . .)*. 2 vols. João Pessoa: Editôra Universitária, Universidade Federal da Paraíba, 1977.

Maeyama, Takashi. *Familialization of the Unfamiliar World: The Família, Networks, and Groups in a Brazilian City*. Ithaca: Cornell University Press, 1975.

Maia, N. Freire, and A. Freire Maia. "The Structure of Consanguineous Marriages and Their Genetic Implications." *Annual of Human Genetics* 25 (1961):25–29.

Marcílio, Maria Luiza. *A cidade de São Paulo: Povoamento e população, 1750–1850*. São Paulo: Livraria Pioneira Editôra, 1974.

———. "Mariage et remariage dans le Brésil traditionnel: Lois, intensité, calendrier." In *Marriage and Remarriage in Past Populations*, edited by J. Dupâquier, E. Hélin, P. Laslett, M. Livi-Bacci, and S. Sogner, pp. 363–73. New York: Academic Press, 1981.

———. "Variations des noms et des prenoms au Brésil." *Annales de Demographie Historique* (1972):345–53.

Mariz, Celso. *Apanhados historicos da Parahyba*. Parahyba: Imprensa Oficial, 1922.

———. *Cidades e homens*. João Pessoa: *A União* Editôra, 1945.

———. *Evolução econômica da Paraíba*. João Pessoa: *A União* Editôra, 1939.

———. *Memória da Assembléia Legislativa*. João Pessoa: Imprensa Oficial, 1946.

Martins Filho, Amilcar. "Clientelismo e representação em Minas Gerais durante a Primeira República: Uma crítica a Paul Cammack." *Revista de Ciências Sociais* [Rio de Janeiro] 27, no. 2 (1984):175–97.

Matta, Roberto da. "As raizes da violência no Brasil: Reflexões de um antropólogo." In *Violência brasileira*, by Maria Celia Paoli, Roberto da Matta, Maria Victoria Benevides, and Paulo Sérgio Pinheiro, pp. 11–44. São Paulo: Brasiliense, 1982.

McDonough, Peter. *Power and Ideology in Brazil*. Princeton: Princeton University Press, 1981.

Mesquita, Eni de. "Uma contribuição ao estudo da estructura familiar em São Paulo durante o período colonial: A família agregada em Itú de 1780 a 1830." *Revista de História* [São Paulo] 105 (1976):33–45.

Mesquita Samara, Eni de. "A família na sociedade paulista do século XIX (1800–1860)." Ph.D. diss., University of São Paulo, 1980.

Miller, Charlotte. "The Function of Middle-Class Extended Family Networks in Brazilian Urban Society." In *Brazil: Anthropological Perspectives*, edited by Maxine L. Margolis and William E. Carter, pp. 305–15. New York: Columbia University Press, 1979.

———. "Middle-Class Kinship Networks in Belo Horizonte, Minas Gerais." Ph.D. diss., University of Florida, 1976.

Mitchell, Simon, ed. *The Logic of Poverty*. London, Boston, and Henley: Routledge & Kegan Paul, 1981.

Moura, Margarida. *Os herdeiros da terra*. São Paulo: HUCITEC, 1978.

Murillo de Carvalho, José. "Barbacena: A família, a política e uma hipótese." *Revista Brasileira de Estudos Políticos* 20, 1 (1966):153–94.

———. "A composição social dos partidos políticos imperiais." *Cadernos do Departamento de Ciência Política* [Universidade Federal de Minas Gerais] 2 (Dec. 1974):1–34.

———. "Elite and State-Building in Imperial Brazil." Ph.D. diss., Stanford University, 1974.

Murphy, Robert F., and Leonard Kasdan. "The Structure of Parallel Cousin Marriage." *American Anthropologist* 61 (1959):17–29.

Naro, Nancy Priscilla. "Brazil's 1848: The Praieira Revolt." Ph.D. diss., University of Chicago, 1982.

Nicholas, Ralph W. "Factions: A Comparative Analysis." In *Political Systems and the Distribution of Power*, edited by Michael Banton, pp. 21–61. London: Tavistock Publications, Ltd., 1968.

Nie, Norman H., Dale H. Bent, and Hadlai Hull. *Statistical Package for the Social Sciences*. New York: McGraw-Hill Book Company, 1970.

Nóbrega, Apolônio. "Chefes do Executivo Paraibano." *Revista do Instituto Histórico e Geográfico Brasileiro* 249 (Oct.–Dec. 1960):45–145.

———. *História republicana da Paraíba*. João Pessoa: Imprensa Oficial, 1950.

Nóbrega, Humberto. "João Suassuna—O estadista." *Revista do Instituto Histórico e Geográfico Paraibano* 18 (1971):8–23.

Nóbrega, Trajano Pires da. *A família Nóbrega*. Biblioteca Genealógica Brasileira 8. São Paulo: Instituto Genealógico Brasileiro, 1956.

Nunes Leal, Vitor. *Coronelismo, enxada, e voto*. 2nd ed. São Paulo: Editôra Alfa-Omega, 1975.

Oliveira Torres, João Camilo de. *A democracia coroada; Teoria política do Império do Brasil*. 2nd ed., rev. Petrópolis: Editôra Vozes, 1963.

Oliveira Vianna, [Francisco José de]. *Instituições políticas brasileiras*. 2 vols. Rio de Janeiro: José Olýmpio Editôra, 1955.

———. *Populações meridionais do Brasil*. 2 vols. Rio de Janeiro: Paz e Terra, 1973.

Otávio, José. *A Revolução estatizada; um estudo sobre a formação do centralismo em 30*. Mossoró, Rio Grande do Norte: Edições Escola Superior de Agricultura de Mossoró/Fundação Guimaraes Duque, 1984.

Pang, Eul-Soo. *Bahia in the First Brazilian Republic*. Gainesville: University Presses of Florida, 1979.

———. "The Changing Role of Priests in the Backlands of Northeast Brazil, 1889–1964." *The Americas* 30 (Jan. 1974):341–72.

———. "*Coronelismo* in Northeast Brazil." In *The Caciques: Oligarchical Politics and the System of Caciquismo in the Luso-Hispanic World*, edited by Robert Kern, pp. 65–88. Albuquerque: University of New Mexico Press, 1973.

———. "The Politics of Coronelismo in Brazil: The Case of Bahia, 1890–1930." Ph.D. diss., University of California, Berkeley, 1970.

Pearse, Arno. *Brazilian Cotton*. Manchester: International Federation of Master Cotton Spinners & Manufacturers' Association, 1923.

Pereira de Queiroz, Maria Isaura. *Cultura, sociedade rural, sociedade urbana no Brasil*. São Paulo: Livros Técnicos e Científicos Editôra, S.A. & Editôra da Universidade de São Paulo, 1978.

———. *O mandonismo local na vida política brasileira e outros ensaios*. 2nd ed. São Paulo: Editôra Alfa-Omega, 1976.

Pessoa, Epitácio [Lindolfo da Silva]. *Obras completas de Epitácio Pessoa*. 25 vols. Rio de Janeiro: Instituto Nacional do Livro, 1955–1965.

Pessôa Raja Gabaglia, Laurita [Irmã Maria Regina do Santo Rosário]. *Epitacio Pessôa*. 2 vols. Rio de Janeiro: José Olýmpio Editôra, 1951.

Pinto, Estevão. *História de uma estrada-de-ferro do nordeste*. Rio de Janeiro: José Olýmpio Editôra, 1949.

Pinto, Irineu Ferreira. *Datas e notas para a história da Paraíba (Reprodução da edição de 1908)*. 2 vols. João Pessoa: Editôra Universitária/UFPB, 1977.

Pinto, Luiz. *Síntese histórica da Paraíba*, 2nd ed. Rio de Janeiro: Gráfica Ouvidor, 1960.

Prado Junior, Caio. *The Colonial Background of Modern Brazil*. Translated by Suzette Macedo. Berkeley and Los Angeles: University of California Press, 1969.

———. *História econômica do Brasil*. 21st ed. São Paulo: Brasiliense, 1978.

Ramos, Donald. "Marriage and the Family in Colonial Vila Rica." *Hispanic American Historical Review* 55, no. 2 (May 1975):200–225.

Rebelo Horta, Cid. "Famílias governamentais de Minas Gerais." In *Segundo Seminário de Estudos Mineiros*, pp. 45–91. Belo Horizonte: Universidade de Minas Gerais, 1956.

Ribeiro Coutinho, Renato. "História da Associação Comercial da Paraíba." Associação Comercial de João Pessoa, João Pessoa, Paraíba, 1958. Typescript.

Richards, A. I. "Matrilineal Systems." In *Kinship: Selected Readings*, edited by Jack Goody, pp. 276–89. Baltimore: Penguin Books, 1971.

Robock, Stefan. *Brazil's Developing Northeast: A Study of Regional Planning and Foreign Aid*. Washington, D.C.: The Brookings Institution, 1963.

Rodrigues Pereira, Lafayette. *Direitos de família*. Rio de Janeiro: B. L. Garnier, 1869.

Romero, Sylvio. "As oligarchias e sua classificação." In *Provocações e debates*, pp. 401–16. Porto: Livraria Chardron de Lello & Irmão, 1910.

Sá, Antônio e Fernando Nóbrega. *Em defesa de uma memória: O Ex-Presidente João Suassuna perante os tribunários revolucionários*. João Pessoa: Livraria São Paulo, 1931.

Salzano, Francisco M., and Newton Freire-Maia. *Problems in Human Biology: A Study of Brazilian Populations*. Detroit: Wayne State University Press, 1970.

Santos Coelho Filho, J. *Impostos na Paraíba (Contribuição ao estudo do regime tributário)*. João Pessoa: *A União* Editôra, 1946.

Schneider, Peter. "Honor and Conflict in a Sicilian Town." *Anthropology Quarterly* 42, no. 3 (1969):130–54.

Schusky, Ernest L. *Manual for Kinship Analysis*. New York: Holt, Rinehart, and Winston, 1965.

Schwartz, Stuart. *Sovereignty and Society in Colonial Brazil*. Berkeley and Los Angeles University of California Press, 1973.

Schwartzmann, Simon. "Back to Weber: Corporatism and Patrimonialism in the Seventies." In *Authoritarianism and Corporatism in Latin America*, edited by James M. Malloy, pp. 89–106. Pittsburgh: University of Pittsburgh Press, 1977.

———. *São Paulo e o Estado Nacional*. São Paulo: Difusão Européia do Livro, 1975.

Shirley, Robert W. *The End of a Tradition: Culture Change and Development in the Município of Cunha, São Paulo, Brazil*. New York and London: Columbia University Press, 1971.

———. "Law in Rural Brazil." In *Brazil: Anthropological Perspectives*, edited by Maxine Margolis and William E. Carter, pp. 343–61. New York: Columbia University Press, 1979.

———. "Patronage and Cooperation: An Analysis from São Paulo State." In *Structure and Process in Latin America*, edited by Arnold Stricken and Sidney M. Greenfield, pp. 139–58. Albuquerque: University of New Mexico Press, 1972.

Shorter, Edward. *The Historian and the Computer*. Englewood Cliffs, N.J. Prentice-Hall, 1971.

Silva, Hélio da. *1922—Sangue na areia de Copacabana*. Rio de Janeiro: Editôra Civilização Brasileira, 1964.

Smith, T. Lynn. *Brazil: People and Institutions*. 2nd ed., rev. Baton Rouge: Louisiana State University Press, 1963.

Smith, T. Lynn, and Alexander Marchant, eds. *Brazil: Portrait of Half a Continent*. New York: The Dryden Press, 1951.

Soares de Galliza, Diana. *O declínio da escravidão na Paraíba, 1850–1888*. João Pessoa: Editôra Universitária Federal da Paraíba, 1979.

Souza, Amaury de. "The *Cangaço* and the Politics of Violence in Northeast Brazil." In *Protest and Resistance in Angola and Brazil*, edited by Ronald H. Chilcote, pp. 109–31. Berkeley and Los Angeles: University of California Press, 1972.

Stein, Stanley. *The Brazilian Cotton Manufacture: Textile Enterprise in an Underdeveloped Area, 1850–1950*. Cambridge: Harvard University Press, 1957.

Stolke, Verena. "The 'Unholy' Family: Labour Systems and Family Structure—The Case of São Paulo Coffee Plantations." Paper presented at the Symposium on Latin American Kinship Structure, sponsored by the Social Science Research Council, Ixtápan de la Sal, Mexico, September 1981.

Tiller, Ann Quiggins. "The Igniting Spark—Brazil, 1930." *Hispanic American Historical Review* 45, no. 3 (1965):385–92.

Topik, Steven. *The Political Economy of the Brazilian State, 1889–1930* Austin: University of Texas Press, in press.

———. "State Intervention in a Liberal Regime: Brazil 1889–1930." *Hispanic American Historical Review* 60, no. 4 (1980):593–616.

———. "The State's Contribution to the Development of Brazil's Internal Economy: 1850–1930." *Hispanic American Historical Review* 65, no. 2 (1985):203–28.

Uricoechea, Fernando. *The Patrimonial Foundations of the Brazilian Bureaucratic State.* Berkeley and Los Angeles: University of California Press, 1980.

Varnhagen, Francisco Adolpho de, Visconde de Porto Seguro. *História geral do Brasil . . . antes de sua separação e independencia de Portugal.* 2nd ed. 2 vols. Rio de Janeiro: E. & H. Laemmert, 1977.

Vidal, Ademar. *João Pessoa e a Revolução de 30.* Rio de Janeiro: Edições GRAAL, 1978.

———. *1930; historia de João Pessoa e da Revolução na Parahyba.* São Paulo: Cia. Editôra Nacional, 1933.

Wagley, Charles. "Luso-Brazilian Kinship Patterns: The Persistence of a Cultural Tradition." In *The Politics of Change in Latin America,* edited by Joseph Maier and Richard W. Weatherhead, pp. 174–89. New York: Praeger, 1964.

Waterbury, John. *The Commander of the Faithful.* New York: Columbia University Press, 1970.

Watson, James L. "Chinese Kinship Reconsidered: Anthropological Perspectives on Historical Research." *The China Quarterly* 92 (Dec. 1982):589–622.

Webb, Kempton. *The Changing Face of Northeast Brazil.* New York: Columbia University Press, 1974.

Willems, Emílio. "The Structure of the Brazilian Family." *Social Forces* 31, no. 4 (1953):339–45.

Williams, H. E., and Roderic Crandall. *Mappa dos Estados do Ceará, Rio Grande do Norte e Parahyba.* Rio de Janeiro: Ministerio da Viação e Obras Publicas, 1910.

Wirth, John. *Minas Gerais in the Brazilian Federation, 1889–1937.* Stanford: Stanford University Press, 1977.

Wolf, Eric R. "Aspects of Group Relations in Complex Societies." *American Anthropologist* 58 (1956):1065–76.

———. "Kinship, Friendship, and Patron–Client Relations in Complex Societies." In *The Social Anthropology of Complex Societies,* edited by Michael Banton, pp. 1–22. London: Tavistock Publishers, 1968.

Wolf, Eric R., and E. C. Hansen. "*Caudillo* Politics: A Structural Analysis." *Comparative Studies in Society and History* 9, no. 2 (1967):168–79.

INDEX

Library of Congress Cataloging-in-Publication Data

Lewin, Linda, 1941-
Politics and Parentela in Paraíba.

Bibliography: p. Includes index.
1. Paraíba (Brazil : State)—Politics and government. 2. Oligarchy—Brazil—Paraíba (State)—History. 3. Family—Brazil—Paraíba (State)—Case studies. 4. Pessoa family. I. Title.
JL2499.P372L48 1987 306'.2'098133 86-42850
ISBN 0-691-07719-3 (alk. paper)